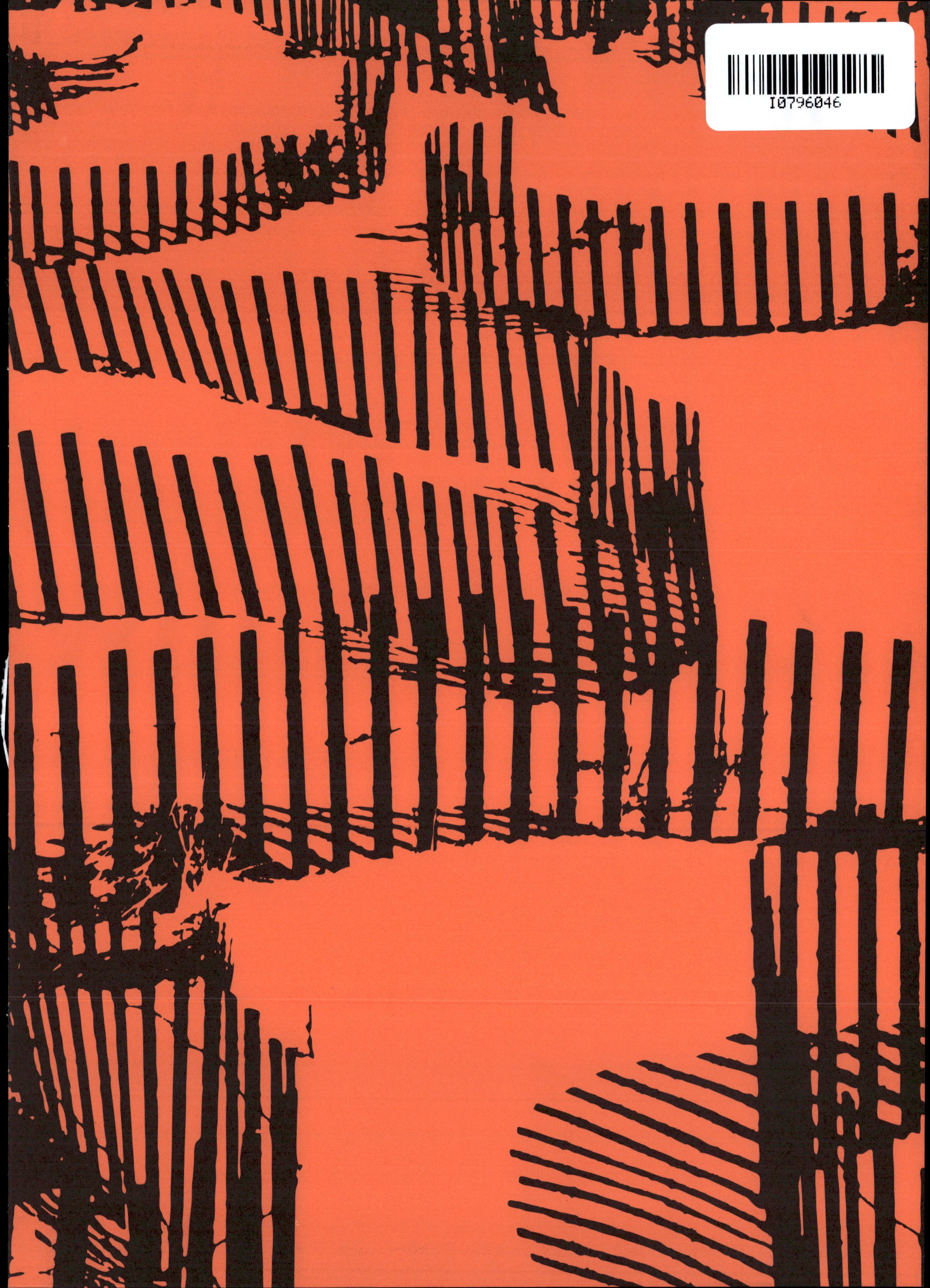

I0796046

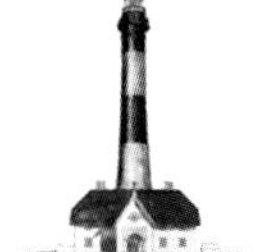

FIRE ISLAND MODERNIST

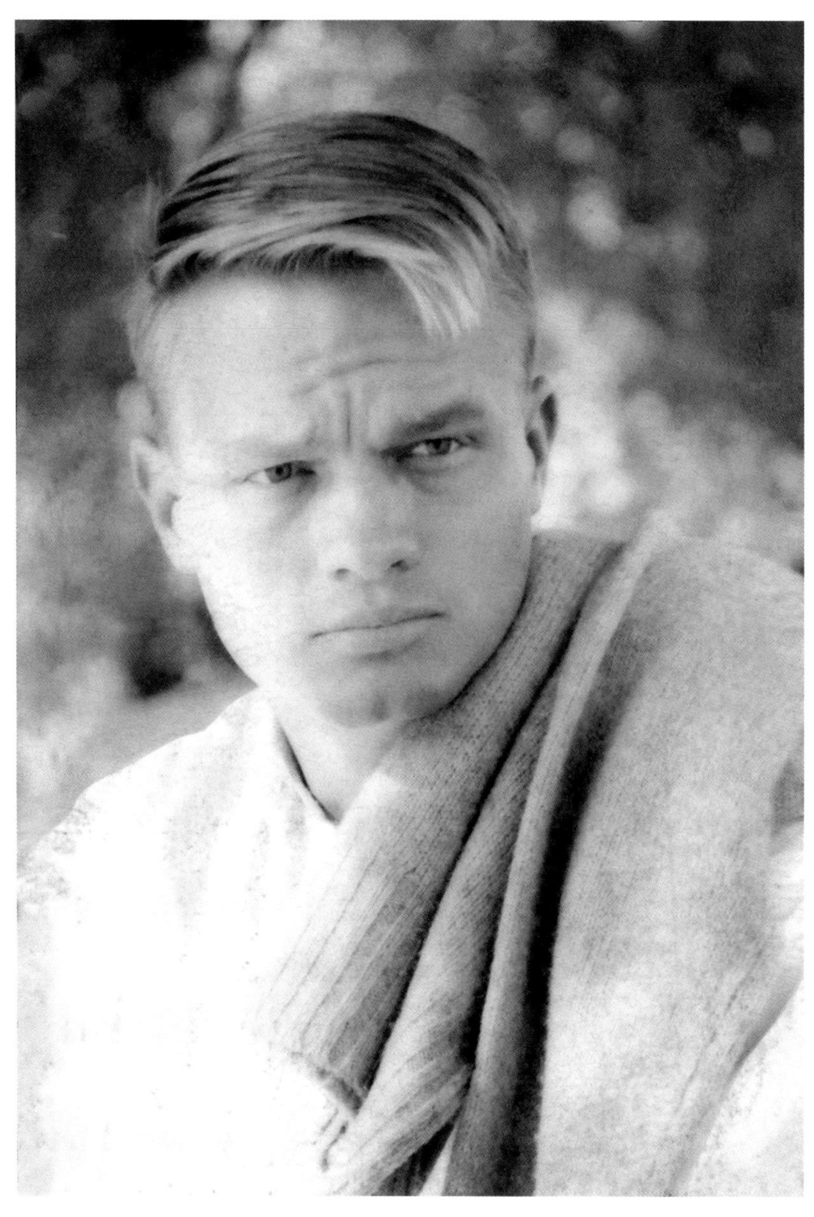

You will now have twenty closets to come out of.
—Horace Gifford, 1965

FIRE ISLAND MODERNIST

Horace Gifford and the Architecture of Seduction

EXPANDED EDITION

Christopher Bascom Rawlins

Foreword by Alastair Gordon
Afterword by Charles Renfro

Metropolis Books/Gordon de Vries Studio

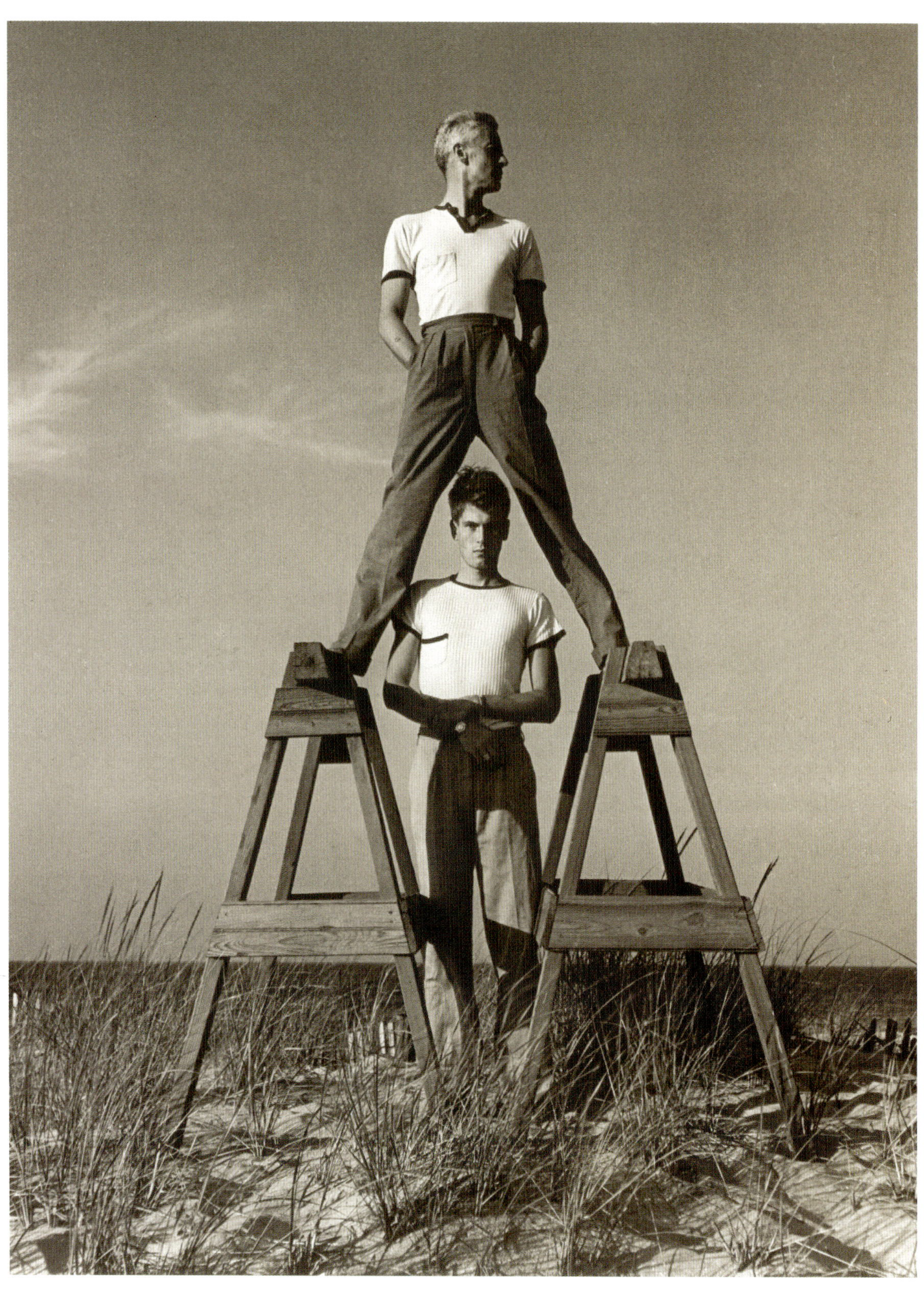

CONTENTS

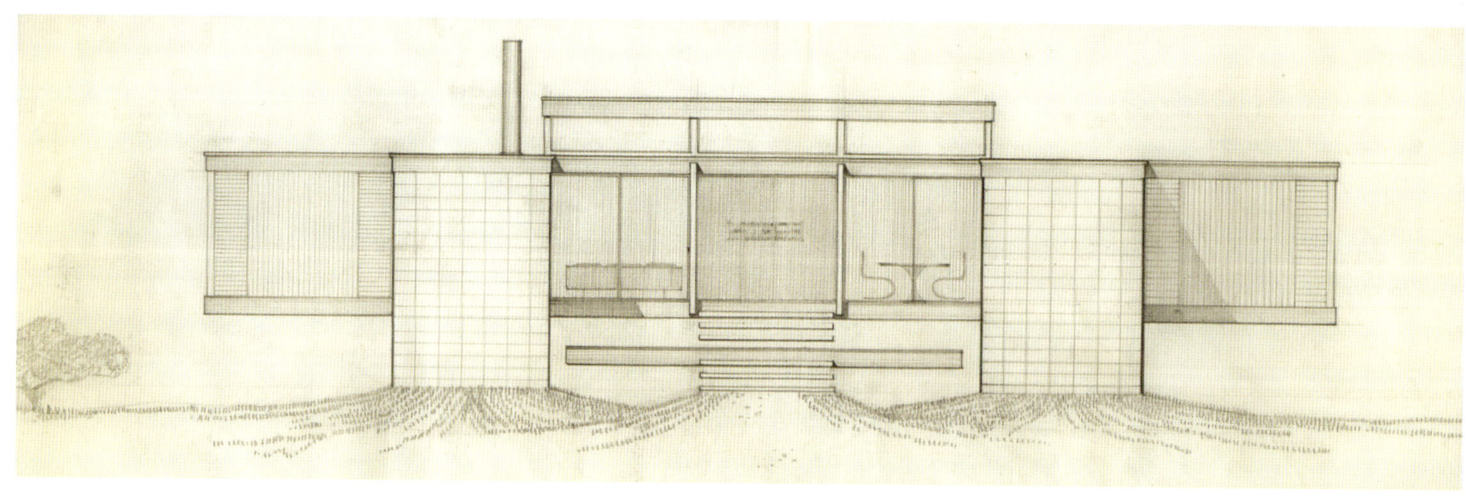

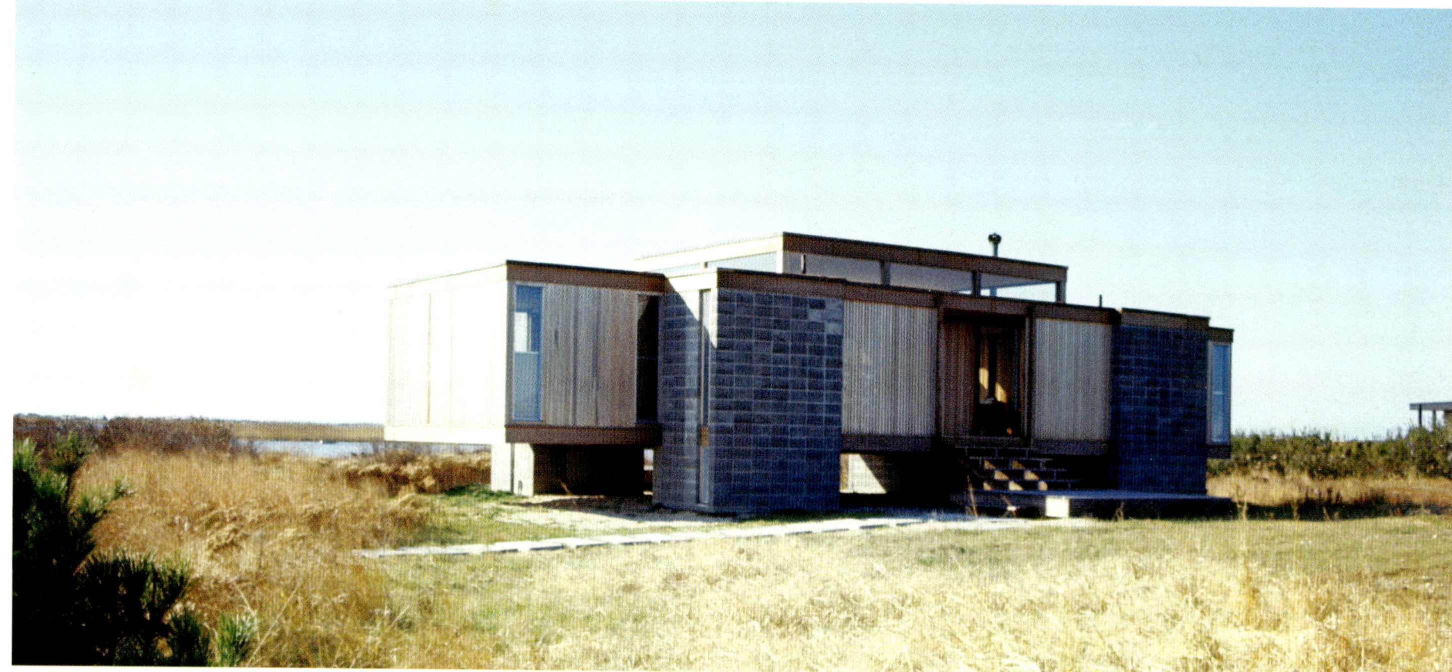

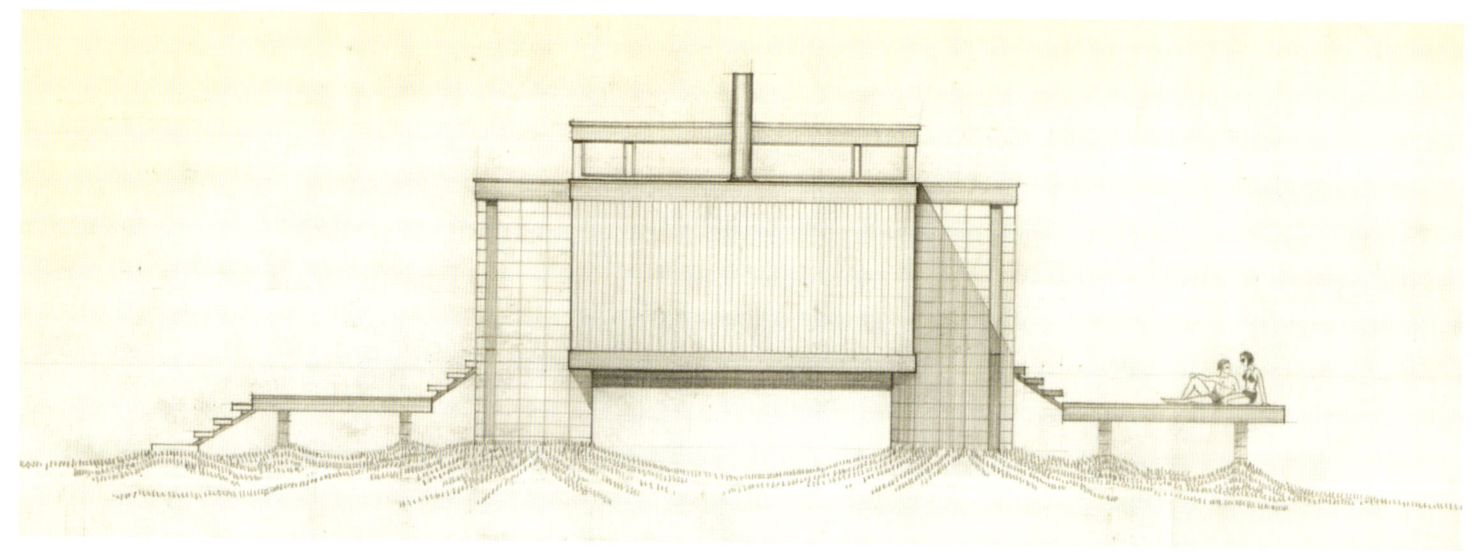

Lines of Sight

Foreword by Alastair Gordon

Everything, everything is free and natural.
—Marlo Sloan, owner of a Gifford House[1]

PAGE 4:
Horace Gifford, ca. 1960

PAGE 6:
Photo by Paul Cadmus. Portrait of George Platt Lynes and Jonathan Tichenor, Cherry Grove, NY, 1940

OPPOSITE:
Luck House, Bridgehampton, NY, 1967

Back in the 1990s, when I was driving all over Long Island conducting research for *Weekend Utopia*, I stumbled upon a small modernist dwelling, little more than a shack by today's standards, and it perched, ever so lightly, on a wetlands site in Bridgehampton, just off Job's Lane, near a little bridge where Sam's Creek drains into Mecox Bay. Boarded over for the season, or maybe forever, it was overgrown with bayberry and an orange vine that crept up the walls and made it feel like a poignant ruin of summers lost.

I wanted to include it in my book, but no one seemed to know anything about it. A local historian guessed that it might be by Peter Blake, since Blake had designed the neighboring house (his own), but that didn't make sense. This house lacked the hovering, "barely there" illusion that made Blake's work so distinctive and instead had its own kind of earthy integrity. Indeed, there was something almost stoic about the way it clung to its site with twin piers of concrete block, as if it had been abandoned there, like a shipwreck, and taken root.

When I asked Blake himself, he scoffed and made some dismissive remark about "forgeries." An East End realtor told me it was a spec house by an unknown architect, a failed Blake imitation, but this turned out to be hearsay, more local mythology, and the authorship remained a mystery for several more years. Then, Christopher Rawlins, a young architect (and author of this revelatory study), called me up and told me about Horace Gifford. The name sounded vaguely familiar. I'd seen it mentioned in some of the architecture magazines that I'd combed through during my research. Most of his beach-house designs from the 1960s and 1970s had been built on Fire Island, but a few were in the Hamptons, including one that Rawlins thought was on or near Mecox Bay. Some months later, Sarah Medford asked me to write a story about the rescue of an early-modern beach house for *Town & Country*, and it turned out to be the mystery dwelling. A trend-setting couple—art consultant Kim Heirston and her husband, the entertainment lawyer, Richard Evans—had just bought the property and were restoring it and furnishing it with contemporary art and vintage pieces by Charlotte Perriand and Arne Jacobsen.

"My immediate impression was that this was a real modernist gem, and I wanted to preserve it as it was," said Evans, who'd managed to uncover more information about the house and its provenance. He'd even found the original plans and some correspondence between architect and client confirming that, indeed, it was designed by Horace Gifford and built in 1967 for Dr. David Luck, a cell biologist at Rockefeller University. Luck died in 1998 and the house was bought by Charles Urstadt, chairman of the Battery Park City Authority, who then sold it to Heirston and Evans in 2006.

They invited me over for lunch and allowed me to snoop around without feeling like an intruder. The roadside facade still seemed pretty dour, with hardly any windows, just vertical slits, and a small entry court designed by Ward Bennett that had been added in the 1970s. Unlike the overblown ego statements of the past twenty years, the architecture was understated, almost a simple wood-framed box, stretched and cantilevered at either end with glassed-in overhangs resting on steel I-beams. There were hints of Marcel Breuer and Louis Kahn and a breezy echo of Paul Rudolph's iconic beach houses from the 1950s. (As I would later learn, Gifford grew up in Florida and fell under Rudolph's spell at an early age.) As soon as I walked inside, the rhythms changed and I could see the plan's originality. The modest dimensions and materials were part of a staged illusion that deferred generously to nature. After such a narrow entryway, the living room ballooned into an effervescent well of light that expanded through a wall of glass to the bay beyond, and a narrow boardwalk that turned into a dock. Interior walls were made from vertical, V-joint, cedar siding, and the floor was pale oak. There was a simple open kitchen with a concrete counter and behind it a small guest room; the primary bedroom was at the opposite end. The layout couldn't have been simpler. It was all about the sea-flecked light that flooded through windows and skylights, almost blindingly, through the pop-up roof and wrap-around clerestory that saturated the interior with a liquid glow and gave everyday objects a spectral sense of otherness. The owners really didn't need anything more. "We get up in the morning and watch the swans glide up to our deck," said Heirston. "It's my dose of sunshine: happy, open, and nature driven." The light served as a constant reminder, a companion and guide to living in the natural moment. The light was the real art and furniture—the primary reason for being there.

Gifford's simple plan turned prosaic summer architecture into a poetic experience: an odd out-of-body sensation that made one feel as if the house had slipped its moorings and drifted out among the plovers and overlapping reflections of the bay.

As I gradually learned more about Gifford, I was intrigued by the number of houses he'd designed in such a relatively short amount of time: more than sixty on Fire Island alone, and about a dozen in the Hamptons, yet he remained virtually unknown. (As Rawlins points out in his text here, so many of his clients, so many of his champions, died prematurely and couldn't promote his legacy.) There'd been a brief flash of recognition in 1968 with a six-page spread in *Progressive Architecture* that presented his work as a kind of pattern book for modern beach-house living, with playful variations on a basic plan. Some of the houses featured saw-toothed roofs. Others were horizontal slabs, cedar-sided boxes and towers, or shingled blocks tucked into other blocks like Russian dolls, twisting and turning around central sun courts, some with flat roofs (like the Luck House), some shed-roofed, others floating on the dunes, stepped down, or nestled among clumps of windblown pines.

"The site usually suggests what the house wants to be as a form in space," said Gifford, who followed this maxim throughout his career, taking his cue from the beach, inventing new forms while honoring the fragile ecosystem of Fire Island, the slender sandbar that straddles the south shore of Long Island, only 20 miles west of the frenetic, social-climbing Hamptons. His wood-framed architecture echoed the landscape and the culture of the place: simple and low-maintenance, designed for easy weekend living. "The house is like summer to us," said one happy owner. "Everything, everything is free and natural."[2]

But while, on first glance, Gifford's work appears to fit neatly into the same weekend utopia school as Blake, Andrew Geller, George Nelson, and Robert Rosenberg, there was a cultural twist, an alternate narrative that was slightly skewed from the Hamptons version of postwar leisure. As Gifford warned a prospective client: "I'm gay and I'm manic-depressive," and these were aspects of the man's personality that shaped his work: houses that expressed the longings of a culture that had transformed Fire Island into a free-fire zone of social and sexual discovery, especially along the beaches of the Pines.

A protected part of the National Seashore Preserve had become known as the "Meat Rack," an all-night, back-to-nature bacchanal. The handy *Pines Phone Directory* listed residents by first name. *Boys in the Sand*, a famous gay porn film of 1971, was shot there, and some of the intimate scenes were staged in the Frank House, a modernist glass-and-wood cube by Andrew Geller. "Orgy is a grand old tradition on Fire Island," wrote journalist Albert Goldman in 1972. Fittingly, Rawlins titled one of his chapters "Form Follows Foreplay," and here he describes the lavish parties and characters, and how Gifford's architecture echoed their liberated lifestyle.

Gifford, the architect, was also quiet and withdrawn. He suffered blinding bouts of self-doubt, followed by uplifts of giddy well-being and would walk to meetings in a bathing suit. His best work was more pathological than those simple, one-stroke pavilions of the 1950s and 1960s. While this was due in part to rising real estate values, lack of privacy, and an extended season that saw homeowners investing more money and wanting less Spartan, more comfortable escape pods with full kitchens, bathrooms, and extra guest rooms, it was also due to a shift in the whole idea of weekend leisure, both gay and straight, and how it was growing more fraught with urban angst and personal entanglements.

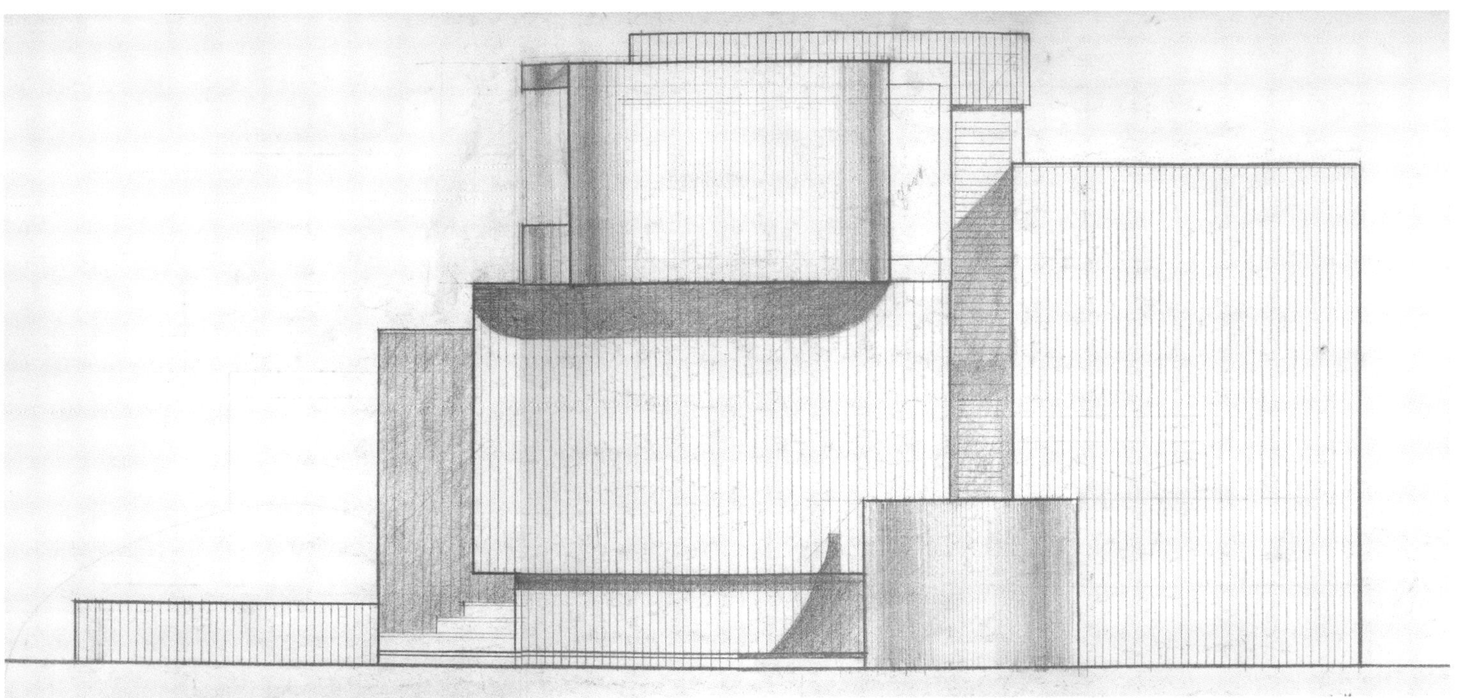

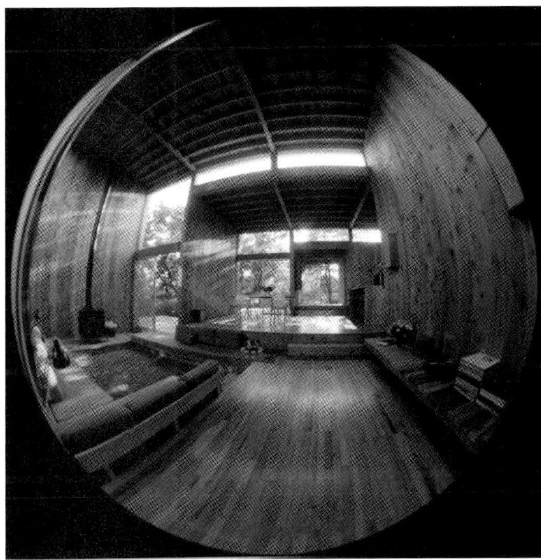

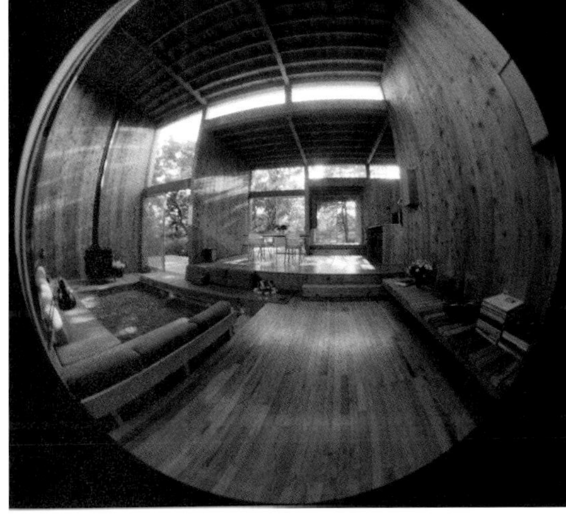

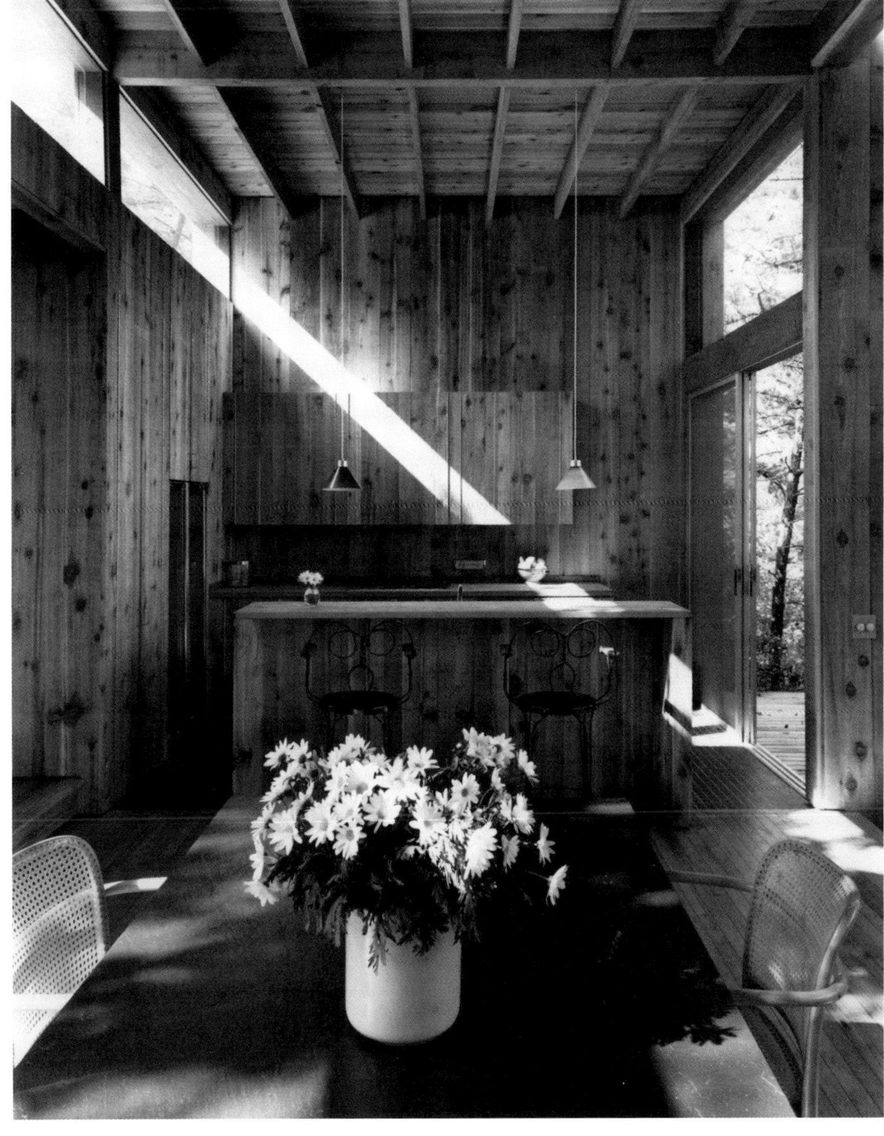

TOP:

Globus House, Corneille Estates, NY, 1966. Elevation depicting curved additions, 1971

ABOVE::

Bonaguidi House, Fire Island Pines, NY, 1968, peephole perspective

RIGHT:

Bonaguidi House, interior

Seismic social changes were reflected in the architecture of the moment, both by Gifford and other architects. The simple, mid-century box pushed out into odd angles and flaring floor plans that shielded, revealed, twisted, and turned programmatic elements to fit tiny building lots while still providing a degree of privacy amid cheek-by-jowl dunescapes and bigger sundecks, eccentrically shaped overhangs, telescoping canopies, and cedar-clad towers that rose higher to capture increasingly elusive ocean views. The mid-1970s saw an even more complex play of geometric configurations, almost puzzlelike, as in Gifford's designs for the Lipkins, Pilson, and Sloan houses, with broader expanses of opaque surfaces and bulky forms with rounded corners, elliptical openings, and lozenge-shaped decks to hide the Jacuzzis.

It was an architecture of seduction, with hide-and-seek expanses of glass, skylights, floor-to-ceiling mirrors, prurient lines of sight, sunken living rooms and lurid conversation pits—not to mention the exposed outdoor showers and ironic lack of closets—that turned Gifford's houses into Kabukiesque stage sets for concealment and exposure, light and shadow, inviting voyeuristic tendencies, while indulging a taste for flamboyance within the limits of an informal modernist vocabulary and a tight budget. His domestic interiors erased spatial hierarchies and eased them open with loosely flowing spaces that nurtured a wildly divergent array of experimentation. Indeed, some of the houses were so saturated and transparent that they seem, in retrospect, to be like overexposed Polaroids, blurred and buckling around the edges.

A house that Gifford designed for Stuart Roeder in 1969 was a masterwork of narcissistic modernism as it stretched the notion of "functionalism" to a new extreme. Sensually bulging forms and knotty wood siding concealed a soaring den of iniquity with a brightly upholstered maxicouch conversation pit circling a central fireplace and affording views, upward, of Roeder's infamous "make-out loft" that hung suspended overhead,

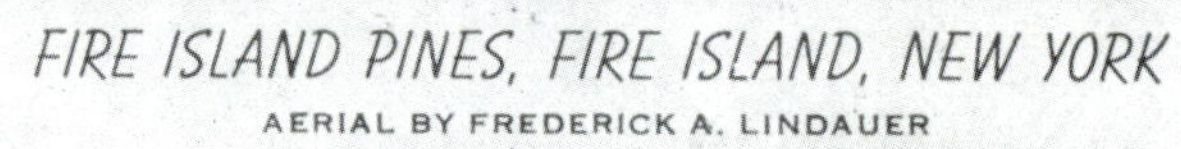

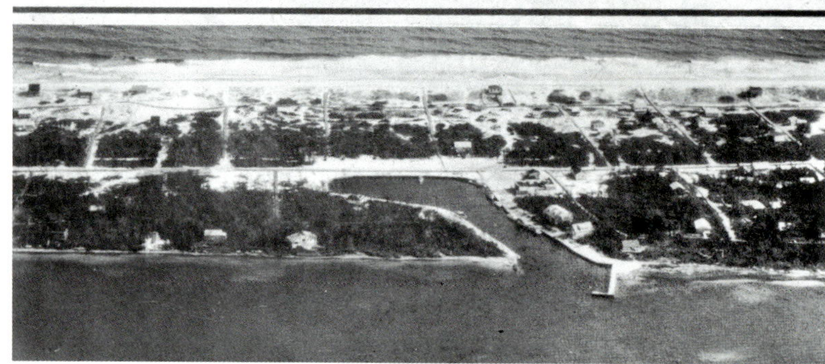

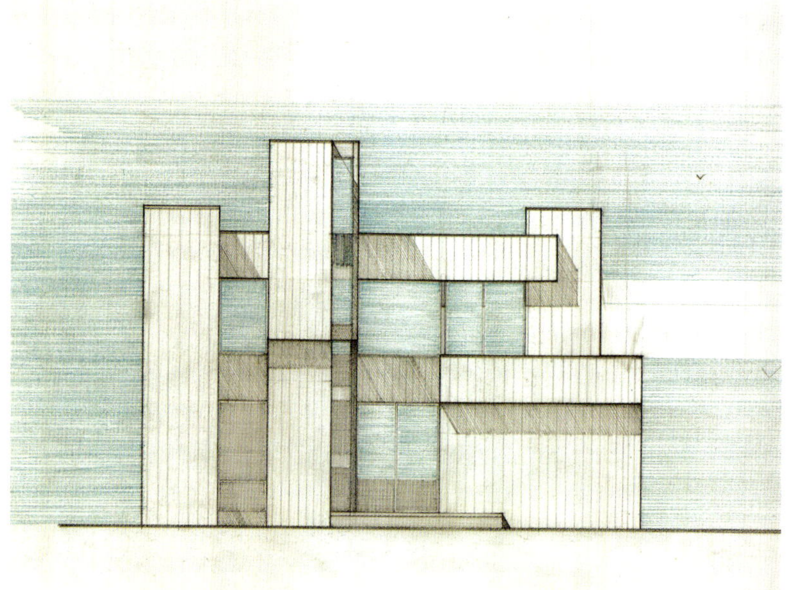

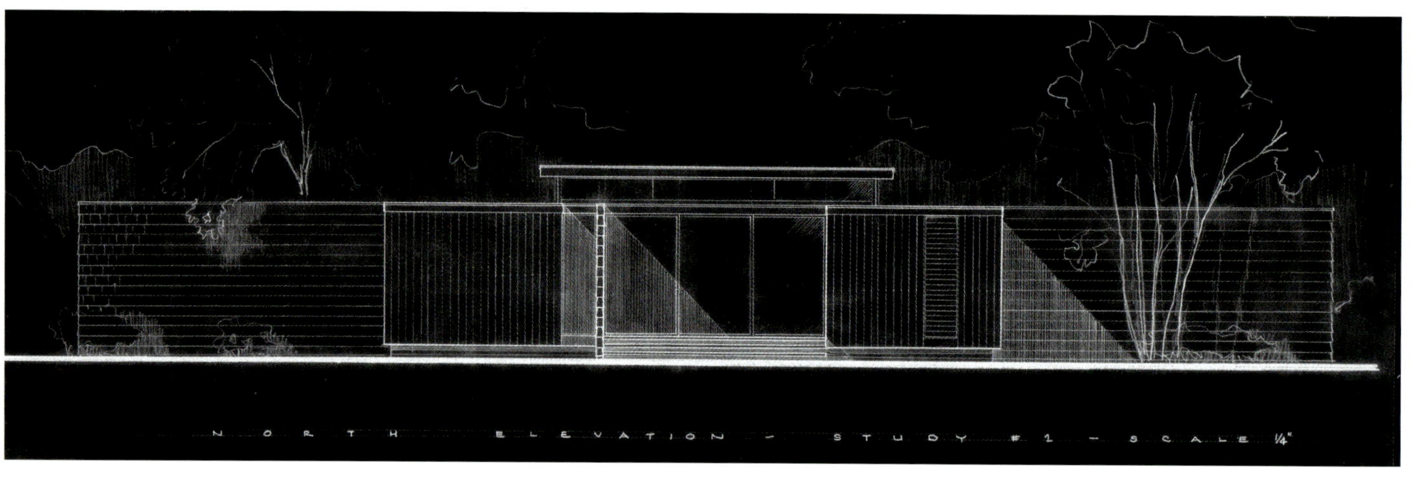

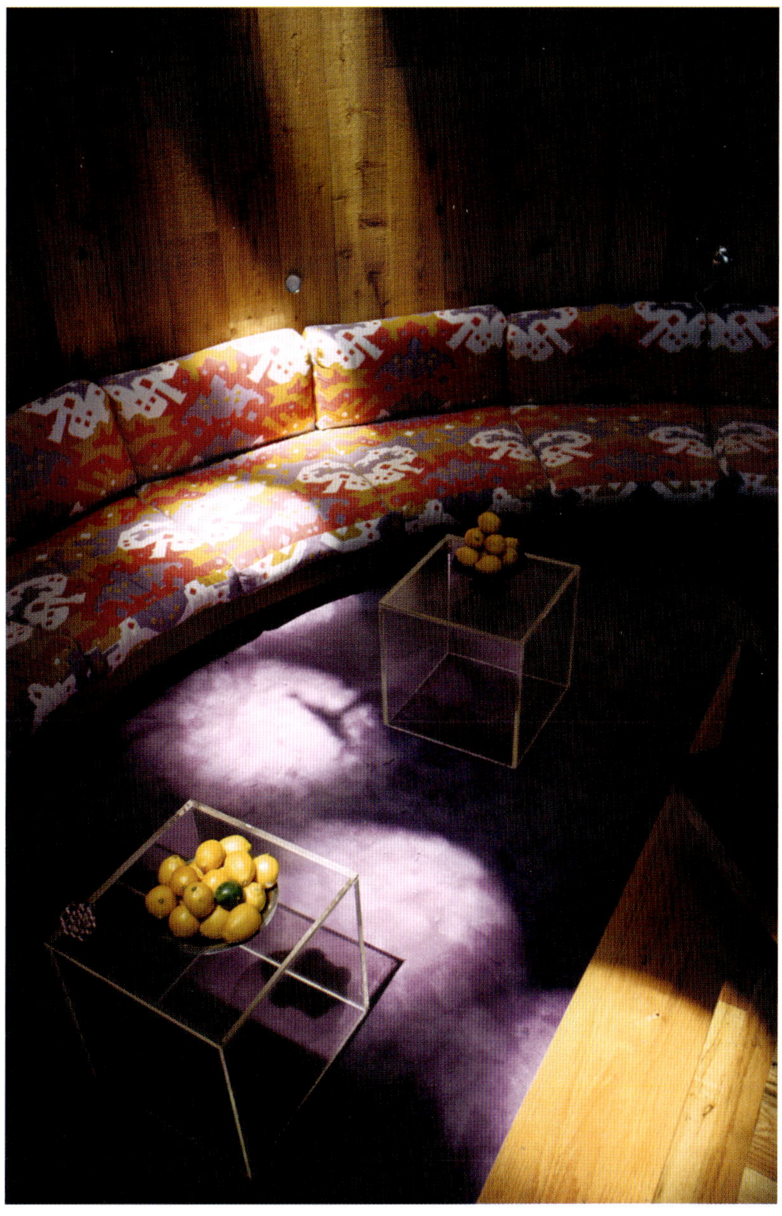

OPPOSITE ABOVE:
Fire Island Pines, NY, aerial view, early 1950s

OPPOSITE MIDDLE:
Chasas House (unbuilt), elevation, 1971

OPPOSITE BELOW:
North elevation, unknown house, undated

ABOVE:
Roeder House, Fire Island Pines, NY, 1969

draped with shaggy flokati rugs and reached by a spiral staircase. "A fur-lined loft? Sure, for this is a beach house with an owner who's enormously *gregarious,*" read the understated feature in *House Beautiful* from July 1972. A ring of portholes in the roof created a speckled pattern of sunlight splashing across the rough-hewn interior, further enhancing the otherworldly ambience of Roeder's lair. The free-spirited, out-of-the-closet era would ultimately end with the AIDS epidemic of the 1980s and 1990s, claiming Gifford himself as one of its victims. (He died of complications from the disease in 1992.)

Chris Rawlins' admirable and doggedly persistent research on a man who sometimes seems to have preferred obscurity has brought to light one of the missing links in mid-century modern architecture. His legacy seems more important today than ever, and it's a revelation to see these photographs and drawings pulled together for the first time and presented as a complete body of work. Suddenly, Gifford's imprint seems not only substantial but also significant and timely, in the deferential scale and proportions of his dwellings, in his doing less with more (as in Buckminster Fuller's sense of "ephemeralization"), and in the innovative, almost manic engineering of minimal spaces to suit maximal needs.

Gifford relied on a certain amount of intuition and an intimate, one-to-one relationship with nature that he forged through an understanding of the ever-shifting sandscape of Fire Island. Though tiny by today's standards—an average Gifford beach house was about 1,000 square feet—they expanded outward through oversize windows, decks, sun courts, and walkways, and seemed more spacious than they really were, all part of the forgotten art of "entasis," a kind of sleight of hand, dating from antiquity, that Gifford introduced into his practice.

With all the flash and extravagance of the Gay Renaissance and Gifford's part in it, this unlicensed architect was also something of a recluse, a quiet outsider who seemed to be searching for a sense of completion and personal resolution through more subtle undertones of social choreography and craftsmanship. He pursued the mysteries of light, shadow, and space as a poet might, and he would continue to struggle with light, shadow, and space—practically and metaphorically—throughout his sadly truncated career. The more lyrical side of Gifford's character might have been lost in the glare of a gratuitous exhibitionism, but Rawlins made every effort to seek out the private and vulnerable man through correspondence and interviews, giving us a more human view of this architect and his considerable achievement.

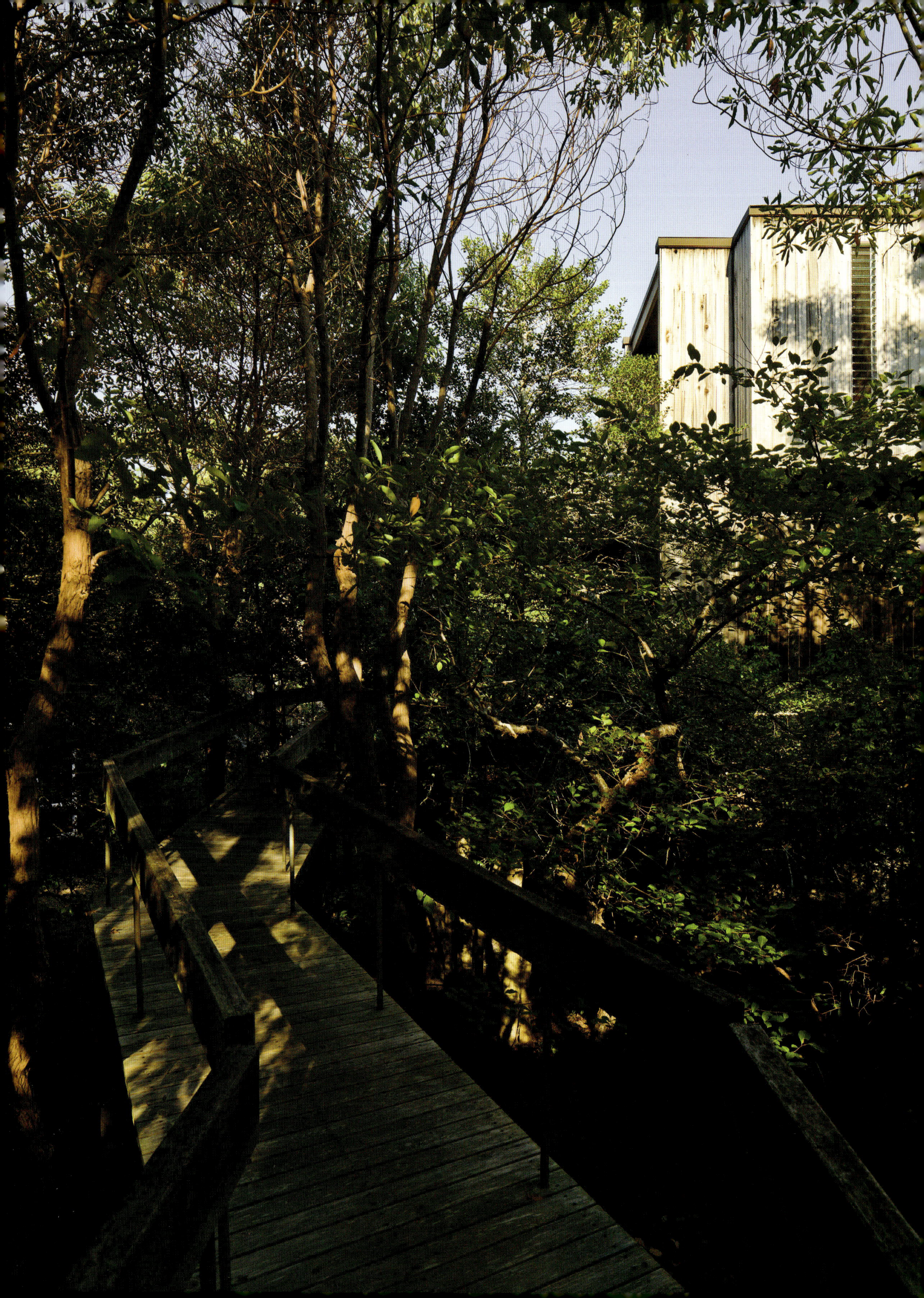

Refracting Prism

Introduction by Christopher Rawlins

There are two things you should know about me. I'm gay, and I'm manic-depressive.
—Horace Gifford[3]

Something kept drawing my eye through that particular tangle of holly trees. A meandering wooden bridge, suspended high above a hillside, threaded its way to a house seemingly floating among the treetops. By night, attenuated slivers of illuminated glass confirmed that the place was inhabited. Other odd and seductive homes invited exploration with the hook of a soaring roofline, a breezeway cut through the middle, or a dance of platforms artfully dodging the trees. None looked alike but all seemed to be part of an extended architectural family. I began knocking on doors.

"Who designed this place?"
"Horace Gifford."
"Who?"

I was a student of modern architects. Why didn't I know this one? In every case, homeowners offered alternately poetic and salacious accounts of the young, handsome, and fiercely talented architect who once had the run of this island.

I was exploring the Pines, one of about eighteen coastal communities dotted along the narrow slip of land known as Fire Island, which protects the south shore of Long Island from the Atlantic Ocean, forming the Great South Bay. It is thirty-one miles long, barely a quarter of a mile wide, and rewards the effort of reaching it with car-free boardwalks and expanses of protected dunes. Fire Island Pines—often just called the Pines—is accessible only by ferry or chartered seaplane, and it is hard to imagine a setting more removed from the skyscrapers of Manhattan that loom fifty miles to the west.[4] Yet the Pines is very much an urban invention, possessing a rustic-chic aesthetic that only a city dweller could conjure. In fact, the entire island is a place where urbanites of every conceivable stripe have perfected very particular takes on the weekend getaway. As journalist Albert Goldman put it in 1972:

> Fire Island appears to be designed by the cunning hand of nature to allow New Yorkers to escape the Melting Pot...Hot Jewish girls rub shoulders with coy gentile fags. Hot faggot queens bump up against chilly Jewish matrons. It's always Forbearance Week in New York City...Like a refracting prism, Fire Island takes your glaring white New York light and bends it into eighteen neatly demarcated bands, ranging from the bright pink of Cherry Grove and the lovely lavender of the Pines to the suburban Dutch Boy of Seaview and Ocean Ridge to the grungy shades of Ocean Beach and Fair Harbor, until the spectrum ends in the sterling-silver, goyim-gray of Saltaire and Point O' Woods.[5]

Soon, I found myself renting a Horace Gifford home in the Pines, a slightly rundown affair that still managed to delight with its clutch of cedar towers that spun around a glass-walled living room. A drafting table and a monogrammed T-square revealed this to have been Gifford's own residence. Yet no one outside of the Pines seemed to know anything about him. How could an architect of such evident appeal have vanished from the collective consciousness? I was feeling rather overlooked myself at the time, and fuss-

OPPOSITE:
Cashel House, Fire Island Pines, NY, 1969

ing over someone else's career proved to be an agreeable distraction. Many months of snooping delivered me to the snowy driveway of Edward DiGuardia, a Long Island artist who befriended Horace Gifford in his final years. Edward led me to a garage packed with thousands of drawings, magazine clippings, and slides. Here sat a life's work, hastily rescued from the bloodless ministrations of estate liquidators during the chaotic nadir of the AIDS epidemic.[6] That evening, under the flicker of an old-fashioned slide projector, dozens of ingenious homes flashed before me, tucked into lightly settled, utopian dunescapes. I was smitten, and determined to introduce this work to a broader public.

Horace Gifford built his first Fire Island beach house in 1961. As the 1960s became the "sixties," a remarkable series of beach houses performed a transformation of terrain and culture. Growing up on the beaches of Florida, Gifford forged a deep connection with coastal landscapes. Pairing this well of sensitivity with jazzy improvisations on modernist themes, he perfected a sustainable modernism in cedar and glass, as attuned to natural landscapes as our animal natures. His biography and that of his clients are essential to decoding the work. In rediscovering Gifford's architecture, I also found a portal to a lost generation, truncated by AIDS and winnowed by the passage of time, but still resonant with artistic and cultural significance.

I learned that Marilyn Monroe, Elizabeth Taylor, Diahann Carroll, and Montgomery Clift once spurned Hollywood limos for the rustic charm of Fire Island's boardwalks. Truman Capote wrote *Breakfast at Tiffany's* here. Diane von Fürstenberg showed off her latest wrap dresses for an audience that included Halston, Giorgio Sant'Angelo, Calvin Klein, and Geoffrey Beene. Jerry Herman's piano reverberated with the crashing surf. Composer Ned Rorem was moved by the staccato rhythms of the new, modern beach houses "architected by Horace Gifford so that you live simultaneously indoors and out."[7] Today, an equivalent talent roster evokes the aloof, gated compounds of the Hamptons or Malibu. But these celebrities lived in modestly scaled homes alongside middle-class vacationers, all with equal access to Fire Island's natural beauty. For both the famous and the obscure, Gifford turned heads as he strode down the beach from meeting to meeting "wearing a Speedo and carrying an attaché case," an amused client recalled.[8]

The beach house might seem an unlikely vehicle for social change, but Gifford's little homes exerted a considerable influence upon their inhabitants. His architecture resisted the creeping acquisitiveness of mid-century America, and his injunctions to clients reflected Gifford's respect for the inherent fragility of America's coastlines. Unlike many architects, Gifford attempted to reduce the size of his structures. "Sometimes the client's ideas must be challenged...Usually they can be reduced in cost and size, and still satisfy them."[9] In the car-free milieu of Fire Island, he choreographed a ritual of stepping down off of the public boardwalk, physically reconnecting with the landscape, and proceeding through a winding path before entering a home. He resisted fences. He left doors off closets to limit the stockpiling of possessions. He discouraged washers and dryers. He urged clients to tote little baskets of toiletries to the bathroom. He loathed painted surfaces, clipped lawns, and all of the brute force involved in tending a typical suburban home. There was a conspicuous lack of accommodation for televisions. Bedrooms remained small to focus activity within the public spaces. Life in a Gifford home prescribed an artful form of camping.

Some clients balked at Gifford's enforced simplicity. Others reveled in the generosity of his liberated and libertine spaces. Graciously appointed, open-plan kitchens invited group participation. Interior space passed almost imperceptibly into, or cantilevered thrillingly over, the dunes. Soaring ceilings extracted grandeur out of the smallest footprints. Sleek "piano" hinges eliminated lumpen displays of hardware while keeping doors exceptionally stable in houses that drifted with the sands. Light switches positioned knee-high on the walls minimized their visibility. Grooves between horizontal and vertical surfaces created shadow lines that allowed each plane to float in space. Exposed ceiling joists spun precise and elaborate traceries.

Over time, an element of seduction entered into his work. The majority of his clients were queer men, a demographic that came into full visibility for the first time during Gifford's twenty-year reign as a prolific beach-house architect. These two decades were roughly bisected by the Stonewall Rebellion of 1969, the Greenwich Village revolt against pervasive police harassment at gay establishments. Out of this watershed moment, the Gay Pride Movement ascended and social constraints fell away. Gifford's serene 1960s pavilions provided refuge from a hostile world, while his exuberant post-Stonewall, pre-AIDS masterpieces orchestrated bacchanals of liberation. Sculpted outdoor shower stalls evoked cedar orgasmatrons. Cushions on Gifford's built-in sofas sidled into their adjacent conversation pits to create tailored love nests. In the early 1970s, Gifford carved a sheepskin-lined pit into his own 1965 residence, a fitting surface for a wolf on the prowl. The make-out loft entered the architectural lexicon via Horace Gifford. Such embellishments were of a piece with the broader countercultural cur-

OPPOSITE, UPPER LEFT:
Evans-DePass House, Fire Island Pines, NY, 1965

OPPOSITE, UPPER RIGHT:
Cashel House, Fire Island Pines, NY, 1969

OPPOSITE, BELOW:
Wittstein-Miller House II, Fire Island Pines, NY, 1963

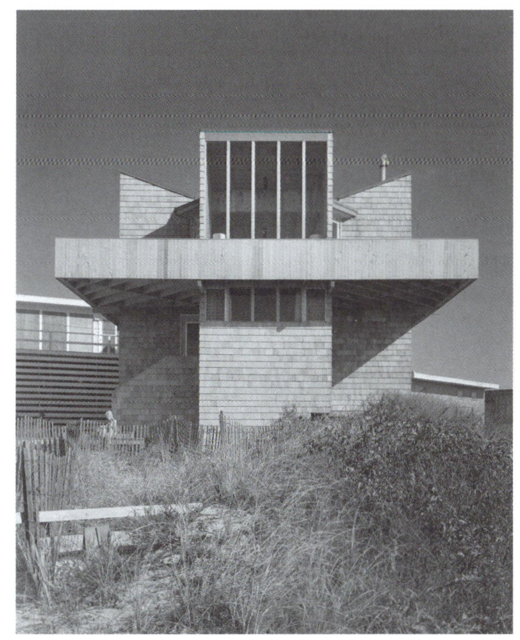

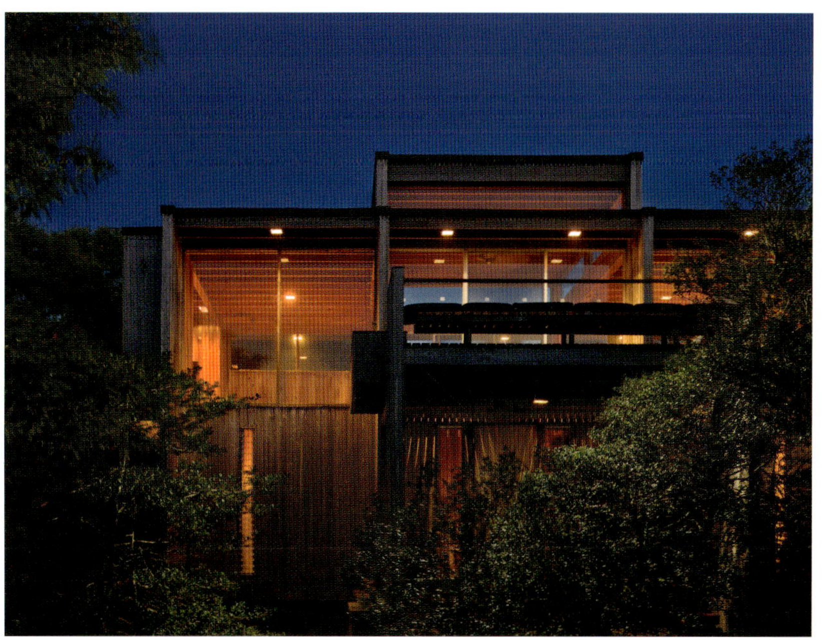

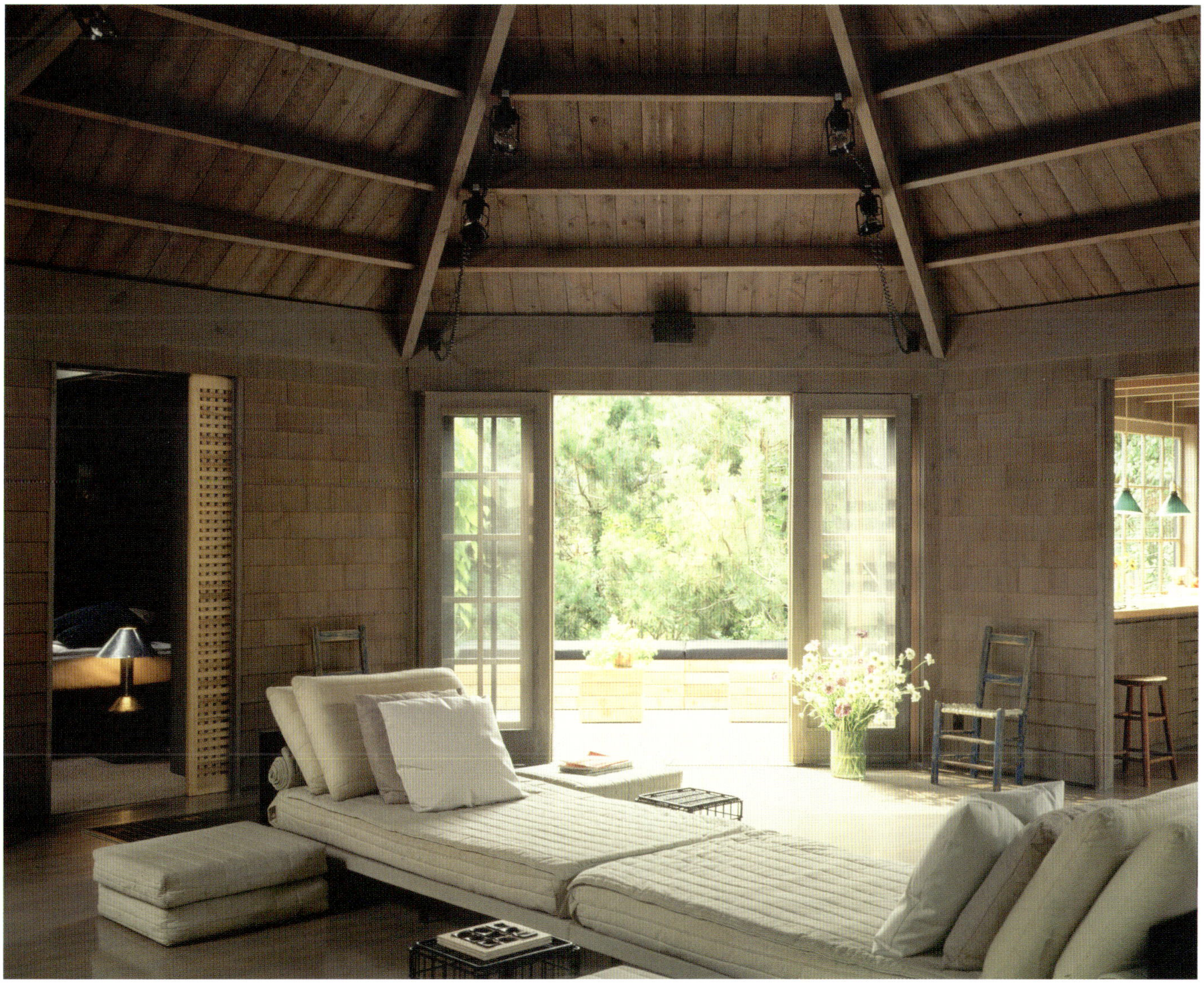

rents that ran through his work. Bathrooms that traded mirrors for glass walls invited prurience on occasion, but they also drew the inhabitant's gaze away from himself toward an increasingly threatened nature.

Gifford's grounding in both the natural world and the art of construction buffered him against the more bombastic tendencies of his field. A series of revolutions in taste marked the history of architecture in the twentieth century, and each revolution required the abandonment of all that the previous generation had wrought. Gifford practiced in an evolutionary spirit, transcending an earlier beach-shack vernacular while maintaining the virtue of simplicity. He did not fetishize the notion of originality, and freely borrowed from mentors, colleagues, and the local vernacular on his journey to realizing a unique body of work. Of his beach houses, he required only that "They must excite me" and "Let them look undated in twenty years."[10] It was the agenda of a man with sufficient confidence to be modest.

Living in a Gifford home, as I did, invites certain psychological assumptions about the man who invented it: a light-flooded interior; a thoughtfully conceived plan; a symbiotic connection to all around it; everything in its place. But the resemblance of the man to his architecture is illusory. Horace Gifford was haunted by specters personal and political. His life followed the operatic arc of repression, liberation, and despair that befell a lost generation. Through it all, he responded with optimistic, forward-looking dwellings that "reach out and grab for light."[11] The seventy-eight modern homes that he created between 1961 and 1981, for an audience that would perish before properly recognizing his achievements, constitute a unique contribution to twentieth-century domestic architecture.

Gifford's beach houses are revealing artifacts of their time and place. But they also speak to the perennial notion—dating back to Hadrian's Villa and perhaps before—that crafting a more direct relationship with the natural world will lead to a restorative existence. The fact that this notion, and this architecture, is often sustained by the artificial and acquisitive life of the city remains one of its many paradoxes. But the longing for Eden persists, and the work in these pages bears the mark of a restless search for that illusory place. So perhaps the architecture reveals the man after all. Gifford liked to say that "someday we will learn to live *with* nature instead of living *on* nature."[12] In their simplicity, sustainability, and sensual delight, the beach houses of Horace Gifford ennoble that wish and speak to us today with renewed power and purpose.

POSTSCRIPT TO THE FIRST EDITION

I first ventured to Fire Island Pines in 1998, knowing almost nothing about the place. My most vivid recollection from that day is holding my boyfriend's hand in public without fear. That freedom was followed by lifelong friendships cultivated in a shared house and a continuing exploration of its architecture. Yet I found that this enclave was often dismissed for its hedonistic ways and shallow muscle boys, an outlook most tenaciously espoused by those who had never traveled there. As far as I was concerned, hedonism had never curtailed *my* reading list; the Athenians were rather fond of muscles, too. My resistance to this critique of Fire Island softened as I came to understand my relative privilege within the gay community. The truth is that a place of such natural and man-made beauty can be intimidating. And queer people can be fierce gatekeepers. My work, as I see it, is to nudge the gates open with a spoonful of exaltation and a dash of demystification.

The critical and popular reception to *Fire Island Modernist* surpassed my wildest hopes. Horace Gifford now features in the architectural canon, and he is rightly seen as a forerunner of the sustainability movement. The study of "queer space," previously confined to ephemeral cruising spots, defunct bars, and movie sets, can now focus on a robust body of work created by, and for, us. Others have recently applied their expertise to this once-overlooked utopia. A literary history of Fire Island, a nine-episode podcast, and an art-historical survey exemplify the new bounty.[13] Handsome renovations of Gifford's homes abound, aided by his archive of original drawings. I founded Pines Modern, a nonprofit that further documents Fire Island Pines' mid-century legacy, and my architectural firm is currently restoring five of the homes found in these pages. There is much to celebrate.

However, Fire Island's once-sleepy real estate market has doubled in value since the pandemic. The resulting development pressures reveal the limits of public education. Diminutive homes, tailored to individual sites in communion with nature, now compete with a rental revenue formula that prescribes identical and enormous bedrooms, all with en suite bathrooms. Without legal protections, Gifford houses continue to be torn down or radically altered.[14] Even well restored homes often hide behind massive fences, forsaking the communitarian ethos that forms the radical heart of his work. We have embraced Horace Gifford's aesthetic, but not his values. Perhaps this last critique is a quibble, given the complete destruction that climate change portends for this glorified sandbar. This new edition of *Fire Island Modernist* remains a love letter, but it is also a call to action. There is still work to be done.

OPPOSITE, ABOVE:
Men of the Pines, ca. 1968

OPPOSITE, BELOW:
Men of the Pines, ca. 1977

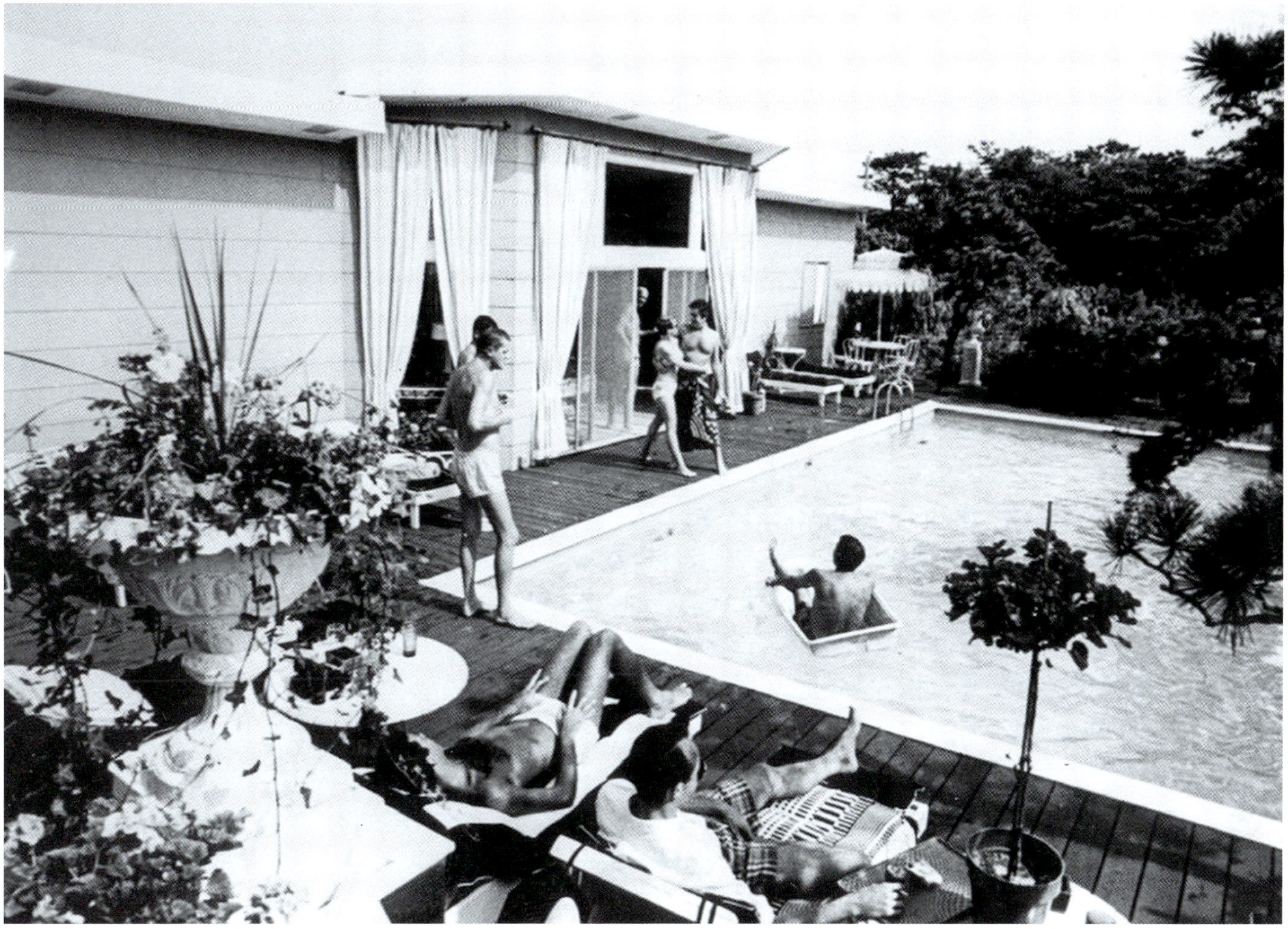

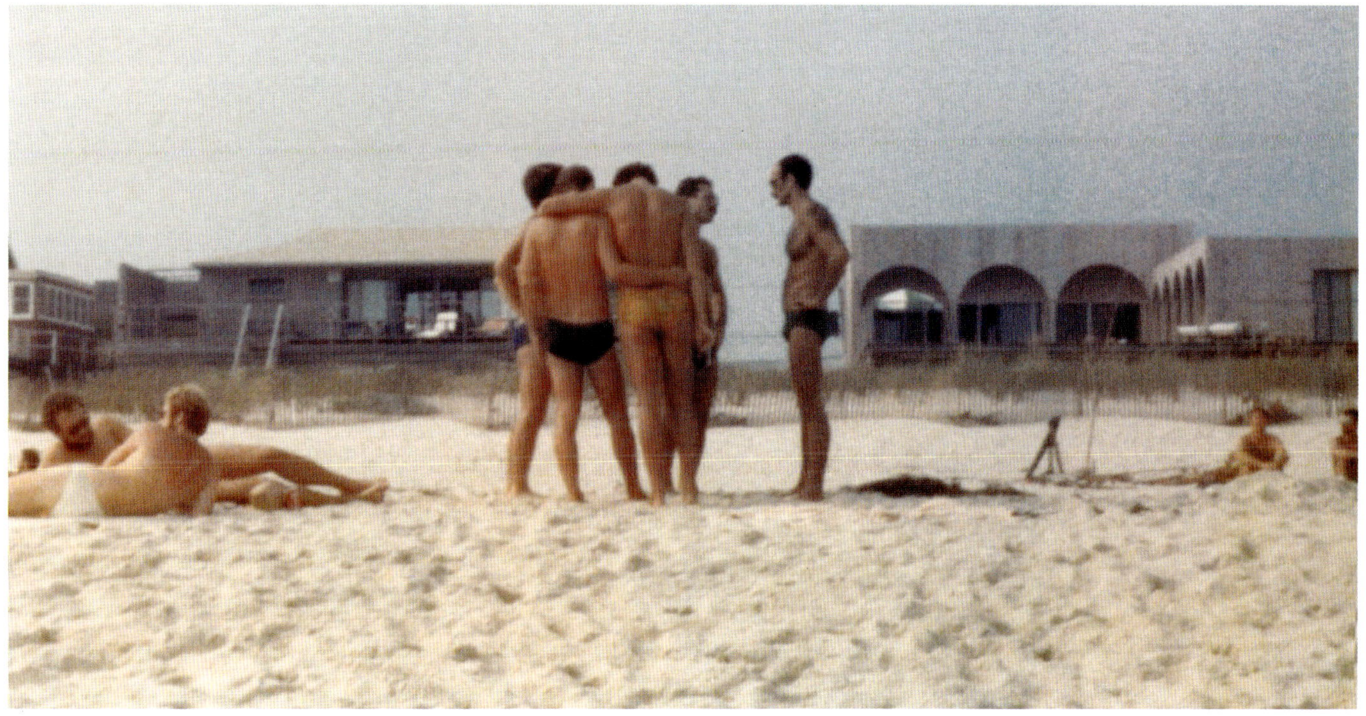

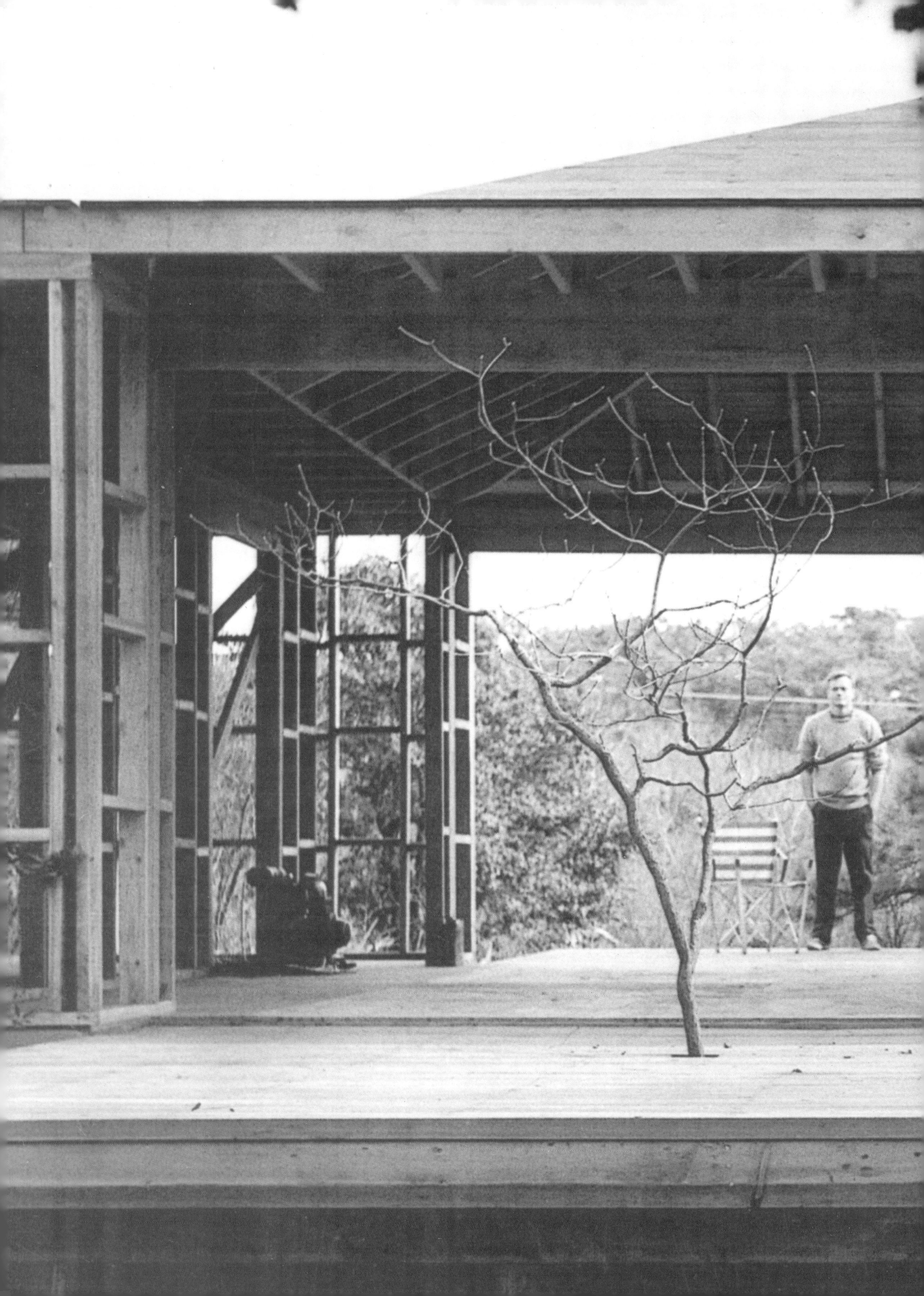

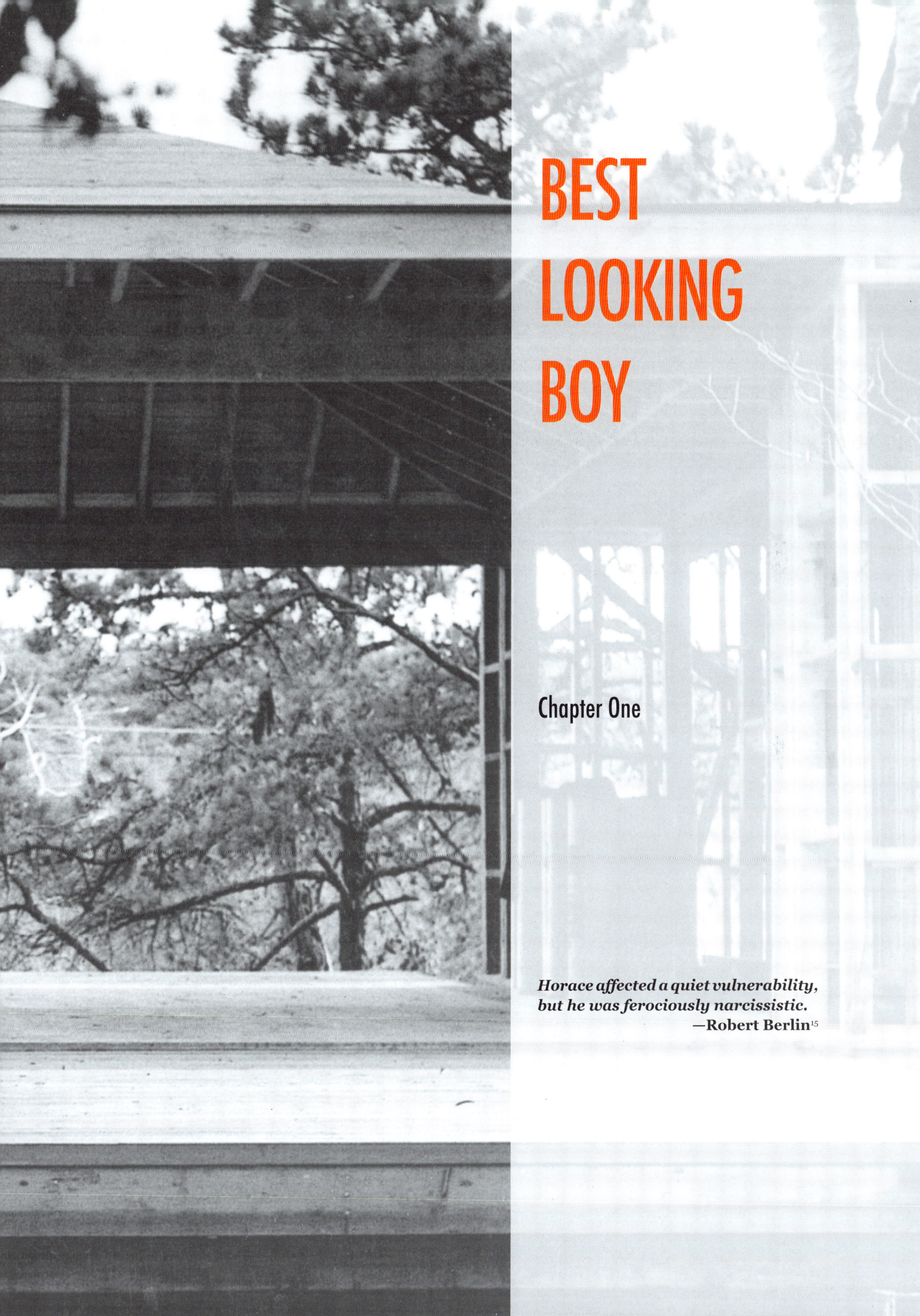

BEST LOOKING BOY

Chapter One

Horace affected a quiet vulnerability, but he was ferociously narcissistic.

—**Robert Berlin**[15]

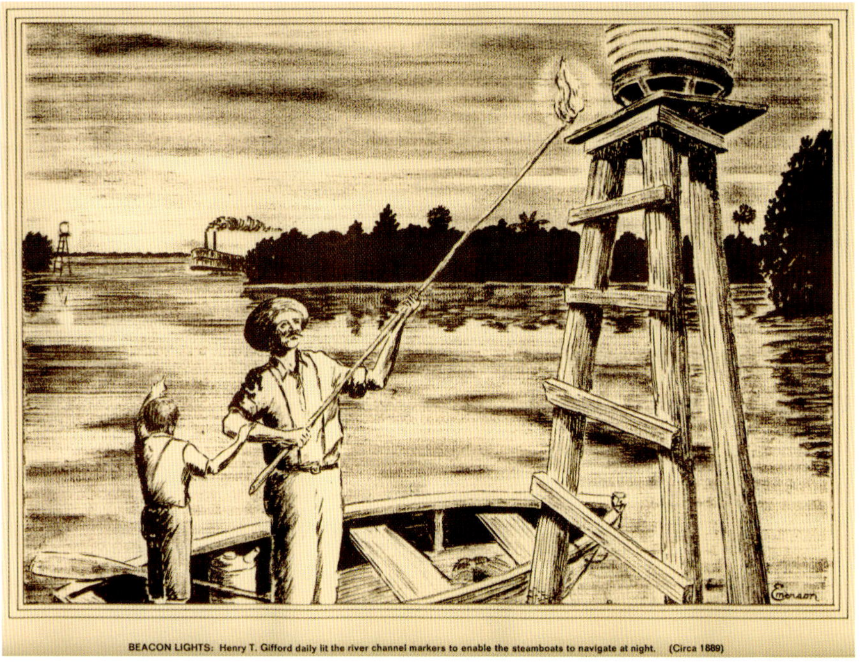

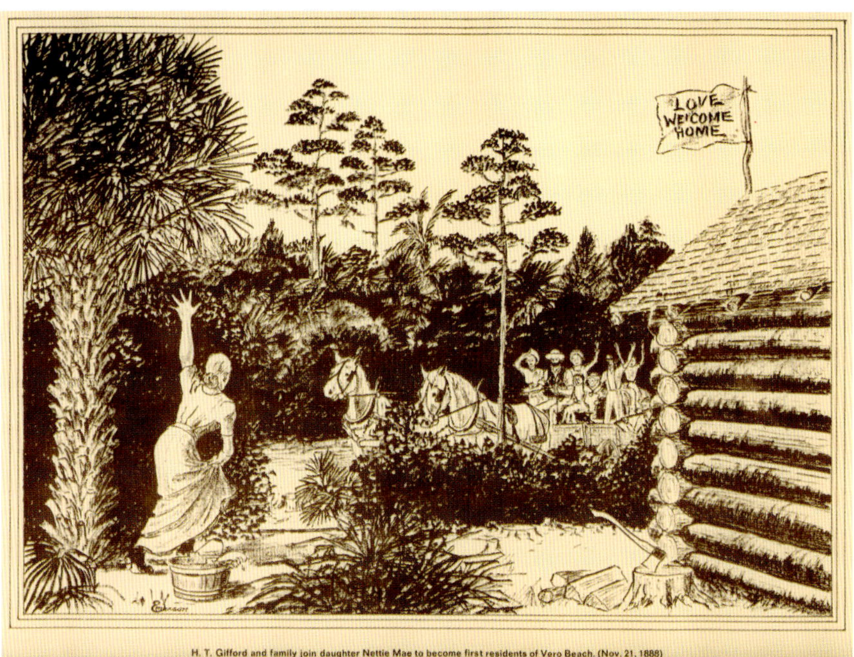

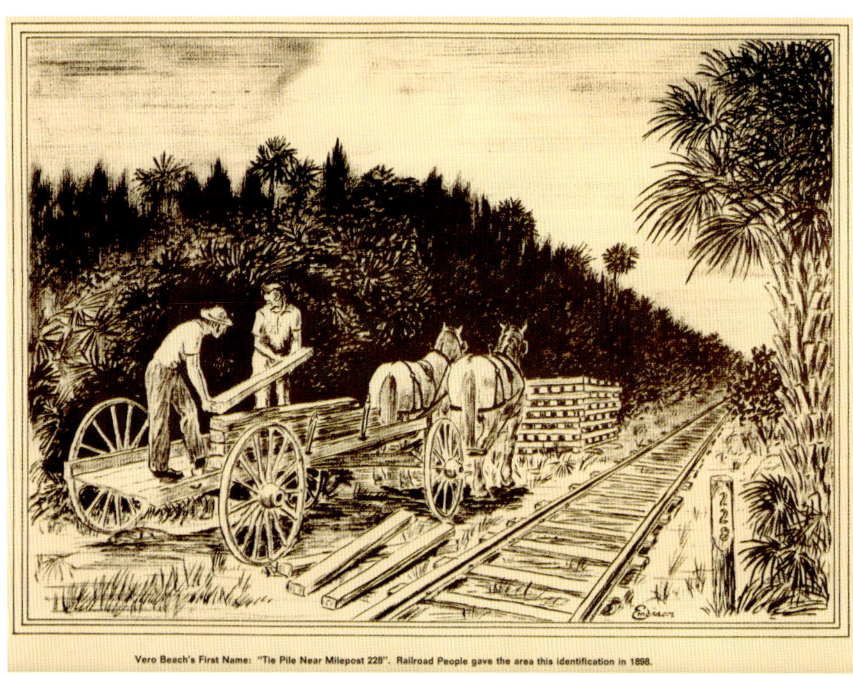

PAGES 20–21:

Horace Gifford at Gifford House under construction, Fire Island Pines, 1961

ABOVE:

Great-grandfather Henry T. Gifford and grandfather Friend Gifford light the channel markers of Vero, FL, ca. 1889, to help steamboats navigate at night.

CENTER:

Nellie Mae Gifford, Horace Gifford's great-aunt, greets her family from Vermont as they arrive, November 1888. The family lived in a self-built log cabin.

BELOW:

Grandfather Friend Gifford helped to lay Vero's nascent railroad.

OPPOSITE, LEFT:

Gifford and younger brother J. Charles, ca. 1935

OPPOSITE, RIGHT:

Gifford as an adolescent, ca. 1946

There is a photograph of Horace Gifford during the construction of his first beach house that, like the man himself, is both revealing and enigmatic. Striding from house to house along the boardwalks of Fire Island, he took hundreds of slides of his projects and the people that built them. Only once did he pause to train the camera on himself. In the background, partially obscured by tree branches, he stands casually dressed, hands in pockets, looking proud but diffident: the young architect staking his claim. As a roofer toils overhead, he appears to gaze straight into the camera. The exact contours of his expression are too far in the distance to be in focus. In this photograph, as in Gifford's work, nature occupies the foreground. Like a lens, the architecture in the middle serves chiefly as a frame of the view beyond. Its upturned roof inscribes the space below with a perfect square. Unshorn tree trunks bear the weight of his creation. A sapling—today a towering presence but then just a trifle—wriggles through the decking, as if to remind us that nature eventually reclaims all that man creates. Leaves blur the top of the frame. Gifford was only twenty-eight years old when he drove his first piling into the lightly settled sands of Fire Island, yet his work already possessed clarity and conviction. How a young man could emerge so fully formed remains somewhat mysterious, but his early life provides some clues.

A child of the Great Depression, Horace Henry Gifford II was born on August 7, 1932, in Vero Beach, Florida, to a family of middling means but high social standing. His great-grandfather Henry T. Gifford was a founder of the hamlet of Vero in 1887, having made the trip south from his native Vermont, leaving his wife to join him later. Henry served as Vero's first postmaster, and also illuminated the Beacon Lights, channel markers that enabled steamboats to navigate the shoals by night. These were constructed of three angled pilings, twelve to fourteen feet high, with a lantern set on top that had to be refreshed every other day. Henry's wife, Sara, arrived the next year after a grueling journey that entailed riding a covered wagon to New London, Connecticut, followed by three steamer boats, two trains, and a sailboat. Sara is credited with naming the frontier settlement "Vero," Latin for "to speak the truth."

Henry's son (and Gifford's paternal grandfather, Friend Gifford) carried on the role of postmaster and helped build the nascent railroad before becoming a citrus farmer. He lived long enough to see his grandchildren become adults. It was a self-reliant clan: they hunted their own game, grew their own crops, and built their own homes. "People were rough and one didn't ask too many questions as to why they came here,"[16] Friend recalled of his fellow pioneers who ventured south to take advantage of affordable land offered by the federal Homestead Act of 1862. Friend married a teacher named Fannie, whose father, N. N. Penny, had distinguished himself as a sea captain and Florida pioneer of ferocious repute. In 1903, Friend and Fannie's son Horace became the first male child born in Vero.

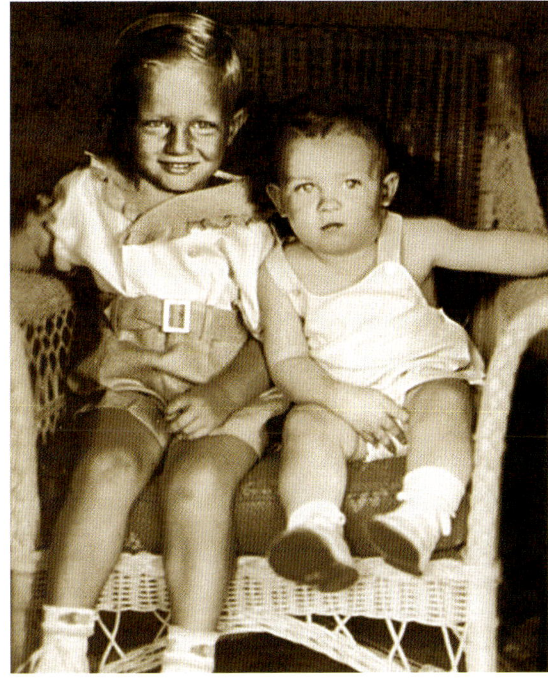

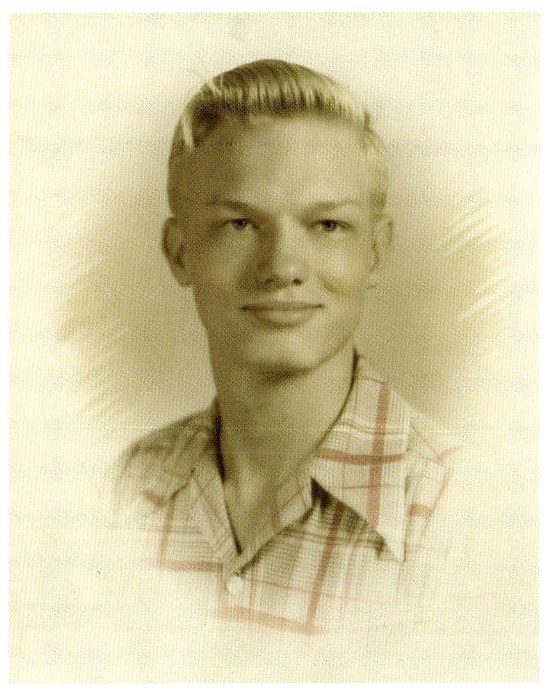

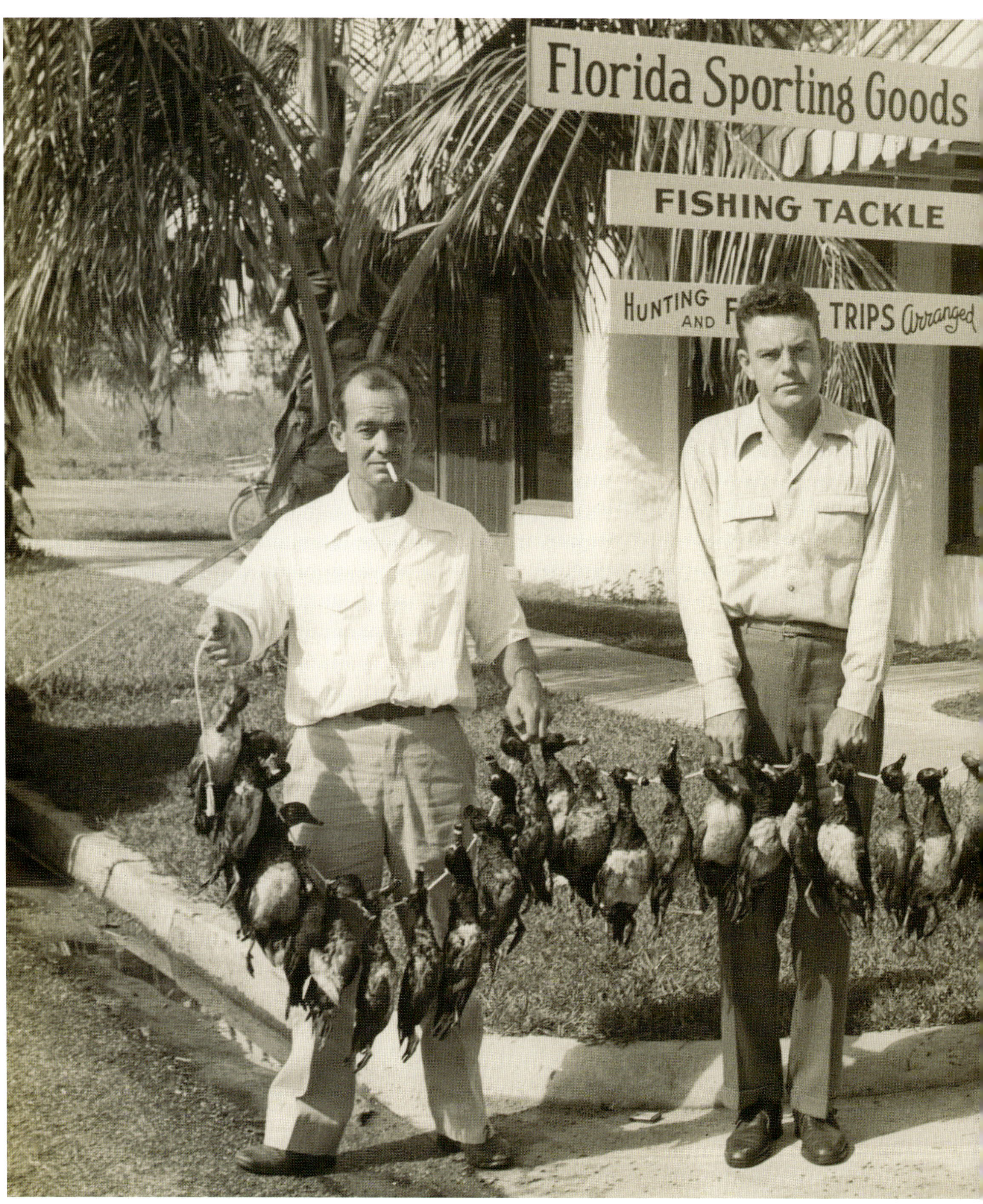
Florida Sporting Goods
FISHING TACKLE
HUNTING AND
TRIPS Arranged

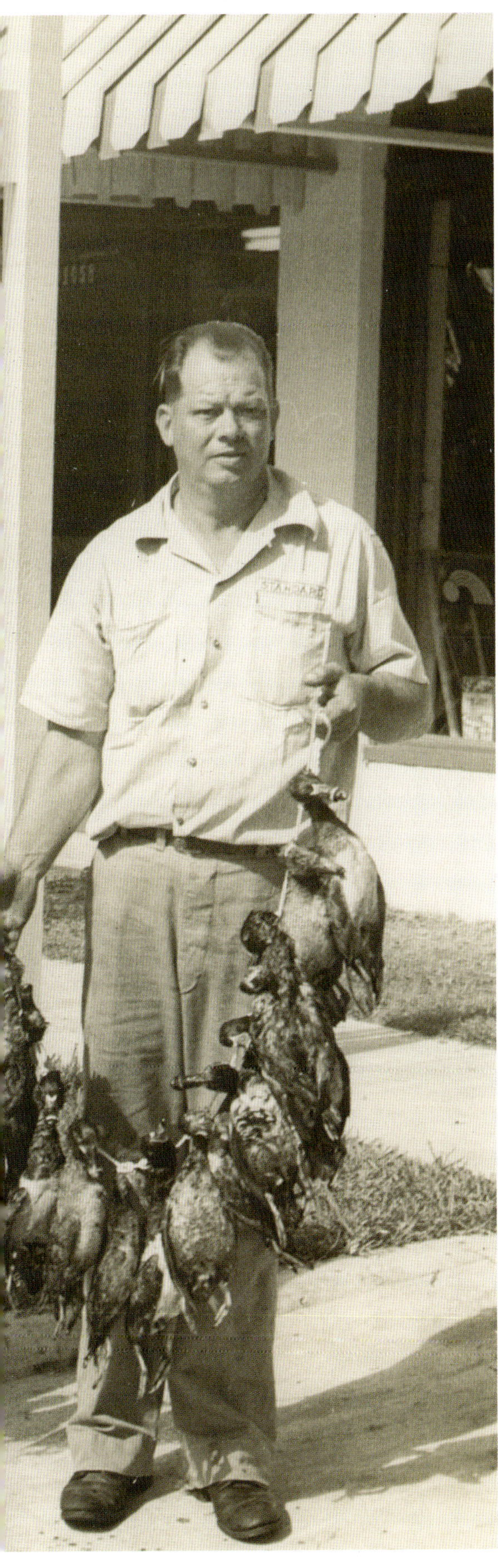

By the time Horace Junior was born, in 1932, the newly named Vero Beach was no longer a frontier, but it remained a small town of 2,500 people,[17] sprinkled with low-rise wooden structures in a smattering of vernacular styles. On narrower lots, one found "shotgun" houses, so named because they were one-room wide and a gunshot could pass through each room from front to back. Horace had an older half-sister, Jean, who remained his lifelong confidante. His younger brother, J. Charles, was born in 1934. Bookish, quiet, and strikingly handsome, Horace was an unlikely namesake for his father. The elder Gifford was an avid sportsman, local politician, and "simple steak and potatoes man,"[18] as his son described him. For twenty years, Horace Senior owned a filling station before becoming a partial owner of the Florida Sporting Goods Company, which supplied the professional baseball teams that practiced nearby in the winter. Young Horace worked in the store, affecting nonchalance in the presence of the celebrity athletes who patronized it. Both parents were educated, however, and encouraged their son to pursue his studies. Sometime in his childhood—perhaps to distinguish him from his father—people began calling Horace Junior "Giff," and the nickname stuck for his entire life.

As a teenager, Giff developed a love of music and theater, acquiring a sizable trove of albums that would rival the book collection in all of his subsequent dwellings. In high school, Giff was an overachiever—class president, coeditor of the yearbook, band officer, president of the student Kiwanis Club, and such a thespian that, according to the yearbook, he could navigate the school theater with his eyes closed. Fellow classmates voted him "Best Looking Boy."[19]

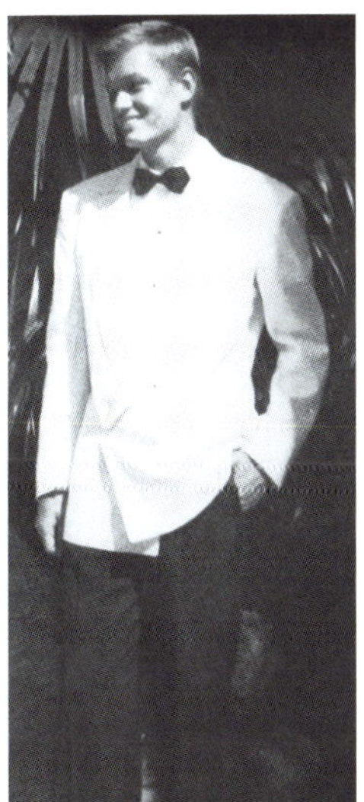

LEFT:
Horace Gifford Sr., right, poses with friends in front of his sporting goods store after a duck hunt, 1950s.

RIGHT:
Gifford in a high school yearbook spread that declared him "Best Looking Boy"

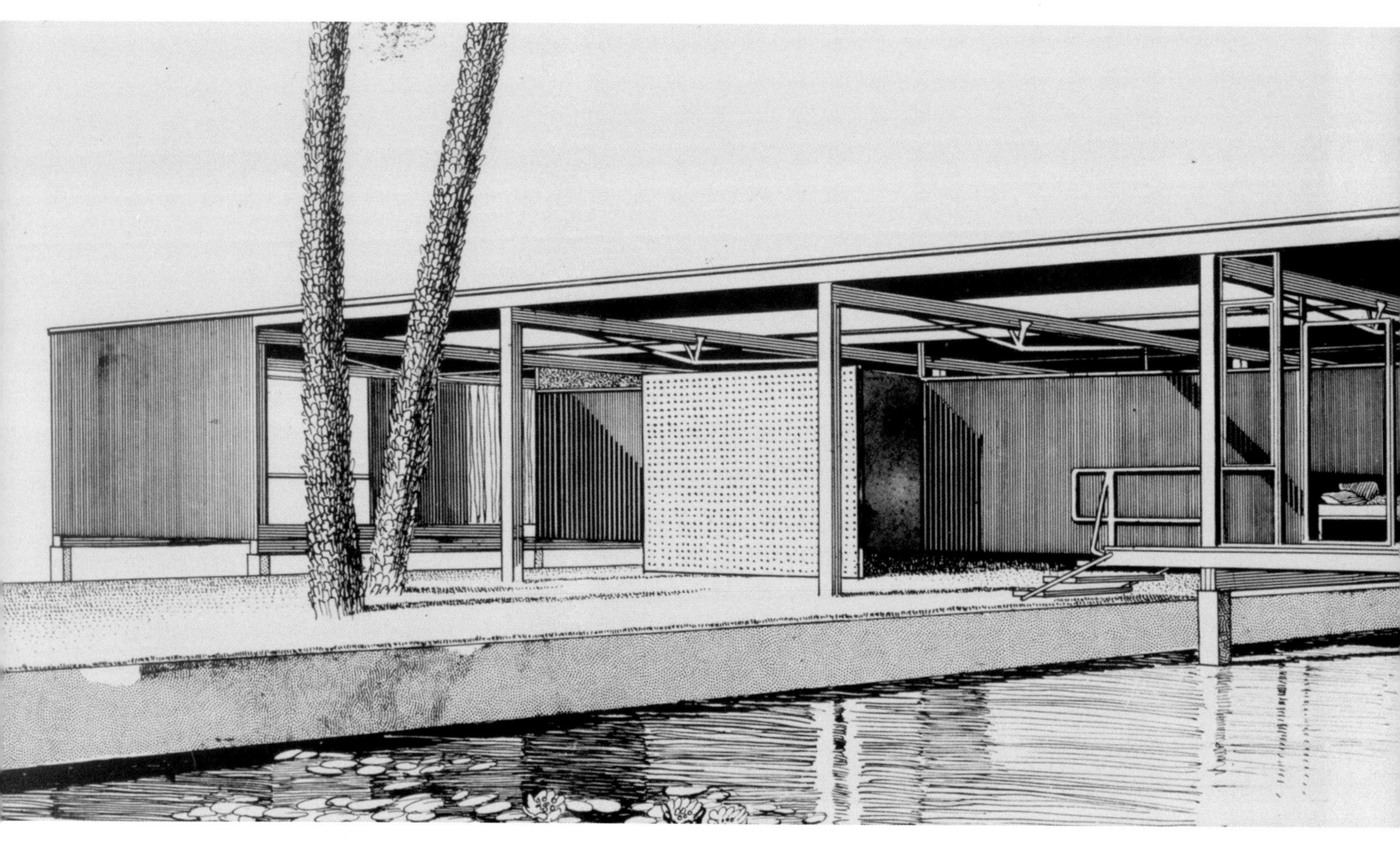

His uncle Fred Gifford, a respected physician, influenced Giff's decision to enter the University of Florida at Gainesville as a premed student, but he soon switched to architecture. Younger brother J. Charles resembled Giff in appearance, but the boys shared little else in common and maintained a distant relationship as adults. A football star in high school, Charles became an undertaker and spent virtually his entire life in Vero Beach.[20] The Giffords' home life was outwardly conventional but strained by the periodic depressions of both parents, a trait passed on to at least two of their three children.[21] Giff found solace in the beautiful beaches and thrilling swamps all around him, where he once stepped on an alligator. His favorite activity was swimming, and he was occasionally joined by porpoises on his long dips in the ocean. He was, as one friend described, "addicted to water," and an increasingly impressive physique betrayed his passion.[22] During college, he swam laps every day in the Olympic-size pool.

Although Gifford's undergraduate work has not survived, a classmate recalled an "intense, dedicated, and sensitive student" in thrall to the kinetic facades and minimalist means of the young Paul Rudolph.[23] Beginning in the late 1940s, the Kentucky-born Rudolph attracted a following as the author of modernist winter homes along the coast of Sarasota, Florida. These homes shared much in common with other International Style dwellings, such as the Case Study Homes in California: modularity and prefabrication, a fluidity between indoor and outdoor spaces, and open floor plans. Rudolph's designs staked out new ground with movable shading devices and louvered "jalousie" windows that imbued the homes with a climatic dexterity appropriate to the hot and humid coastline. He further distinguished them with innovative materials that he discovered while serving in the U.S. Navy. These theatrical interior spaces were a departure from the sober functionalism of his Harvard training, incorporating sybaritic touches that would later be associated with the bachelor pads that coincided with the sexual revolution. Early in his career, in Florida, Rudolph had realized a compelling, regionally inflected modernism. These light and seemingly impermanent pavilions, set amid an exotic and unsullied landscape, resonated with the optimistic postwar aspiration for carefree outdoor leisure. Both Rudolph and his business partner Ralph Twitchell lectured at the University of Florida while Horace was a student there. In his Fire Island summer houses, Gifford would effect a plausible transplantation,

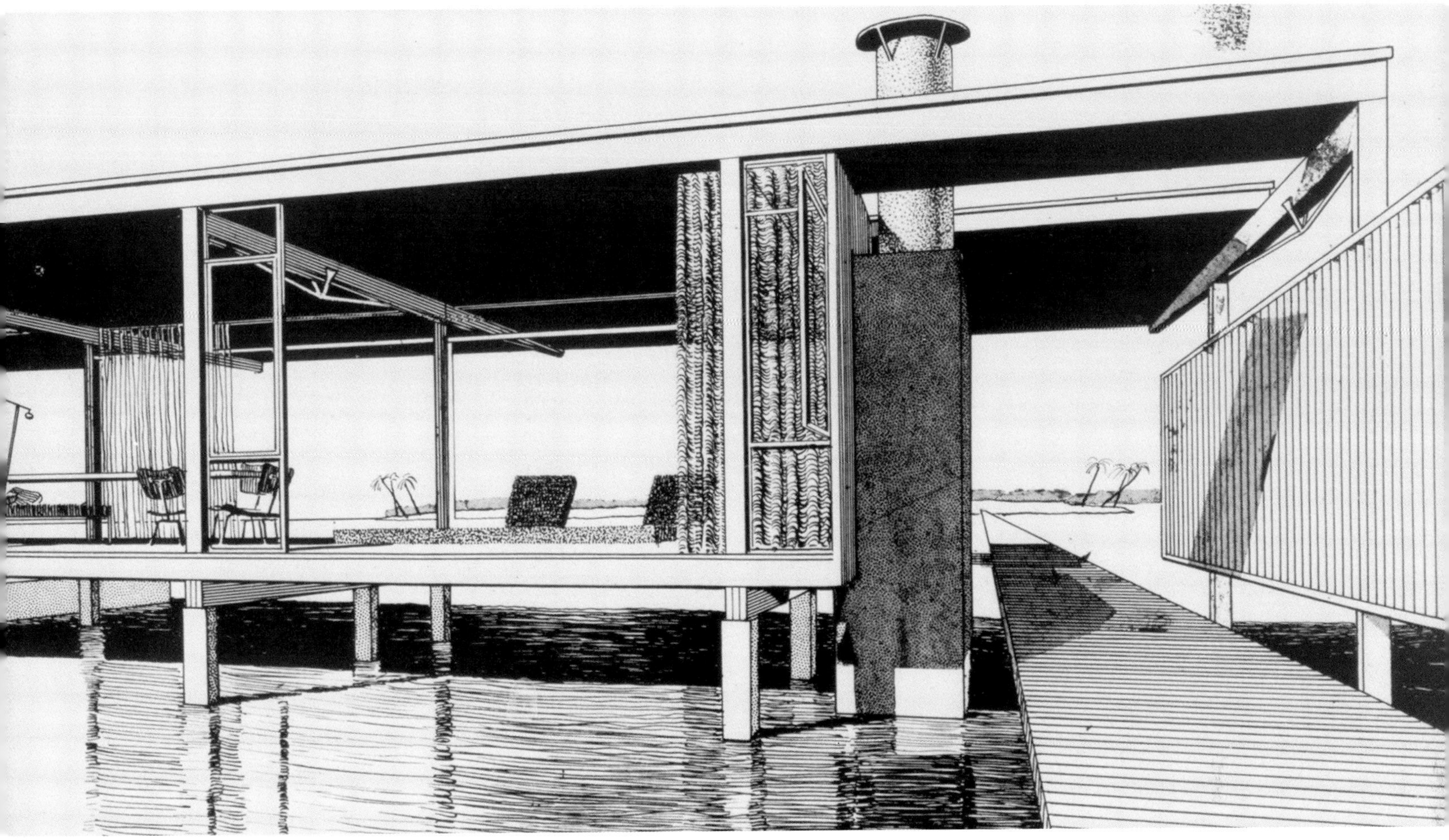

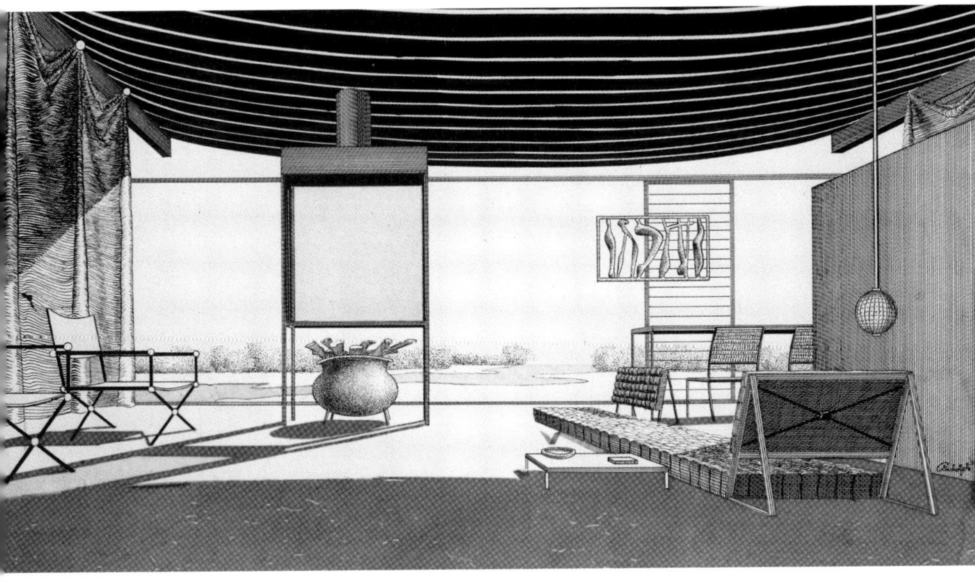

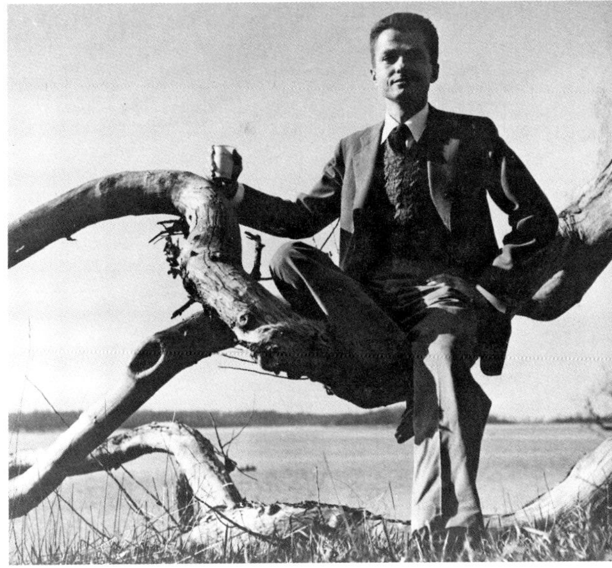

ABOVE:
Paul Rudolph and Ralph Twitchell, Finney Guest House, Siesta Key, FL, 1950

LOWER LEFT:
Paul Rudolph and Ralph Twitchell, Cocoon House, Siesta Key, FL, 1950

LOWER RIGHT:
Paul Rudolph, ca. 1950

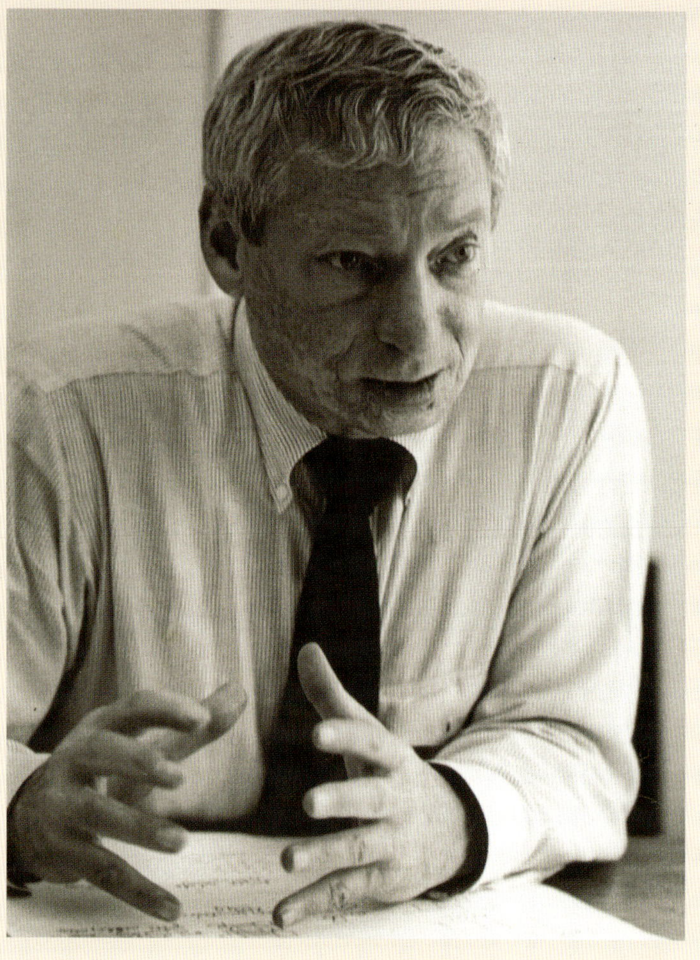

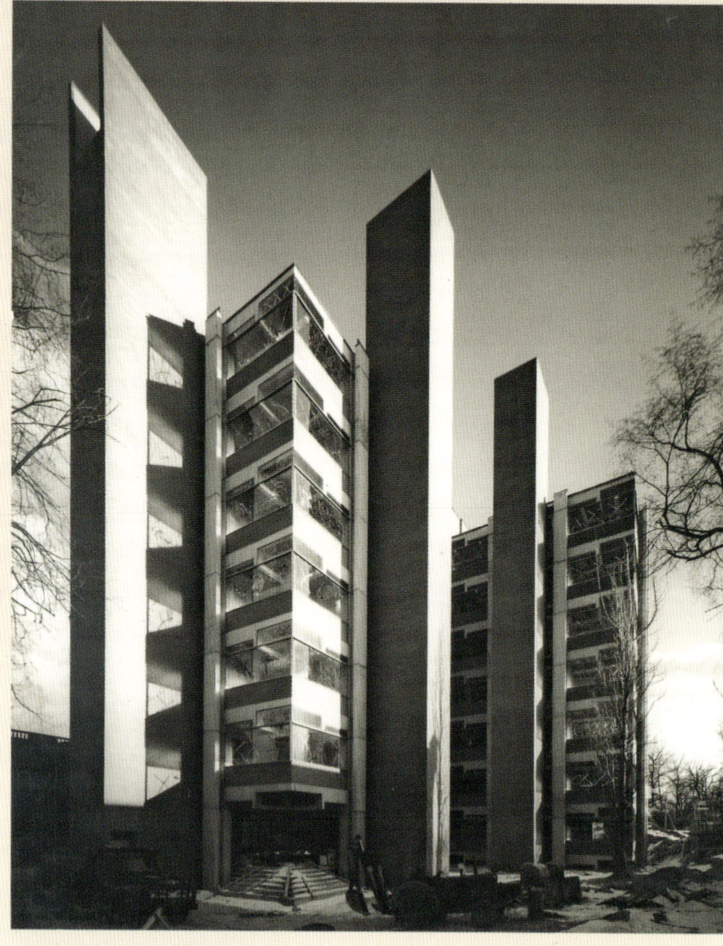

UNIVERSITY of PENNSYLVANIA

PHILADELPHIA 4

Office of Scholarships and Student Aid

April 3, 1958

Mr. Horace Gifford
3929 Pine Street
Philadelphia 4
Pennsylvania

Dear Mr. Gifford:

We are delighted to learn that you wish to accept the scholarship offered to you for study in the Graduate Division of the School of Fine Arts during the Fall semester of the next academic year.

You may obtain your scholarship voucher at this office, 200 Logan Hall, when you register in September. We look forward to seeing you then.

Sincerely,

Douglas Root Dickson

DOUGLAS ROOT DICKSON
Director

DRD/bd

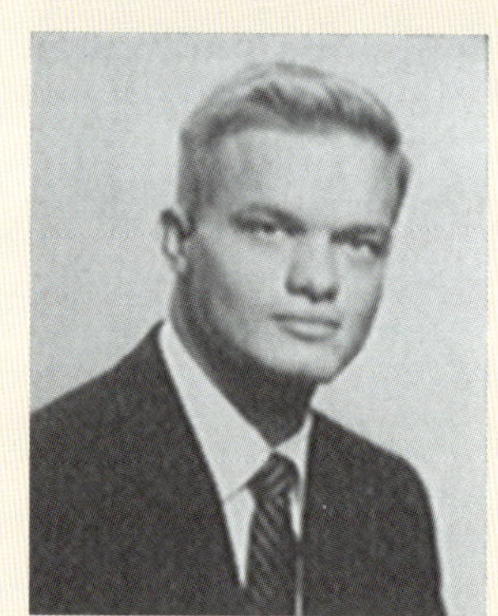

across the latitudes, of many ideas that informed Sarasota's winter homes.

Though it lacked the prestige of northeastern schools such as Harvard and Yale, the University of Florida benefited from older faculty members who ventured south after being forced to retire at sixty-five from the Ivy League. It was also invigorated by Alfred Browning Parker, a young modernist under the spell of Frank Lloyd Wright, who helped define Miami's postwar architectural scene. As a student, Gifford honed a supremely confident and stubborn manner. The architecture school had a display space on which students pinned up their best projects. Asked to design a gathering place, Gifford produced a spare, open-air composition of artfully arrayed flagstones and retaining walls. His uncomprehending instructor scrawled: "Where is the architecture?" on his presentation, followed by a "D."[24] This was the project that Gifford chose to display.

He was also openly gay in college, a briefly tenable stance in the permissive university atmosphere that existed during the early to mid-fifties. Newly liberated and out of the family fold, Gifford discovered that he possessed a natural charisma. Robert Berlin, a psychology major and a close friend, found him to be a fascinating study. "He affected a quiet vulnerability, but he was anything but. He was ferociously narcissistic...and naturally blonde, but he kept it just a few shades lighter."[25] Gifford's talent for architecture developed in tandem with his skill at seduction. His classmate recalled observing Gifford at work in the local "mixed" club. "During the holiday, he would be sitting there at the bar, and appearing not to look left or right, and after a few minutes he would get up and tap somebody on the shoulder and say 'Let's go.'"[26]

The university's free thinkers in matters sexual and otherwise were routed by a McCarthyesque investigation in 1958, and the same political winds soon brought Sarasota's architectural renaissance to a close. To live his life, and to realize his ambitions, Horace Gifford completed his degree in 1955 and moved to Manhattan. He struggled at first to fulfill his talents, writing to his friend that, "I'm working for a dull architect, making a good salary, but I don't know for how long."[27] For a time he even flirted with a modeling career. But a new architectural hero reignited Gifford's single-minded focus. His name was Louis Kahn.

Kahn's buildings crystallized into mysterious clusters of forms with a hierarchy of "served" and "servant" spaces, one type dedicated to artful inhabitation and the other reserved for services and transitions. Shimmering glass and steel, the twentieth century's architectural totems, receded in Kahn's work in favor of stone, concrete, and brick, all powerfully composed with monumentality, geometric rigor, and structural clarity to evoke abstracted ruins. Kahn distinguished himself as a conjurer of poetic and literal gravitas, and students flocked to his lectures and studios at Yale University. In 1957, Paul Rudolph was appointed director of the Yale School of Architecture. As if to mark his territory, one of Rudolph's first official acts was the "renovation" of Kahn's celebrated Yale Art Gallery, obscuring its carefully exposed construction details with drywall. Then he forced the resignation of Kahn's close colleague Josef Albers.[28] Yale proved too small to contain the two giants, and Kahn decamped for the University

OPPOSITE, UPPER LEFT:
Louis Kahn, ca. 1965

OPPOSITE, UPPER RIGHT:
Louis Kahn, Richards Medical Research Building, Philadelphia, PA, 1957–65

OPPOSITE, LOWER RIGHT:
Gifford in a 1955 University of Florida yearbook portrait

OPPOSITE, LOWER LEFT:
Letter to Horace Gifford from the University of Pennsylvania granting him a scholarship for his second semester, 1958

RIGHT:
Frank Lloyd Wright, Unity Temple, Oak Park, IL, 1905–08

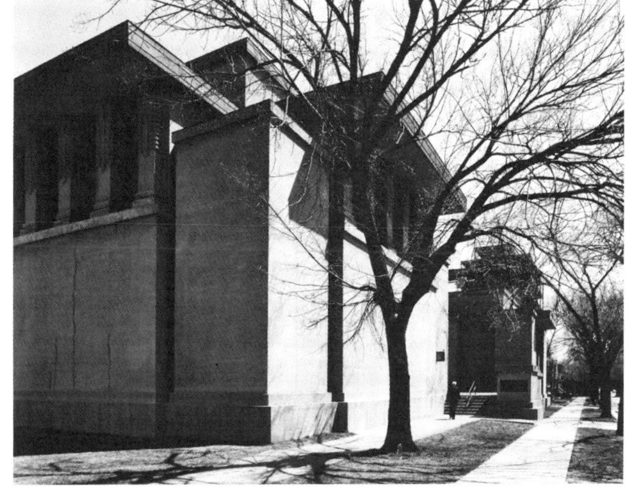

of Pennsylvania. This transpired just as Horace Gifford was accepted for graduate studies at Yale, and now he had a decision to make. He chose to follow Kahn, and began a one-year master's program at the University of Pennsylvania in the spring of 1958.

Gifford's choice of Kahn over Rudolph marked the first of his catholic oscillations between the sensibilities of two very different icons of modern architecture. Whereas Kahn embraced gravity, Rudolph, and his cantilevers, defied it. If the plan was essential to understanding a Kahn building, the cross-section was the key to understanding a Rudolph. But while having significant differences, they shared a common architectural forebear in Frank Lloyd Wright. Kahn sometimes incorporated the exact dimensions of Wright's interior spaces within his own projects. Rudolph recognized Wright's superiority in matters of interior space and siting. Wright's Larkin Administrative Building and Unity Temple in particular exercised a profound influence upon both Kahn and Rudolph. And this trio of formative figures would situate Gifford's own work within a particularly American strain of modern architecture.

For reasons he never explained, Gifford dropped out of the University of Pennsylvania with a single semester remaining and a scholarship in hand. Kahn exerted a cultish influence over his students, yet Gifford was never a "joiner." It would not be the last time that he made a life-altering decision on impulse. Gifford returned to New York, reestablishing the employment with architect J. Gordon Carr that began shortly after his arrival from Florida. Carr had worked for both Raymond Hood and Raymond Loewy before distinguishing himself as a partner with William Lescaze. Together, he and Lescaze designed high-profile projects such as the Aviation Building at the 1939 World's Fair. By the 1950s, though, the firm was best known for its corporate interiors. Gifford rarely mentioned his employment with Carr. It was a "day job" that afforded him the opportunity to experiment with his own projects and engage in a prolific nightlife that traded on his confidence and his passions for architecture, music, and the theater. Soon, his social wanderings took him fifty miles east to Fire Island Pines, where talent, cunning, and excellent timing conspired to set a career in motion.

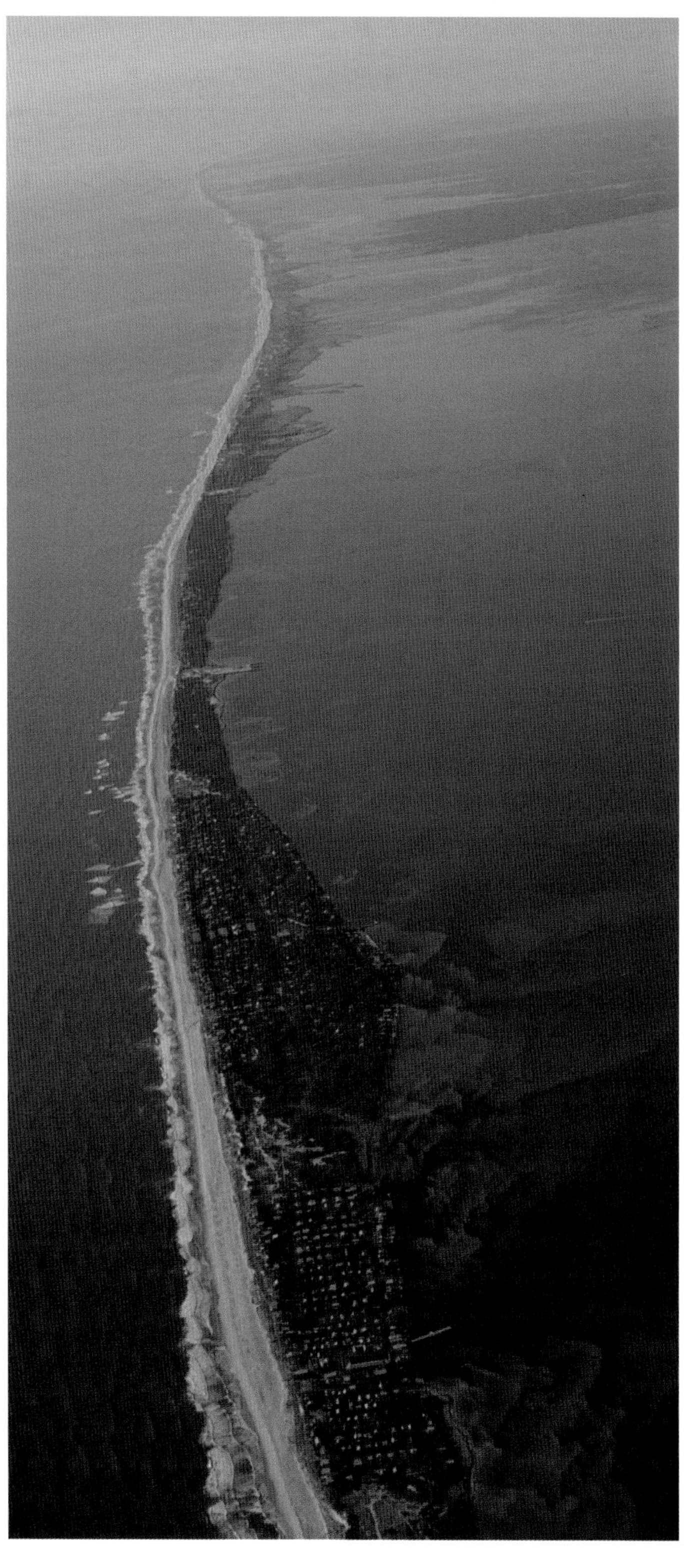

ABOVE:
Aerial photograph of Fire Island, NY, 1990s

OPPOSITE:
Horace Gifford, ca. 1960

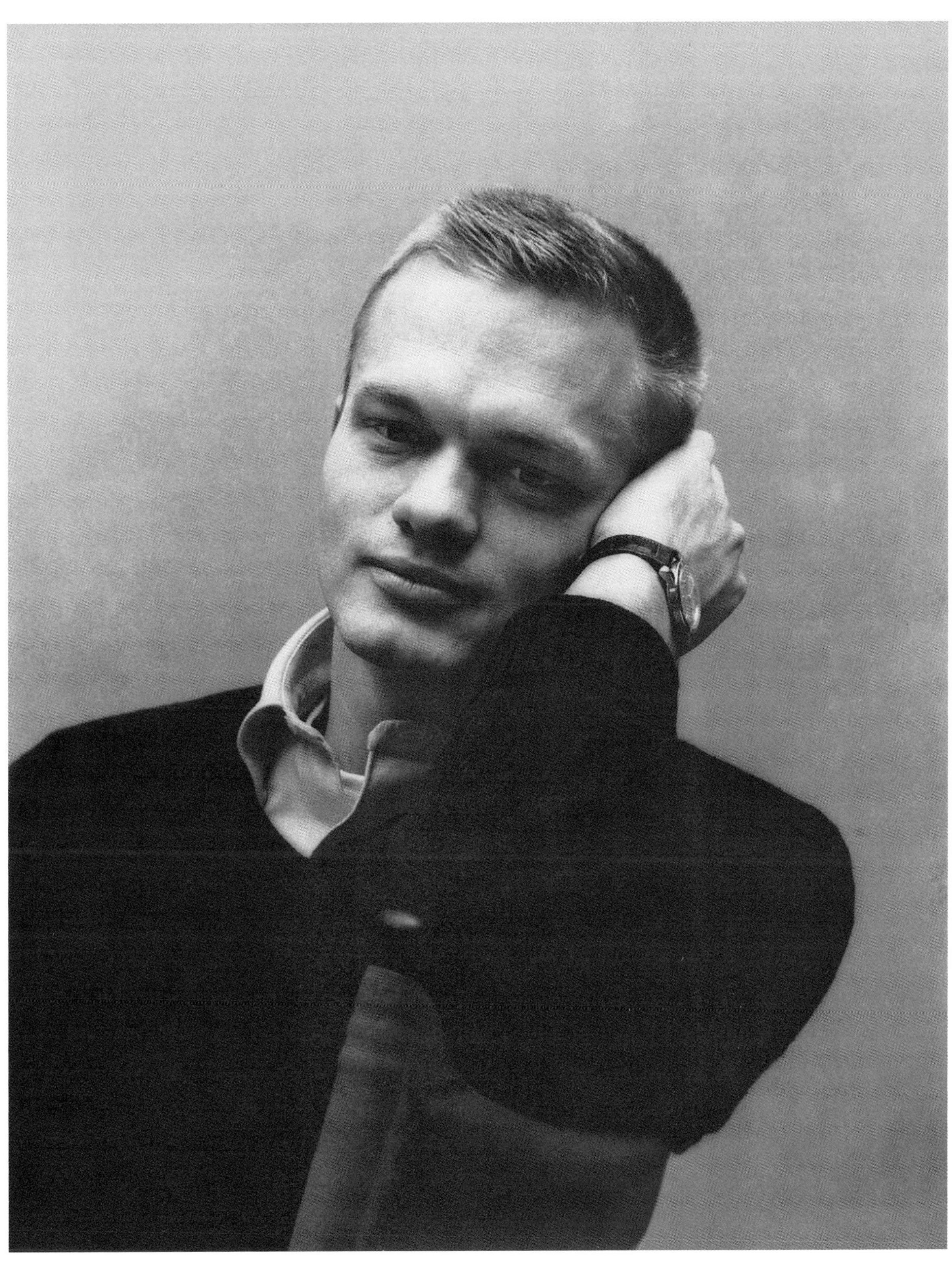

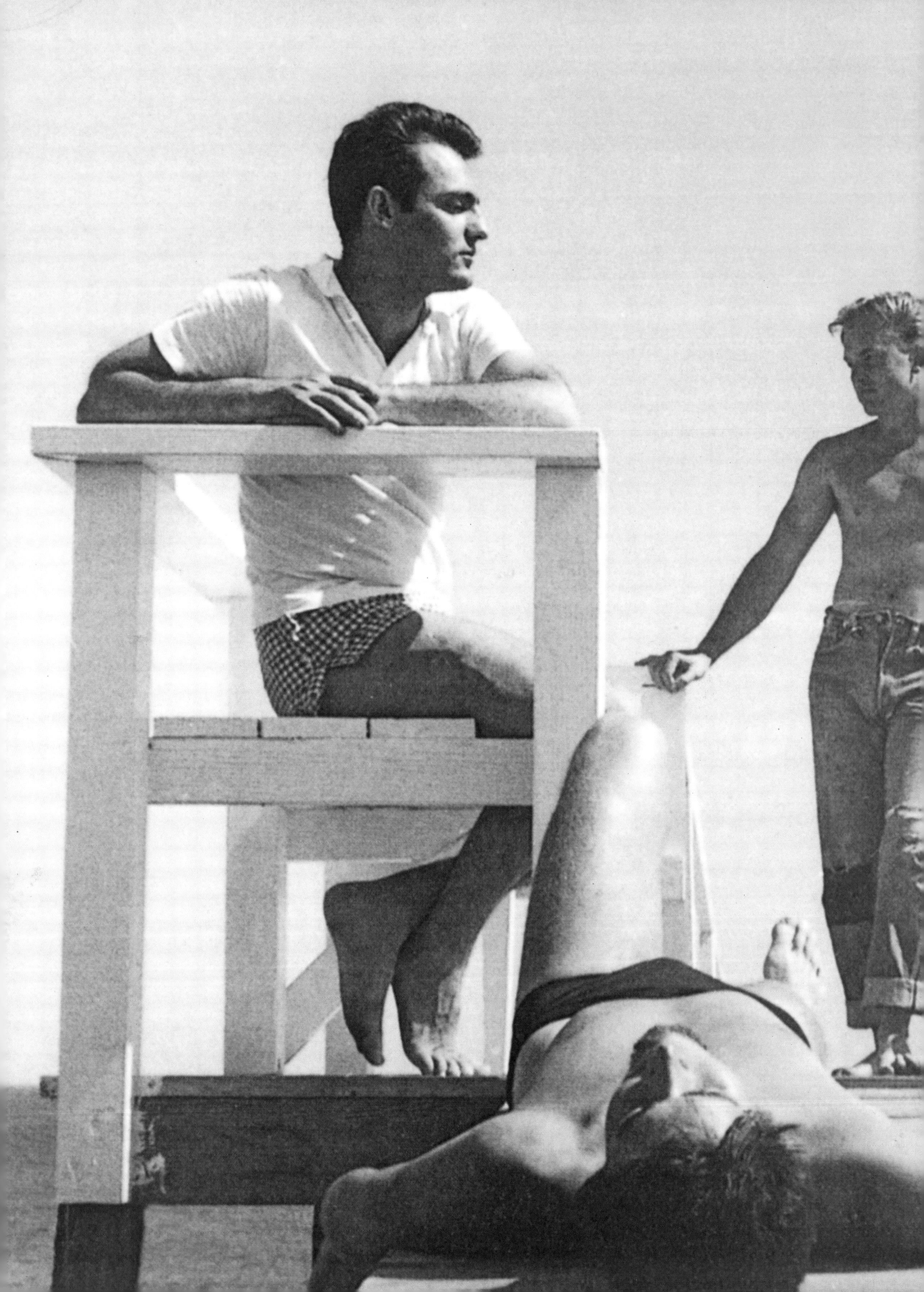

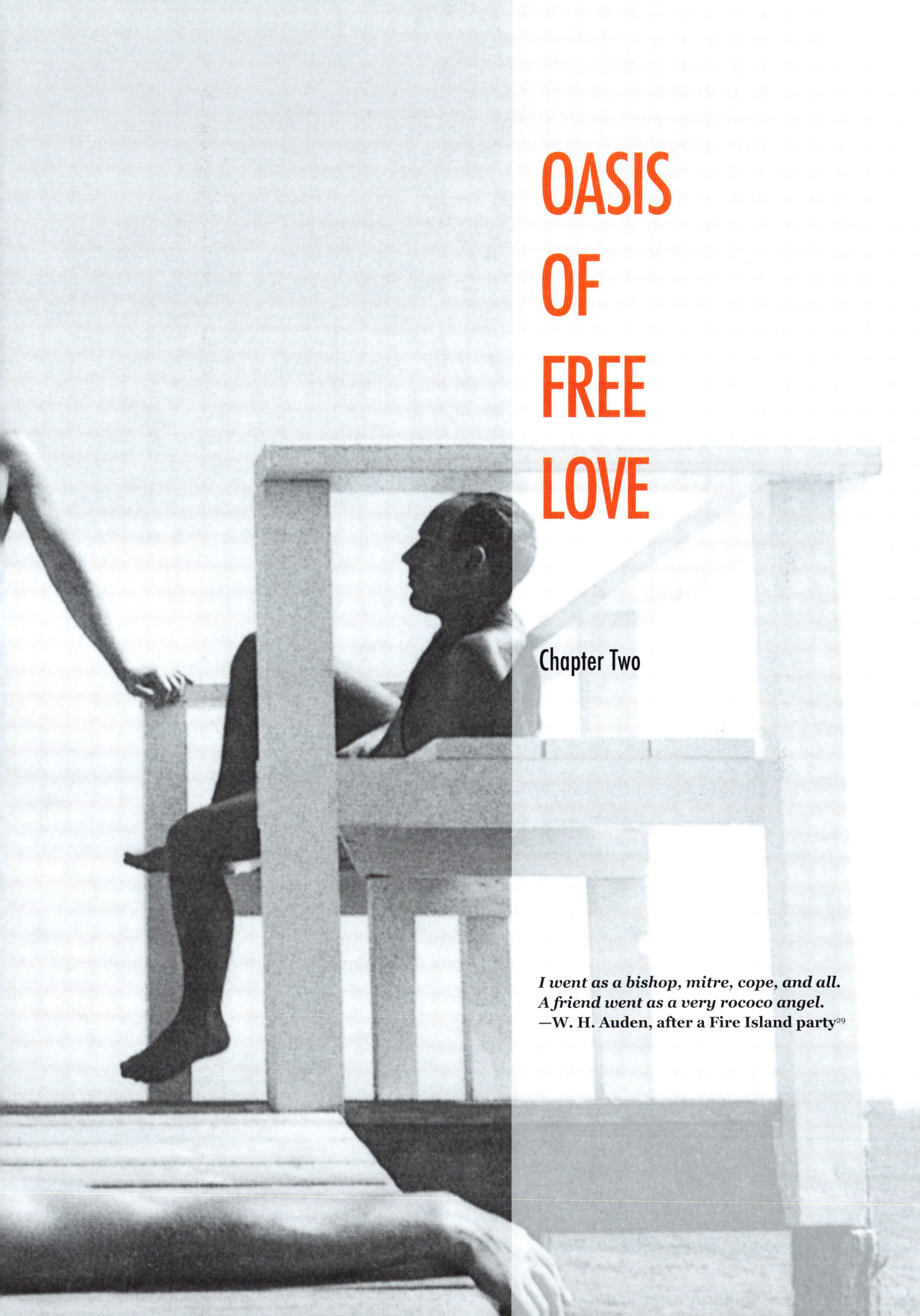

OASIS OF FREE LOVE

Chapter Two

I went as a bishop, mitre, cope, and all.
A friend went as a very rococo angel.
—W. H. Auden, after a Fire Island party[29]

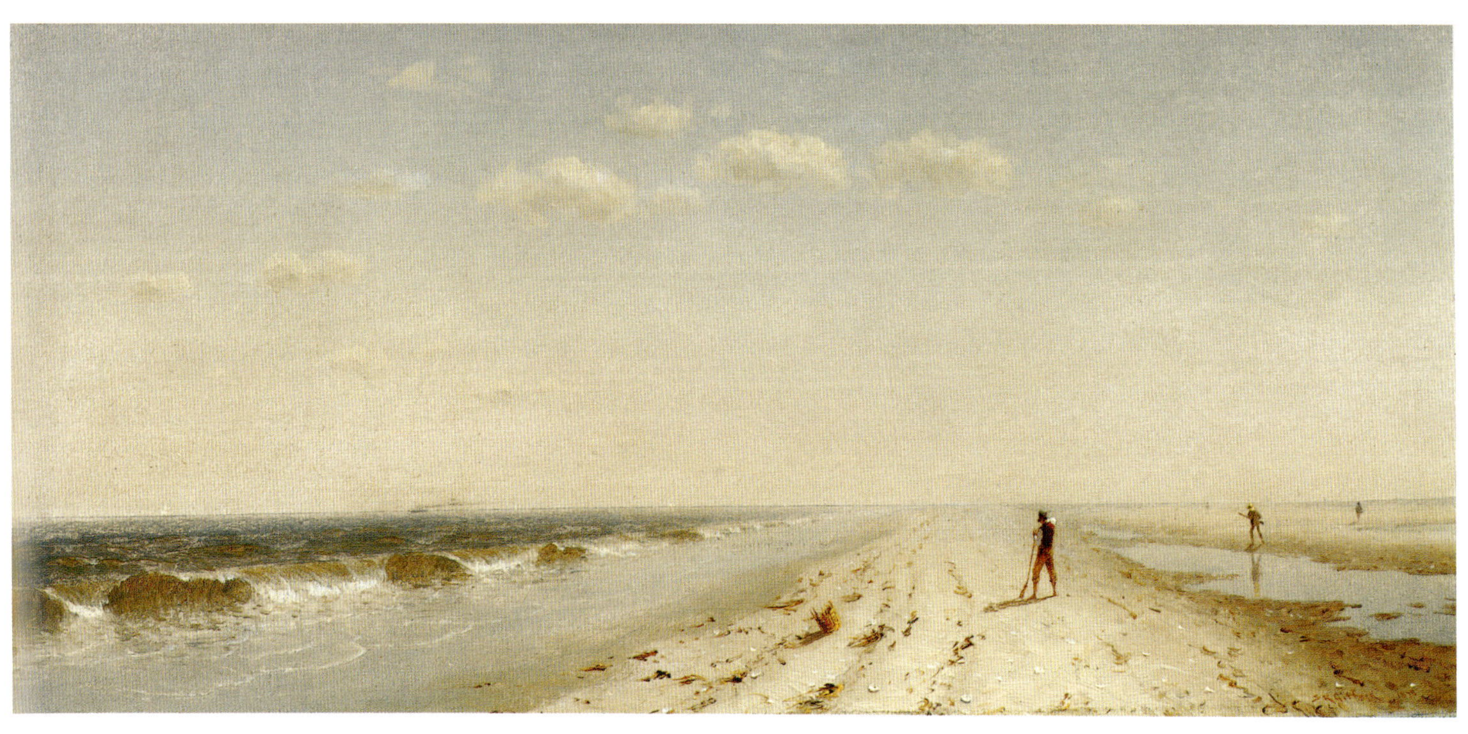

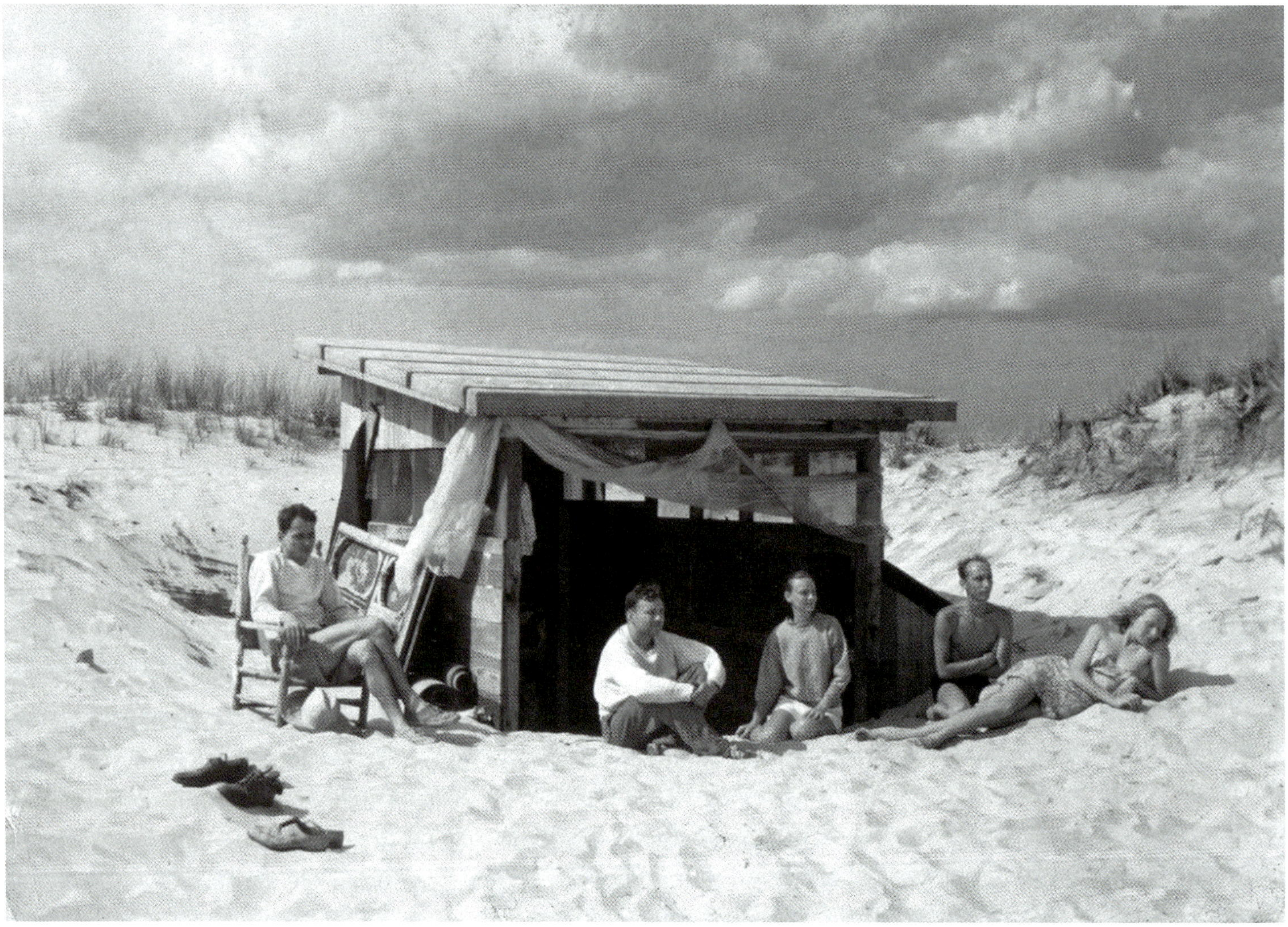

Fire Island remained a wild and unruly place long after its surrounding geographies were subdued by European settlers. Storms periodically sliced right through it, uniting the Atlantic Ocean with the Great South Bay. Some contend that Fire Island's name comes from the blazes that were set on its shores to guide ships to inlets. Others cite a transcription error from seventeenth-century English maps that christened the battered archipelago "Five Islands," or Dutch maps that called it *Vier* (Four) Islands.[30] Whatever the origins of its name, Fire Island has never really been one place but rather a collection of locales in varying degrees of separation from one another. It functions as a sacrificial barrier island, five miles out to sea from the mainland, and its resulting turbulent landscape has always been an edgier proposition for habitation than Long Island's flat and verdant plains. As such, its early residents tended toward the intrepid, the rustic, the foolhardy, and the criminal. Before 1850, it was known chiefly as a site of Native American wampum production and as a pirate's lair.

Fire Island's reinvention as a leisure destination dates to 1855, when the Surf Hotel opened at the western edge of the island. This was followed by the Perkinson Hotel, established in what is now the hamlet of Cherry Grove. Perkinson's was sufficiently renowned by 1882 to host Oscar Wilde, who recorded in his diary that Cherry Grove was "one of the most beautiful resorts he had ever visited."[31] Beginning in the early 1900s, other tiny communities dotted the island's thirty-one-mile length. Like Cherry Grove, these were resorts rather than towns, with small local populations that swelled with seasonal city vacationers who arrayed themselves in tiny demographic slivers across the island. After deed restrictions were lifted in 1928, Jews were free to congregate in Seaview, while Roman Catholics favored Saltaire.[32] *Social Register* WASPs fenced themselves into a restricted community called Point O' Woods. There were no roads to speak of, just boardwalks.

Just east of Point O' Woods, the community of Cherry Grove subsisted without a church or local police force, lending it the charm of a rustic setting without the prying eyes of a small town. Its tiny lots were populated with modest New England–style cottages. Private generators were the sole source of electricity, possessed by only a few wealthy residents. By the 1930s, it attracted a bohemian theater crowd whose members included many queer people. The influx rankled some of the more established families, and the last straw was a hurricane in 1938; it devastated the community and caused many longtime residents to depart. Yet one demographic's catastrophe was another's boon. Cherry Grove's newly cheap real estate and the relative safety accorded by geographic isolation conspired to create America's first predominantly and openly gay community. In a hostile world, there emerged an oasis of free love.

Unsurprisingly, Cherry Grove attracted a number of creative artists. The poets W. H. Auden and Stephen Spender vacationed together there with the novelist Christopher Isherwood through the 1940s. Lincoln Kirstein, a brilliant polymath who cofounded the New York City Ballet, captured them in a 1947 oceanfront photo (page 38). Another trio of artists that arrived in 1937 and stayed for twenty years was Paul Cadmus, his lover Jared French, and Jared's wife, Margaret French. Under the acronym PaJaMa (Paul-Jared-Margaret), their collaborative photographs taken in Cherry Grove set slyly erotic poses within architectural compositions. George Platt Lynes worked in a similar vein, pressing his lover Jonathan Tichenor into service as a model (both are pictured on page 6).

PAGES 32–33:
Photo by Paul Cadmus. Joe Santoro, Peter Buckley, Jensen Yow, and Fred Melton, Fire Island, NY, 1954

OPPOSITE, ABOVE:
Sanford R. Gifford, Fire Island Beach, NY, 1878

OPPOSITE, BELOW:
Beach-shack squatters, Lone Hill, NY, 1940s

RIGHT:
Postcard of Cherry Grove, NY, 1930s

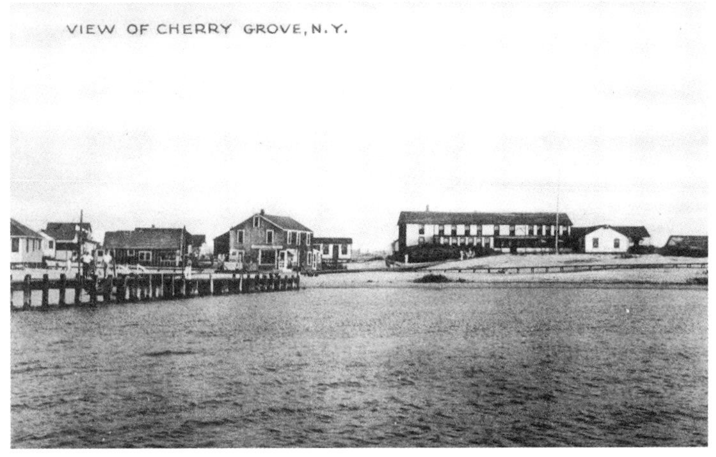

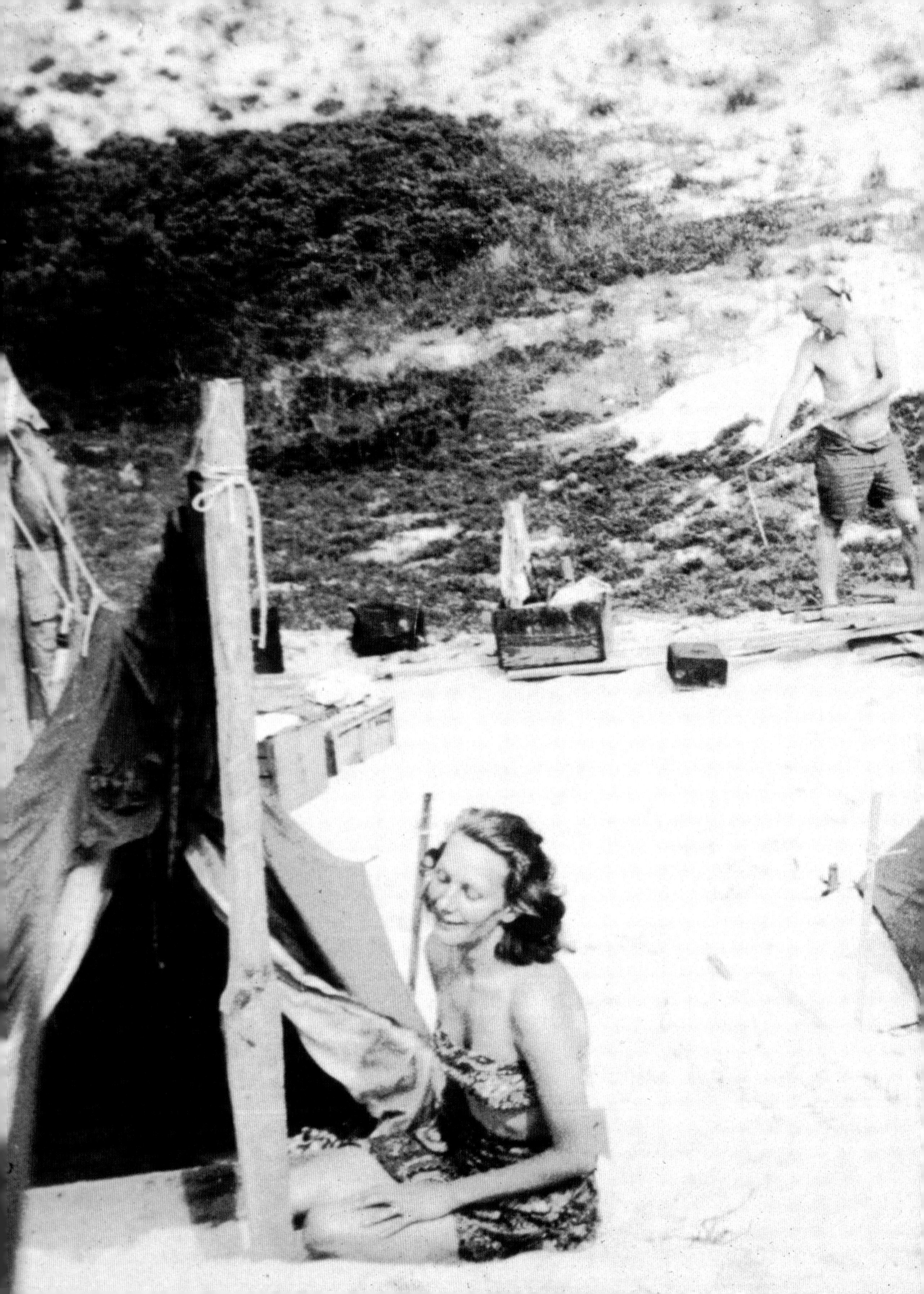

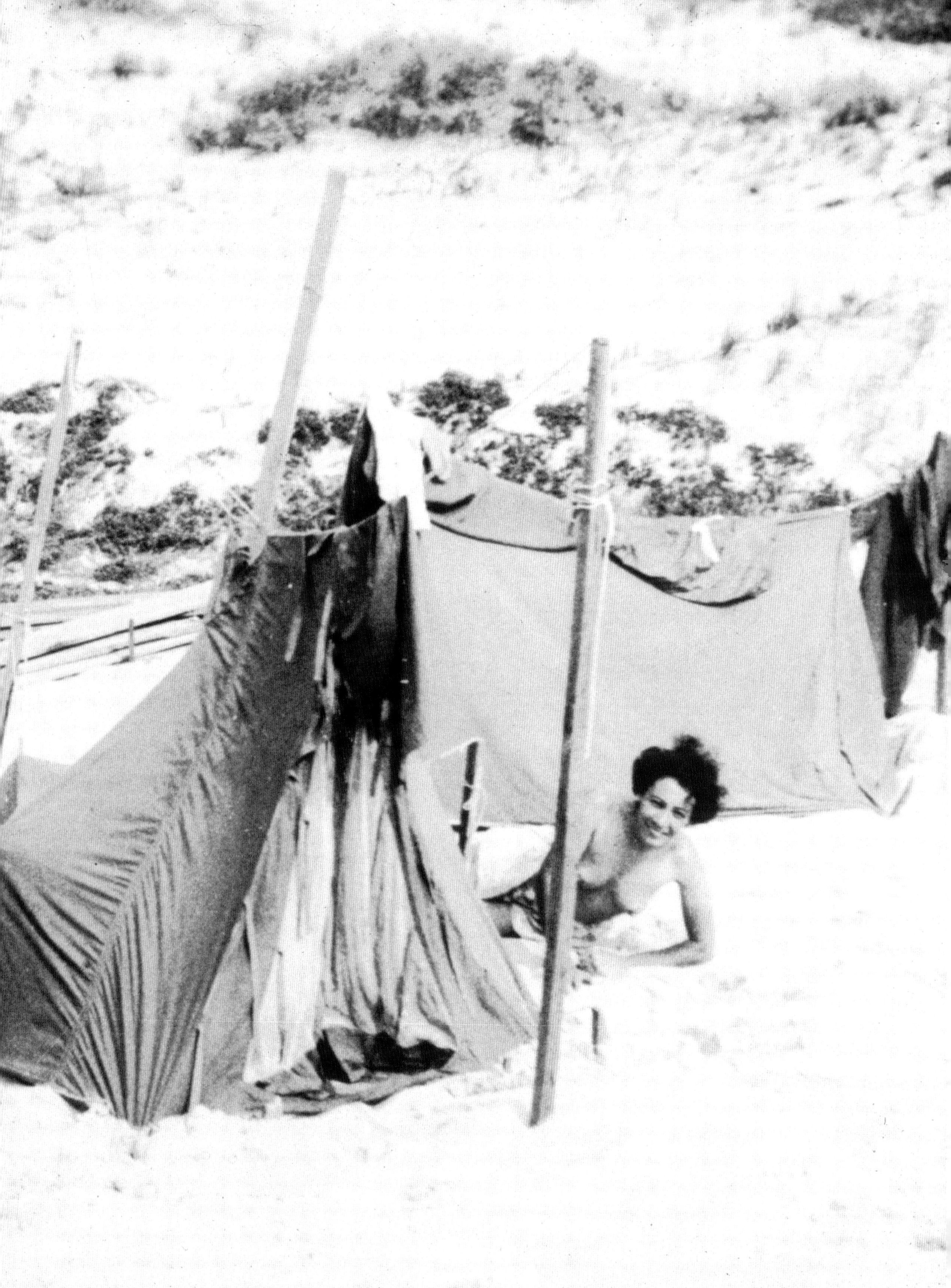

Richard Avedon arrived in 1946, sharing a cottage with his wife, Doe, his *Junior Bazaar* colleague Lillian Bassman, and her bisexual husband, Paul Himmel, himself a talented photographer. Friday evenings commenced at Duffy's Hotel, where Avedon would devour two meals, drink with abandon, and dance barefoot for hours before washing it all off with a predawn dip in the ocean.[33] His first cover for *Harper's Bazaar* in January 1947 drew upon his summer exploits. The bohemian atmosphere was both titillating and fraught for the scandal-weary, respectably married photographer. According to Lillian Bassman, "Avedon's real fascinations were androgyny and theatricality."[34]

For all of its photographic talents, the artistic medium that most defined Cherry Grove was the stage. Increasingly elaborate gender-bending local productions led to the creation of the Arts Project of Cherry Grove, a professional theater operation. Its campy ways soon spilled over into every aspect of the Grove's social life. The Arts Project began sponsoring Beach Day, a Fourth of July event that pitted women in old baseball uniforms against men in women's hats and bras. Parties took on decadent themes. Auden attended one event dressed "as a bishop, mitre, cope, and all," while his companion accompanied him "as a very rococo angel."[35]

Within walking distance of Cherry Grove were the uninhabited, windswept vistas of Lone Hill. During the 1940s, out-of-sight but accessible beaches became a favored haunt for nudists and the occasional beach-shack squatter. A few crude structures made from hurricane wreckage provided a bit of shade but little else. By 1952, the postwar appetite for weekend getaways prompted the Home Guardian Company to sweep in and create 600 lots measuring 60 feet wide by 100 feet deep—compact but, by Cherry Grove's standards, luxurious. As its name suggested, Home Guardian strenuously touted its new development as a *family* destination ("The children will love it here!").[36] Lone Hill was rechristened Fire Island Pines, and oceanfront lots began selling for $800.

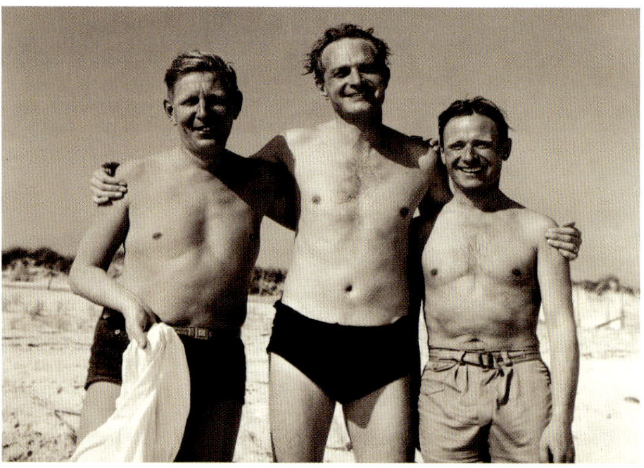

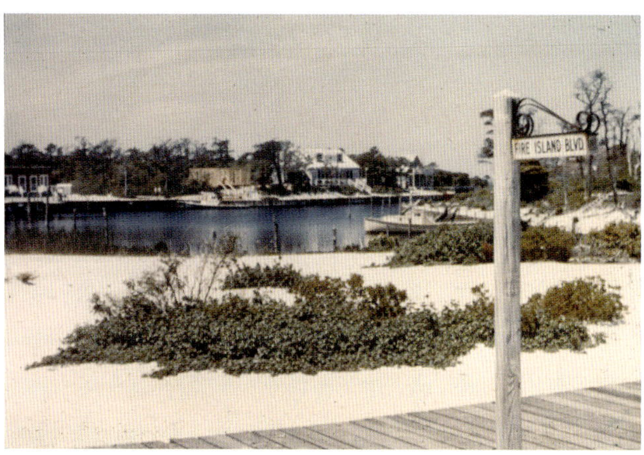

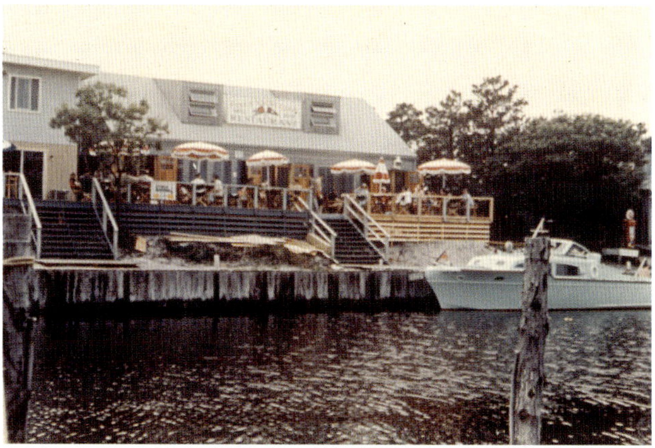

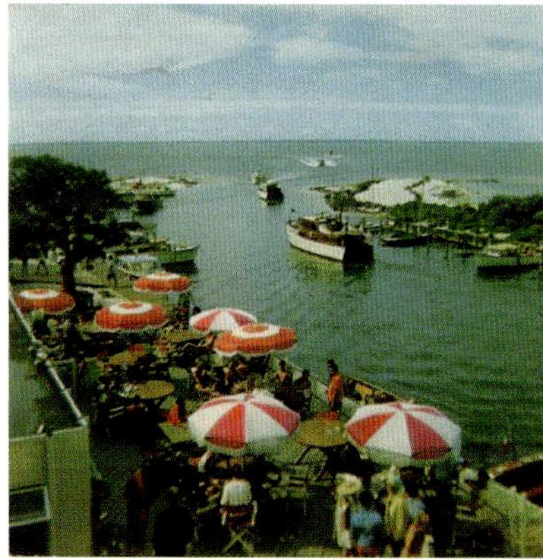

Peggy Fears

PINES YACHT CLUB

AND

BOTEL

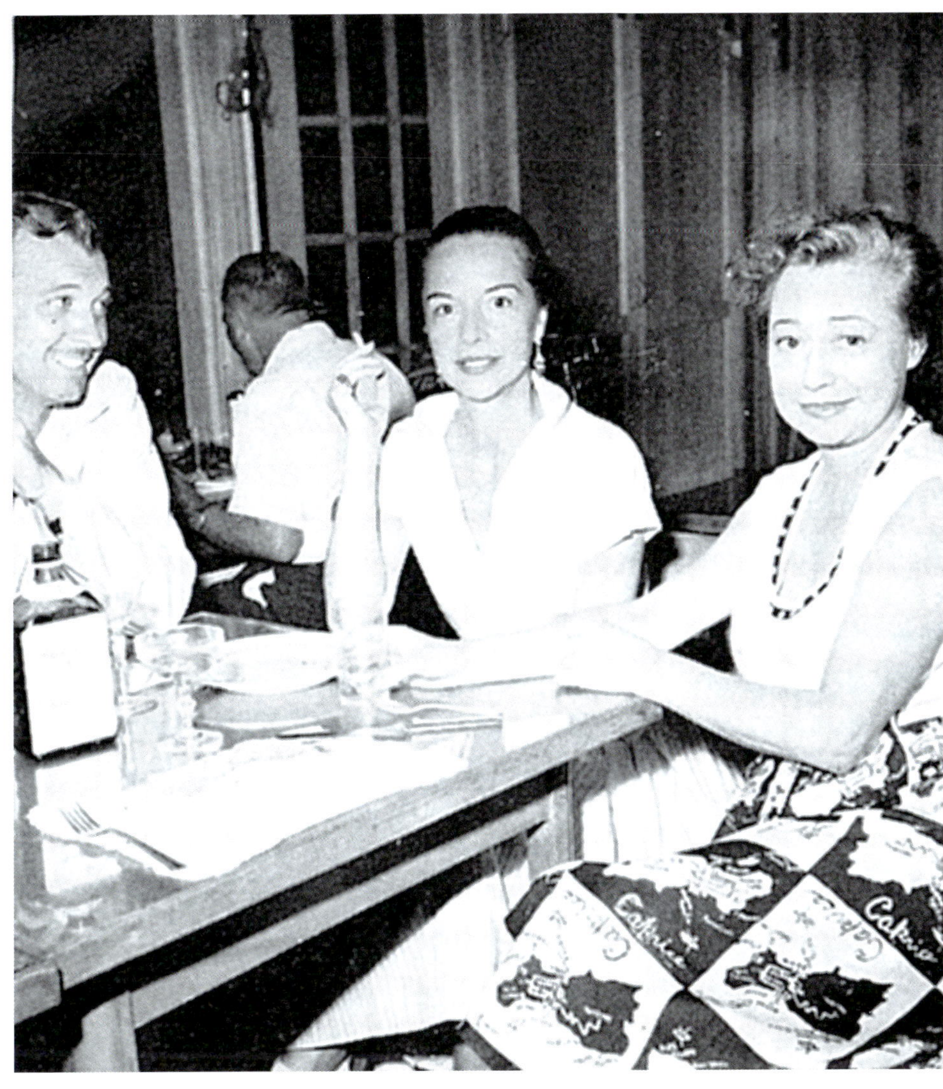

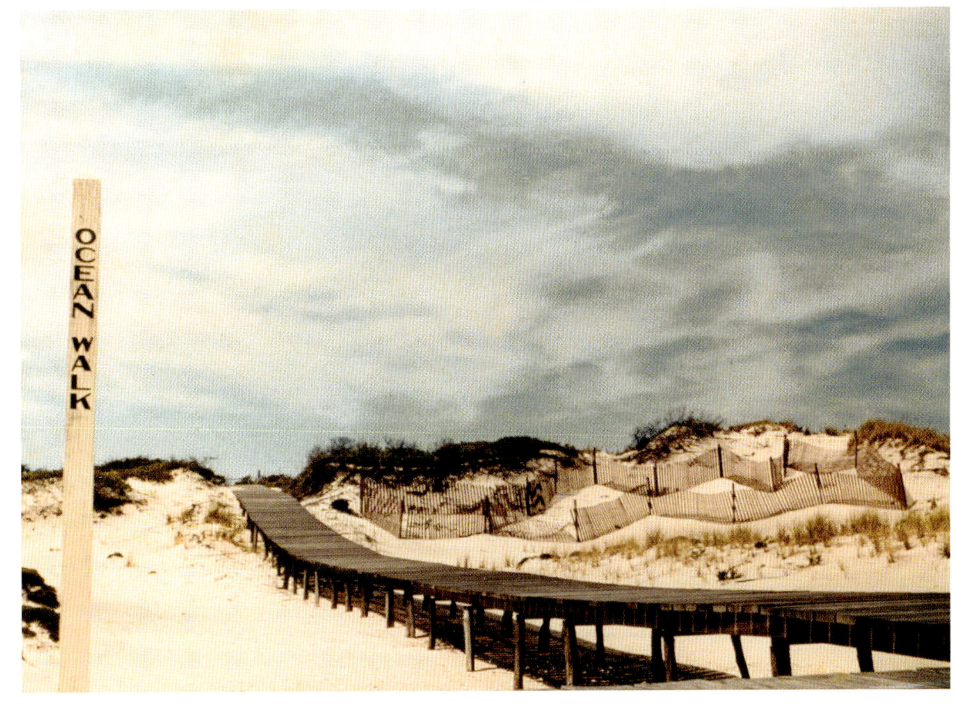

PAGES 36–37:
Nudist campsite in Lone Hill, NY, 1940s

OPPOSITE, ABOVE:
Left to right: W. H. Auden, Stephen Spender, and Christopher Isherwood pose for Lincoln Kirstein in Cherry Grove, NY, 1947

OPPOSITE, 2ND.
Fire Island Boulevard, ca. 1958

OPPOSITE, 3RD:
Peggy Fears Yacht Club and Botel, 1950s

ABOVE:
Peggy Fears (center) with friends Zachary and Ruth Scott, late 1950s

RIGHT:
Fire Island Pines boardwalk, 1958

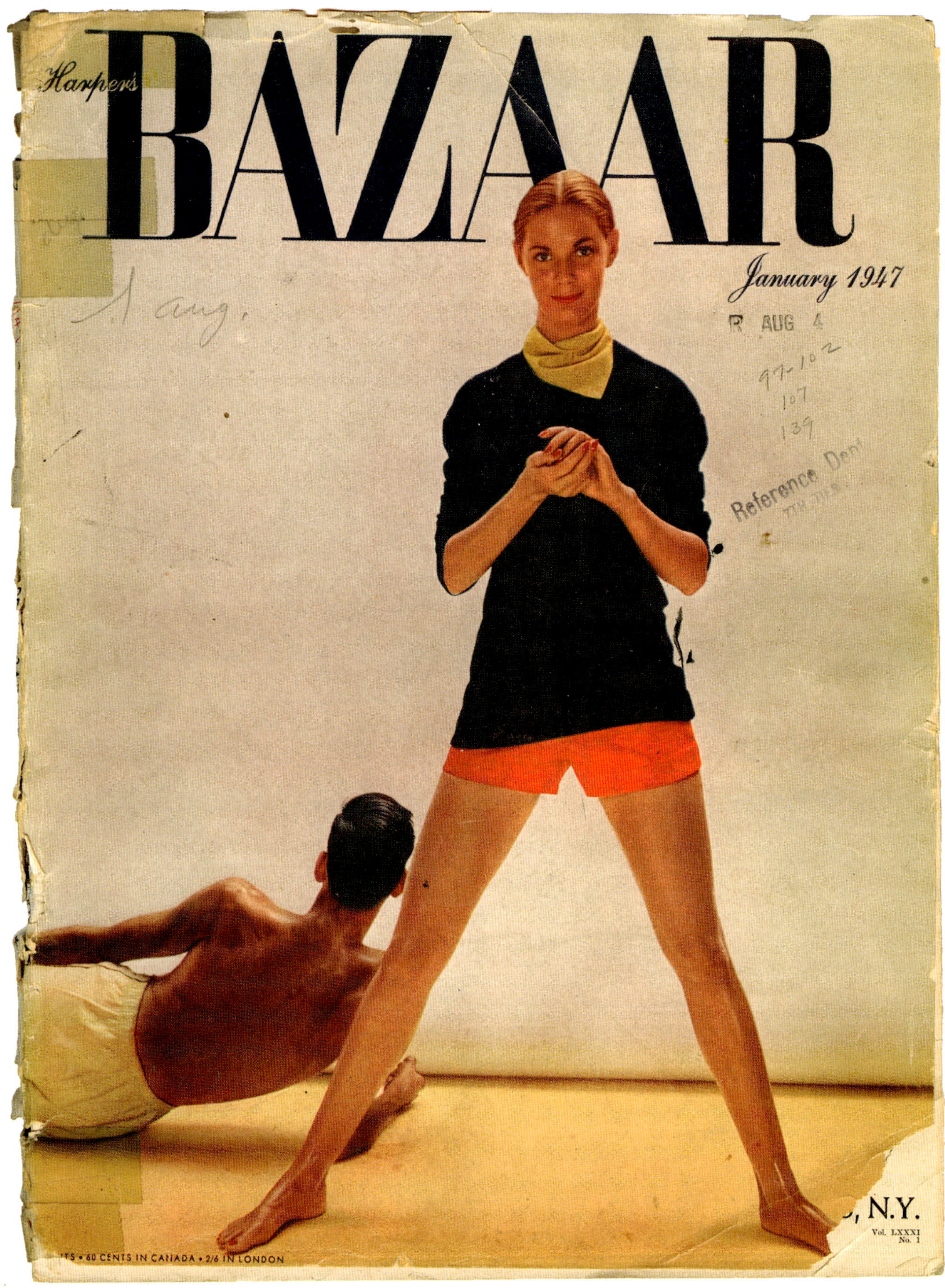
Harper's
BAZAAR
January 1947
, N.Y.
Vol. LXXXI
No. 1
60 CENTS IN CANADA • 2/6 IN LONDON

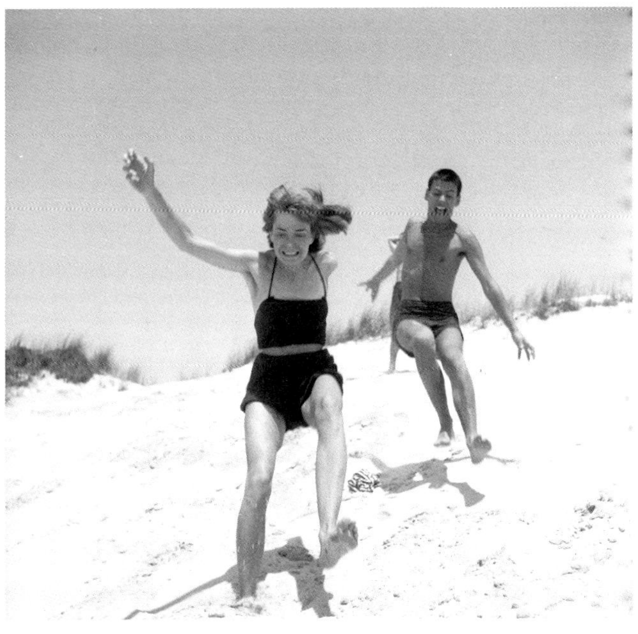

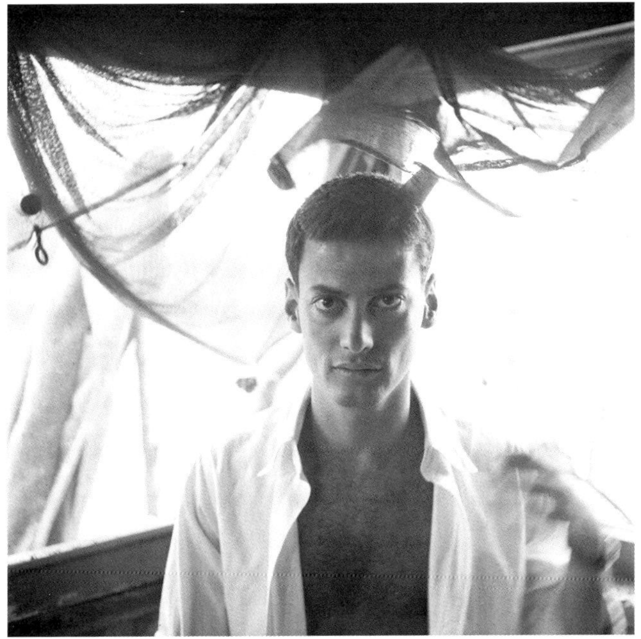

Commercial activity confined itself to a picturesque bayside harbor, where ferries from Long Island made their rounds. By 1956, Peggy Fears, a Cherry Grove transplant, former Ziegfeld Follies showgirl, Broadway producer, and discreet lesbian, was holding court at her rustic Yacht Club. Fears introduced a show-business undercurrent to the Pines that persists to this day. In her unmistakable style, she recounted how a prominent Cuban fashion designer, his model wife, and famous actors staffed her grand opening:

> I invited a few close friends—Luis and Betty Estevez, Zachary and Ruth Scott, Joan McCracken, oh, a small group...I drove out from town with another car full: there was a boy who was being trained to play the Prince of Wales for Paramount, and Burt Martinson (you know, Martinson's Coffee), Jerry Tishman, and several others. When we got there, we found that fifty-five people had turned up! Well, Betty got a speedboat and tore across the harbor to get me a piano, (the boy who was going to be the Prince of Wales said he would play), and Zachary began taking orders for drinks...It was one of my nicest productions.[37]

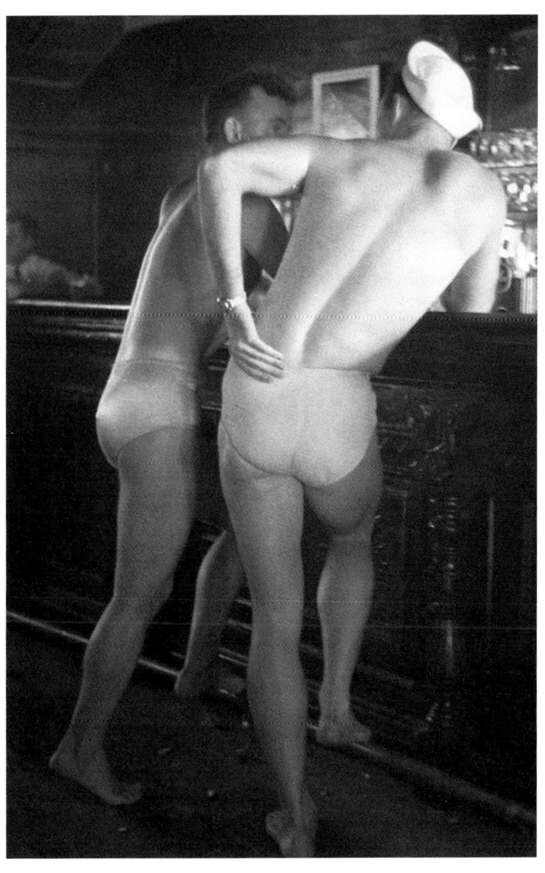

OPPOSITE.
***Harper's Bazaar,* January 1947 cover by Richard Avedon**

ABOVE:
Photo by Paul Himmel. Richard and Doe Avedon, Cherry Grove, late 1940s

MIDDLE:
**Photo by Paul Himmel.
Richard Avedon, Cherry Grove, late 1940s**

RIGHT:
Photo by Paul Himmel. Duffy's Hotel, Cherry Grove, late 1940s

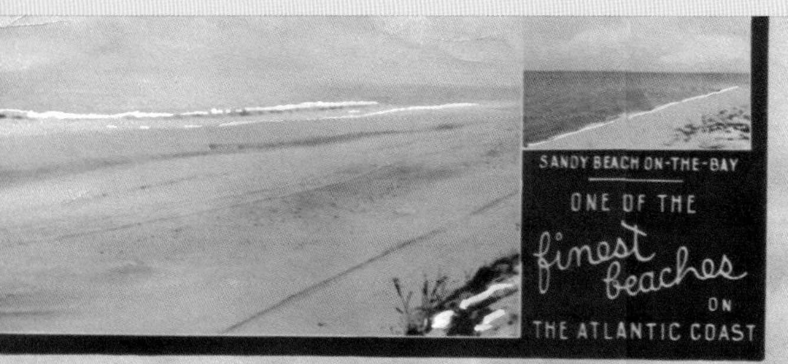
SANDY BEACH ON-THE-BAY
ONE OF THE
finest beaches
ON
THE ATLANTIC COAST

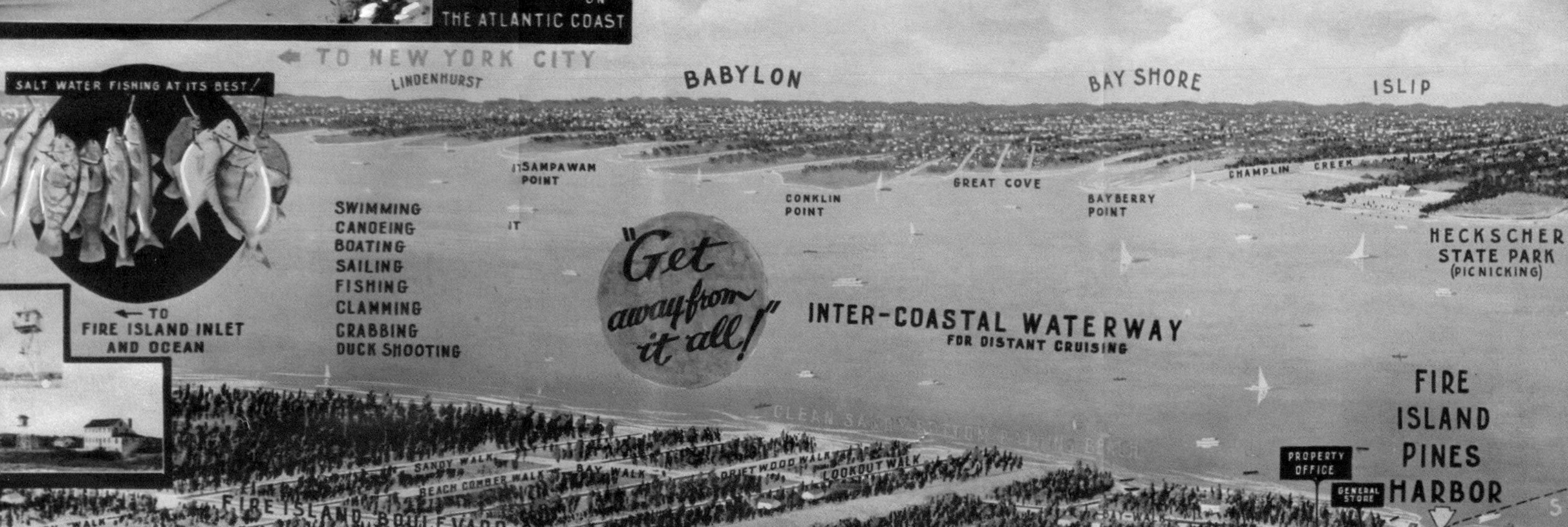
To really enjoy Aquati
LIVE IN FIRE ISLAND PI
← TO NEW YORK CITY
LINDENHURST
BABYLON
BAY SHORE
ISLIP
SALT WATER FISHING AT ITS BEST!
SAMPAWAM POINT
CONKLIN POINT
GREAT COVE
BAYBERRY POINT
CHAMPLIN CREEK
HECKSCHER STATE PARK (PICNICKING)
SWIMMING
CANOEING
BOATING
SAILING
FISHING
CLAMMING
CRABBING
DUCK SHOOTING
"Get away from it all!"
INTER-COASTAL WATERWAY
FOR DISTANT CRUISING
← TO FIRE ISLAND INLET AND OCEAN
FIRE ISLAND PINES HARBOR
PROPERTY OFFICE
GENERAL STORE
SANDY WALK
BEACH COMBER WALK
BAY WALK
DRIFTWOOD WALK
LOOKOUT WALK
FIRE ISLAND BOULEVARD SITE
OCEAN WALK
BEACH HILL WALK
MIDWAY
PICKETTY
CEDAR WALK
WIDGEON WALK
ATLANTIC WALK
HARBOR WALK
SCAUP WALK
NEPTUNE WALK
SITE
STEPS
← TO THE INLET
SAND DUNES
Deep sea fishing at its best!
ATLANTIC OCEAN
OCEAN BATH
TROLLING
BOATING
One of the finest bea

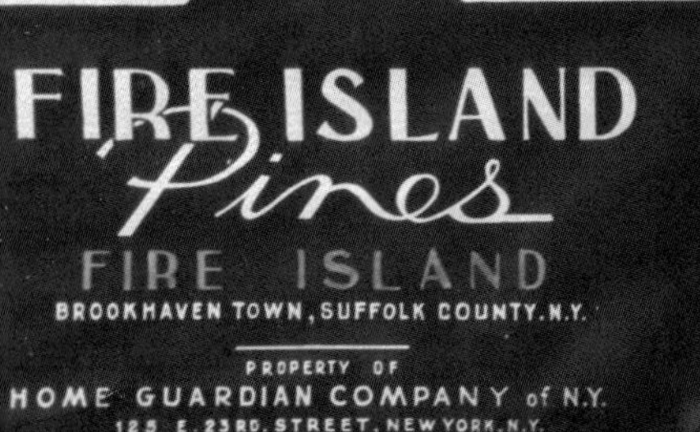
FIRE ISLAND
Pines
FIRE ISLAND
BROOKHAVEN TOWN, SUFFOLK COUNTY, N.Y.
PROPERTY OF
HOME GUARDIAN COMPANY of N.Y.
125 E. 23RD. STREET, NEW YORK, N.Y.
HARRY A. CHANDLER
Map
570 7TH AVENUE
NEW YORK 18, N.Y.

sports

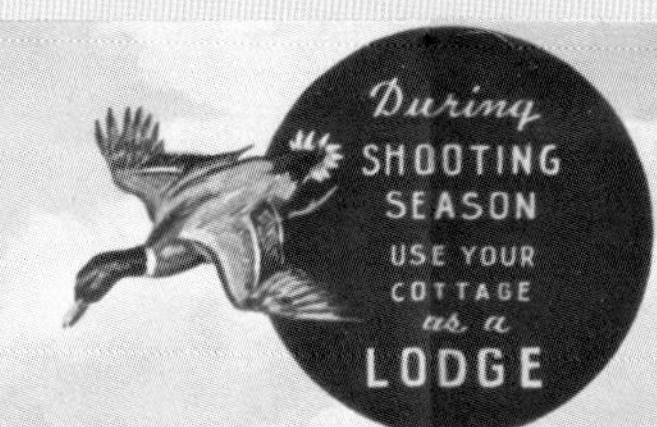

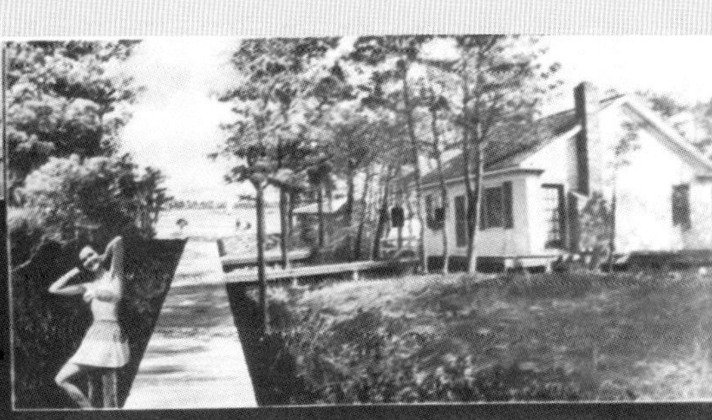

SAYVILLE RR. STATION

LONG ISLAND'S GREAT PARKWAY SYSTEM

SAYVILLE

BAYPORT

LONG ISLAND R.R.

CONNETQUOT RIVER

FOSTER AVE

BROWN CREEK

HOMANS CR.

PATCHOGUE BAY

GREENE POINT

GREENS BROOK

FISHING BOATS FOR HIRE

STEINS FERRY TO FIRE ISLAND PINES

BLUE POINT

TO PATCHOGUE ➡

Here Summers are Unforgettable!

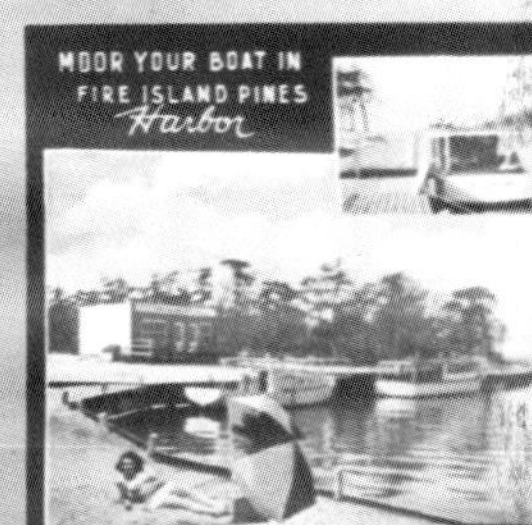

GREAT SOUTH BAY

"A Sportsman's Paradise"

BOAT RACING

CLEAN SANDY BOTTOM BEACH

TO MORICHES INLET ➡

HOLLY WALK

BAY WALK

SHADY WALK

FLORAL WALK

BASS WALK

PORGIE WALK

SNAPPER

CROWN WALK

SUNBURST WALK

SHELL

FIRE ISLAND BOULEVARD SITE

PATH

OZONE WALK

SKY WALK

TARPON

OCEAN WALK

FISHERMENS

OCEAN WALK

SAIL WALK

STEPS

All plots face a boardwalk!

WIDE CLEAN SANDY BEACH

and SURF CASTING

STEPS

SAND DUNES

STEPS

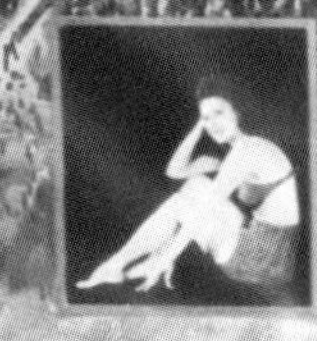

...es on the Atlantic Coast!

TO MORICHES INLET ➡

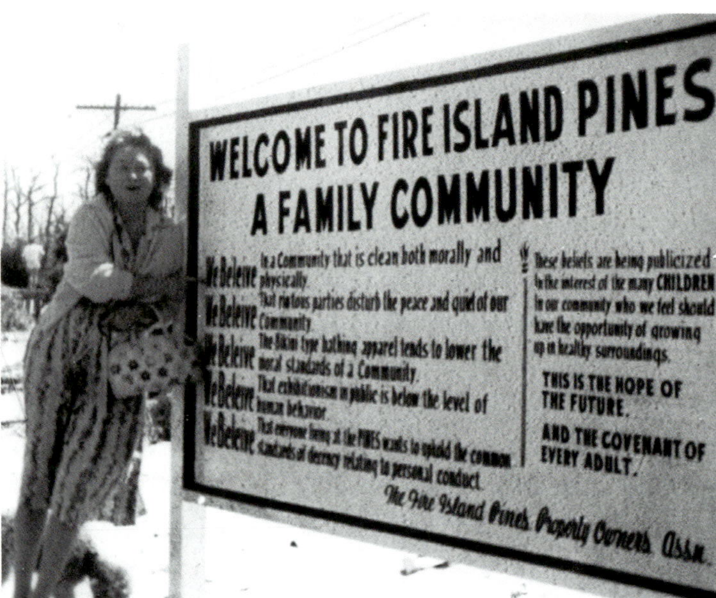
WELCOME TO FIRE ISLAND PINES
A FAMILY COMMUNITY
We Believe In a Community that is clean both morally and physically.
We Believe That riotous parties disturb the peace and quiet of our Community.
We Believe The Bikini type bathing apparel tends to lower the moral standards of a Community.
We Believe That exhibitionism in public is below the level of human behavior.
We Believe That everyone living at the PINES wants to uphold the common standards of decency relating to personal conduct.
These beliefs are being publicized in the interest of the many CHILDREN in our community who we feel should have the opportunity of growing up in healthy surroundings.
THIS IS THE HOPE OF THE FUTURE.
AND THE COVENANT OF EVERY ADULT.
The Fire Island Pines Property Owners Assn.

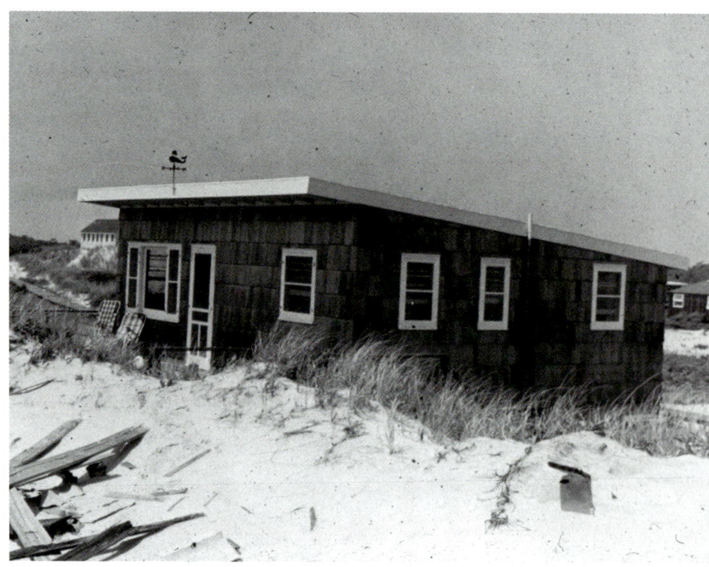

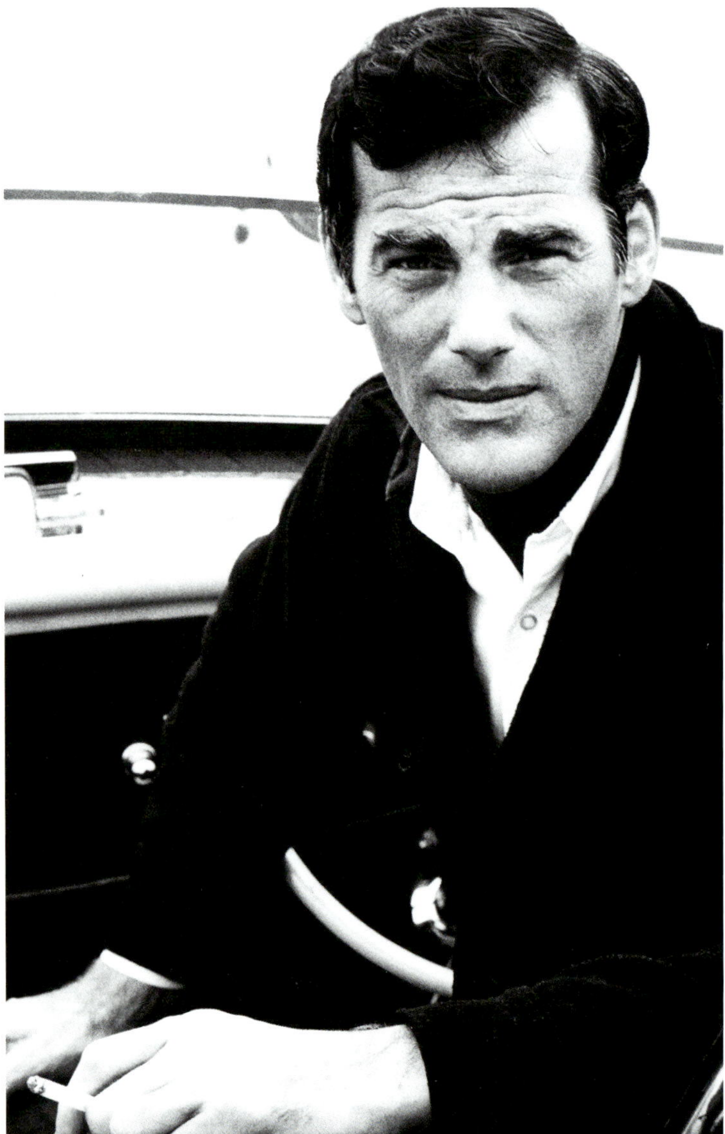

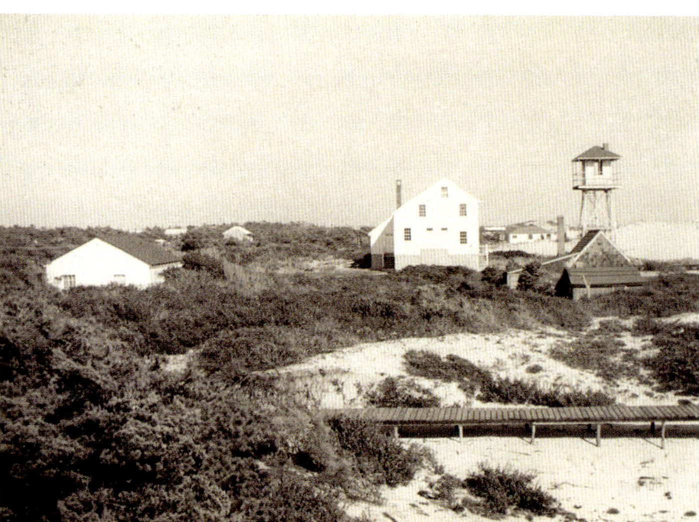

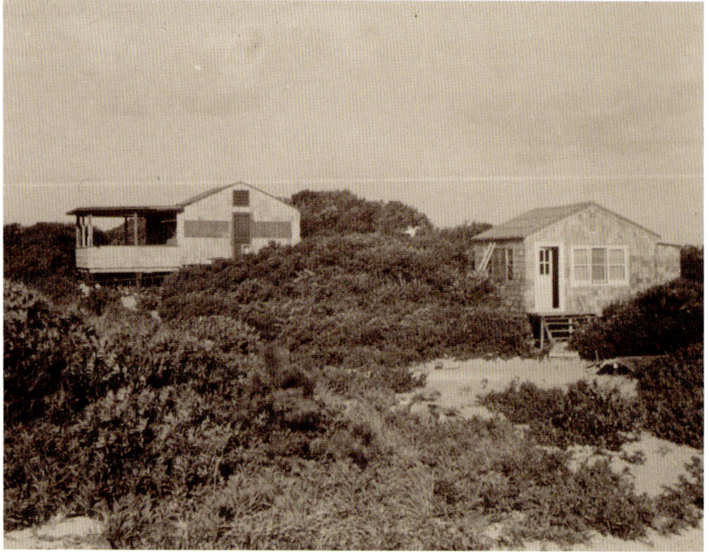

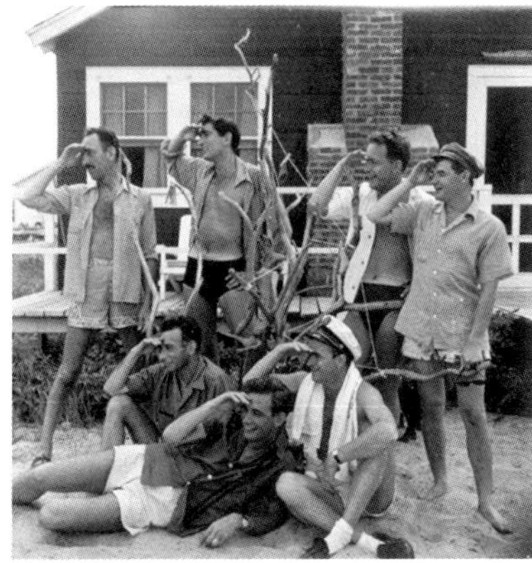

PAGES 42–43:
Home Guardian Company promotional poster for Fire Island Pines, NY, ca. 1953

OPPOSITE, UPPER LEFT:
Real estate broker Arden Catlin poses in front of the infamous "Family Community" sign, Fire Island Pines, NY, early 1960s

OPPOSITE, RIGHT:
Typical Fire Island Pines beach houses, 1950s

OPPOSITE, LOWER LEFT:
John Burlingame Whyte, ca. 1962

ABOVE:
Men of Fire Island, ca. 1960

Cherry Grove bore the stigma of being a queer enclave, but more cautious vacationers discovered that they could maintain an untainted address in the Pines, only a stroll away from the beach to unite them with the forbidden pleasures of Cherry Grove. They soon found that not all of the Pines' residents hailed from the permissive world of showbiz. Worldly New Yorkers might have countenanced the occasional homosexual in their midst, but a tectonic shift in orientation was quietly rippling through the Pines. Fears sold her real estate holdings in 1962, and the Property Owners Association redoubled efforts to stave off the undesirables. Soon, an imposing sign was erected in the harbor that read:

> WELCOME TO FIRE ISLAND PINES,
> A FAMILY COMMUNITY
> We Believe: In a community that is clean both morally and physically.
> We Believe: That riotous parties disturb the peace and quiet of our community.
> We Believe: The bikini-type bathing suit apparel tends to lower the moral standards of a Community.
> We Believe: That everyone living at the PINES wants to uphold the common standards of decency relating to personal conduct.
> These beliefs are being publicized in the interest of the many CHILDREN in our community who we feel should have the opportunity of growing up in healthy surroundings.
> THIS IS THE HOPE OF THE FUTURE. AND THE COVENANT OF EVERY ADULT.
> The Fire Island Pines Property Owners Association

These developments might have spelled the end of the Pines' nascent bohemianism, except that the buyer of the Peggy Fears Yacht Club and Botel was John Burlingame Whyte, a fashion and cigarette model who parlayed his earnings into real estate. Over the next several years, Whyte steadily acquired most of the Pines' commercial venues. His entourage of photographers and fellow models added even more glamour and gaiety to the mix of vacationers. Whyte presided over his tiny empire from an austere modern house on the ocean, becoming one of many tastemakers who would define the Pines as an experiment in domestic living.

Yet the architecture of the Pines was a drab backdrop for all of this local color. Many of the homes erected during the 1950s were mean, prefabricated wooden cottages with tiny windows, delivered on barges and dragged across

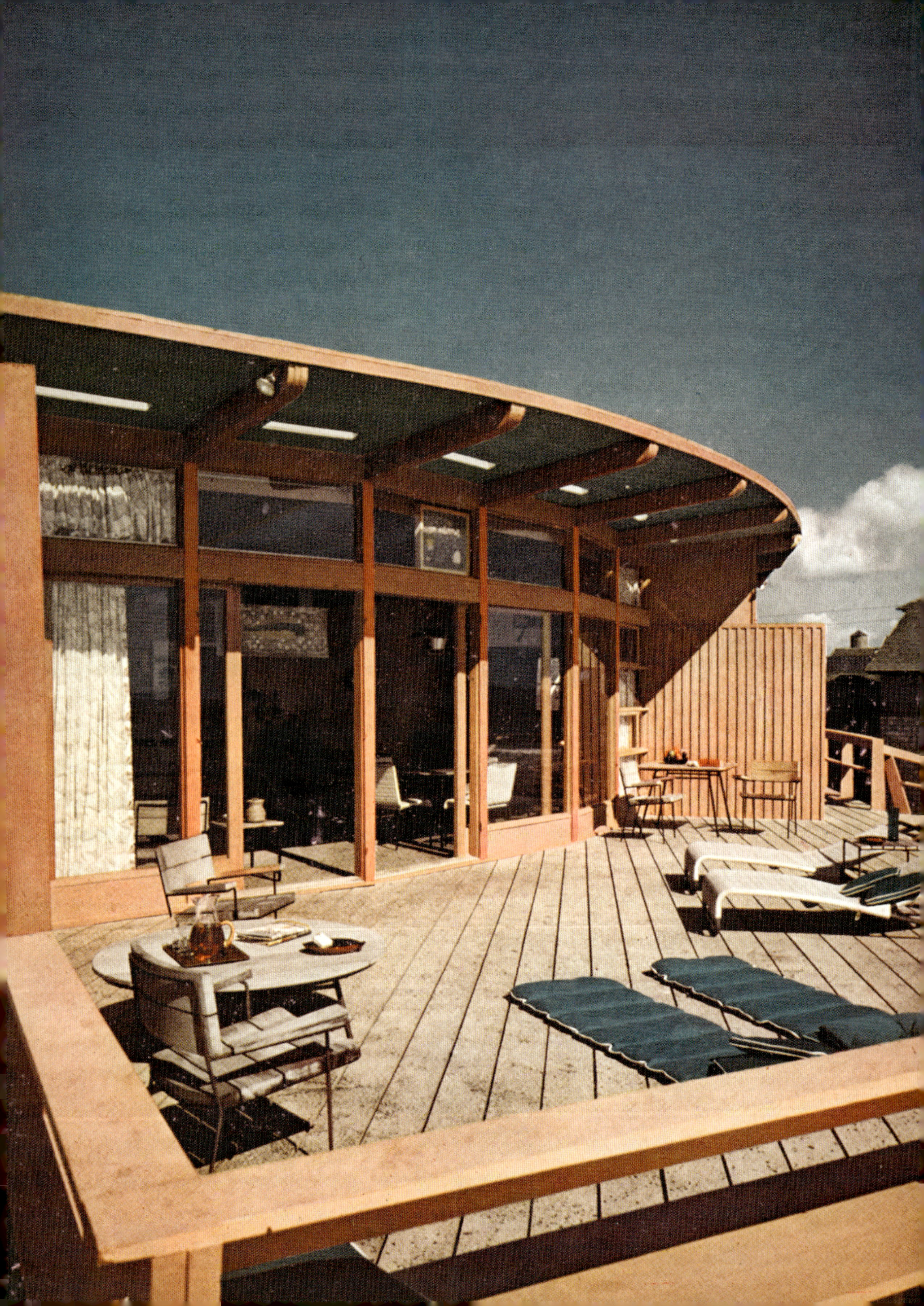

the fragile dunes to rest upon scrums of skinny wooden pilings. What was left of the dunes was often scraped away to "improve" views, leaving the Pines vulnerable to storms and erosion. Distinctive architecture, modern or otherwise, could be found only further afield.

The first modern home on Fire Island was built in the community of Seaview for George Marek, a classical-music critic who also contributed to *House Beautiful*. In 1951, the magazine decided to see how modern architecture might suit a man of traditional tastes and temperament. Marek proved up to the challenge once the magazine offered to build the home at cost. Veteran architect Eldridge Snyder set out to create a home that maximized ocean views while maintaining privacy on a public beach. He accomplished this with a high, twenty-four-foot-deep deck that launched over the crest of a dune. Floor-to-ceiling glass, set well back from the deck rail, was scarcely visible from the oceanfront below. Outdoor furniture was used throughout the house, blurring traditional distinctions of enclosure. The ceilings were even painted pale blue to merge with the summer sky. A clever floor plan, inspired by the radiating lines of a clamshell, allowed each room to enjoy ocean views. But the implicit tease of the home's rakish roofline and hidden spaces undermined its claims to privacy. As Marek's son Richard recalled, "The house was so unusual that people used to walk up a ramp to the deck and peer in the windows, at 7:00 in the morning. My father used to chase them away with a broom."[38]

In 1959, Guy J. Rothenstein added to Seaview's fledgling architectural pedigree with a diminutive "plastic house" for his family that tested technologies he acquired as a specialist in factory-produced housing for Skidmore Owings & Merrill. A German architect who trained in Le Corbusier's Paris office before fleeing war-torn Europe, Rothenstein maintained the Corbusian view of housing as a mass-produced agent of social change. It was an idea that never really took hold in the United States, but Rothenstein extracted a surprising degree of humanity and artistry from his semisynthetic cube on the dunes. He clad a conventional wooden frame with asbestos panels, vinyl floors, and plastic laminate cabinetry. On the roof, a circular, translucent fiberglass solarium for private sunbathing relieved the modular boxiness of the structure below. Honeycombed fiberglass screens divided the living area from the deck, but pivoted up and over to become sunscreens for a combined indoor/outdoor space. Their multicolored cells bathed the space in a prismatic, twentieth-century interpretation of stained glass.

As a theater for innovation, Fire Island's small lots and relative isolation made it a place of "soft openings" for young architects who were still practicing their lines. Both Charles Gwathmey and Richard Meier designed their first houses on Fire Island. Harry Bates spent the sixties working in the Pines before focusing on the Hamptons where his successor firm, Bates + Masi, still

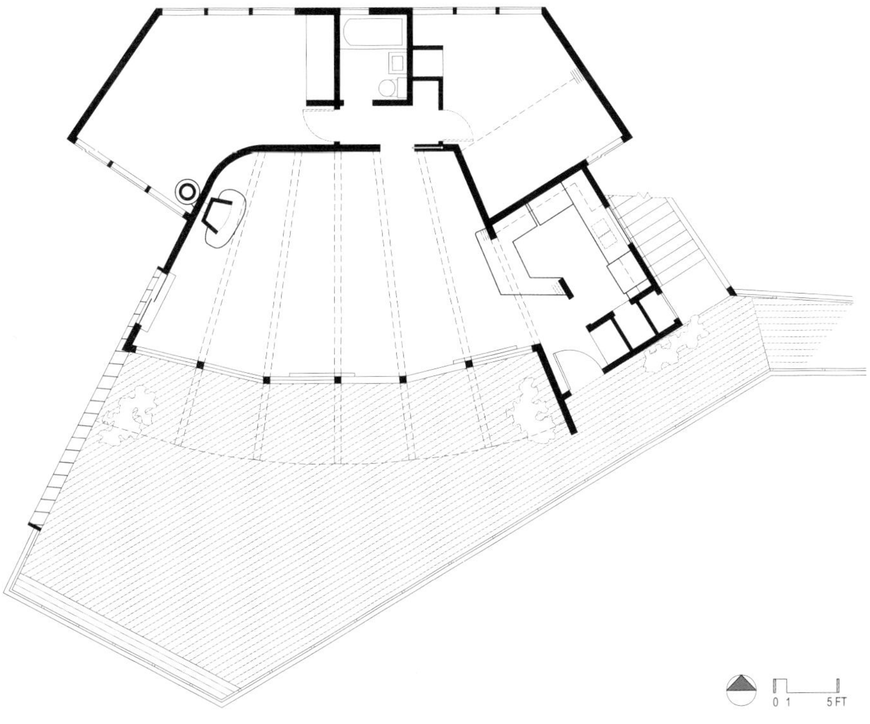

OPPOSITE:
Eldridge Snyder, Marek House, Seaview, NY, 1951

RIGHT:
Marek House, floor plan

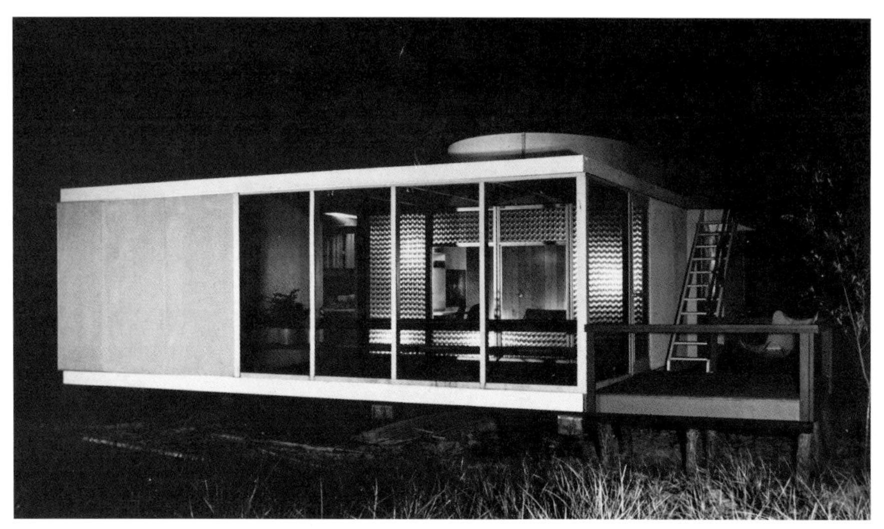

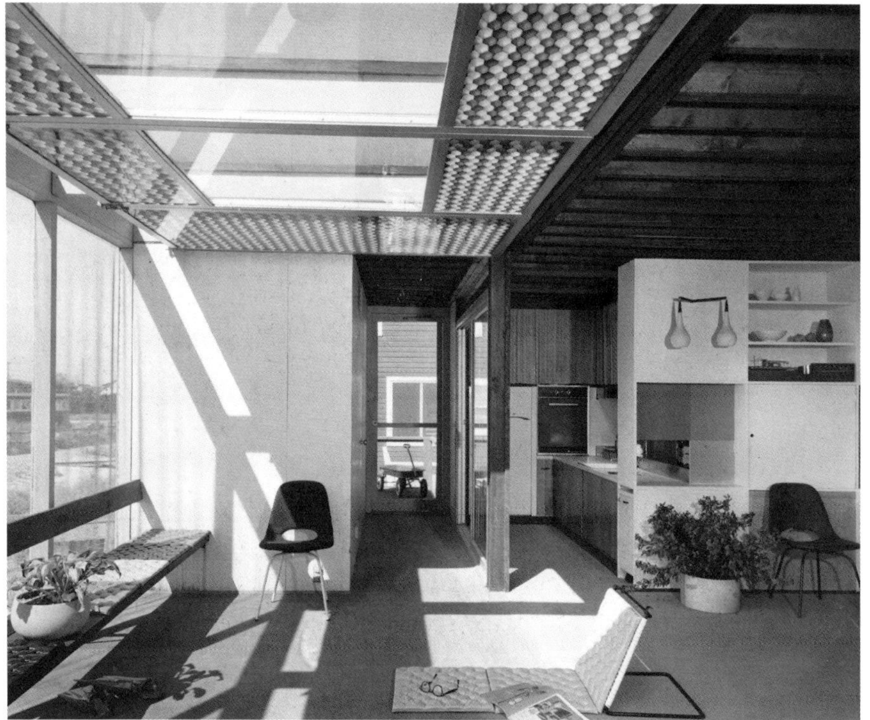

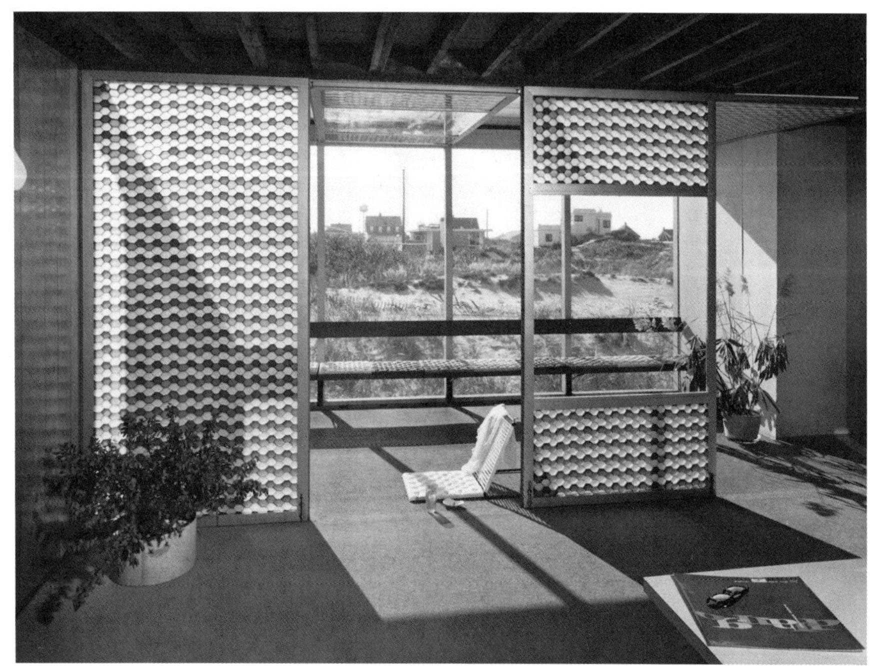

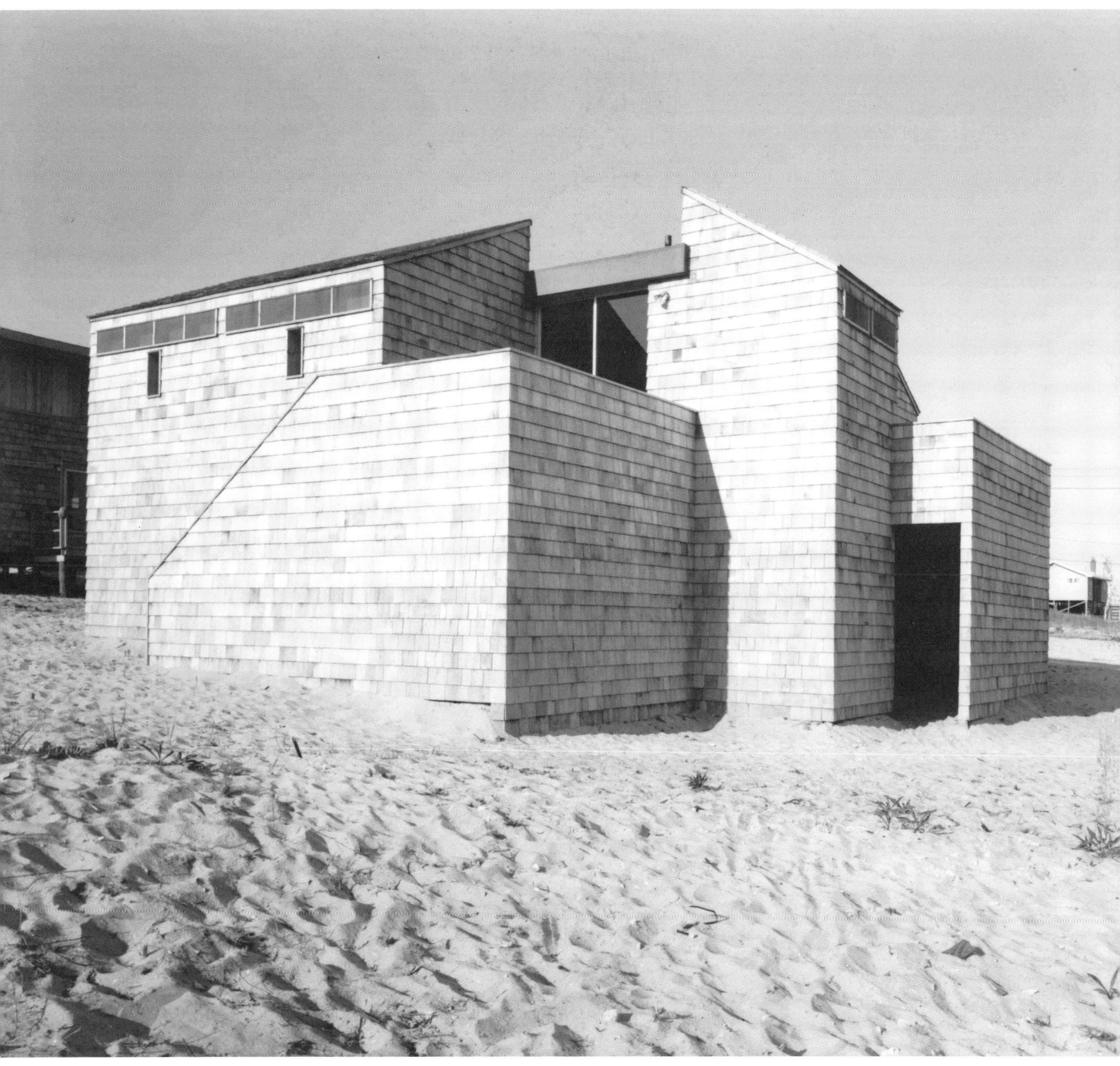

OPPOSITE, ABOVE:
Guy Rothenstein, Rothenstein House, Seaview, NY, 1959

OPPOSITE, MIDDLE:
Rothenstein House, interior

OPPOSITE, BELOW:
Rothenstein House, interior

ABOVE:
Charles Gwathmey, Miller House, Fair Harbor, NY, 1964

thrives today. But at the dawn of the 1960s, the only architect with a high profile practicing on Fire Island was Andrew Geller.

Geller began to turn Fire Island's architecture literally on its head in 1958 with quirky and endearing beach houses that revealed "how far a little plywood and a lot of guts will take you."[39] Geller's immersion in industrial design conferred a gadgetlike quality to his houses that made them accessible to the sort of men who tinkered with Chevys but shied away from the "feminine" arts of high design and decor. The Irwin and Joyce Hunt House, located in the Fire Island community of Ocean Bay Park, aimed its leading edge like a missile into the wind, demonstrating Geller's theory that an "aerodynamic" house was the best form to withstand a hurricane.

By 1960, Geller had completed seven well-publicized homes across Fire Island but none in the architectural backwater of the Pines, where plentiful lots and a seemingly ideal audience awaited his imprint. That changed in 1961, when Rudy and Trudy Frank, an ice-cream executive and a painter, built a Geller-designed home on one of the highest dunes in the Pines. It was a refined composition, inspired by the truncated pyramids that the Franks had recently explored in Mexico. Their house rose at the exact moment when Gifford began to build his own home a few hundred feet away.

While Gifford's modest debut barely registered from the public boardwalk, the Frank House towered over its surroundings—a commanding work by a seasoned master—and it should have established Geller as the preeminent architect of the Pines. Soon, the Franks' close friends Edwin Wittstein and Robert Miller decided they, too, wanted to be inspired rather than simply housed. Wittstein and Miller had found each other and career success as very young men in the 1950s, Miller as an art director and Wittstein as a set designer. Wittstein was flush with the proceeds from his work on 1960's *The Fantasticks*, which became off-Broadway's longest-running show. The commission for their beach house was Geller's for the taking—that is, until the upstart Gifford brazenly seduced Wittstein, thereby landing his first Fire Island client. Wittstein recalled the affair fifty years later with lusty relish, while a mischievously approving Robert Miller looked on.[40] Andrew Geller never built another home in the Pines. Like a scene right out of *All About Eve*, Gifford stole Geller's show.

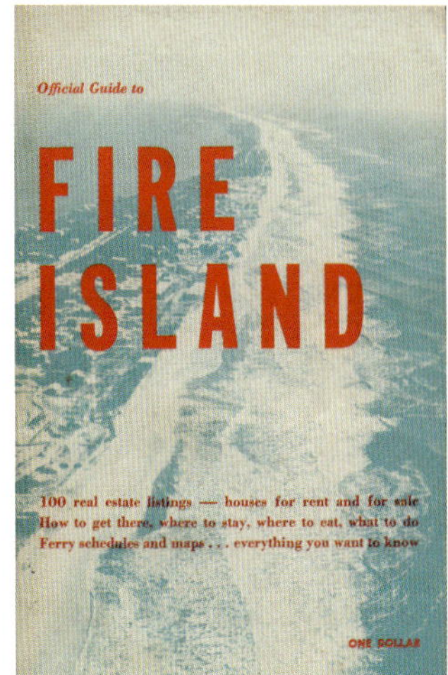

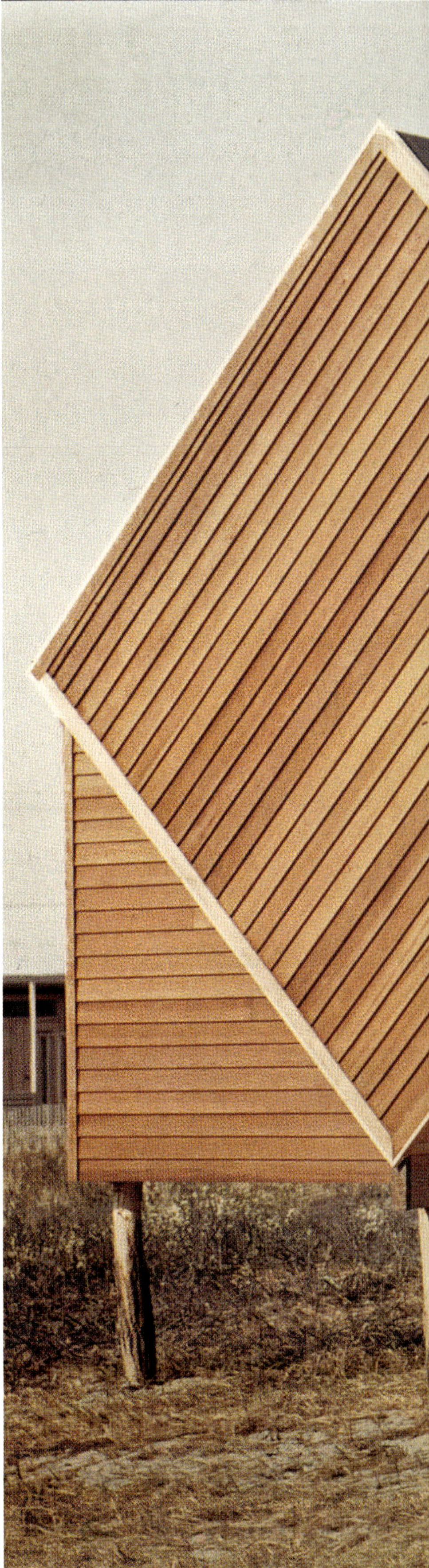

ABOVE:
Real estate guide to Fire Island, 1963

OPPOSITE:
Andrew Geller, Hunt House, Ocean Bay Park, NY, 1958

PAGES 52–53:
Horace Gifford (right) and Robert Miller, photographed by Edwin Wittstein, 1963

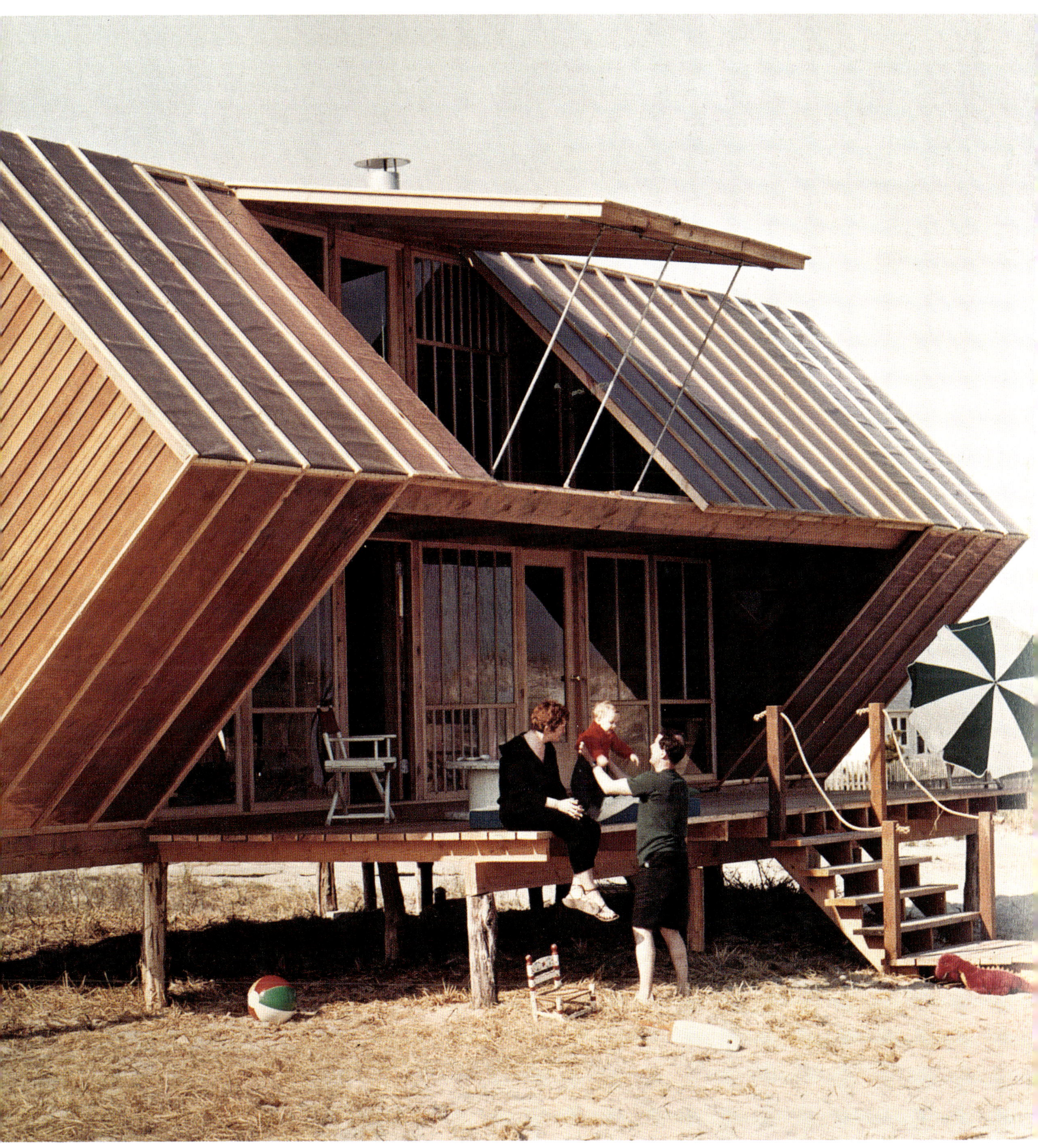

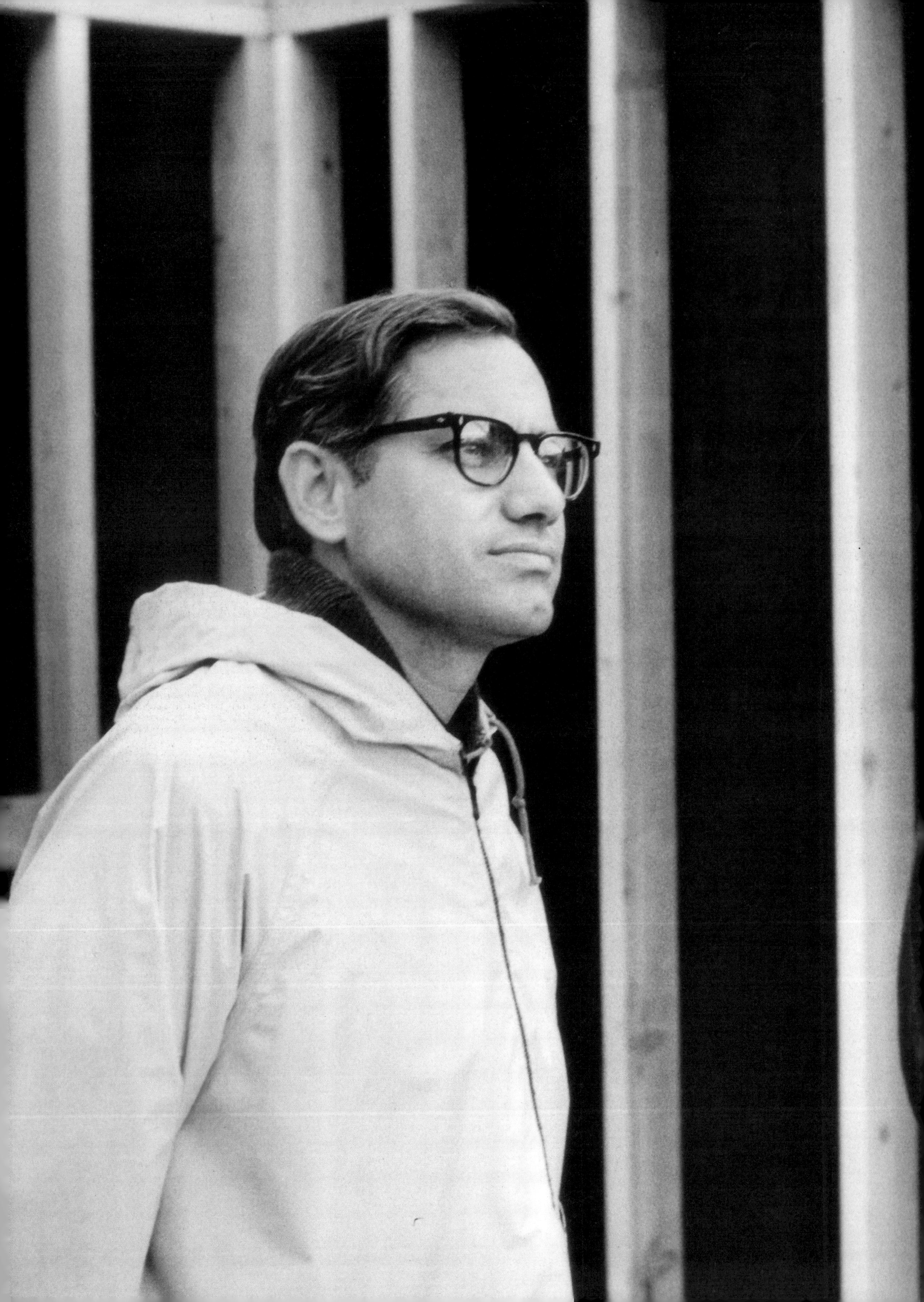

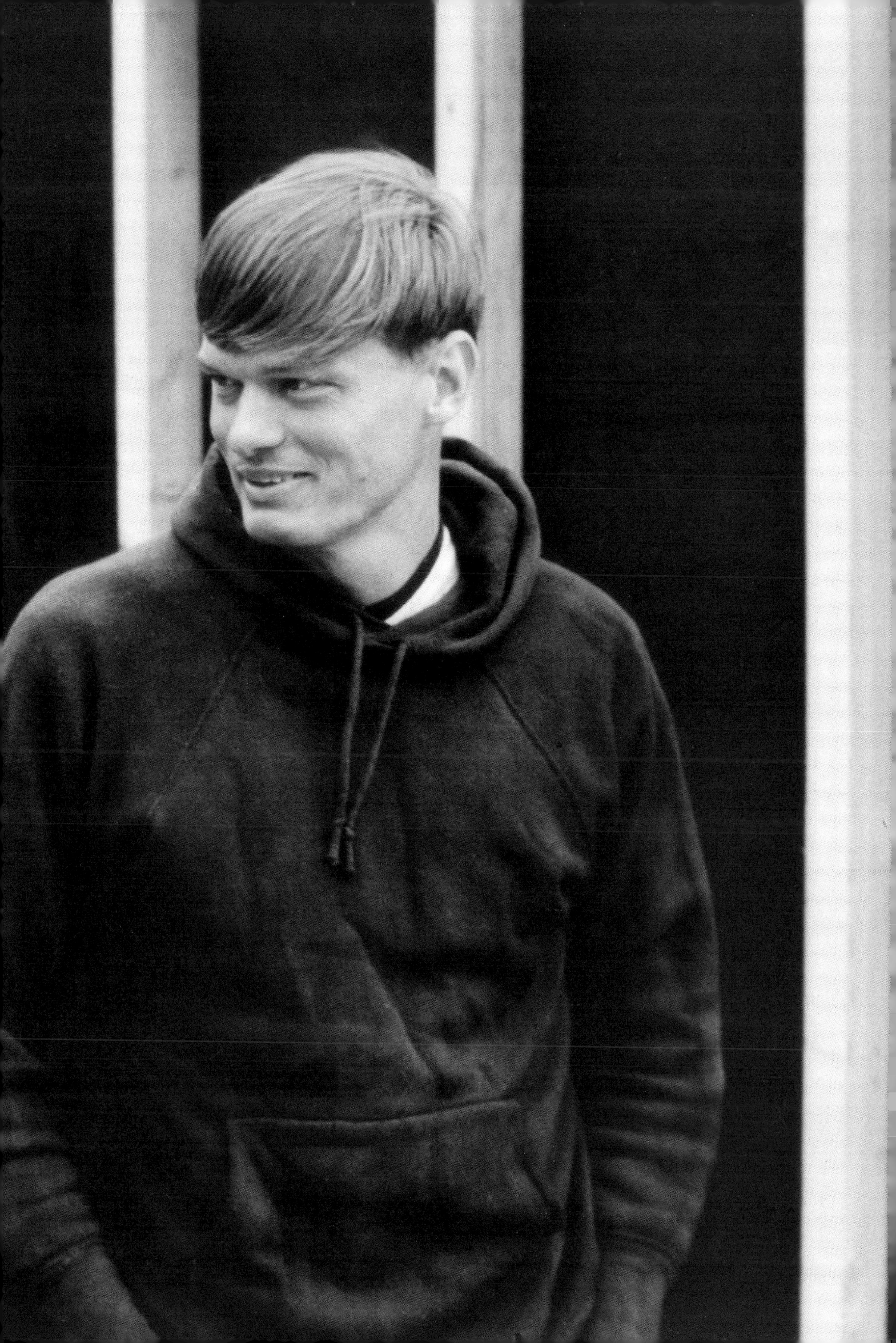

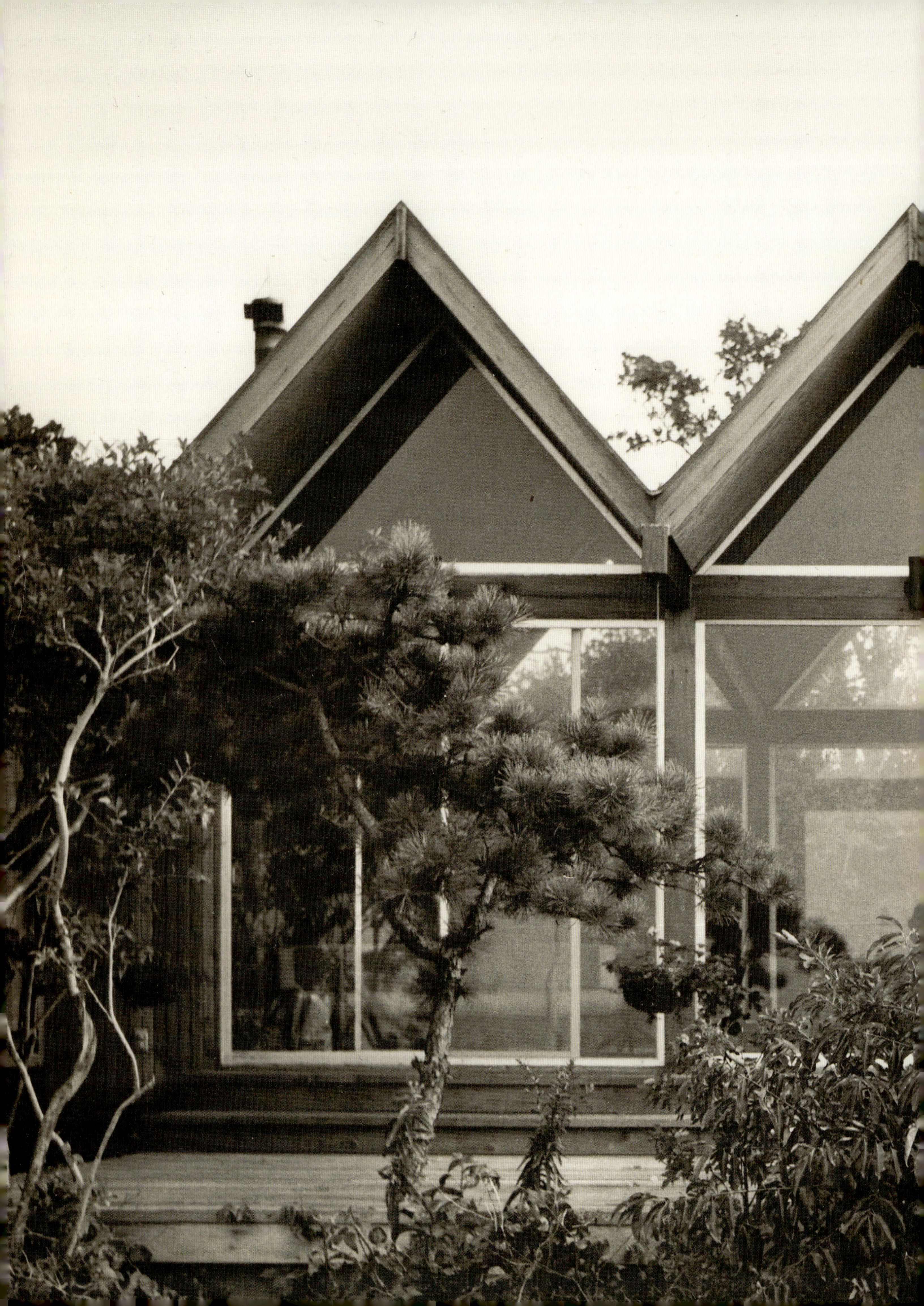

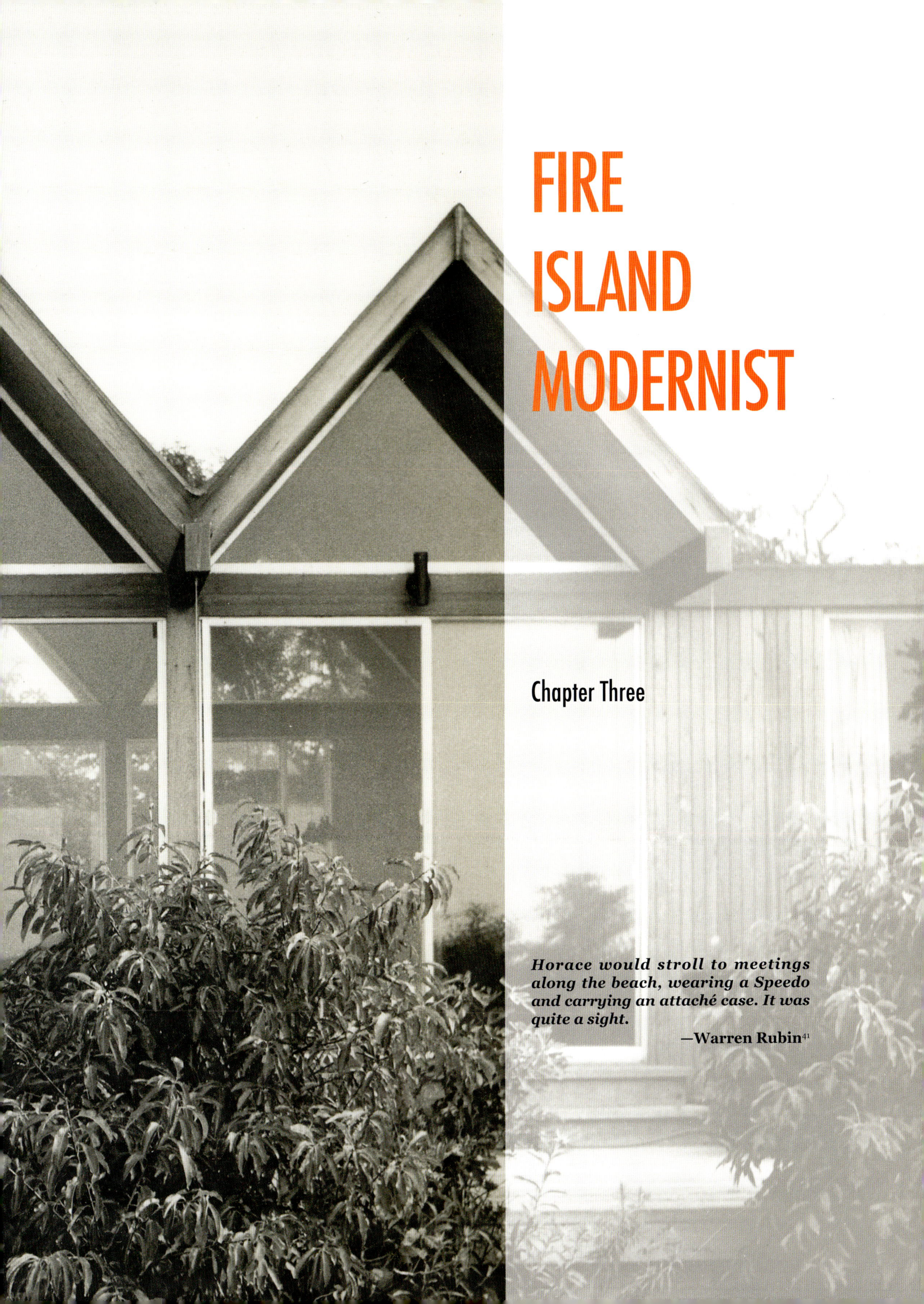

FIRE ISLAND MODERNIST

Chapter Three

Horace would stroll to meetings along the beach, wearing a Speedo and carrying an attaché case. It was quite a sight.

—**Warren Rubin**[41]

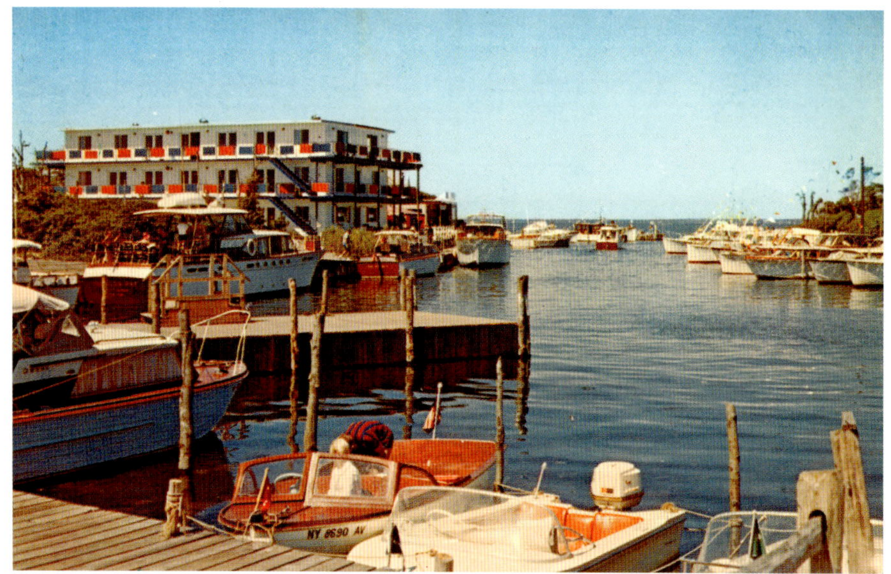

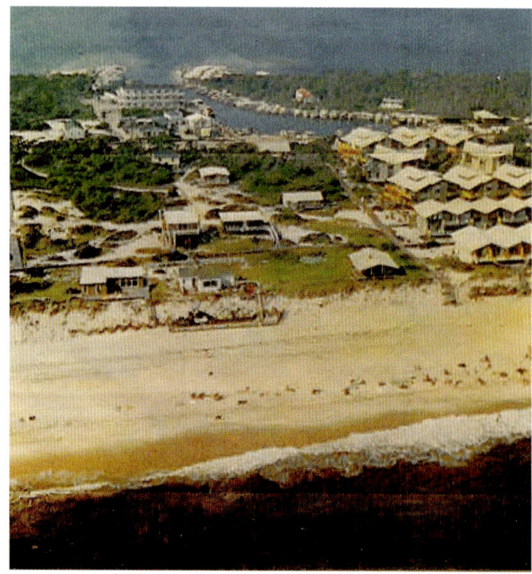

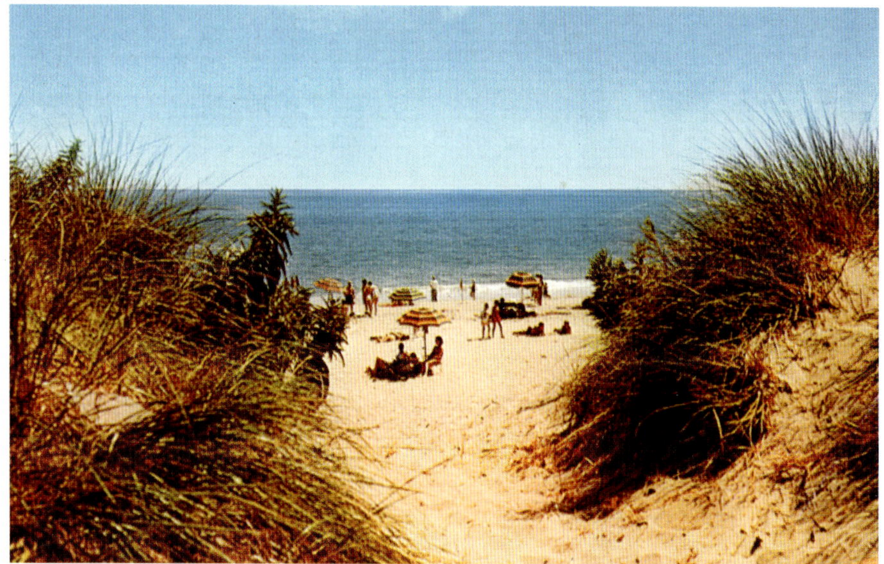

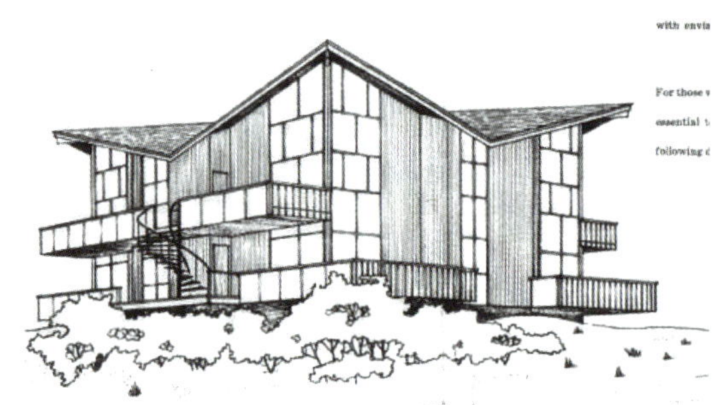

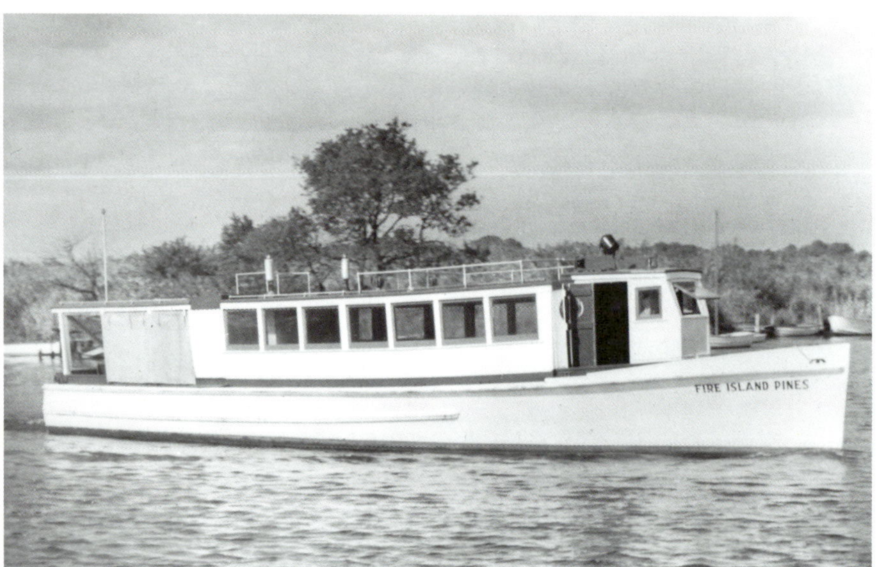

PAGES 54–55:
Wittstein-Miller House, Fire Island Pines, NY, 1962

UPPER LEFT:
Fire Island Pines Harbor, showing rebuilt Botel, ca. 1962

UPPER RIGHT:
Fire Island Pines aerial view, overlooking the new Island Pines Apartments at right, 1962

ABOVE:
Island Pines Apartments, rendering, 1960

MIDDLE LEFT:
Fire Island postcard

LOWER LEFT:
Fire Island Pines Ferry, 1958

OPPOSITE:
Gathering at Fire Island Pines Harbor, 1960s

"I am building myself a nice beach cottage. I hope you'll come up and visit," read the casual aside in Gifford's letter to a college friend in 1961.[42]

A series of letters written by Gifford from the mid-fifties to the early 1960s were peppered with tales of romantic conquest, naughty double entendres, pithy observations on theater performances, and a Floridian's struggle to understand the "cosmopolitan attitude in New York."[43] They paint a picture of a happy-go-lucky young man busily absorbing all that New York had to offer. By day, he worked full-time for another architect. By night, he designed a home in Houston for his sister, dabbled as a theatrical set builder, and leveraged his looks as a model. At the same time, the young architect set out to do for Fire Island what Paul Rudolph had done for the beaches of Sarasota.

"Where's that favorite relaxation spot of yours? Mountains? Seashore? Or a tranquil lake where the big ones never get away?...When you find that place, make your second home as wonderful as this one: handsome, tough, completely carefree," wrote *Better Homes and Gardens* about Gifford's first Fire Island home in 1962.[44]

Gifford once told a reporter that "It is not until forty, maybe forty-five that an architect does work of real monument."[45] At twenty-eight he saw himself as a student, not a master, of architecture. Accordingly, Gifford's first beach house adapted the forms of his teacher Louis Kahn's Trenton Bathhouse to life on the dunes. The bar-shaped home was anchored by a central, glassed-in space sheltered by a pyramid-shaped roof. Juxtaposed with this vaulted space were modest flat-roofed bedrooms on either side. Sundecks to the north and south created a crisscrossing floor plan. Like the Southern vernacular homes of his youth, it was raised several feet above the ground to capture breezes, but not high enough to break through the tree line, making it nearly invisible from the public walkway. Its approach consisted of a narrow, meandering boardwalk that traversed a small pond, dappled with tiny lily pads and populated with snapping turtles. The first glimpse of the home revealed an opaque corner, clad in redwood that weathered to a barklike patina. *Better Homes and Gardens* published images of the house in 1962 and sold the plans to readers. Two virtual replicas were soon built in the Pines, and the avant-garde architect Charles Renfro purchased one in 2013. Its sleek yet restrained renovation speaks to the resonance of these elemental dwellings for a new generation.

The Gifford residence's sophisticated site choreography, combined with elegant details, reveal an architect remarkably precocious for his age. The essential grammar of a Horace Gifford house could already be seen: the home was held

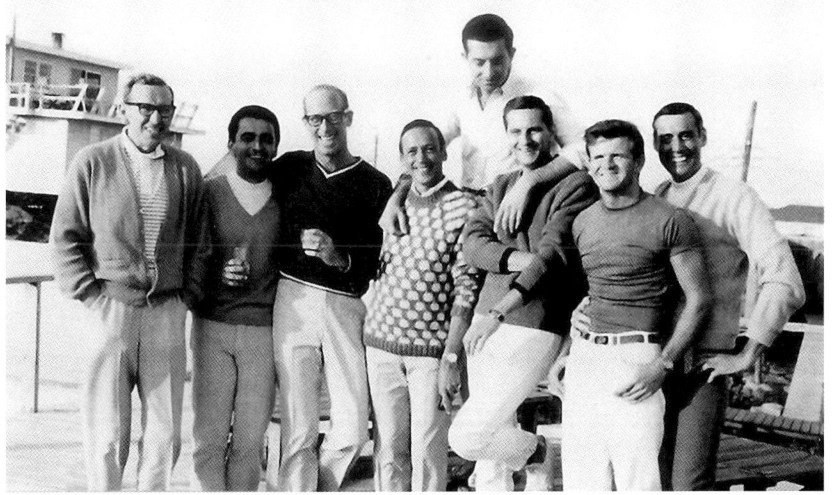

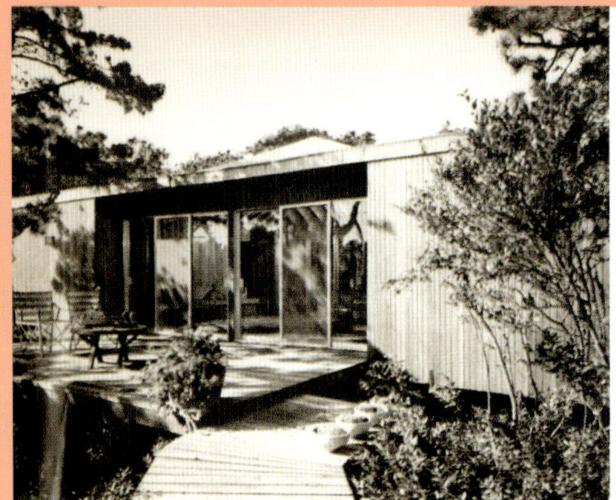

FIVE STAR HOME 3208
YOU CAN BUY PLANS *SEE PAGE 10*

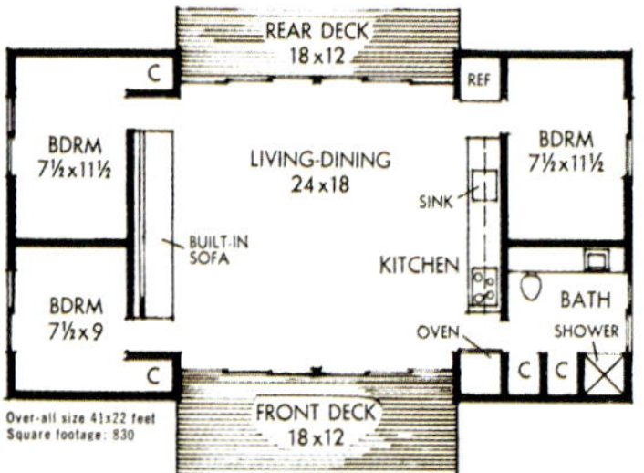

Troubles stay behind

By John D. Bloodgood

Where's that favorite relaxation spot of yours? Mountains? Seashore? Or is it a tranquil lake where the big ones never get away? Wherever it is, there's a place there to build your vacation home—one that will be waiting for you and your family every weekend you want to slip away.

When you find that place, make your second home as wonderful as this one: handsome, tough, completely carefree.

The exterior is as uncomplicated as vacation life itself—and so's the upkeep. That first staining of the tongue-and-groove redwood siding lets you forget it for years. The approach side is the same as the view side—it has no unwelcoming back to turn either way. Wide decks on each side stretch the living space to nearly crowd-size capacity.

Up goes the ceiling of the living room (below)—the peak inside follows the exterior roofline, to make the big living-dining-kitchen area more exciting. Construction is simple, and the exposed rafters create a cozy, relaxed atmosphere; it even makes cooking seem easier in the along-the-wall kitchen.

Continued on page 10

Photographs: Lisanti. Designer: Horace Gifford. Data: Jane Price

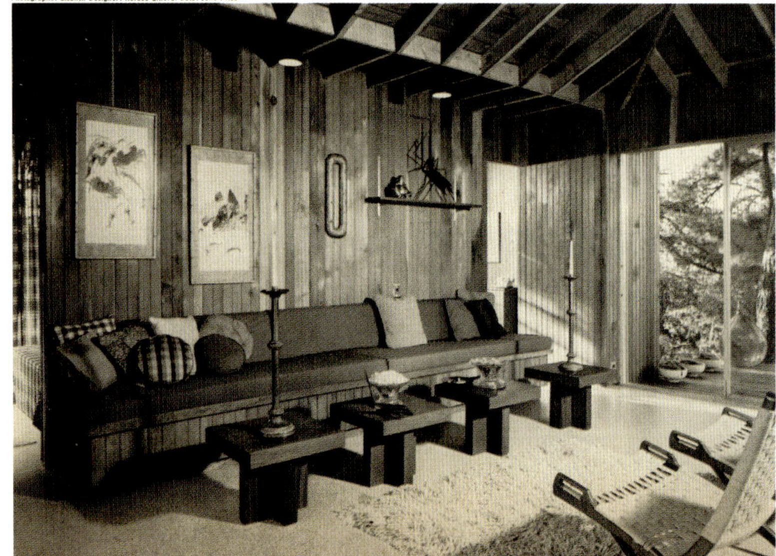

Let troubles stay behind

Continued

Simplicity—both in construction and in maintenance—is particularly important when you build your vacation house. This one uses the same material inside as on the outside walls—tongue-and-groove redwood siding. Easy to apply both places, it has a wax finish inside that doesn't turn play time into housekeeping time.

Sliding glass doors do the entire ventilating and daylighting jobs, in addition to providing access to the outdoors. They double as windows in the bedrooms (in the bath, too, with obscured glass) and make the wall framing go fast.

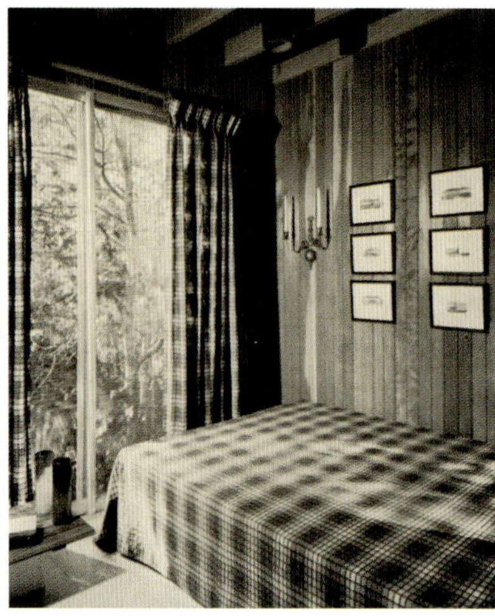

Even the smallest bedroom—this one is just 7x9 feet—is completely comfortable when the outdoors is only inches away and in full view. And with the sliding glass open, you're cooled by a floor-to-ceiling breeze.

The wood paneling lends as much atmosphere to the bedrooms as it does to the daytime living areas.

How to get plans for FIVE STAR homes

Five Star Home, 3208, shown on page 6, is one of a monthly series for which you can buy complete plans with the following features:

- ★ **Designs by America's foremost architects** in styles from Cape Cod to Contemporary.
- ★ **Detailed working drawings,** from which your home will be erected. The cost is $18 for the first set; $18 for the second set; $9 for the third and additional sets ordered at the same time.
- ★ **Complete specifications** outlining quality of materials and workmanship.
- ★ **Builder-owner agreement,** a suggested legal contract to assure home is built as specified.
- ★ **Cost-finding list of materials.** (List available at 25 cents purchased separately.) With this list, a builder or building-materials dealer can estimate costs.

These Five Star home plans may be ordered directly from Better Homes & Gardens Five Star Home Plan Service, 1700 West Hubbard Street, Chicago 22, Illinois. In many localities you can order plans through your building-materials dealer.

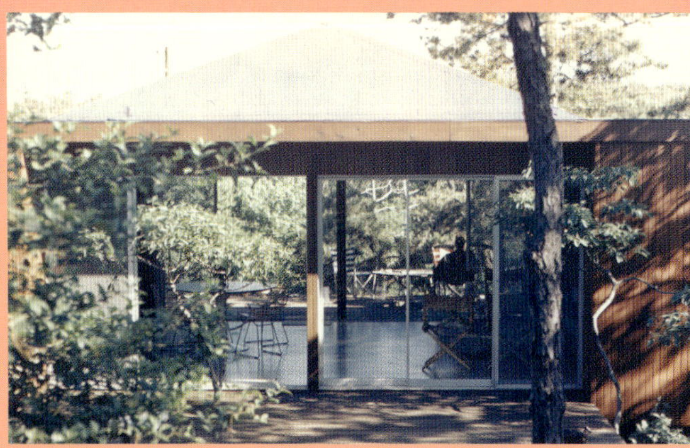

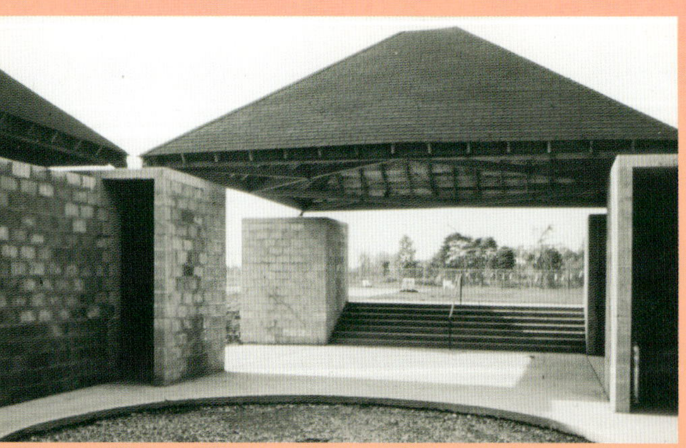

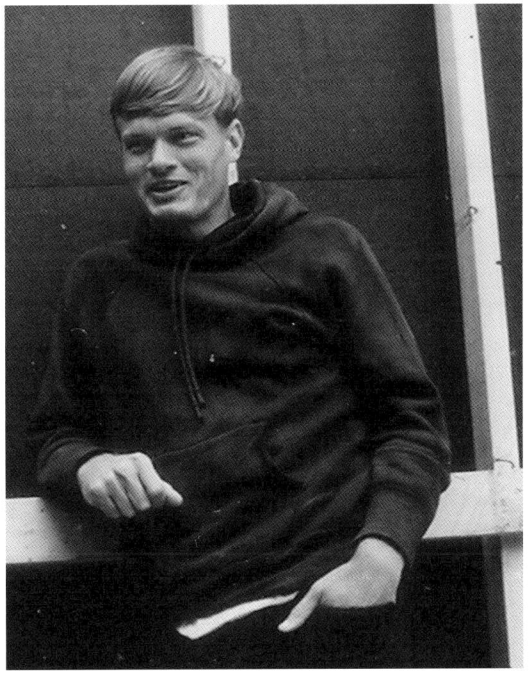

aloft on tree trunks or locust posts, ensconced in multiple sundecks, clad with naturally weathering cedar and redwood, tailored with built-in furniture, and framed by an untouched landscape. Some of these qualities could be found in his contemporaries' work in the Hamptons, but there was one totem of modern architecture that Horace Gifford decisively rejected.

At the time, prefabrication represented a kind of holy grail for the architectural profession. It was the ultimate fulfillment of industrialization's promise and a means to make well-designed homes accessible to the middle class. While architects dreamed of design dividends that might accrue from the economies of industrialized housing, all but a few builders harnessed this technology to churn out "ticky-tacky little boxes" that "all look just the same," in the words of the folk song made famous by Pete Seeger in 1963.[46]

The built reality of the dune-dragged, prefab cottages already pocking the Pines did not go unnoticed by Gifford. Prefabrication was ill-suited to the transportation challenges of an island accessed by ferries and traversed by "roller-coaster" boardwalks, so Gifford rethought the whole enterprise for this unique setting. Structurally, his methods differed little from the stick construction that characterized earlier beach shacks. In order to have the least possible impact on the landscape, he specified that all materials be made of wood and carried to the site by hand. His houses still rested on friction pilings, but Gifford composed and selectively clad his to ensure a robust connection to their site. He considered the design of the base to be as important as the dwelling above it.

Naturally weathering, low-maintenance cedar comprised the primary cladding material, inside and out. Gifford, essentially, treated all surfaces like floors, with planks that flexed with the inevitable movements of a house on stilts. He then interspersed solid volumes with walls of glass set into the thinnest possible aluminum frames to merge with the outdoors. Most furniture was built-in. What remained of the site, at least two-thirds, he left untouched, save for a winding path to reach the house. Construction relied on a somewhat standardized catalog of hardware and joinery techniques, allowing Gifford to focus on deft siting and sculptural presence.

OPPOSITE, ABOVE:
Gifford House, Fire Island Pines, NY, 1961, published in *Better Homes and Gardens*, August 1962

OPPOSITE, LOWER RIGHT:
Louis Kahn, Trenton Bathhouse, Ewing Township, NJ, 1955

OPPOSITE, LOWER LEFT:
Gifford House

ABOVE:
Horace Gifford, 1963

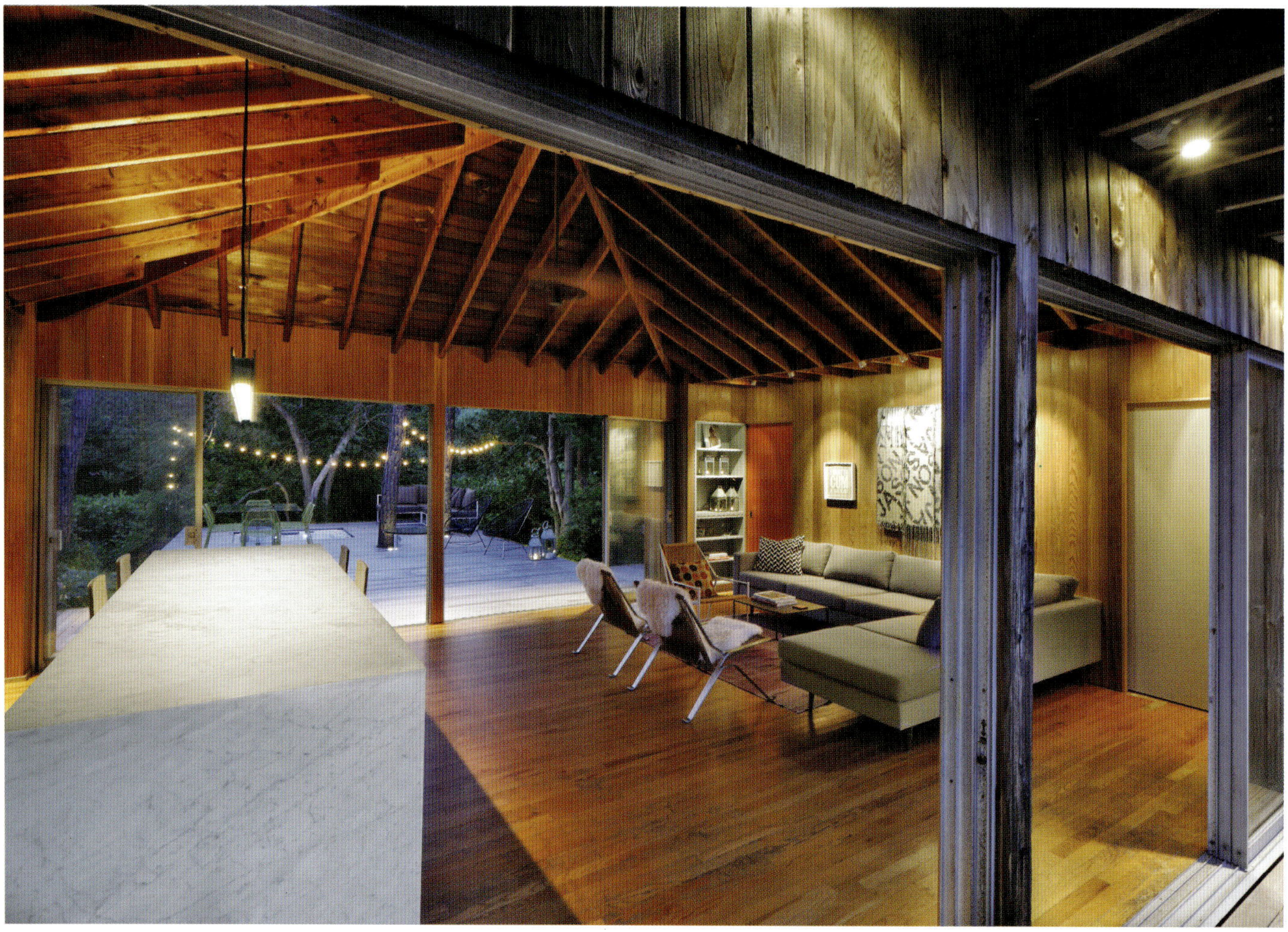

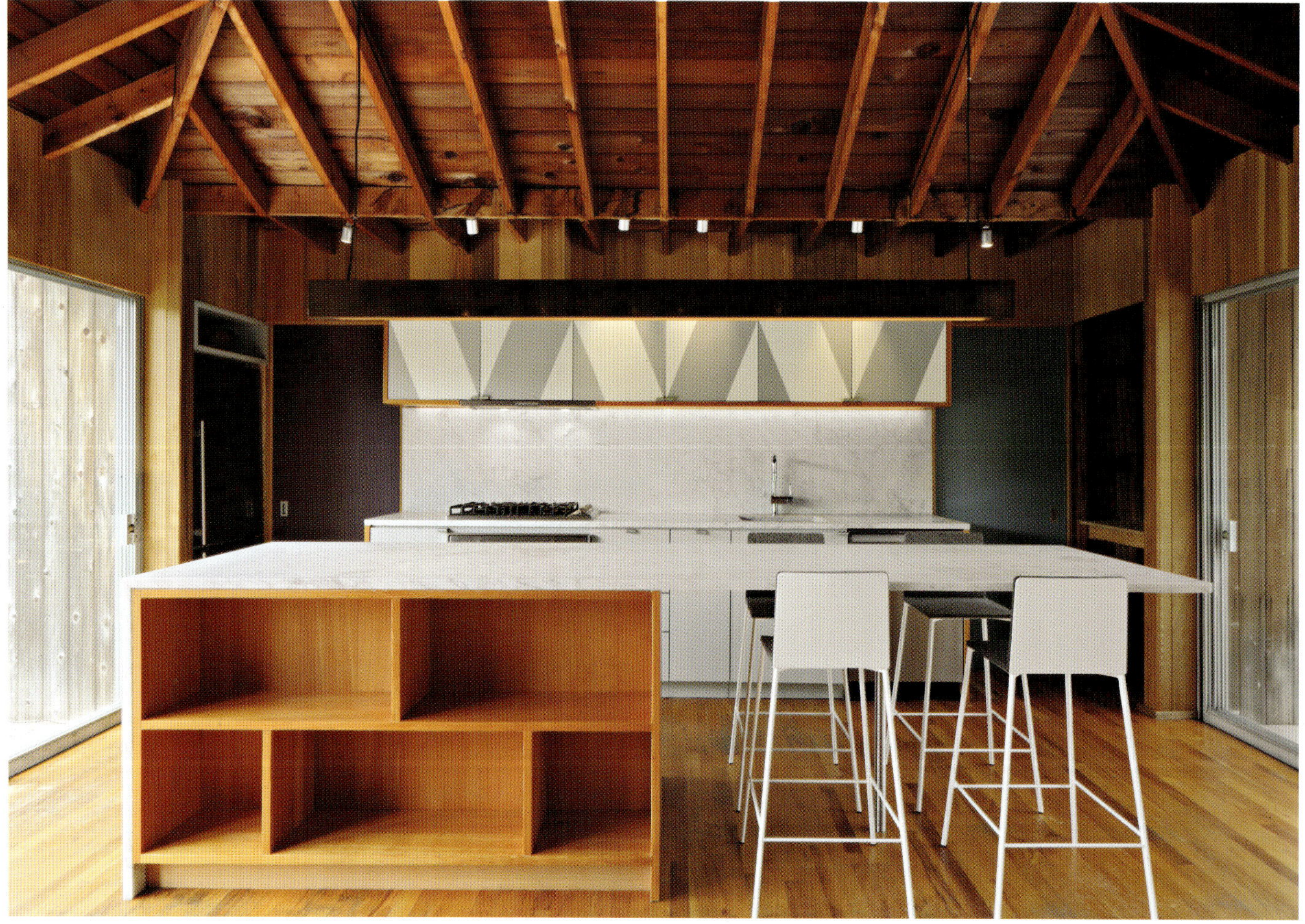

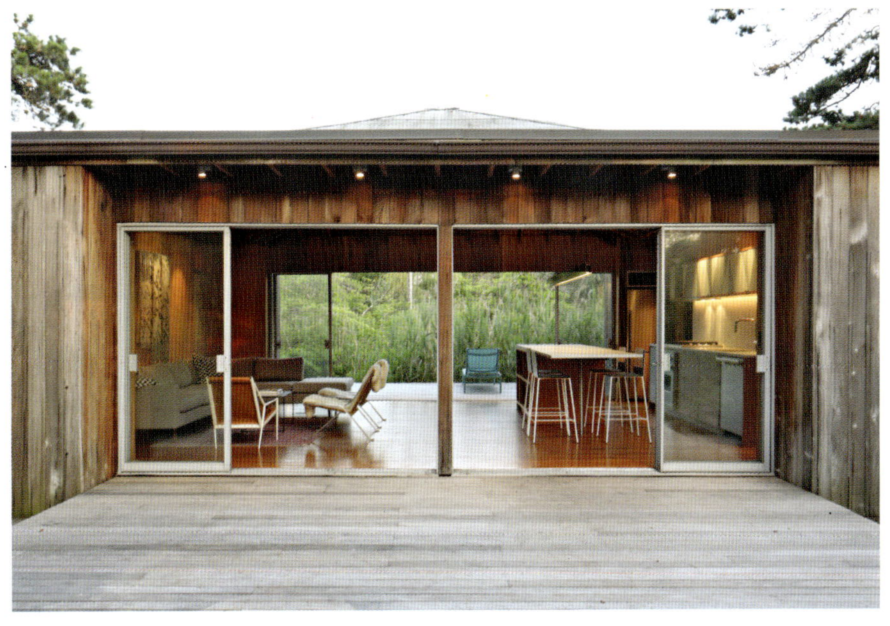

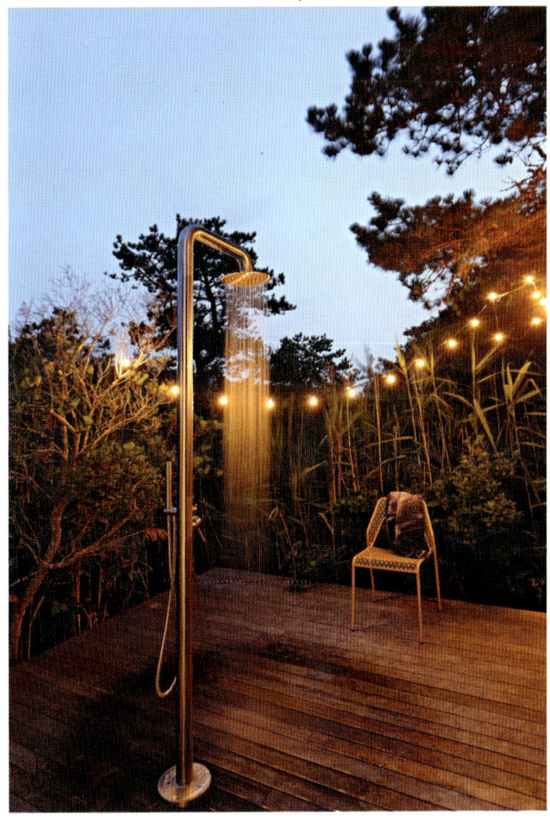

OPPOSITE AND ABOVE:
Renfro House, Fire Island Pines, NY, 1961, renovated 2014

PAGES 62–63:
Wittstein-Miller House, Fire Island Pines, NY, 1962, published in *The American Home*, April 1964

Gifford was practicing in the spirit of Frank Lloyd Wright's Usonian homes, which shared a common constructional grammar that was flexible enough to allow for formal and spatial variety.[47] The Usonian experiment was hampered by its far-flung geography, forcing Wright to engage novice builders across many states, and this affected both the quality and cost of these nominally middle-class homes. Gifford's physical proximity to most of his commissioned houses enabled a hands-on approach, so he personally trained local builders until he had developed a shortlist of the most capable hands.

Gifford spent all available funds for his house in the Pines, obtaining a mortgage on the basis of a trumped-up savings account that was temporarily padded by his mother. Yet in spite of his resourcefulness, he found himself the owner of a home that he could not afford to live in. Edwin Wittstein resolved his new paramour's dilemma. For the summer of 1962, he secured renters for Gifford's residence, while the architect joined Wittstein and Robert Miller in the new home he had just designed for them.

The architect-with-benefits arrangement produced a dynamic house. It retained the cruciform plan of Gifford's own residence but shook off its strict symmetry. In place of a brooding pyramid roof, Wittstein and Miller were sheltered by a serrated roofline that flooded the interior with light. Smooth mahogany ceiling panels set against gray-stained redwood beams drew the eye upward and outward, toward the bay to the north and the forest to the south. Trees freely penetrated the south deck, shading it during the summer, while a rustic cast-iron stove warmed the interior. The three-bedroom home of 1,150 square feet cost only $12,500.[48] It was published in the *New York Times*, followed by *The American Home*, which made it the cover feature for its 1964 "vacation homes" issue.

Gifford secured a second commission from Wittstein and Miller by sketching a plan in the sand for his delighted clients. This new lot lacked the sea and forest contrasts of their first home, so Gifford changed tack. This time, he designed a vast octagonal space supported by rectangular decks and rooms alternating across each of its eight sides, celebrating all views equally. Sheltered by its great roof, the house remains one of the most sociable and alluring spaces that Gifford ever created. For their second home, Wittstein and Miller proved to be reluctant modernists. They insisted on traditional wooden casement windows and French doors, lending a lodgelike feeling to the home, which they filled with antiques.

2 FACED HOUSE

Here is a vacation house that neatly solves the old either/or dilemma of whether you should go to the sea or into the forest for rest and rejuvenation. The choice here becomes as simple as deciding whether to walk out the one side of the house onto the beach or out the other into the trees that grow to the edge of the deck. (In fact, in some places they grow *through* the redwood platform.) The designer took full advantage of the site and chose to orient the house so it capitalizes on all possibilities. There is no main side or front to this house. The symmetry of the plan lends itself to this and permits the direct contrast of light and shade, interior and exterior, beach and forest. The sharply pitched gables over the central section give a heightened sense of shelter and enclosure in an otherwise open structure. Bedrooms, studio, and bath are grouped at the sides of the living area right under the low, flat sections of the roof, which gives them a more cozy feeling. The windows and doors in these side rooms are located so that there is a clear passage of light from a window on one side of the house to the opposite window. The secluded location on Great South Bay, New York, makes draperies on the wide windows unnecessary. By night the house is visible only from the sea. By day trees shade the bright southern exposure. A natural air conditioning effect is produced by opening the wide windows to the cool north breeze or the warm south, as desired. The dramatic architectural design needs only the most restrained interior decorating. Varied wood tones, large open walls, and clerestory windows are dramatically accented by aluminum frames. No paint breaks up the natural materials. The house is mainly redwood. Charcoal stain on the roof frame adds contrast. The roof facing is mahogany; flooring is stained pine. The wood cabinets are designed without hardware. Spot lighting in the beams can be thrown up to light the peaks or turned down into the room.

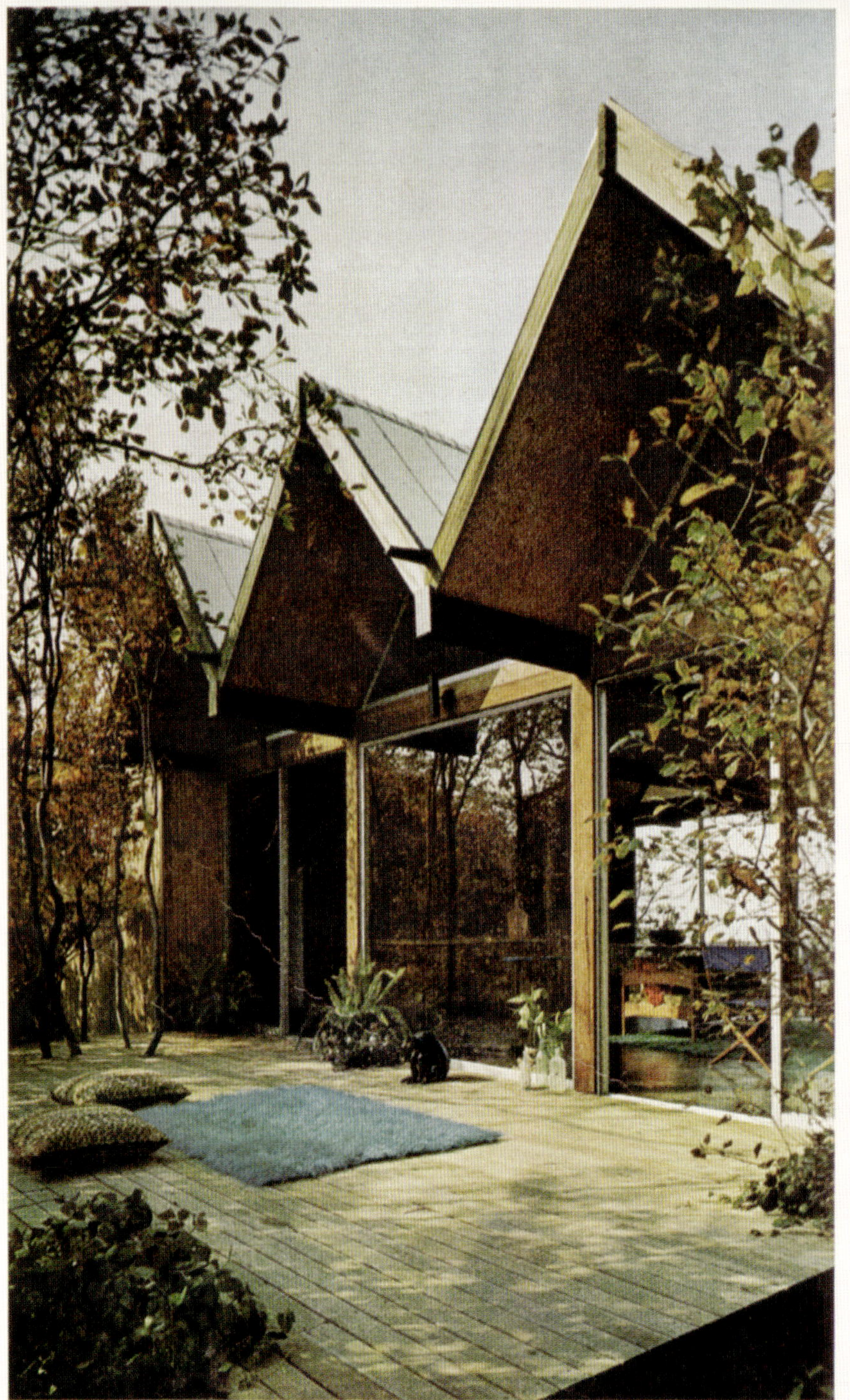

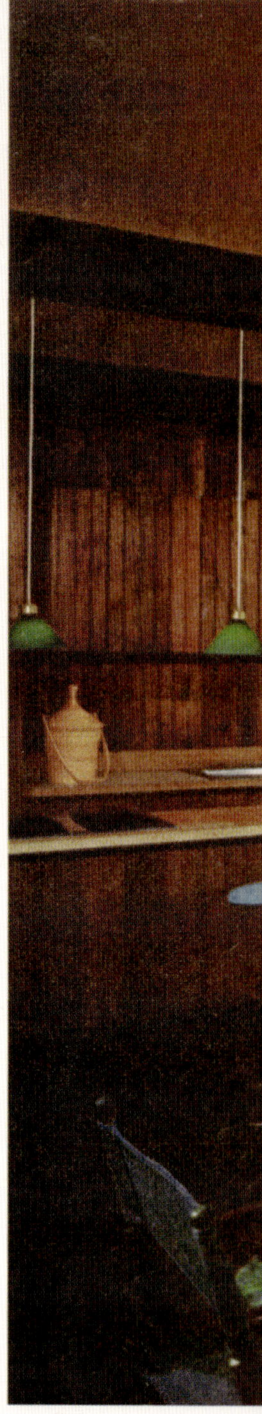

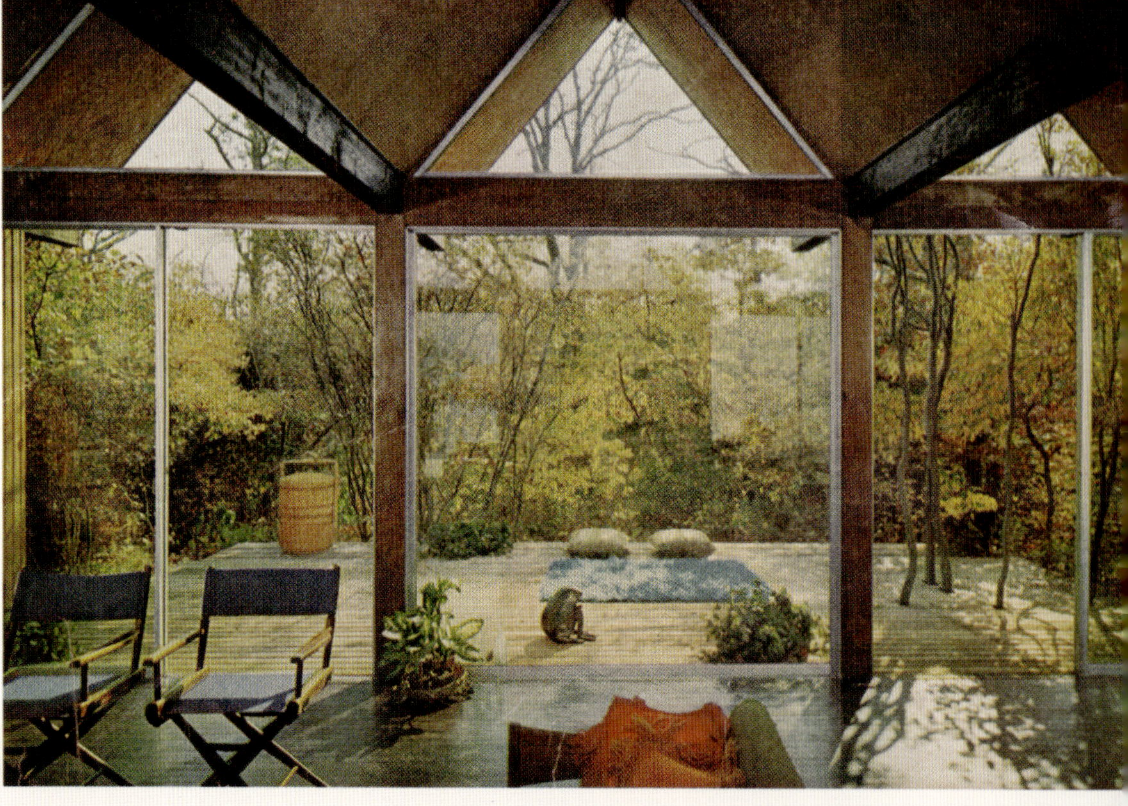

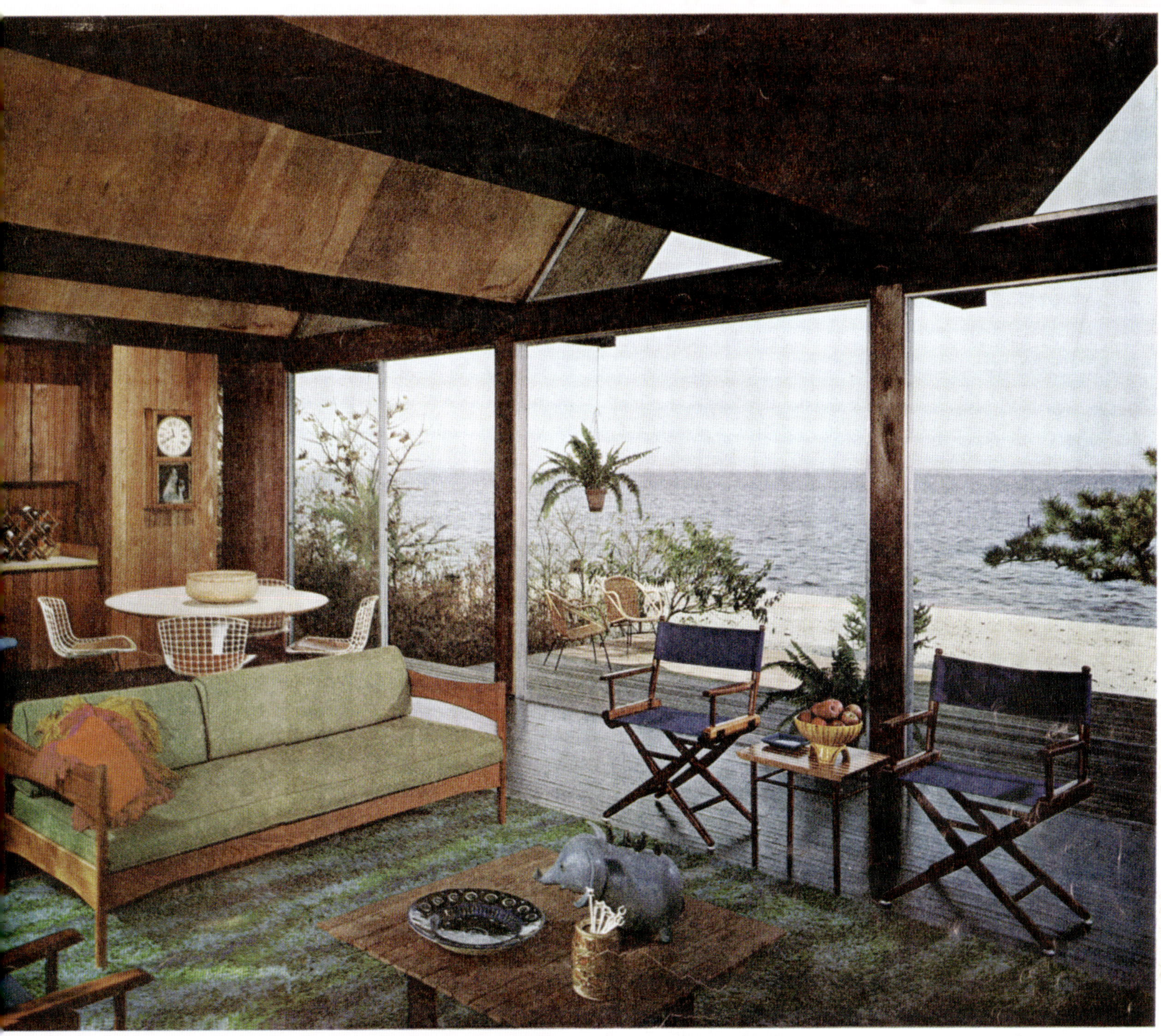

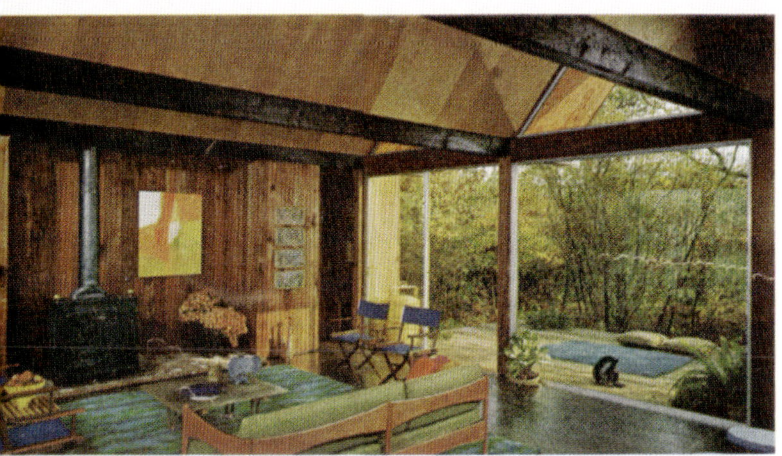

tographs show peaked roof and 20x25′ living-ng area which faces both forest and beach. Two vs at left show trees poking through the deck. ol blue and green are used with warm wood es. Open kitchen and free-standing counter are one end of living area. Franklin stove at other keeps chill out in cool weather. At right, a view bar with bath beyond as seen from the kitchen a. Plan shows relationship of open and private as with deck on both sides. Bedrooms face beach.

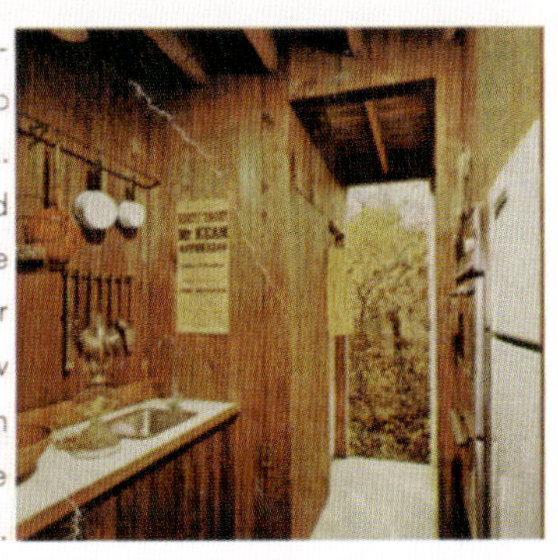

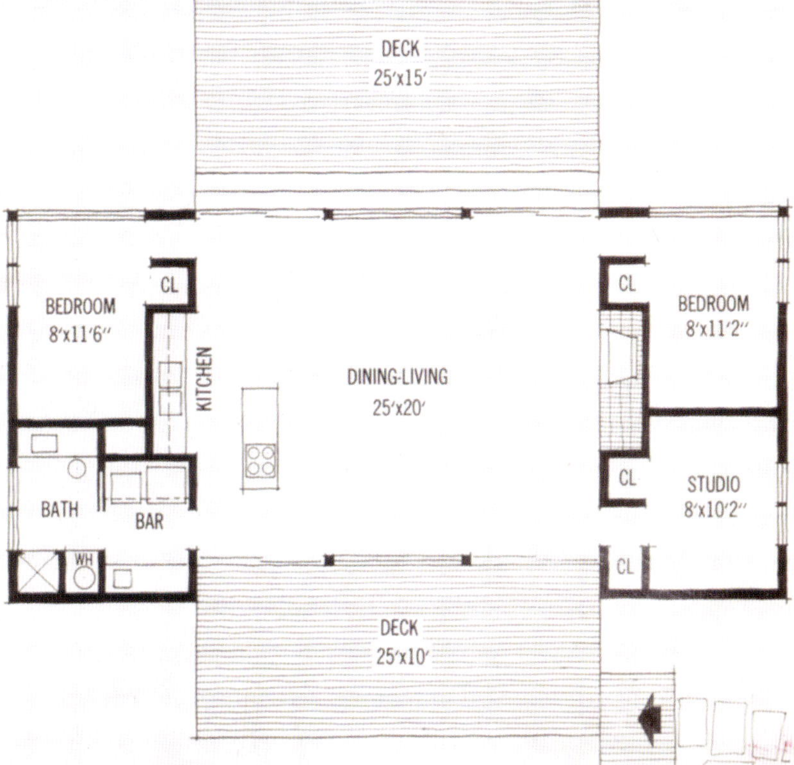

The architect's relationship with Wittstein and Miller cooled after the pair built a third Pines home on a prime ocean lot but designed it themselves, without Gifford's help. The home's frequent misattribution to Horace Gifford only deepened the rift. When passing by, he ostentatiously turned his back to the house before offering a slim greeting. All was forgiven a few years later, when Gifford needed investment partners for oceanfront property in his hometown of Vero Beach.

Prior to this drama, Wittstein and Miller recommended Gifford to their friend Kenneth Leedom, director of the National Academy of Television Arts and Sciences. Leedom's treeless lot in the Pines lay low in the dunes, soon to be surrounded by other homes. Without views to exploit, Gifford created his own. A courtyard bounded by separate living and sleeping structures created a protected outdoor space. Enormous sliding doors that tucked into pockets shut out the encroaching construction (and prying eyes) all around, while long, narrow jalousie windows facing east and west balanced privacy with cross ventilation. Yet another feature in *The American Home* brought the Leedom-Cott residence to a national audience, entitled "An Open and Shut Case for Privacy." Indeed, privacy was still essential for gay pioneers quietly infiltrating the Pines in 1963. In the background of the double-page spread loomed a pokey knockoff of Gifford's first, pyramid-roofed residence. After just two years in the Pines, Gifford already had lesser imitators.

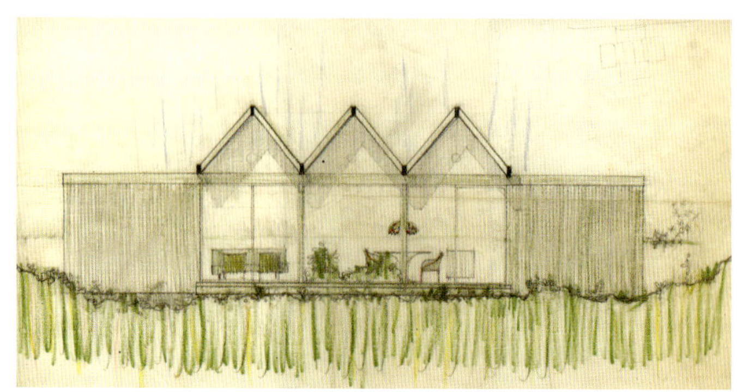

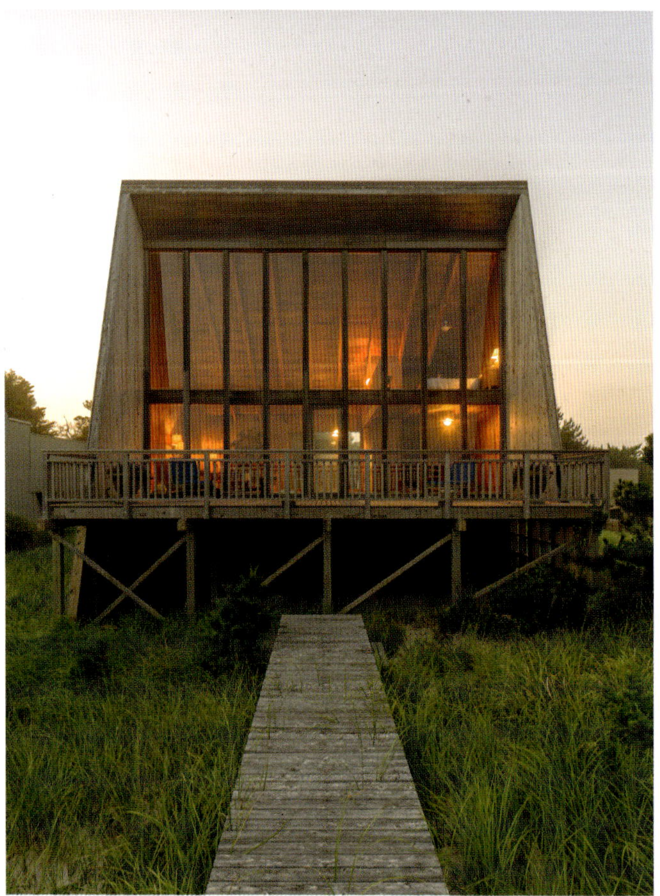

ABOVE:
Wittstein-Miller House, Fire Island Pines, NY, 1962, sketch

LEFT:
Wittstein-Miller House 3, designed by Wittstein and Miller, Fire Island Pines, NY, 1967

OPPOSITE:
Wittstein-Miller House on the cover of *The American Home*, April 1964

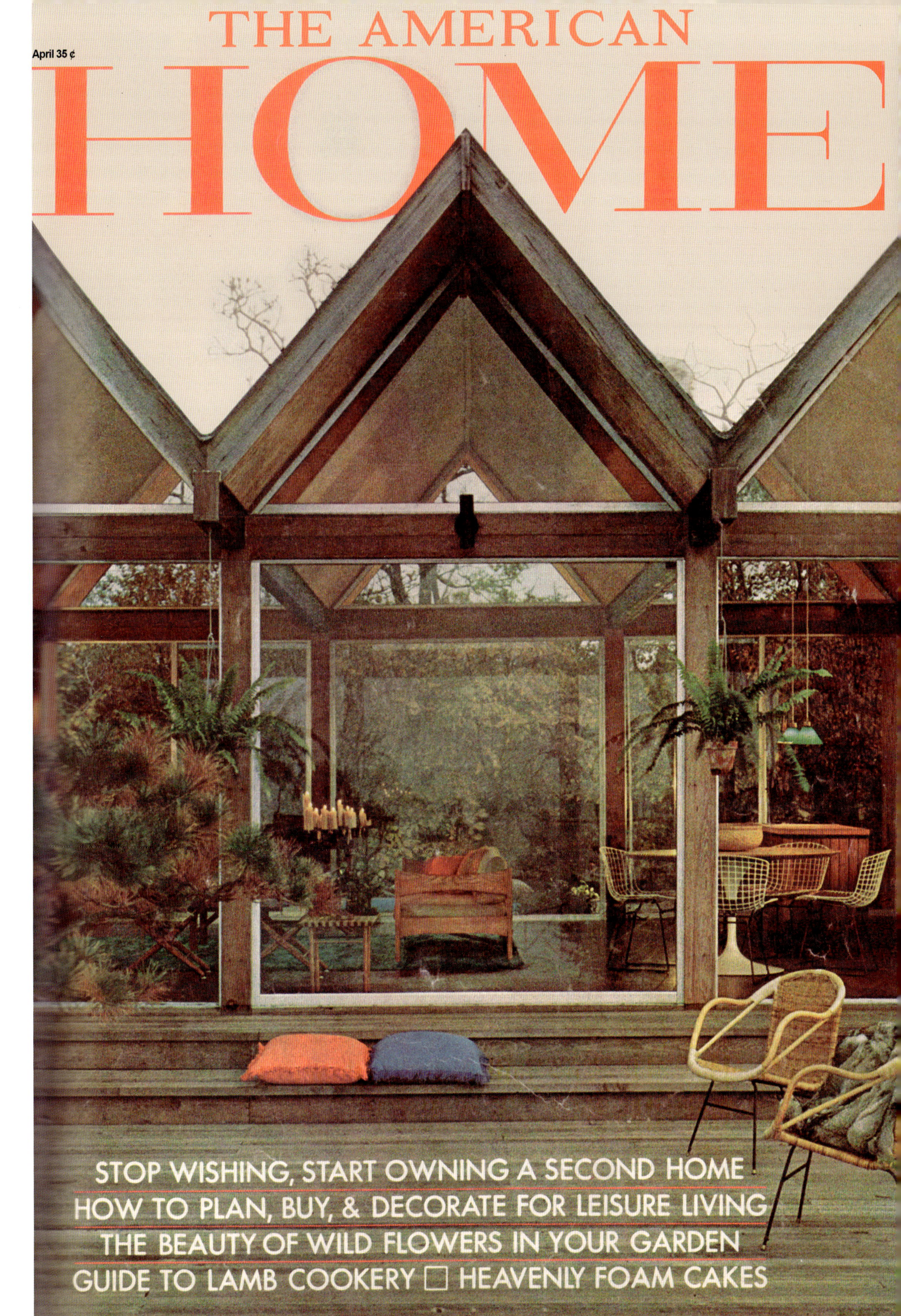
THE AMERICAN
HOME
April 35¢
STOP WISHING, START OWNING A SECOND HOME
HOW TO PLAN, BUY, & DECORATE FOR LEISURE LIVING
THE BEAUTY OF WILD FLOWERS IN YOUR GARDEN
GUIDE TO LAMB COOKERY □ HEAVENLY FOAM CAKES

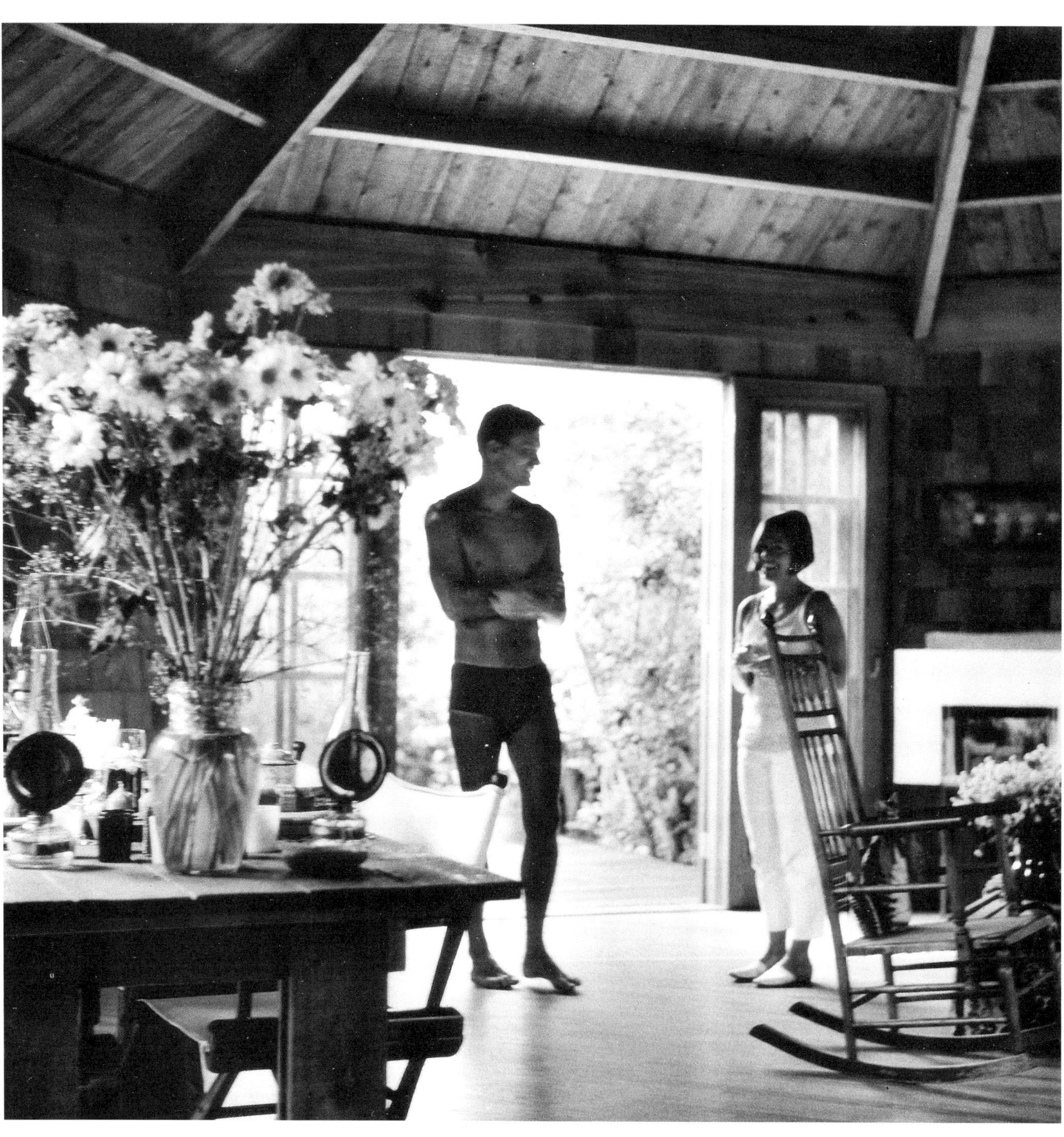

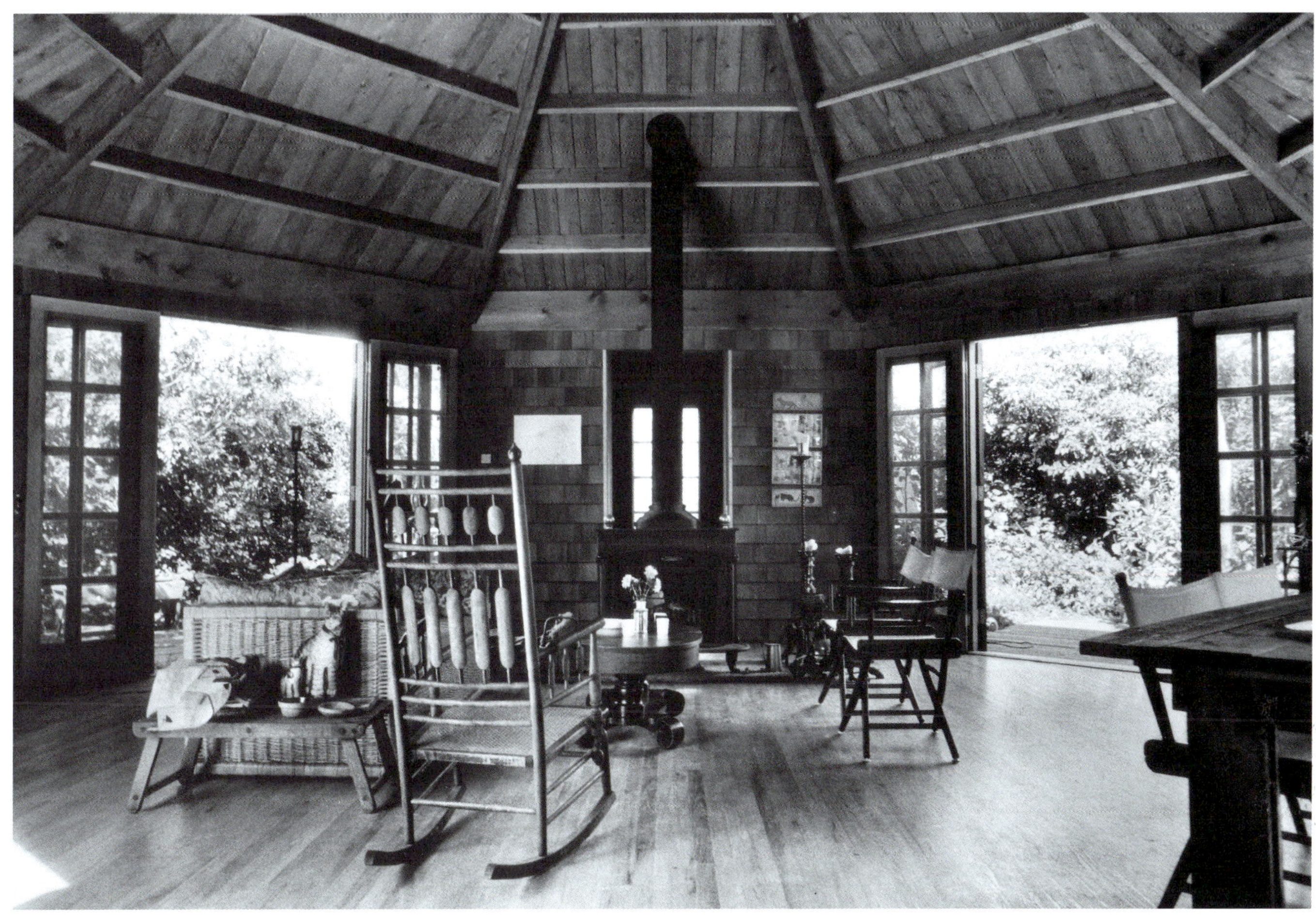

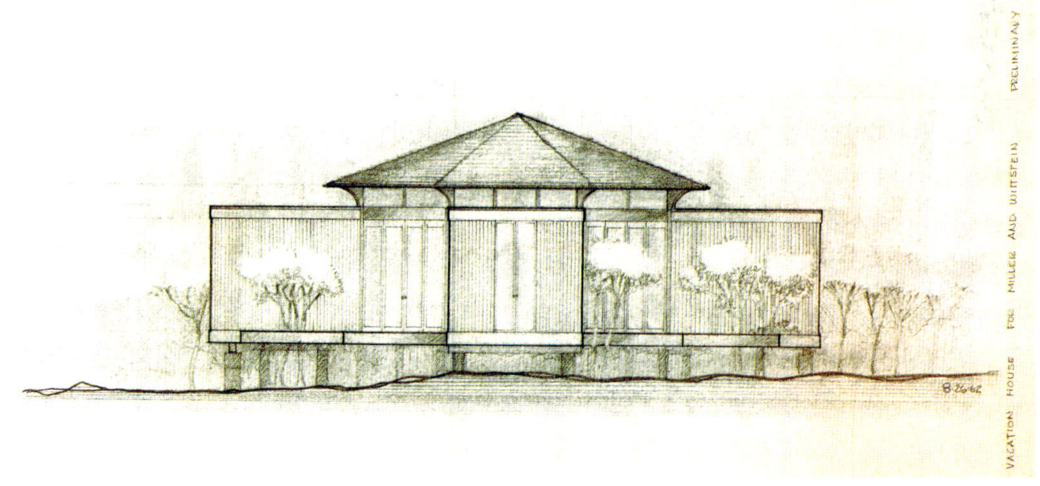

OPPOSITE:
Horace Gifford and Trudy Frank at Wittstein-Miller House II, Fire Island Pines, NY, ca. 1964

TOP:
Wittstein-Miller House II, Fire Island Pines, NY, 1963

ABOVE:
Sketch of Wittstein-Miller House II, Fire Island Pines, NY, August 1962

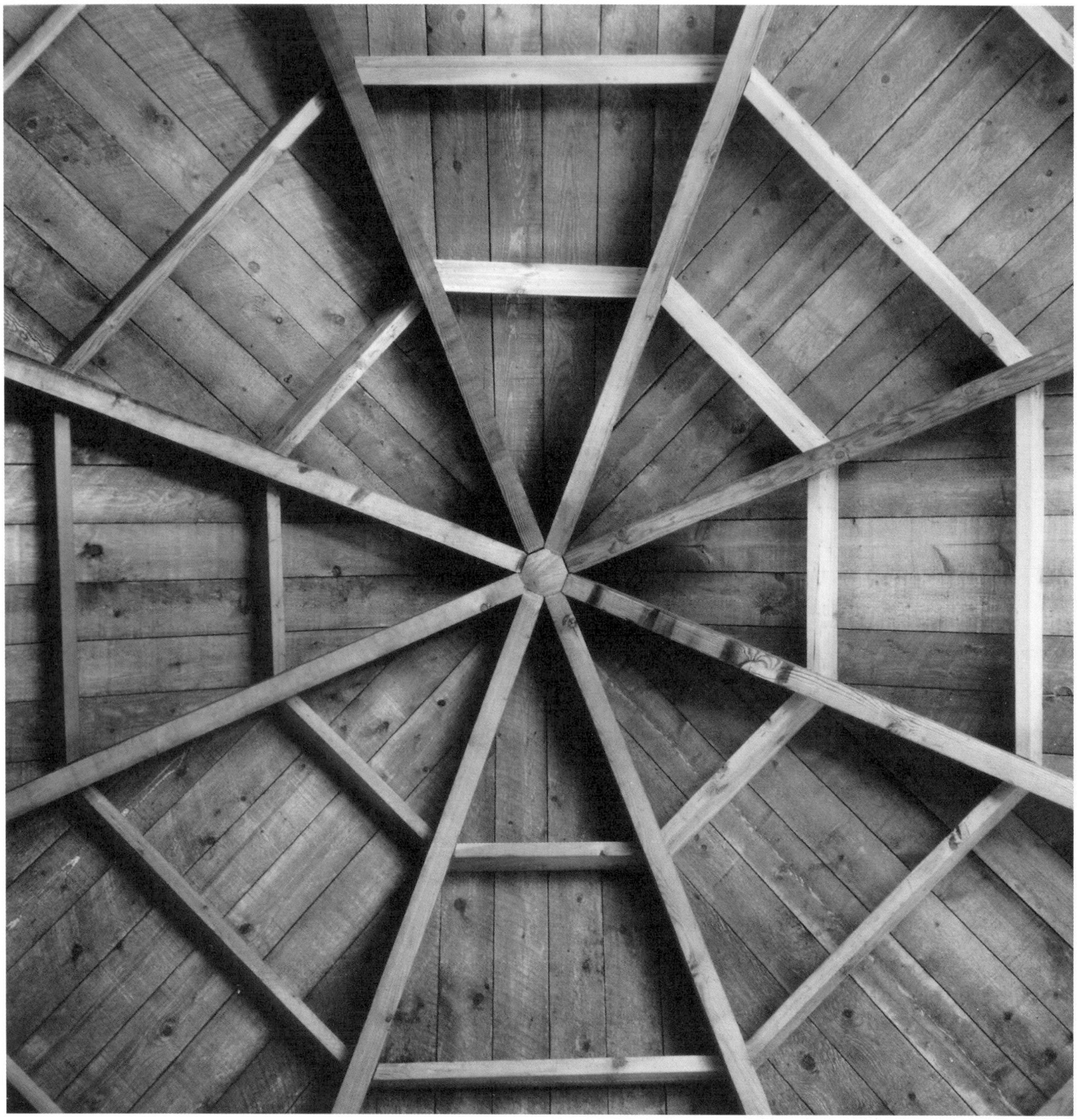

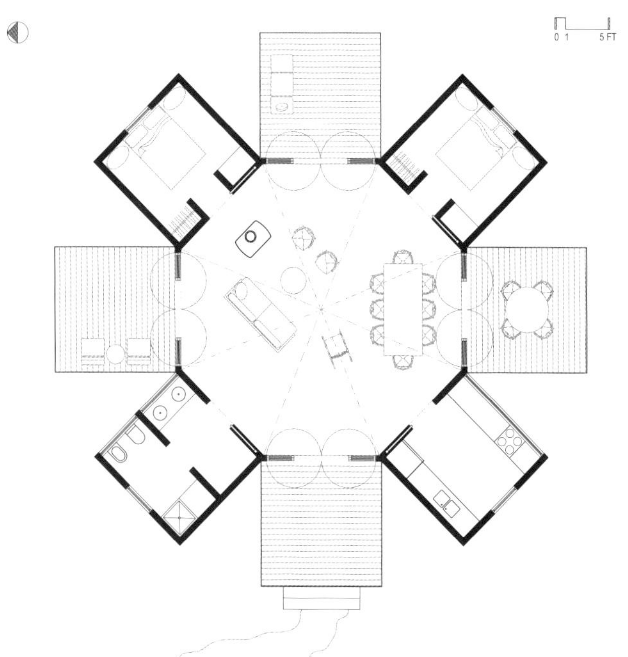

ABOVE:
Wittstein-Miller House II, ceiling detail

LEFT:
Wittstein-Miller House II, floor plan

OPPOSITE, ABOVE:
Wittstein-Miller House II

OPPOSITE, LOWER RIGHT:
Robert Miller (left) with a friend during Wittstein-Miller House II construction

OPPOSITE, LOWER LEFT:
Edwin Wittstein, Wittstein-Miller House II, interior. Robert Miller sits at head of table.

PAGES 70–71:
Leedom-Cott House, Fire Island Pines, NY, 1963, published in *The American Home,* April 1964

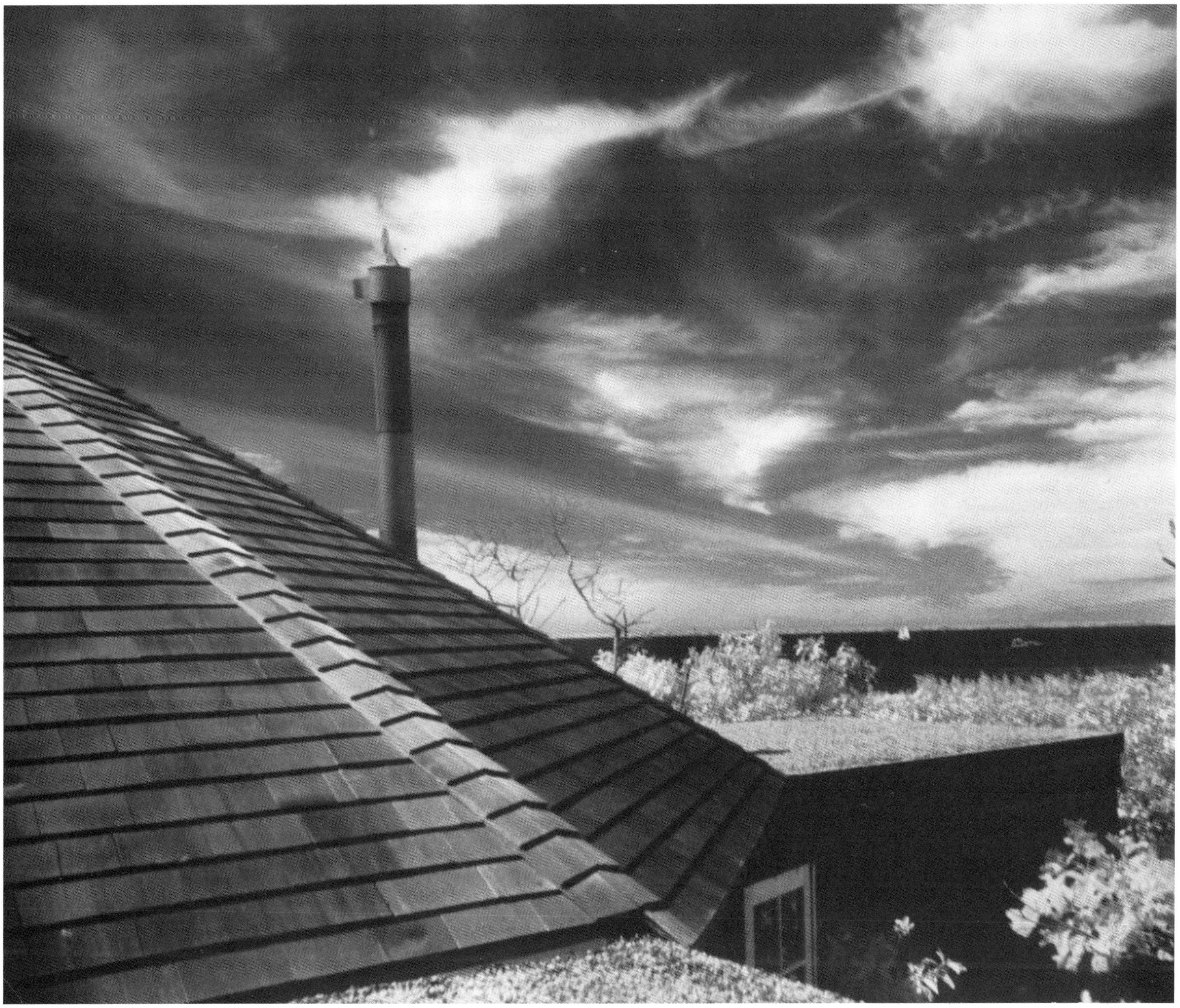

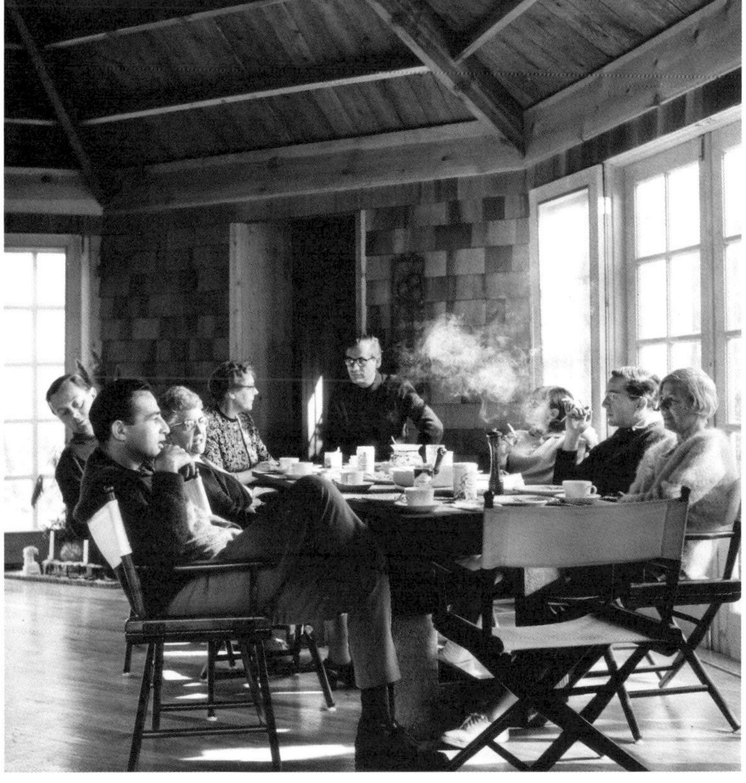

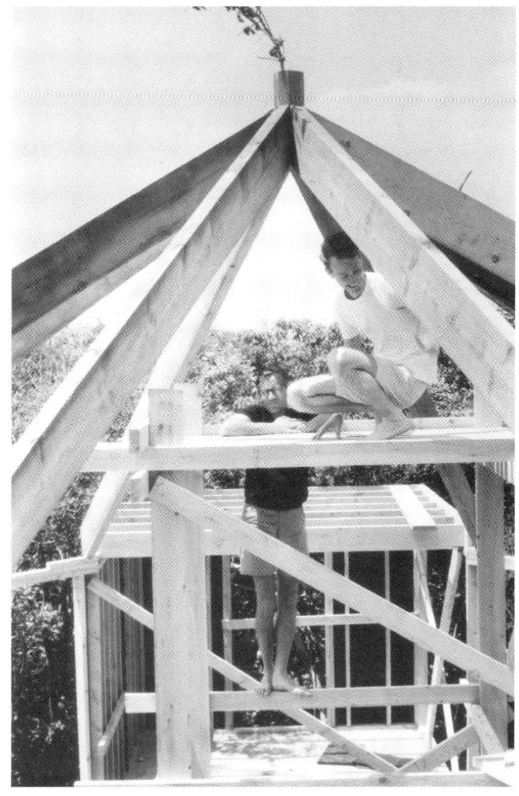

from it all. Unfortunately, it's often impossible to find a site that is remote enough yet doesn't interfere with comfort and convenience. Worse yet, one's apt to find that dozens of others have already discovered the spot, or soon will. One happy solution is seen in this house at Fire Island Pines, New York, which will retain its privacy regardless of present or future surroundings. This house on a low exposed lot is built around an open central court. Living areas are on one side, bedrooms and bath on the other. Sliding glass doors separate the rooms from the court. The entrances to the court itself can be closed of from the wind, sun or people with heavy wooden panels resembling boxcar doors. The only windows opening directly to the outside are narrow louvered ones on the ends. Al others face the cout. Easy-maintenance materials contibute to the slef sufficiency of this structure. The inexpensive, unstained rough-sawn siding which weathers very well fits the character of the unembellised grassy site.

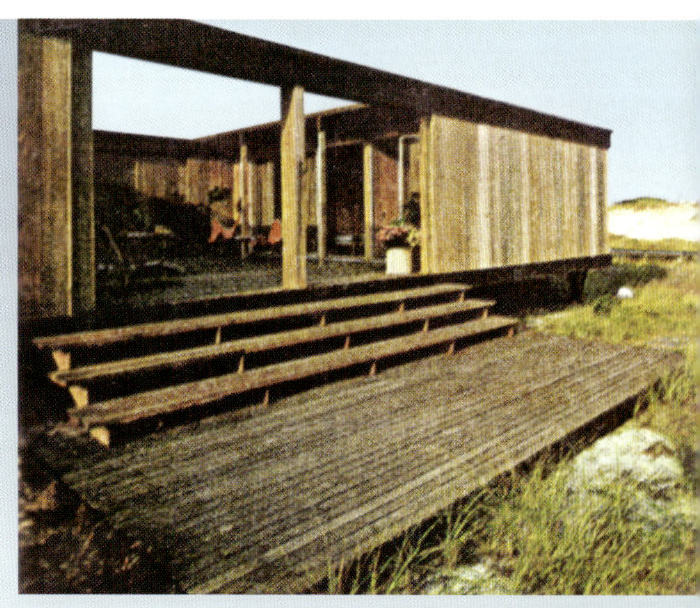

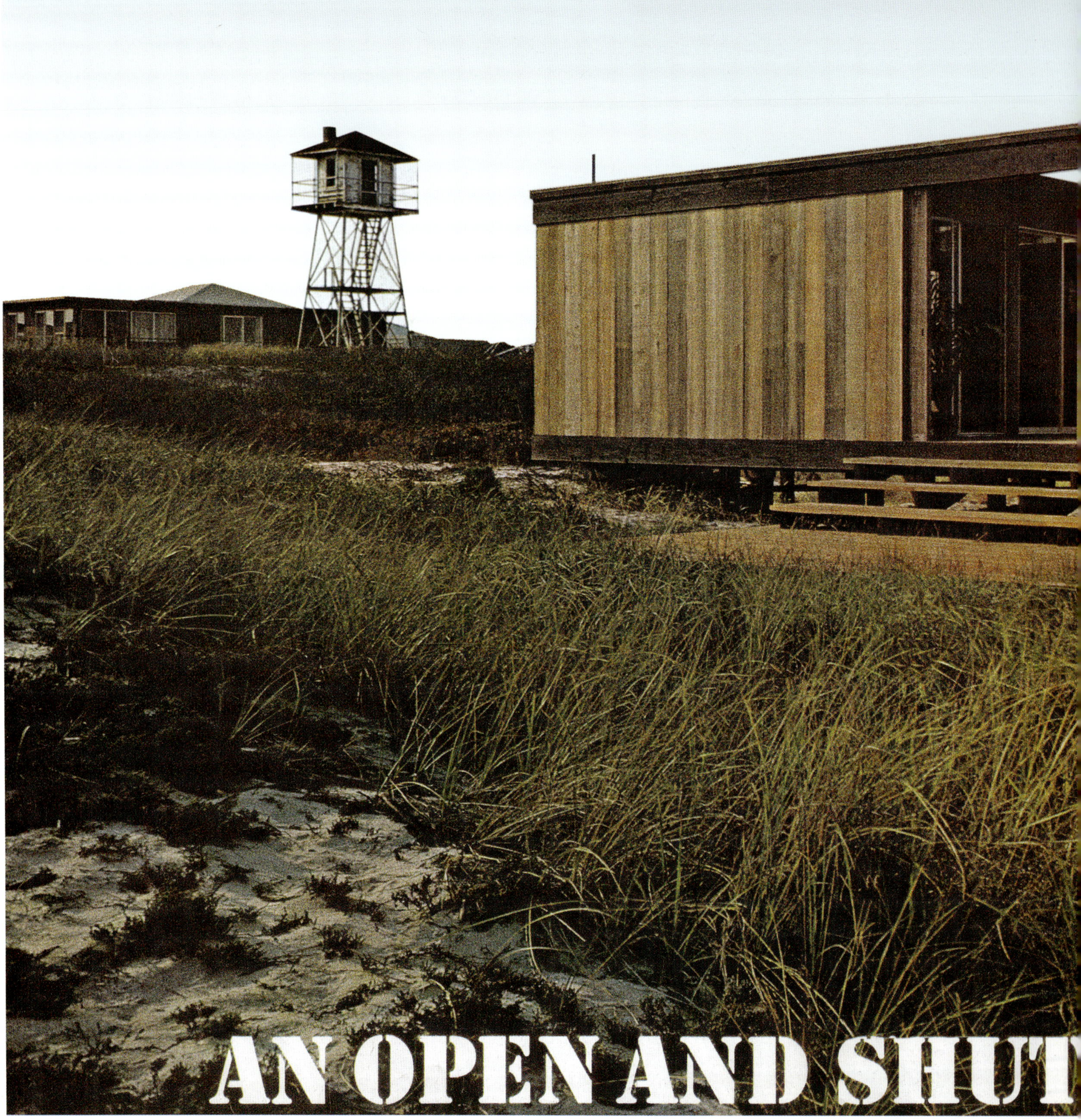

AN OPEN AND SHUT

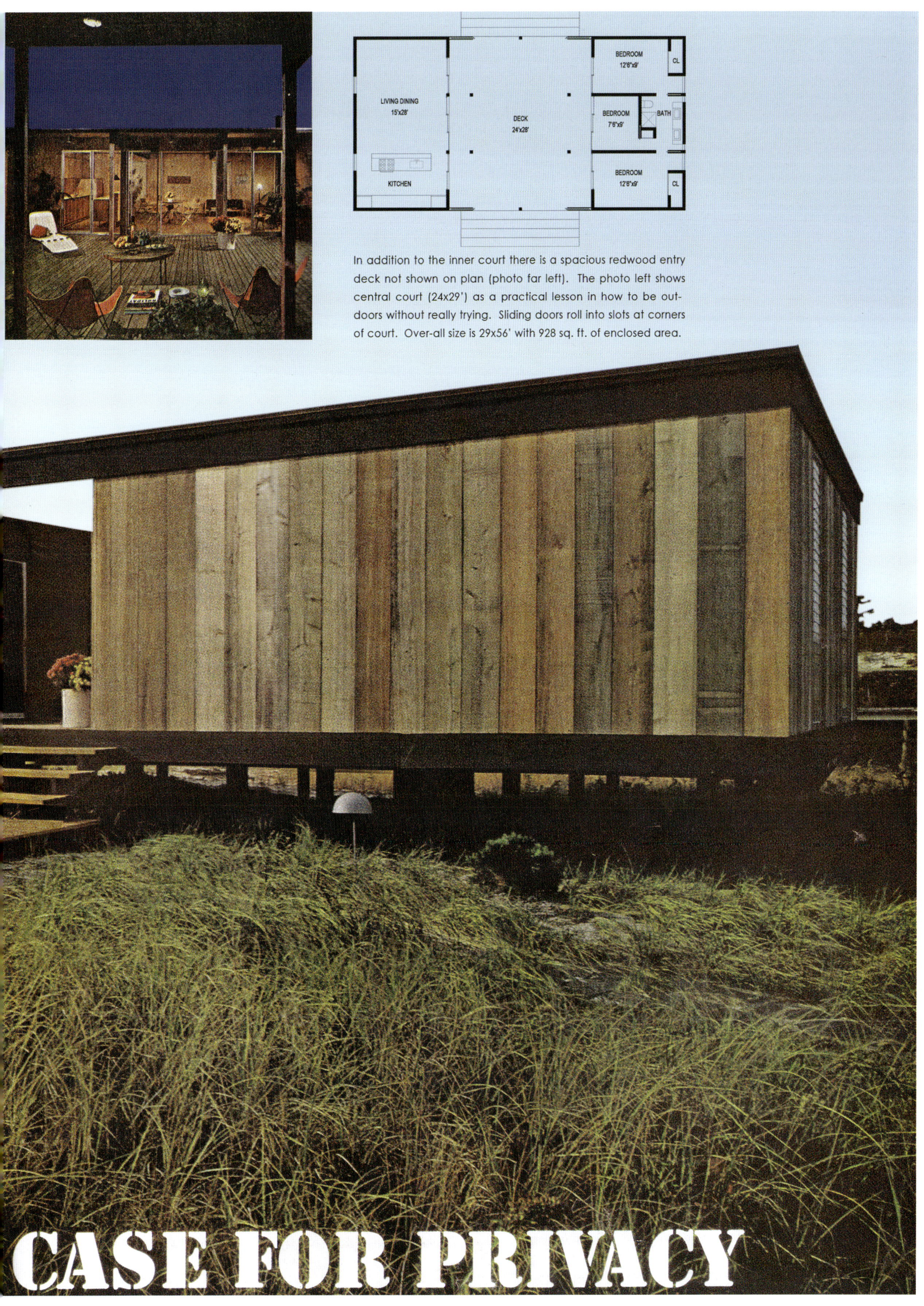

In addition to the inner court there is a spacious redwood entry deck not shown on plan (photo far left). The photo left shows central court (24x29') as a practical lesson in how to be outdoors without really trying. Sliding doors roll into slots at corners of court. Over-all size is 29x56' with 928 sq. ft. of enclosed area.

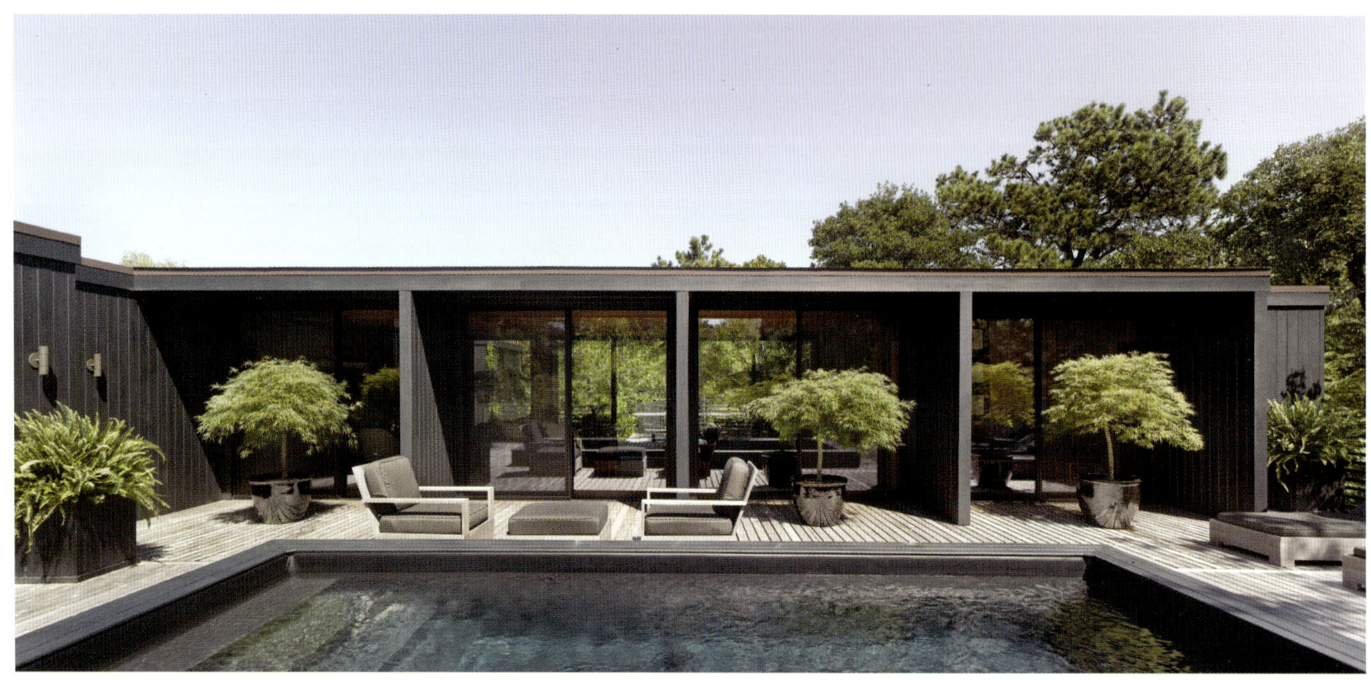

ANOTHER SMART VACATION IDEA

When Marjorie Dell closes up her vacation home in Fire Island, New York, she does it alone and in about five minutes—from start to finish. Whether it be for a week or for the season, the task is simple; the method, practical. And it costs little to achieve in construction dollars. The secret is in the way the designer, Horace Gifford, of New York City, integrated large, hinged panels into the total design of the house to protect the sliding glass doors when the house isn't being used. The panels are shut and locked from the inside except for the last one to be closed, which is then locked from the outside with lock and key. Panels are kept fixed in the open position by standard garage-door sliding bolts at the bottom. With the panels open, the large decks on both sides of the house become an extension of the living areas inside, shaded by the roof overhang. Sliding doors are used throughout the house as windows.

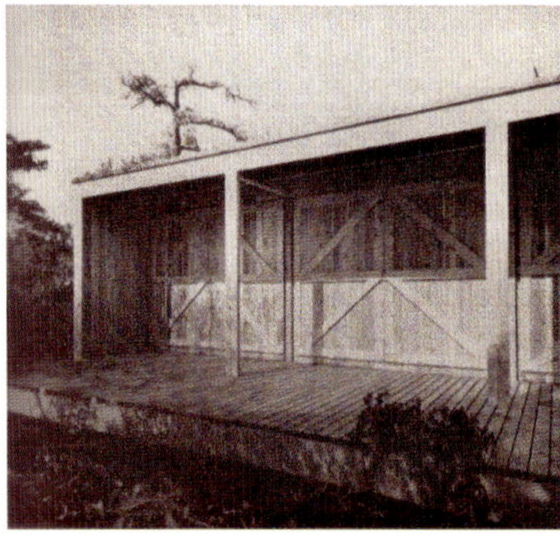

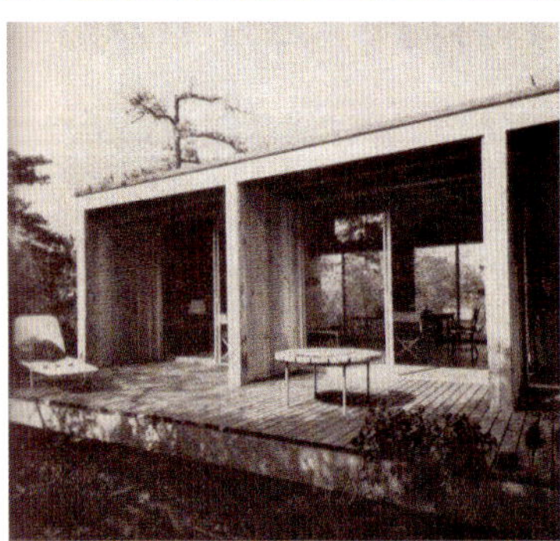

THE AMERICAN HOME, APRIL, 1965

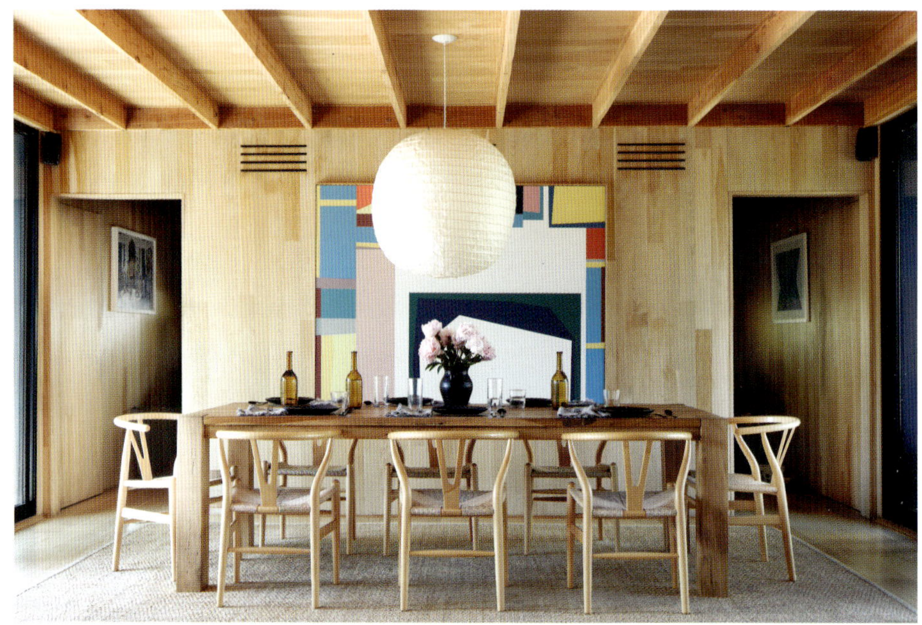

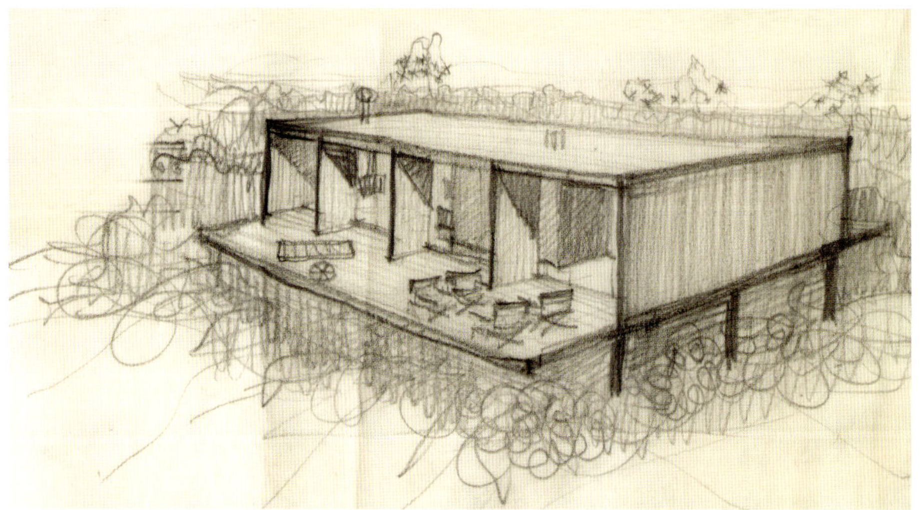

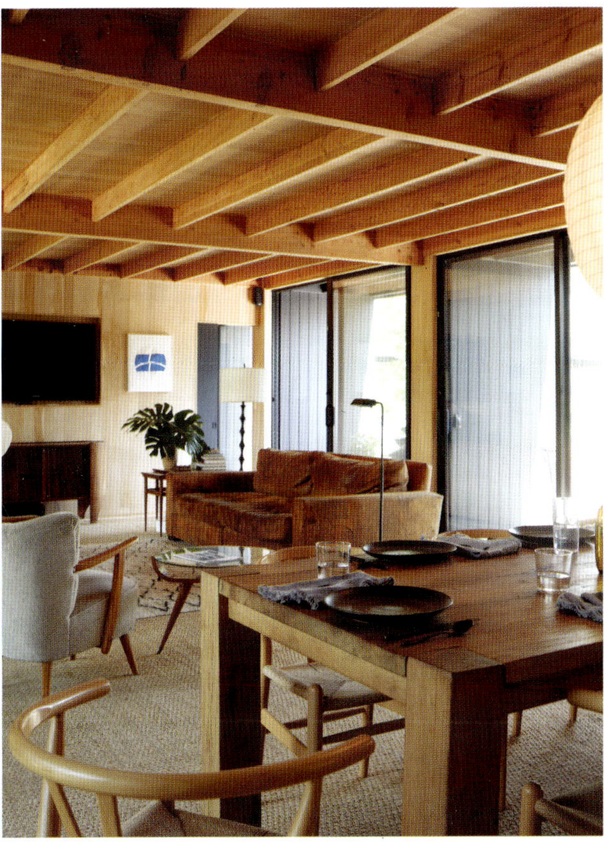

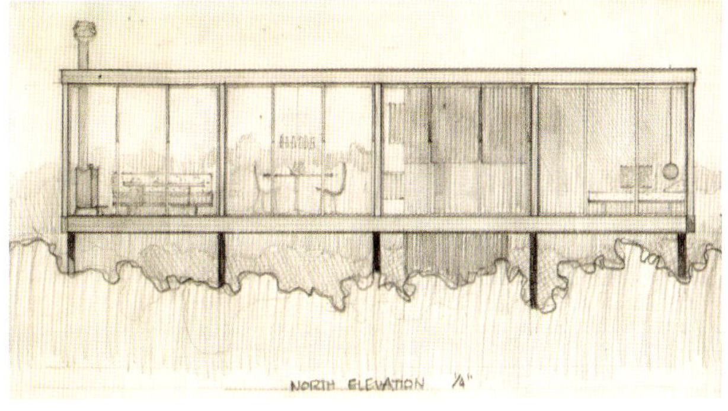

OPPOSITE TOP:
Dell House, Fire Island Pines, NY, 1963

OPPOSITE BOTTOM LEFT:
Dell House, published in *The American Home*, April 1965

OPPOSITE MIDDLE:
Dell House, interior

OPPOSITE BOTTOM RIGHT:
Dell House, sketch

TOP:
Dell House, interior

ABOVE:
Dell House, elevation sketch

The kinetic minimalism of the Leedom House also features in a dwelling for Marjorie Dell, a no-nonsense single woman who worked in theater. It comprised four bays, each measuring nine feet wide by nine feet tall by twenty-seven feet deep, with floor-to-ceiling sliding doors and deep overhangs. Hidden, ingenious shutters incorporated into the piers allowed Dell to completely secure her home against the elements in five minutes.

The Peter and Nan Schultz House revisits the themes of Gifford's own residence, a final riff on his professor Louis Kahn's iconic Trenton Bath House. It is a refined but conservative 1964 effort compared with the experimental forms that emerged the following year: *A Hard Day's Night* rather than *Rubber Soul*. While it appears low-slung today, when built it enjoyed ocean views. During the 1970s, these views were framed with Moorish arches by its new Moroccan owner.

Angelo Donghia, a rising star in the interior design world, also turned to Gifford in 1964 to create a bayside retreat for himself and his best friend, the couture fashion designer Halston. Like Gifford, Donghia was a precocious talent who made his mark at an early age, rising swiftly through the ranks of the Yale Burge atelier. Burge was a society decorator and early Pines resident who advised Jacqueline Kennedy on the renovation of the White House. In 1966, on the heels of Donghia's acclaimed interiors for the Opera Club at Lincoln Center, he was made a full partner and the firm was renamed Burge-Donghia. He took the company to new heights by pioneering the practice of licensing his name for home furnishings and accessories. By the 1970s, Donghia was a household brand, having established a mass-market business model that would be emulated by Ralph Lauren and Martha Stewart.

Donghia's eclecticism and opulent taste were at odds with Gifford's austerities, and the client's classicizing influence is apparent in the broad boardwalk that was centered on the home, a gesture in direct opposition to the winding path favored by Gifford. Three arched bays delineated a symmetrical plan with a clear front and back. Paint and plaster made a rare appearance in this residence, abetting black-and-white Donghia furnishings. Green glass pool-table pendants custom-fabricated by Gifford illuminated the kitchen, as they would in virtually every Gifford home. A lowered, flat ceiling across the home's midsection brought curved clerestory windows to both ends of the living room and the bedrooms, diffusing the light across the rounded ceilings. Artist Hans Namuth immortalized the home with black-and-white photos that were published first in the *New York Times* and then *House and Garden*.

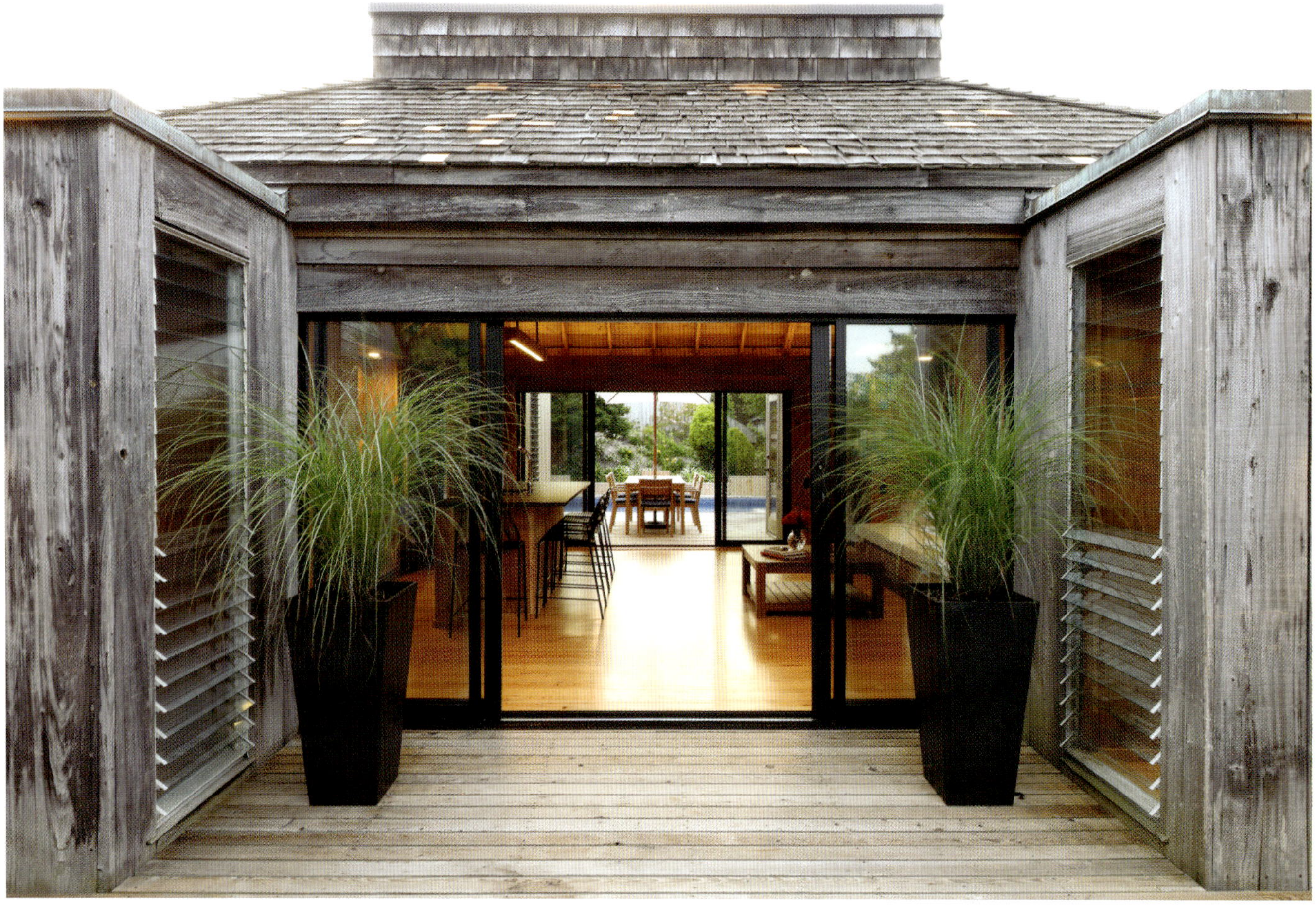

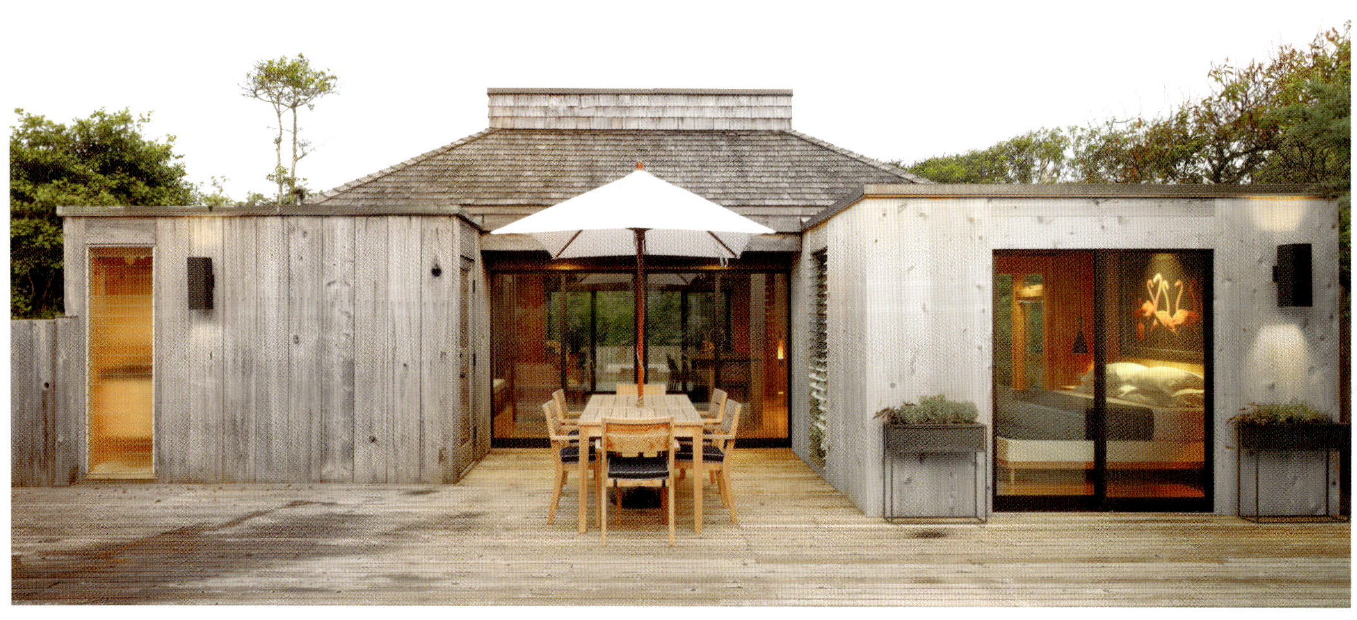

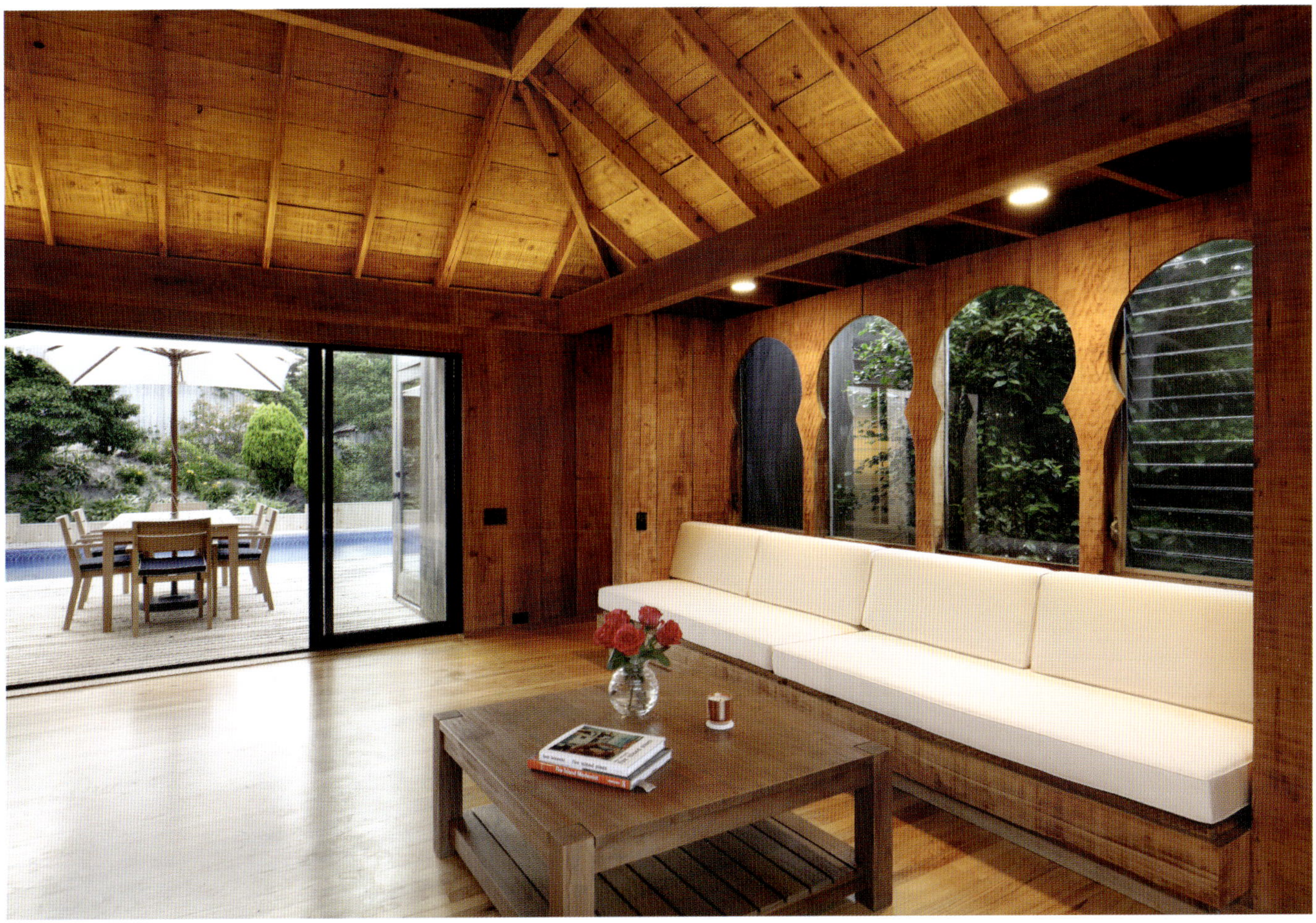

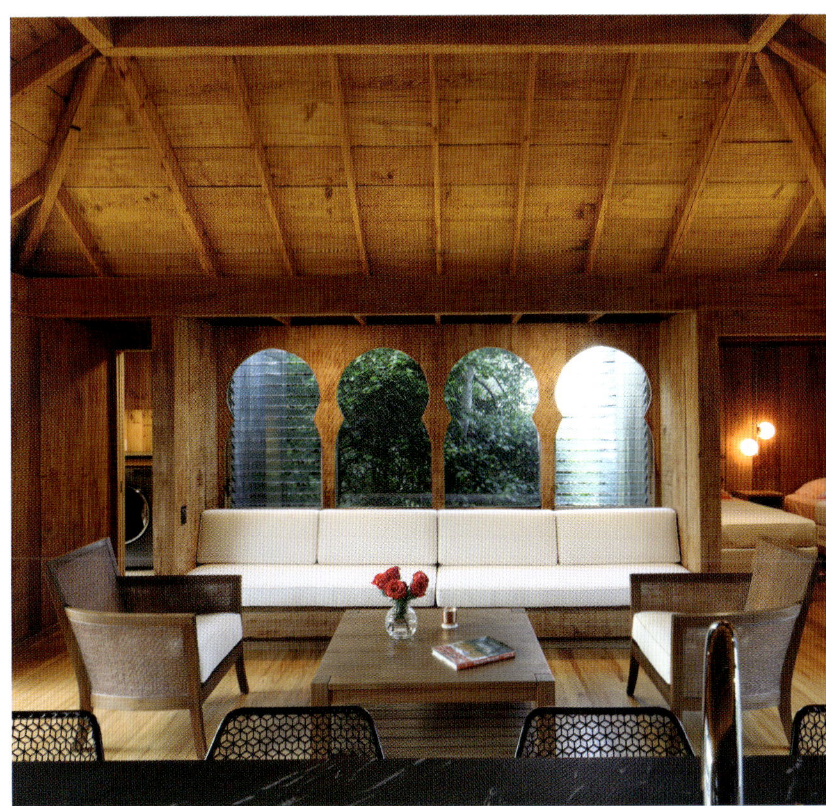

OPPOSITE ABOVE:
Schultz House, Fire Island Pines, NY, 1964

OPPOSITE BELOW:
Schultz House, back yard (bedroom at right has been expanded)

THIS PAGE:
Schultz House, interior

The clashing taste of the two designers was not the only difference between them. Donghia was the son of a tailor from Vandergrift, Pennsylvania. He never possessed the society connections that launched the elite ateliers that dominated the interior design field. To be perceived as an equal to his wealthy clients, Donghia affected the imperious manners of those who are unaccustomed to having their judgment questioned. In a television interview, Donghia explained: "You would not go out and have cocktails with your doctor. It's very important that they take what I'm saying as a business arrangement and not something that becomes a friendly conversation."[49] Gifford persevered, but a second commission from Donghia in 1973 turned acrimonious. He filed that project away with an angry red scrawl, under the heading of "MISS DONGHIA."

The Pines and Cherry Grove were not the only creativity-infused hamlets on Fire Island. Showbiz types also gravitated toward Fair Harbor, and the burgeoning field of television was well represented there. After the Pines, Fair Harbor would boast the largest number of Gifford homes on Fire Island. The first was for Dr. Benjamin Kauth, a podiatrist to stars of the stage and screen. At first glance, the Kauth residence was much like the architect's earlier efforts, yet it contained new subtleties. Gifford carved his first conversation pit into the living area, sheltered by an encircling clerestory that directed dramatic shafts of eastern and western light into the space. A painterly arrangement of windows prioritized water views, while covered porches introduced a new degree of enclosure to the mix.

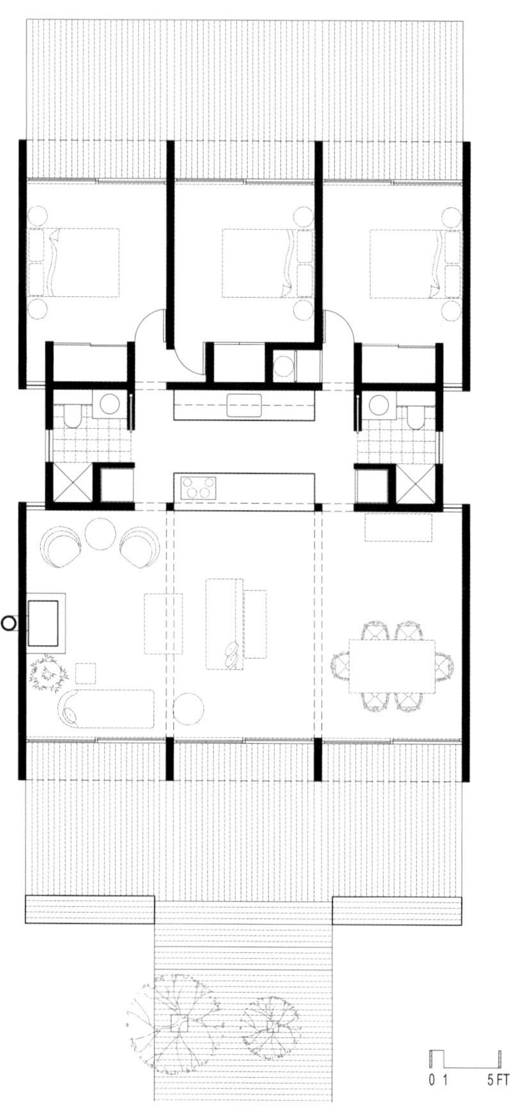

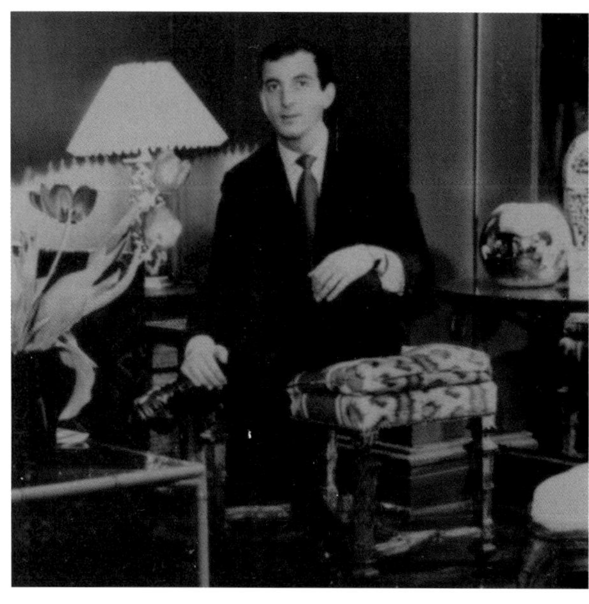

ABOVE:
Donghia House, Fire Island Pines, NY, 1964, floor plan

LEFT:
Angelo Donghia, ca. 1965

OPPOSITE:
Donghia House, exterior facing Great South Bay

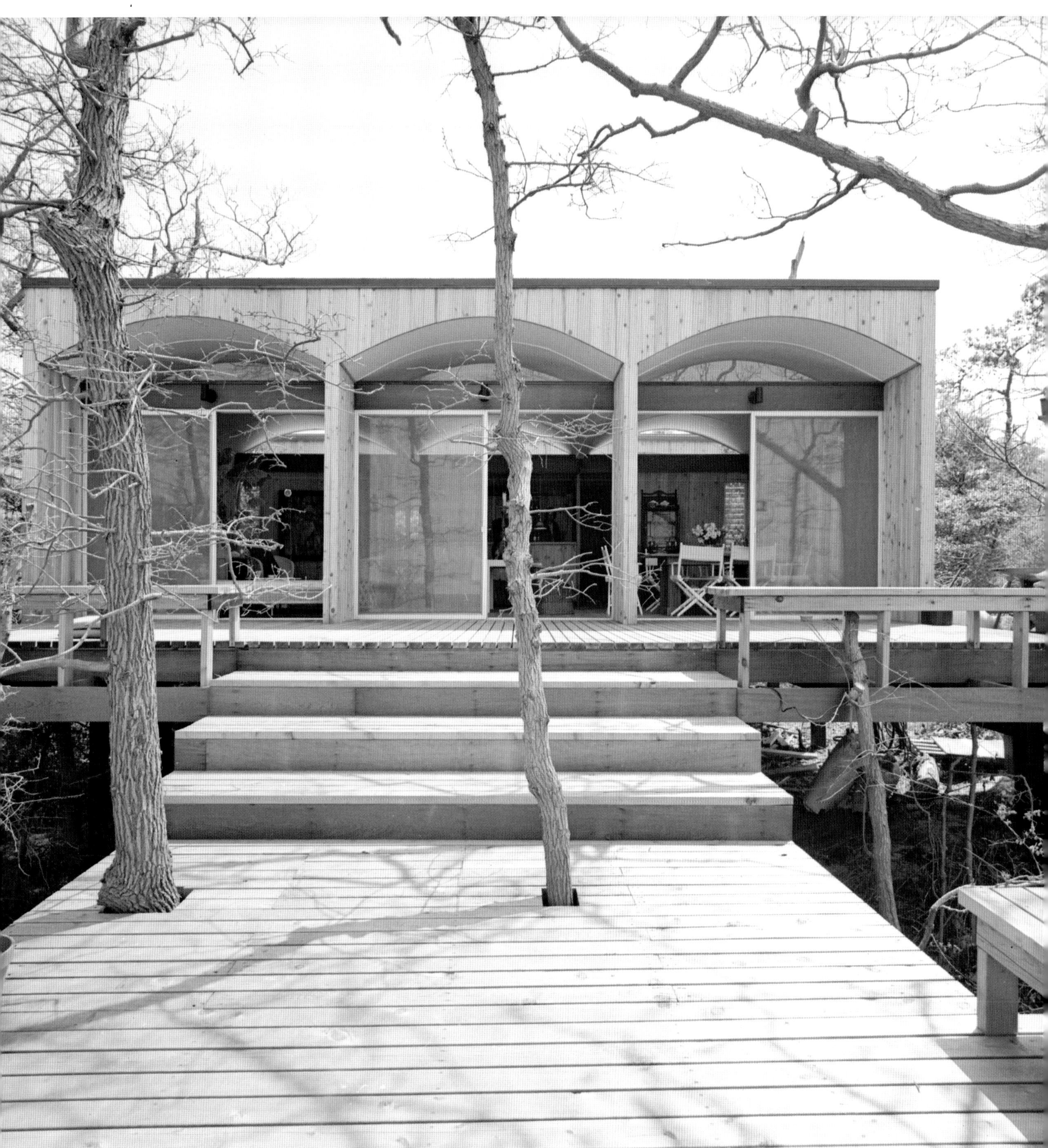

tled, 1965. Photograph by Hans Namuth.

Untitled, 1965, Photograph by Hans Namuth.

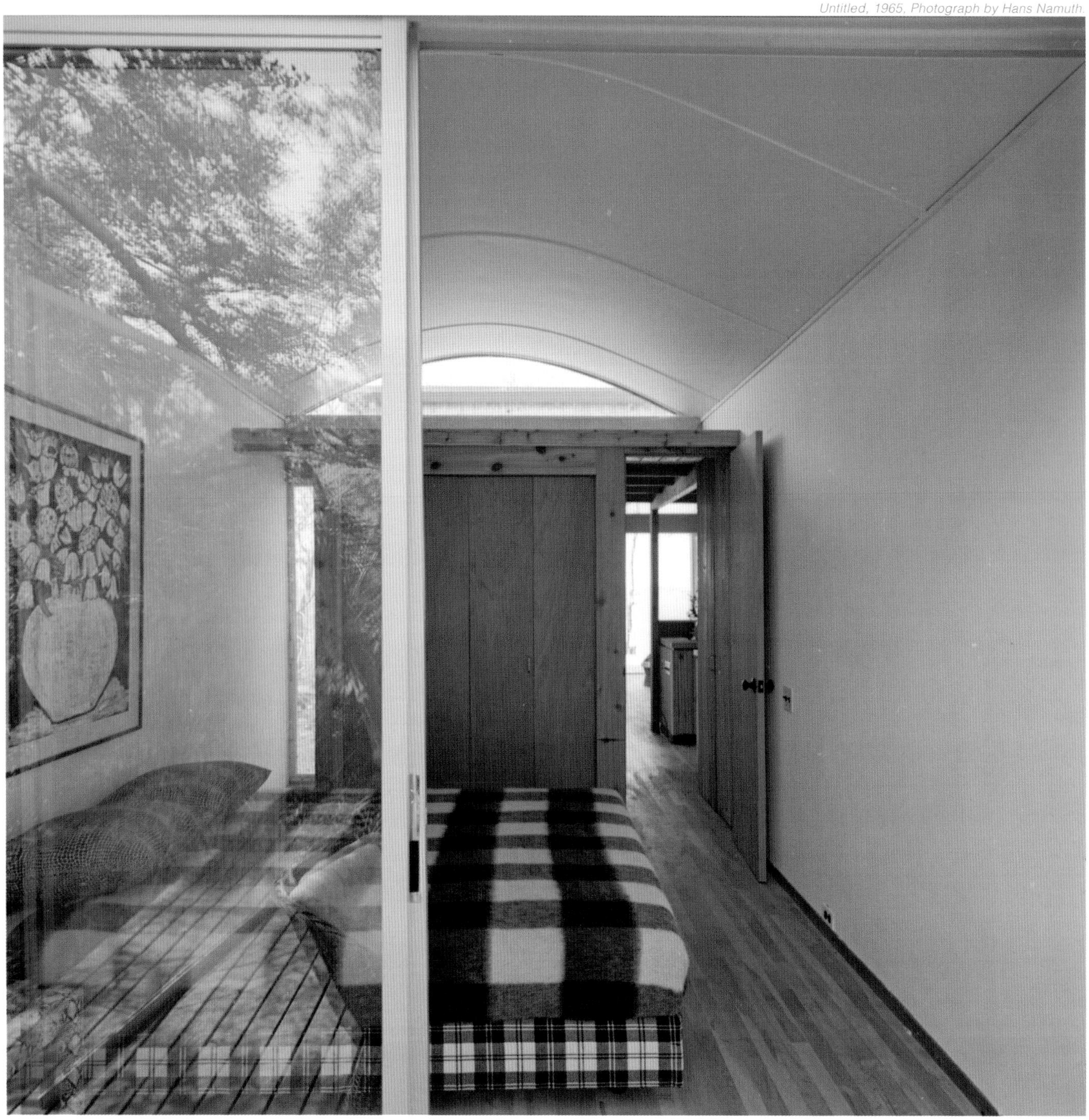

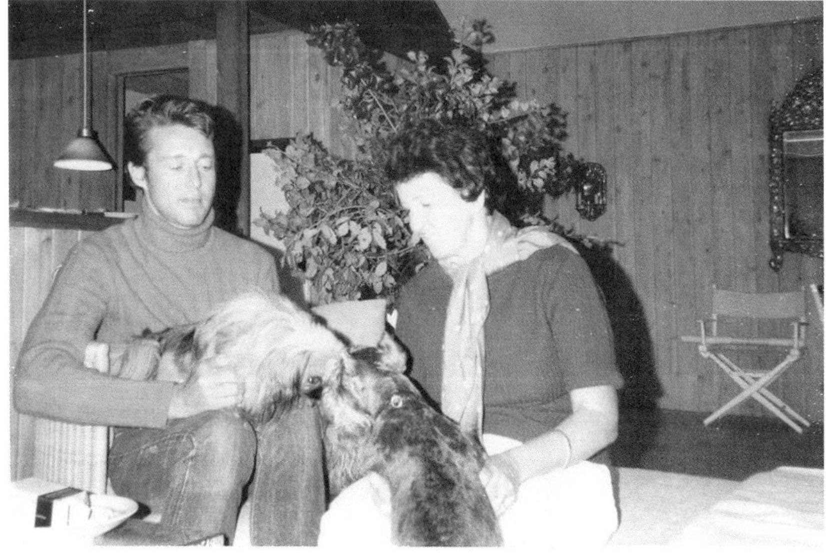

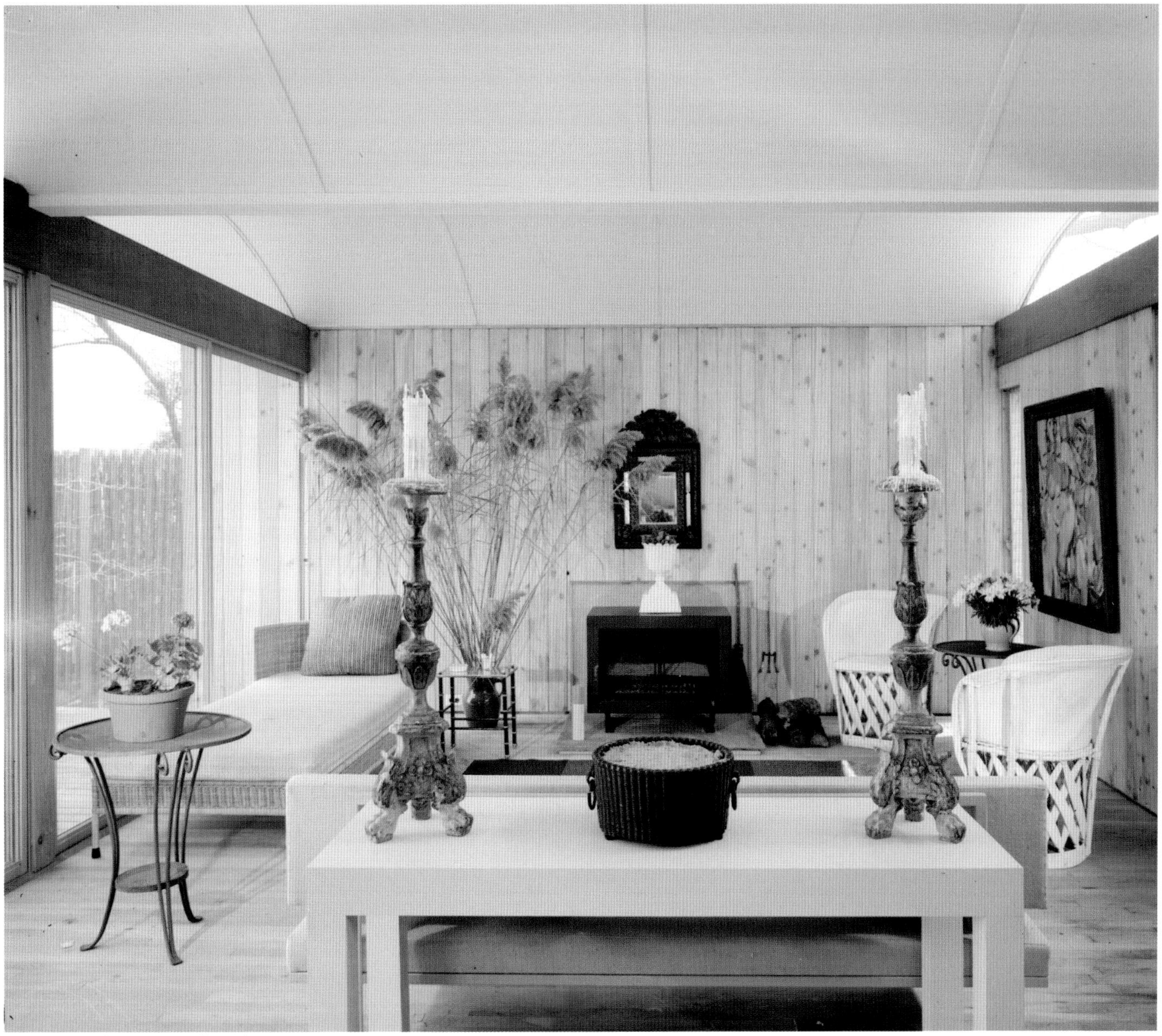

Untitled, 1965. Photograph by Hans Namuth.

OPPOSITE, ABOVE:
Donghia House, bedroom

OPPOSITE, BELOW:
Halston and Donghia's mother at Donghia House, ca. 1965

ABOVE:
Donghia House, living room

RIGHT:
Donghia House, kitchen

PAGES 80–81:
Kauth House, Fair Harbor, NY, 1964, exterior facing Great South Bay

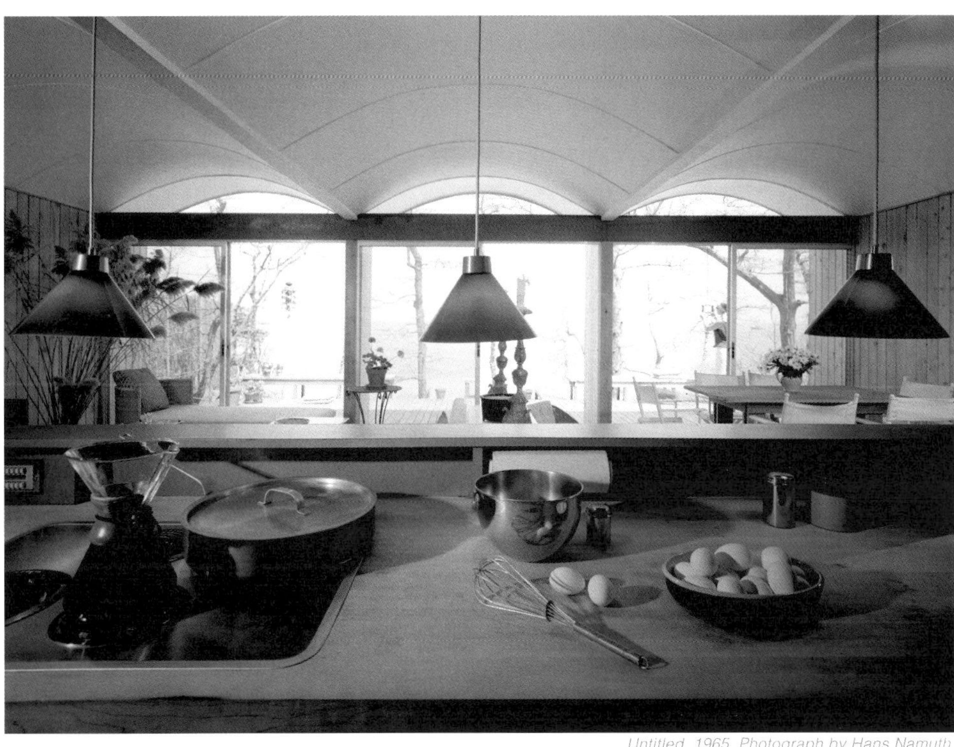

Untitled, 1965. Photograph by Hans Namuth.

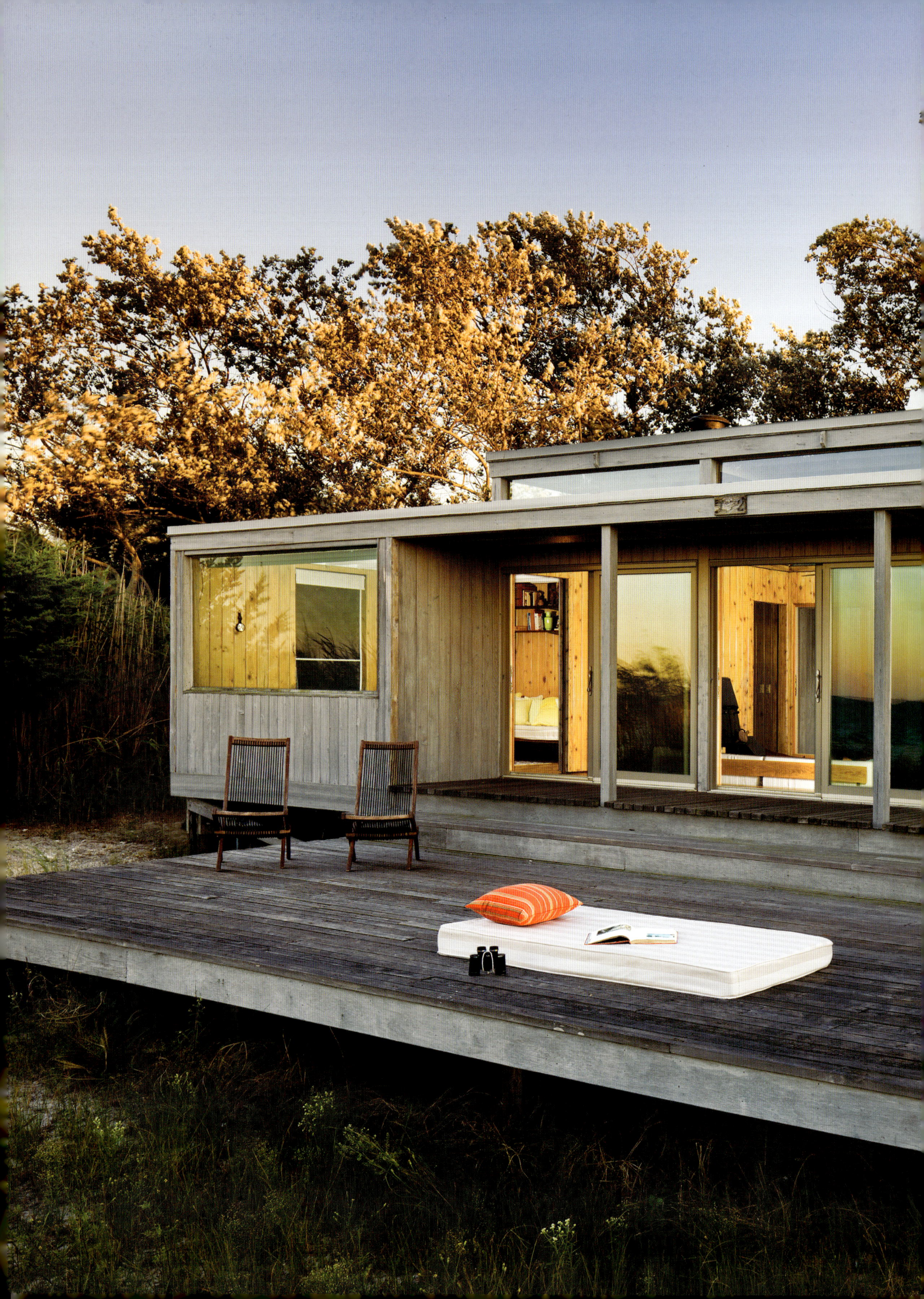

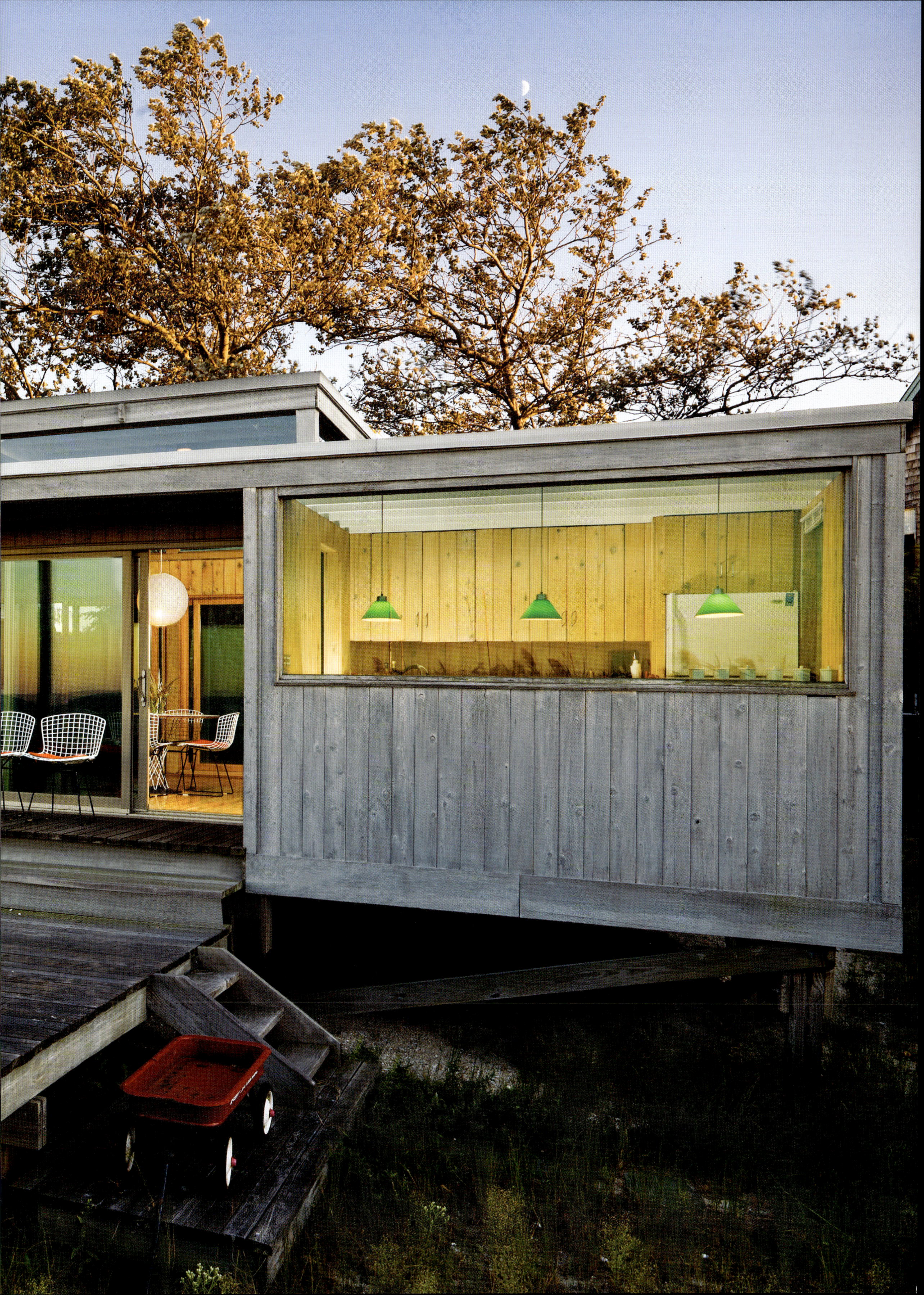

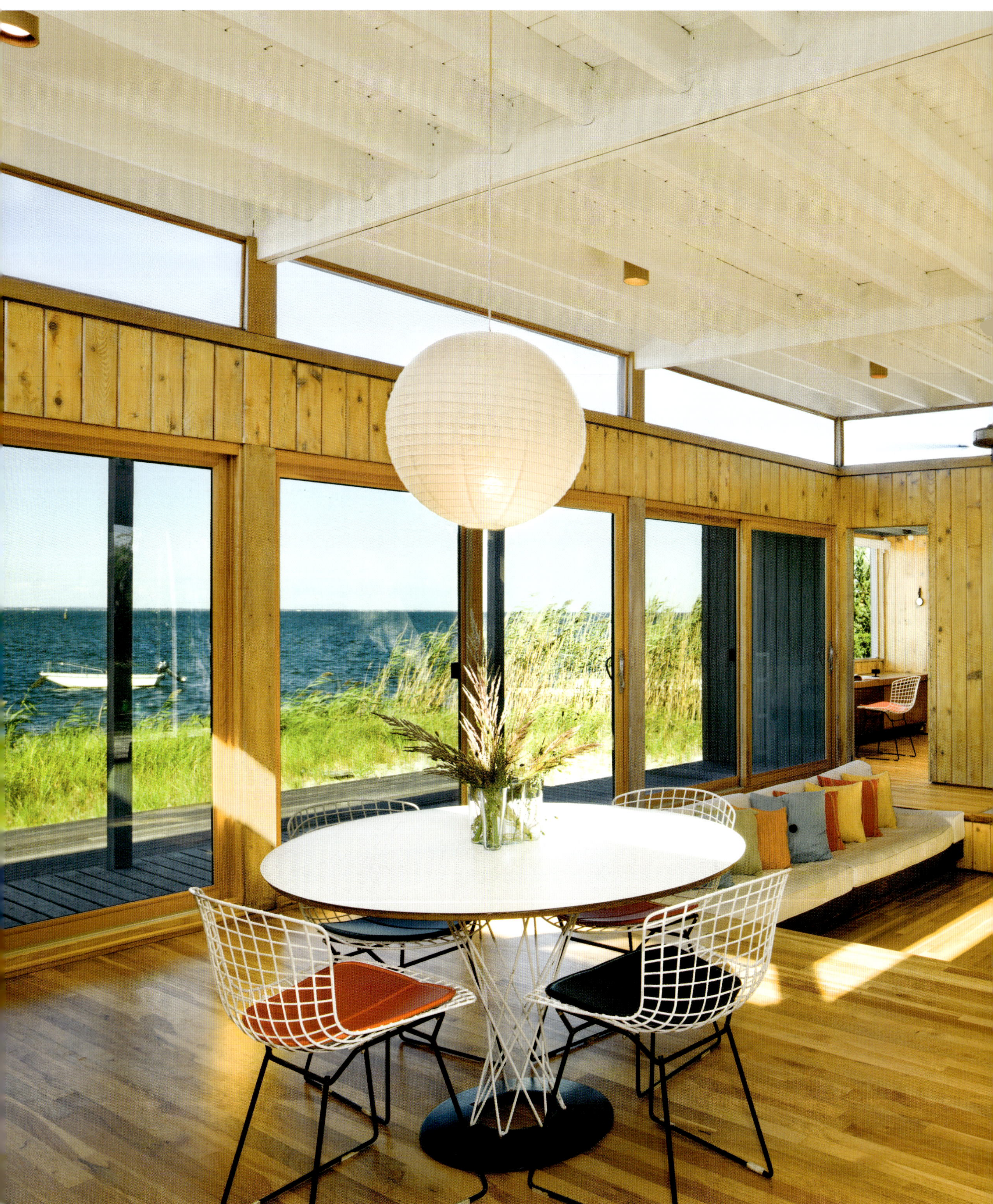

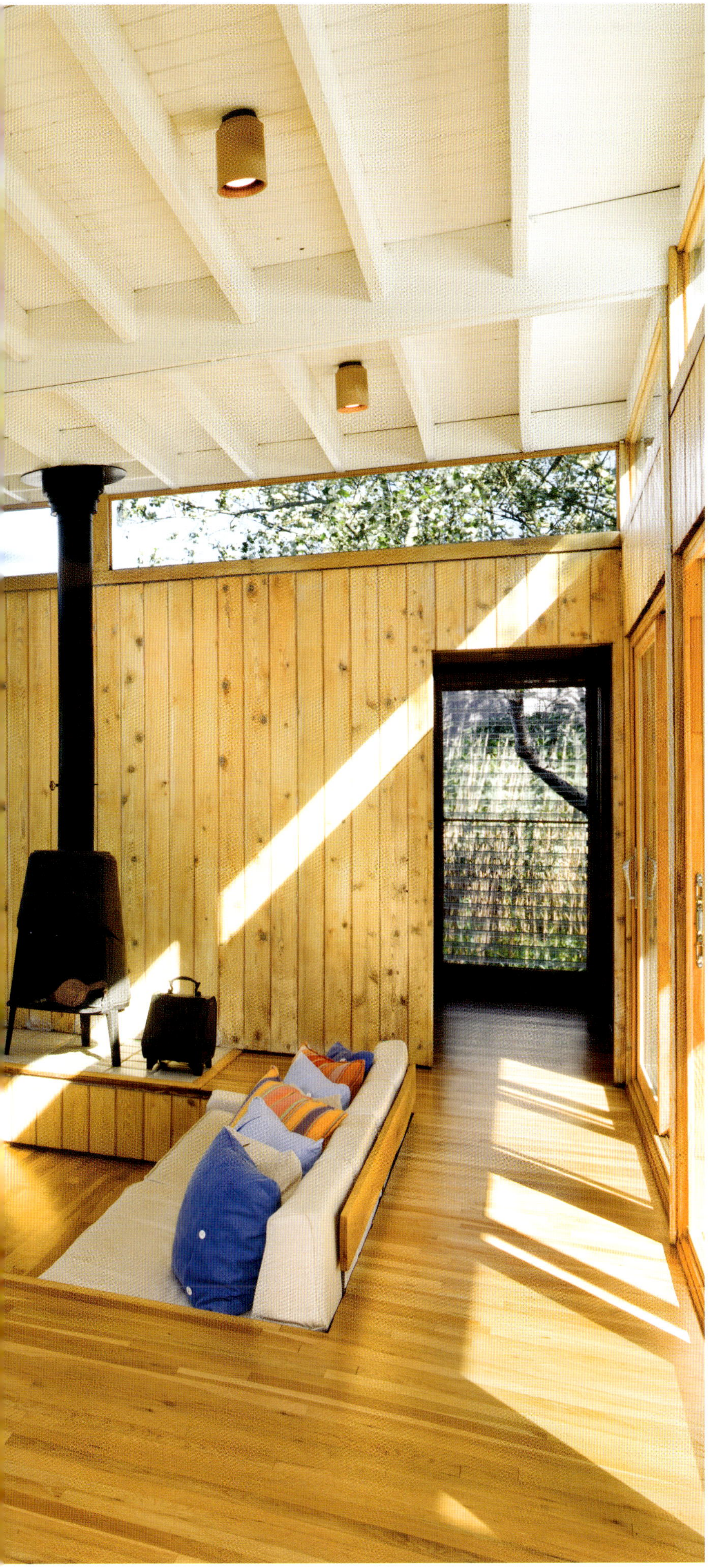

LEFT:
Kauth House, interior with sunken seating area

BELOW:
Kauth House, kitchen

PAGES 84–85:
Kauth House at sunset

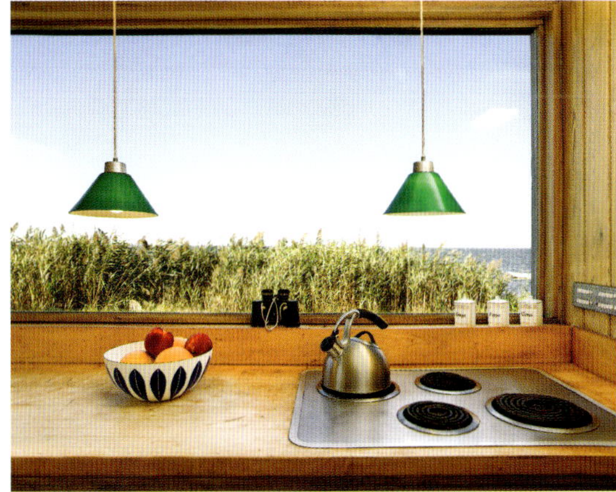

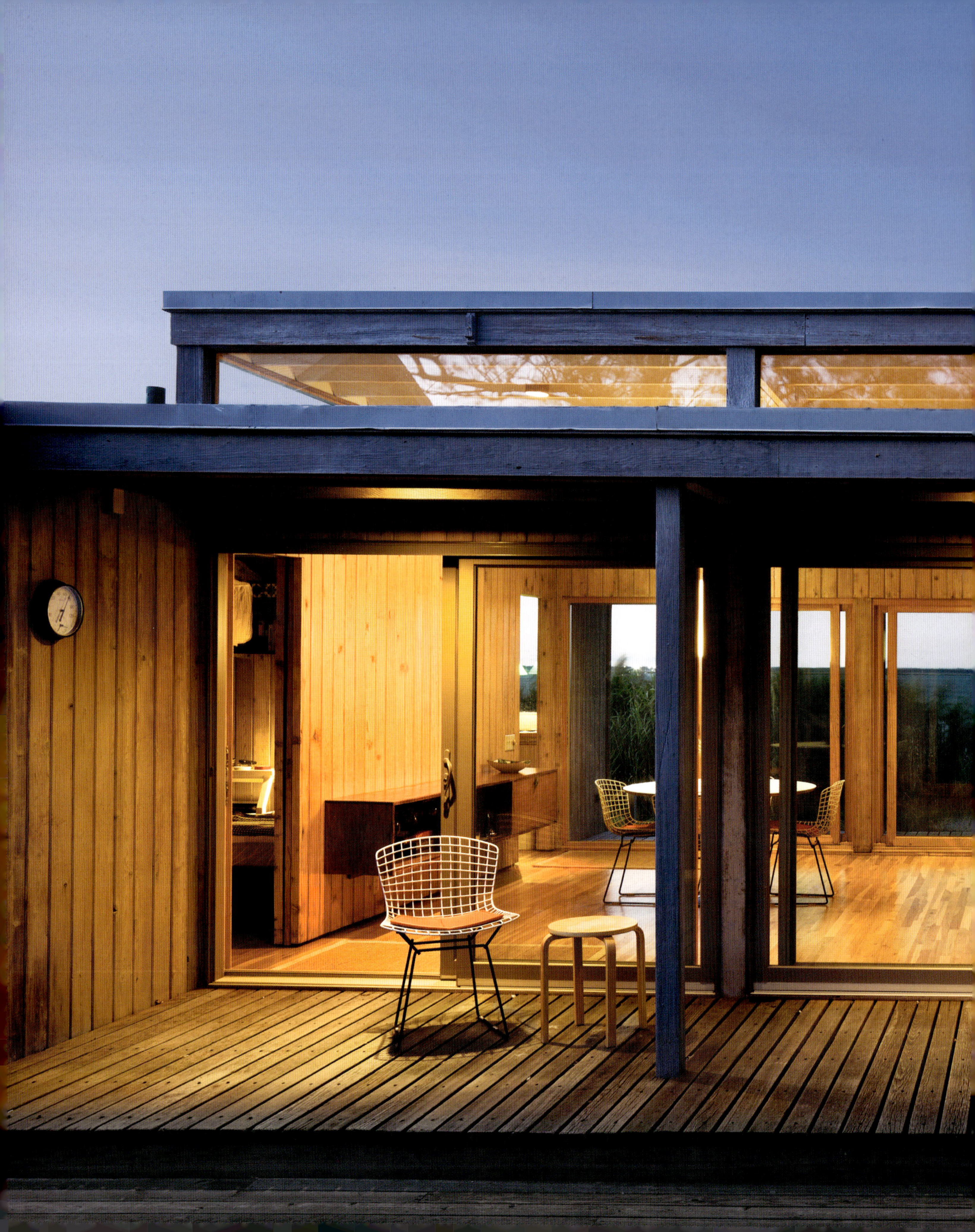

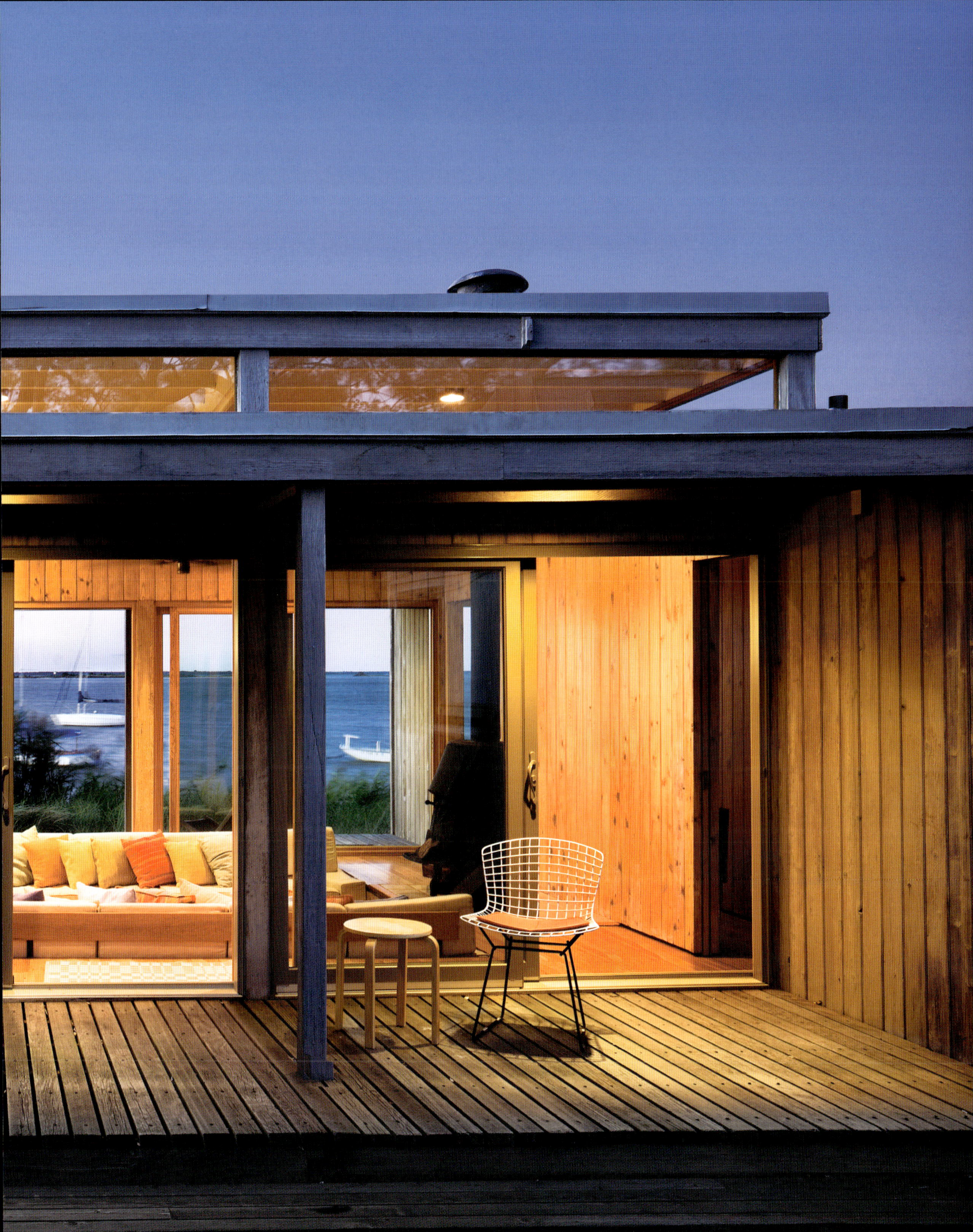

In just three years as a freelancer, Horace Gifford designed fourteen homes on Fire Island, surpassing all rivals to become its most sought-after architect. There were limits to his reach, however. He would eventually design forty homes in the Pines and twenty-three more across Fire Island, but Cherry Grove proved immune to Gifford's charms.[50] Though seemingly bound by sexual orientation, the Pines and Cherry Grove were actually divided by class and culture. The bigger lots, varied topography, and safely ambiguous orientation of the Pines had siphoned off much of Cherry Grove's artistic and intellectual sheen in the years since Isherwood and Auden summered there. A parallel universe of two gay cultures ensued.

John Whyte, the commercial dean of the Pines, had an equally entrepreneurial and influential counterpart in Cherry Grove—the hotelier John Eberhardt. In 1956, Eberhardt built the Belvedere Guest House, a faux-Venetian confection decked out in a delirium of urns, frescoes, and fountains. Campy excess was his stock in trade. His many Cherry Grove rental properties were similarly festooned with painted curlicues that quickly flaked away in the sea air. It was architecture in drag. Locals referred to Eberhardt as the "Lady Builder."[51] Drag was popular with Cherry Grove's working-class population. But a new, less ghettoized generation of gay men began to disdain this practice, much as assimilated children roll their eyes at the manners of their immigrant parents. Horace Gifford's stripped-bare creations in cedar and glass suited an upwardly mobile generation that traded muumuus for muscles, and mascara for mustaches. His architecture was butch. But in its muscular austerity, free of domesticating bric-a-brac, a hypermasculine form of drag could also be discerned. His occasional incorporation of vintage porthole windows, stained glass, and Palladian transoms offered a wry, backward glance at all the new generation was leaving behind.

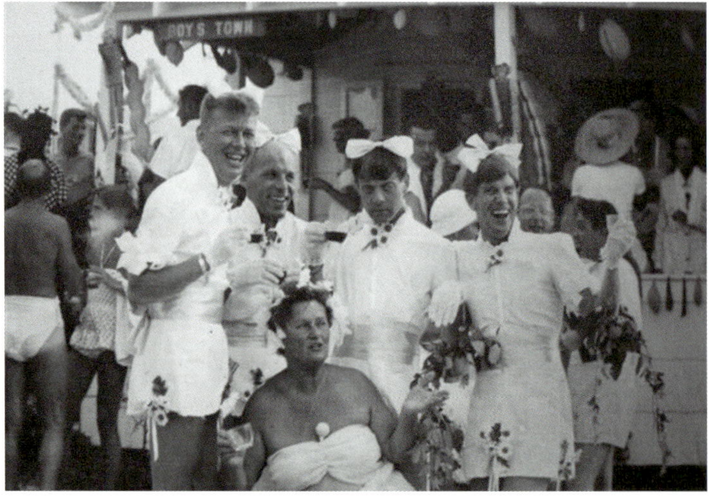

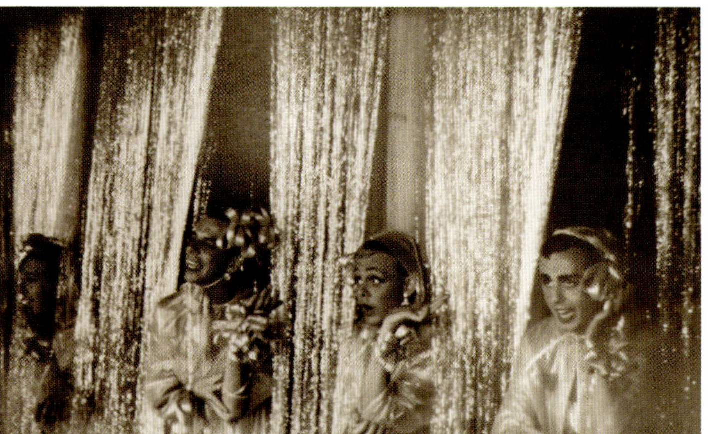

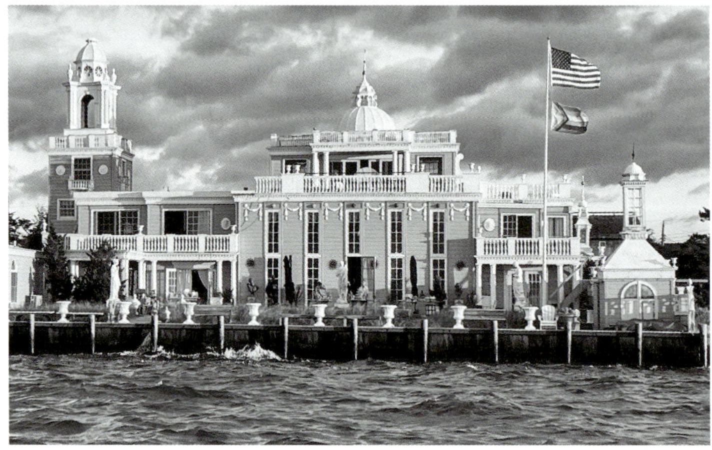

TOP:
Cherry Grove theme party, late 1950s

MIDDLE:
Cherry Grove theater production, ca. 1948

ABOVE:
Architecture of Drag: John Eberhardt, the Belvedere Guest House, Cherry Grove, NY, begun in 1956

OPPOSITE:
Tom Bianchi, Untitled, SX-70 Polaroid, 1970s

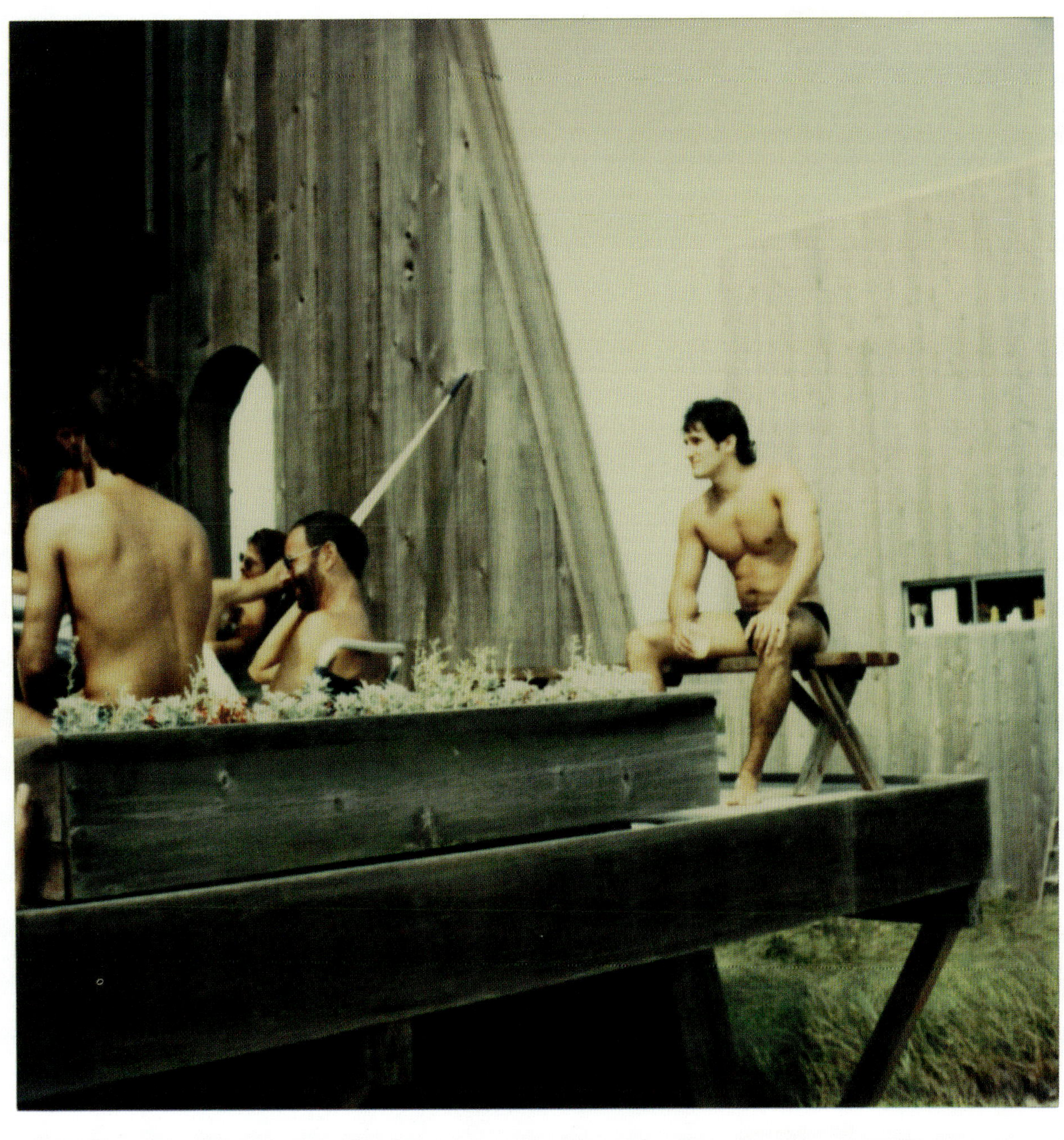

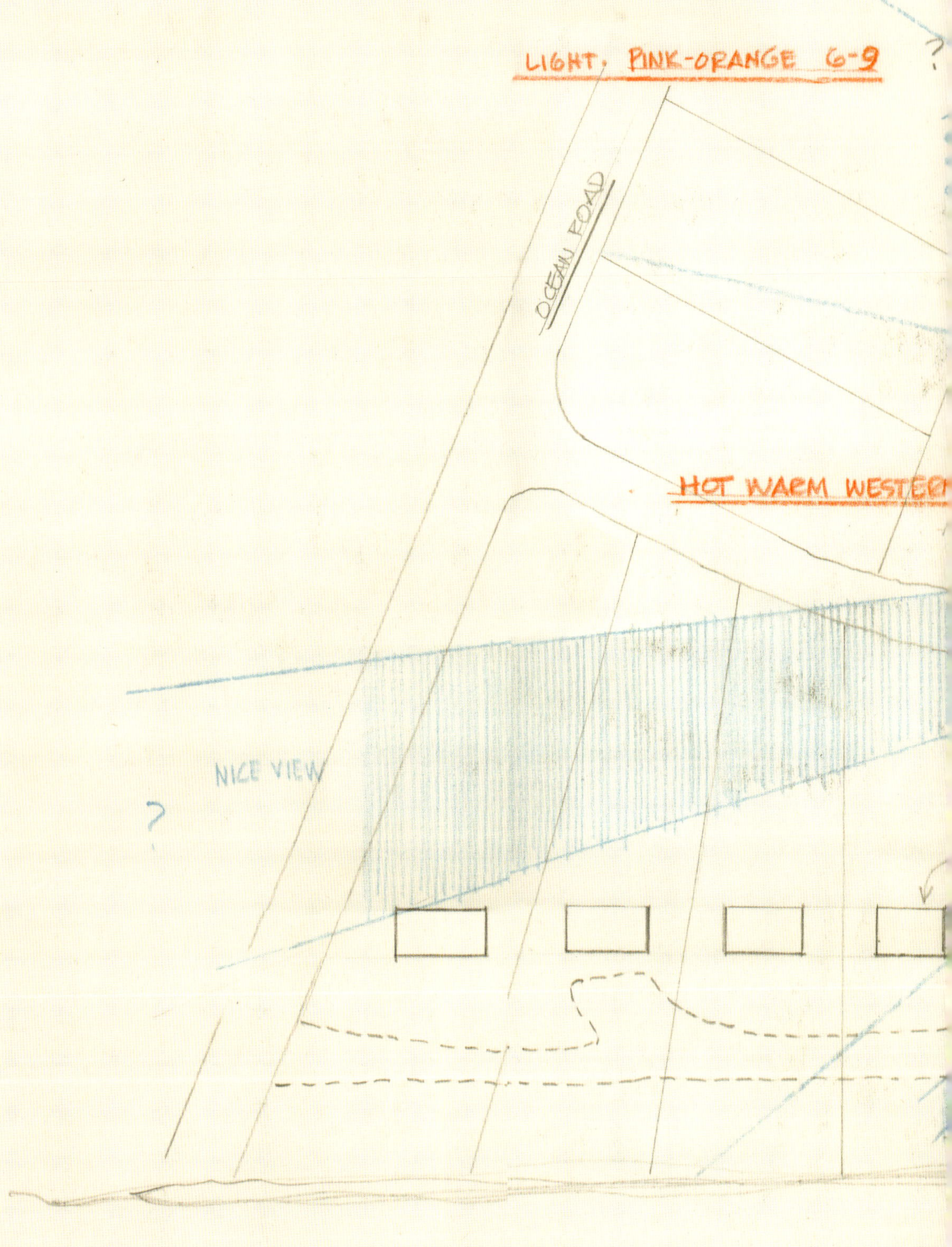

A SITE TUDY IN TERMS OF PROJEC

THIS IS A DIAGRAMAT

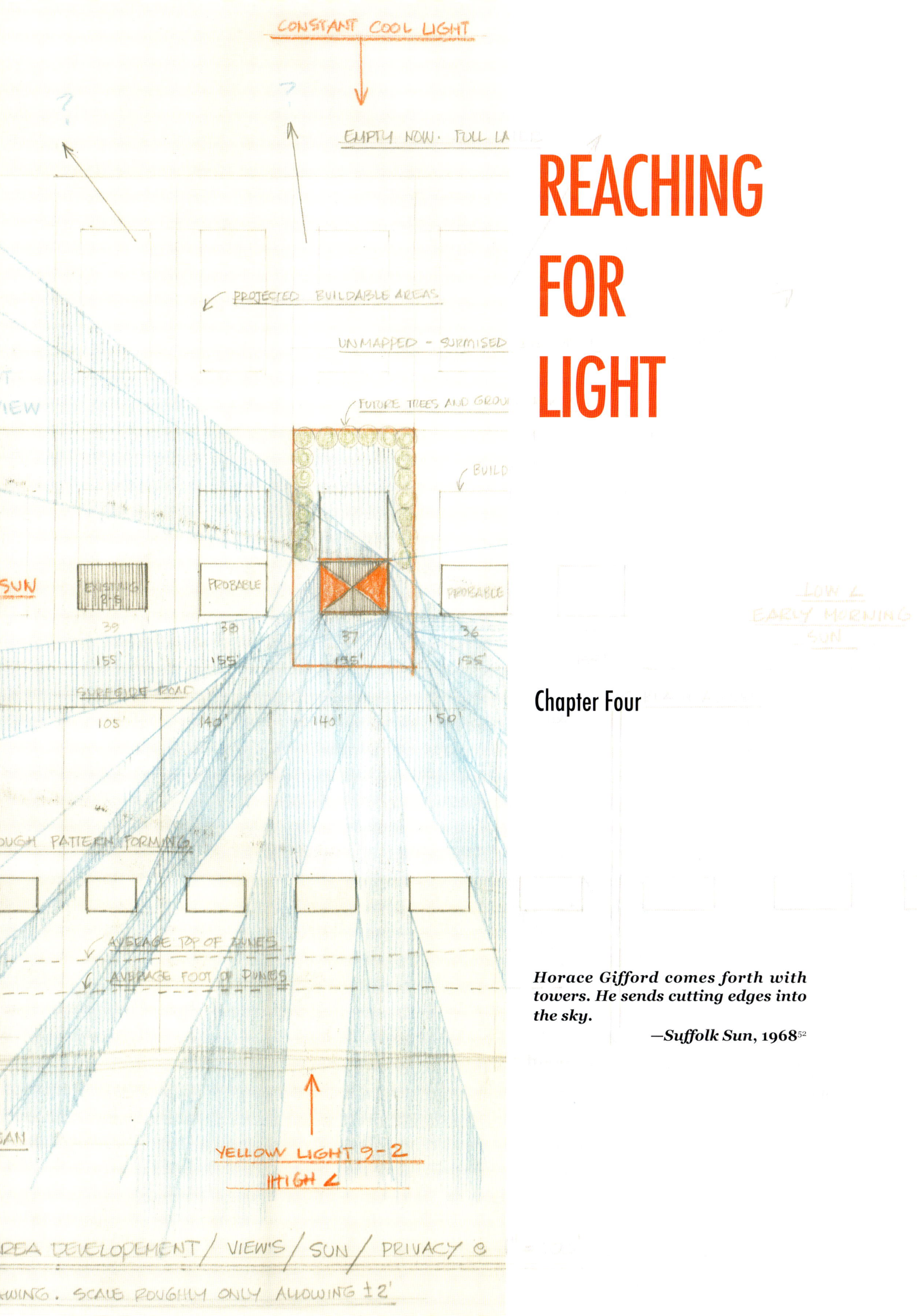

REACHING FOR LIGHT

Chapter Four

Horace Gifford comes forth with towers. He sends cutting edges into the sky.

—*Suffolk Sun*, 1968[52]

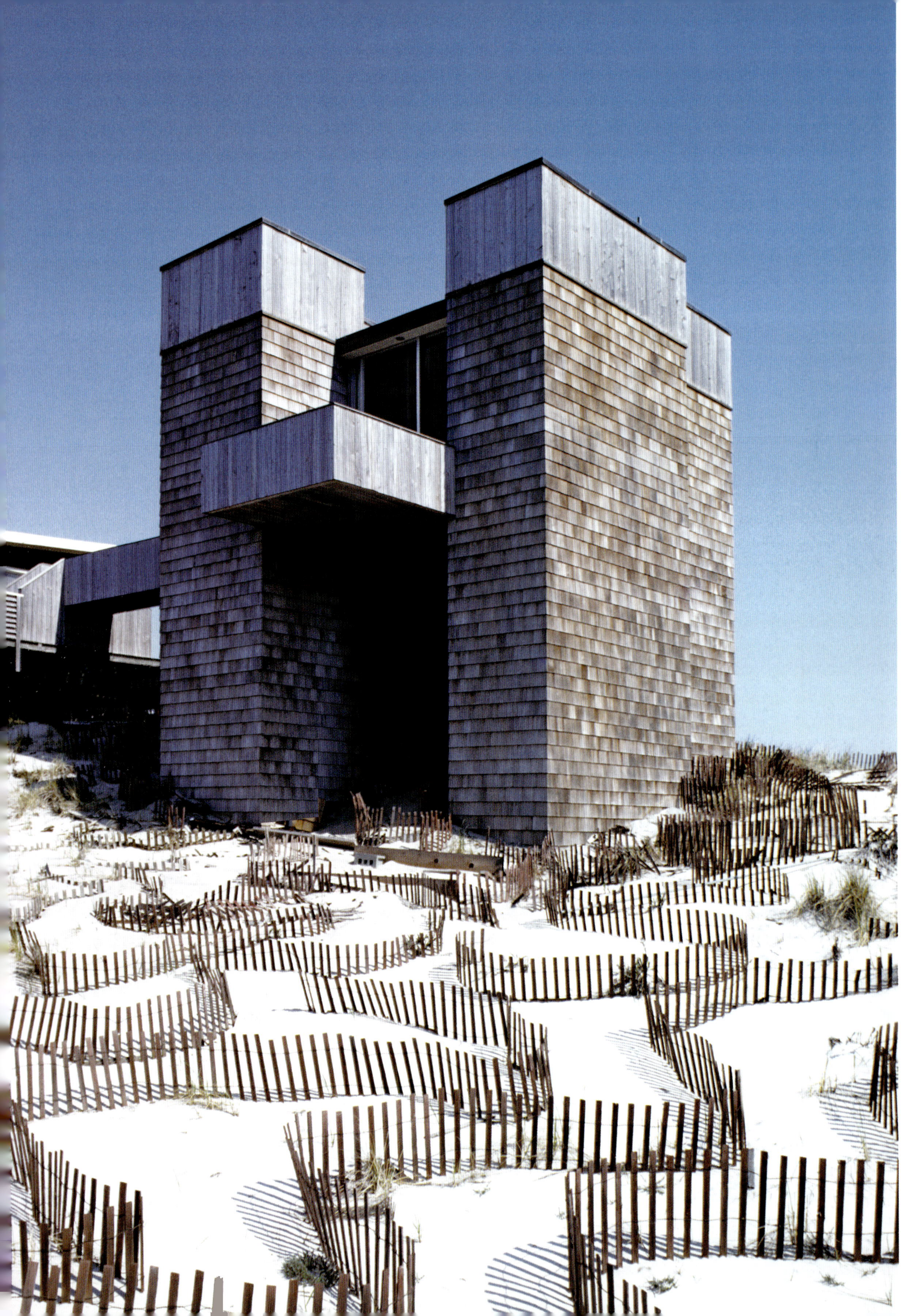

PAGES 88–89:
DeSwaan House, Bridgehampton, NY, 1968 (unbuilt), site sketch

BELOW, LEFT:
Pines beachfront with Burge Pavilion in the foreground, ca. 1967

BELOW, RIGHT:
Frank Lloyd Wright, Larkin Company Administration Building, Buffalo, NY, 1906

OPPOSITE:
Burge Pavilion, Fire Island Pines, NY, 1965

PAGES 92–93:
Sprague-Geller House, Fire Island Pines, NY, 1965, published in *The American Home*, May 1966

It took a certain suspension of disbelief to build anything on Fire Island in the early sixties. Robert Moses, the ruthless and multititled director of New York state's housing, transportation, and parks departments, had long desired a parkway to cross the length of the island. Such a road would have flattened a series of autonomous, diverse communities into an anonymous strip. Moses liked to think big, and what can only be described as a fetish for auto transport made him openly scornful of Fire Island's small-by-design, carless ways. He seemed unstoppable. Early, laudable works of his, such as Jones Beach, shored up a base of support with the public, while a mastery of legislative chicanery unleashed a cascade of funding that only added to his power. Whatever reformist impulses had launched his career in the 1920s had long since calcified into an arrogant determination to remake New York State into an endless suburbia, traversed by an infinite swirl of highways and bridges.

"Fire Island's most hated man" finally met his match in the form of enraged homeowners who pressured Governor Nelson Rockefeller and Secretary of the Interior Stewart Udall to designate Fire Island as a unique natural environment worthy of protection.[53] The eighteen communities dotted across the island had evolved organically, with idyllic expanses of dunes and forest separating many of them. The Fire Island National Seashore Act of 1964 permanently inscribed this form. The act forbade development between the communities and maintained the ban on cars, while allowing existing hamlets to build within their borders. Storms may have sliced through the island every few decades, but its population became emboldened to put down more ambitious roots with this extraordinary defeat of Robert Moses in 1964. Moses had finally lost a battle, allowing Fire Island's most ambitious architectural era to begin.

While working on the Kauth residence in Fair Harbor, Gifford encountered the Miller House, Charles Gwathmey's first commission (see page 49). It drew heavily on Gwathmey's own "Lou Kahn education,"[54] as he recalled. A central living area, shielded by a pinwheel of shed-roofed spaces and sundecks, maintained privacy in a crowded landscape by selectively framing unobstructed diagonal views at the edges of neighboring properties. But the trope and the shingled aesthetic of this 1964 project were quickly abandoned. In subsequent projects, Gwathmey revived the sleek interwar modernism practiced by Le Corbusier, producing extroverted cubist compositions across the dunes and potato fields of the Hamptons. In 1965, Gifford performed a series of variations on Gwathmey's discarded debut. His Sprague-Geller residence harvested the pin-wheeled plan of the Miller House and elevated it an entire story off the ground. Views from the internal living space were diagonally directed and framed by encircling towers. Narrow slit windows and enclosed, cantilevered decks maintained privacy within the low-lying, hemmed-in site. Gwathmey's squat, shed-roofed appendages became bold towers in Gifford's hands. Elevating the house had a financial benefit as well, allowing a lower floor to be inexpensively added at a later date. Robert Sprague, a textile executive, marveled at how his home emerged from a freehand sketch that embroidered prevailing winds, sightlines, landforms, and sunlight studies. The publication of the Sprague-Geller residence marked Gifford's debut in the critically acclaimed journal *Arts & Architecture*, where it appeared opposite a Case Study House by Marcel Breuer.

The neofeudal aura of the Sprague-Geller residence reached its zenith with a pavilion for the interior designer and antiques purveyor Yale Burge, the senior business partner of the up-and-coming Angelo Donghia. Burge and his wife,

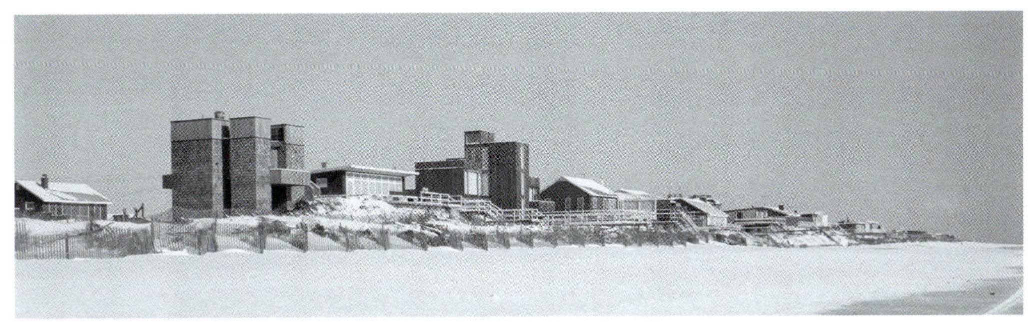

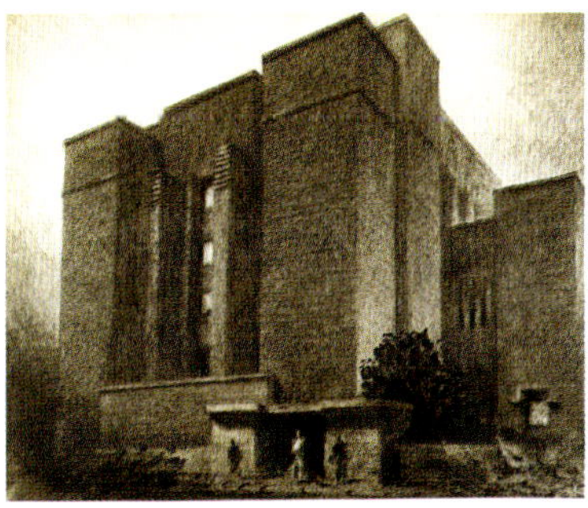

SAND CASTLE VACATION HOUSE

Our sand castle we'd say is introverted. Though the living room has a wide view of the beach, other rooms are shut off for privacy. (The house on the following pages is just the opposite, all open.) The striking design is completely modern with its multiple towers and platforms. They serve very practical purposes, though, of overcoming disadvantages of the site. The lot, 300 feet from the ocean on New York's Fire Island, is surrounded by other houses. The four towers, shingled in red cedar, provide privacy. The design appears complex, but is really just an unusual way of wrapping the exterior walls around the four corners to form the towers and floating the living room pavilion between them. Decks with wide glass doors jut out from the living room on four sides and give an open feeling. The tall, narrow jalousie windows set into the corners provide light. The house, which was designed by Horace Gifford, was built at a moderate cost.

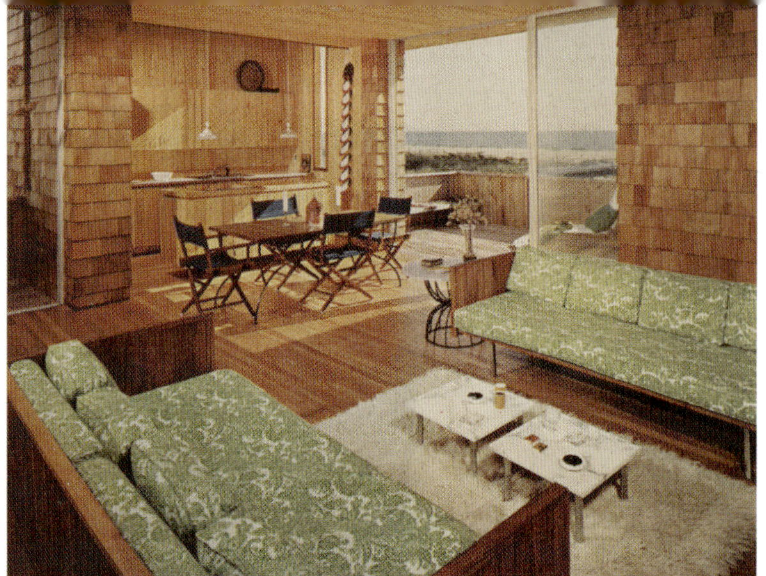

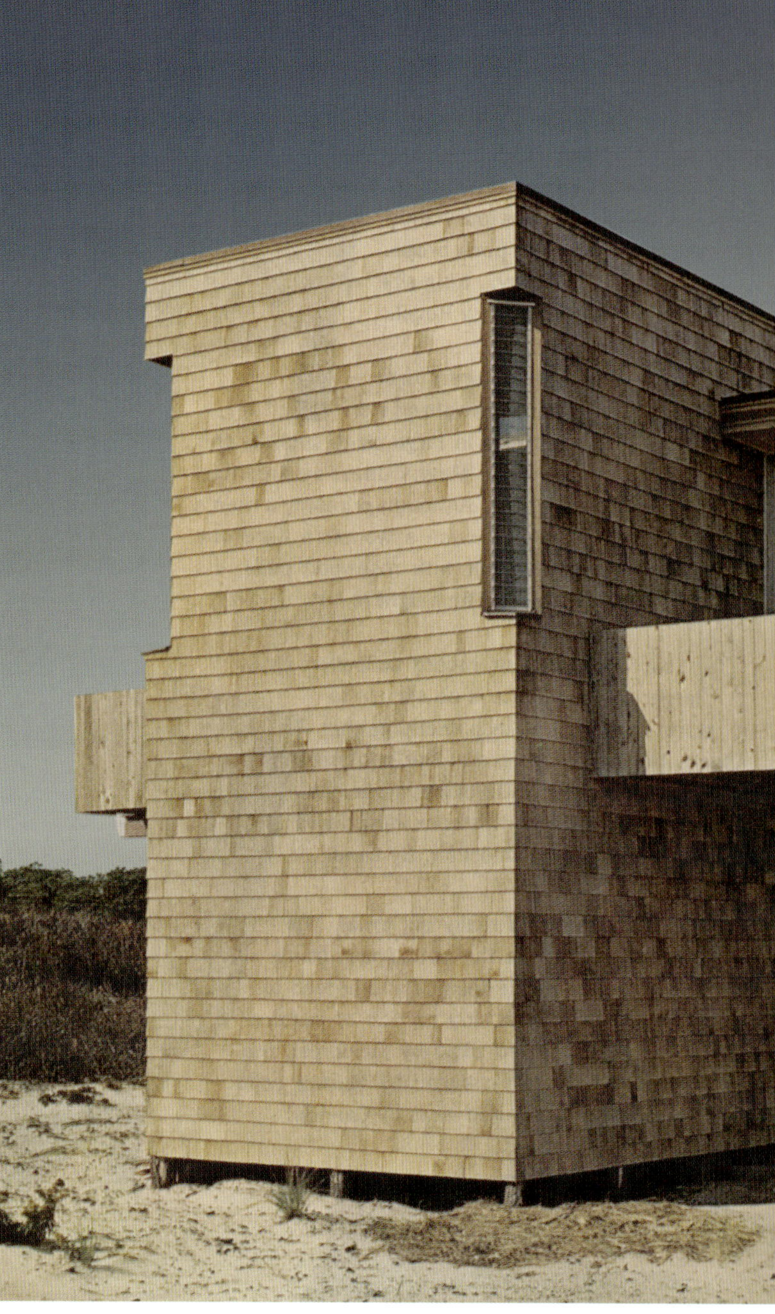

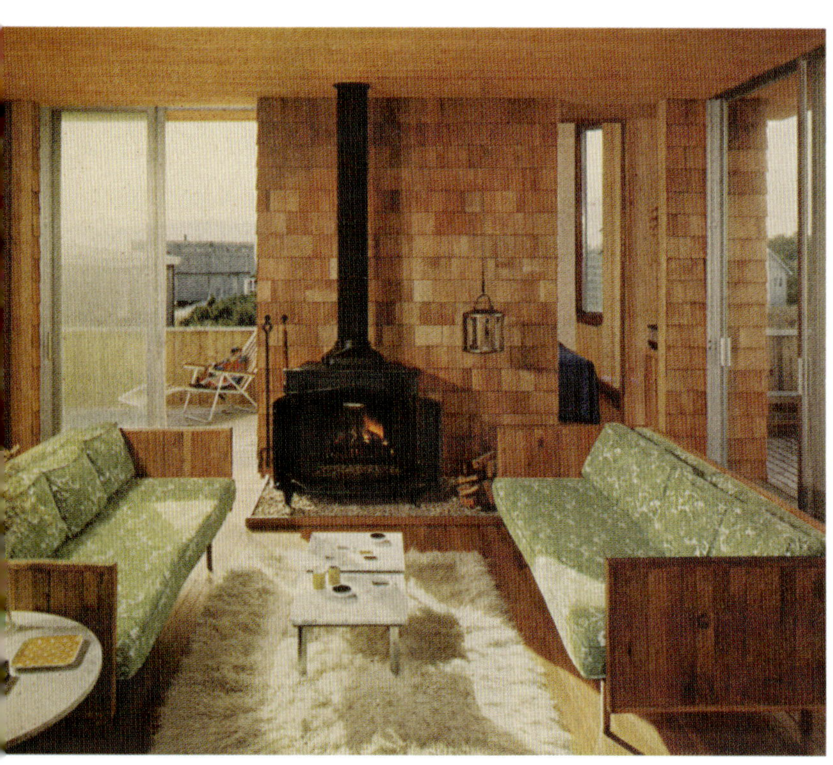

View from living room shows how close other houses are, but relatively high railing of deck allows a clear view from inside or on the decks. The wood-burning Franklin stove is at home in its contemporary setting. Bedroom behind fireplace wall gets light from windows set into corners.

The living room is cool and serene. Slight roof overhang on the decks works to visually extend the room. Same cedar shingles as outside are used on some of the walls. The major pieces of furniture were designed by the architect. The kitchen cabinets and counter were built of the same wood as rest of house.

The plan shows how the subsidiary rooms fit into the towers, with the living-dining area between them. The lower level of one of the towers is used as a utility room. In the future, two bedrooms and another bath will be put in the lower level of the three other towers.

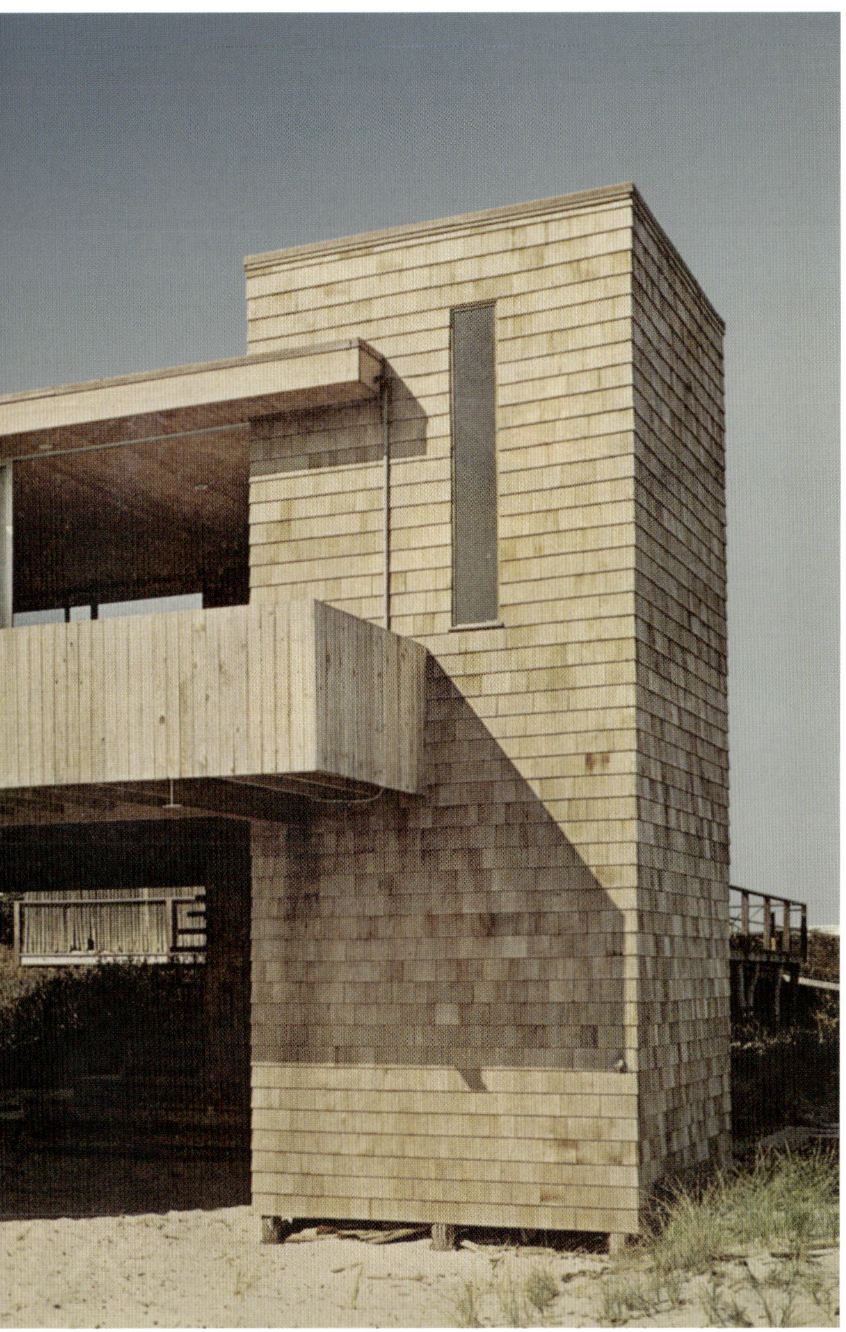

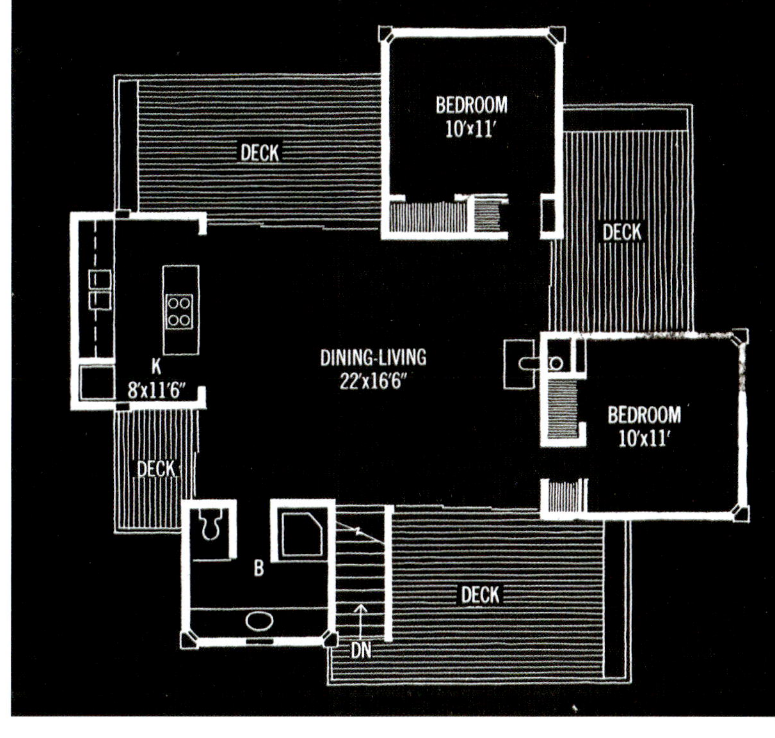

Exterior of house is a combination of the closed-in and the opened-up. Living room is in wide-windowed section between the towers. House has the locust-post foundation system typically used in the area, but surface of towers hides the posts with shingles.

The entryway (right) leads dramatically under the main living level of the house and then up to it. Platforms in the sand guide visitors to the cantilevered stairs. House is raised above ground level to get the view and the breeze.

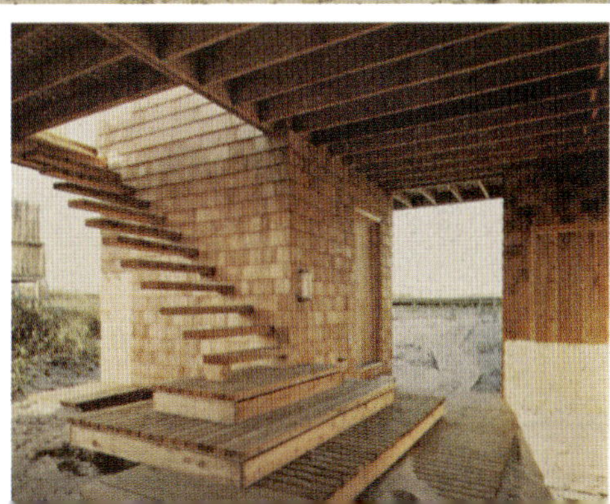

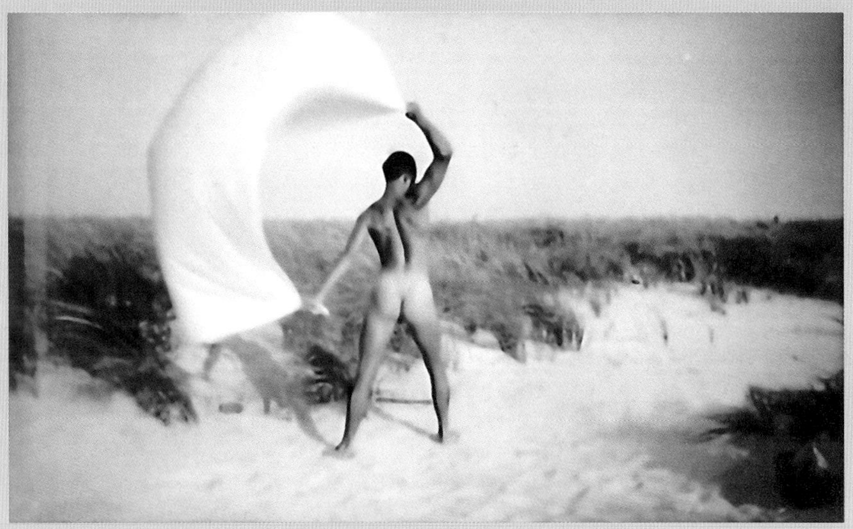

A-4563-65

POLICE DEPARTMENT
COUNTY OF SUFFOLK
ARREST REPORT

Central Complaint No.	Date of Arrest	Command Reporting	Ident. No.
65-93,591	8-8-65	235	7232

Classification	Code	Place of Arrest	Sector	
A	27od	5th	510	01-135

Charge: Disorderly Conduct Sec. 43 P.L. — Time of Arrest: 0300

Last Name	First	Middle	Place of Arrest
Gifford	Horace	Henry	Cherry Grove, Fire Island Pines

Nicknames/Aliases: ----------- — Occupation: Architect

Address: 330 East 33rd Street, New York City — Employer: Self-employed

Brief Details of Offense:

Did with the intent to commit a Breach of the Peace, whereby a Breach of the Peace was likly to occur, did loiter in a public place for immoral purposes.

CERTIFIED
CENTRAL RECORDS SECTION
SUFFOLK COUNTY POLICE DEPARTMENT

Final Charge(s)	Disposition & Date
Same	8-8-65 Fined $50.00 and 30 days-suspended jail sentence

Court & Location	Magistrate
Brookhaven Town	William Underwood

Teletype Mesa No.	Date	Reporting Officer
12929	8-8-65	Det. Kiechlin

Police Pick A Pansy Bouquet At U-No-Wear

(This is no fairy tale)

At midnight Saturday, Suffolk County Police made one of their infrequent raids at Cherry Grove, and by the time their quarry had donned their pretty apparel, 22 males had been arrested for outraging public decency. The raid also extended into Fire Island Pines.

The 22, along with three others who were arrested on other charges, paid fines totaling $1,170 before Brookhaven Town Justice of the Peace William Underwood Jr. in a court session held in the Davis Park Firehouse.

As usual, practically all of those arrested came from the New York City area, and one hailed from Texas.

Those charged with outraging public decency were each fined $50 and given a 30-days' suspended sentence. Two others were fined $25 each on disorderly conduct charges, and one was fined $20 for trespassing.

As the 22 left to return to their frolicking on the beach, one courtroom observer, having heard about the male bathing beauty fashion show recently held at Cherry Grove, remarked, "Boys will be girls."

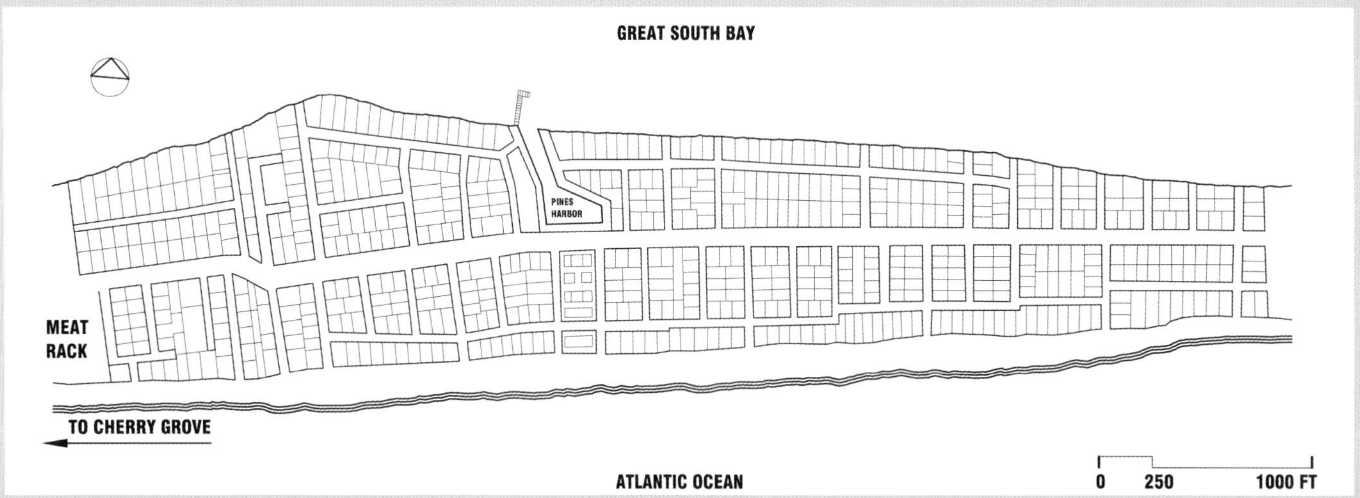

Elizabeth, resided in an unassuming oceanfront cottage for a time, but the availability of the lot next door offered a unique expansion opportunity for their young family. The first generation of Fire Island builders heedlessly flattened the dunes to accommodate cookie-cutter cottages. At the Burge Pavilion, slender, skylit towers soared above carefully preserved dunes, with an elevated bridge to connect the new structure to the old house. The existing workaday beach cottage housed two children and a nurse, while Gifford's folly preserved a sphere of sybaritic style for the parents behind its austere shell. "Only when you have entered this seemingly stark stockade are you aware that Mr. Burge has designed a velvet lining for his iron glove," noted *House and Garden*.[55] A travertine table, thick patterned carpets, and antiqued wood finishes complemented Gifford's rustic walls and skylit alcoves.

Beyond their shared business interests, Burge and Donghia maintained a close friendship. Summer afternoons were happily frittered away together with long lunches that alternated between Donghia's bayside retreat and Burge's towers by the sea. Burge's children preferred "Uncle Angelo's" home, where they could go clamming in the shallow bay waters. Upon Burge's untimely death in 1972, Donghia purchased Burge's folly and enlisted Horace Gifford to enlarge it.

Gifford's early homes were delicately situated into the landscape, their rooflines arcing just above the trees. His tower houses were less self-consciously beautiful and more demanding, echoing tumult both personal and societal. The gables, hips, and arcs of Gifford's early confections gave way to a more abstract vocabulary that relied exclusively upon flat and shed roofs. Scale became intentionally ambiguous, as his influences veered toward monumental sources. Sixty years earlier, Frank Lloyd Wright was the celebrated architect of hip-roofed "Prairie" houses, but large commercial projects eluded him. The Larkin Company Administration Building, completed in 1906, relieved Wright's pent-up ambition, and he composed it with grand and austere service towers relieved only by a single band of decorative stone. A side-by-side glance at the Burge residence and the Larkin building reveal Gifford channeling Wright's first towers, transposing them to the scale of the beach.

The architect realized nine homes in 1965. With the impending departure of fellow modernist Harry Bates, Gifford's continuing primacy in the Pines was secured. On summer weekends, friends gathered at the home he now shared with Tom Prentiss, an artist who found his niche as a principal illustrator for *Scientific American*. An articulate polymath, Gifford's partner was equally at home discoursing on modern music or drawing the eggs of a squid. To a far greater extent than Gifford, Prentiss was at ease in the heart of New York's artistic and literary scene. His closest friend was the celebrated composer Ned Rorem, who often stayed with the couple in the Pines. Like Gifford, Prentiss was tall, blond, muscular, and handsome. He was also an ardent nudist. The couple presided amiably over cookouts and conversation, "looking like gods" as one reverent client recalled.[56] Gifford's friend Robert Berlin described the "beautiful people" that passed through their home. "I'm not talking about those boys on the beach," he said. "I'm talking about Ivy League young men, both students and graduates, cultivated, well-spoken people, very different from most of the Cherry Grove crowd...all affable and very sociable, mostly unaffected and quite self-confident."[57]

That summer, Gifford toiled on a new beach house for Prentiss and himself that would transcend anything he had yet created, the perfect shelter for a hitherto charmed life. He looked forward to his thirty-third birthday—a Saturday in August—fitting for a child of the sun and sand. It was a celebration that would conclude with

OPPOSITE, UPPER LEFT:
At the Meat Rack, n.d.

OPPOSITE, UPPER RIGHT:
Local newspaper account of Meat Rack raid that ensnared Horace Gifford, August 13, 1965

OPPOSITE, BELOW:
Map of Fire Island Pines, showing Meat Rack at its western edge

OPPOSITE, MIDDLE LEFT:
Horace Gifford's arrest report

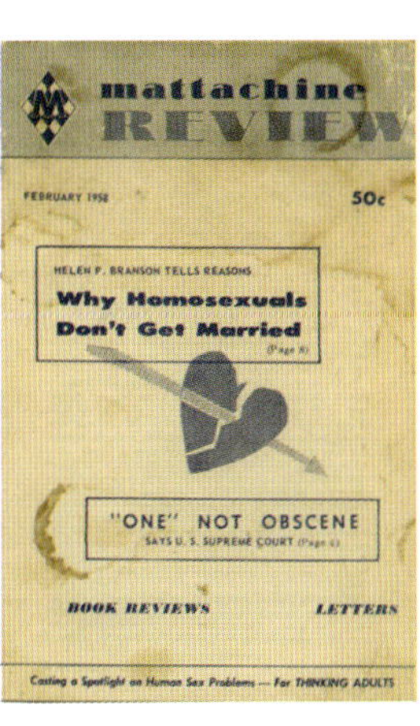

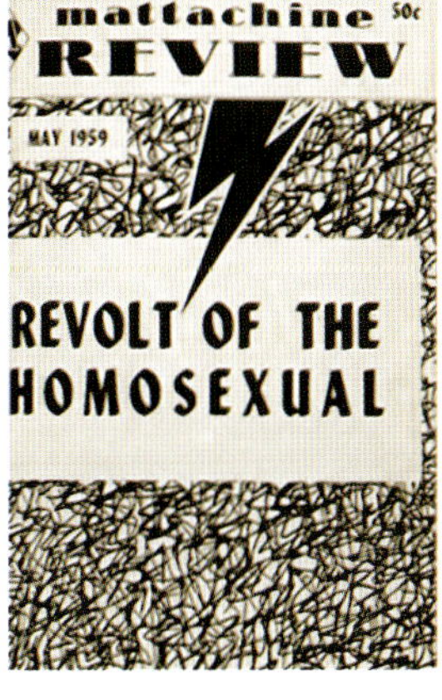

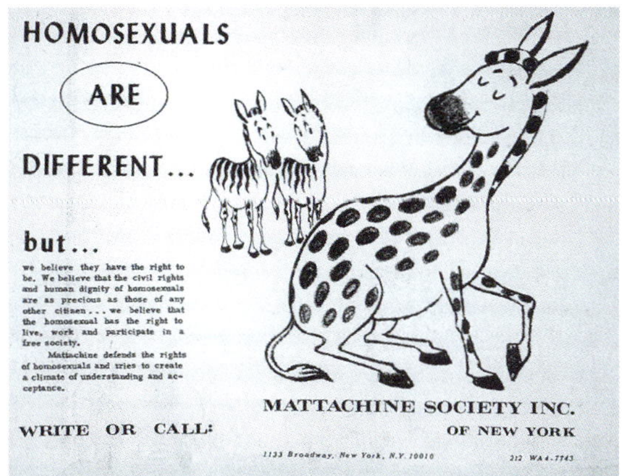

LEFT:
The *Mattachine Review*, February 1958

CENTER:
The *Mattachine Review*, May 1959

RIGHT:
Mattachine Society advertisement, n.d.

Gifford in handcuffs: he was arrested in the dunes separating the Pines and Cherry Grove, and he wasn't innocent.

They called these particular dunes the Meat Rack. Men's cruising areas had developed spontaneously in the byways of Cherry Grove throughout the 1940s, only settling in this particular locale as the development of the Pines shifted the geography of gay life on the island.[58] As clothes were shed under the moonlight, so, too, were the cultural and class divides between the two communities. Freedoms so fiercely denied to homosexuals everywhere else found their ultimate release in this radicalized domain.[59]

However, the spoils of the sexual revolution exacted a dear price for the gay population of the Pines and Cherry Grove, since the mainland police department with jurisdiction over the two communities did not share their joie de vivre. Undercover agents, sometimes dressed absurdly and wearing perfume, entrapped and arrested men in raids on the Meat Rack throughout the 1960s. Police dangled the threat of felony sodomy charges over anyone who challenged their misdemeanor arrests. Names were published in newspapers. Careers ground to a halt. As one enraged Gifford client recalled, "They would entrap and beat the crap out of the guys, then drag them down the boardwalks and corral them at the harbor-front like dead fish!"[60]

Gifford's ten years of employment with J. Gordon Carr came to an end around this time, possibly due to his arrest. That was not the real problem, however. In a state where licensed professionals had to be "of good moral character,"[61]

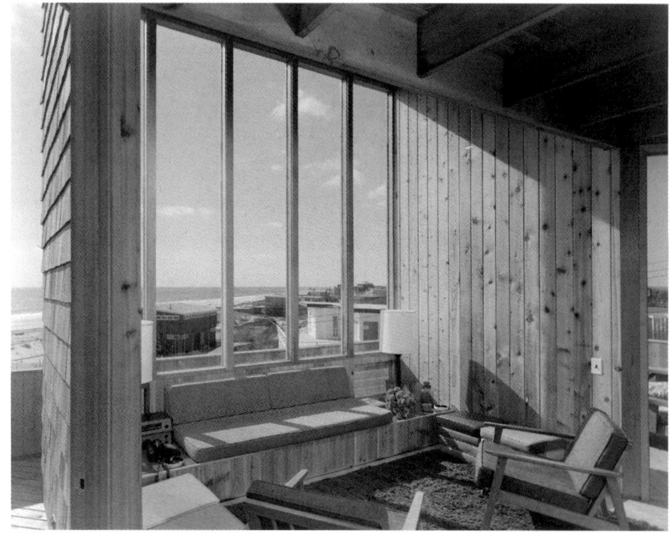

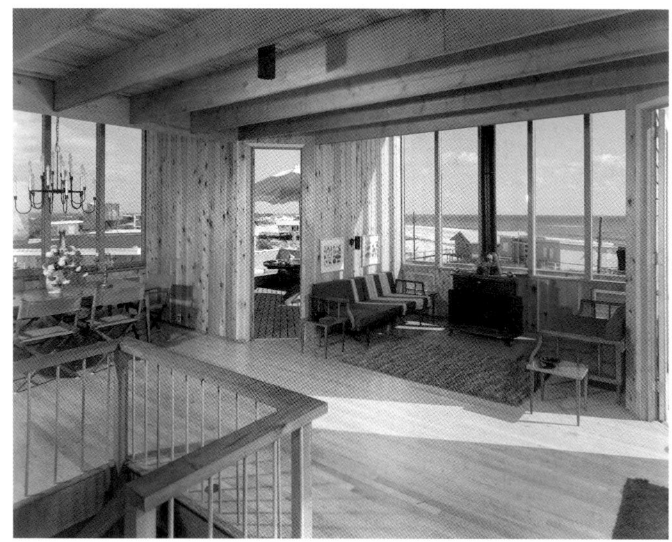

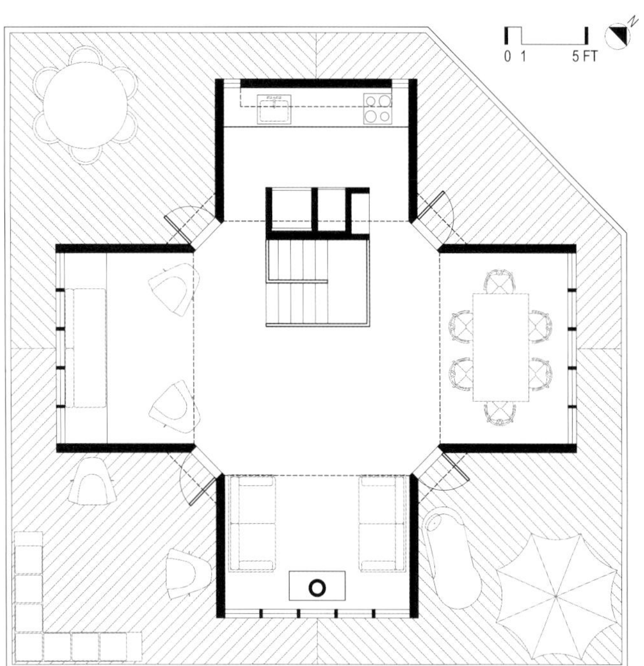

TOP:
Evans-DePass House, Fire Island Pines, NY, 1965, interior

ABOVE:
Evans-DePass House, interior

LEFT:
Evans-DePass House, floor plan

OPPOSITE:
Evans-DePass House

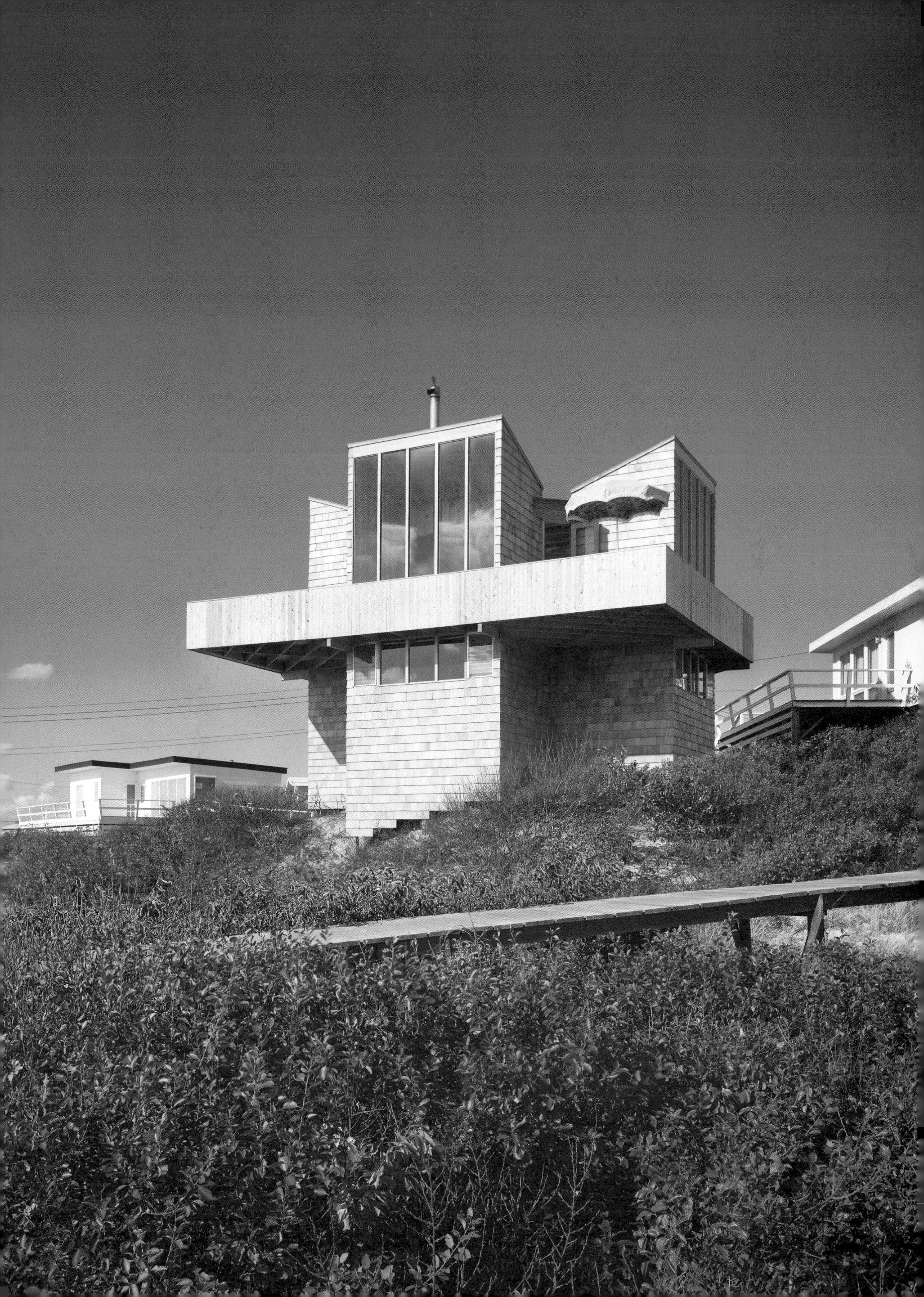

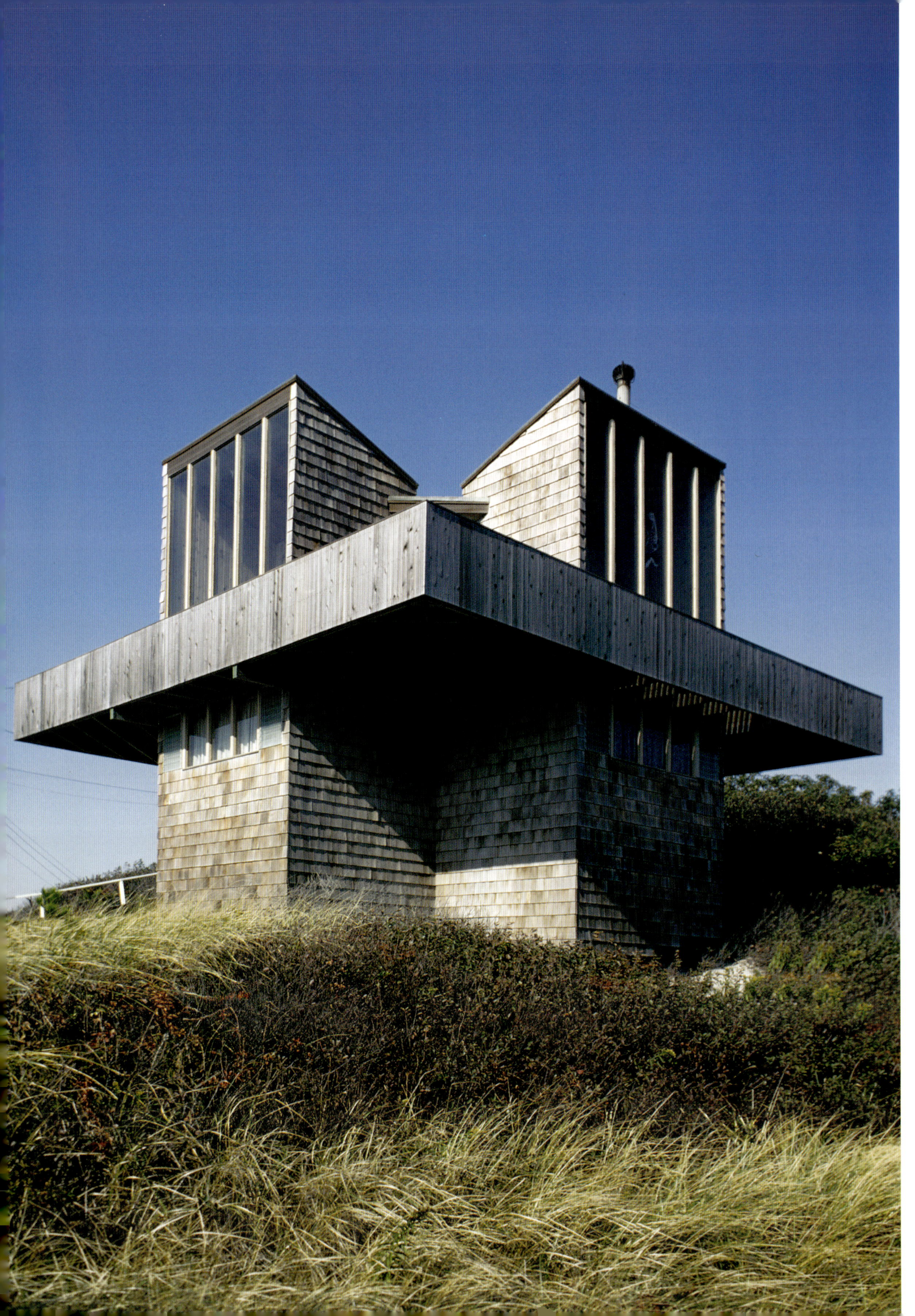

Gifford found himself barred from obtaining his license to practice architecture.[62]

Raids on the Meat Rack supplied easy kills for the Brookhaven police, generating revenue and political theater at the expense of disenfranchised citizens. The Mattachine Society, an underground "homophile" rights organization founded in 1951, came charging out of the closet during the sixties and took up the cause of the raids. They found an unlikely advocate in a conservative, cigar-smoking man named Benedict Vuturo, president of the Suffolk County Criminal Bar Association. Vuturo's civil libertarian streak was offended by New York State's "garbage statute" against "deviate conduct," and he coveted a chance to have it declared unconstitutional.[63] Defending twenty-seven raid victims in 1968, Vuturo turned in a masterful performance: "The cops literally beat the bushes to find the queers. They're not bothering anybody... until the cops find them in the bushes and then it's the cops who are disturbing the peace."[64]

With Vuturo and the Mattachine Society at their vanguard, Cherry Grove and the Pines slowly awoke from a fearful slumber to the possibility of their own political empowerment. Vuturo won case after case, demanding jury trials that exhausted the courts. By September 1968, the Meat Rack raids came to an end. This victory established the notion of autonomous gay jurisdictions that could devise their own standards of conduct outside of bourgeois notions of respectability. An entire class of oppressed citizens had finally established a beachhead, but for Gifford the damage was done. For the remainder of his career, the accomplished "designer" would pay others to stamp his drawings, rather than risk reopening the humiliations of that cruel summer.[65]

In the midst of this turmoil, Gifford created some of his strongest work to date with a second series of tower houses. In these, he retained the shed-roofed rooms but projected rooflines outward, commanding rather than retreating from the landscape. The Evans-DePass residence was delicately tethered to the landscape on its slender tower bases, a "space ship," as Gifford described it, hovering over its earthbound neighbors.[66] The octagon of the second Miller-Wittstein residence merged with the early cruciform plans to create a flared cross in both plan and elevation. Three spacious decks facing due west, south, and east chased the sun. From a seated position, the solid deck rail created a filtered, idealized horizon line where ocean meets sky. The central living space was left open, for dancing. Two living areas, a dining room, and a kitchen claimed the four tower niches.

Gifford's second personal residence formed a pinwheel of shed-roofed towers around a living area that exploded into voyeuristic stages for living. Glass doors opened wide in the public spaces to create a breezeway through which birds flew, achieving a remarkable tension between the openness of the flat-roofed public spaces and the high-waisted sentinels housing the bedrooms, bathroom, and kitchen. On this low-lying site, Gifford conjured "towers that reach out and grab for light."[67] As he told *Newsday* in 1966, "I planned it for sun, but when the moon goes around the house, it is so beautiful."[68] A shifting ceiling plane acted as an ever-changing foil to a floor plan that was consistently composed using "golden section" proportions.

With this home, Gifford perfected the transition from nature to architecture. Upon stepping off the common boardwalk, a leaf-strewn path threaded between two trees and ascended two exterior decks, which progressed to two interior stages, and culminated in a fifth outdoor level at the other end of the inhabitable breezeway. This progression formed a multitude of spatial experiences, from leaves and shade toward western

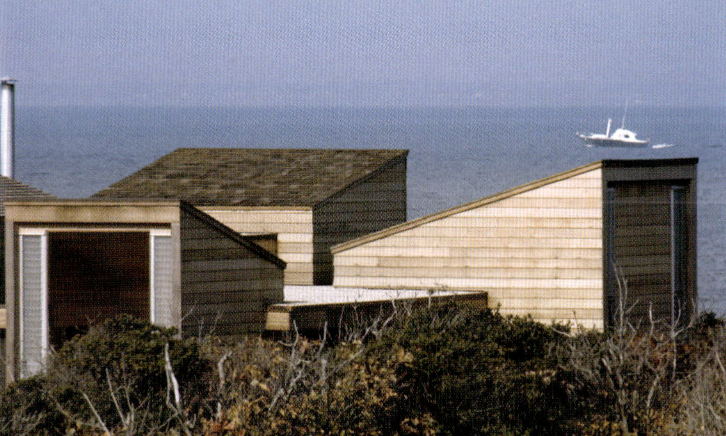

OPPOSITE:
Evans-DePass House, Fire Island Pines, NY, 1965

RIGHT:
Gifford House II, Fire Island Pines, NY, 1965

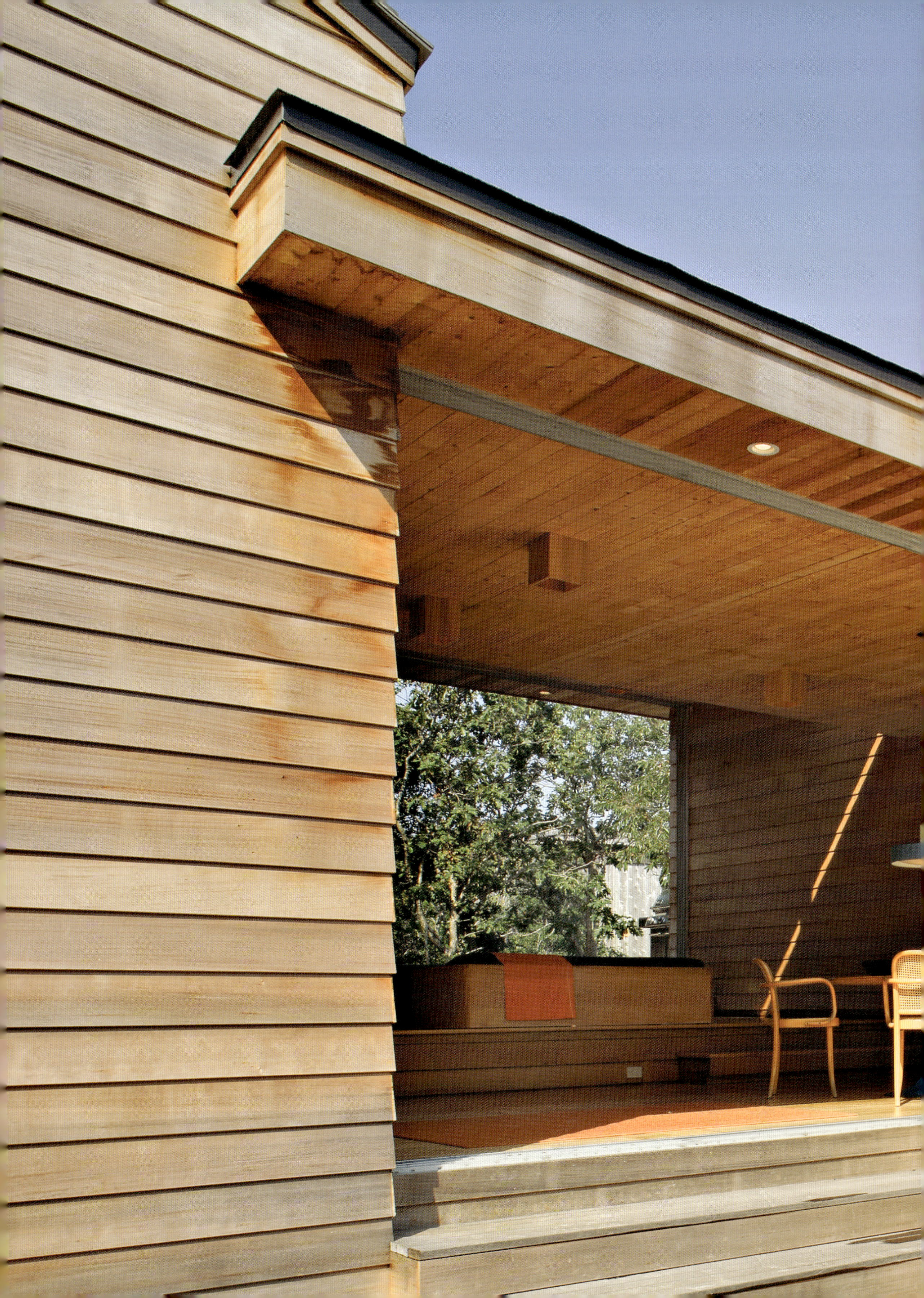

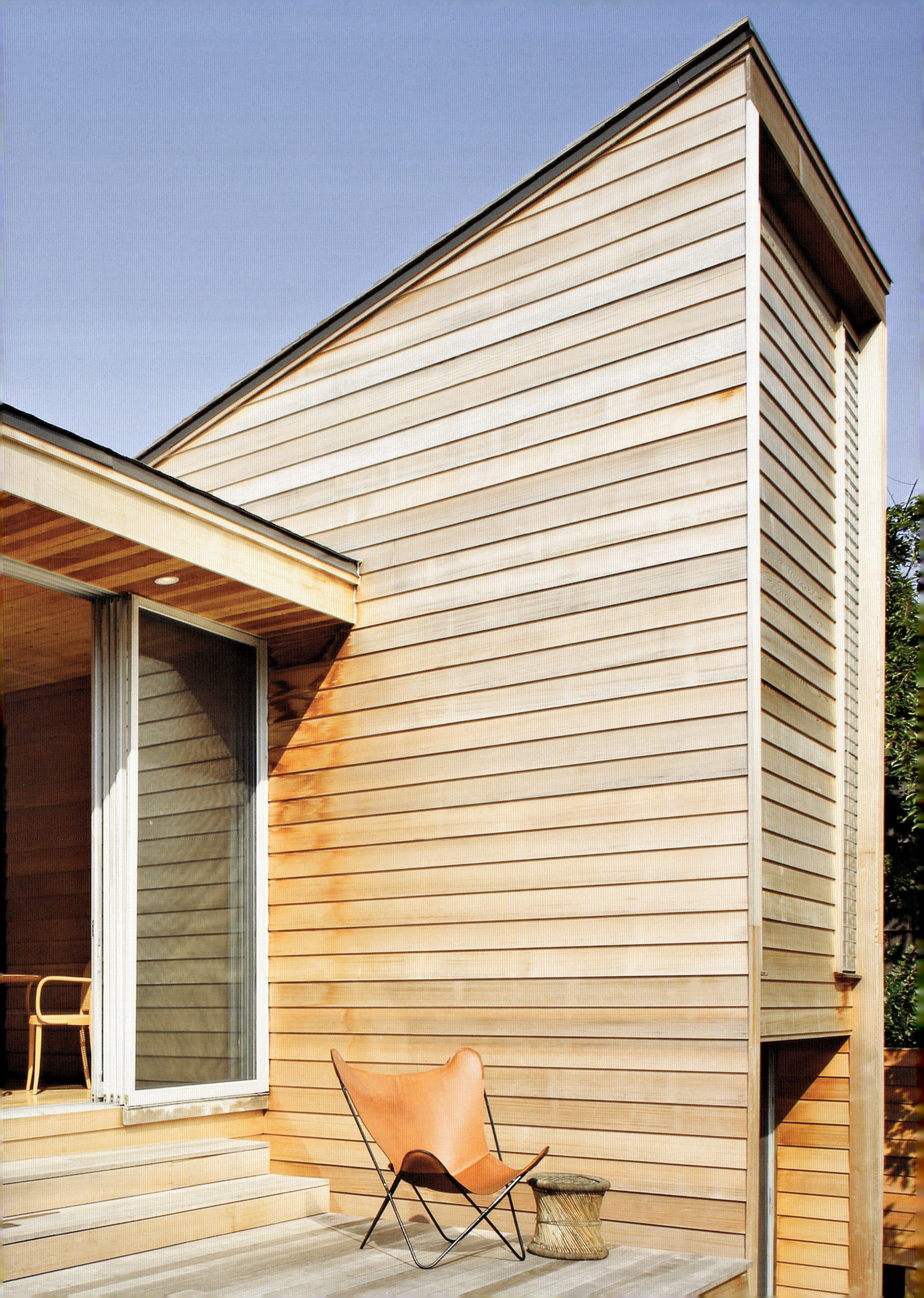

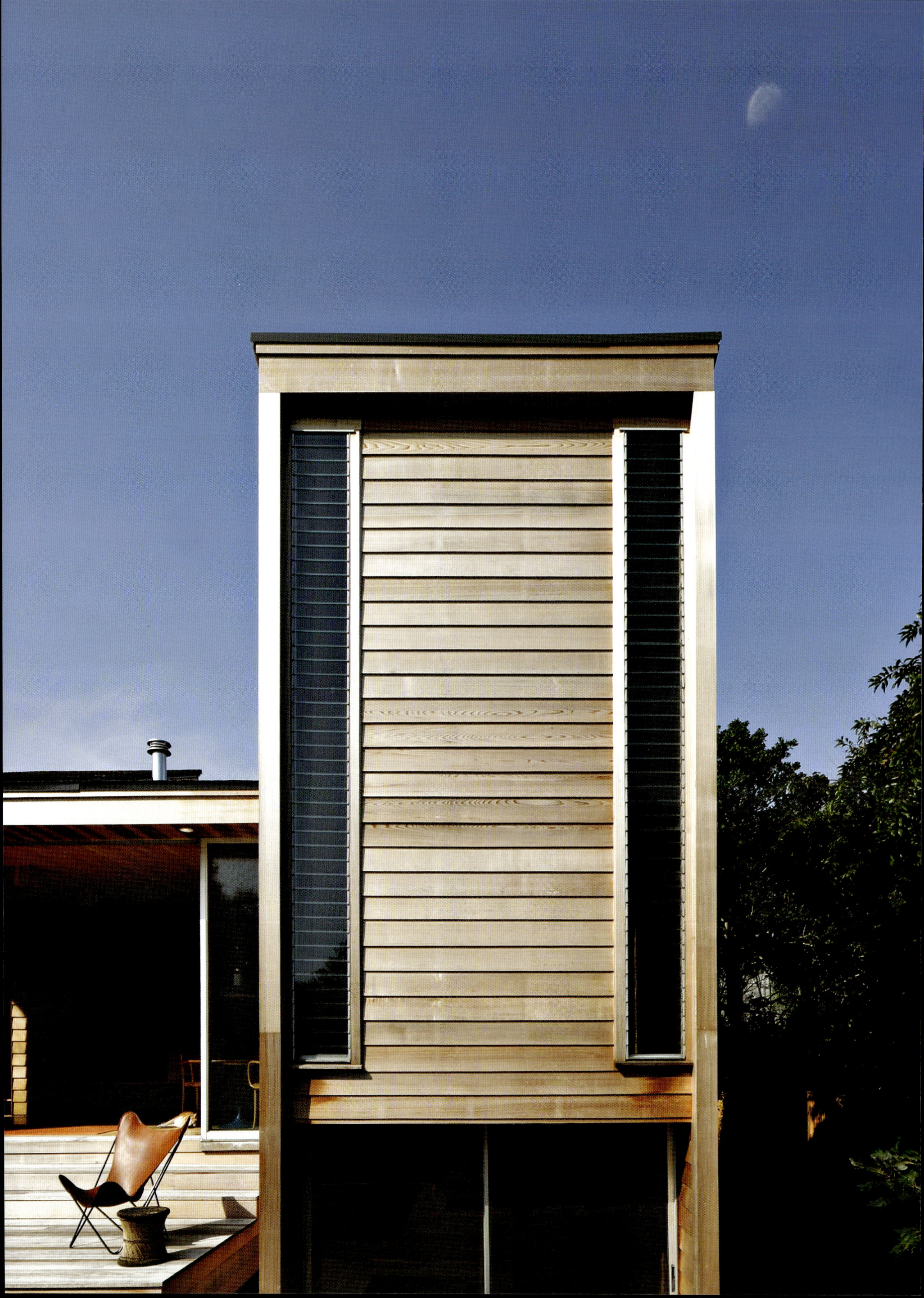

light, treetops, and a water view. Gifford was so proud of this project that he sent photographs to Louis Kahn; his mentor replied, "Horace, you have created a mountain and a valley."[69]

Inside, narrow steps formed thresholds between public and private spaces, compressing the senses before the release of the spare, light-filled bedrooms. Compact in plan, from a reclining position they were expansive. Low furniture exaggerated the sensation of height. The first waking moments witnessed a dance of light skimming across the high, rough-hewn spruce ceiling. Slim, floor-to-ceiling jalousie windows in the primary bedroom fostered an interior focus in counterpoint with the extroverted public spaces. Wooden wall surfaces were hung with archaic farm implements, a column capital, and the inner workings of a clock. Another found object—the felt-and-wire innards of a piano—watched over the living area, in silent tribute to the musicality of the architecture.

Gifford's new home, built on the opposite end of the Pines as his first home and the Meat Rack, was designed for two but ultimately inhabited by one. All was not well within the union of Gifford and Prentiss, and the denouement was particularly cruel. Prentiss did not simply leave. He left for one of Gifford's clients. Her name was Nan Schultz.[70]

PAGES 100–01:
Gifford House II, Fire Island Pines, NY, 1965

OPPOSITE:
Gifford House II

BELOW:
Gifford House II, cross-section perspective by the author

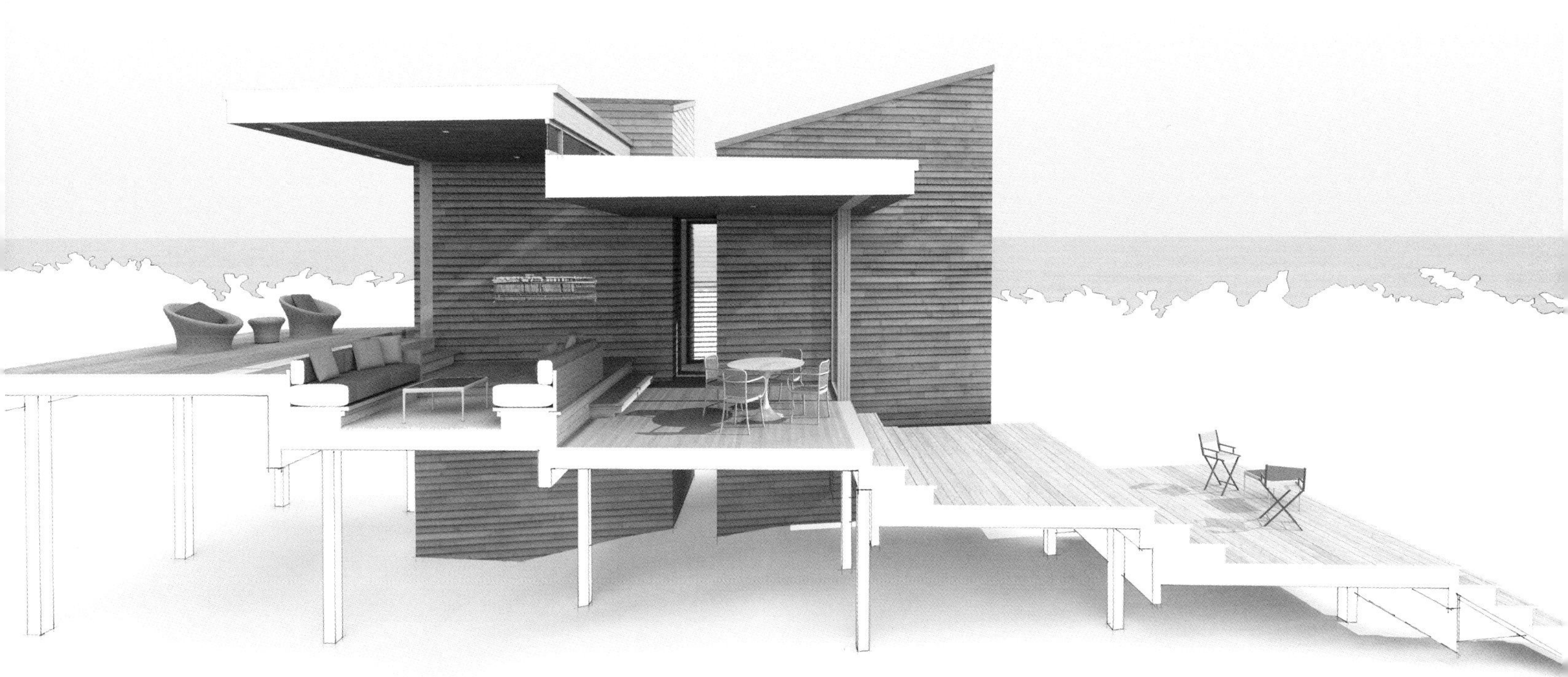

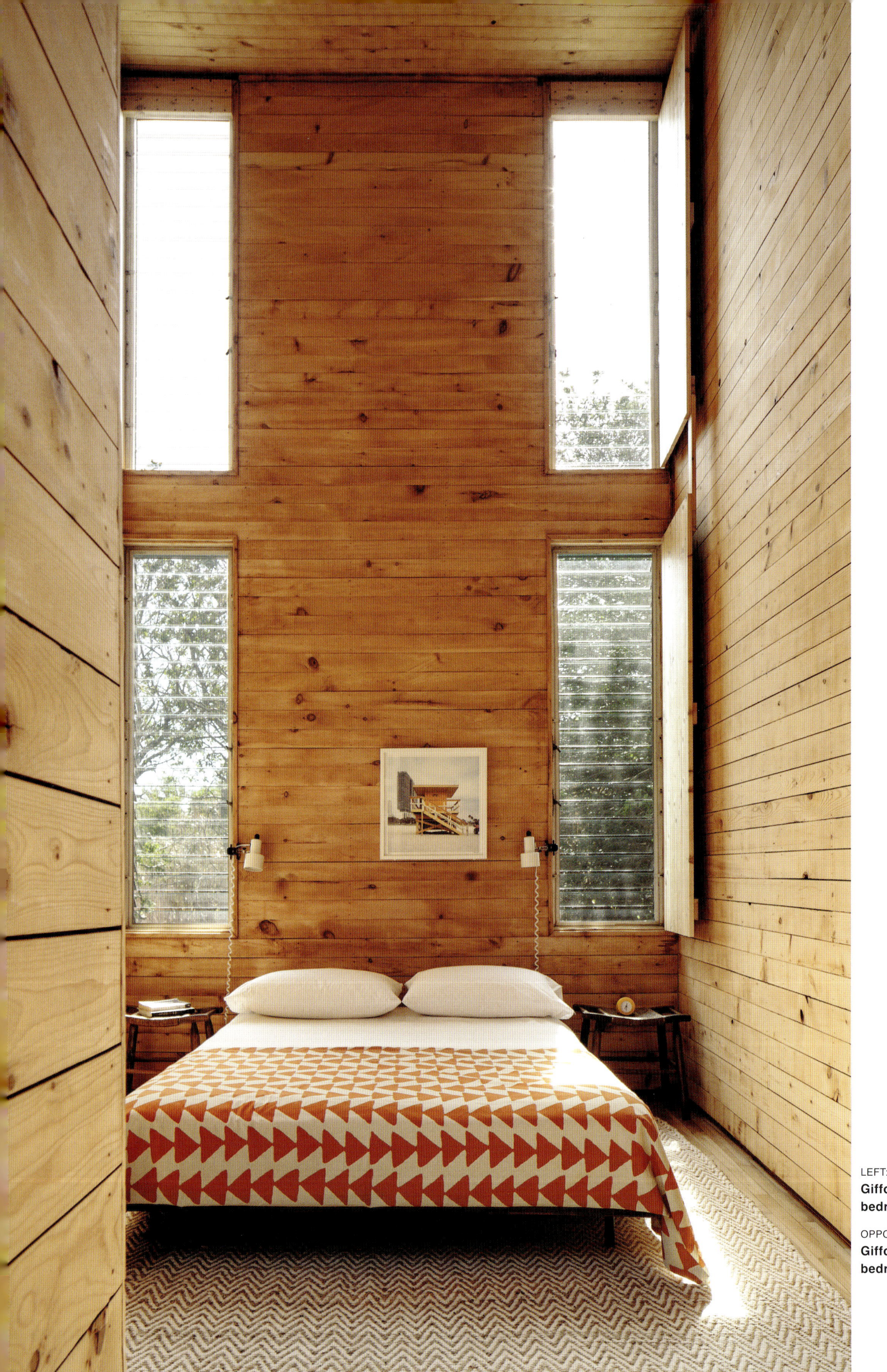

LEFT:
Gifford House II, bedroom

OPPOSITE:
Gifford House II, bedroom

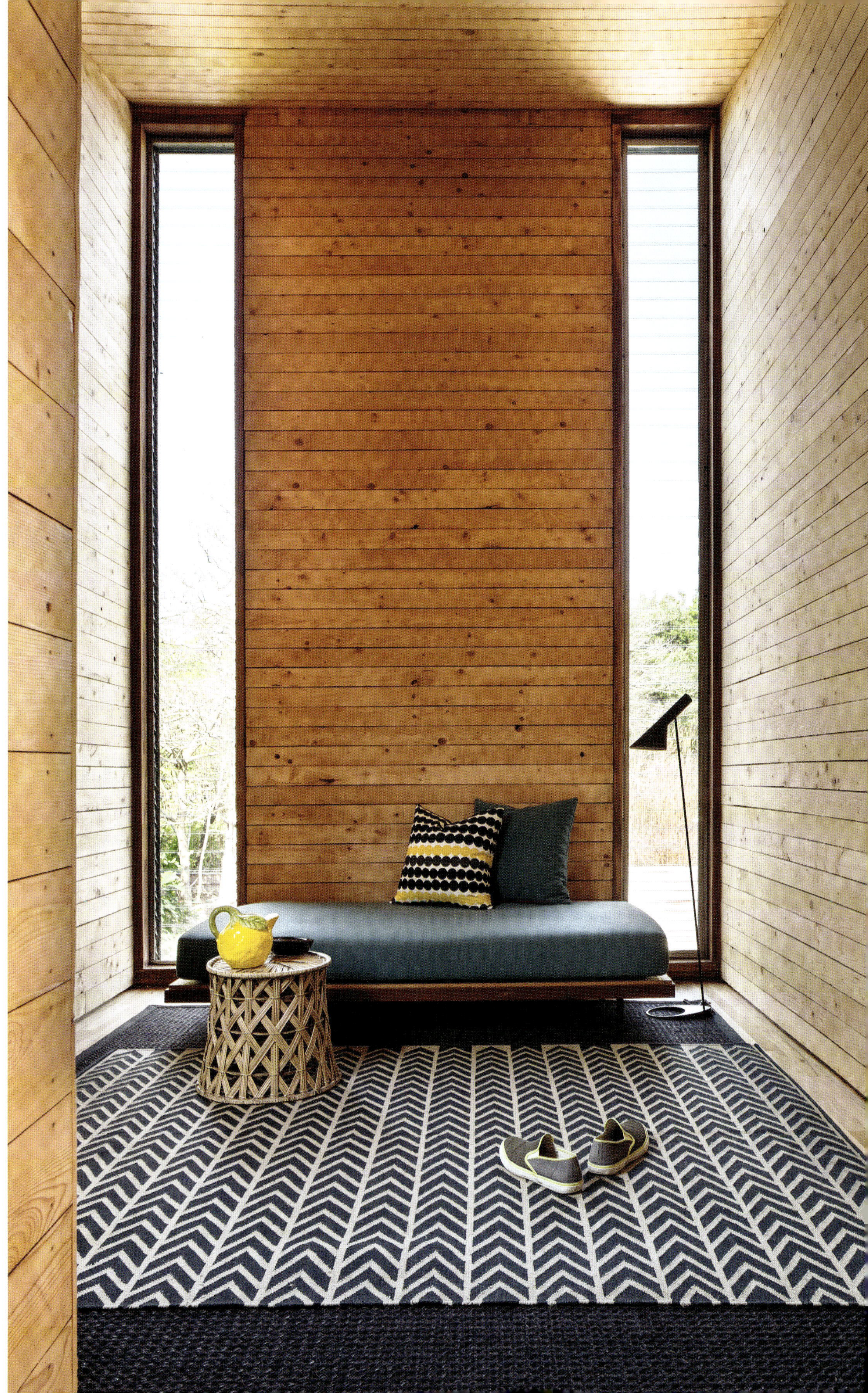

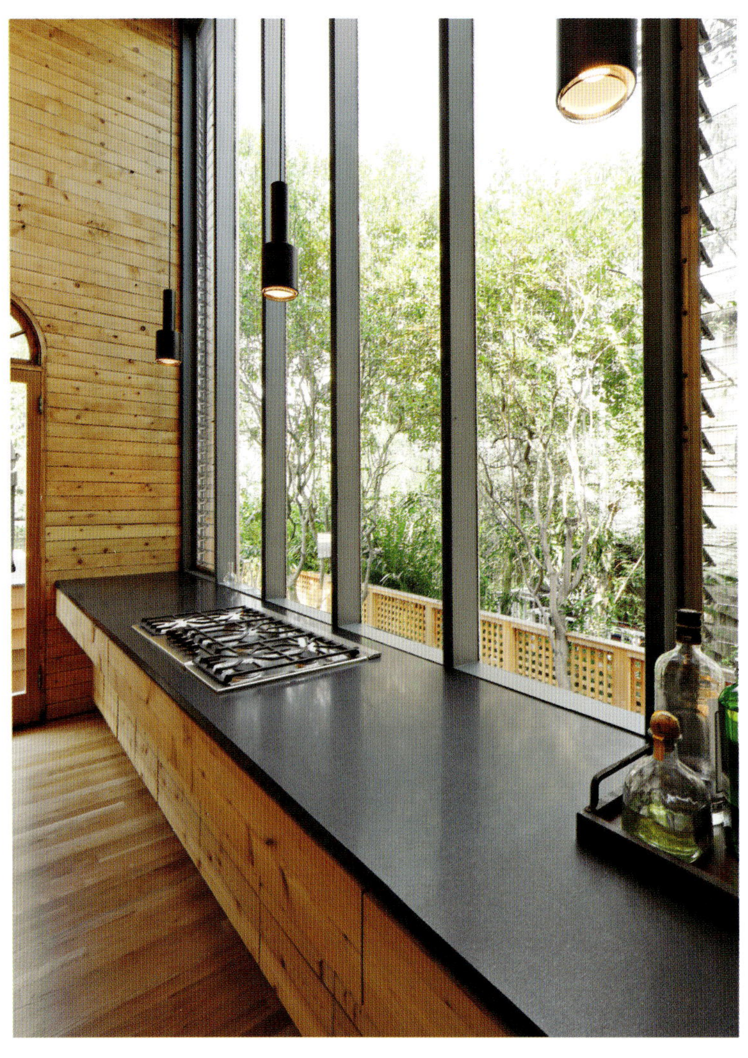

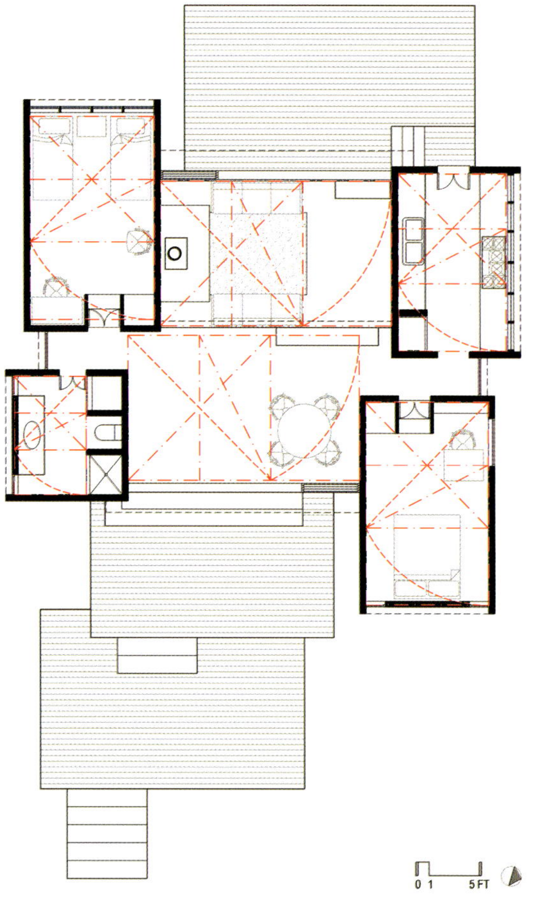

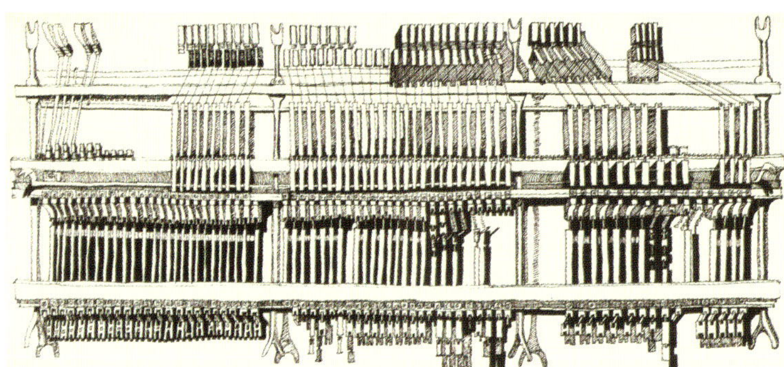

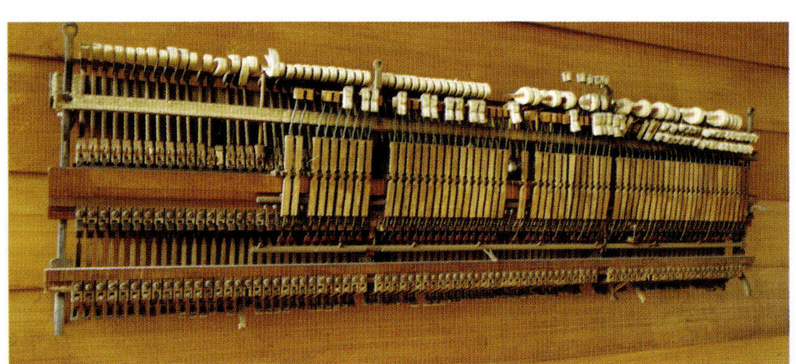

UPPER LEFT:
Gifford House II, kitchen

UPPER RIGHT:
Gifford House II, floor plan, overlaid with golden-section proportions in red

MIDDLE LEFT:
Horace Gifford. Untitled sketch of piano action, 1964

LOWER LEFT:
Piano action hung in Gifford House II

OPPOSITE:
Gifford House II, living area

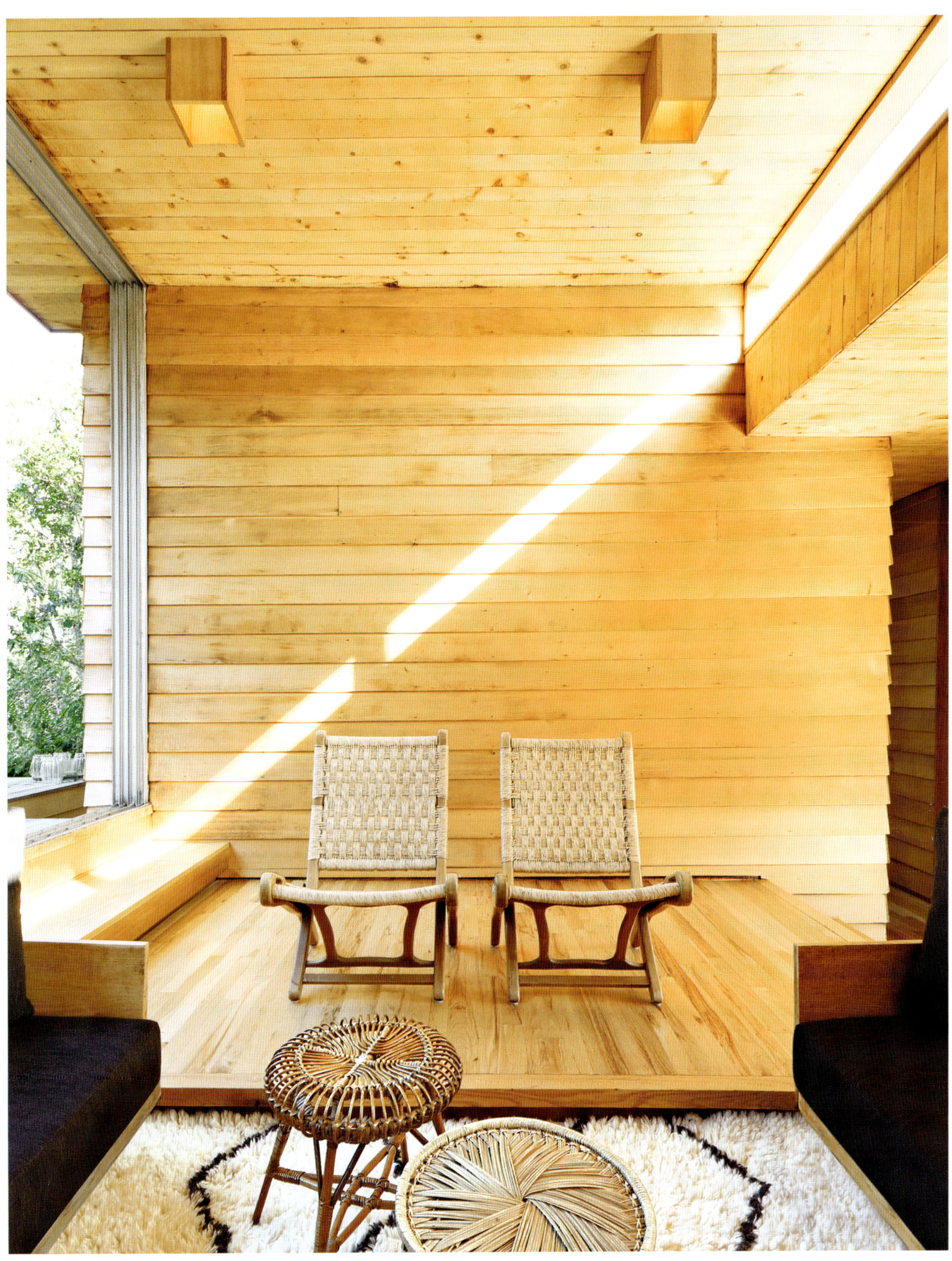

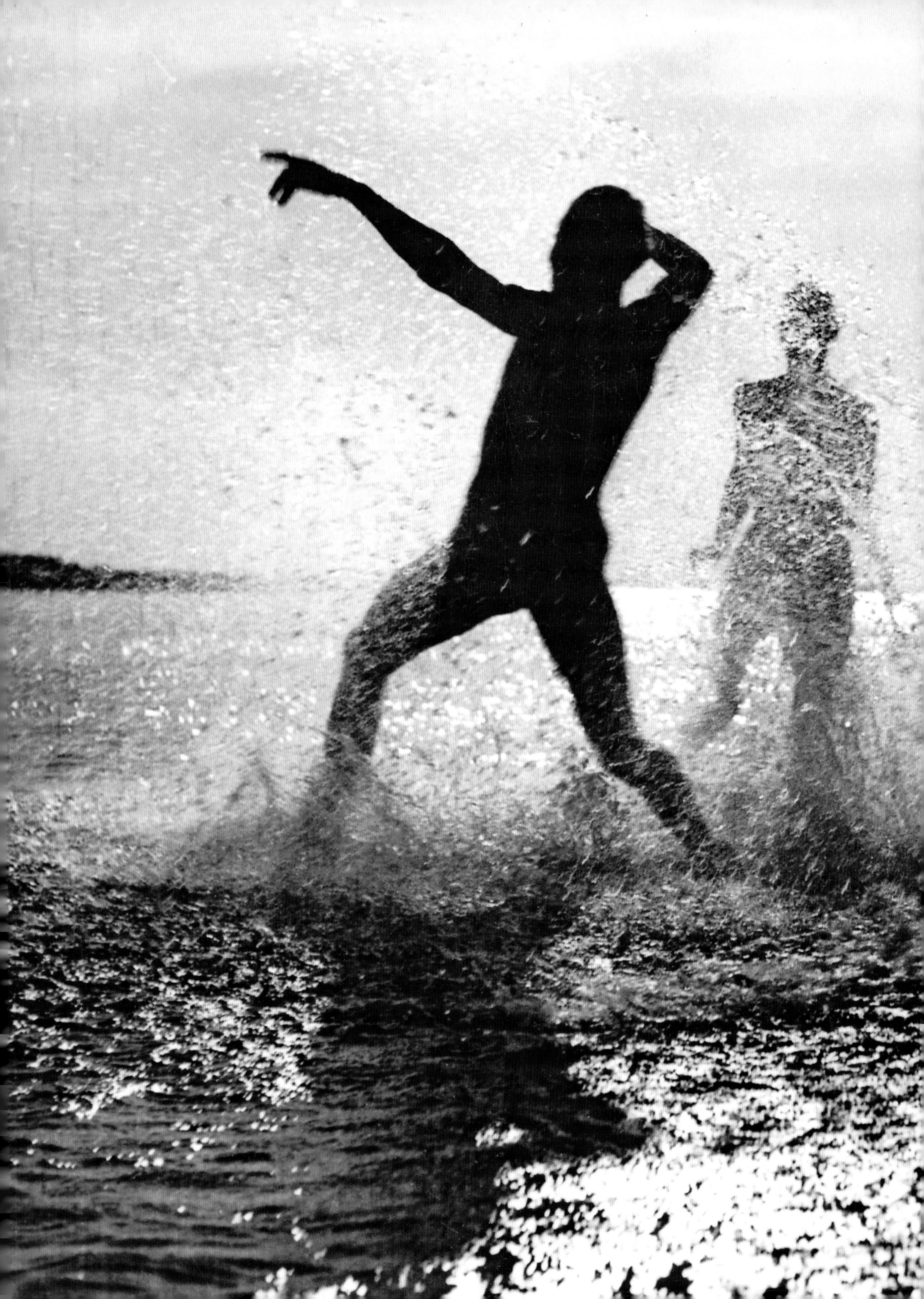

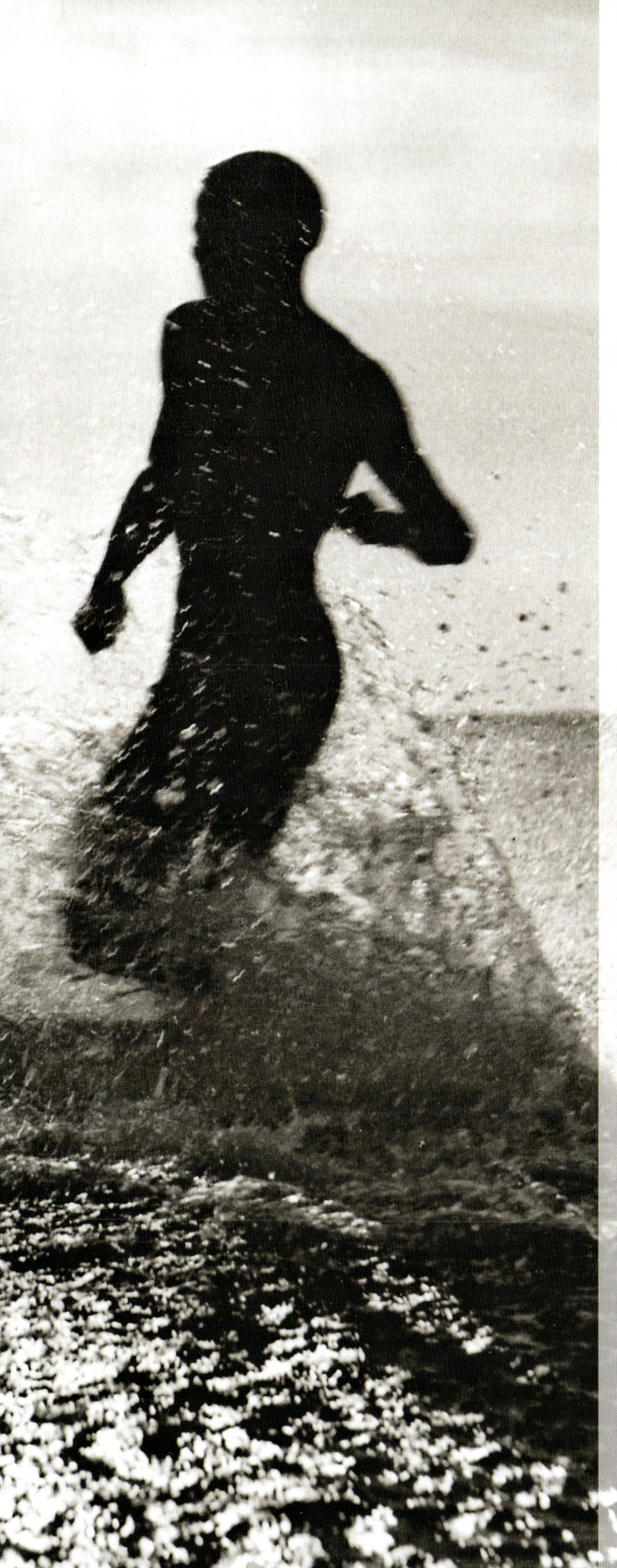

BOYS IN THE SAND

Chapter Five

Orgy is where it's all headed, and orgy is a grand old tradition on Fire Island.

—*New York* magazine, 1972[71]

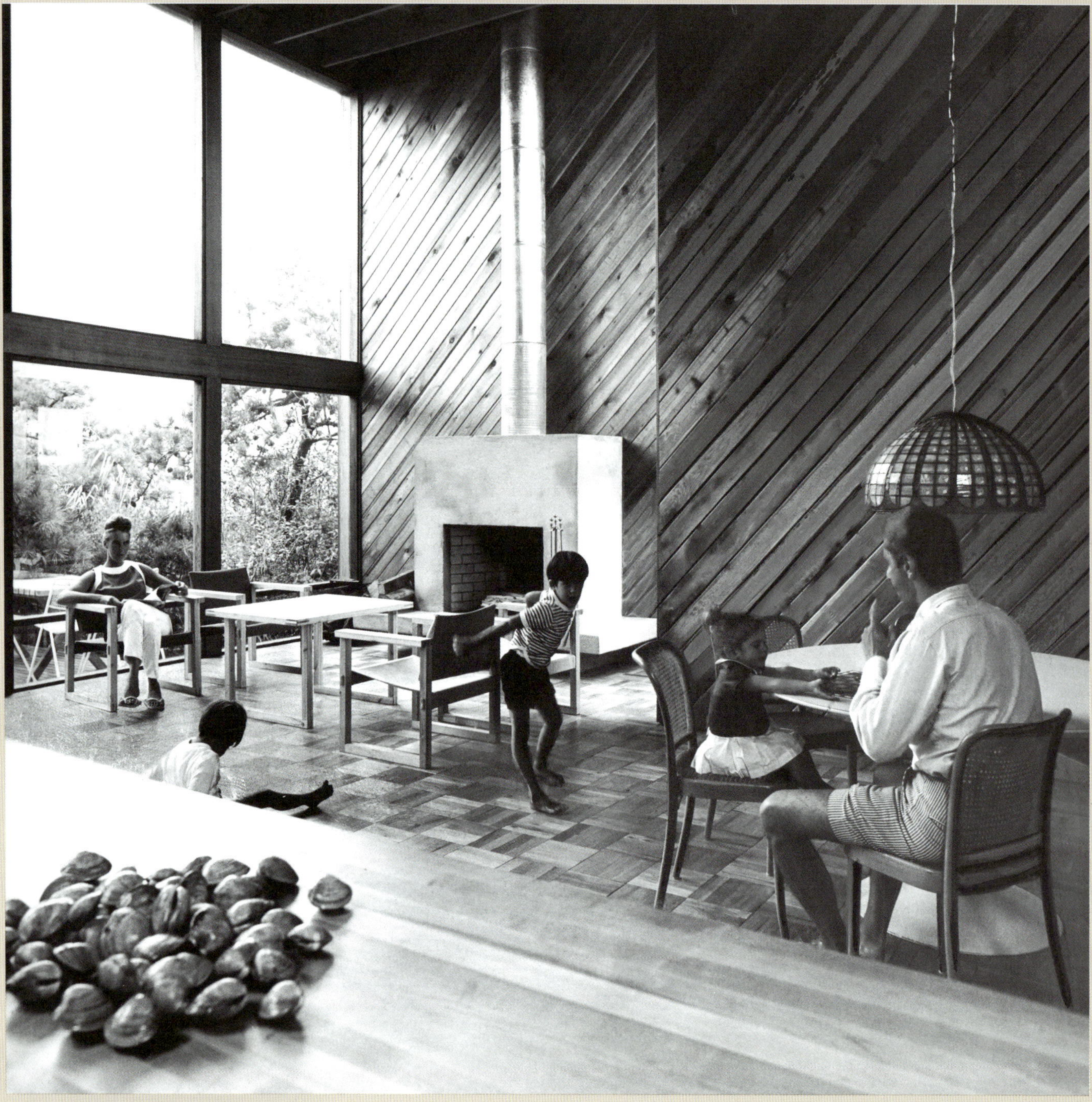

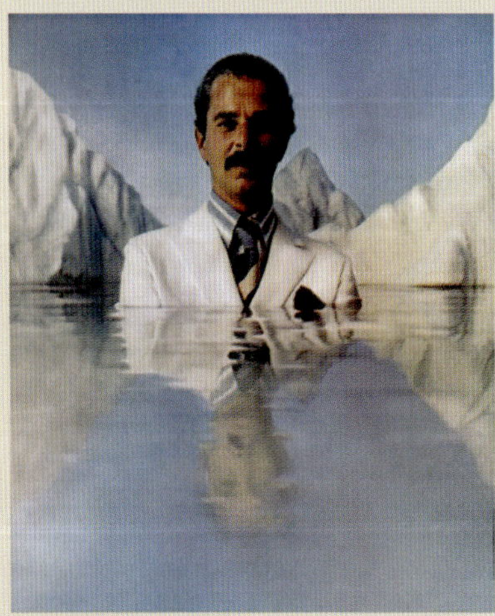

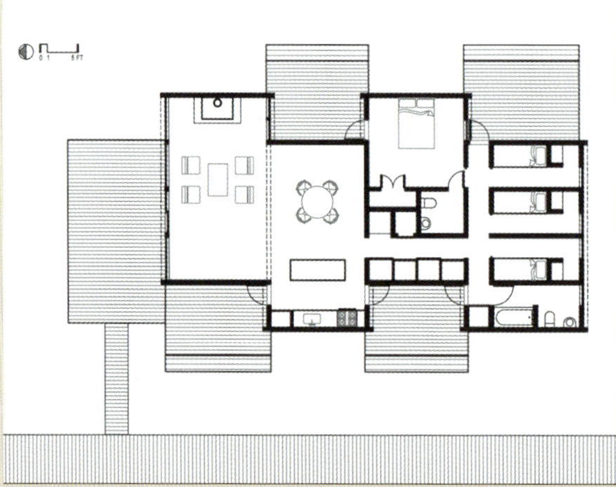

PAGES 108–09:
Herbert List, *Water Games*, 1937

ABOVE:
Scali House, Fair Harbor, NY, 1967

LOWER RIGHT:
Scali House, floor plan

LOWER LEFT:
Sam Scali, 1972

OPPOSITE:
Scali House, elevation

"It has been observed many times by his peers that [he] is a very nice, quiet guy who is almost unflappable. Inside that quiet exterior, however, resides a raging fire of creativity that catches people off guard with its simplicity, directness, and brilliance."[72] The author might have been speaking about Horace Gifford, but the compliment was actually directed toward his client. Sam Scali was a quintessential 1960s Mad Man, a creative director of advertising campaigns for Volvo, Maxell, the *Herald Tribune*, and—most famously—Perdue Farms. Scali's business partner Ed McCabe penned the slogans—in Perdue's case, "It takes a tough man to make a tender chicken"[73]—while Scali obsessively crafted the visual presentation. The font he selected for Perdue was "picked for a specific reason. If you look closely at the inside of the O's, they look like eggs."[74] He spent his free time in equally precise hobbies like winemaking, and the appreciation for subtlety and craft he shared with Gifford made Scali and the architect an ideal match.

Scali and his wife, Joan, an artist, combined several lots in Fair Harbor into one parcel, with bay views at the narrow northern edge, a public boardwalk to the west, and Gifford's serene Kauth residence from 1964 to the east. Gifford responded to this expansive but unsecluded site with a cluster of linked cubes. Four principal functions—living, kitchen/dining, primary bedroom, and children's rooms—were denoted by staggered forms in descending heights of 16, 14, 12, and 10 feet. Each cube lengthened to approximate the 1:1.618 "golden-mean" proportion and they interpenetrated each other. Floor-to-ceiling windows in the gaps created by staggered wall planes assured that interior spaces received a constant wash of light, brought into relief by diagonally oriented, rough-sawn cedar sheathing. Three shiplike bunk rooms housed the Scalis' young children. All windows faced north or south, leaving a blank but playful tumble of cubes to face the public walkway.

This "house that sits on a sand dune looking like an unpainted primary sculpture,"[75] as the *New York Times* noted, marked a decisive contrast with the Scalis' large and tastefully cluttered pseudo-Tudor home in Queens. "After a summer at the beach, the Scalis are confirmed in their original intention to leave the house without anything on the walls or on top of the tables."[76] The only concession to tradition was the stained-glass, Tiffany-style shade that illuminated an Eero Saarinen dining table. Even if just for the weekend, Americans were casting off their heavy armoires along with their suits and wingtips. People were more willing to take a chance in a summer home than a primary residence, and it was precisely this margin of adventure that Gifford mined.

The design of the Scali residence—the way it turned its back to the public thoroughfare but opened up inside with spaciousness and a privately enjoyed view—closely resembled the prevailing template for American housing in the postwar period. The front of a house sheltered an automobile, while the back secluded a nuclear family. Front yards, emptied of pedestrians and shorn of front porches, had lost their social function of stitching a community together. But the Pines was developing into a very different version of the American Dream, and Gifford soon began to play a role in this shift.

Many Pines residents hailed from tiny apartments and demanding careers. In a real sense, a beach house was not merely a second home: it was the *only* home in which the urbanite could cook, garden, and entertain. The Pines was a place for people to perform a version of domesticity that their city apartments and city careers denied them. And perform they did. The pedestrian boardwalks of the Pines created spatial intimacy between home dwellers and passersby that invited socializing, or more. After all, the Pines was a place to meet like-minded people, a place to marvel, as Albert Goldman put it, at the "remark-

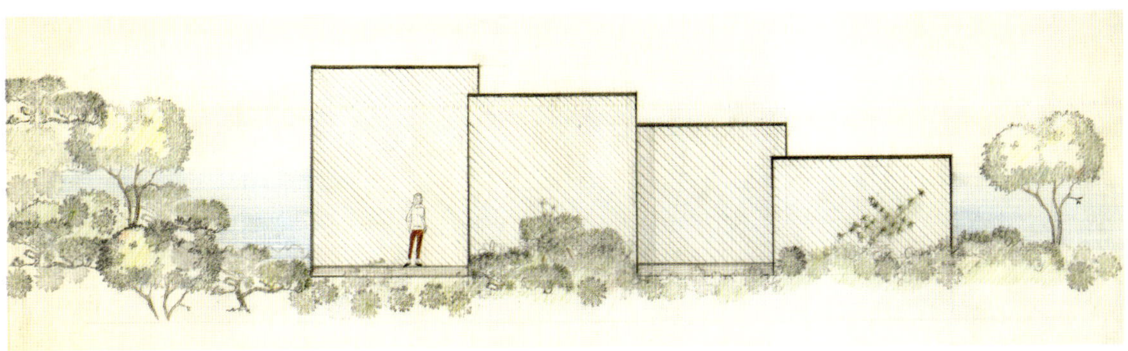

able shorting out of the barriers to interpersonal communication. Cruising along at sunset, with a glass in one hand and a modest pitcher of martinis in the other, you find yourself far more socially acceptable than you ever realized."[77]

Cherry Grove had once been the illicit playground for discreet Pines residents. Now, the social life flowed in both directions. While plenty of straight residents remained in the Pines, its majority-gay population set the tone by the late sixties. As pretenses fell away, Gifford began to rotate glass walls into public view, fashioning voyeuristic vistas from within and without.

A year after the completion of the Scali residence, Gifford revisited the organizing principle of nested cubes. This time, the glass faced the boardwalk. He was designing a home for Lawrence Bonaguidi, a prominent international-relations attorney who purchased a large site in the Pines along a well-trafficked boardwalk. Gifford's first impulse, as revealed in an early sketch, ordered its horizontal surfaces in intricate counterpoint with the ground plane. These diagonally staggered planes dodged existing trees or allowed them to pass through the floor. Eddying around each side of the house, they evoked the nearby but unseen waters of the Great South Bay. While echoing the contours of the land, the decks also hovered weightlessly over it, supported by unshorn tree trunks set back from the edges. The architect folded the roofline into a series of cubes like the Scali residence but with a critical difference—the nested planes of clerestory glass faced east and west, bending the sharply angled light in ways unknown to his earlier houses. Gifford's highest ceiling to date imbued the living room with a grandeur complemented by an intimate, bright red conversation pit. A separate guest house, with a raked roofline, anchored the rear edge of the property.

Gifford presented the house to Bonaguidi as a series of "telescopic"[78] spaces in the landscape, and his inspiration hints at the atmosphere in the Pines at this time. A telescope is a device often used for spying; it elongates when engaged in order to capture objects in its gaze. Once the house was completed, the architect commissioned a "peephole" photograph of the interior, an image that seemed to announce an imminent indiscretion. The Bonaguidi residence marked the opening salvo in Gifford's progression toward a form of modernism with a randy undercurrent.

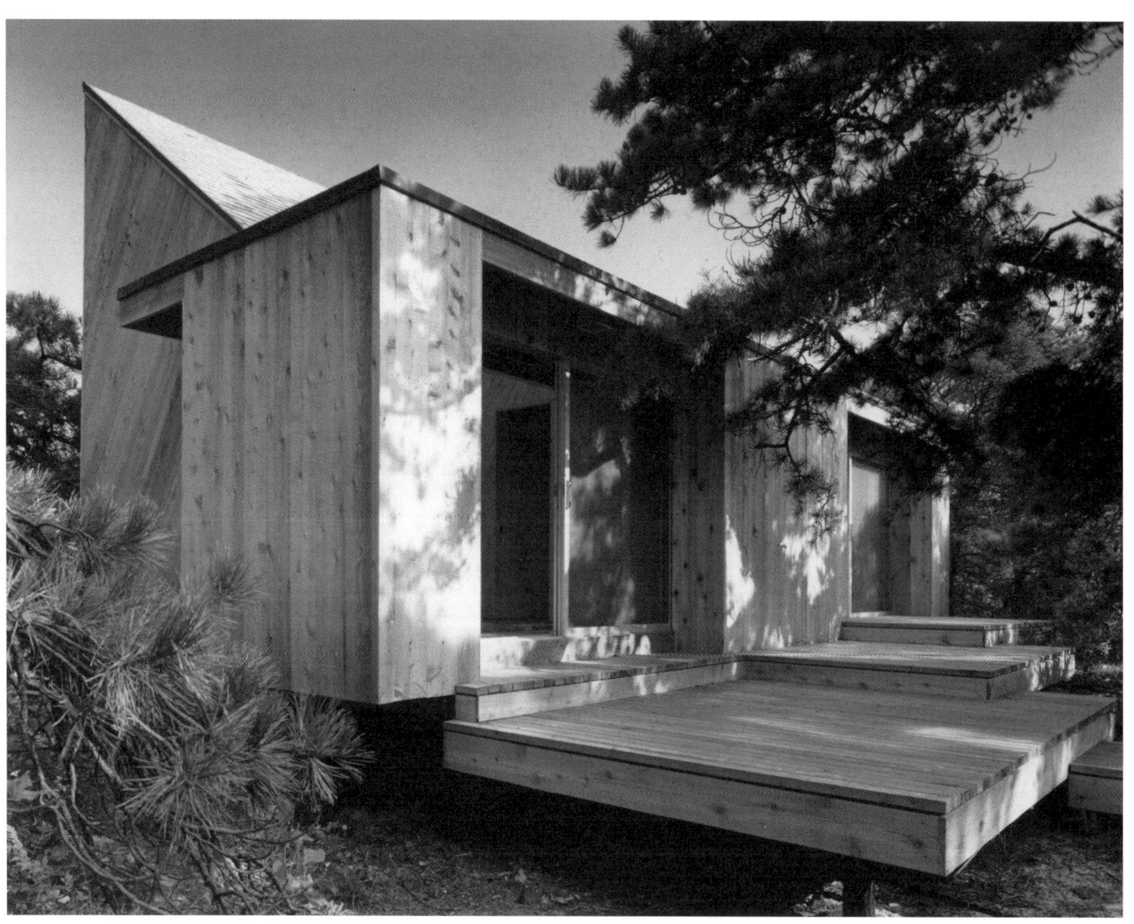

LEFT:
Bonaguidi House II, Fire Island Pines, NY, 1968, guest house

OPPOSITE, ABOVE:
Bonaguidi House, early sketch

OPPOSITE, BELOW:
Bonaguidi House, guest house elevation, by the author

PAGE 114, ALL:
Bonaguidi House

PAGE 115:
Bonaguidi House, interior

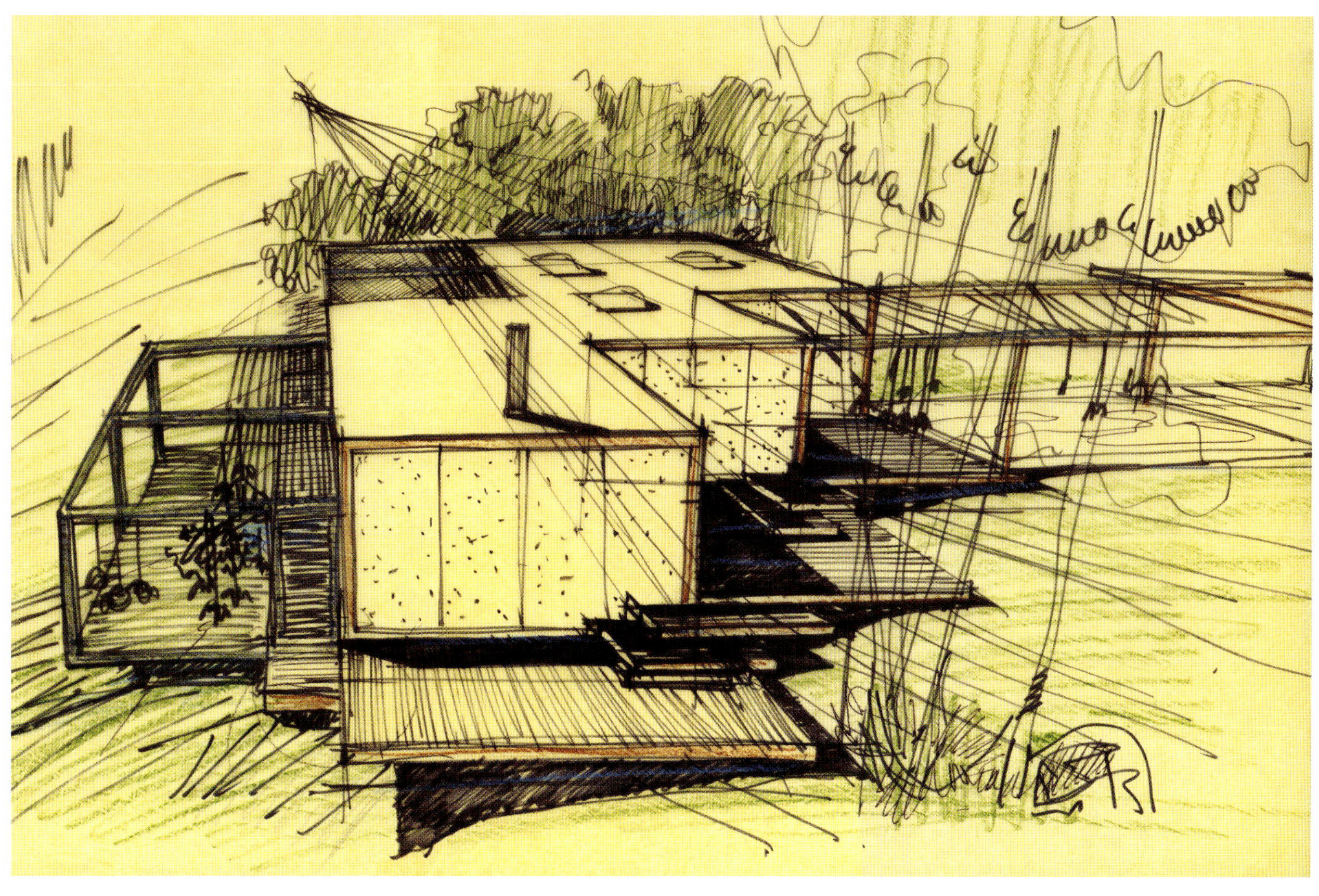

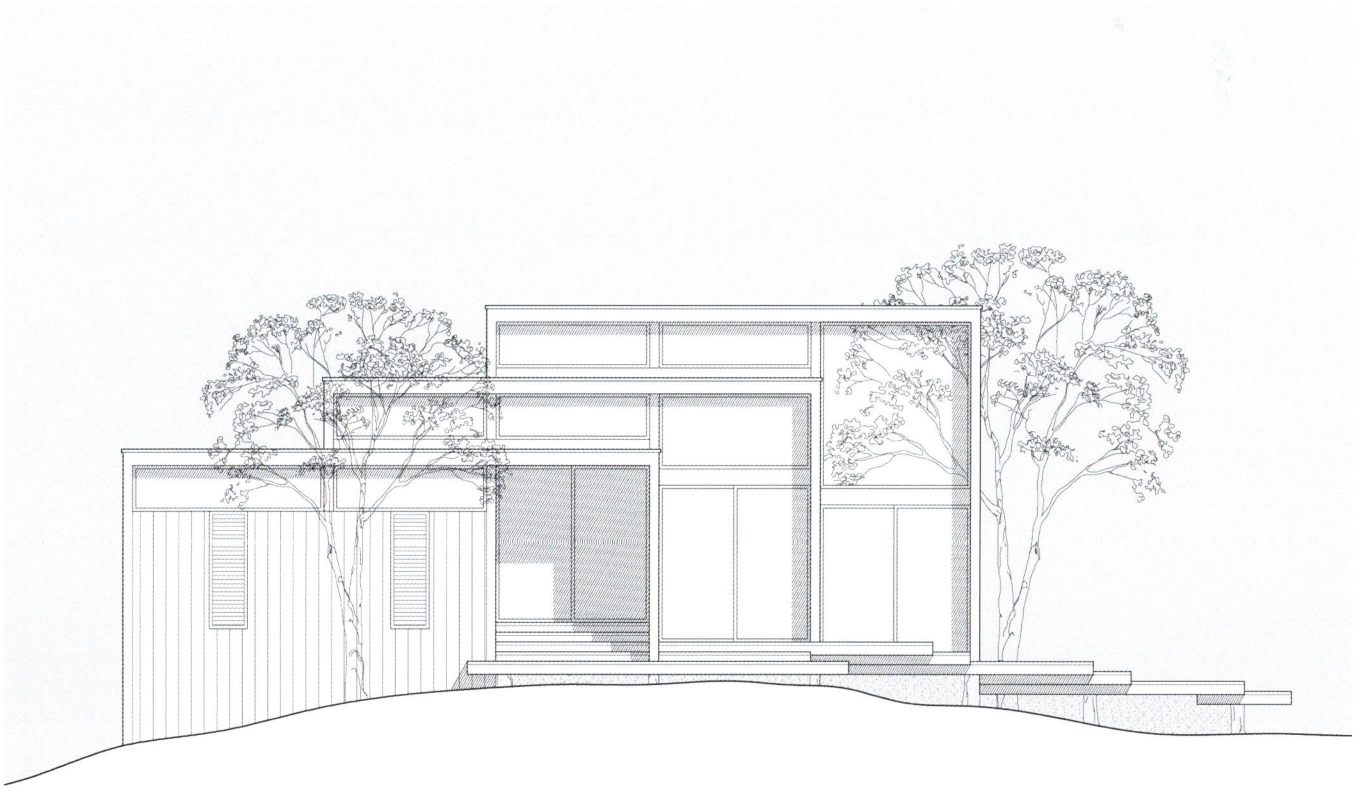

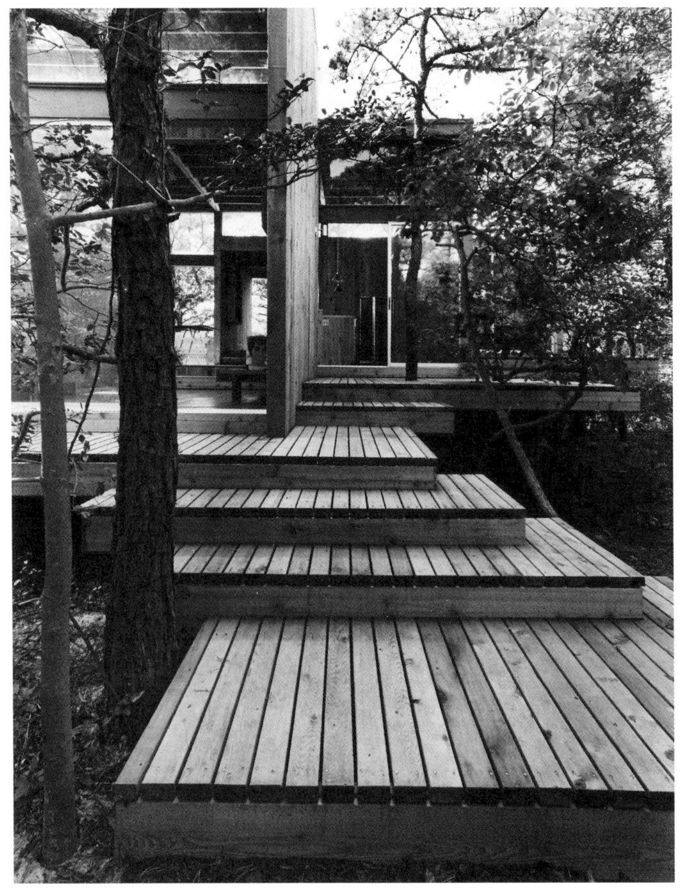
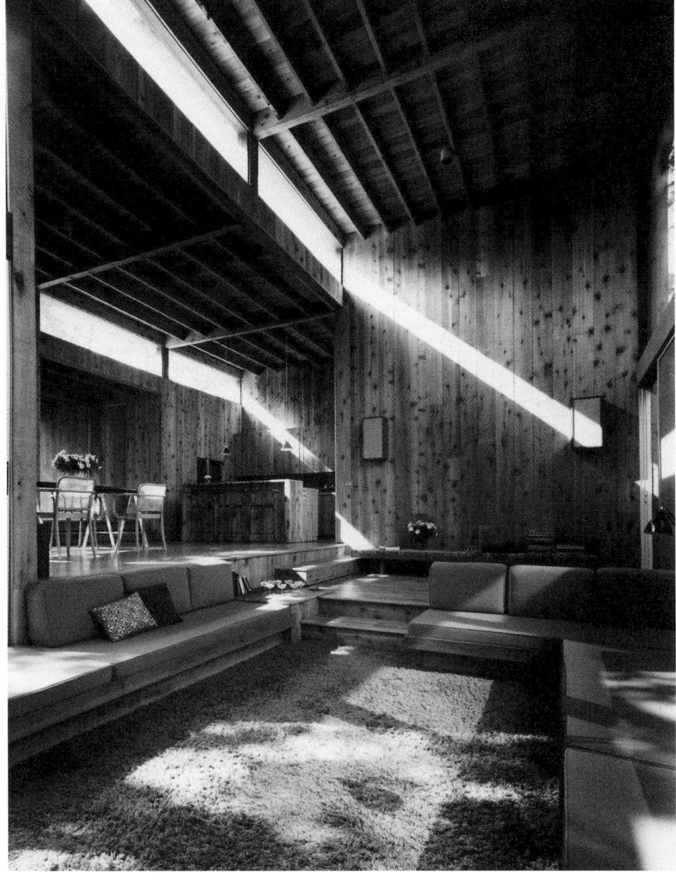
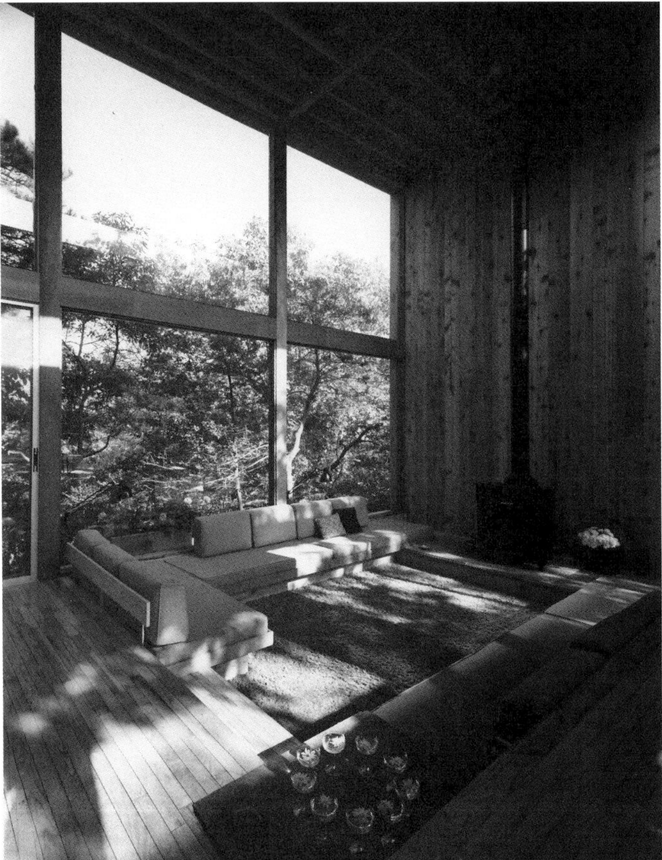
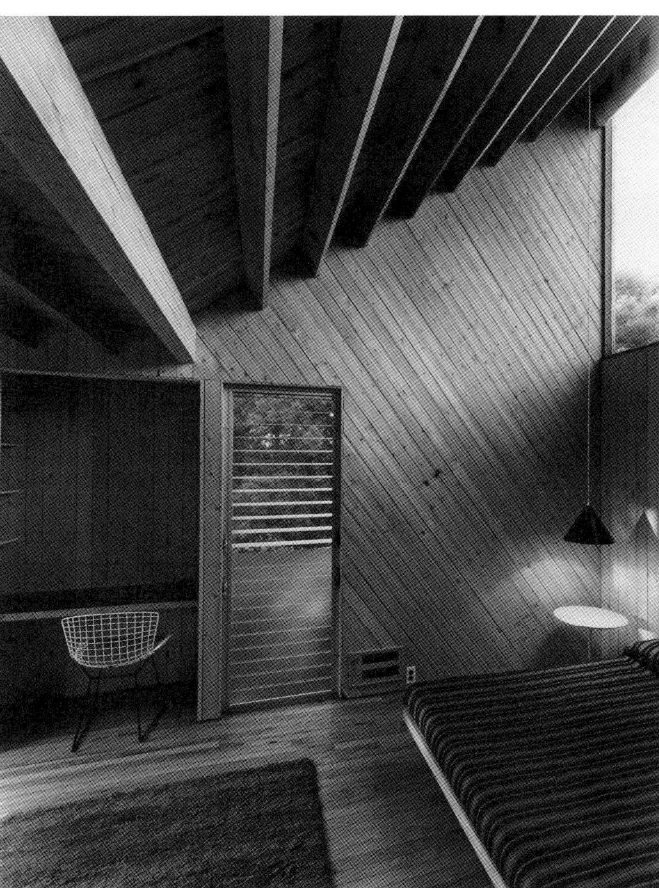

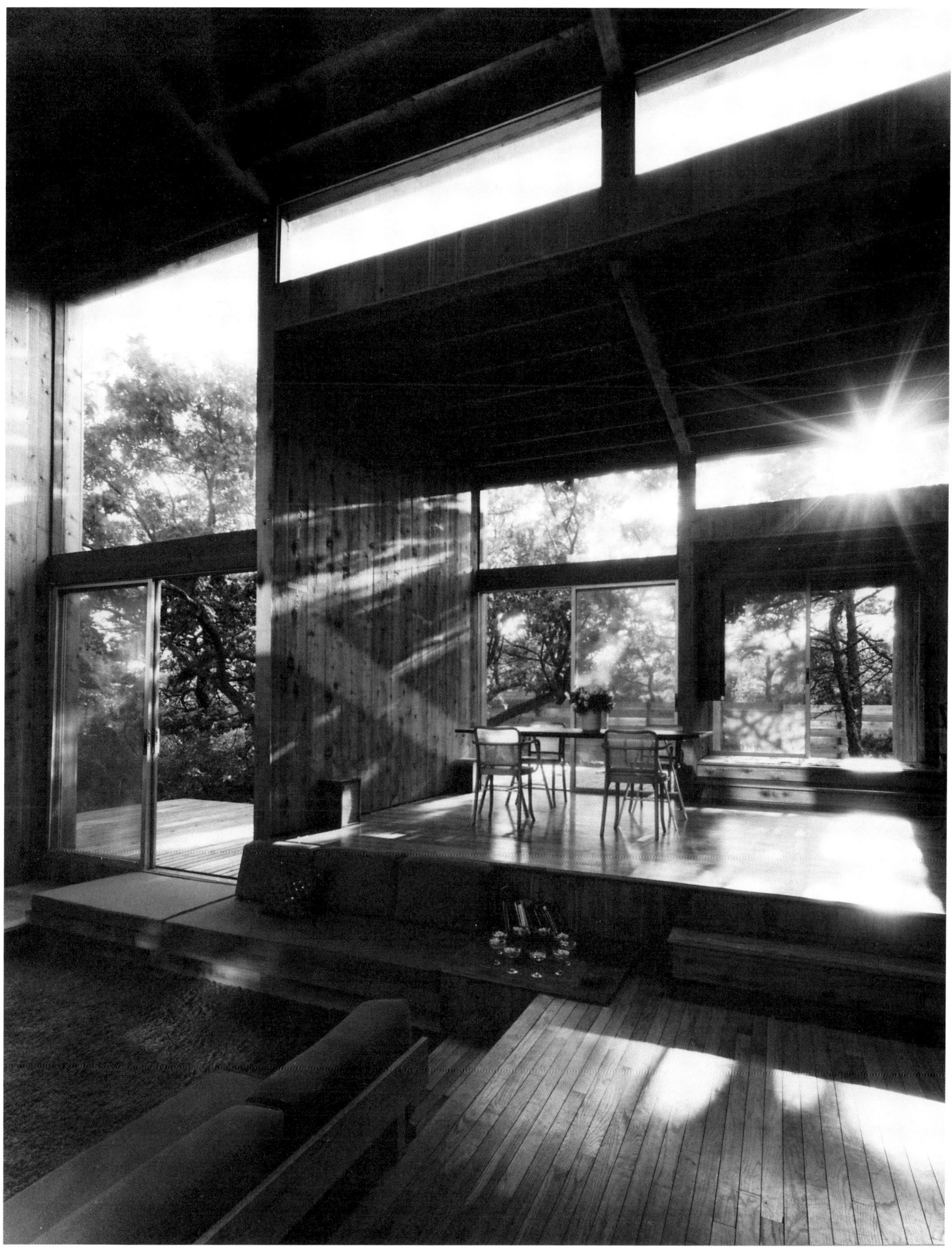

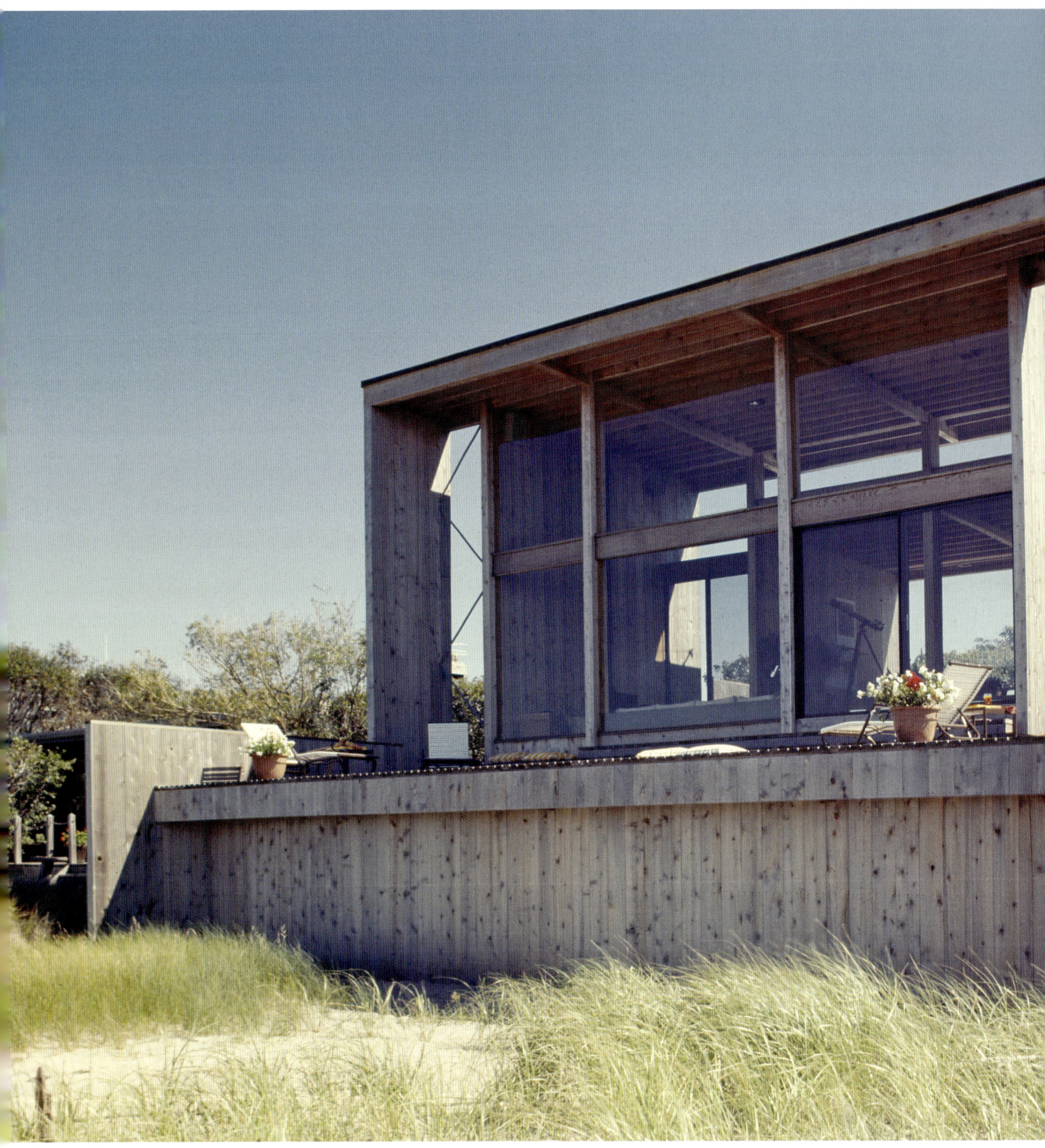

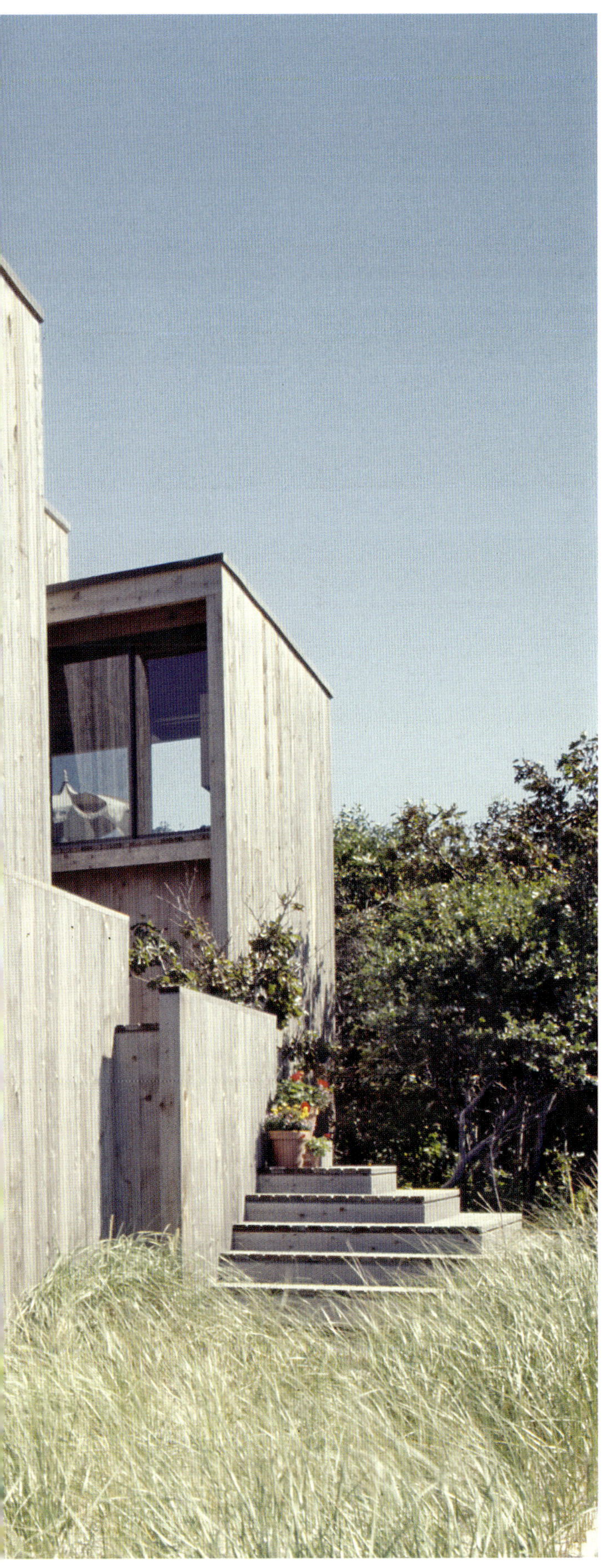

The affluence of new clients like the Scalis and the Rolls Royce–driving Bonaguidi also inflected Gifford's architecture. His earlier homes craned their rooflines for views or cloistered around themselves for privacy, making the most of their middling sites. The telescope houses, uncoiling in a single story across the landscape, were suited to wealthier clients who could afford the best properties. But what strikes one today is that the homes themselves are only a touch bigger and a trifle more expensive than his other efforts. Such restraint was central to what made the communities on Fire Island work, because the picturesque combination of vegetation, boardwalks, and ocean did not entirely obscure an almost urban ensemble of cheek-by-jowl houses on small lots. Gifford exercised this insight to create stretches of homes that would be as aesthetically ordered, scaled, and coherent as the best-preserved brownstone streets in Manhattan.

Gifford was increasingly well-heeled himself. During the early 1960s, he virtually gave away his talents for the opportunity to build, charging just three percent of a home's construction cost for his fee. Six years later, he charged a respectable twelve percent and invested his profits in oceanfront property. "Now, the bank sends cash first and the paper for his signature later. Gifford is good business,"according to a 1968 newspaper profile.[79] With success came selectivity. By 1970, Gifford refused any commission with a budget of less than $50,000. And he got to choose the builder; clients were contractually obliged to use Gifford's hand-picked contractors. This was essential. Gifford's total control of the construction process meant that his homes and his fees remained affordable while his practice remained viable, even lucrative. The blueprints for his increasingly complex Fire Island homes were remarkably simple, in contrast to the more defensive books of drawings for the homes that he created farther afield. At his peak, Gifford realized up to ten homes per year, working out of small home studios with no more than one assistant. By the time Patrick Travis and William Wall sought his services in 1972, the assistant who answered Gifford's phone warned them that he was "very selective" about the sites he took on.[80]

Travis and Wall were hairstylists, and both possessed the gregarious manners this profession rewarded. An increasingly cumbersome permit process for coastal construction along the Great South Bay delayed their house's realization by three highly inflationary years. As the construction cost soared, Travis and Wall pooled their resources with Richard Barry and William Stockmann, investing in what by 1975 was a $72,000 house. They also abandoned an initial design in which all rooms faced the water, instead tucking bedrooms into a lower level and shrinking the home's footprint. But an echo of the larger home persisted in a disembodied facade reminiscent of the oversized shading devices that distinguished Paul Rudolph's Milam residence. Gifford's north-facing brise-soleil provided minimal shade; its function was entirely aesthetic, framing the view, providing an airy complement to the layered opacity of the entry approach, and serving as the "drop-dead" entry threshold requested by Patrick Travis.[81] A stabilizing truss was hastily added to the facade to ensure that this last request remained metaphorical. Gifford's customary descent from the common boardwalk into mulch wound through a thicket of trees, leading to a three-sided staircase. When Travis and Wall arrived for the first time at their new home, they discovered Gifford busily spreading leaves across the freshly scraped pathways. An elaborate swimming pool extension stretching to the Great South Bay was constructed in 1977.

Travis and Wall bonded with Gifford over a meal at a Japanese restaurant that the architect orchestrated to sell his clients on the notion of a sunken dining pit with a built-in glass table. They encountered a modest man with a cutting sense of humor. When his clients thanked him for their home's distinctive design, Gifford readily conceded his influences, explaining that they should also thank a great architect named Paul

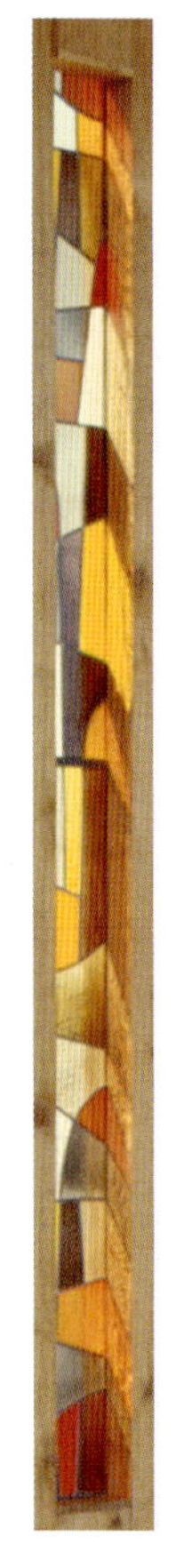

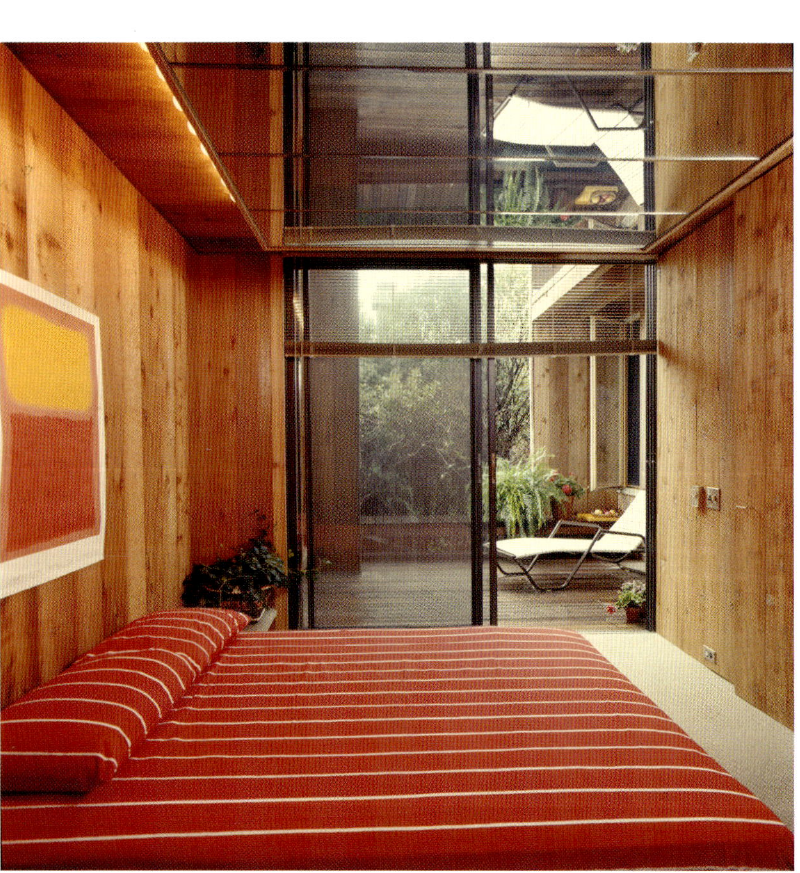

PAGES 116–17:
Travis-Wall House, Fire Island Pines, NY, 1972–75, exterior facing Great South Bay

ABOVE:
Travis-Wall House, stained-glass window, detail

LEFT:
Travis-Wall House, bedroom

OPPOSITE, ABOVE:
Travis-Wall House, interior

OPPOSITE, BELOW:
Travis-Wall House, floor plan with swimming pool added in 1977

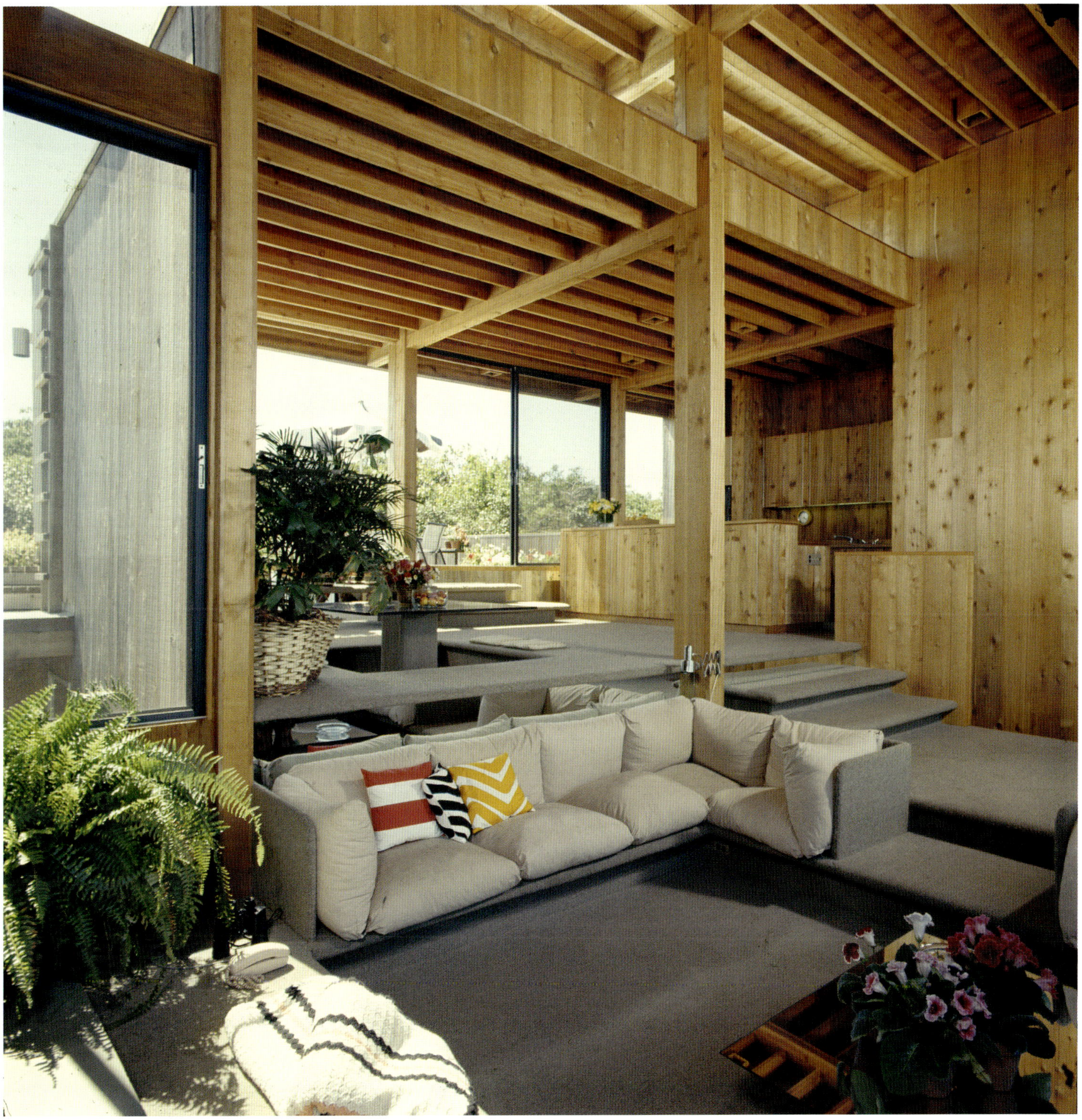

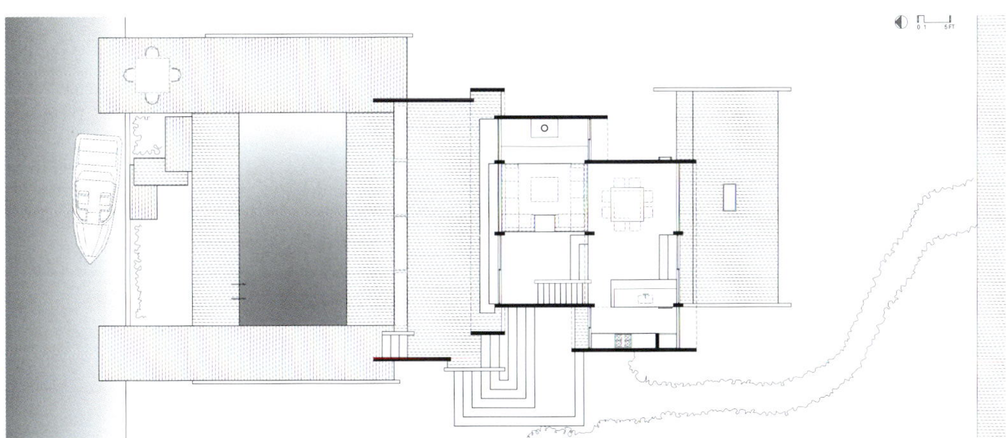

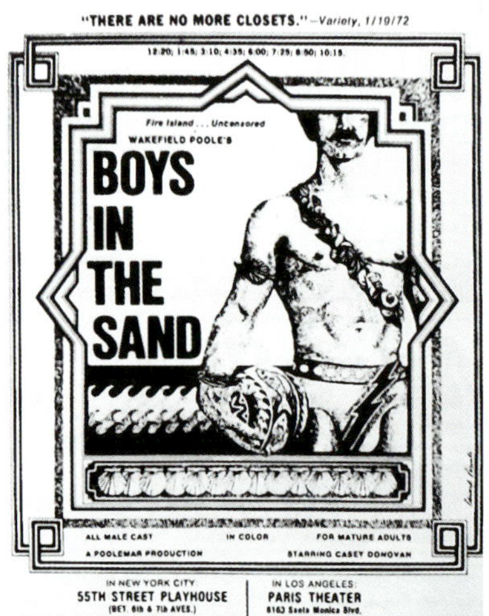

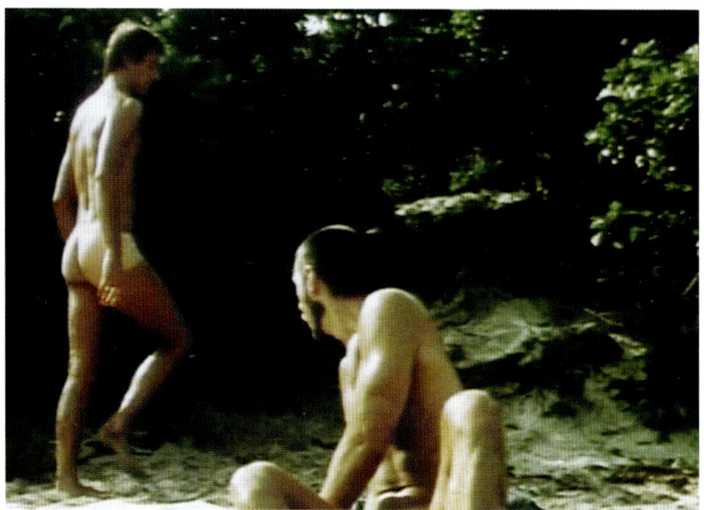

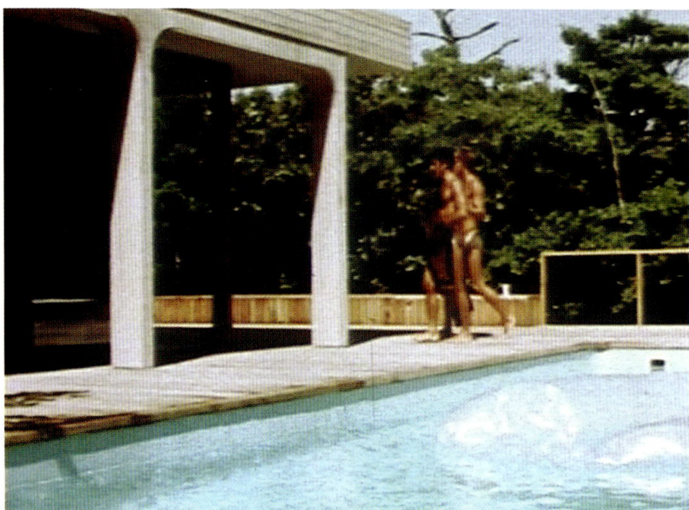

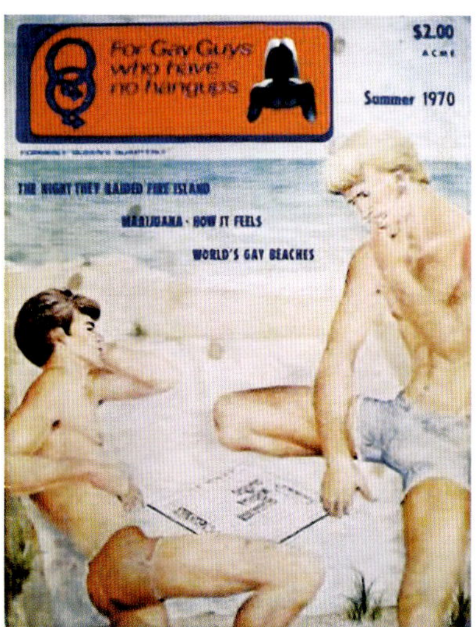

Rudolph. Gifford's housewarming gift to his new friends was an elegant sliver of abstract stained glass, cut to the same width as the vertical siding, transforming the western light that penetrated the living space.[82] His backhand could be just as strong. Referring to his fellow beach-house architect Harry Bates' alleged tendency to ensnare clients with wildly optimistic budget estimates, Gifford renamed his competitor the "Old Bates and Switch" to anyone within earshot.[83]

In plan, the public spaces consisted of a 27-by-27-foot square that was divided in half and slid apart, with varied floor and ceiling heights differentiating the two spaces. A high deck toward the boardwalk and a low deck toward the bay extended the two interior rooms into an ensemble of indoor/outdoor stages, in a reprise of Gifford's second personal residence from 1965. Sand-colored carpet covered the floors. There was not a straight-backed chair to be found. Everything was built-in, including the dining pit that Gifford charmed out of his clients.

If there was an implicit flirtation embedded into the public glass walls of the Bonaguidi residence, the Travis-Wall residence beckoned with a come-hither stare. The primary bath shunned mirrors in favor of plate glass facing the nearby boardwalk. But mirrors abounded everywhere else—as step risers to make objects disappear and as bedroom ceilings to make objects multiply. A multiman shower was illuminated by a large skylight set into the upper deck. All of this tailored informality and frank eroticism reflected a decade of libidinous license, one immortalized in 1971 by Wakefield Poole's *Boys in the Sand*, the first widely seen porn film to exploit the sexual energy of Fire Island and the architecture that housed it.

Poole, a former dancer with the Ballets Russes and a successful Broadway-musical choreographer, seized an opportunity to elevate a coarse medium. Fellow filmmaker Jerry Walker marveled that before *Boys in the Sand*, "we were living in an era where we take a camera into a motel room with two guys that don't have time

UPPER LEFT:
Poster for *Boys in the Sand*, directed by Wakefield Poole, 1971

UPPER RIGHT:
Boys in the Sand

LOWER RIGHT:
***Gay* magazine, summer 1970**

LOWER LEFT:
Boys in the Sand

OPPOSITE:
Tom Bianchi, Untitled, SX-70 Polaroid, 1970s

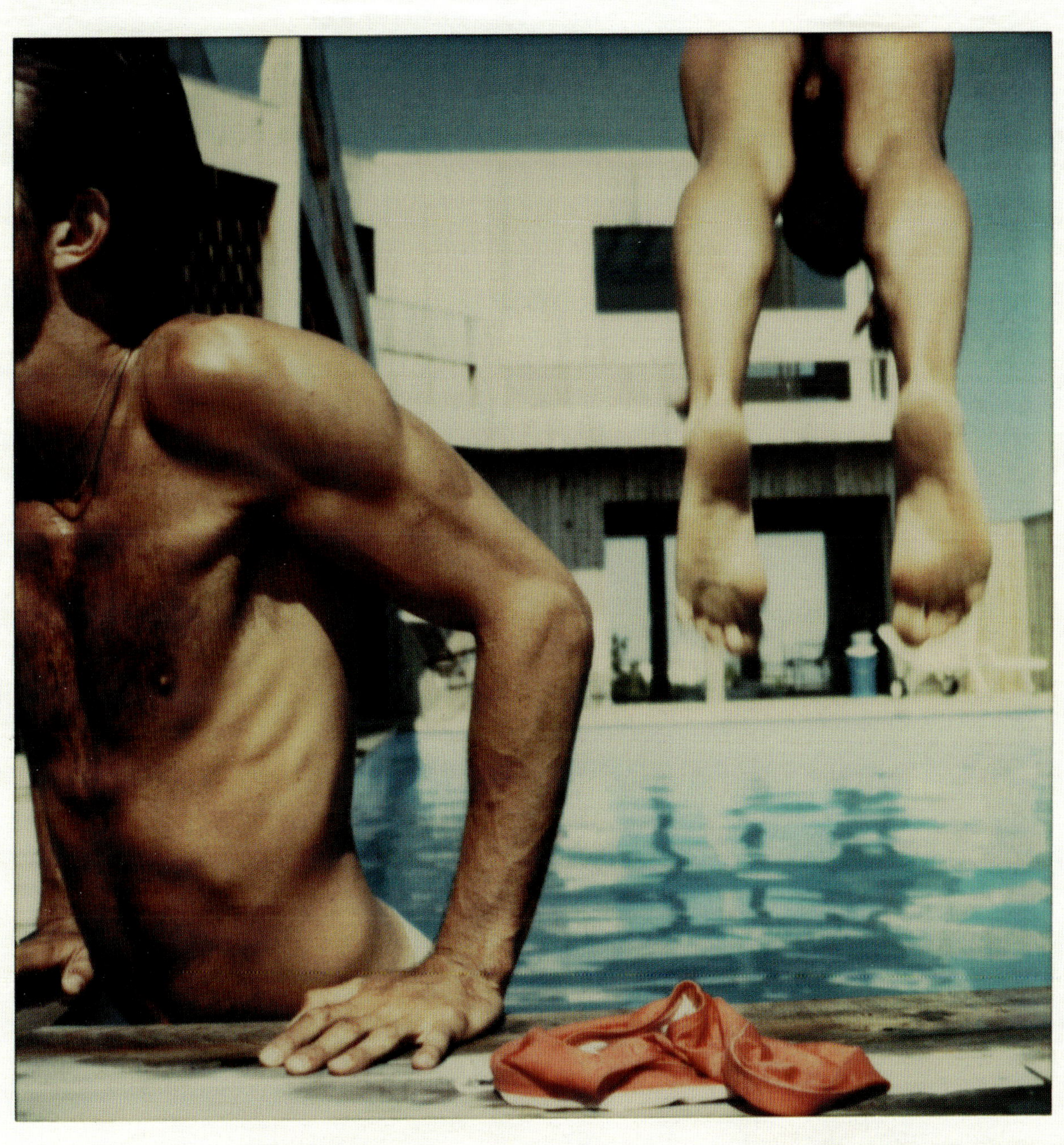

to take their socks off, and shoot them [before you get caught], and run like hell, and sell it to somebody for a dollar and a half."[84] Scored to classical music and brandishing a palette of bronzed skin, stripped-bare facades of cedar and glass, flaxen hair, and shimmering pools, *Boys in the Sand* resituated gay desire in a decidedly upscale, romantic, and aesthetically sophisticated milieu. *Variety* reviewed the first "all-male" film to be promoted in the *New York Times*, declaring: "There are no more closets!"[85]

Filmed in three acts, *Boys* opens with scenes in the Meat Rack before vigorous lovemaking at a modernist home and swimming pool designed by James McCleod. The final act follows a utility worker, who lingers expectantly outside of Gifford's Schultz residence while the nude star cruises him from the window of Andrew Geller's Frank residence. *Boys in the Sand* didn't exactly discover Fire Island, but it heralded its early-seventies transformation from an open secret to the storied destination that it remains today. The film also inaugurated the era of "porno chic," one year before *Deep Throat* mainstreamed the genre for heterosexual audiences. Many other filmmakers would indelibly conjoin sex with the aesthetic of Fire Island's beach houses in the years to come, including the filmmaker and porn star Michael Lucas, who moved into the former Travis-Wall residence and made it into a virtual character in his erotic films.[86]

Gifford's telescope houses spread across some of the more generous lots in the Pines, but he achieved other voyeuristic vantage points by stretching upward. When the Home Guardian Company rechristened Lone Hill as the Pines in 1952, the name was largely aspirational. The rather barren and scrubby province of nudists venturing from nearby Cherry Grove could have been called "the Pine" in its southern half. By the mid-sixties, enough homes existed to create a windbreak atop the narrow barrier island, while septic tanks enriched the soil below, in an accidental synergy that forever altered the rolling terrain. Gifford responded to the new lushness with a series of "upside-down" floor plans that stacked sunny living areas on top of shaded bedrooms—tree houses that gazed across an increasingly frenetic cultural landscape.

With his customary dry humor, Gifford began his design presentation to the textile designer Murray Fishman by declaring, "You will now have twenty closets to come out of."[87] Twelve robust columns, containing closets above and below, lifted the Fishman residence into the air. Early Fire Island cottages squatted akimbo upon skinny pilings, evoking the architectural equivalent of "martini legs." Gifford composed

OPPOSITE:
Fishman House, Fire Island Pines, NY, 1965

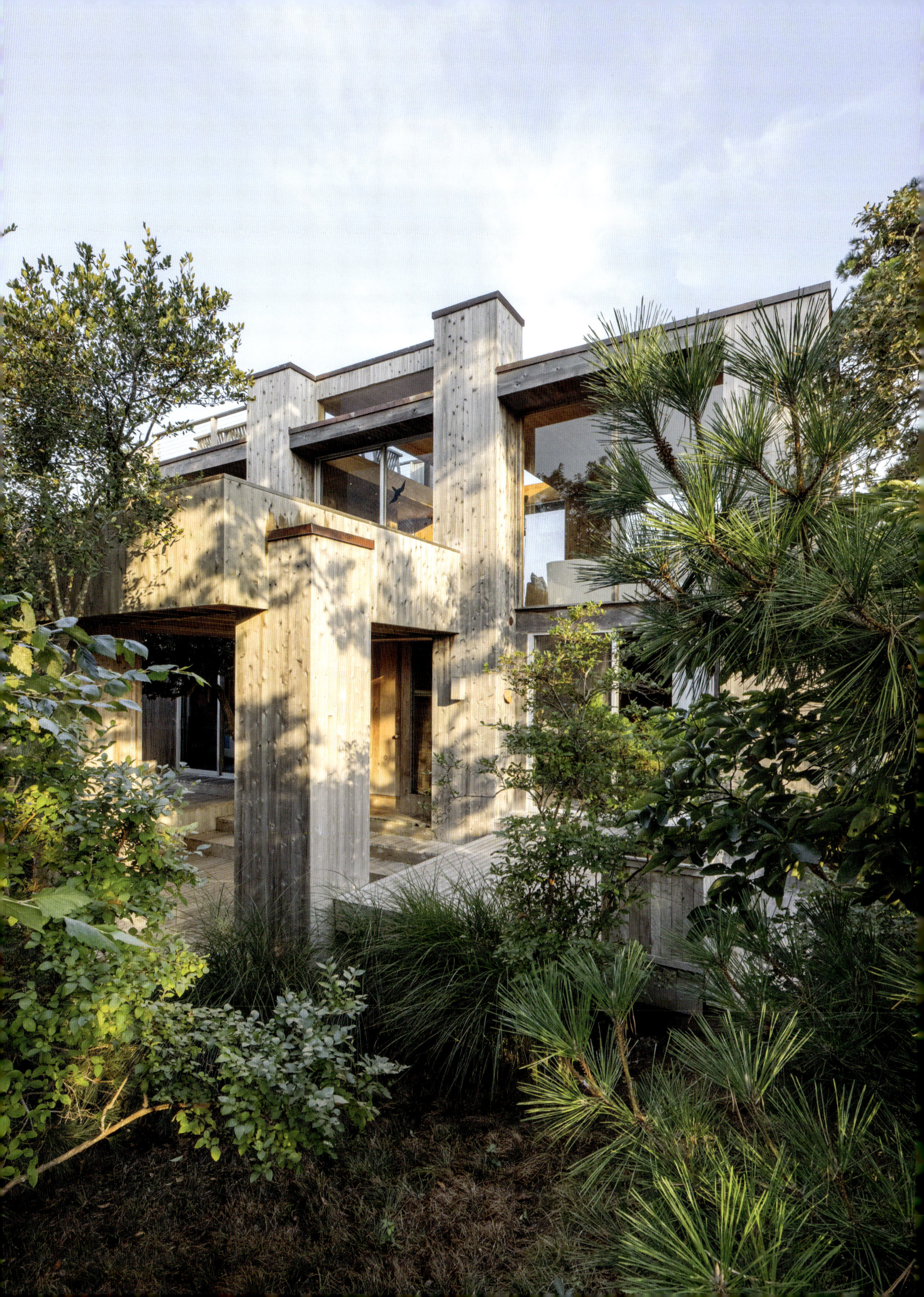

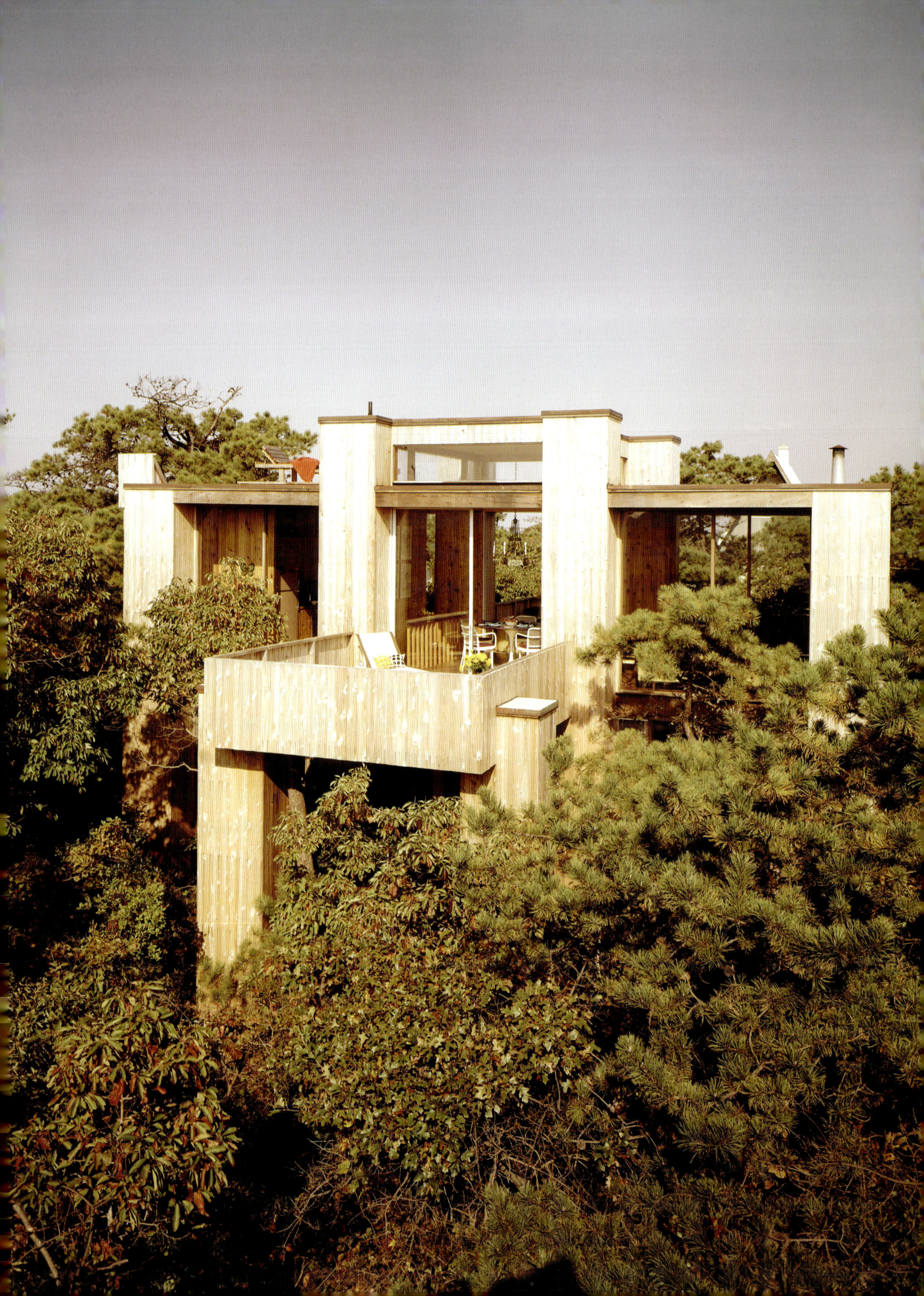

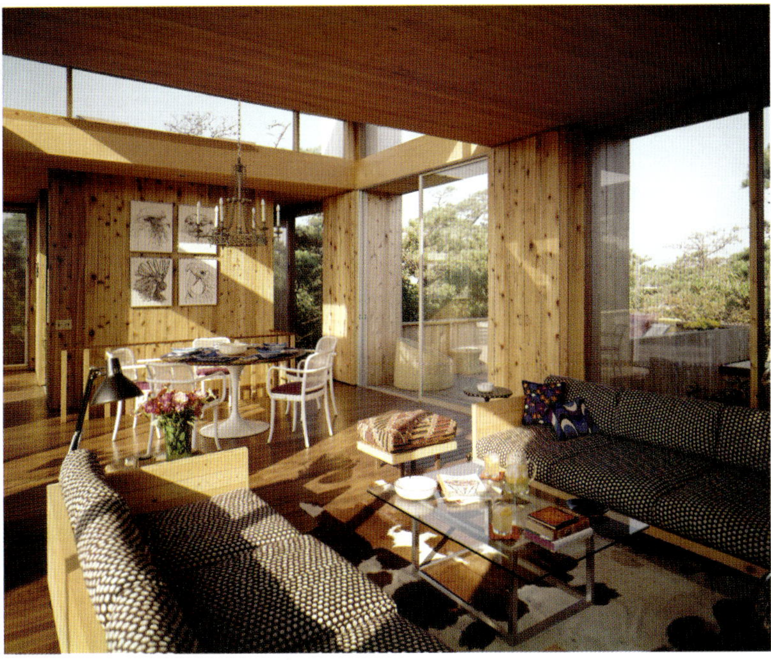

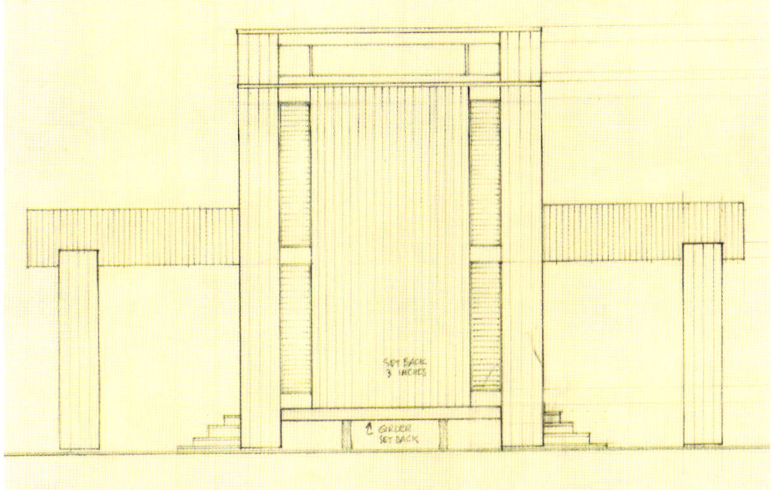

OPPOSITE:
Fishman House

TOP:
Fishman House, interior

MIDDLE:
Fishman House, west elevation

PAGE 126, TOP:
Fishman House, exterior with new pool

PAGE 126, BOTTOM:
Fishman House, plans

PAGE 127:
Fishman House, exterior

and selectively clad his own version of these posts, realizing a muscular base still in harmony with the surrounding architecture. Gifford was indifferent, hostile even, to having all of these closets in a beach house, *except* when they served his desired formal effect. On that basis, the home was a breakout success that made its way into the pages of several magazines and a traveling exhibition sponsored by the American Institute of Architects.

Health issues caused Murray Fishman to sell his home shortly after its completion. Its next occupants were Marvin and Jo Segal, who called on Gifford to add terraces to the ground level. Marvin Segal would distinguish himself as an attorney for the most notorious of defendants, including Nixon Administration Attorney General John Mitchell and numerous Mafia figures. Perhaps his rough-and-tumble milieu made him feel invulnerable, as he neglected to pay Gifford for his work. Undeterred, the architect got his money after a series of characteristically terse and fearless letters demanding payment. Segal's accomplished wife, a fashion editor for *Women's Wear Daily*, *Sports Illustrated*, and *Look*, was part of the Pines' fashion coterie that included John Whyte, Geoffrey Beene, Giorgio di Sant'Angelo, and Diane von Fürstenberg. She also became quite a fan of her architect, organizing the first Horace Gifford house tour in 1975.

The Fishman-Segal residence projected an undeniable sculptural presence, with trunklike columns embodying Gifford's belief that "the site usually suggests what the house wants to be as a form in space."[88] But while it presented a masterly composition of forms, its interior betrayed the rough edges of a prototype. The stair alighted upon a tight landing, facing a closet. Living-room views were curtailed, without purpose, by the bulk of the columns. The kitchen was small and closed off from the living and dining areas, and a hall on the south side of the kitchen disconcertingly dead-ended. On a similar passage north of the kitchen, one passed a tiny powder room on the way to a tacked-on and formally unresolved stair to the roof. It might have worked at a larger scale, but there were limits to how much the architect could cram into a tiny footprint.

An opportunity to perfect the gestures of the Fishman-Segal residence arrived in 1969, when

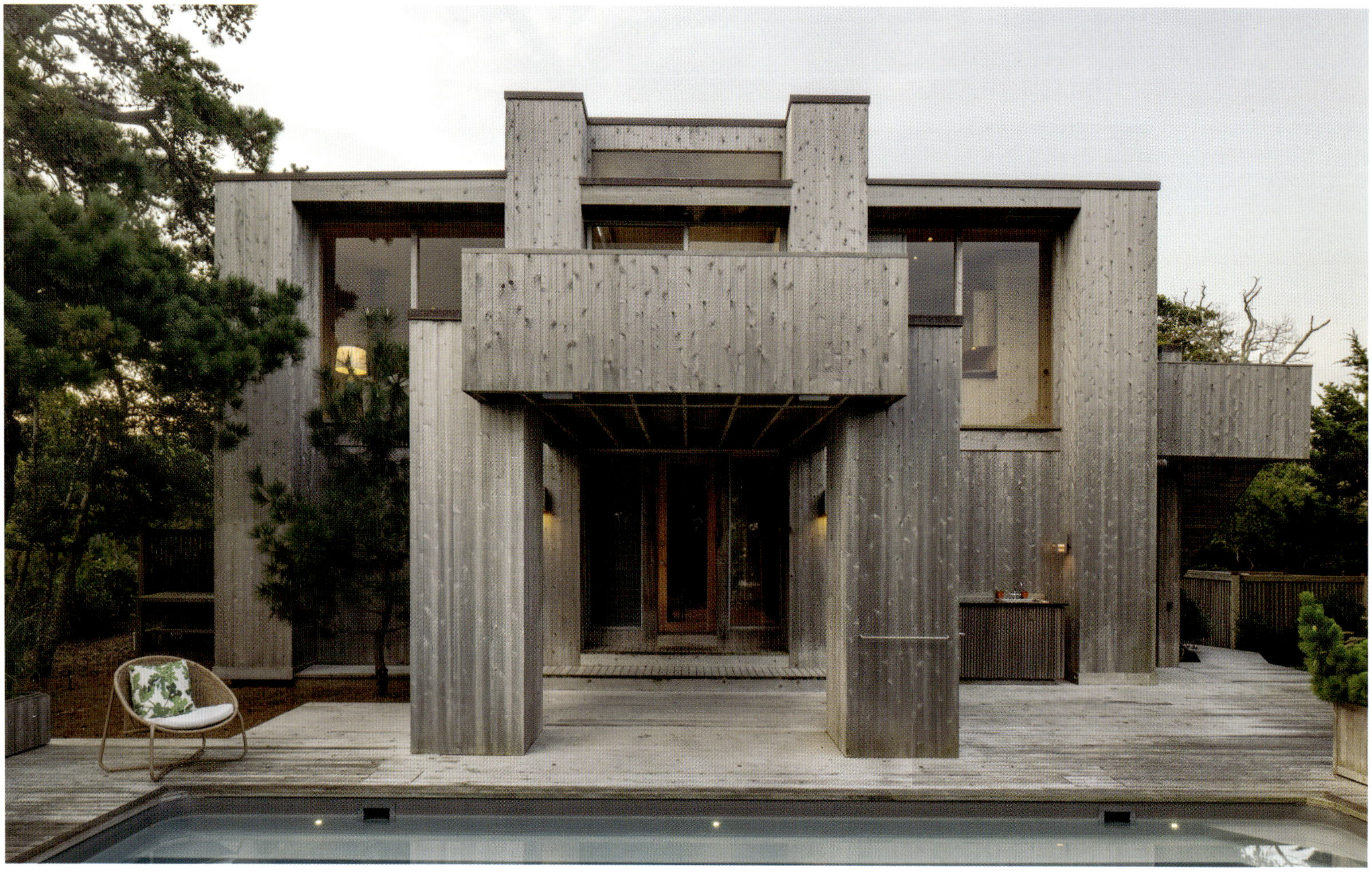

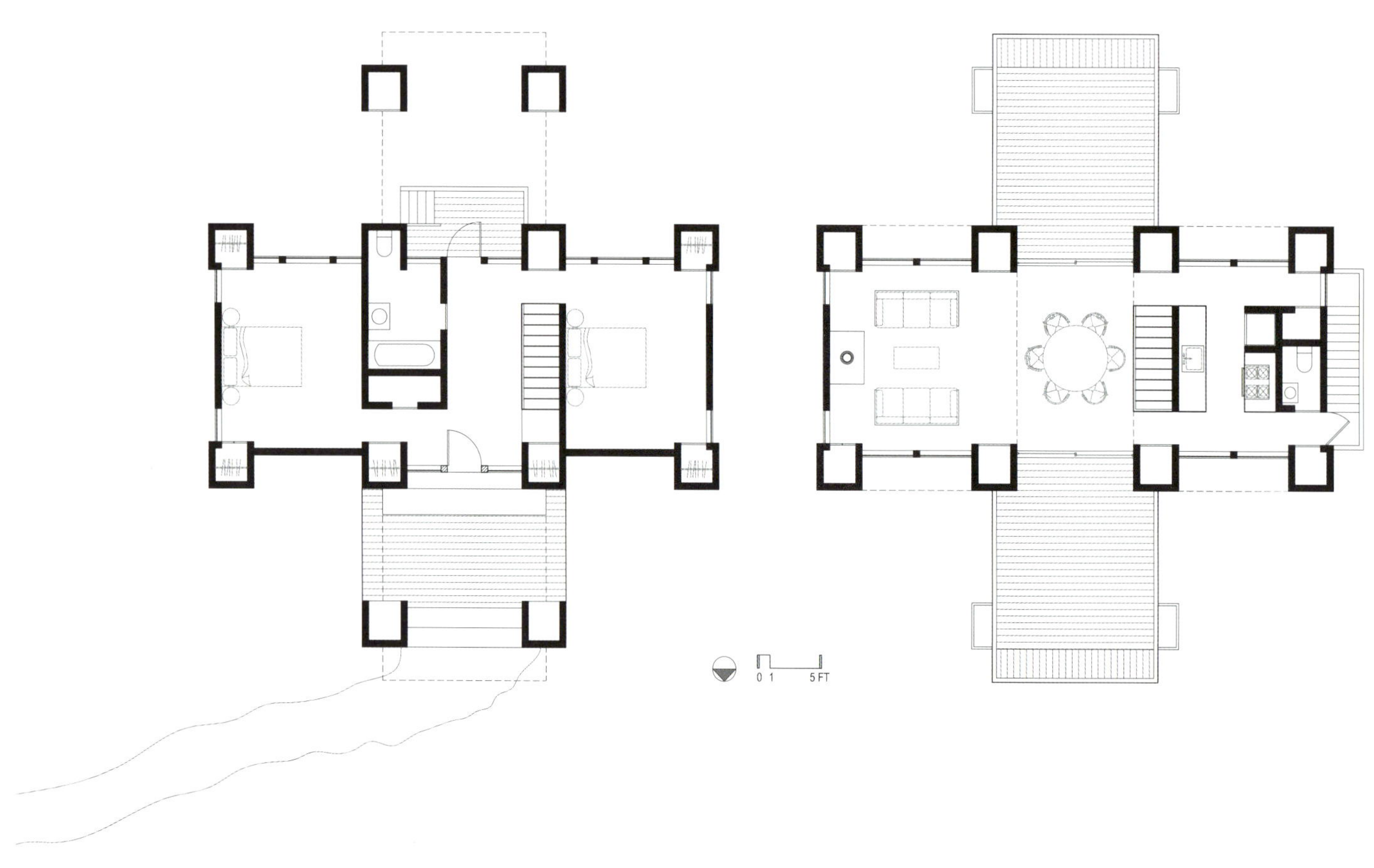
0 1
5FT

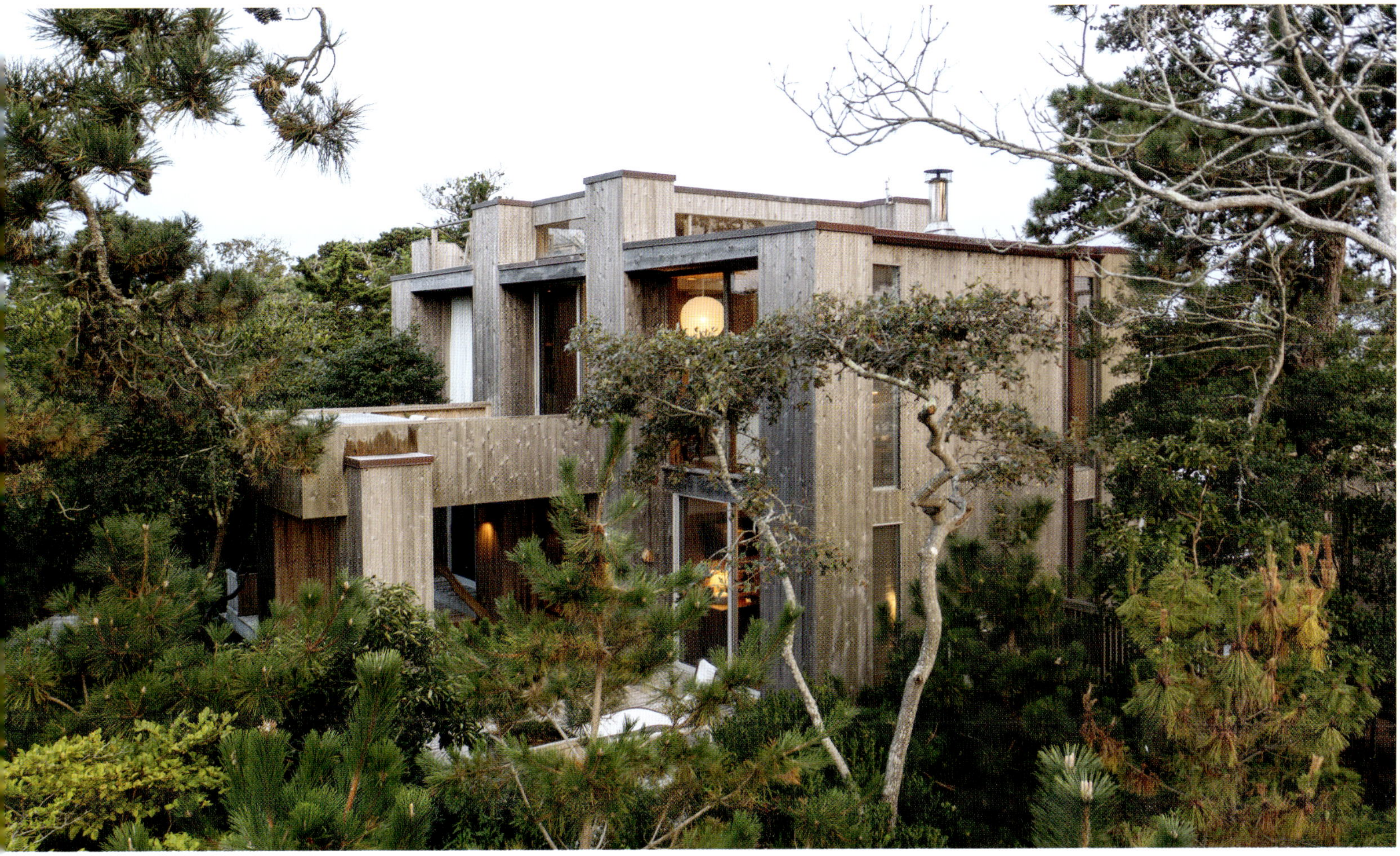

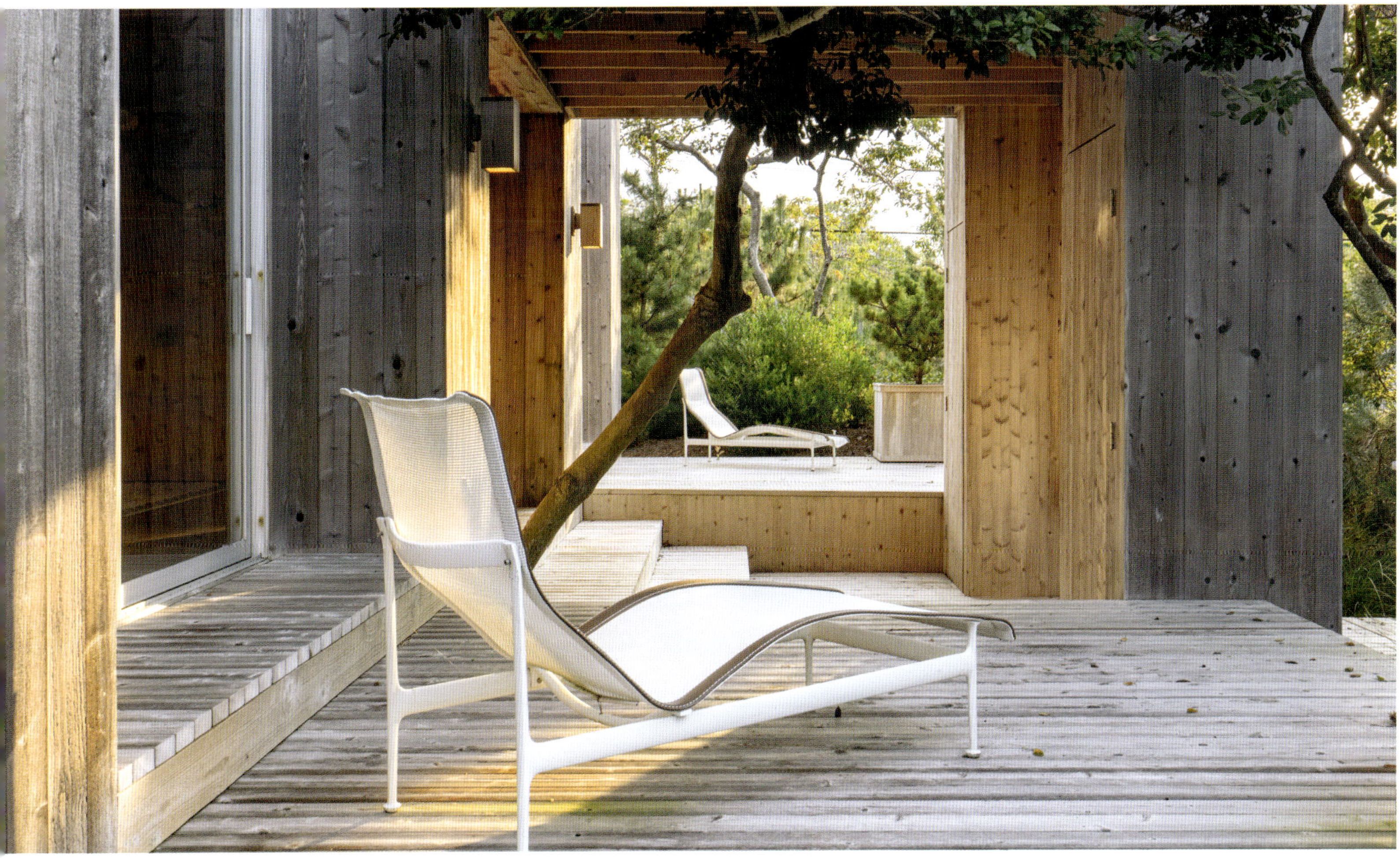

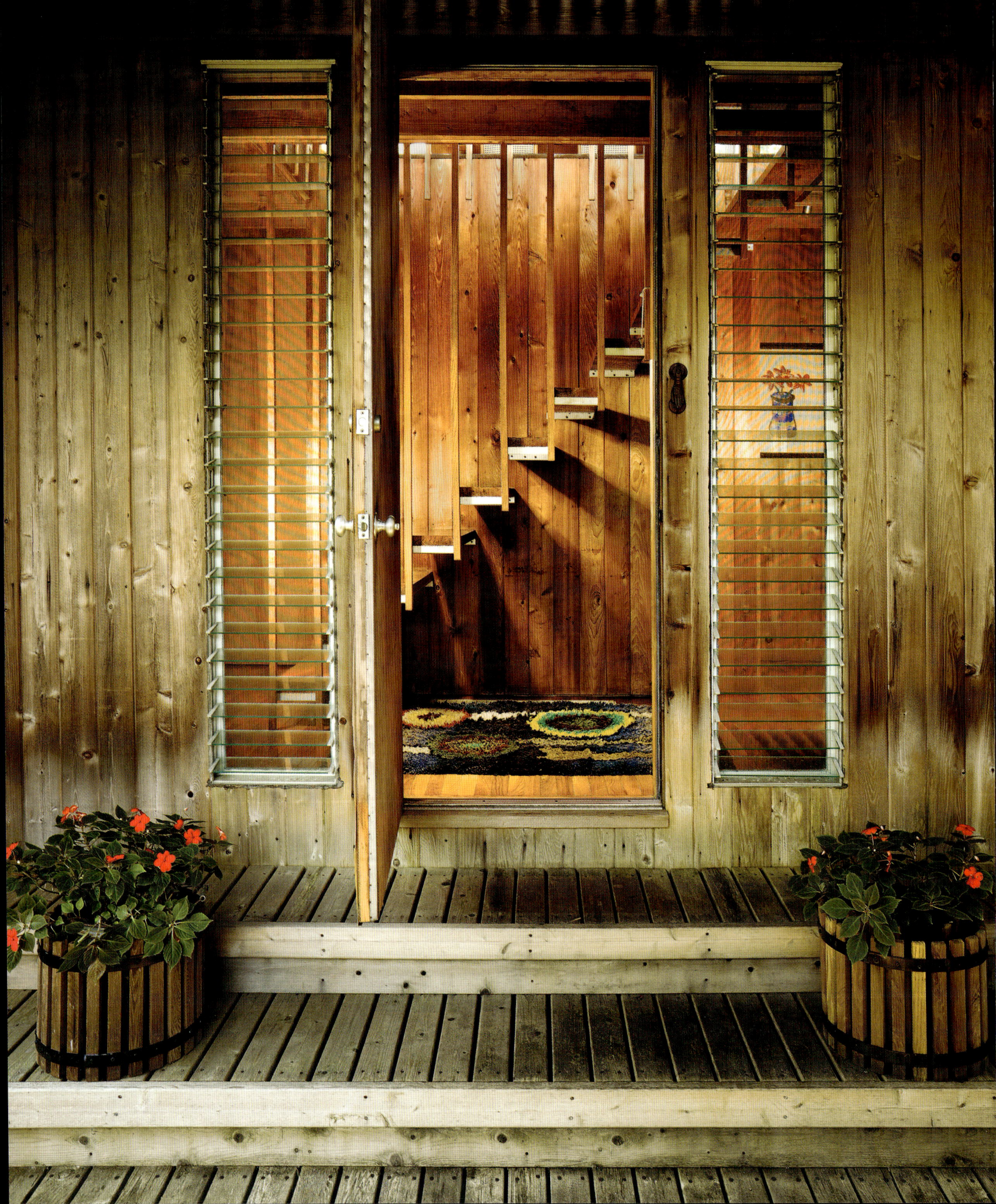

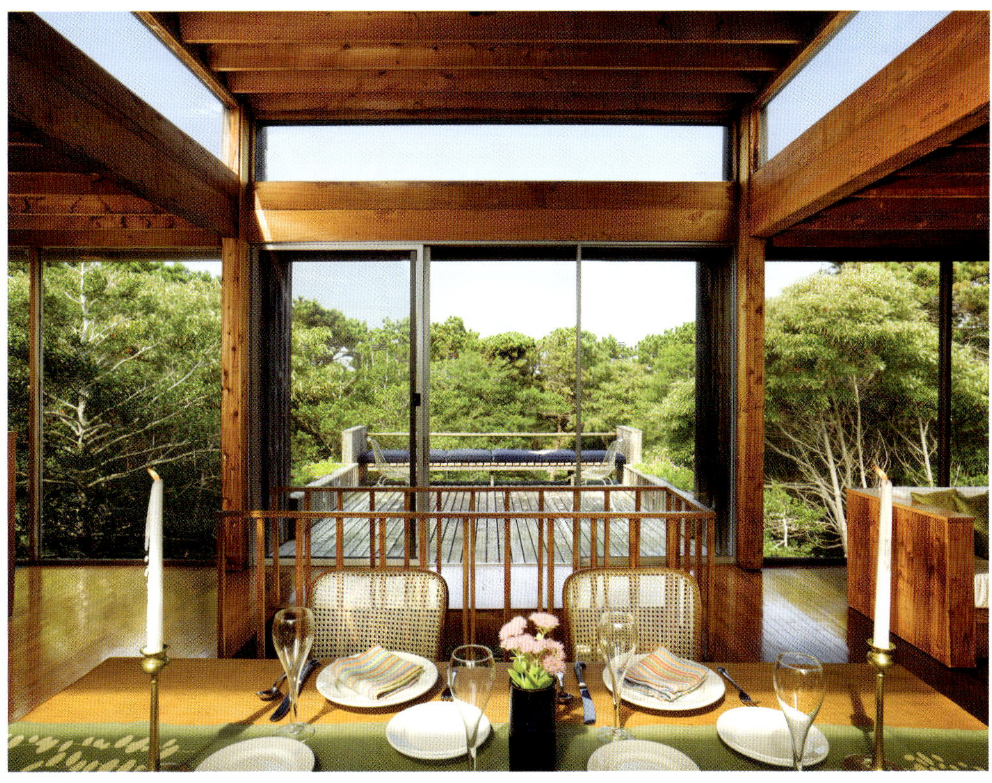

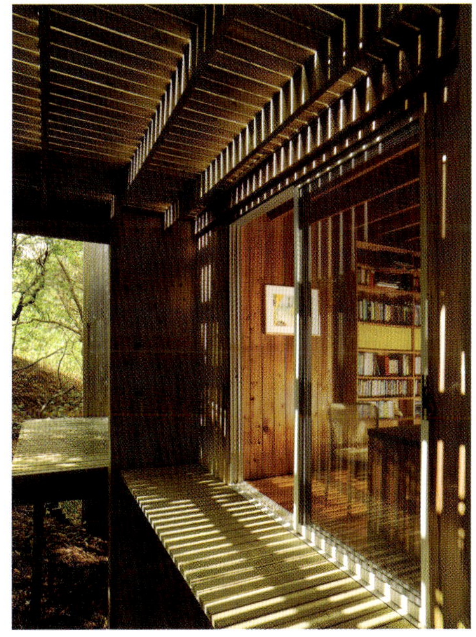

OPPOSITE:
Cashel House, Fire Island Pines, NY, 1969, entrance

ABOVE:
Cashel House, dining area

RIGHT:
Cashel House, the "divorce room"

PAGE 130:
Cashel House, north deck

PAGE 131:
Cashel House, primary bathroom

Gifford designed a home for James Cashel on a high dune. After a curvaceous design for Cashel's steeply sloping site proved too expensive to build, Gifford countered with a tree house entered by a bridge that pivoted around an existing holly grove. Delicately scaled "fin" walls replaced the hollow columns of the Fishman-Segal House, as minimalist benches and cantilevered planters did away with bulky deck rails. Outstretched decks kissed the hillside to the south and ventured high over the landscape toward the north.

The stair—rotated ninety degrees from that of the Fishman/Segal residence and more refined in its detail—created a tighter entry but liberated the space above, much as a steep ladder would foreshadow a treetop aerie. The stair's rotation also allowed for a small third bedroom with a single bed downstairs, christened the "divorce room."[89] An open kitchen acknowledged the home's diminutive scale, joining a single great room with panoramic bay and ocean views. As in several homes from this period, plate glass took the place of mirrors in the primary bath, an intriguing provocation that scorned vanity while inviting prurience and celebrated nature while leading to "unnatural" acts. Cashel, one of Gifford's less flamboyant clients, succumbed to practicality and installed a shaving mirror after Gifford's departure from the construction site.

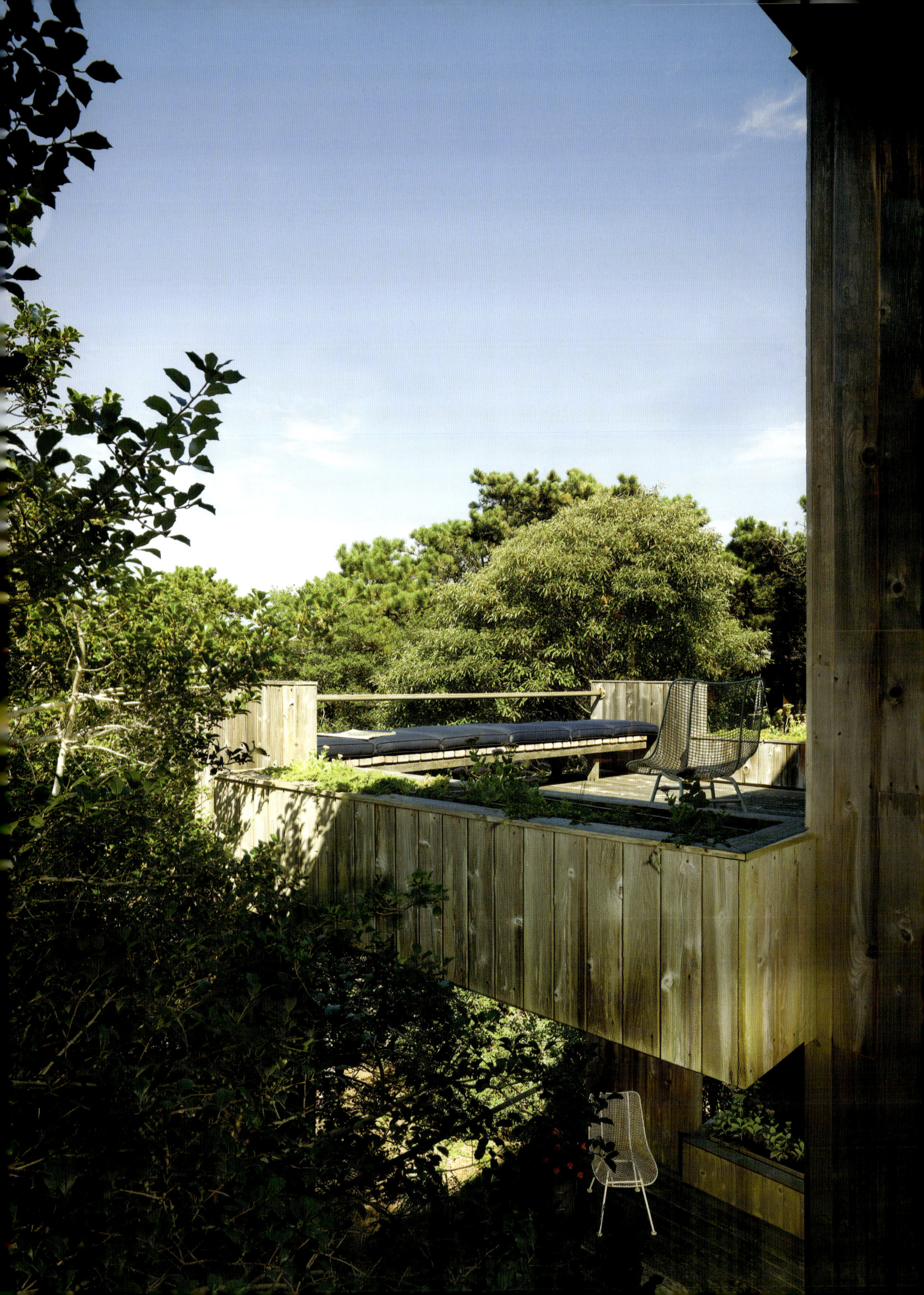

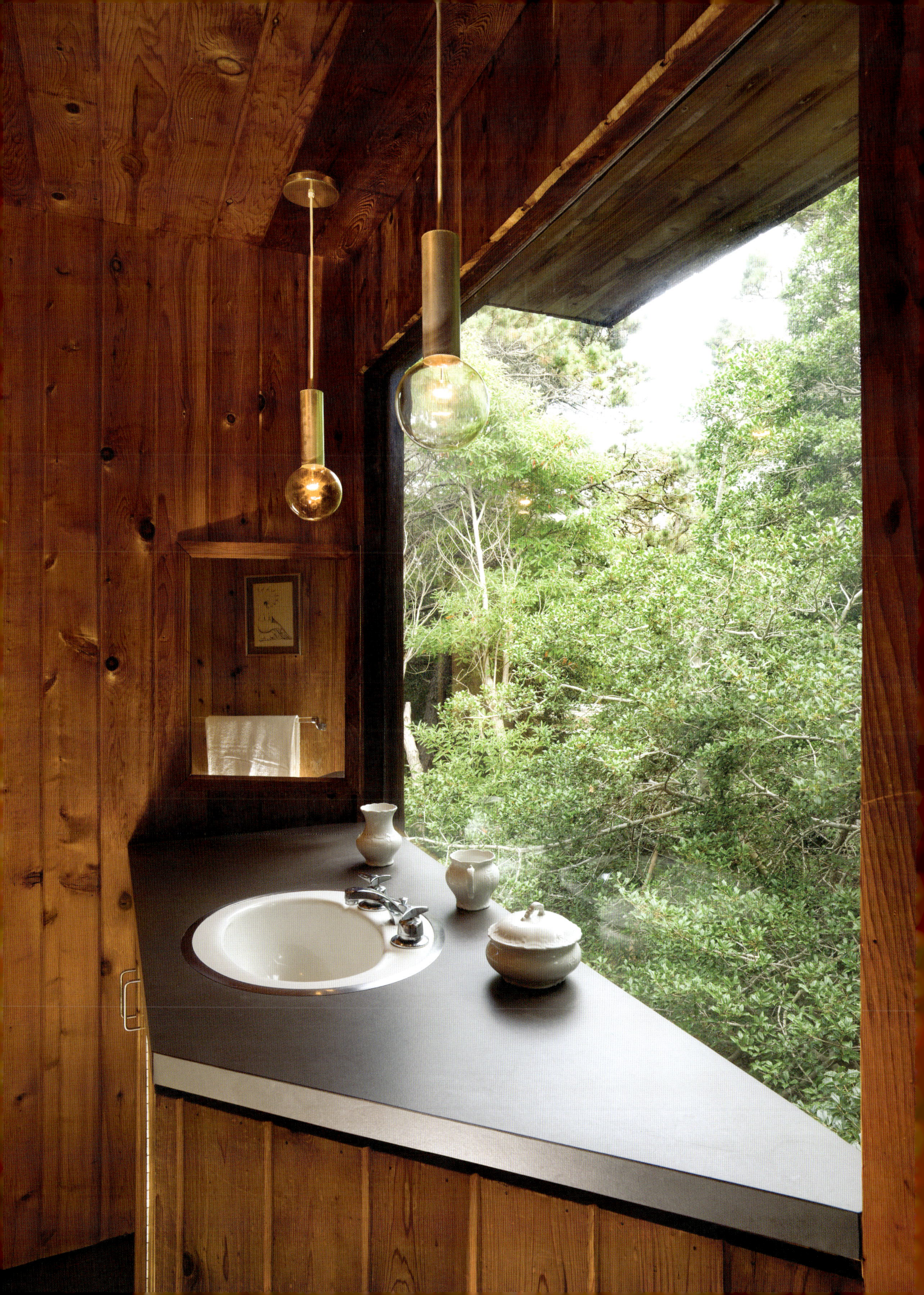

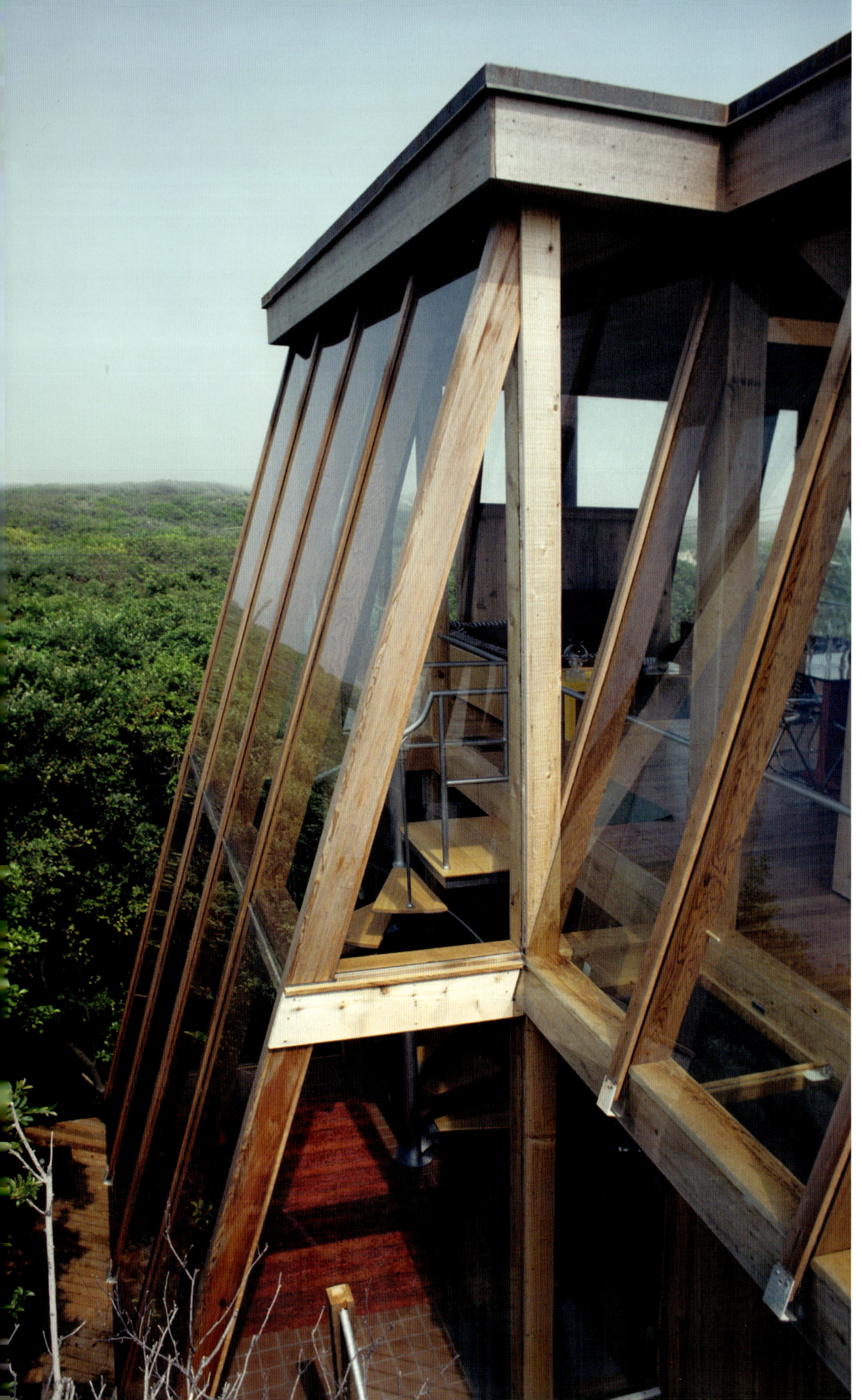

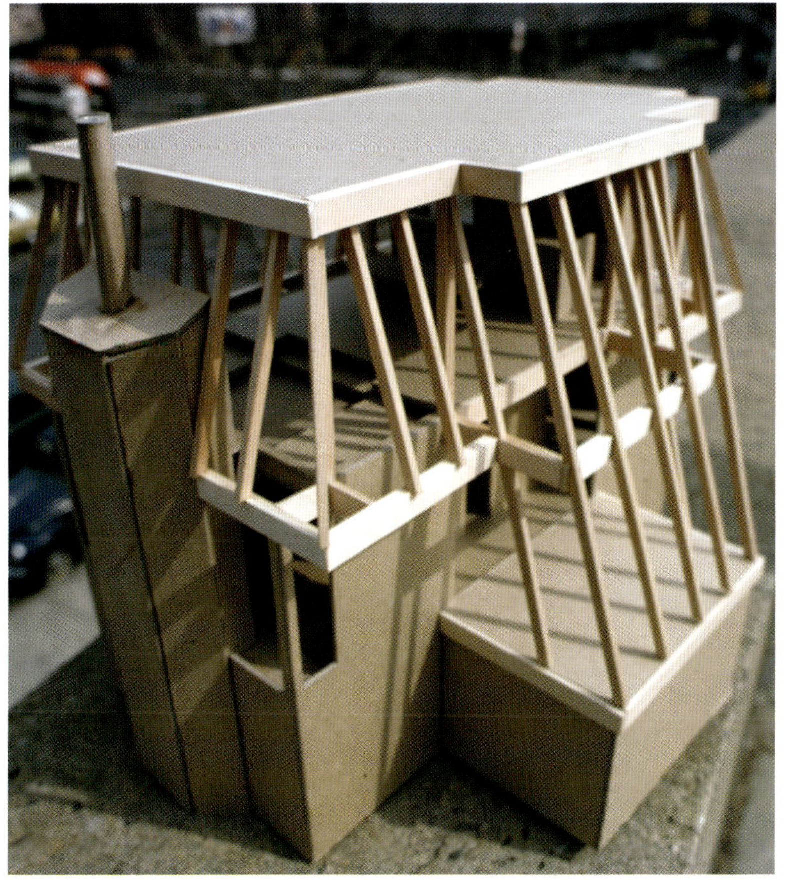

Lawrence Bonaguidi, a repeat client, commissioned Gifford's most innovative tree house, which clung to a dramatic rock outcropping at the eastern edge of the Pines. A twisting stair scaled the steep site, leading to a perfectly square foyer with square tiles. A spiral stair passed the tree line, revealing preserved dunes that stretched eastward. In the gaps created between slanted, clifflike glass walls and the suspended floor, trap doors opened up to ventilate the home, which drew air through a large "chimney" skylight at the center of thc space. The home's remove from the ground, combined with the floor's separation from its glass walls, doubled the gravity-defying excitement of life in the treetops. Two built-in sofas defined a sunken living area, with cushions that slid off their frames to create a fireside love nest. On the north side of the house, the slanted glass careened all the way to the foyer floor. To the south, the sloped glass linked the living area to the primary bath below. Its mirror was positioned so that a primping or showering host maintained a visual connection with the public spaces above.

By the late sixties, the larger world began to notice Gifford's work. So he cast a wider net, undertaking projects in Connecticut, the Hamptons, and Florida. Financial success carved out a calm space from which to create homes for the accelerating pace of summer life. It was a time to sharpen his senses and rethink old certainties. Gifford was in a philosophical mood.

OPPOSITE:
Bonaguidi House II, Fire Island Pines, NY, 1975

ABOVE:
Bonaguidi House II, scale model

RIGHT:
Bonaguidi House II, sketch

PAGES 134:
Bonaguidi House II, with newer lower level rooms and pool

PAGES 135:
Bonaguidi House II

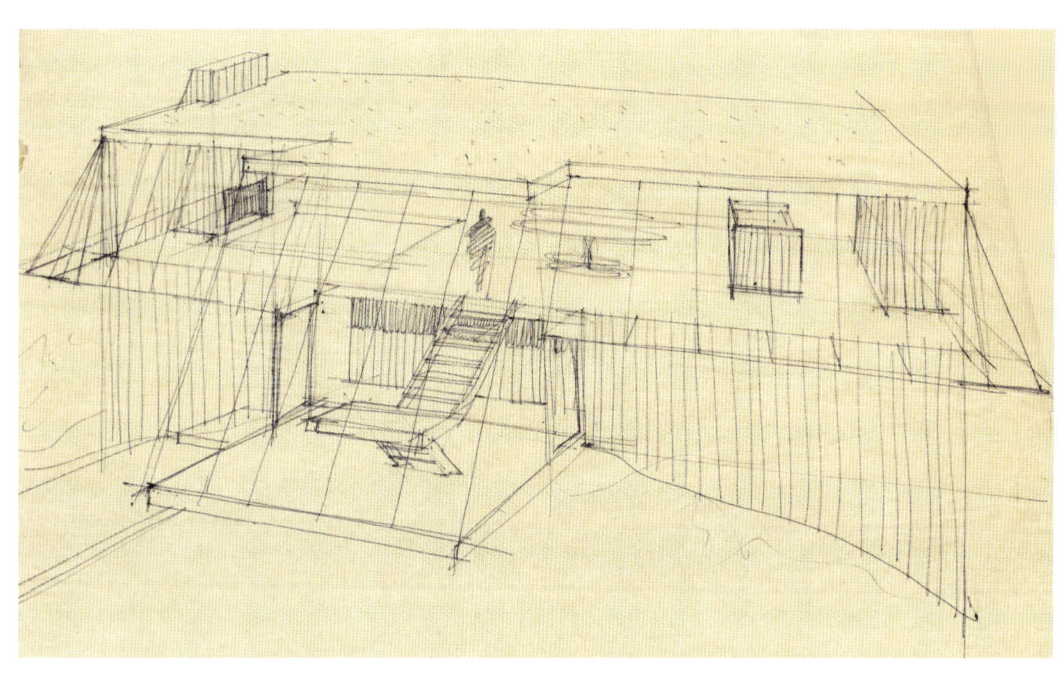

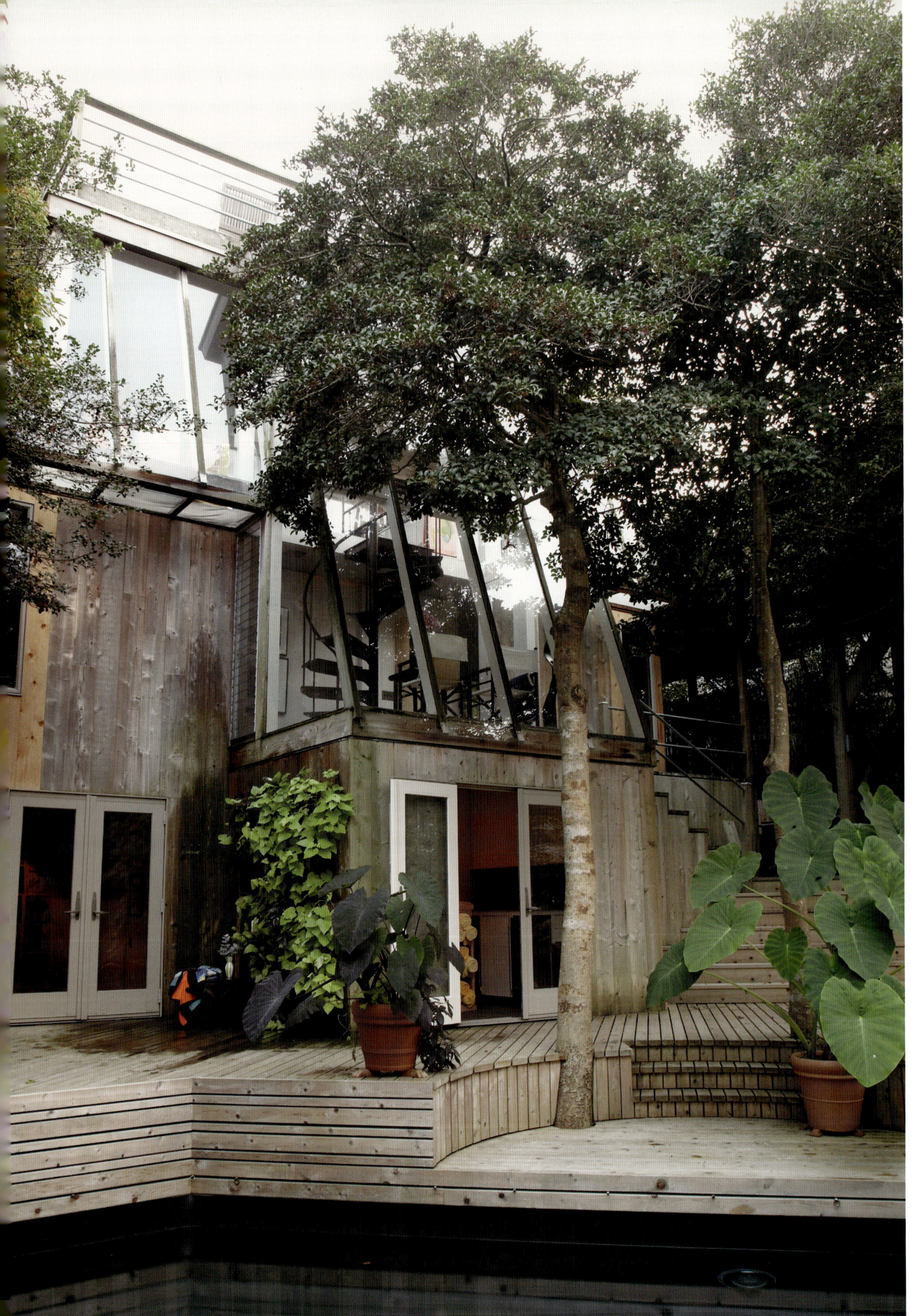

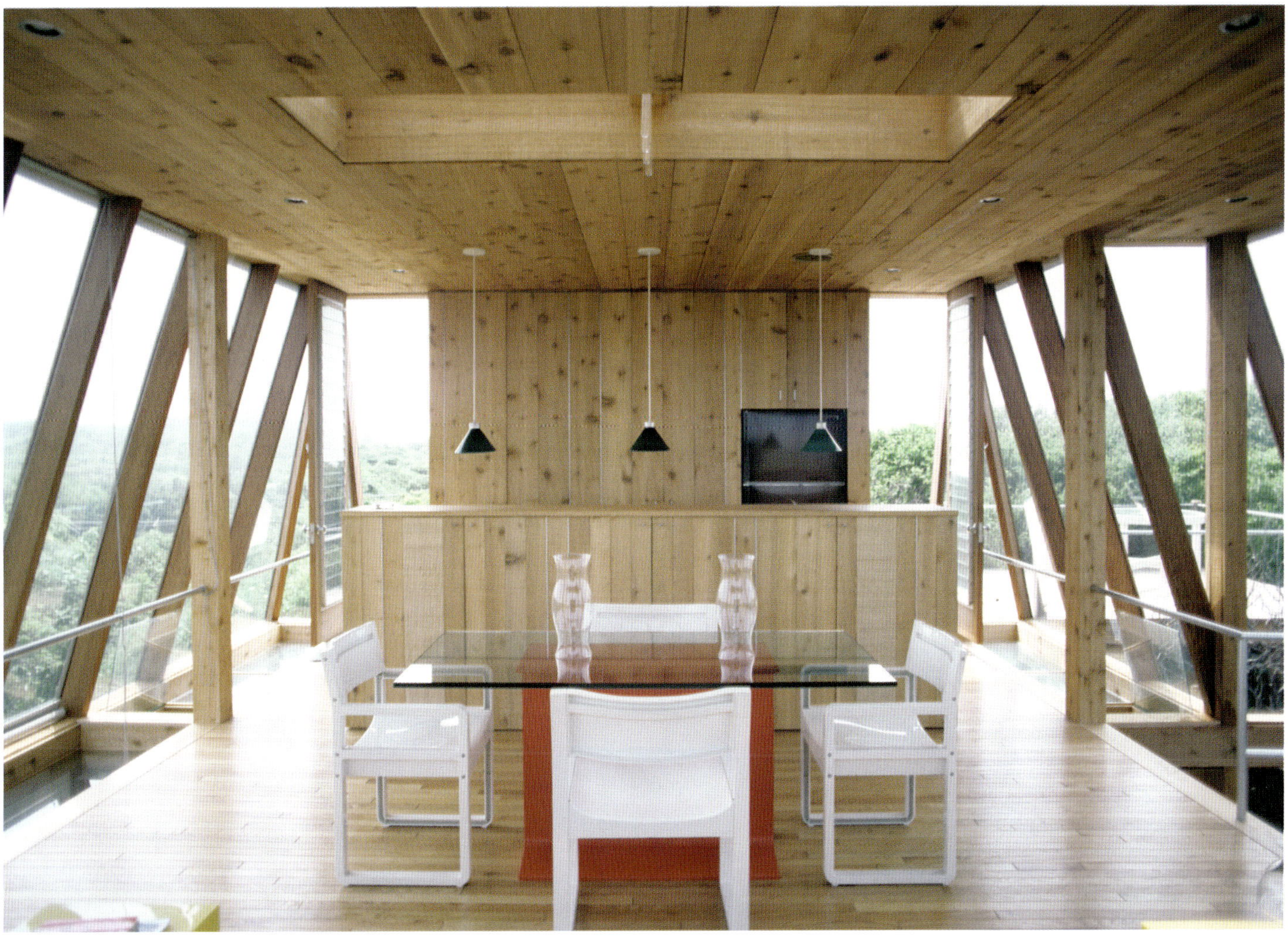

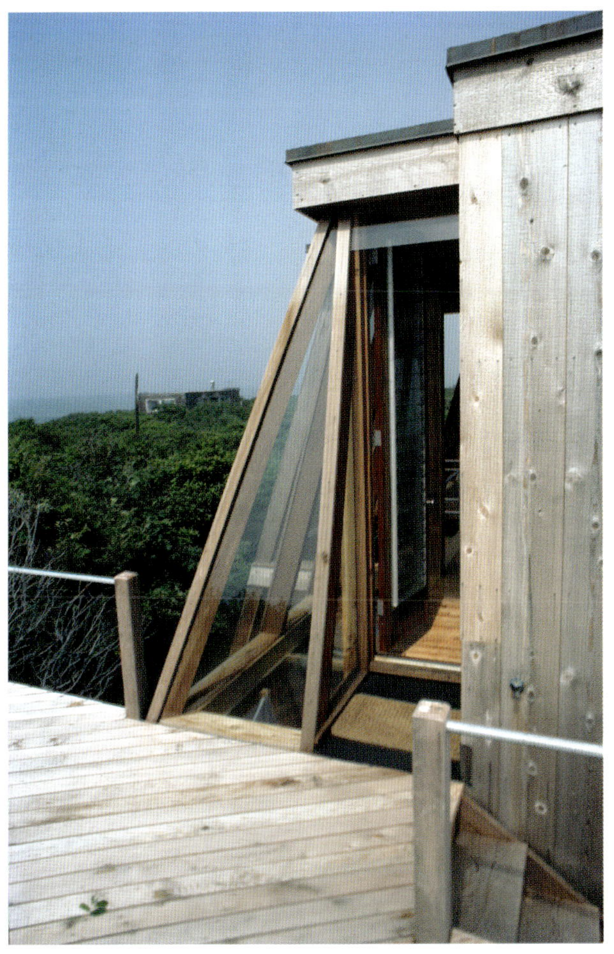

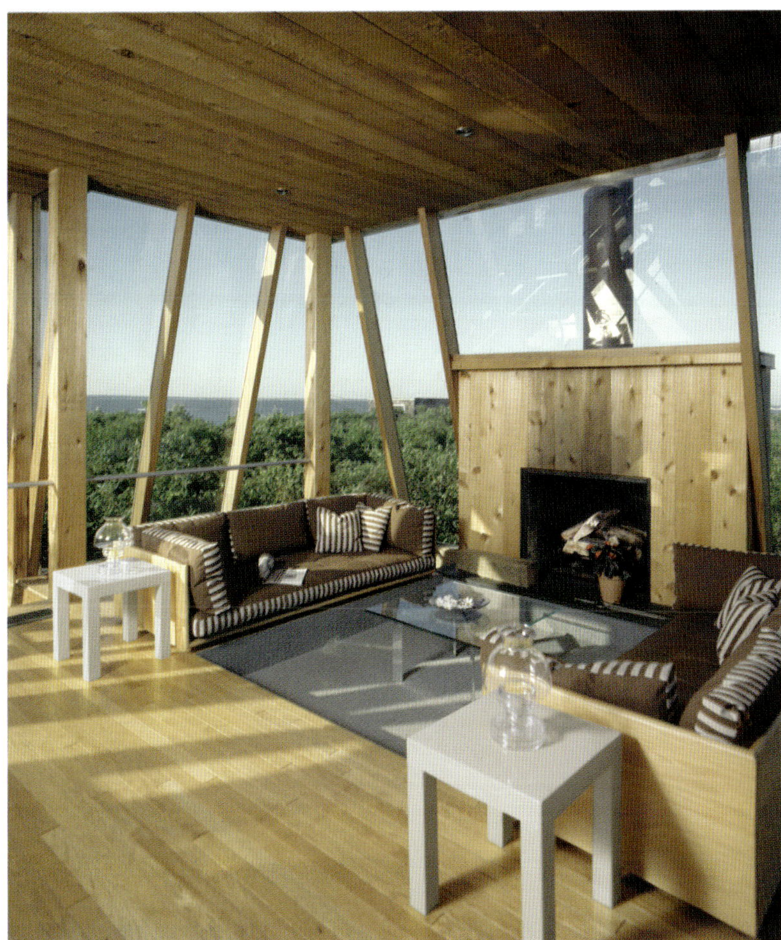

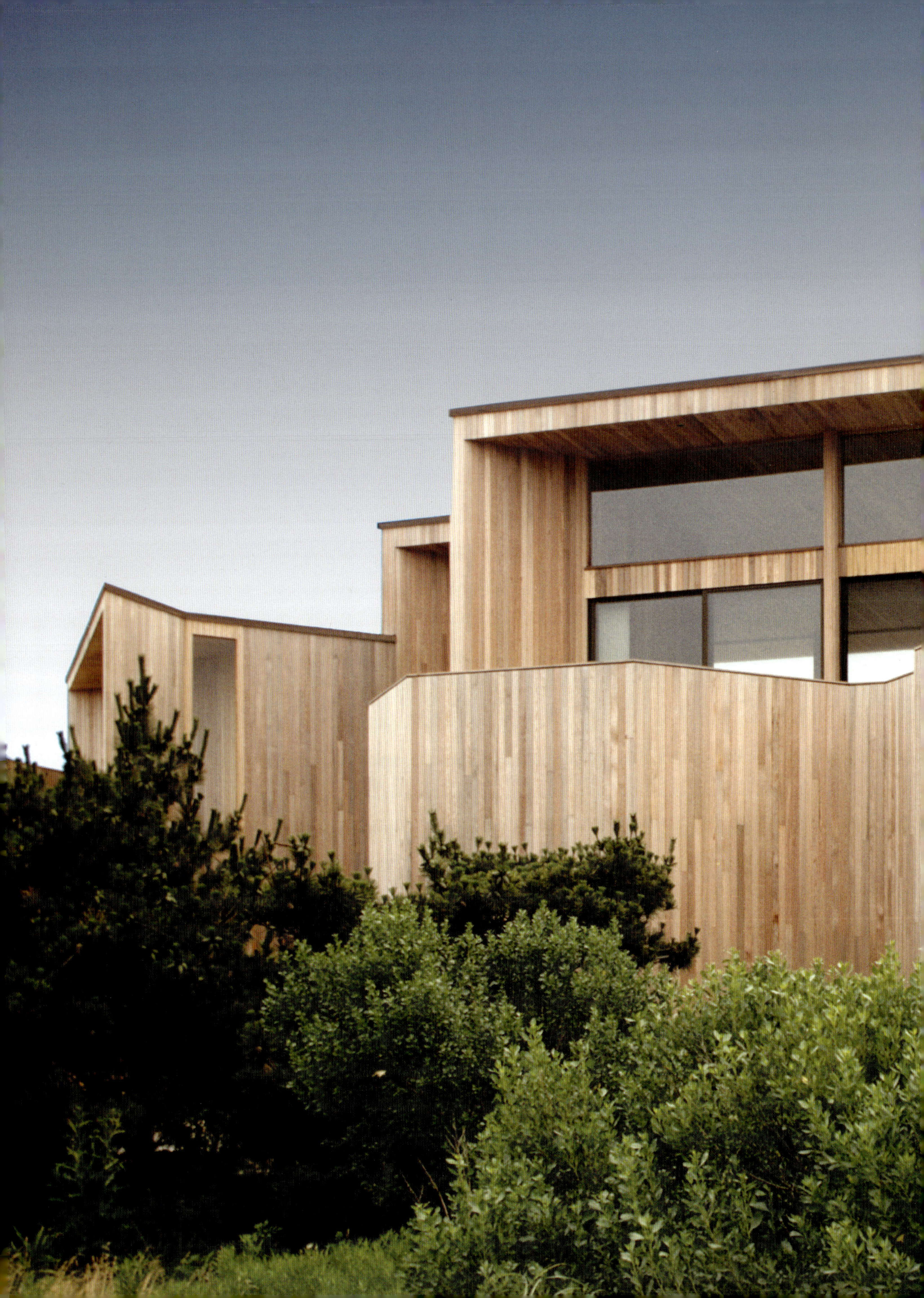

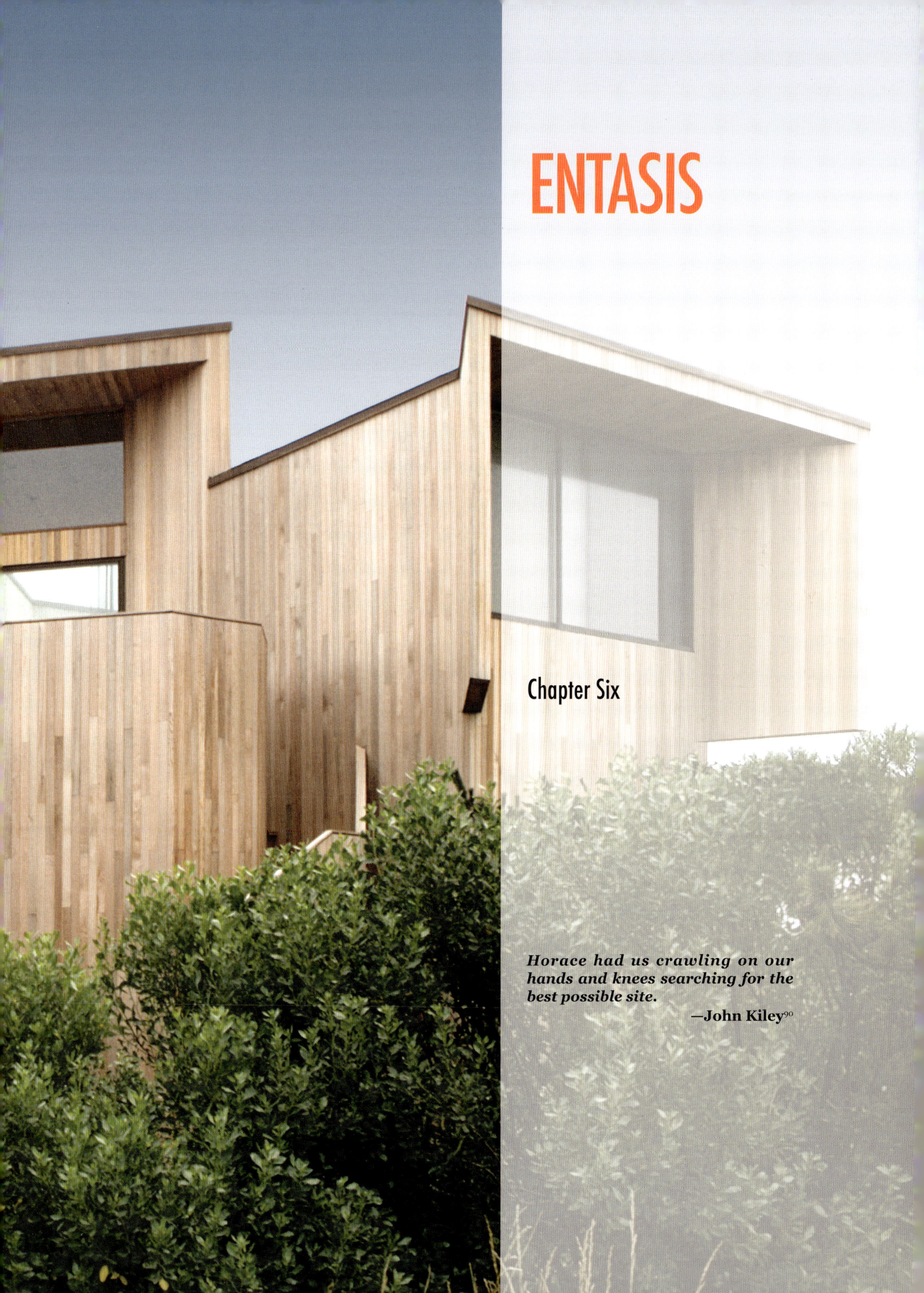

ENTASIS

Chapter Six

Horace had us crawling on our hands and knees searching for the best possible site.

—John Kiley[90]

Designer of numerous beach houses manipulates

VARIATIONS ON A PLAN

In seven years of designing in seven different beach communities on the south shore of Long Island, Horace Gifford has completed a total of 45 vacation houses. Not many designers who do not yet have their registration can make that statement. Still fewer can claim such variety and special elegance as the work of this Florida-trained, New York-based designer shows, despite relatively low cost and speedy construction for modest beach houses.

If there is a single rationale apparent in his development so far, it is the simple one of making variations within established limits. This approach, however, depends on a set of fixed forms or elements or traditions, such as those known formulas the 18th-Century writers and musicians elaborated and ornamented. For Gifford's projects, the constants have been similar sites, similar programs, and similar prices. He has pursued skillful manipulation within these narrow courses, rather than purity of invention or ambitious reaches into unknown areas, and has developed a secure-looking design craft in the process.

The Constants

The sites, all in beach communities within 50 miles of each other, have been approximately the same size. Most are 60′ x 100′, but others have been 60′ x 80′, 80′ x 80′, and 80′ x 100′. Only one has been appreciably larger. Zoning in these areas has permitted most houses to be close, and setbacks are much the same.

The essentially similar programs with which he has worked have called for a large living space, which is also used for dining and sometimes has a kitchen in it, two to four bedrooms, one or two baths, electric heat if any, and ample deck space for sunning. Square footage varying from 800 to 2000 has averaged 1100 sq ft of enclosed space with 600 to 100 sq ft of deck space.

Prices also were fairly constant for any one year, although, as Gifford observes, "Prices have gone up in the last 6 years from $11 per sq ft to $18. Some of this," he adds, "is due to the upgrading of materials and to people's desire for more convenience and comfort in a beach house."

To these basic constants, the designer voluntarily added another — structure. Standard stud construction, set on locust posts, is used throughout. Neither steel, concrete, nor block have been employed, because, first, few of the houses are year round, and, second, transportation of materials is frequently a problem, since at some of the villages all materials have to be hand-hauled the last 200 ft to the site.

The Variations

If these constants were the only determinants, all the houses might look as much alike as those in Levittowns — or like the many shacks in the communities where Gifford himself builds. In fact, a steady progress is apparent in manipulating a basic plan toward some fairly complex environments. Obviously, it is only by sensitive attention to other determinants that such rational variety could have been produced.

"The fact that I had to do so many houses with similar programs, similar budgets, and similar sizes," he says, "brought about a desire to change and vary them as much as I could. So any slight variations in the site or the client's real requirements were eagerly watched for."

Starting with a simple rectangle as a plan, Gifford first divided it into a central rectangular living space and a strip of sleeping and bathing spaces on each end. The living space was open to the out-of-doors through sliding glass doors on both long sides; the sleeping areas were pretty much solidly enclosed.

"In all of the houses," he observes, "the

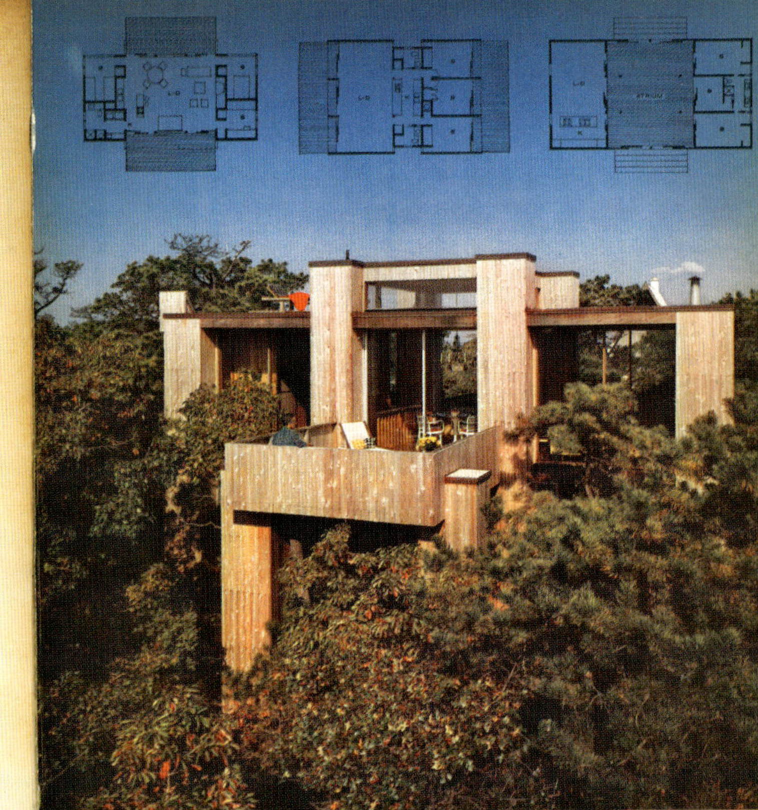

Manipulation of the section was Horace Gifford's first direction in varying the basic rectangle of his beach houses (top of page) from peaked roof (1), to clerestory (2), to folded (3), to arches (4), to atrium-void (5).

Photo credits: (3) Richard Jeffrey. (4) Hans Namuth. [illegible] Courtesy, "House and Garden."

1 2

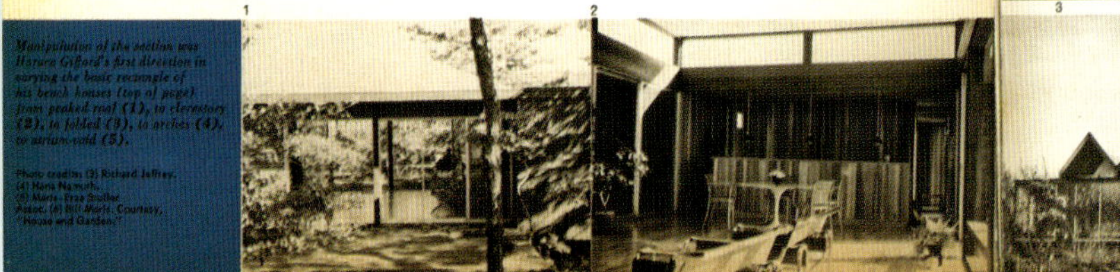

3 4 5 6

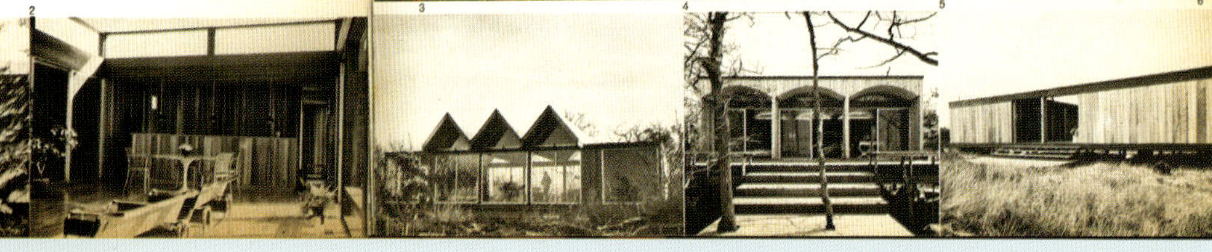

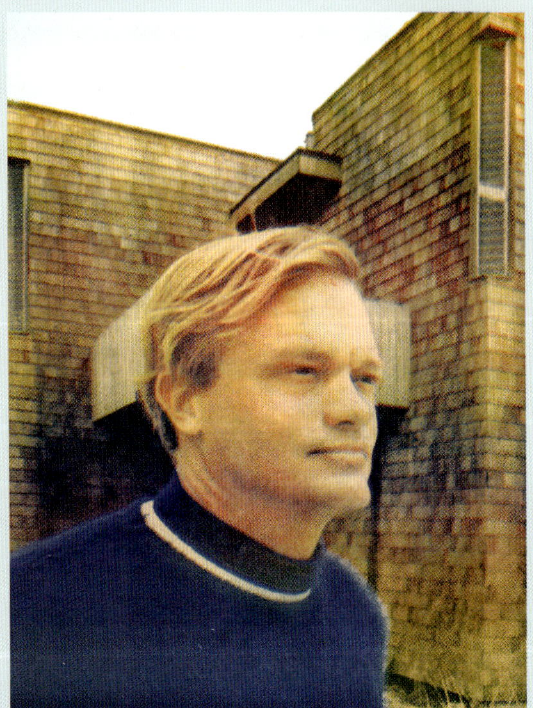

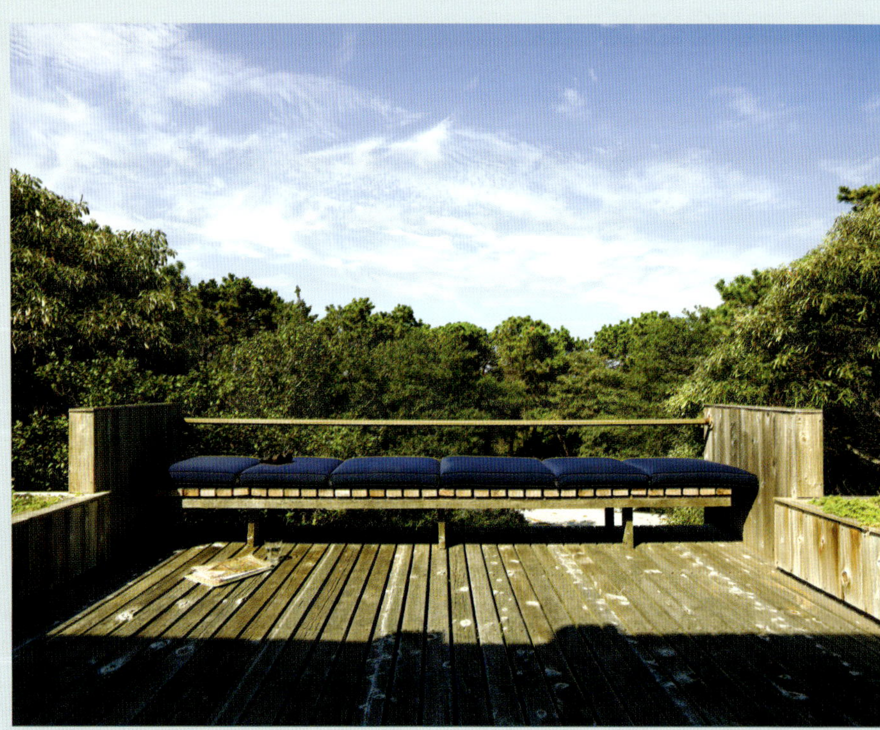

PAGES 136–37:
Pilson House, Westhampton Beach, NY, 1971

OPPOSITE, ABOVE:
Article about Gifford's work in *Progressive Architecture*, May 1968

OPPOSITE, LOWER RIGHT:
Cashel House, north deck

OPPOSITE, LOWER LEFT:
Horace Gifford, 1968

While 1965 delivered a succession of professional advancements and personal setbacks, the world three years later seemed to hold only great promise for Horace Gifford. He was ensconced in his new, thrice-published beach house on Snapper Walk in the Pines. In 1968, the American Institute of Architects included his work in a traveling exhibition focused on vacation homes, even though he never joined the organization. A *New York Times* review of the show singled out the "tree house" effects of his Fishman residence.[91] Other journalists took a more retrospective turn, connecting Gifford's individual works to a larger truth: he wasn't just creating houses, he was helping to invent a *place*. In May 1968, a local newspaper published a spread of his work entitled "He Sends Cutting Edges into the Sky." In it, Gifford held forth on the qualities of his recent work: "My style is becoming more complicated as I learn about light coming into space. The use of entasis. Do you know what that is? Selective ambiguity. I've learned a little about fooling the eye, making spaces bigger than they are," he explained. "It's a way of stretching the dollar, you see."[92]

Deriving from the Greek word for "distension" or "stretching," entasis was a means by which the ancient Greeks manipulated proportions to create a desired effect. The Parthenon's slightly bulging columns dramatized the weight they carried, like a flexed muscle. Ancient Greek theater sets employed exaggerated perspectives to create the illusion of depth. As an inveterate theatergoer, youthful set builder, and child actor, Gifford would draw upon these precedents to choreograph the domestic dramas of his beach houses. The techniques of entasis rarely surfaced in modern architecture, obsessed as it was with straight lines and modularity and industrial "perfection." Entasis was a premodern lie that aspired to a more beautiful truth, and Gifford harnessed it to his own purposes. Towering spaces paired with low-lying furniture belied economical footprints. The dramatic shafts of light that he directed through narrow east- and west-facing clerestories onto straight walls tracked the sun with mathematical precision. But when this light struck curved or mirrored walls, a riot of effects were possible. Floor-to-ceiling openings and a single material used inside and out created an "ambiguity of scale,"[93] as Gifford described it, that allowed his homes to be perceived as abstract sculpture in the landscape.

At this moment of professional maturation, a young critic appeared whose sensibilities were perfectly attuned to the architect's evolving aesthetic. C. Ray Smith's autodidactic expertise in theater design had expanded into a love for architecture, and, by 1968, he was president of the United States Institute for Theater Technology and features editor for the esteemed *Progressive Architecture* magazine. He had a wide-ranging sphere of accomplished friends, including Paul Newman, with whom he had studied acting at Kenyon College. His closest friend was Albert Fuller, the harpsichordist and Early Music Revival pioneer. Smith and Fuller's 1967 excursion to the Pines was a social and architectural revelation. They tracked down Gifford, toured his homes, and soon Gifford was one of Smith's two closest architect friends. The other was Paul Rudolph.

Smith celebrated Gifford's efforts with a retrospective showcasing twenty of Gifford's beach houses in the May 1968 issue of *Progressive Architecture*—a prodigious achievement for a thirty-five-year-old designer without an architecture license. Entitled "Variations on a Plan," it allowed Gifford to hold forth on the variety he managed to wring out of a basic approach:

> In all of the houses, the sleeping and service elements have been used as the solids in the design and the larger elements have been treated as the voids...The fact that I had to do so many houses with similar programs, similar budgets, and similar sizes brought about a desire to change and vary them as much as I could. So any slight variations in the site or the client's real requirements were eagerly watched for.[94]

With forty-five houses to his name, he had already transcended the modest implications of the article's title, for his recent work could no longer be understood with just a floor plan. The feature concluded with Gifford's own Snapper Walk residence, copiously documented to describe its volumetric sophistication. In spite of the changes, Gifford kept what worked—minimally intrusive site plans that saved trees, low-maintenance cedar and redwood detailing inside and out, and a spectrum of sundrenched and shady spaces. But increasingly robust budgets, a more nuanced design agenda, and commissions that strayed from Fire Island ushered in a period of tremendous professional growth.

What would it be like to inhabit a beach house in the rolling countryside of Connecticut? Gene Silbert and John Kiley spent a great portion of the sixties as guests at other people's vacation homes, trying them on for size. Marcel Breuer's houses, which paired floating white cubes with heavy stone bases, impressed them the most, but they also swooned at the modern beach houses that they had encountered in the Pines.

Gene Silbert designed textiles at 80 West Fortieth Street, a grand Beaux-Arts pile built in 1901 with double-height artist studios that surveyed Manhattan's Bryant Park. He often found himself sharing the elevator with a tall, striking, suntanned man. The two chatted and flirted but never exchanged names. This man would step off at the floor occupied by the architects I. M. Pei and J. Gordon Carr, but he disappeared in 1965. Two years later, Silbert and Kiley went to Kips Bay Towers to meet their chosen architect, and the mystery man in the elevator turned out to be Horace Gifford. The revelation was an ice-breaker that inaugurated a lifelong friendship, cemented by weekly design meetings for three homes, two apartments, and offices for John Kiley.

The couple's property in Connecticut was unlike anything Gifford had ever encountered within the confines of Fire Island. Its twenty-five acres spilled across the ridges of Redding, enveloped by a thick tangle of mountain laurel. Gifford stalked the property with a fevered intensity, looking for a sign. The possibilities for such an expansive space seemed endless. "He had us crawling on our hands and knees searching for the best possible site," Kiley laughed. Soon, Gifford discovered a ledge where the mountain laurel gave way to a grove of wild strawberries, indicating a change in soil, light quality, and wind patterns. "Here, we discovered we were at the edge of a cliff with an amazing view of the valley below," Kiley recalled. "On a clear day you could see Long Island Sound in the far, far distance. So that's where we built the house, jutting out from the cliff."[95]

As the clients requested, the plans and materials differed little from Gifford's beach houses. Only the heavy chimney stones, something rarely transported over the boardwalks of Fire Island, betrayed the home's location. The Silbert-Kiley residence presented an opportunity for Gifford to integrate Breuer's earth-hugging form of modernism into his repertoire, and Breuer's influence would reappear in several homes during this period. A subtly landscaped path to the house passed a sinuous courtyard wall that shielded the guest room and study. The T-shaped plan nestled into the shaded hillside to the east, housing a screened-in porch. To the west, a sundeck with low railings hovered bracingly over the edge of the cliff. Glass walls on the north and south facades lent the house a classic modern form, while a barrel-shaped plunge pool, inspired by New York City's iconic water towers, relieved its boxy profile. Inside, Gifford used mirrors and carpeted platforms to introduce optical illusions and a swank undercurrent to the cool minimalism on display. For years, Silbert and Kiley had been guests, and now it was their turn to host, as a seemingly endless stream of visitors arrived.

A play of heavy and light volumes, hinted at in the Silbert-Kiley residence, saw further development in a beach house that Gifford designed in Bridgehampton, New York. David Luck was a cell biologist whose social circle included the architect Peter Blake, the playwright Jerome Robbins, and the designers Ward Bennett and Joe d'Urso. Luck's house was a classic early Gifford layout, with a symmetrical bar-shaped enclosure facing Mecox Bay and a sundeck extending to the front and rear, forming a cross. The Bridgehampton site dictated a different three-dimensional presence, though. Acknowledging the flood-prone nature of the property, Gifford arranged four concrete-block piers that rose from precast cesspits and cantilevered the house to safety.

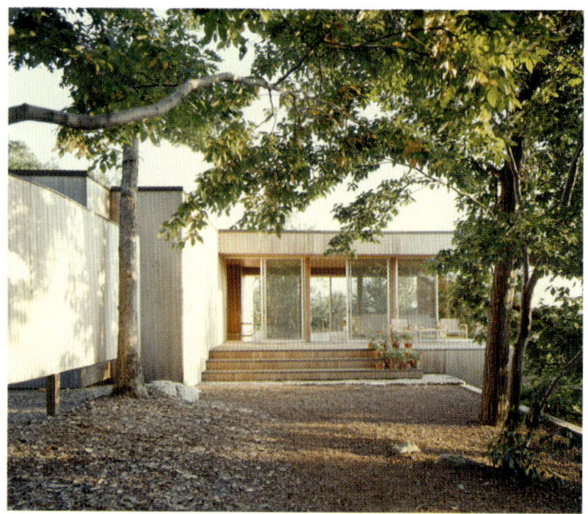

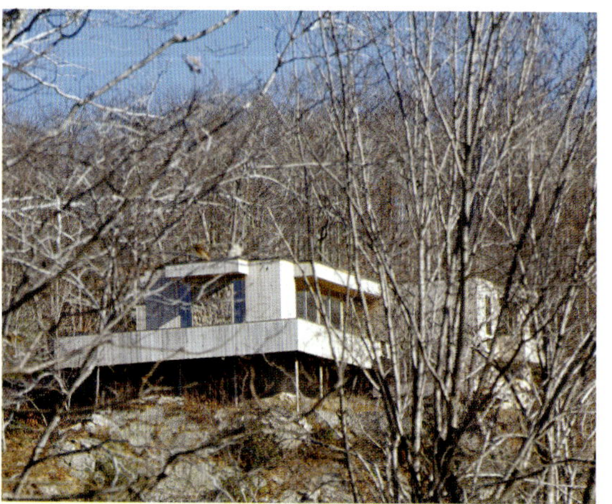

ABOVE:
Silbert-Kiley House, Redding, CT, 1967, approach

LEFT:
Silbert-Kiley House

OPPOSITE:
ABOVE: **Silbert-Kiley House, floor plan;** BELOW, RIGHT: **primary bedroom;** BELOW, MIDDLE: **living area;** BELOW, LEFT: **plunge pool**

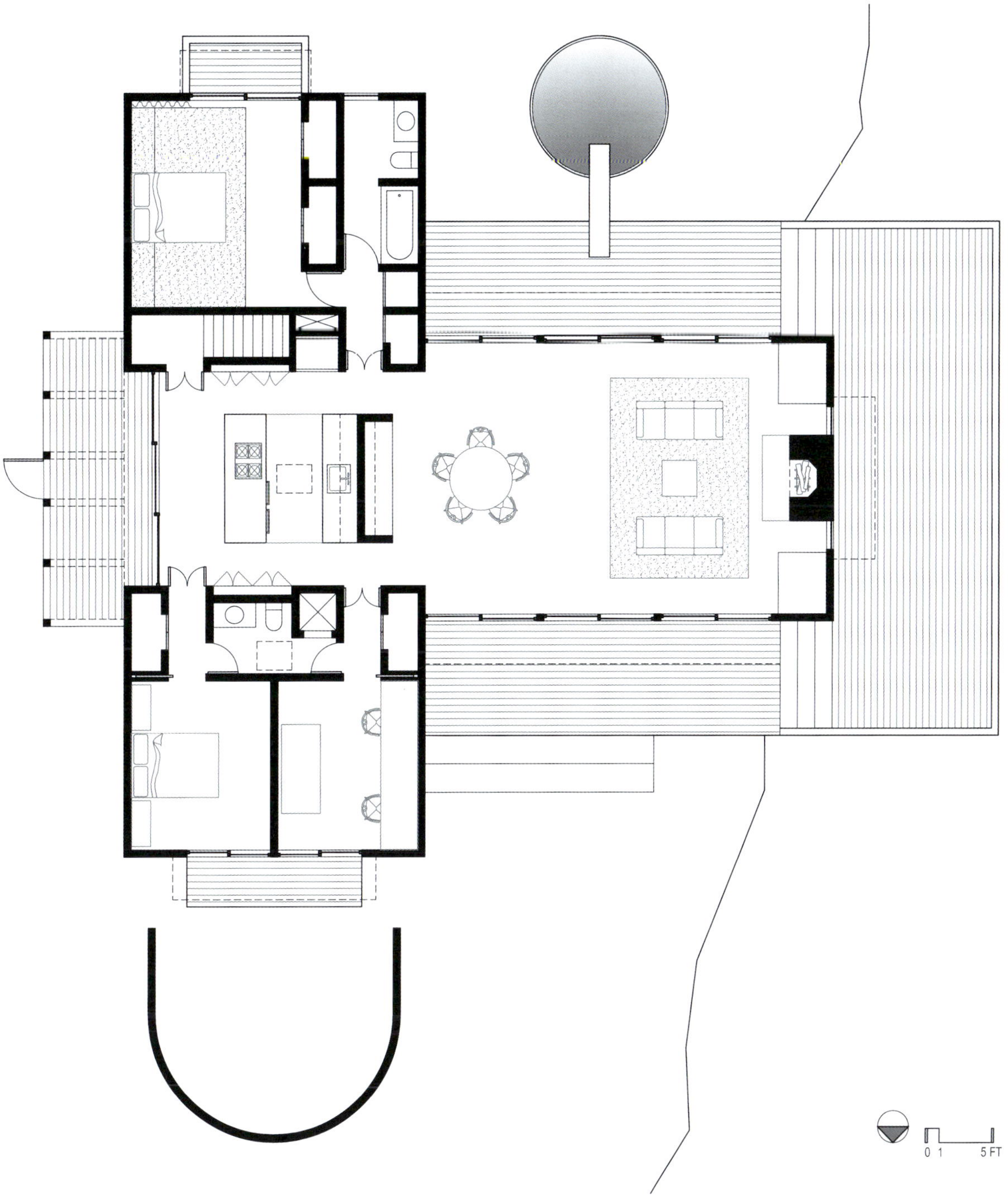

0 1 5 FT

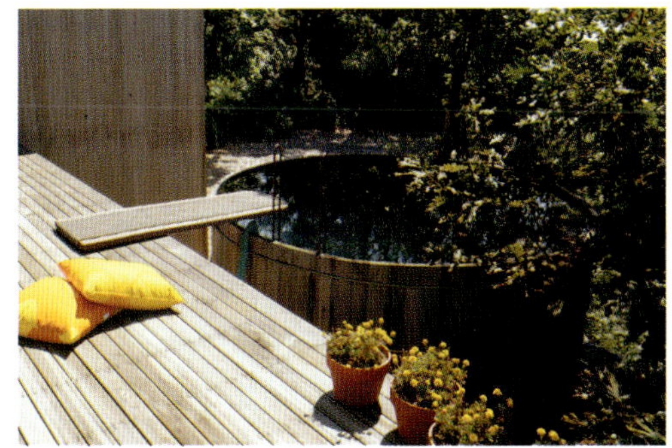

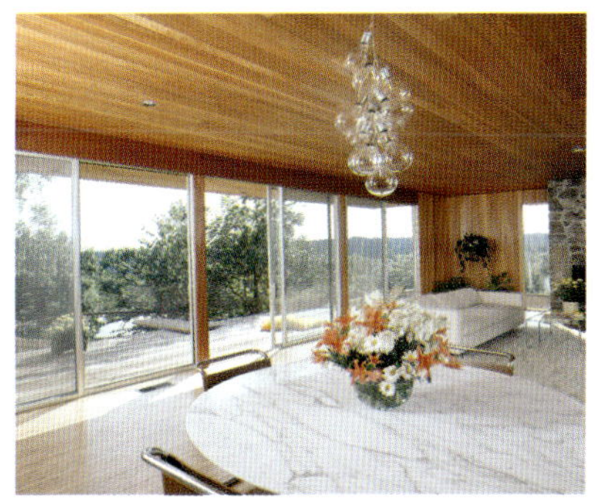

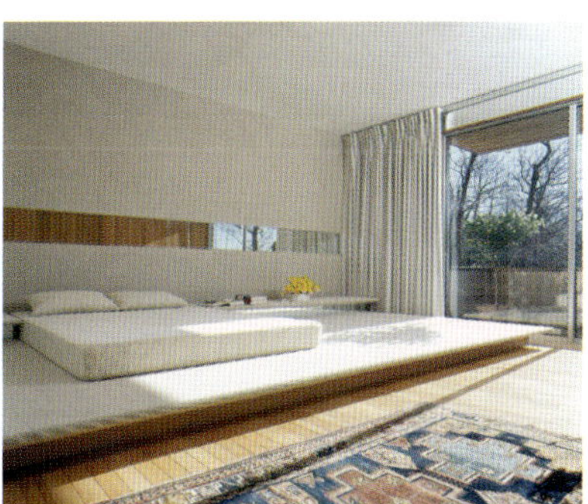

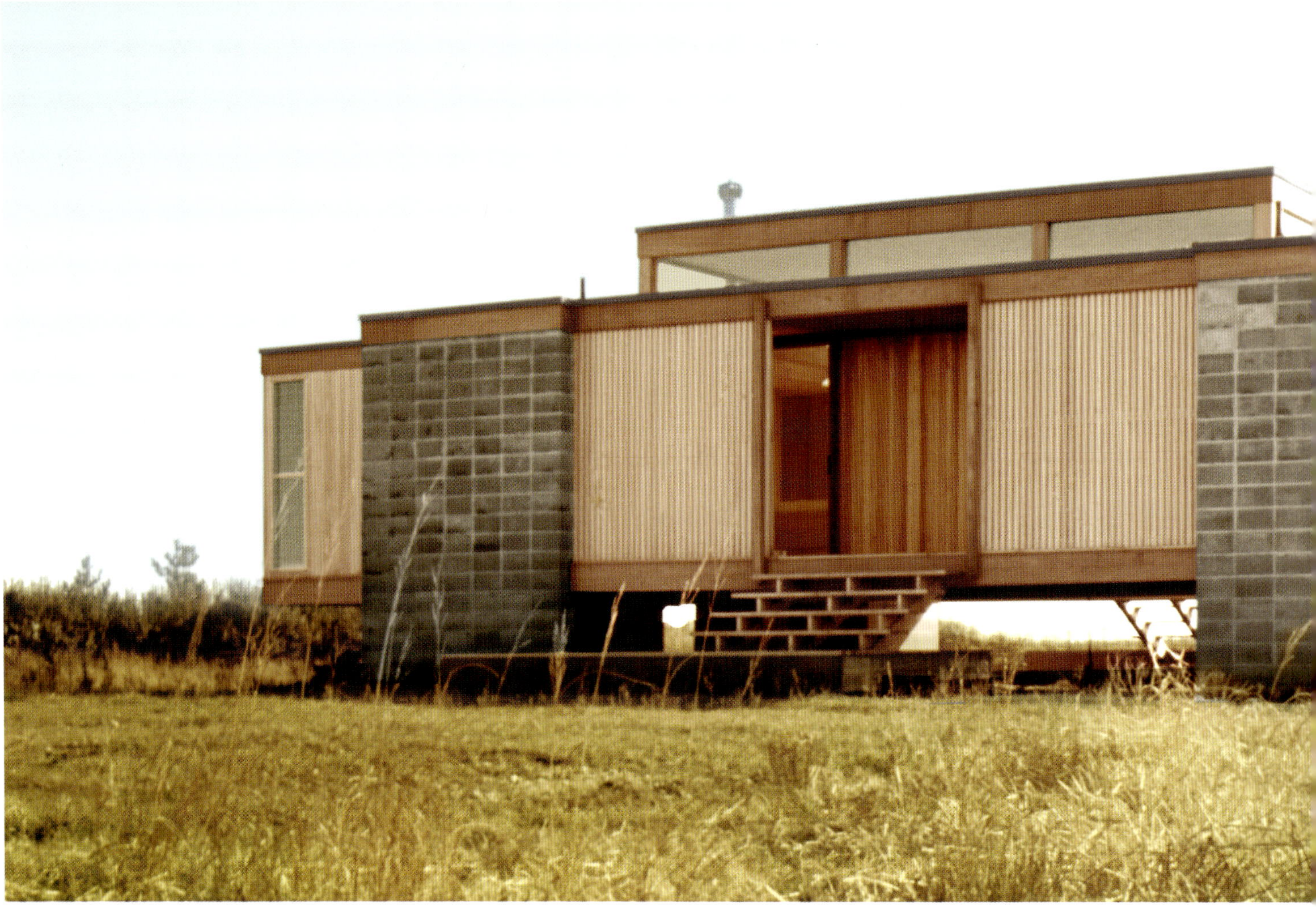

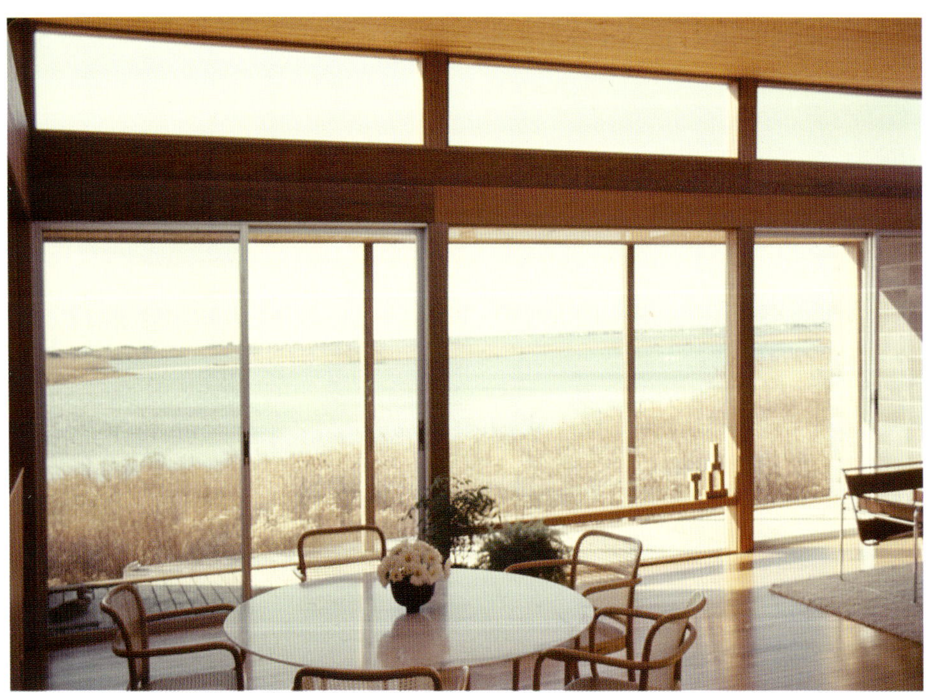

ABOVE:
Luck House, Bridgehampton, NY, 1967

LEFT:
Luck House, living room

OPPOSITE:
Luck House, elevation

PAGES 144–45:
Luck House, renovated interior

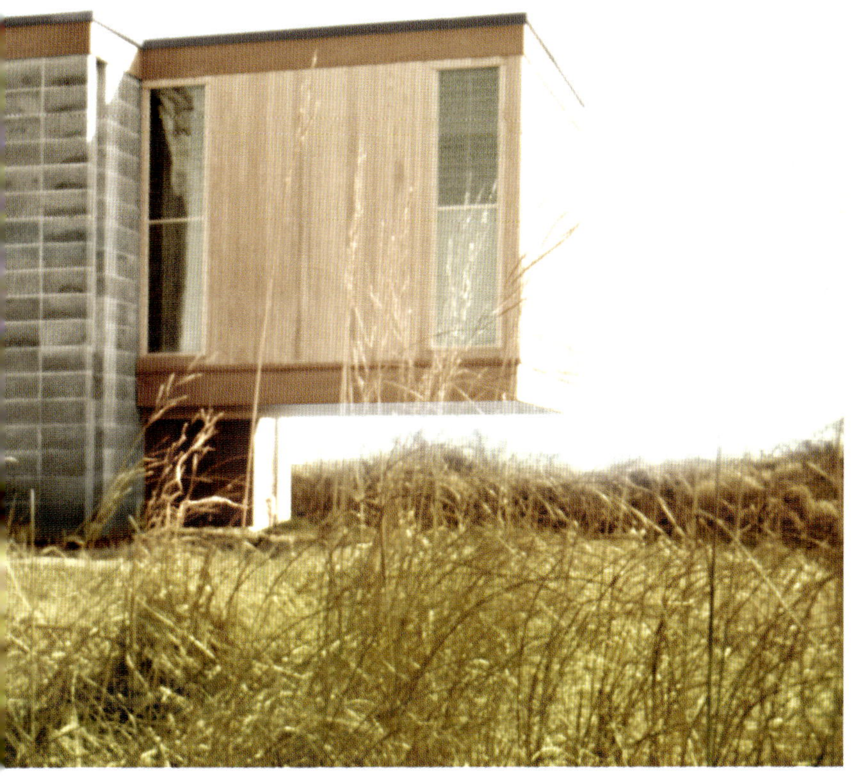

The property was next door to Peter Blake's iconic and eponymous residence from 1960, which hovered serenely over its site like a Miesian dogtrot. The Luck House's carved-out porches, exposed columns, and cladding details all engaged in the sincerest form of flattery toward its neighbor. But its overall profile revisited domestic experiments on the Sarasota coast by Paul Rudolph and his student William Morgan. Gifford's original contributions were found in his now-trademark clerestory windows and elegant details, like slatted pocket doors, tucked into thc concrete piers, that could emerge to draw a dappled wooden curtain across the facade. This grafting of Kahn, Breuer, Blake, and Rudolph could have become a Frankenstein in the hands of a lesser craftsman, but Luck's residence emerged strengthened by its complex genetic code.

Gifford's sister, Jean Slay, and her husband, Clyde, turned to him in 1969 for a new vacation house in Vero Beach. Having enjoyed eight years in her Gifford-designed home in Houston, Jean relished the opportunity to engage the services of her now-seasoned brother. A single square, snipped at its edges and oriented forty-five degrees to the ocean, housed the extended Gifford clan. The intensity of storms along the southeast Florida coast led Gifford to an entirely different constructional approach than the one he was perfecting on Fire Island. Gifford engineered a house of concrete posts and beams, tile floors, and glass so

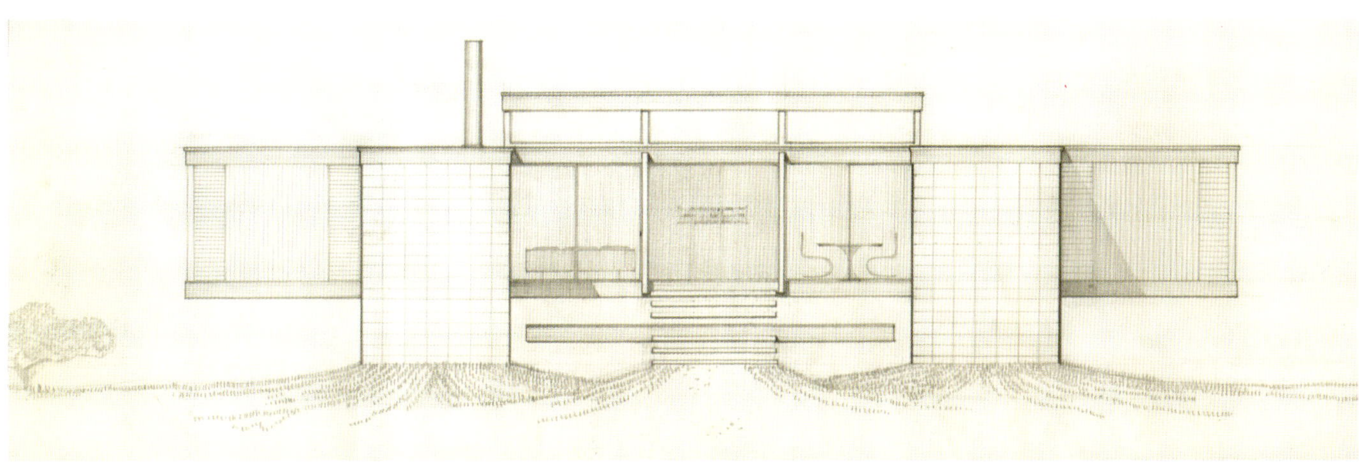

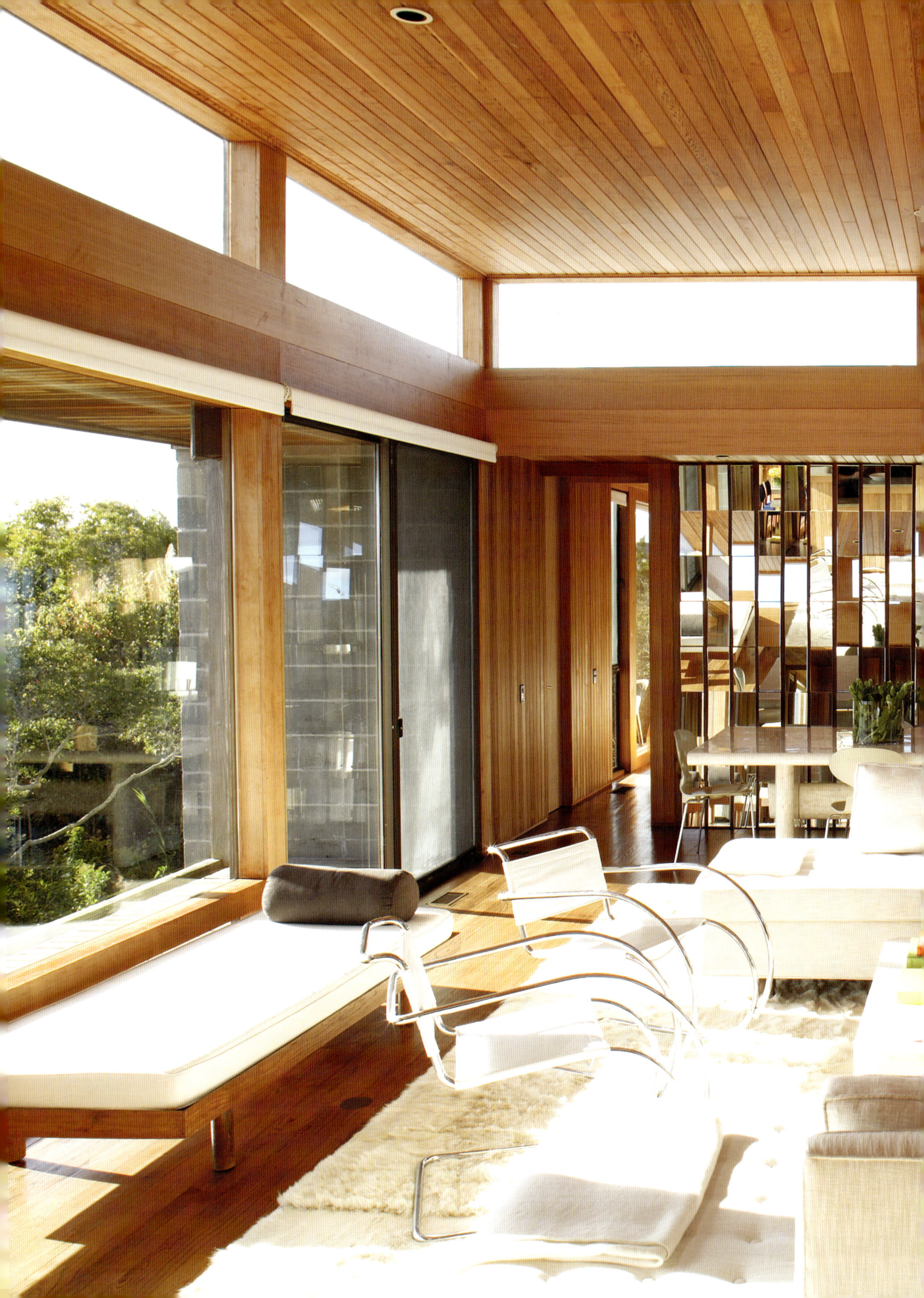

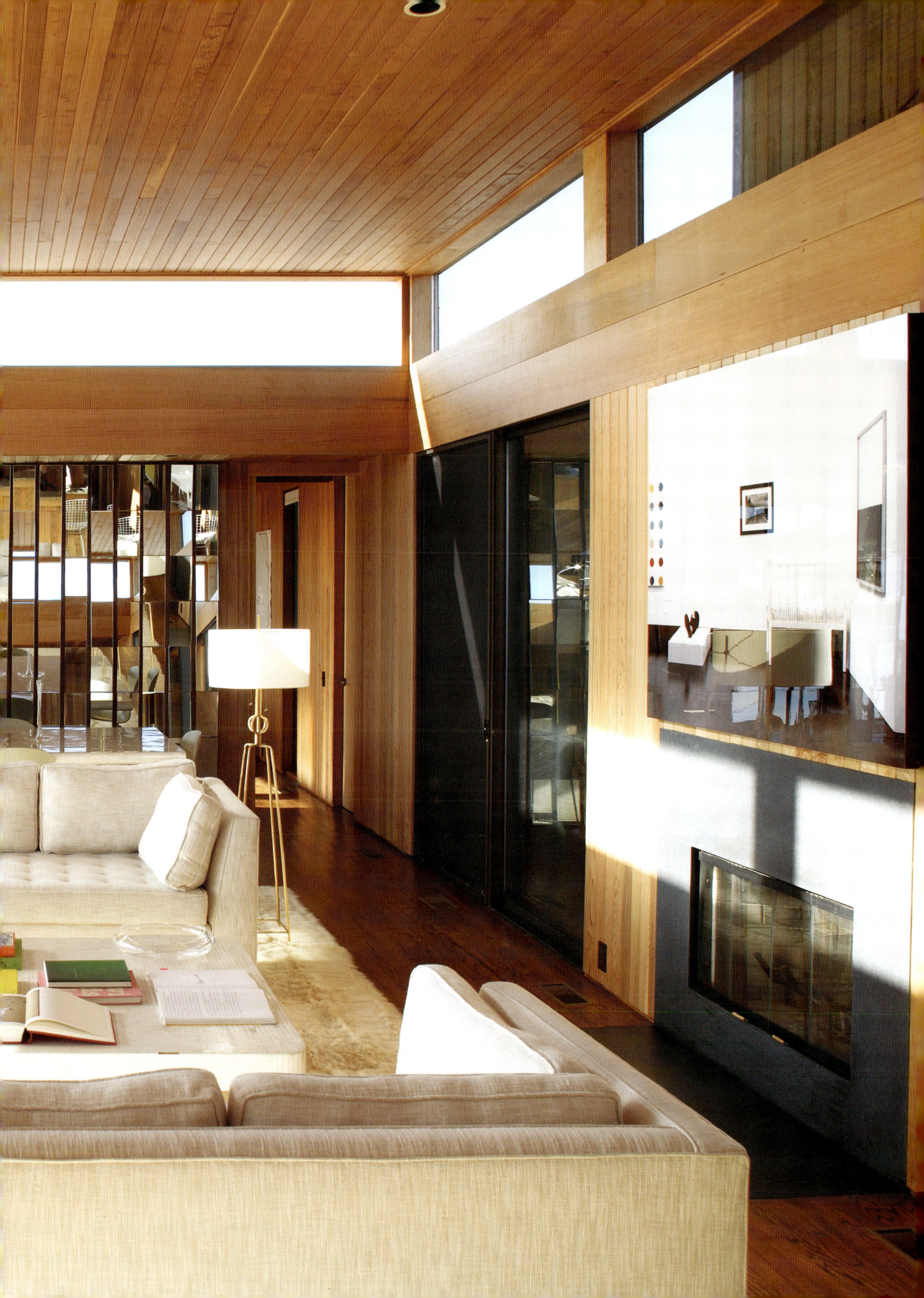

that "water can just sweep through it with little damage," he explained.[96] A concrete-and-tile dining table, as anchored as the architecture, contrasted with lightweight folding captain's chairs and wicker accessories that could be secreted away in double-height closets as storms approached. Sheltering it all was an enormous, solid timber roof in the form of a truncated pyramid, relieved by an eight-foot-diameter skylight in the center.

Back on Fire Island, an inspired synergy with a knowledgeable client led to a rare collaboration for the architect, who usually worked alone. J. Hyde Crawford was a multitalented illustrator, designer of the Bonwit Teller logo, and founder of Quadrille Fabrics. He was handsome and confident, and admired the same qualities in his architect. As Gifford recalled to *House and Garden*, Crawford "was a delightful client who knew exactly what he wanted."[97] Since both men could draw, they exchanged sketches, a twist on the usual process of an architect presenting plans to a client for approval. Three separate high-ceilinged

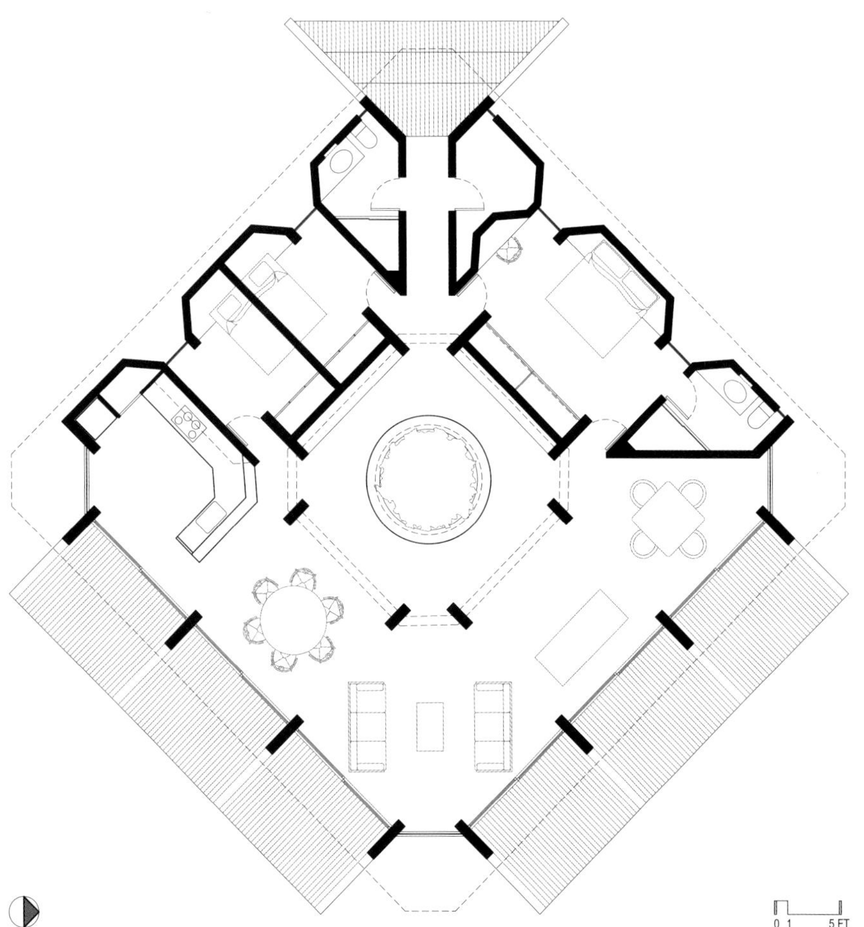

LEFT:
Slay House II, Vero Beach, FL, 1969, floor plan

OPPOSITE:
Slay House II, interior

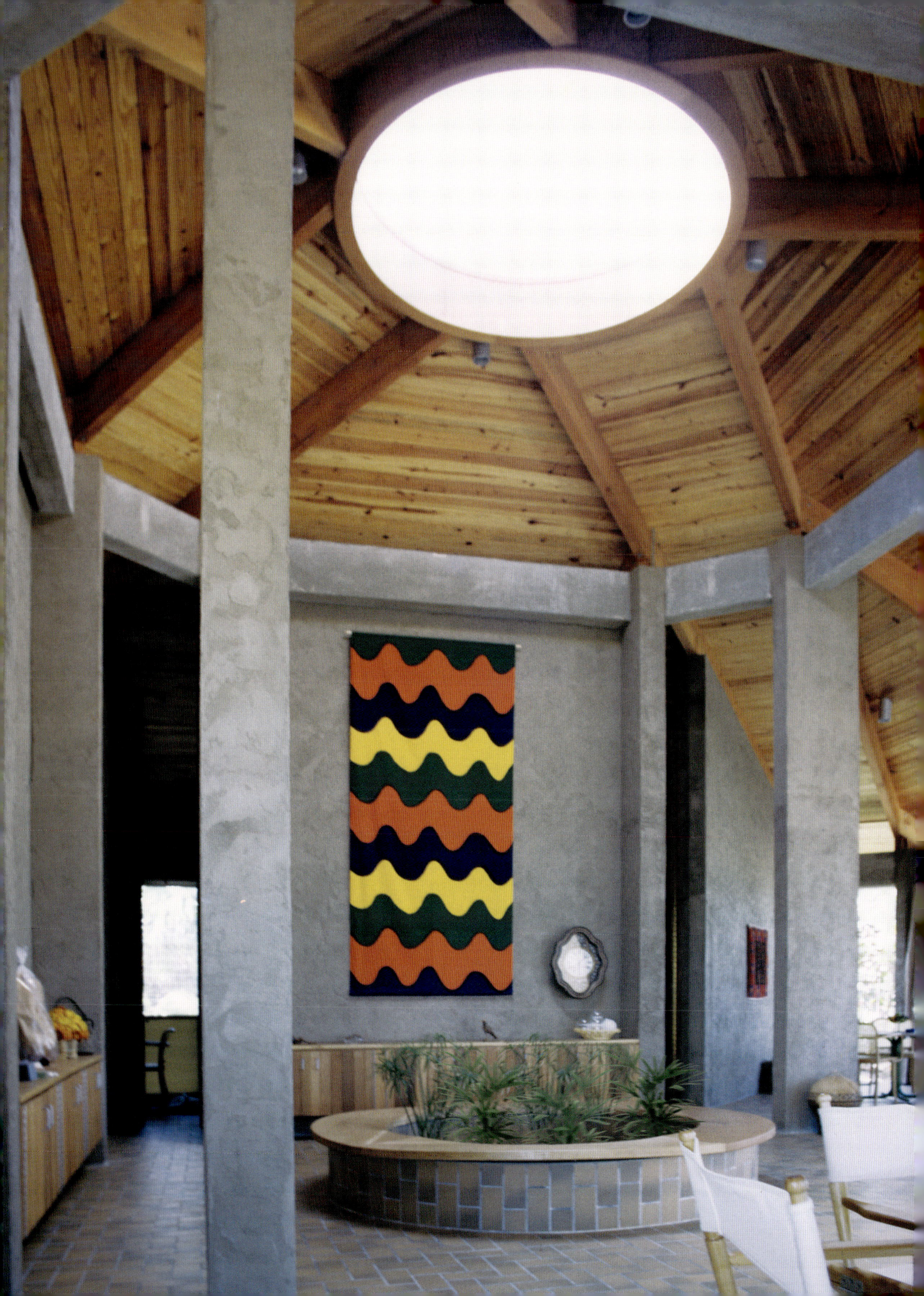

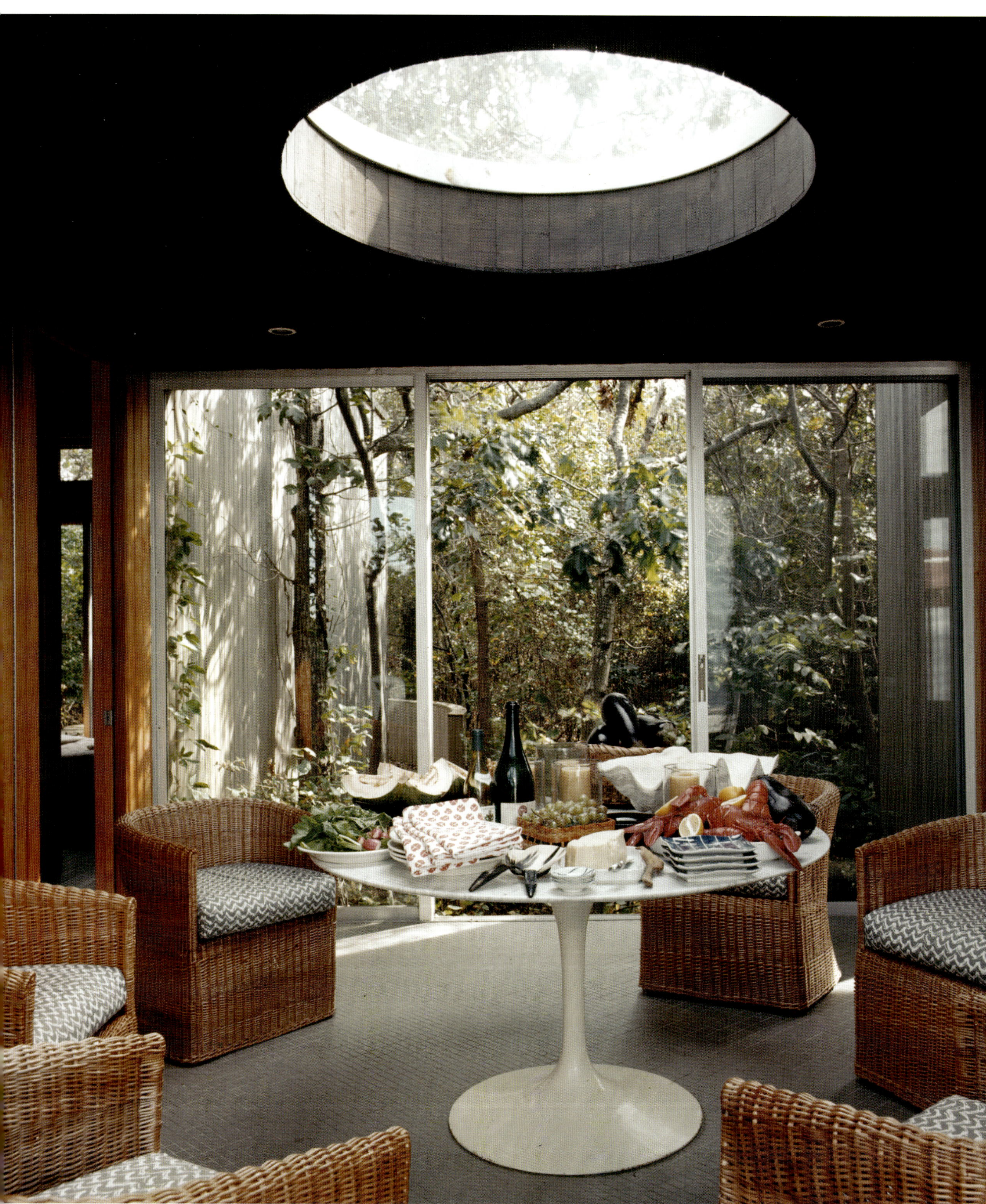

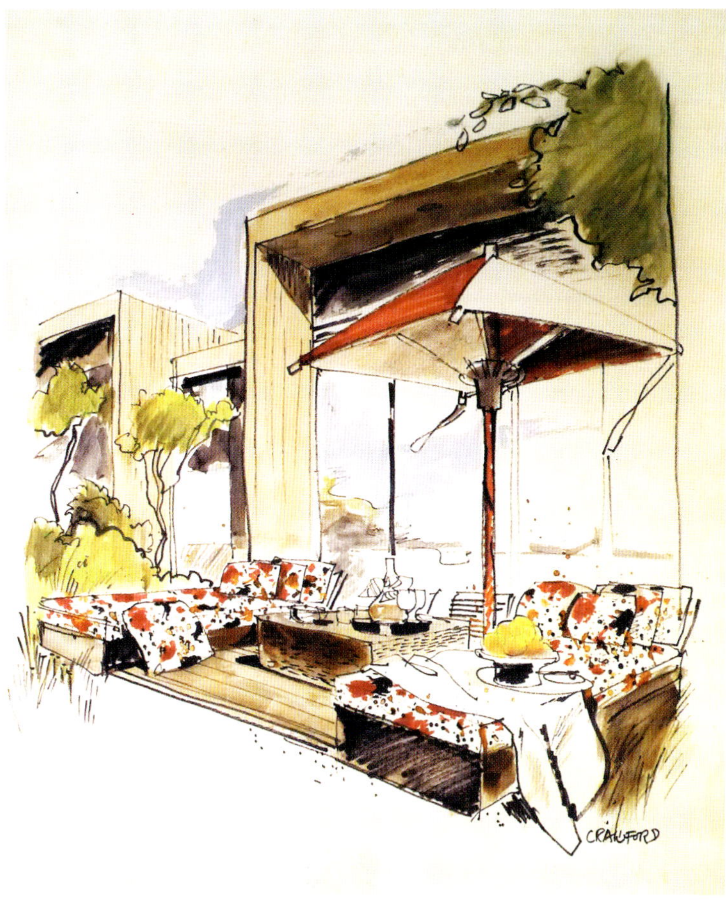

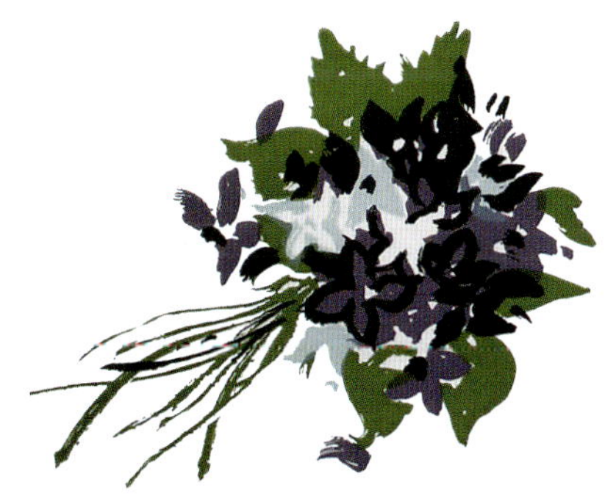

OPPOSITE:
Crawford House, Fire Island Pines, NY, 1969

TOP:
Crawford House, illustration by J. Hyde Crawford

MIDDLE:
Bonwit Teller logo, designed by J. Hyde Crawford

PAGES 150–51:
Crawford House, exterior facing Great South Bay

volumes requested by Crawford housed a guest wing, a living area, and a primary suite. Gifford joined these pavilions with two glass bridges that held a guest bath and the dining room.

Crawford's informed influence nudged Gifford out of his formula of a single grand space surrounded by subservient bedrooms. Every room surprised—even the closets, which were circular and skylit. Asked by *House and Garden* how he could coax such a measure of luxury out of such a modest budget, Gifford explained that "the luxury details are a matter of using standard things in an un-standard way. Simplicity does not mean that variety cannot happen within the given framework."[98] A prefabricated fiberglass unit served as the basis for Gifford's constructing a round shower, which he then embellished with wood cladding and a bubble skylight. He made gray square tiles look fresh by setting them on the diagonal.

Outside, the roofline undulated from room to room, yet a quality of serenity prevailed, since the house was so well integrated into its double lot on the Great South Bay. "The outstanding feature of the house is that we did not diminish the beauty of the site in any way. Glass tends not to enclose—that's why we used so much of it."[99] Windows underneath countertops created the illusion of floating slabs, as circular skylights cast dramatic and unpredictable shadows upon an otherwise orthogonal architecture. "Once we decided to break the rectangles with circular forms—cylindrical showers and closets, round skylights—marvelous things began to happen," said Crawford.[100] The primary bath was the only space that did not face outward, but its circular skylight painted the space with a dramatic, ever-changing ellipse of light.

Before its destruction by Hurricane Gloria, Gifford's oceanfront creation for Robert and Celeste Rubrum was popularly known as the "Plywood House" owing to the prolific use of this finish inside and out. Its materiality owed a debt to the experiments of architect Rudolph Schindler, while its volumes recalled the top-heavy Brutalism of Paul Rudolph and the paintings of Hans Hofmann. The central volume was an airy double-height space, inset with a red conversation pit. Nearly all of the furniture was built-in. A spiral stair ascended to a bridge that connected the two-story wings.

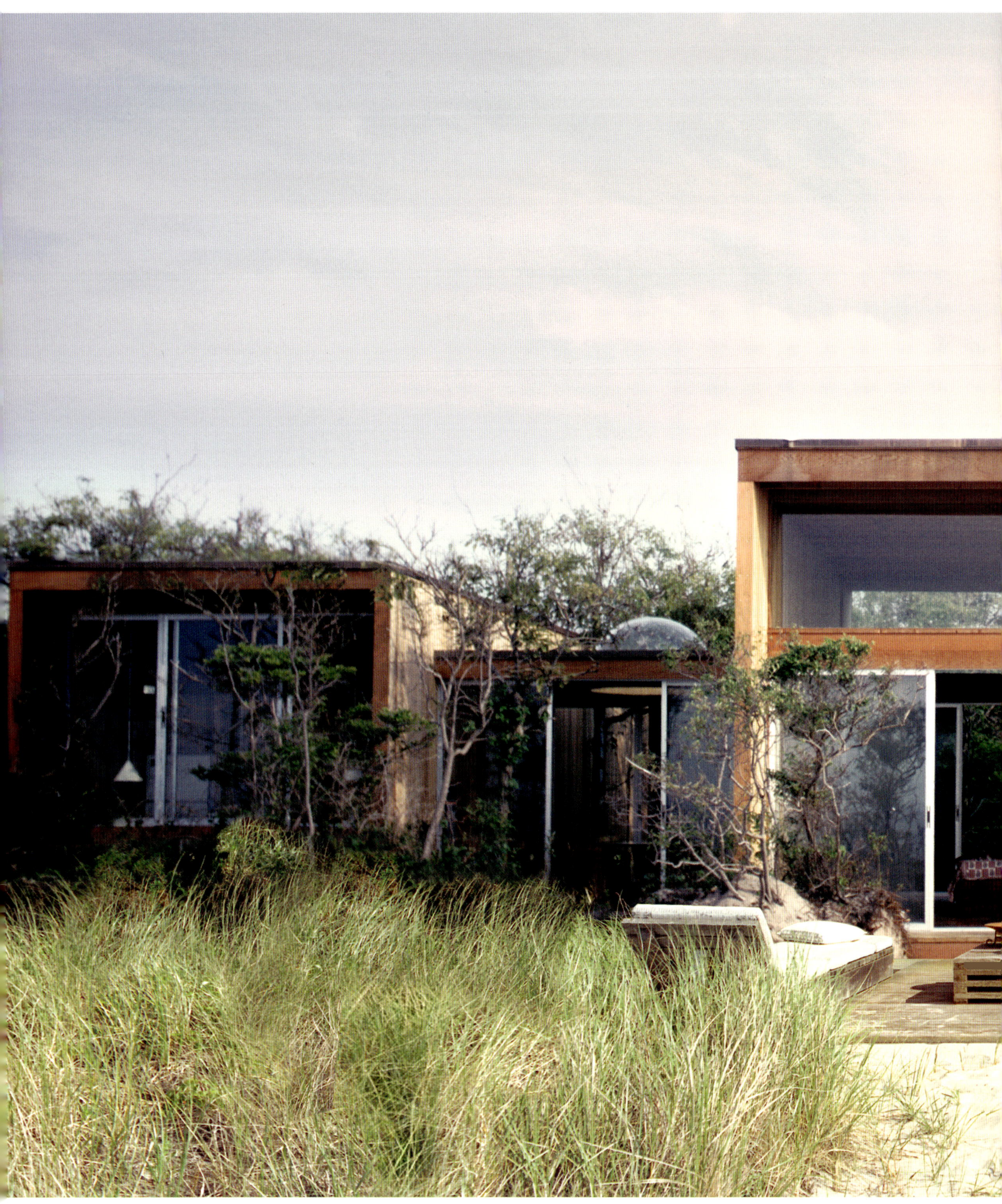

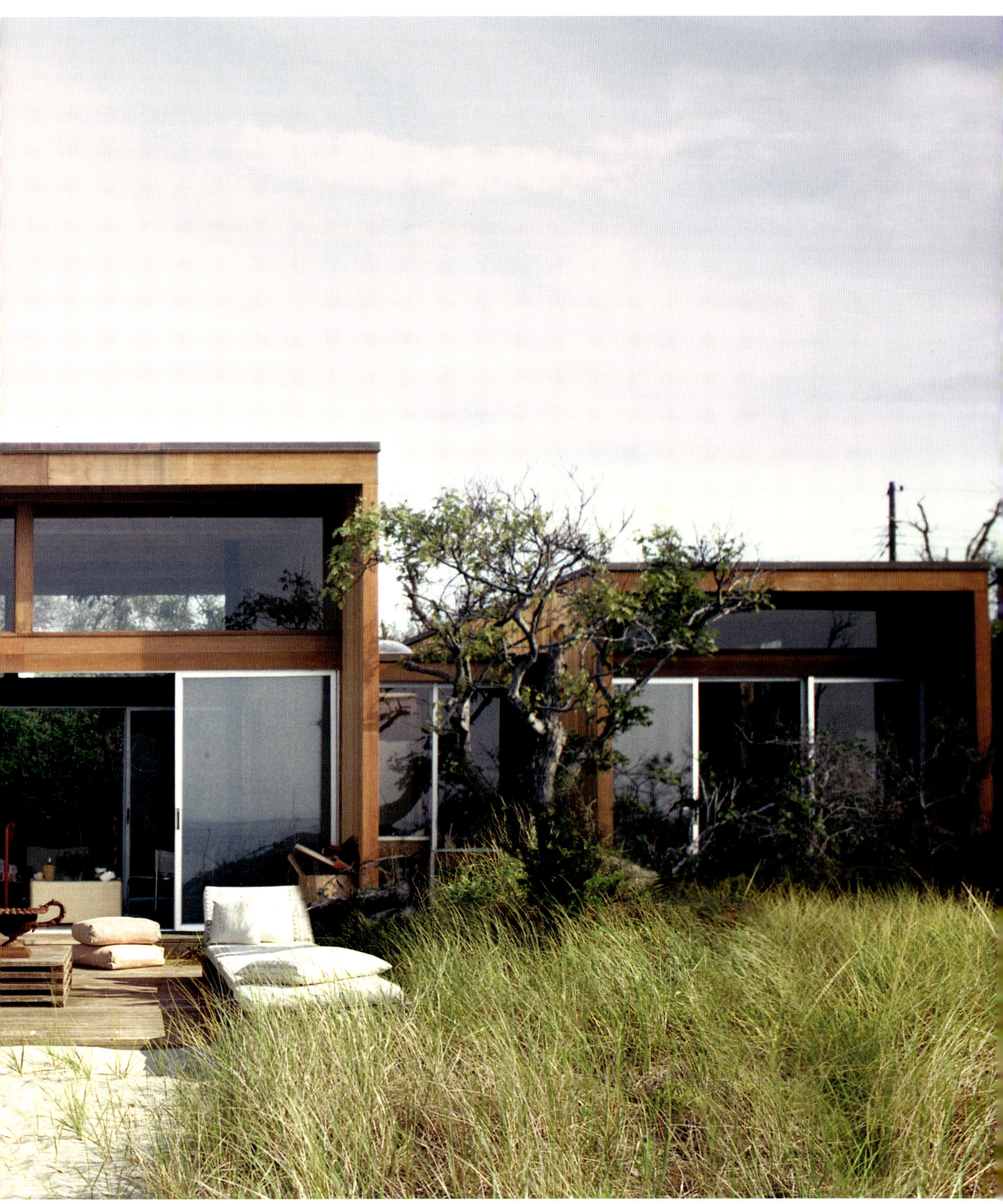

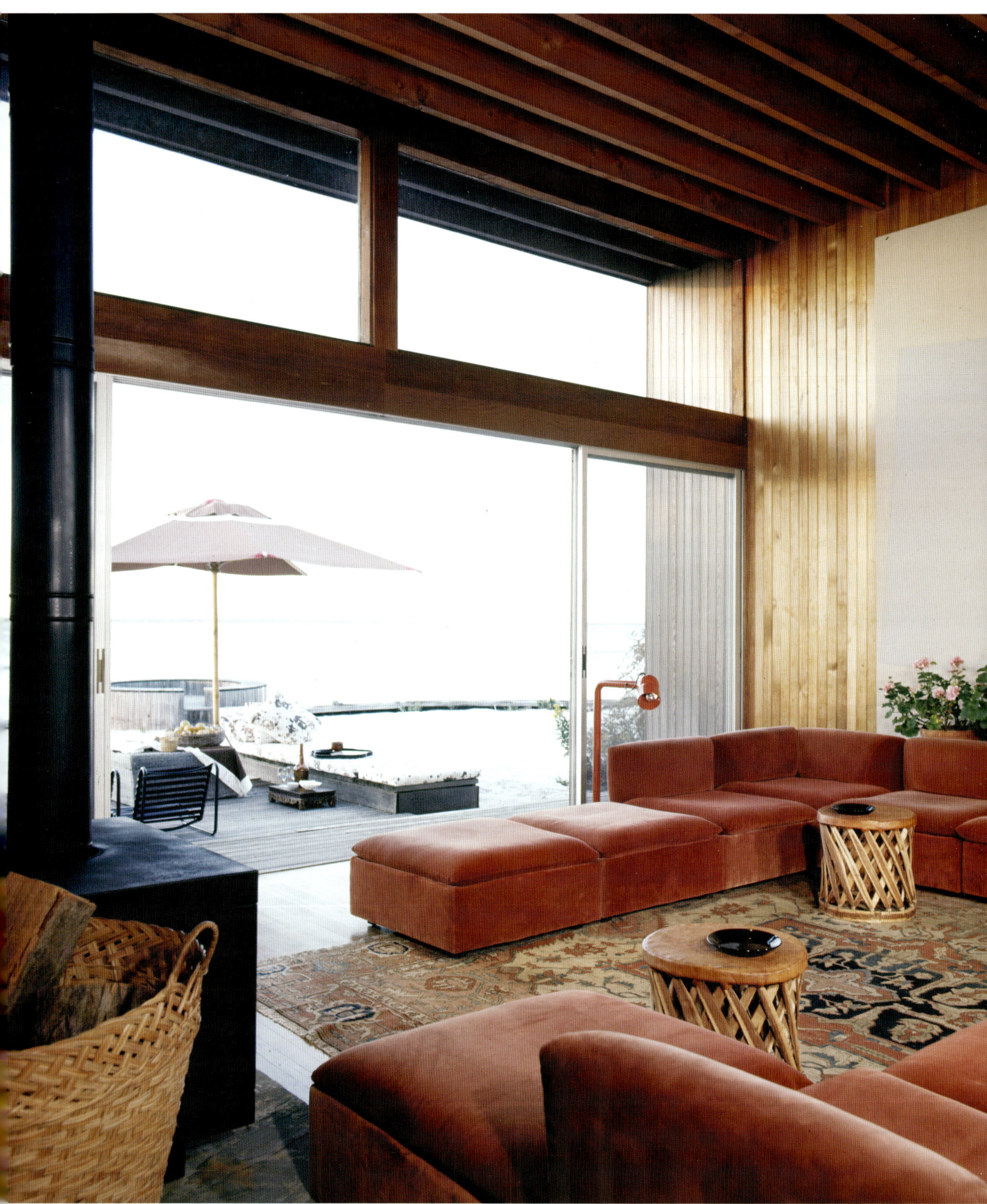

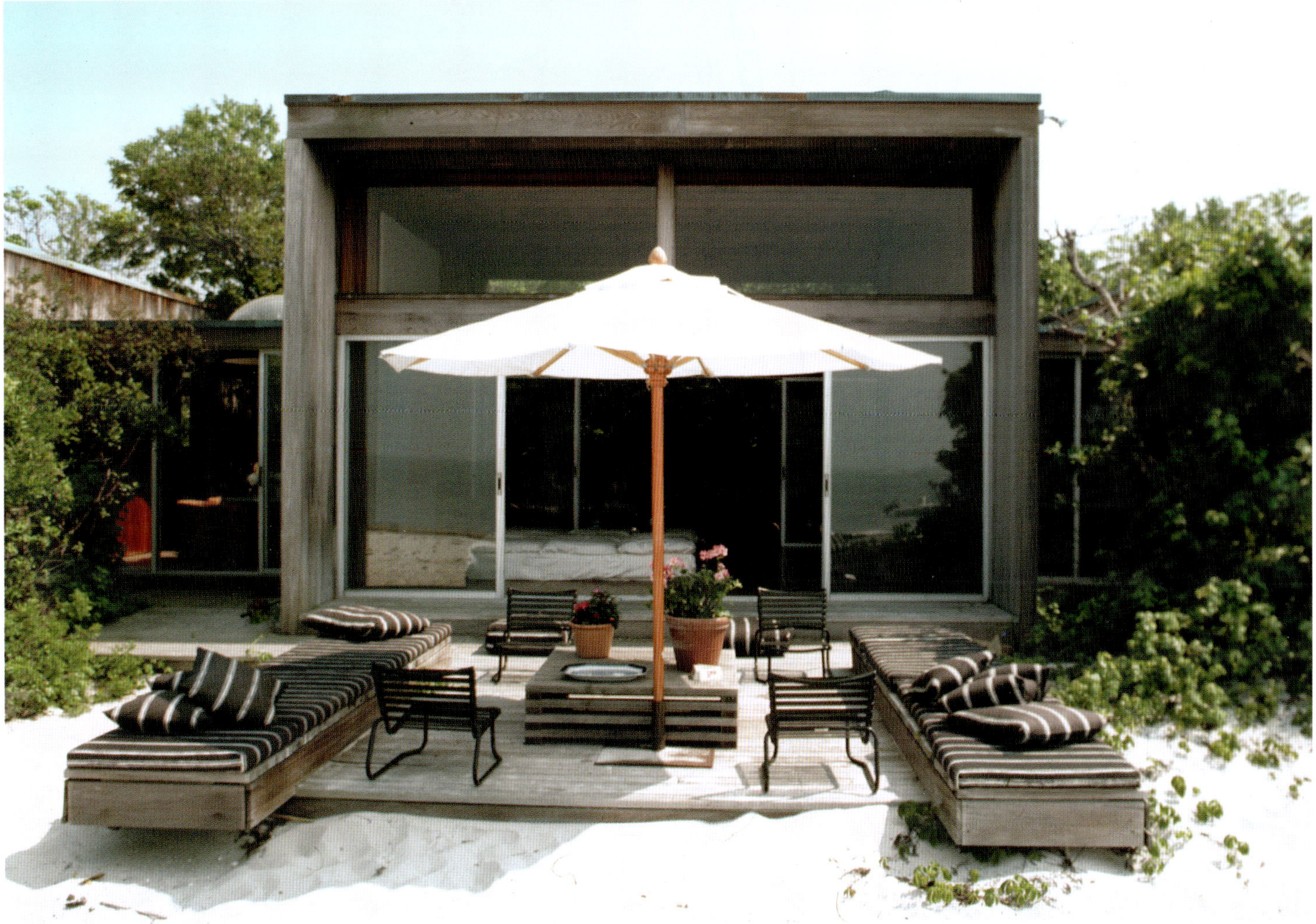

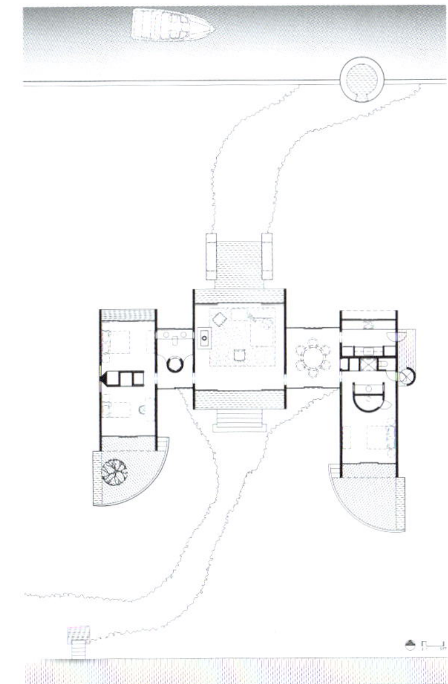

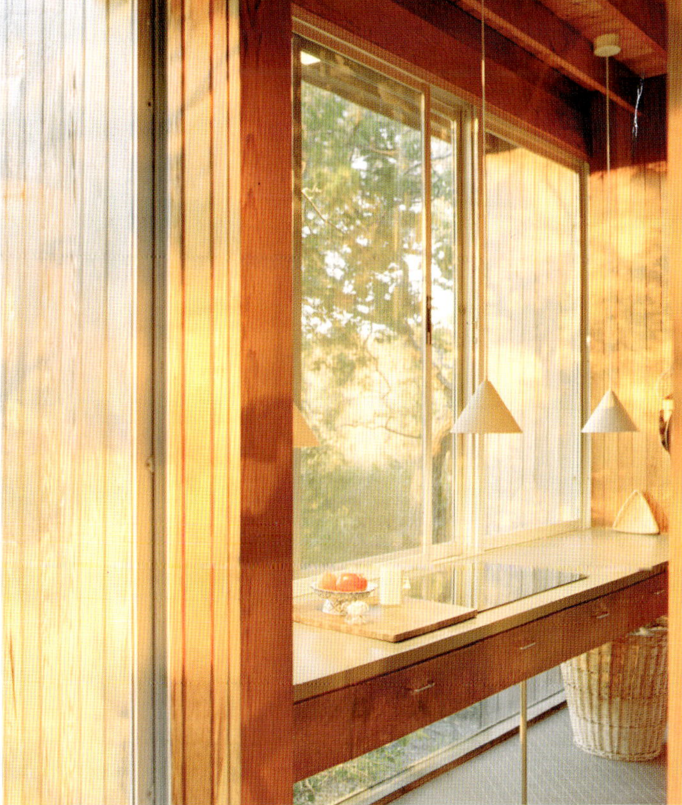

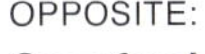

OPPOSITE:

Crawford House, living room

ABOVE

Crawford House, exterior facing Great South Bay

LOWER RIGHT:

Crawford House, kitchen

LOWER LEFT

Crawford House, floor plan

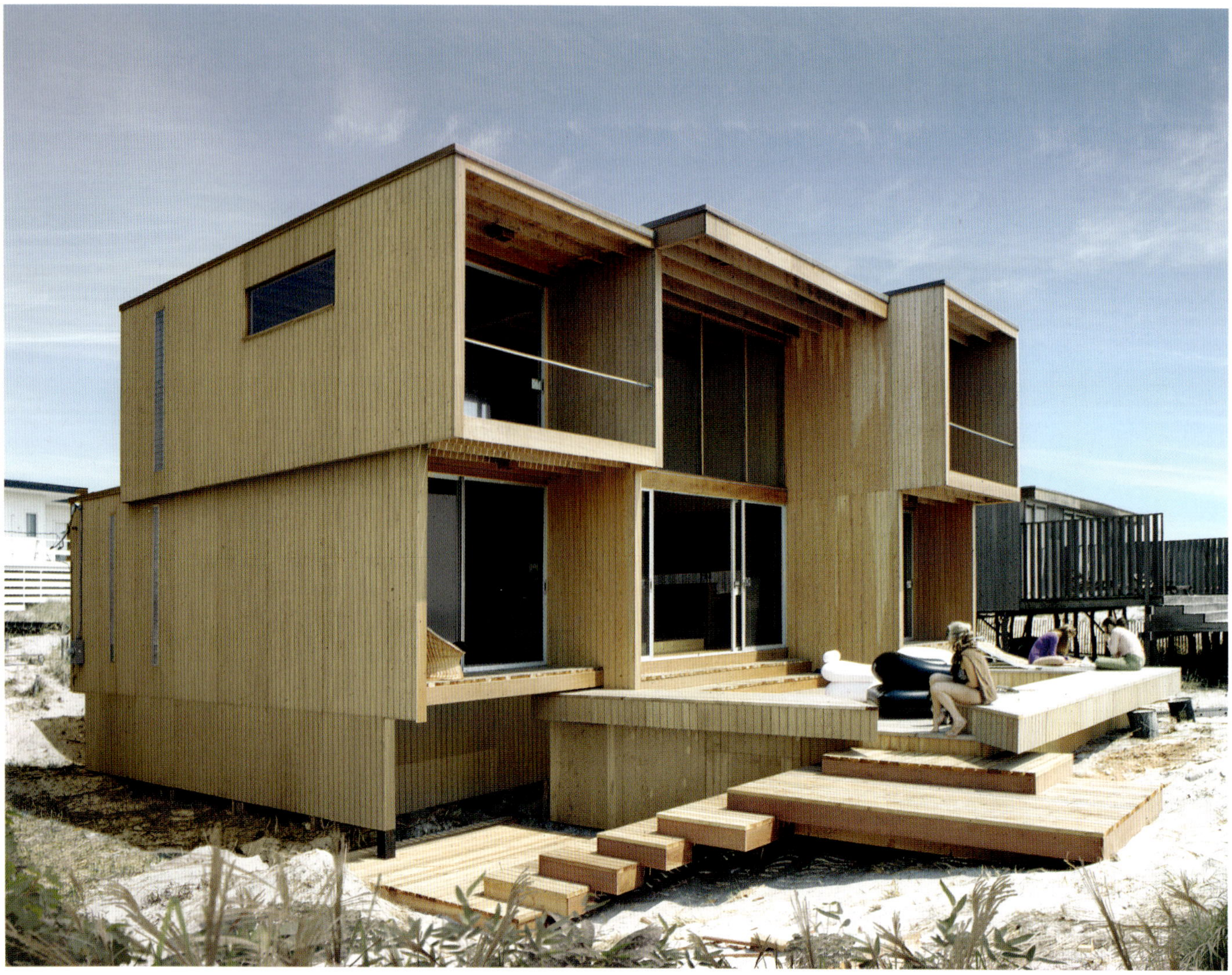

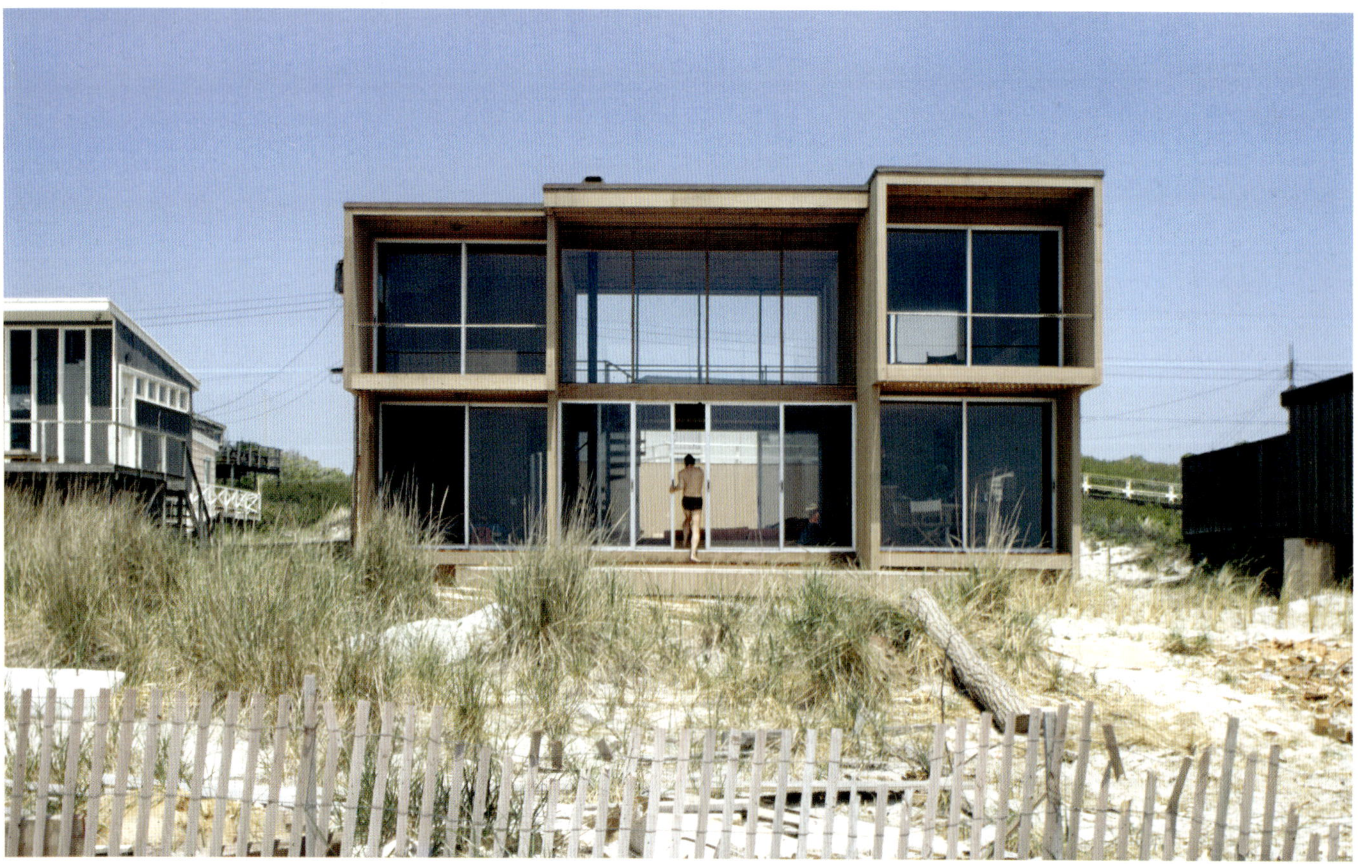

The Rubrum residence added to a growing roster of oceanfront homes that proclaimed the modernist makeover of the Pines. Gifford was hardly the only modern architect working there by this time. Harry Bates and Earl Combs were less prolific but both enjoyed multiple, high-profile commissions there, working in a similar idiom of naturally weathering cedar and glass. Their houses were joined by one-off creations that revealed the eclecticism of late-modern style. By the mid-seventies, whimsical fantasies in cedar and glass traversed the entire beachfront, as captured in artist Ferron Bell's illustration for the *Pines Phone Directory*. More than a mere listing, this was the little black book of social life in the Pines. Residents could be looked up by first name, last name, or address, easing the anxiety of following up on introductions made in a haze of cocktails and marijuana.

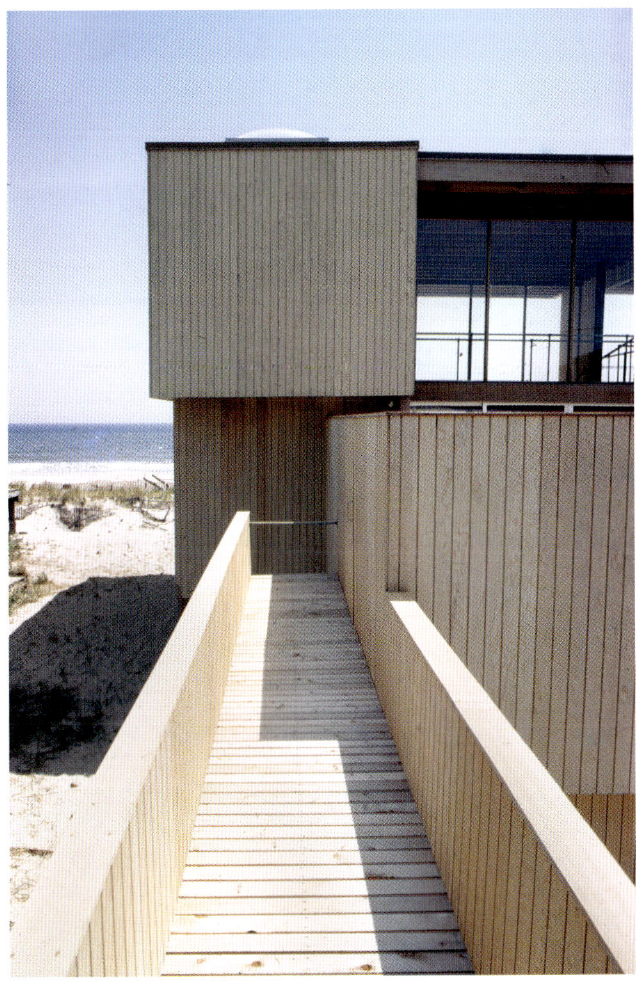

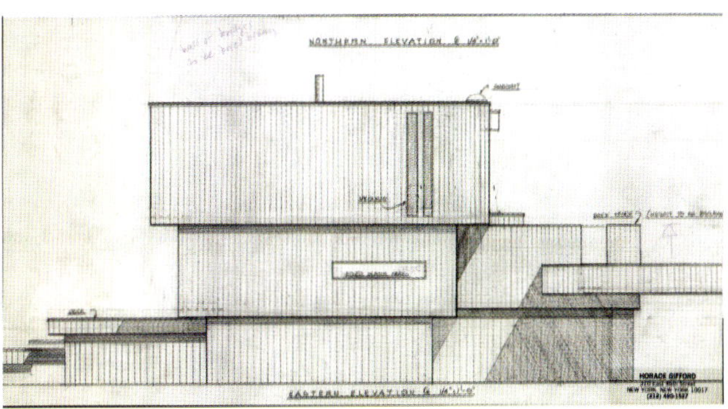

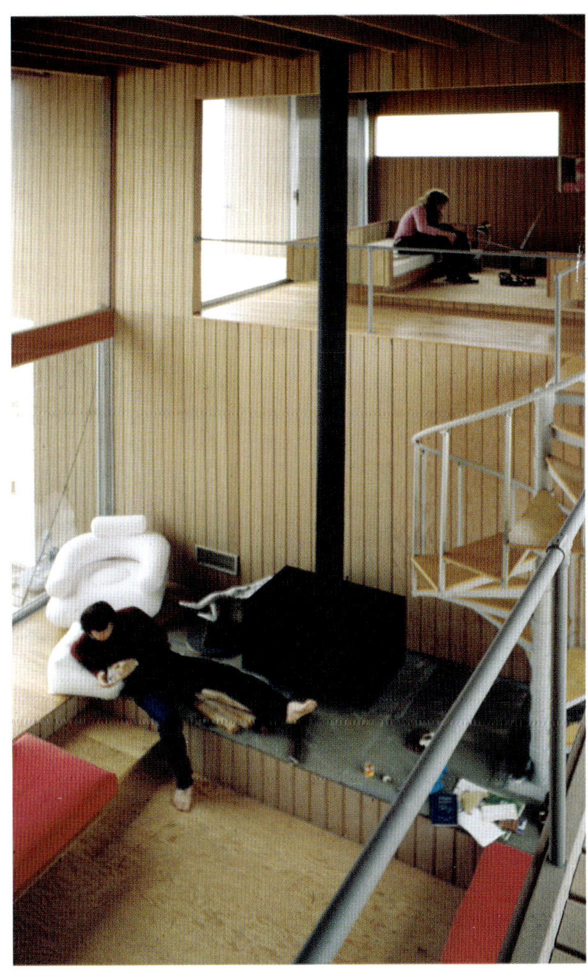

OPPOSITE:
Rubrum House, Fire Island Pines, NY, 1969

TOP:
Rubrum House, approach

ABOVE:
Rubrum House, east elevation drawing

RIGHT:
Rubrum House, interior

A few miles down the beach, in Fair Harbor, Gifford had callers as well. Sam and Joan Scali hired the architect to design a guest house to supplement the spartan bunks of the home Gifford built for them in 1967. Rather than echo the nested cubes of the original structure, he responded with an asymmetrical take on his first pyramid-roofed project. A skylit living area commanded the northwest corner of the site, with rooms poking out as needed to the east and south. Set on a low plinth, with deep overhangs and a *shoji*-like arrangement of glass doors, this home was aptly nicknamed the "Japanese house" by neighbors.

Westhampton Beach, another barrier island directly east of Gifford's usual terrain, resembled Fire Island in many respects, except it allowed cars and was traversed by a two-lane road. Here, the architect found a new client, textile executive Alfred Pilson, and he also explored new geometries. The Pilson residence was sited on a dune, and its most striking features were its "bell-bottom" shading devices, unique in Gifford's oeuvre. Fragmented octagonal decks filled the voids between bedrooms that were expressed as individual forms. A baroque dance of stairs twisted and turned to reach the decks. A bridge supported by telephone poles and punctuated by a waterside perch delivered its occupants to the beach. At first glance, the cacophonous plan seemed to be a break with beach houses past, but there was an underlying order behind the pyrotechnics.

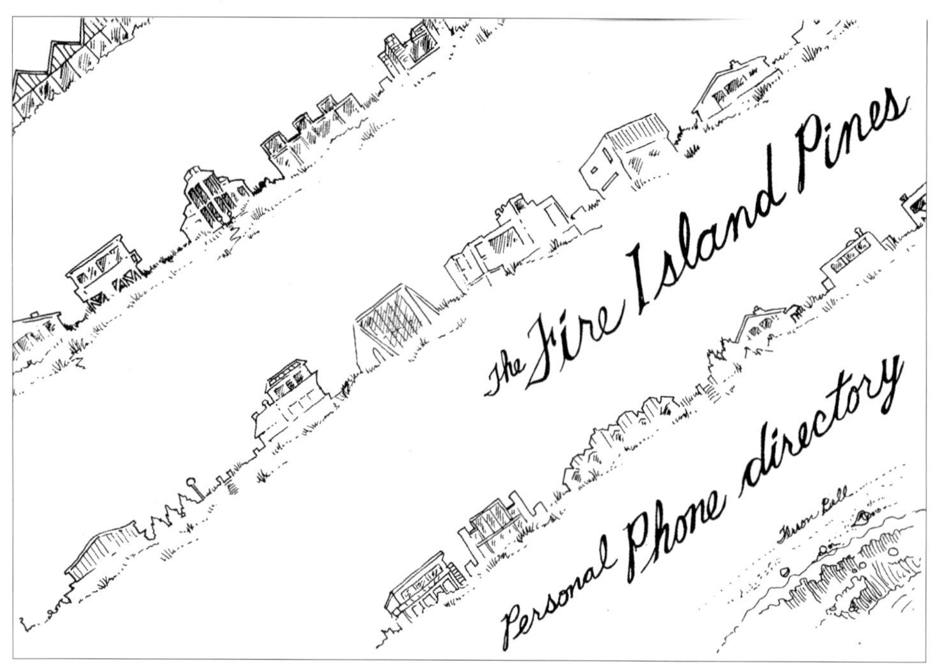

LEFT:
***Fire Island Pines Personal Phone Directory*, cover by Ferron Bell, 1970s**

OPPOSITE, ABOVE:
Men of the Pines, 1968

OPPOSITE, BELOW:
Cartoon by Rick Fiala, ca. 1979

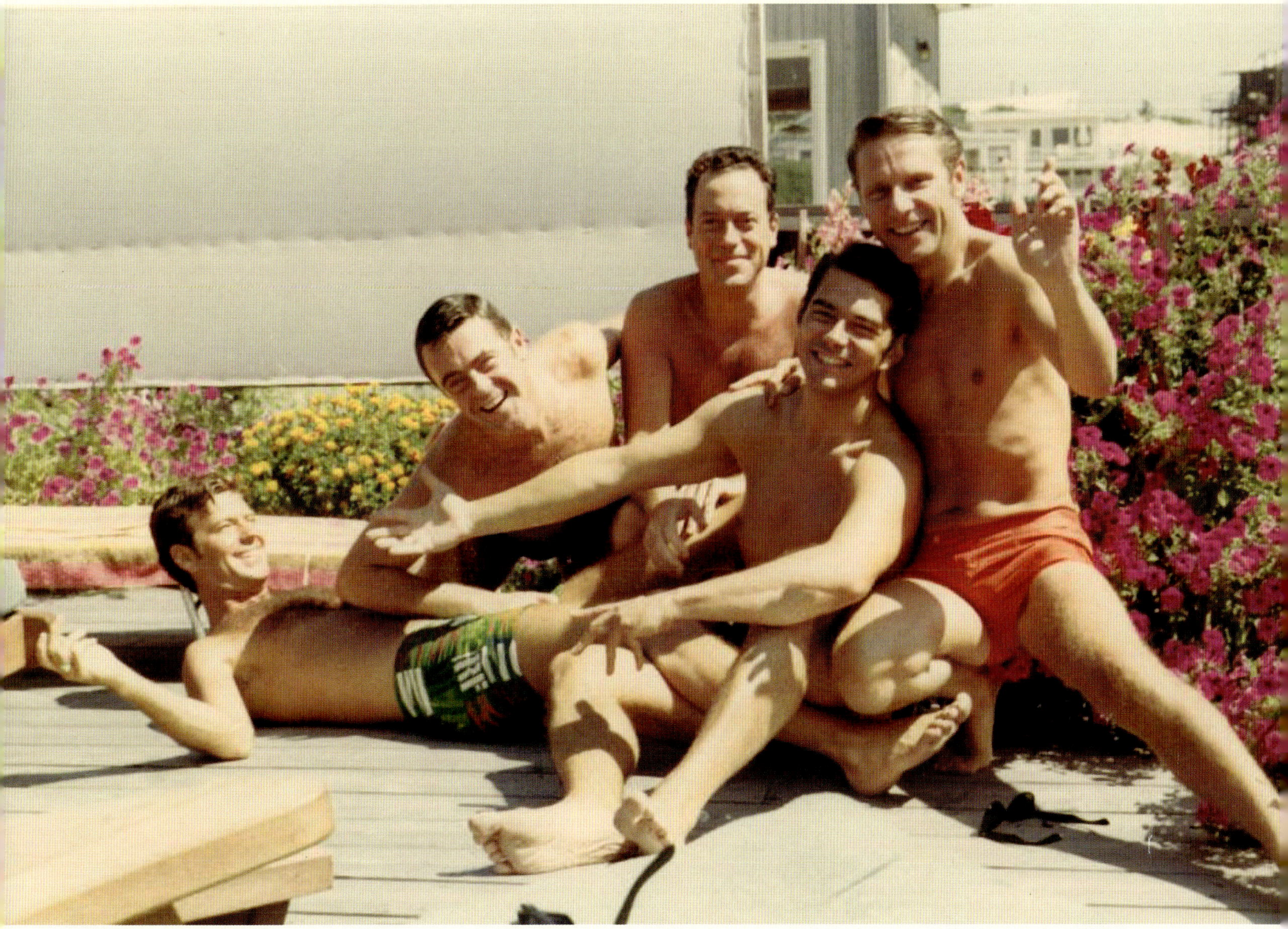

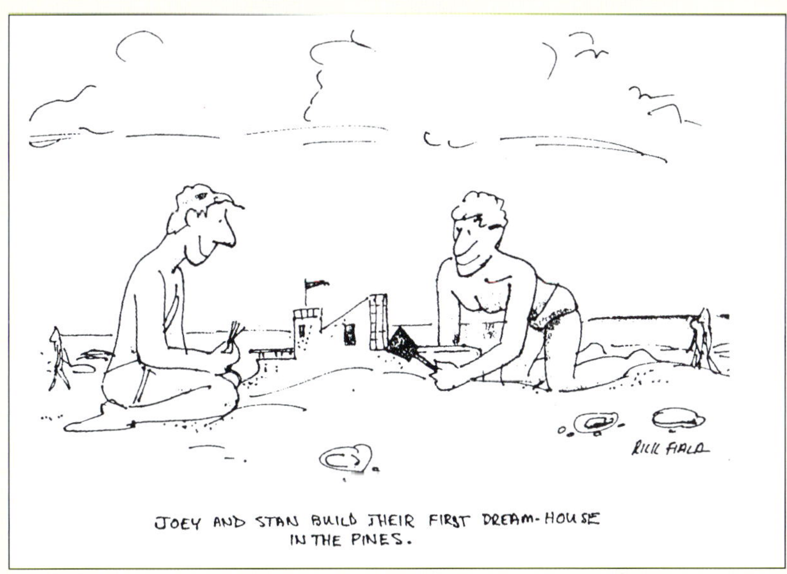

JOEY AND STAN BUILD THEIR FIRST DREAM-HOUSE IN THE PINES.

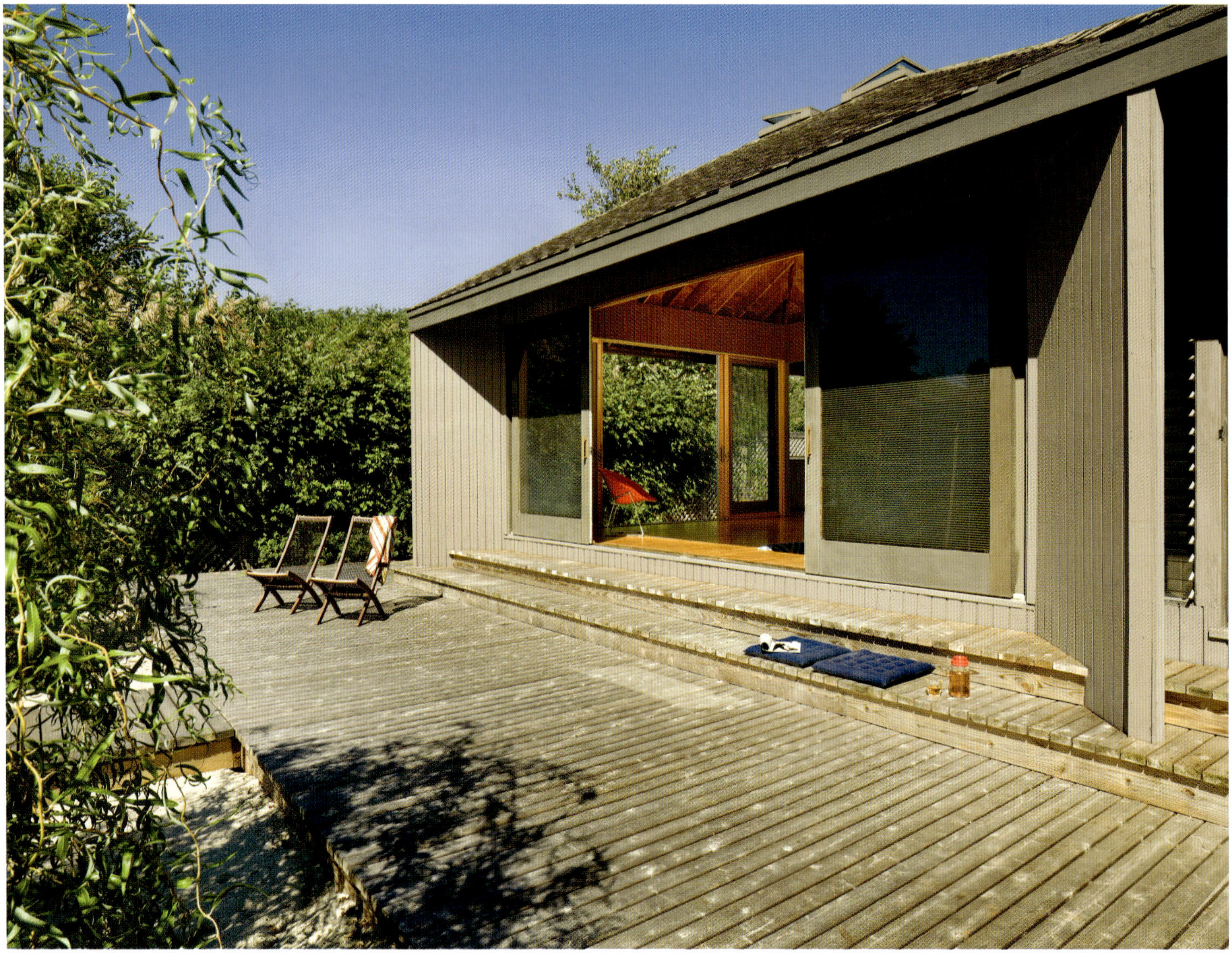

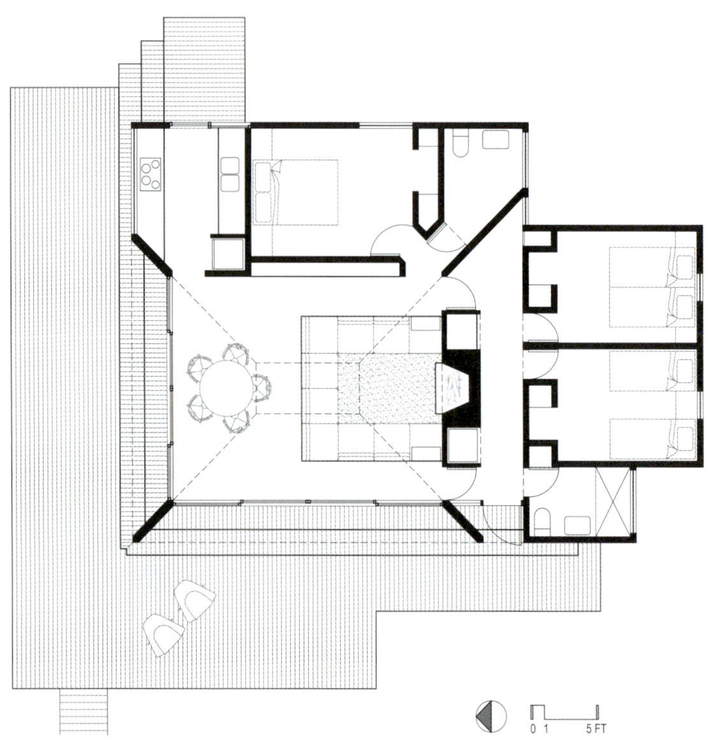

ABOVE:

Scali Guest House, Fair Harbor, NY, 1976

LEFT:

Scali Guest House, floor plan

OPPOSITE:

Scali Guest House, living room with conversation pit

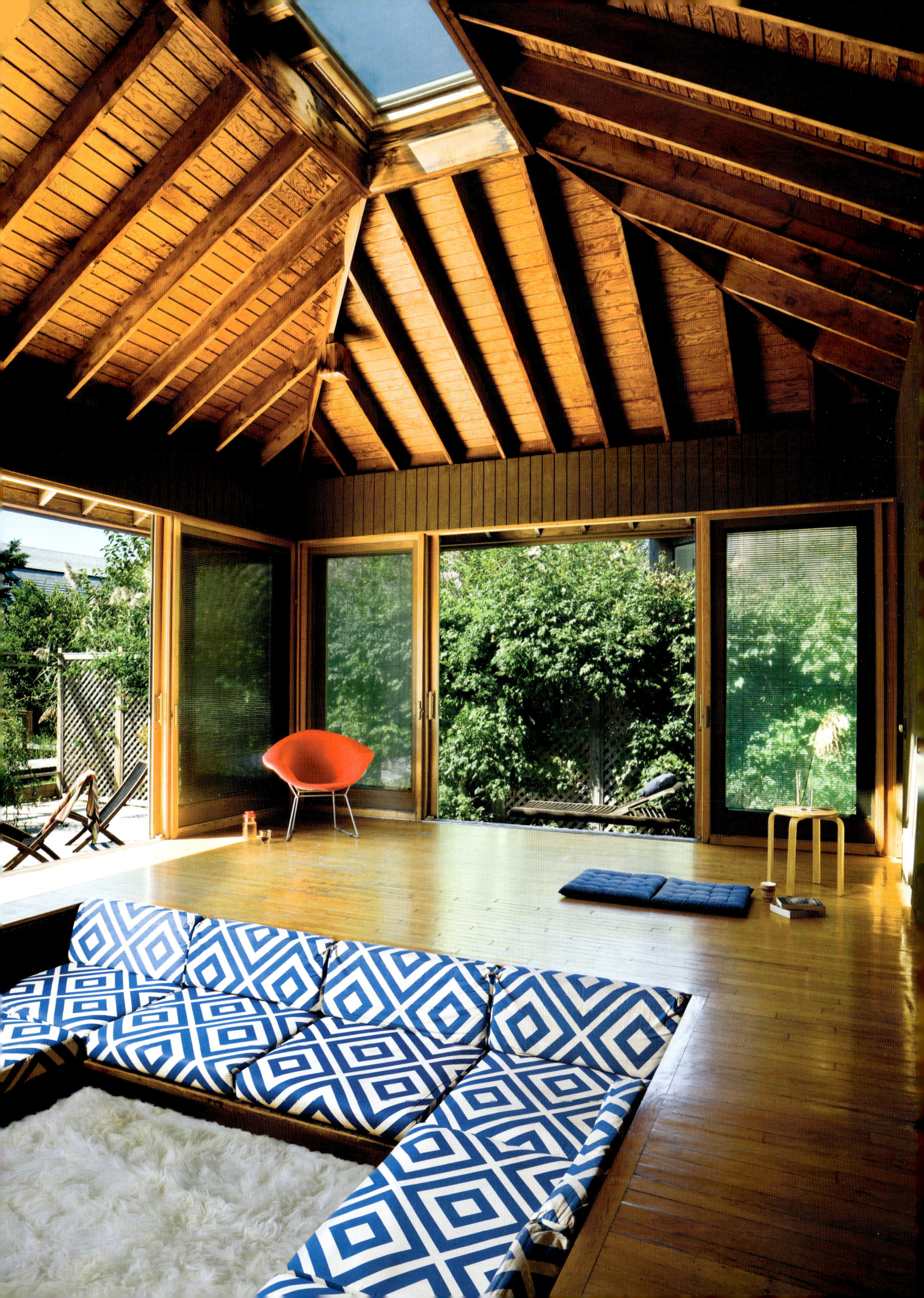

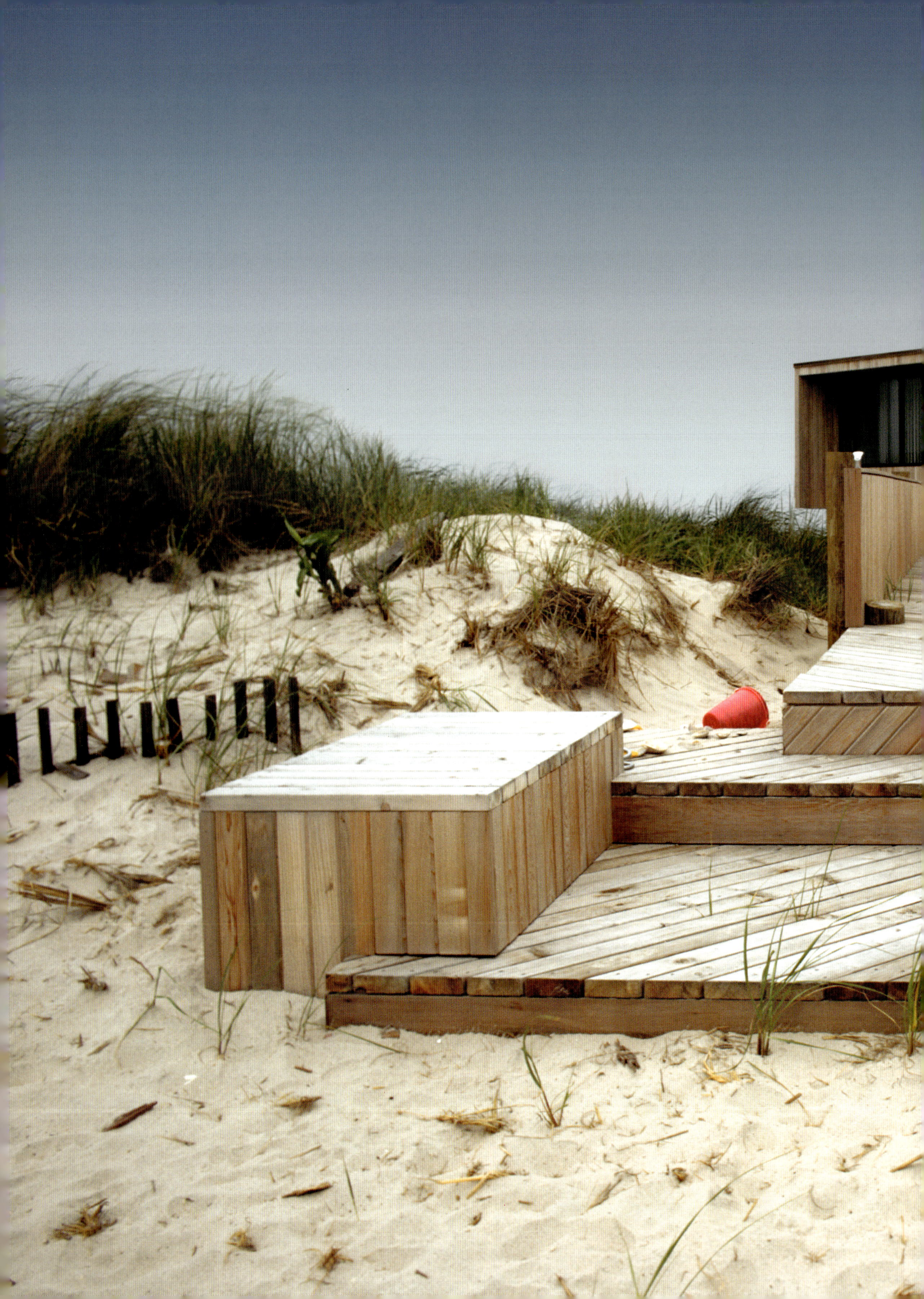

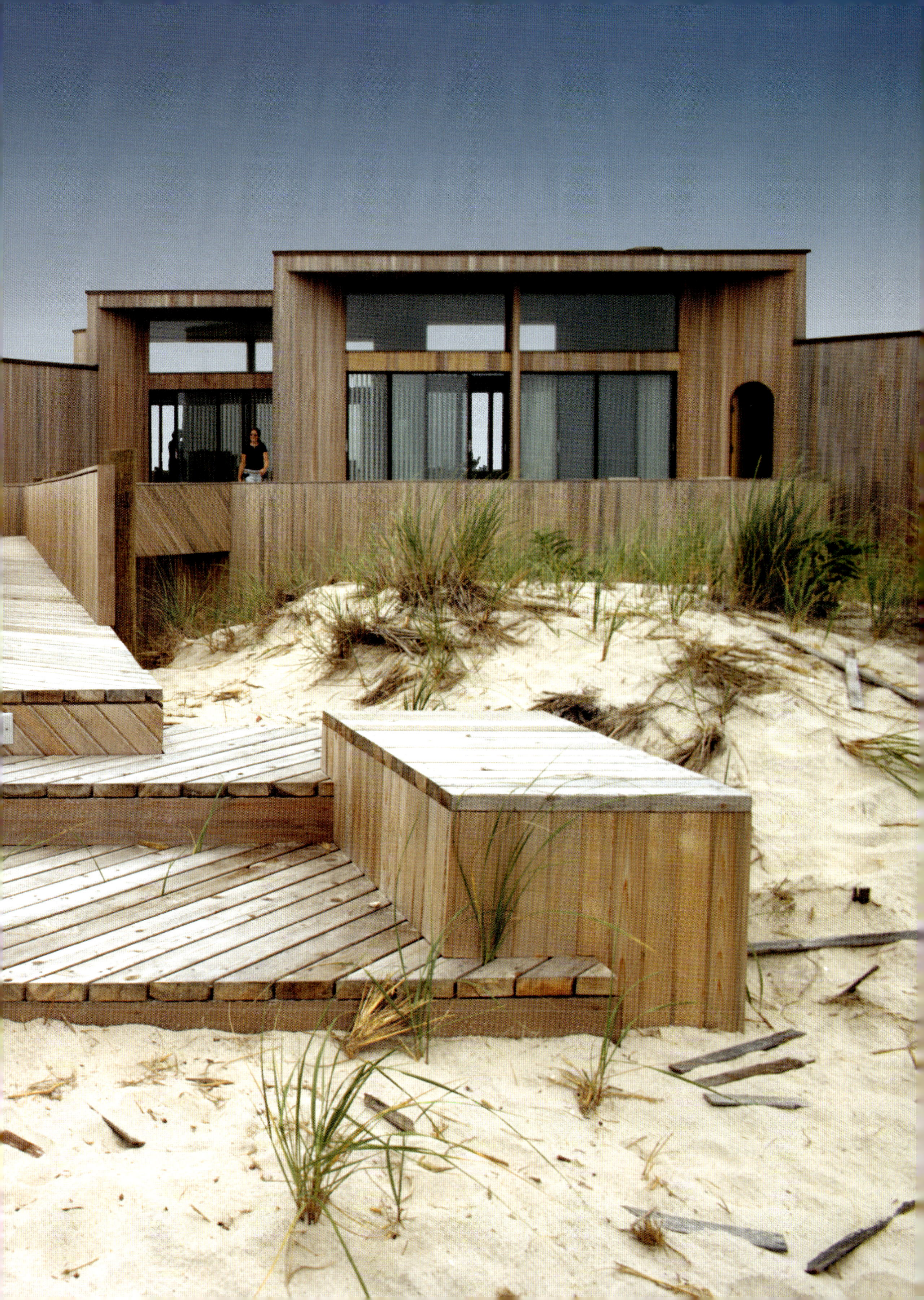

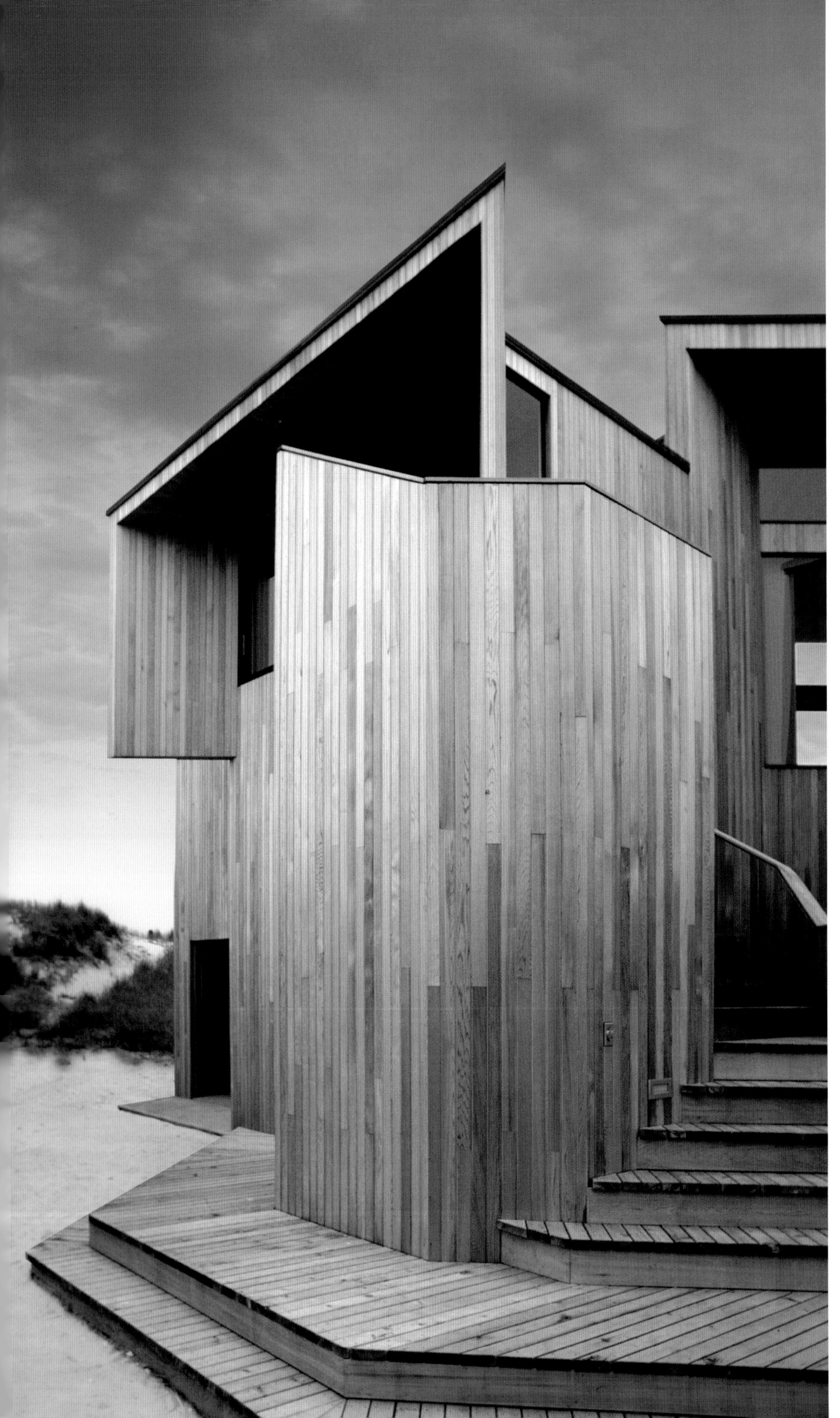

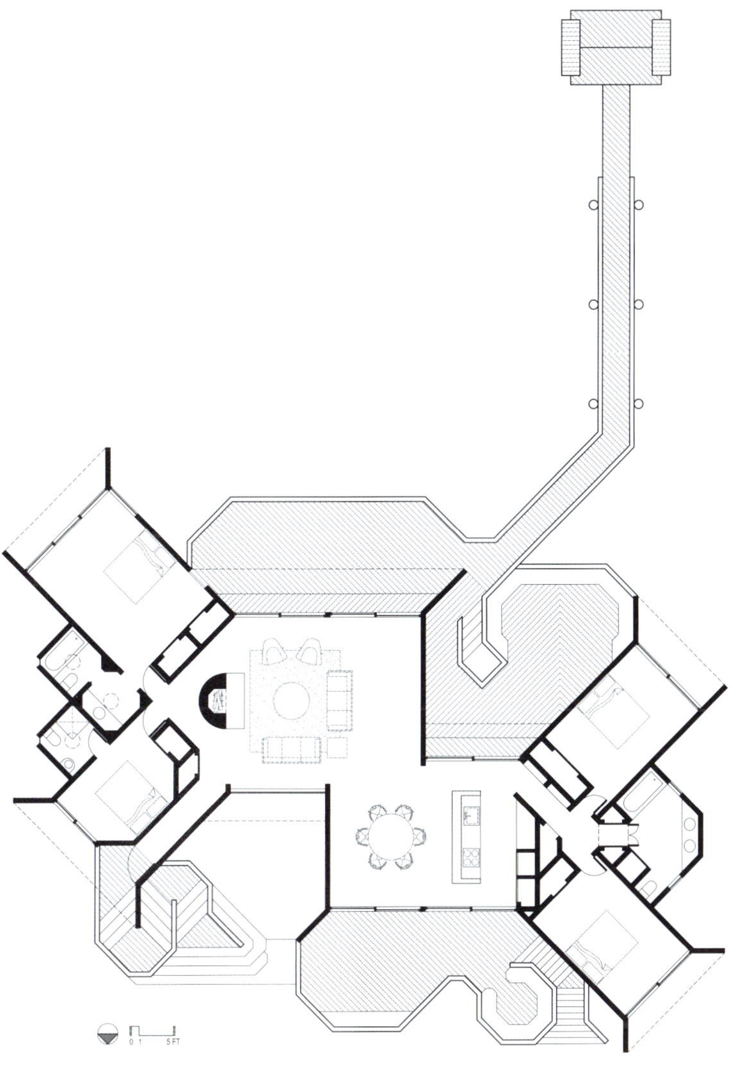

Much like Gifford's earliest work, the house consisted of a glassy central living space flanked by enclosed bedroom wings. But the public space was sheared down the middle, creating distinctive enclosures for the kitchen, dining room, and living area. Its enlarged scale, combined with expensive touches like a round fireplace rendered in stone, foretold a new era for the Long Island beach house.

The complexity of the Pilson residence diagrammed the changing face of the Hamptons in the 1970s. Once, it was a place for city dwellers to get away from it all, but its days as an idyllic setting for tiny houses on large lots were numbered. Entrepeneurial types found East End golf courses and garden parties to be genial settings for approaching captains of industry. Pilson's textile company actually paid for his Gifford beach house as a hub for entertaining clients. Its attention-getting forms and spaces spoke to a new cultural landscape that was less about relaxation and more about cutting deals. The minimalist grammar of modern architecture existed in an uneasy relationship with the language of money and the objects that prove its existence. The Pilson residence revealed Gifford trying to bridge that gap.

In contrast to the Hamptons, Gifford's base in Fire Island Pines remained a sphere of pleasure rather than business. Yet its obsessive pursuit of nirvana, aided by drugs and emboldened by changing mores, made the Pines no less ambitious, in its way, than the Hamptons. The community once served as a cover for discreet homosexuals. In the heady era of gay liberation, the Pines threw open its closets and turned to Horace Gifford to capture the full-blown hedonism of this cultural moment.

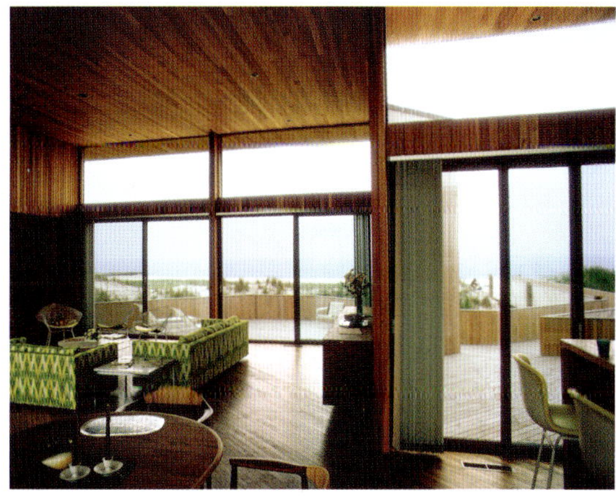

PAGES 160–61
Pilson House, Westhampton Beach, NY, 1971, ocean side

OPPOSITE:
Pilson House

ABOVE:
Pilson House, floor plan

RIGHT:
Pilson House, living room

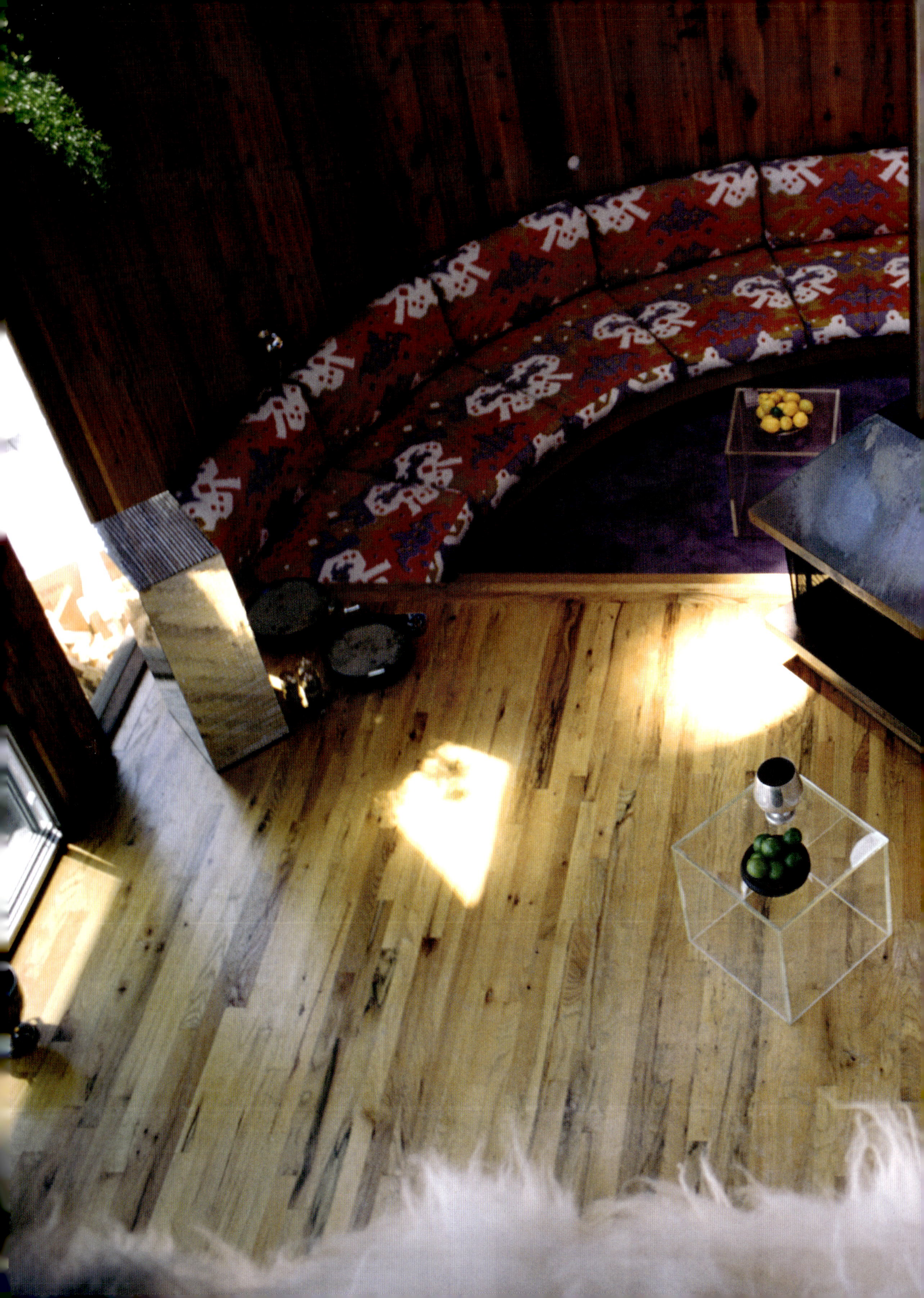

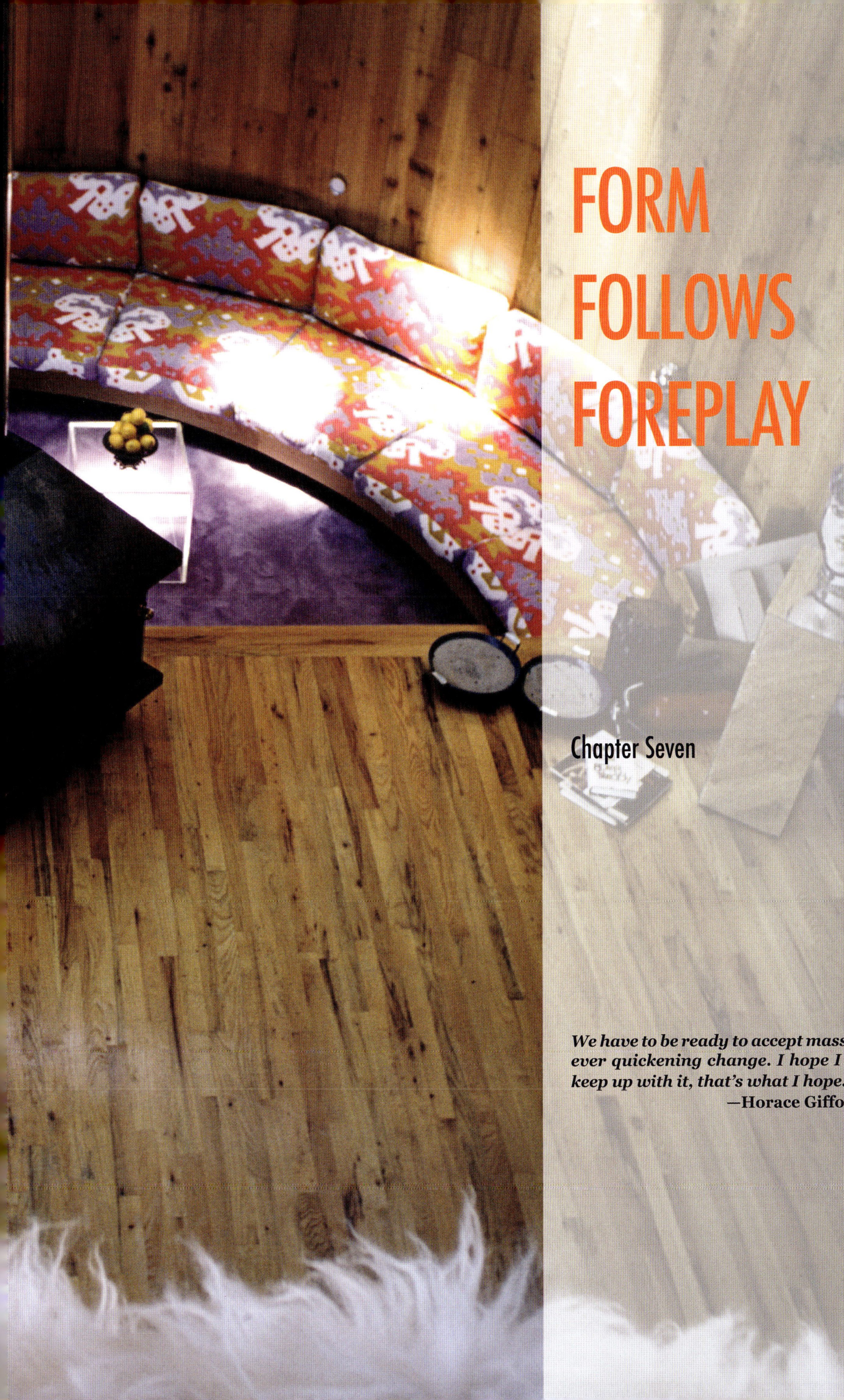

FORM FOLLOWS FOREPLAY

Chapter Seven

We have to be ready to accept massive, ever quickening change. I hope I can keep up with it, that's what I hope.
—Horace Gifford[101]

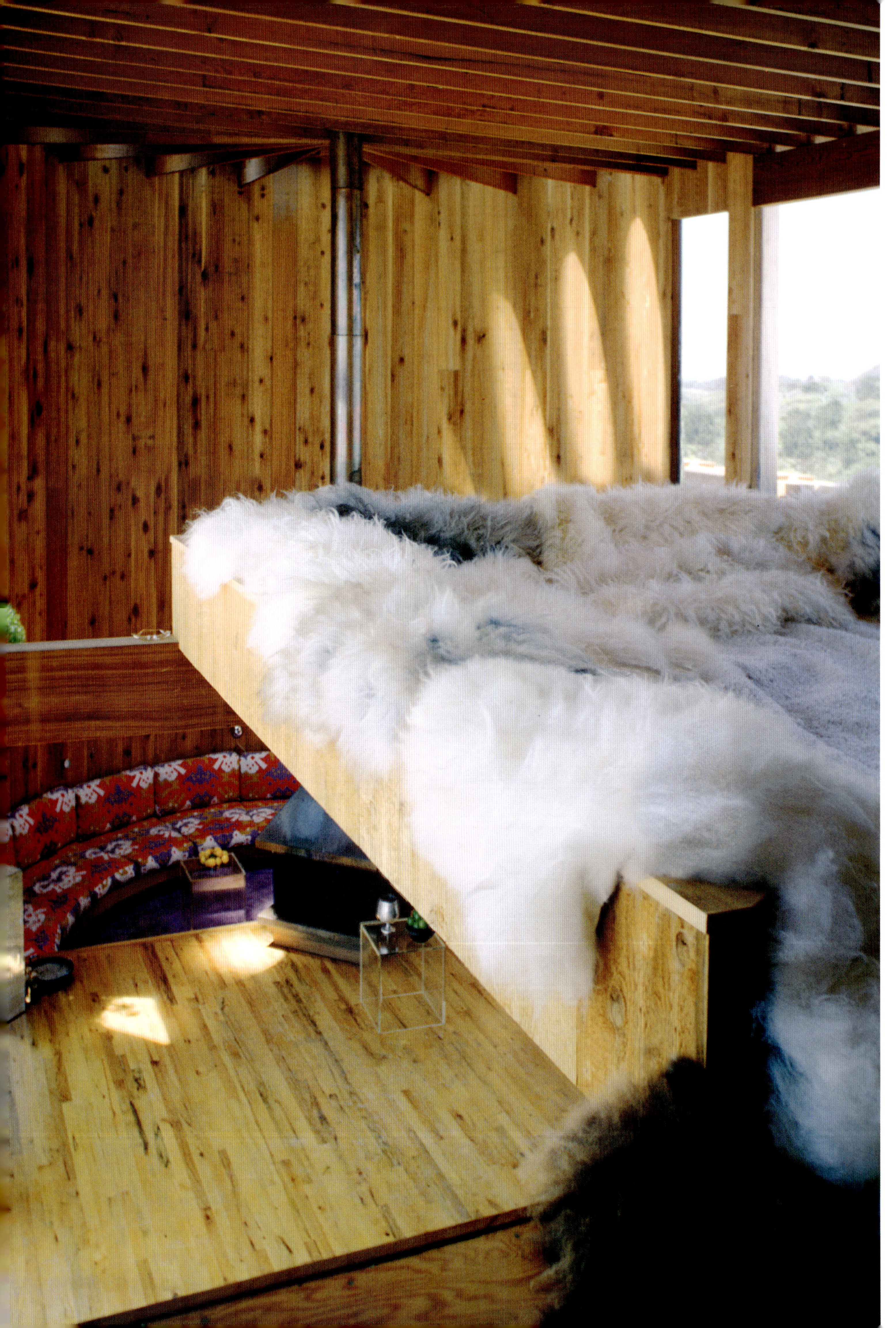

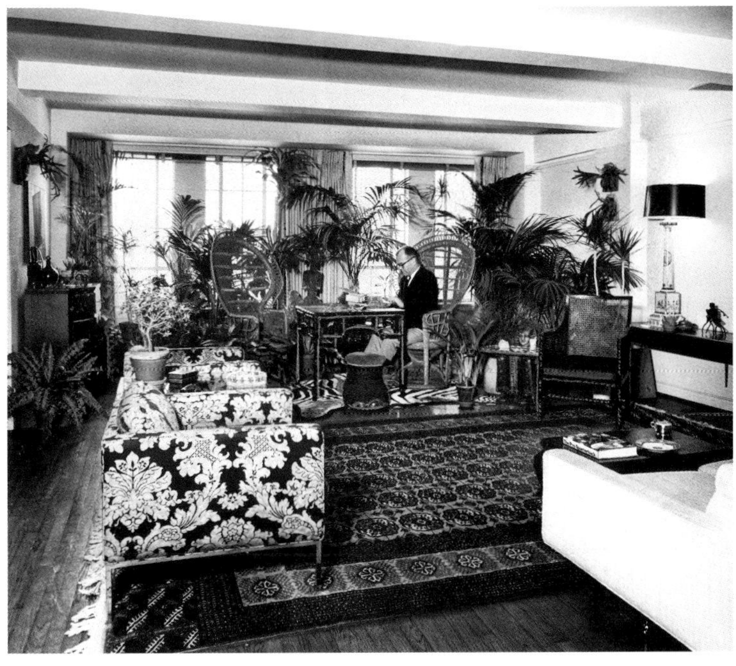

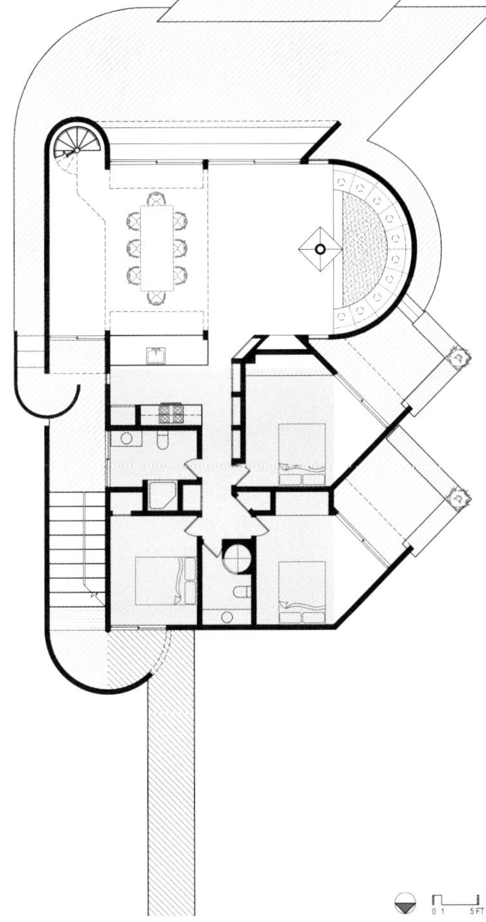

PAGES 164–65:
Roeder House, Fire Island Pines, NY, 1969, view of the maxicouch from the make-out loft

OPPOSITE:
Roeder House, fur-lined make-out loft

ABOVE:
Stuart Roeder in his Manhattan apartment, 1967

RIGHT:
Roeder House, floor plan

Nine months before the Stonewall Rebellion of June 1969, the police raids on the Meat Rack cruising zone ceased when a newly emboldened population fought back. For Fire Island, the Summer of Love had finally arrived. But a fight that was nominally over sex highlighted a broader emotional and political awakening. Suddenly it was okay, even chic, to be gay, while just a few years earlier self-loathing and cultural ostracism had been the norm. Everything was happening so fast. "We have to be ready to accept massive, ever quickening change," Gifford said. "I hope we can keep up with it. I hope I can keep up with it, that's what I hope."[102] This cascade of changes coincided with the mainstreaming of marijuana, acid, and a shower of colored pills, unleashing sensations that couldn't help but influence architecture. Light broke into kaleidoscopic fragments. Space melted. Under the influence, people no longer sat, they lounged. In 1970, an enterprising bar owner in Cherry Grove figured out how to make his lights flicker to the beat of the music, a device instantly copied by John Whyte in the Pines.[103] It was the age of disco, and its erotic undulations enacted on the dance floor what had previously gone on behind closed doors and drawn shades. Expressing one's sexual orientation was increasingly something one did in public.

No one embodied the new pulse of the Pines more than Stuart Roeder, who never lacked for friends or lovers. The public relations man for Warner Brothers made it his business to know everyone, and he entertained lavishly. Lunch for forty was a common occurrence, studded with famous film directors and fashion's leading lights. Kenneth (Battelle), the hairdresser who gained first-name fame as a stylist for Jacqueline Kennedy, Marilyn Monroe, and Lauren Bacall, made frequent visits from nearby Water Island. Diane von Fürstenberg showed off her latest wrap dresses, and Geoffrey Beene would make an appearance whenever he could be lured out of his garden. There was no shortage of party favors. During one well-lubricated fete, roasting birds were briefly reanimated when an exploding oven pelted quail over the astonished crowd. Roeder was the Mad Hatter of the Pines: the writer Felice Picano recalled a dinner in which Roeder set the dining room with giant chairs, dishes, and flatware, reducing guests to childlike proportions.

Roeder's home was actually built around an existing cottage, but Gifford sheathed this 1950s box in a dynamic diagonal wrap that gyrated toward the Meat Rack. Form followed foreplay in the "make-out loft."[104] Lined in sheepskin with reclined edges for bodies in repose, this high place for base desires surveyed the ocean and the psychedelic swirl of the conversation pit below.

Sunlight passed through circular skylights onto a curved wall, creating a trippy light show of ovoid shapes. All bedrooms faced the Meat Rack. In 1970, independent filmmaker Peter De Rome released a pornographic short film called *The Fire Island Kids* that was shot almost entirely within the house.[105] Yet the Roeder residence also possessed quieter virtues, including a dining area intimately scaled by the hovering loft above, superb barrel-vaulted acoustics, a great variety of spaces, and intricate plays of light throughout. For a magazine audience, Gifford primly but not inaccurately described the home's rakish geometries as "view lines that tell you where to look from inside. They turn you away from the town side of the house, toward the sea."[106] Outside, Gifford extolled how his design choreographed the entry of Roeder's guests. "They don't walk smack up to the front door as they do at so many cottages out here," he said. "Instead, we're turning people, bringing them in, introducing them to the interesting design forms of this house in a very deliberate way."[107]

The abstract, sculptural gestures of the Roeder residence and subsequent Gifford designs revealed an affinity with the new Brutalist movement shaped by architects like Paul Rudolph and I. M. Pei. But Gifford skillfully channeled the ponderous concrete forms of Brutalism into light and lyrical wooden structures. Dancing across the sand like divinely inspired driftwood, these houses echoed the fluidity of the cultural revolution that they housed.

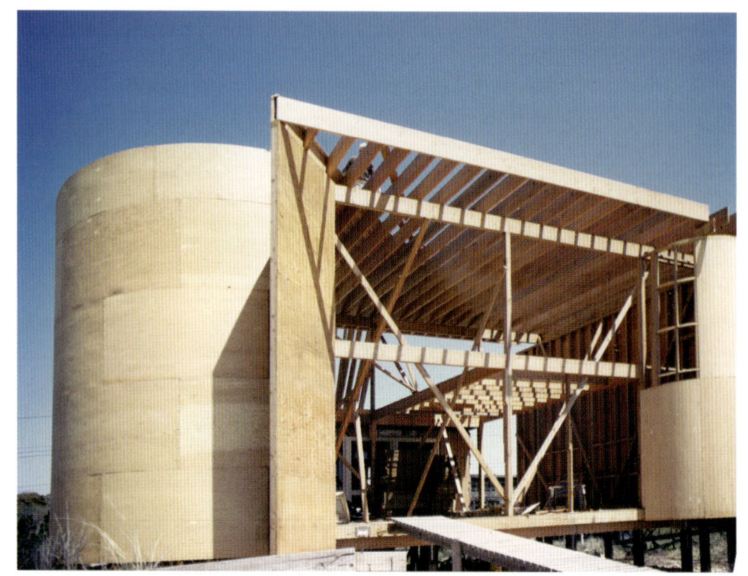

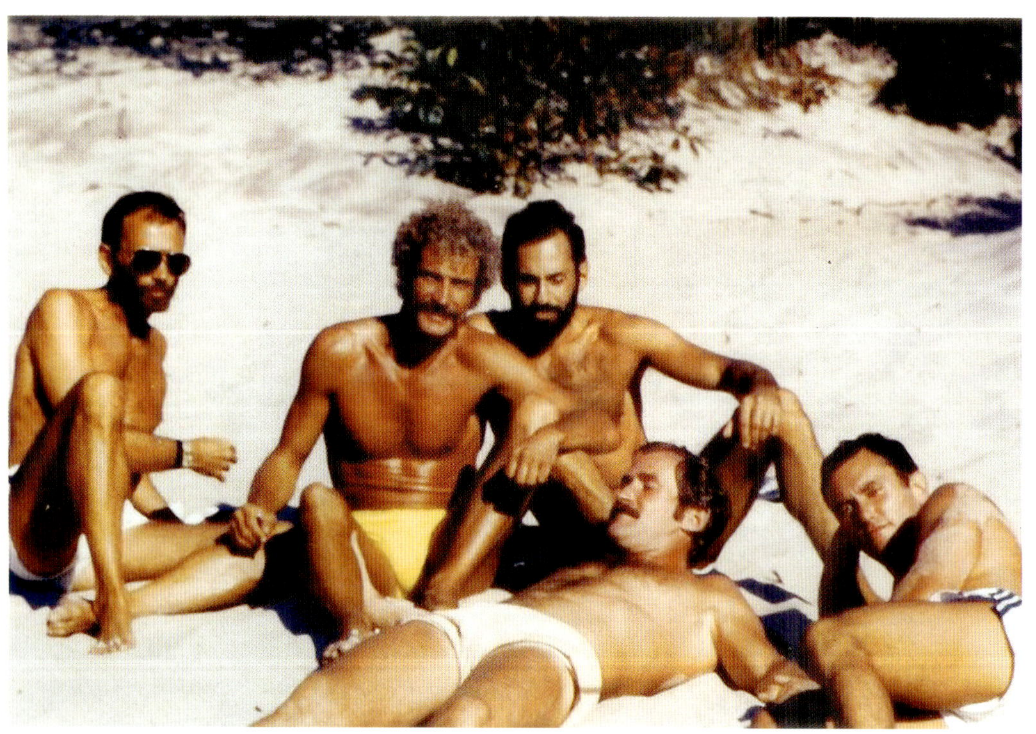

ABOVE:
Roeder House construction

LEFT:
Men of the Pines, 1977

OPPOSITE:
Roeder House

PAGES 170–71:
Roeder House, entry and roof-deck access

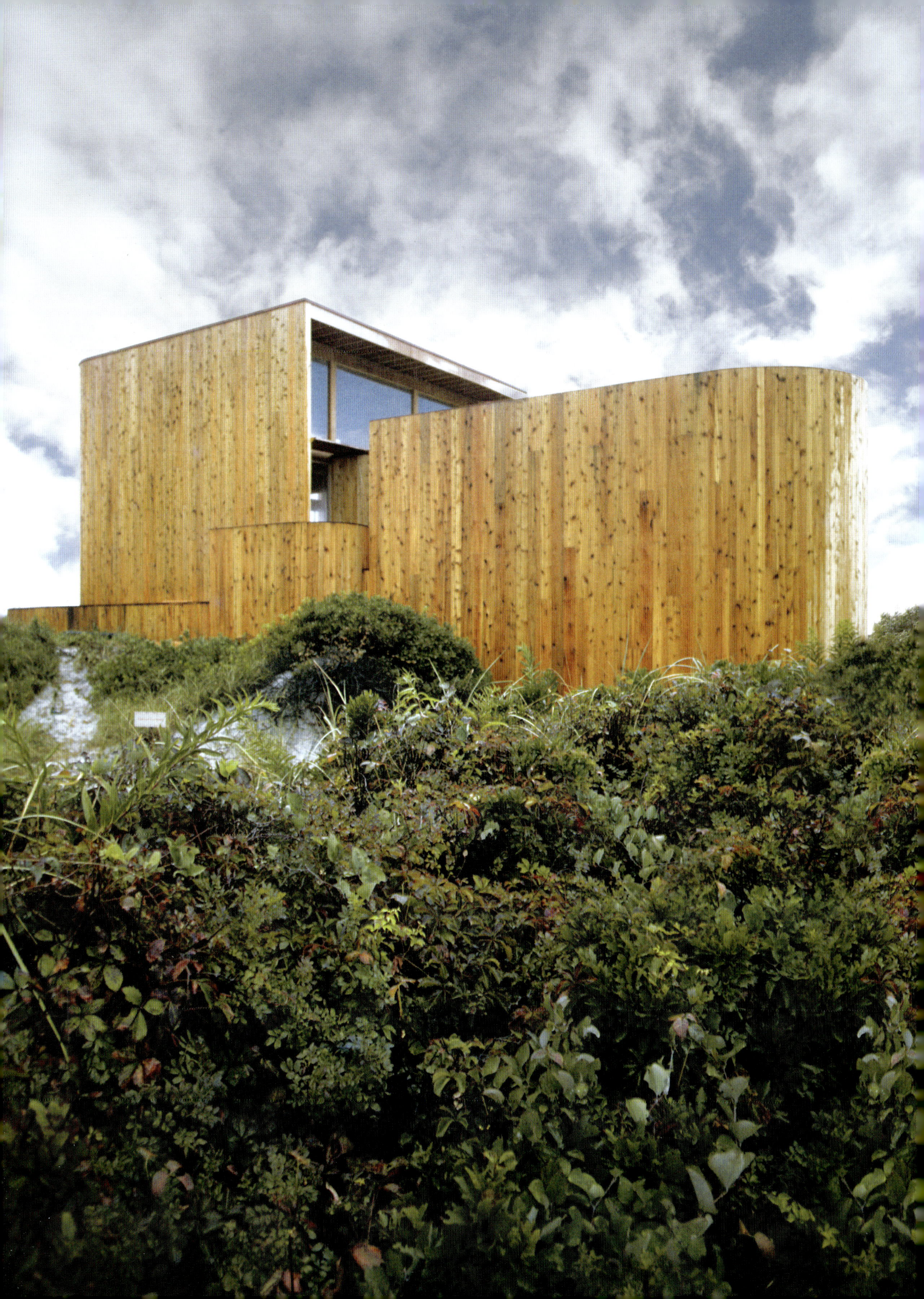

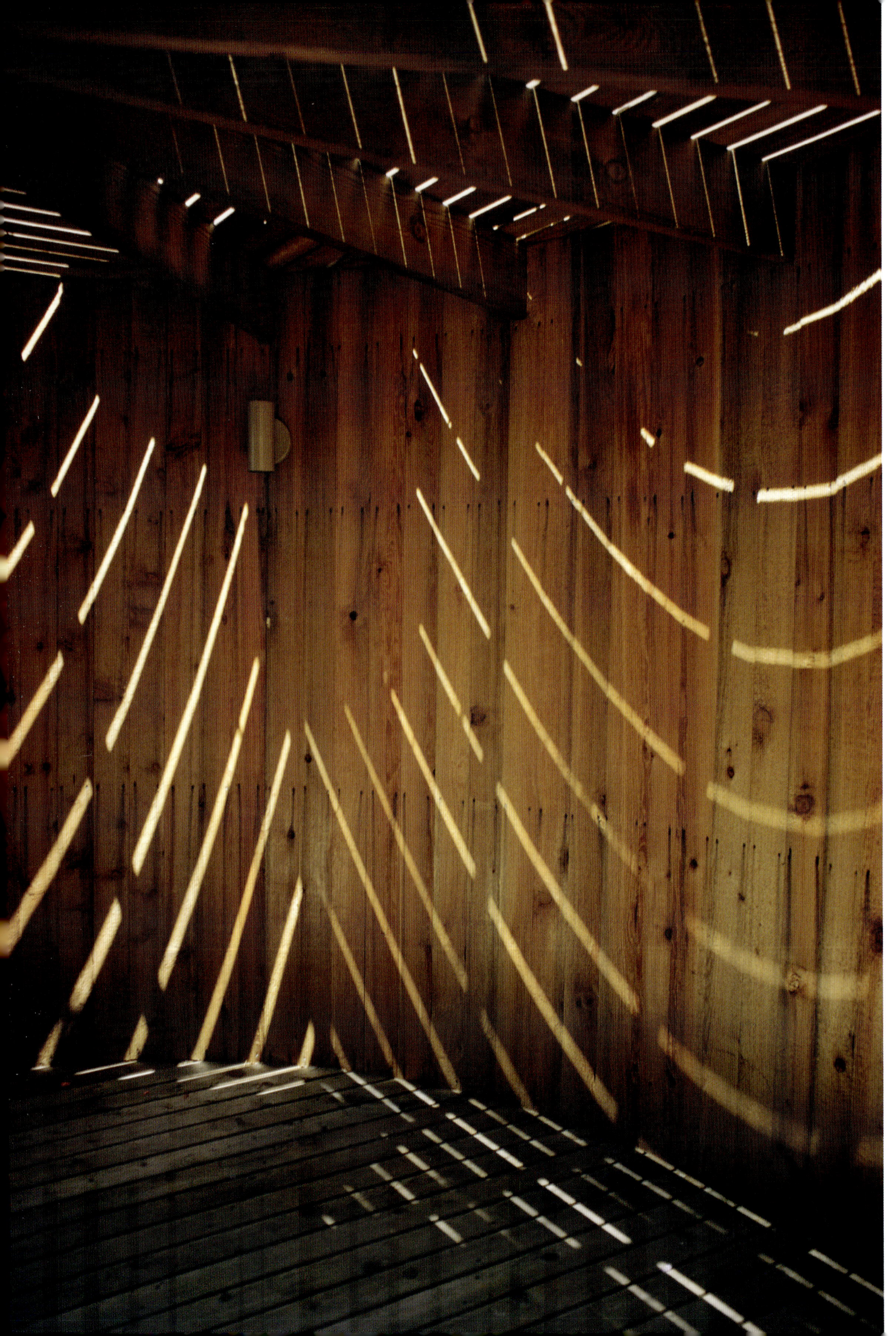

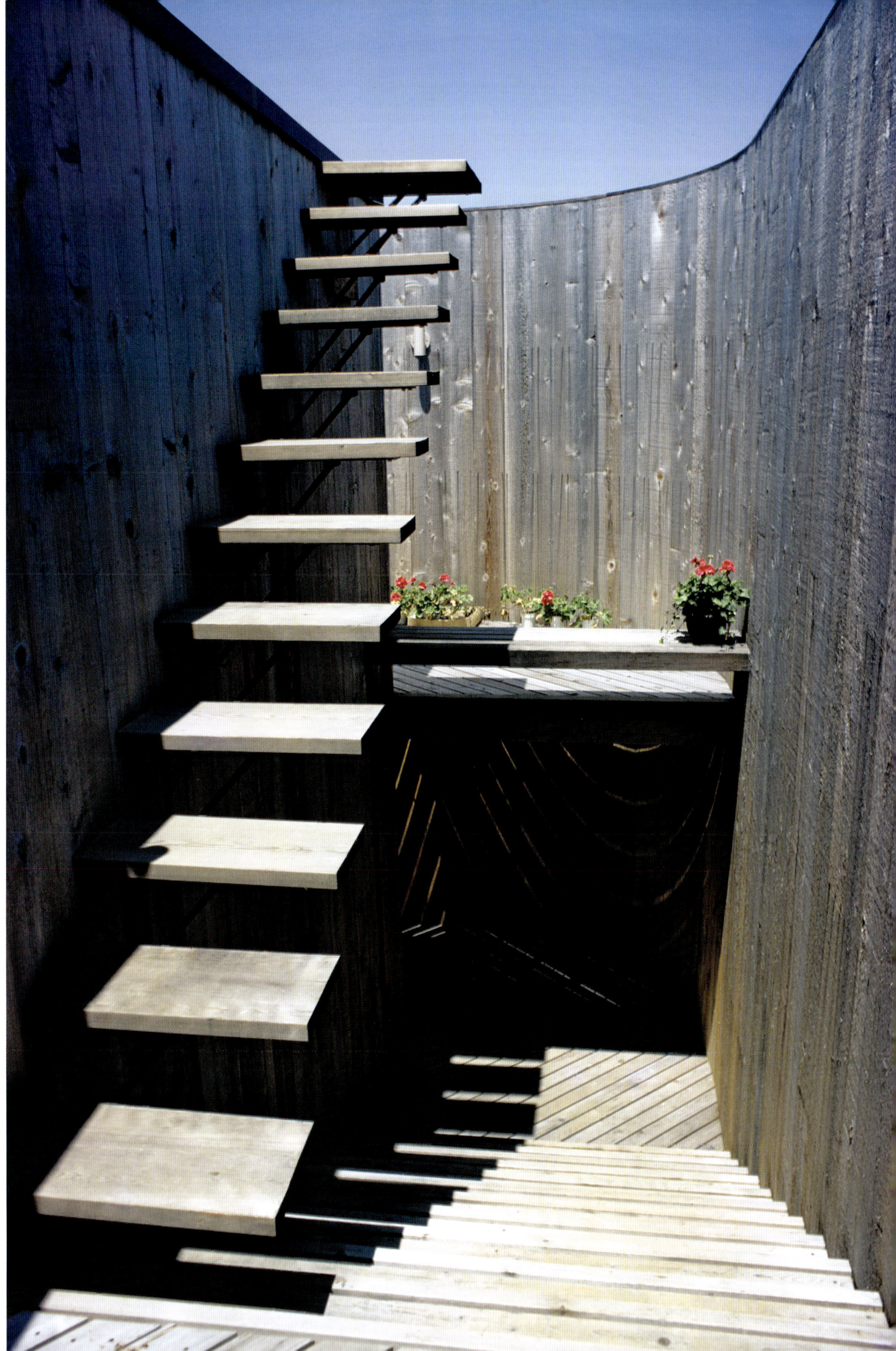

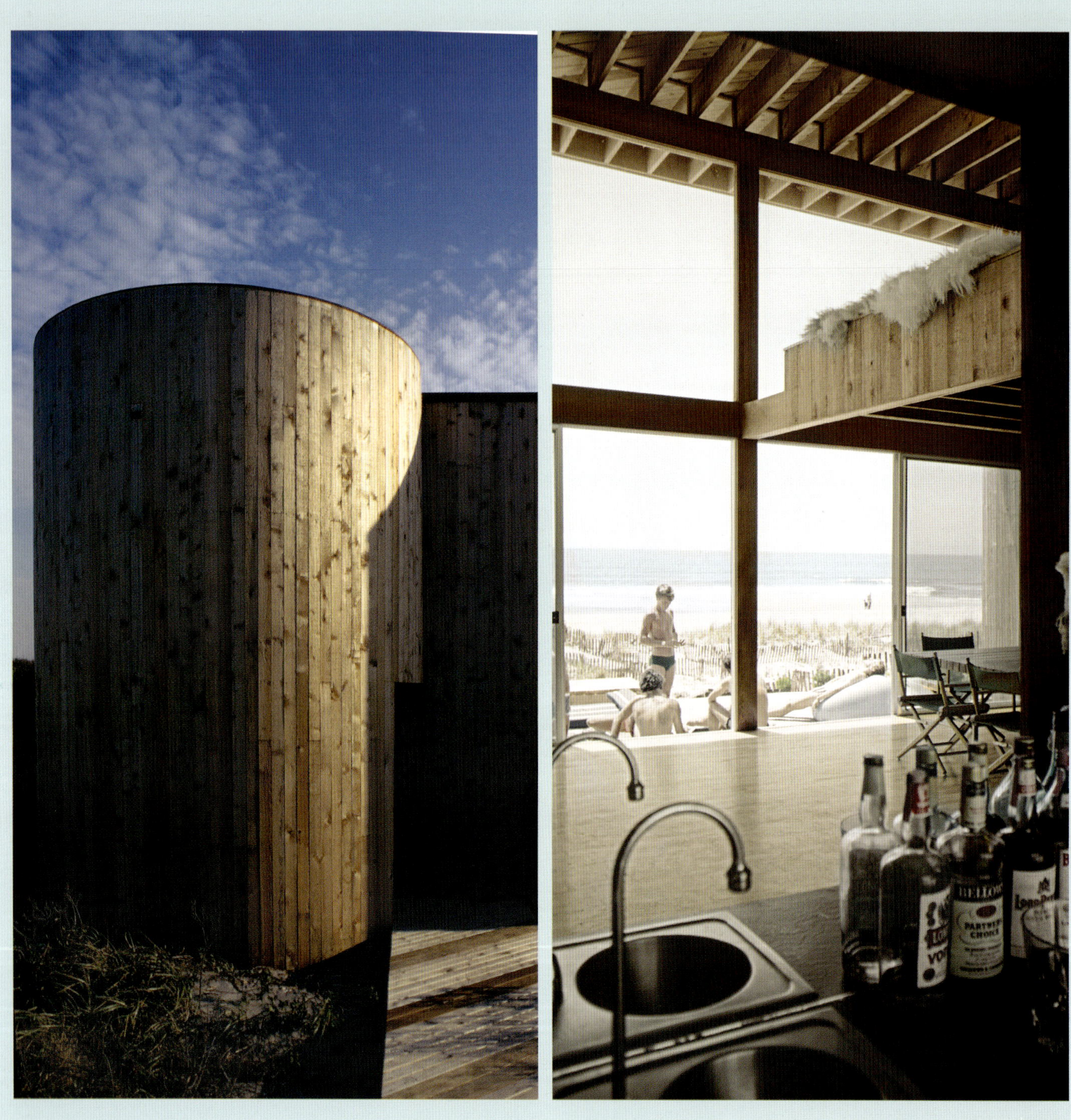

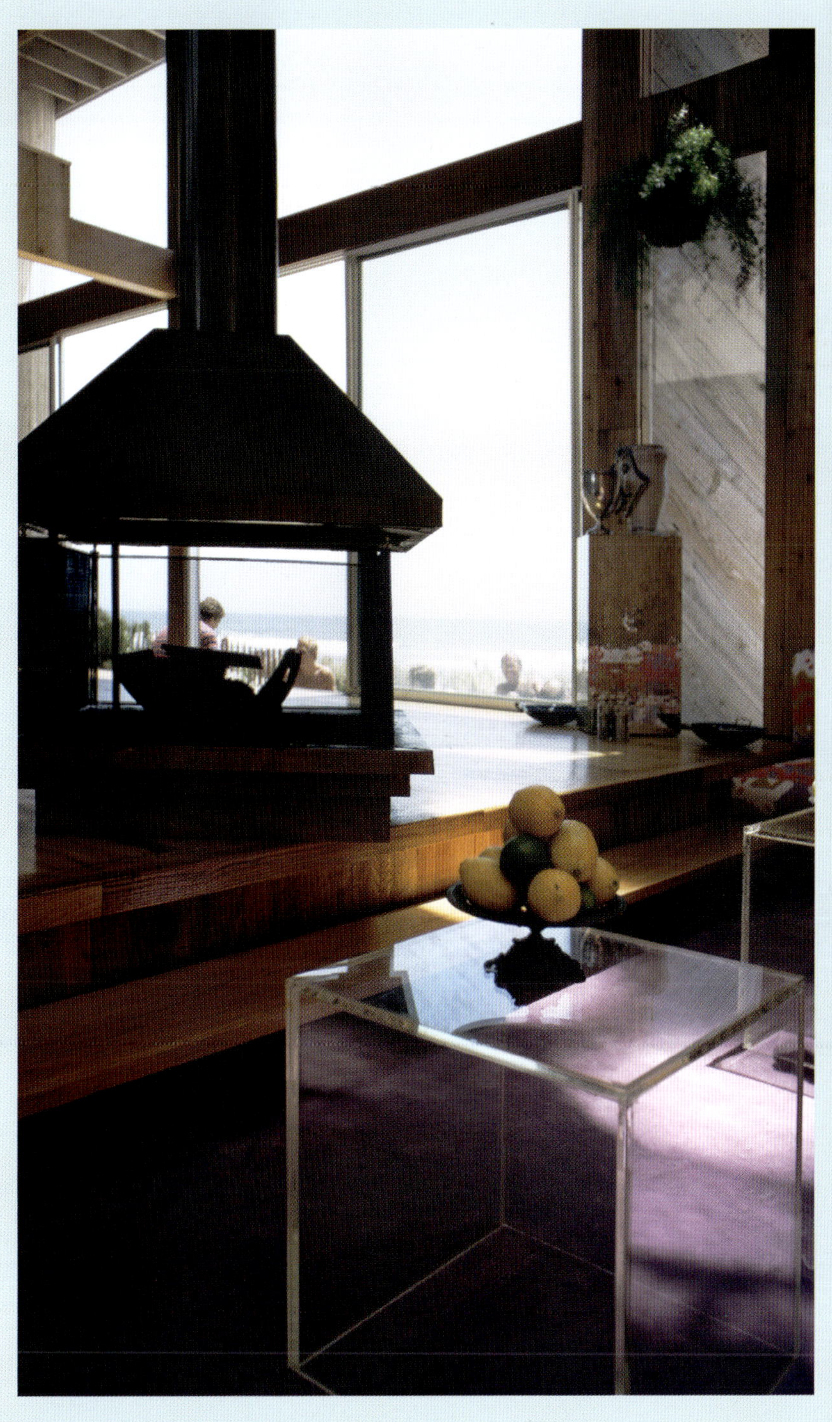
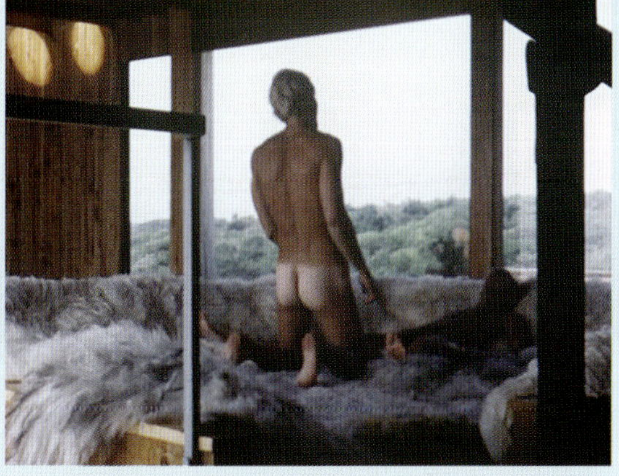
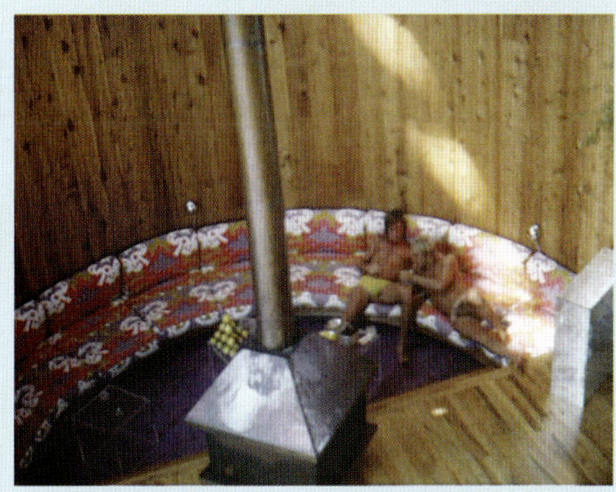
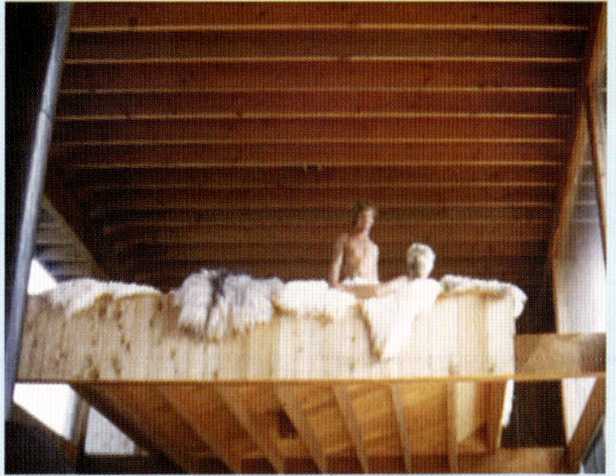
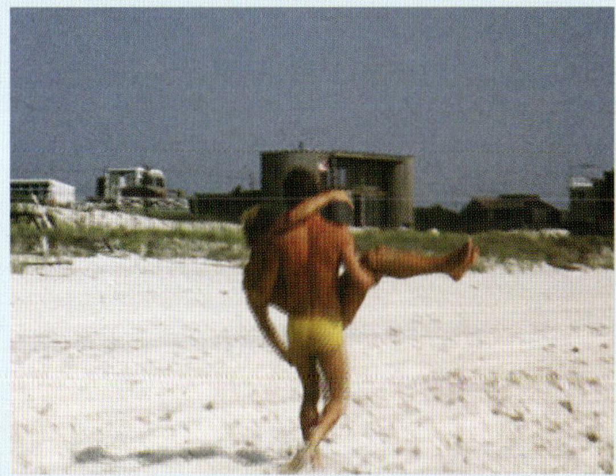

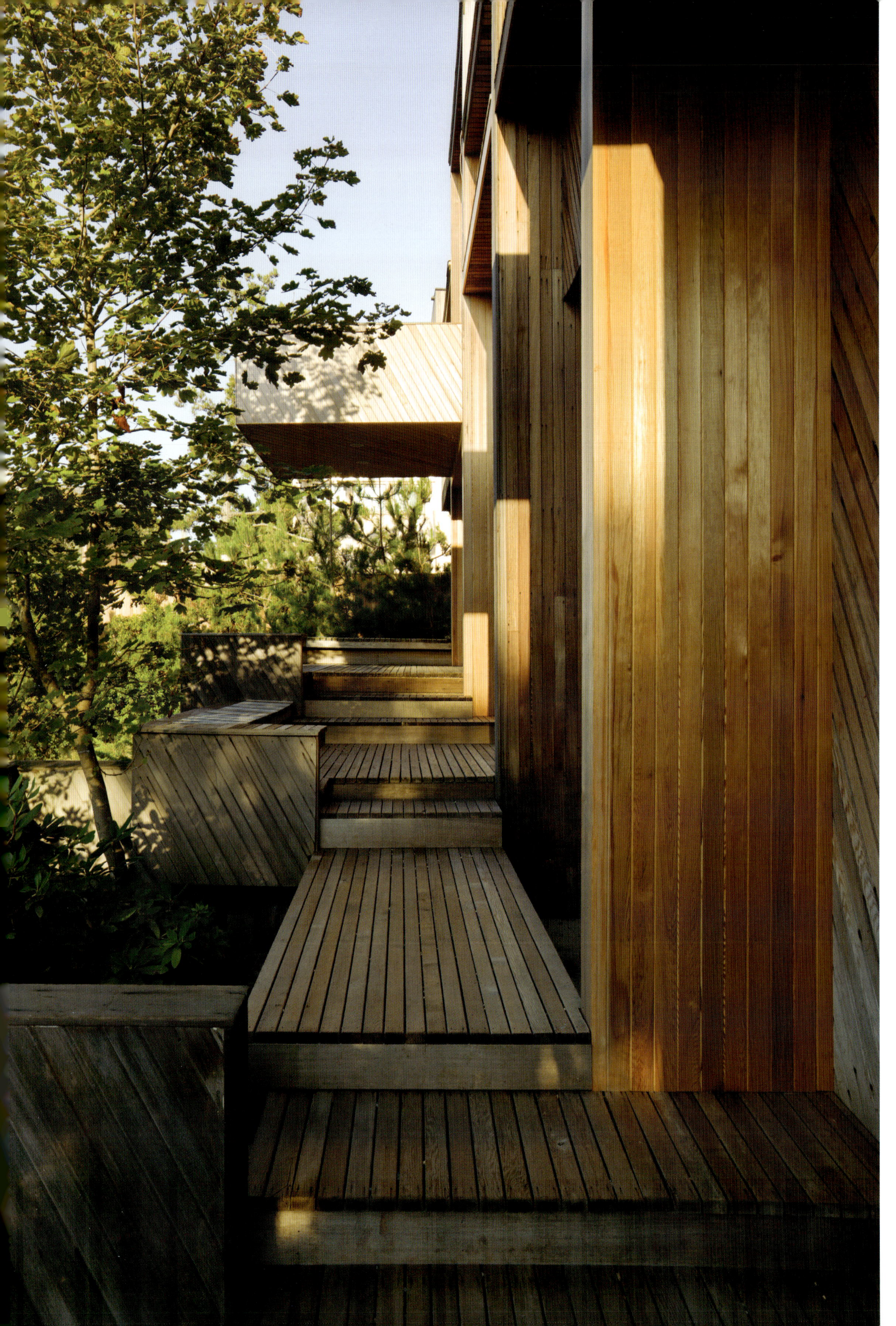

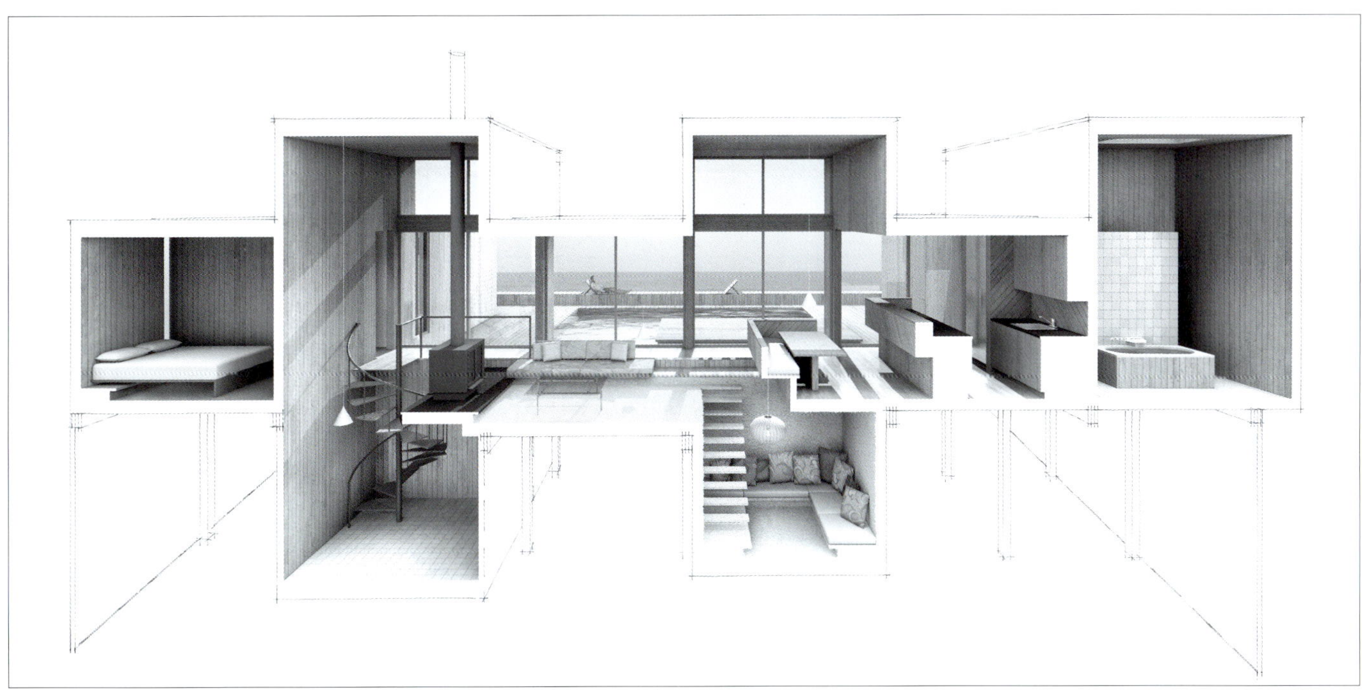

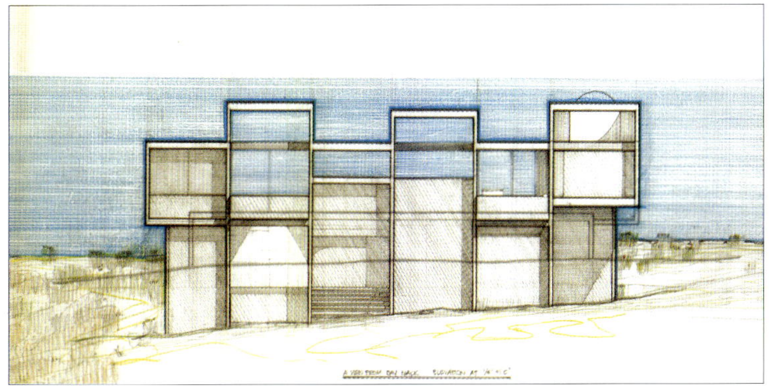

PAGE 172, LEFT:
Roeder House, approach

PAGE 172, RIGHT:
Roeder House, view through bar mirror

PAGE 173, LEFT:
Roeder House, conversation pit

PAGE 173, RIGHT:
Film stills from *Fire Island Kids*, 1970

OPPOSITE:
Lipkins House, Fire Island Pines, NY, 1970, approach

TOP:
Lipkins House, cross-section perspective, by the author

ABOVE:
Lipkins House, elevation drawing

PAGES 176–77:
Lipkins House, front elevation

The Lipkins House conjured a discotheque on the dunes with its pulsating roofline and thrusting cantilevers. All was bared, with floor-to-ceiling glass extending across the entire coastal elevation. Control panels operated a futuristic array of blinking, multicolored lights installed by Broadway Maintenance, the clients' street-lighting company. A sunken living area led down to the "cave," a windowless den of electric blue shag-carpeted walls and oversize pillows. Rechristened the "womb" by its owners, it looked like a sex pit but allegedly functioned as its opposite—a solitary and shadowy retreat from the voyeuristic spaces above.[108]

Six Gifford homes were built in the Fire Island hamlet of Seaview, a historically Jewish enclave. Robert and Gladys Rosenthal were a young, progressive couple—he a doctor, she a genetic researcher—with limited funds but open minds. Gladys had only one requirement: "I didn't want an old house, with all its problems."[109] They had long admired Gifford's nearby Rubin residence, built in 1968 for the founder of Workbench Furniture. Flush with success and eager to head off conflict-laden commissions, Gifford effectively interviewed the Rosenthals, volunteering more than most architects would dare. "You should know two things about me," he told them. "I'm gay, and I'm manic-depressive."[110] He then demanded complete design control, down to the color of the sofa cushions.

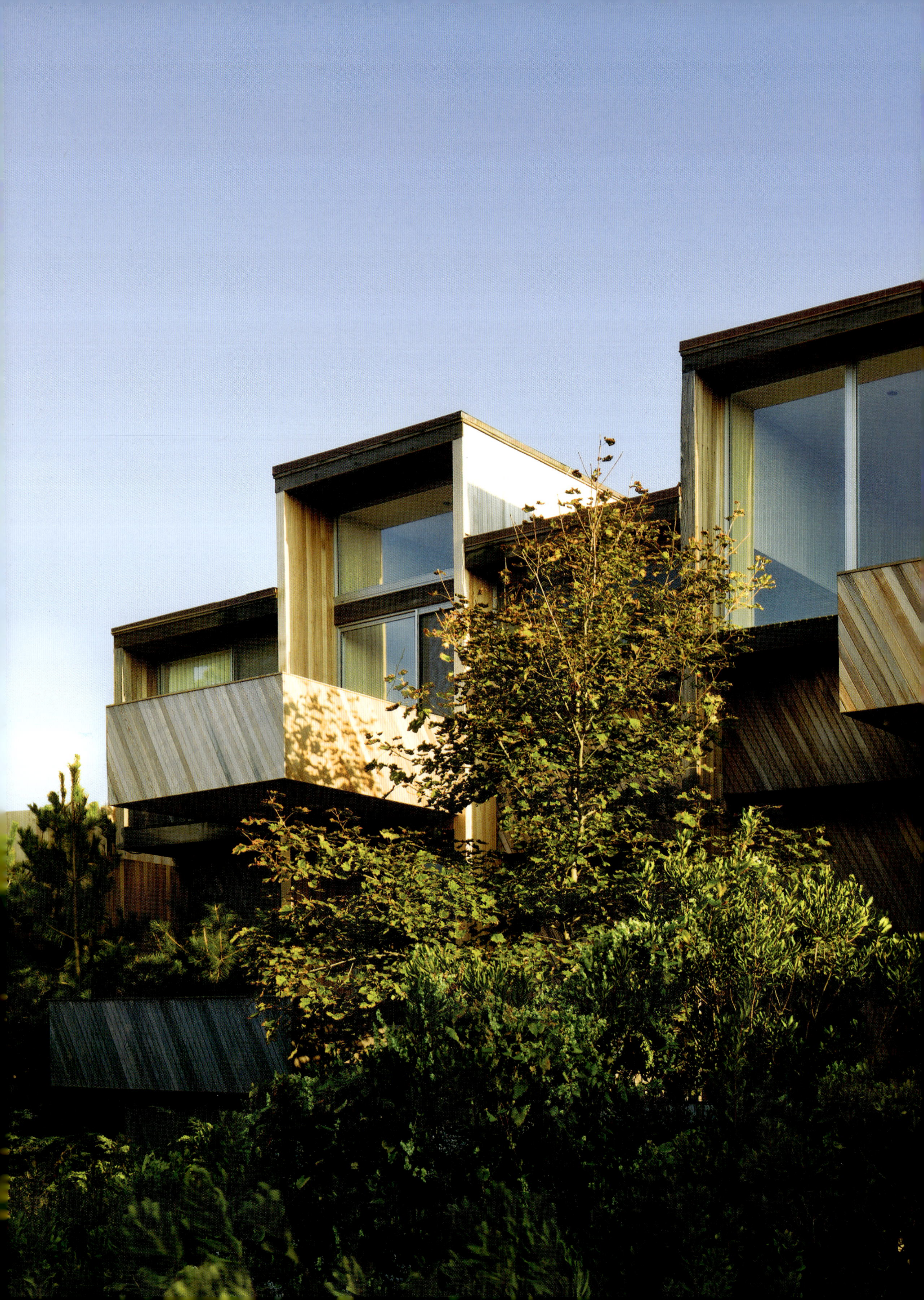

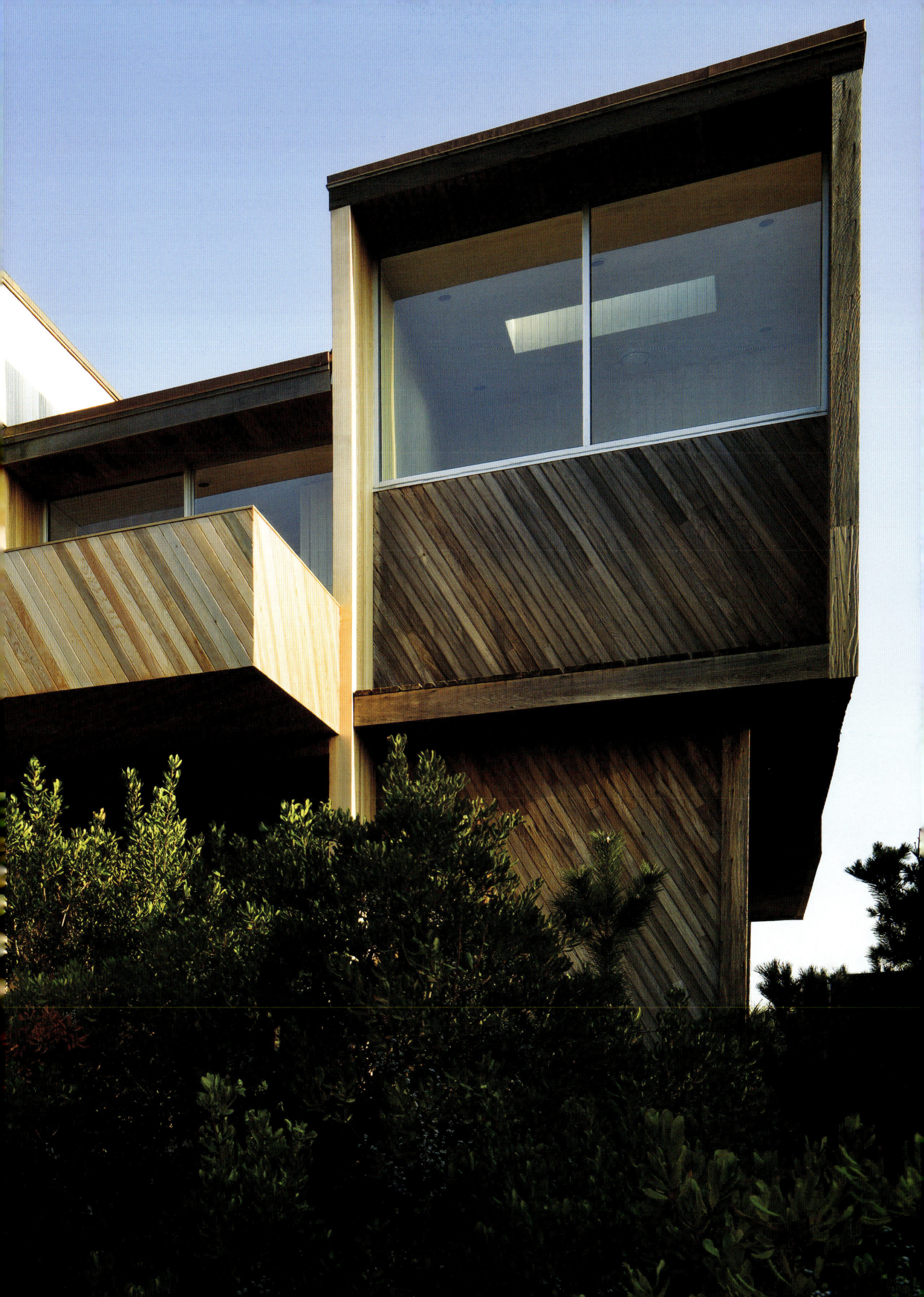

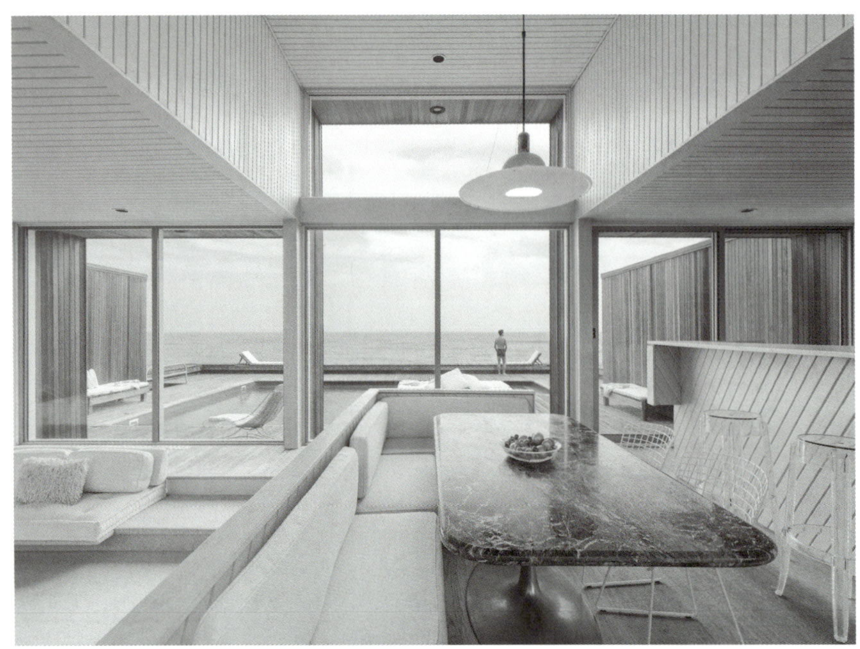

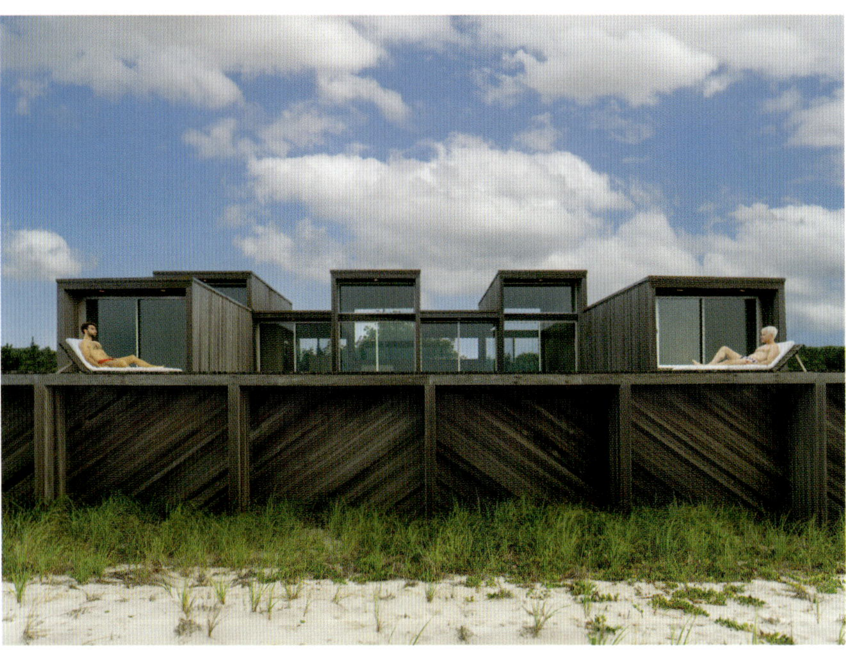

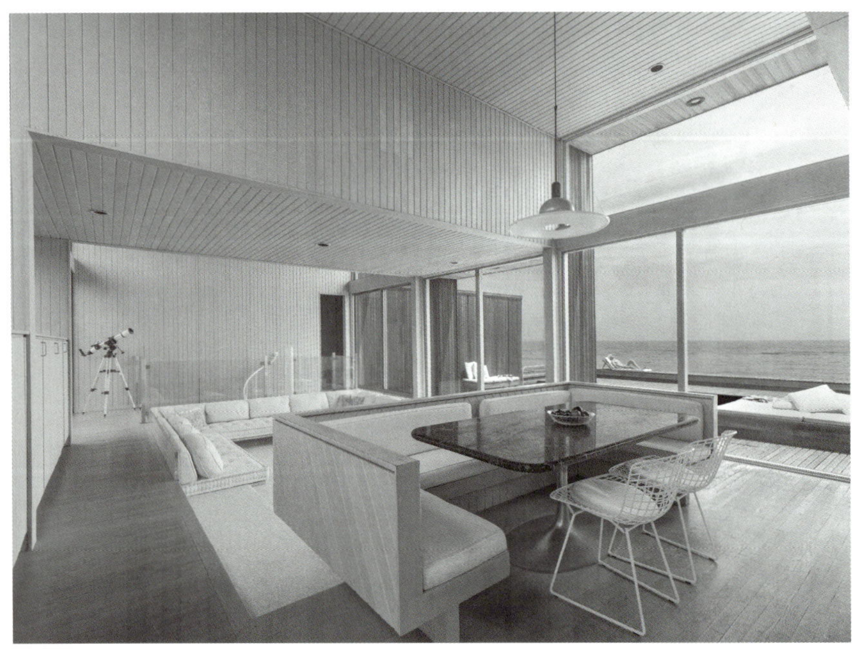

ABOVE AND BELOW:
Lipkins House, interiors

MIDDLE:
Lipkins House, oceanfront exterior

OPPOSITE :
Lipkins House pool

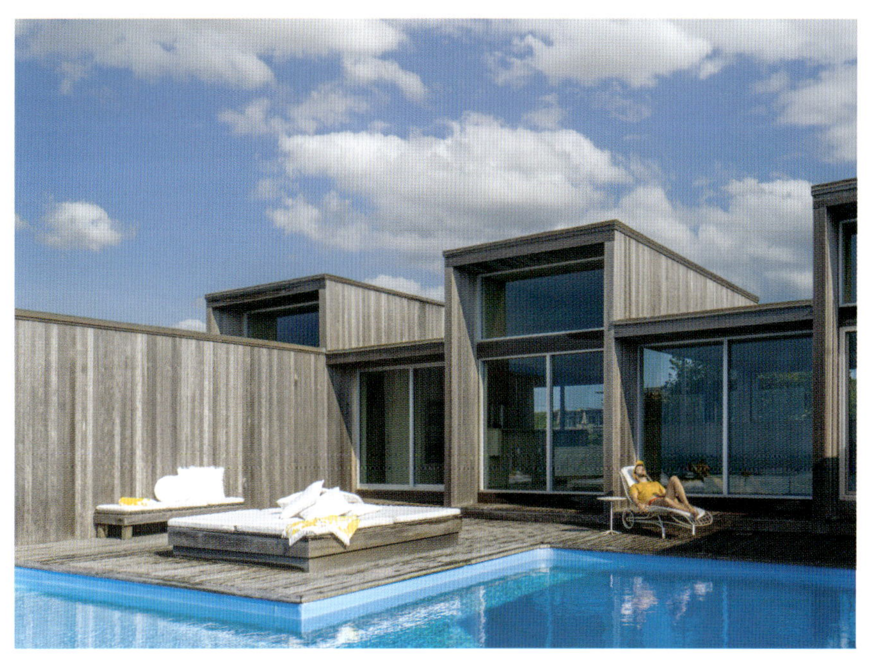

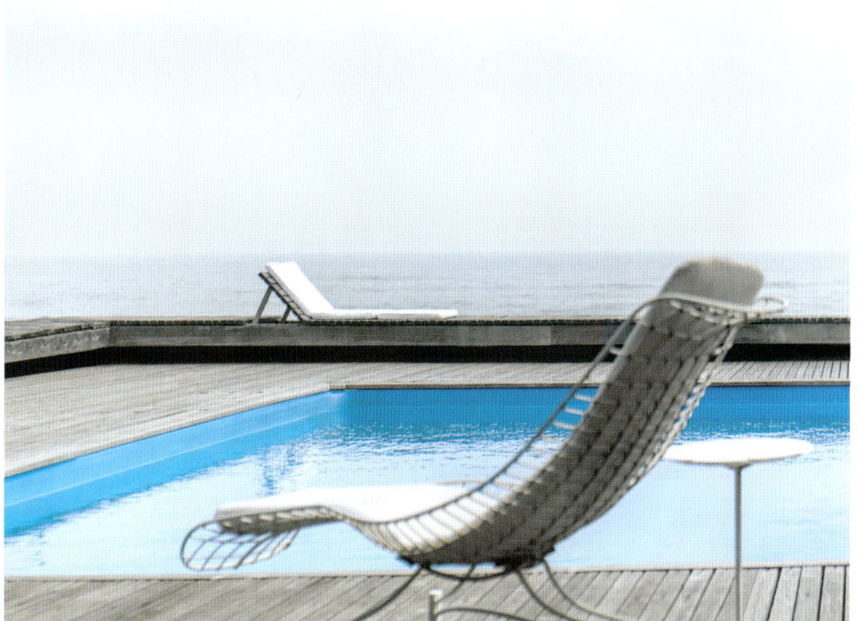

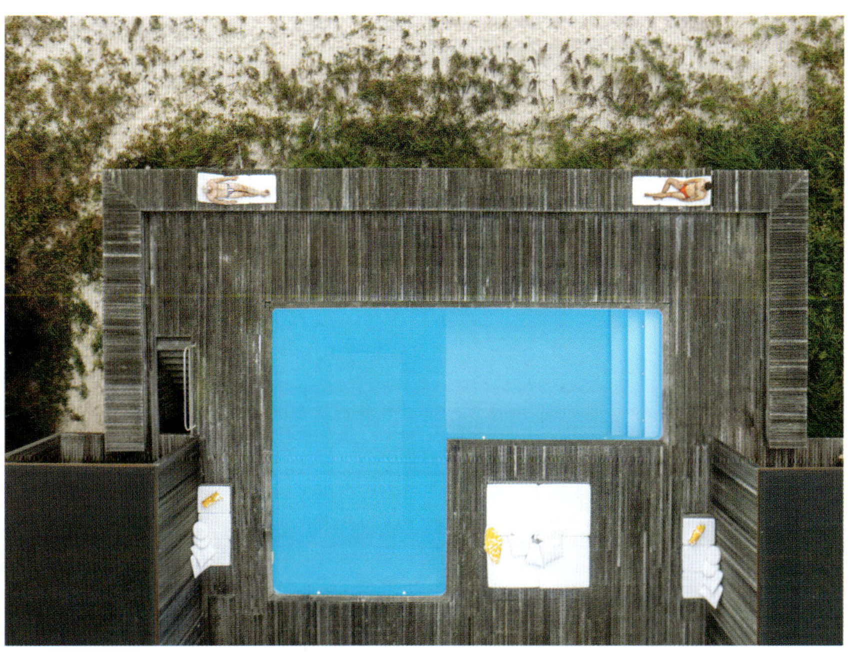

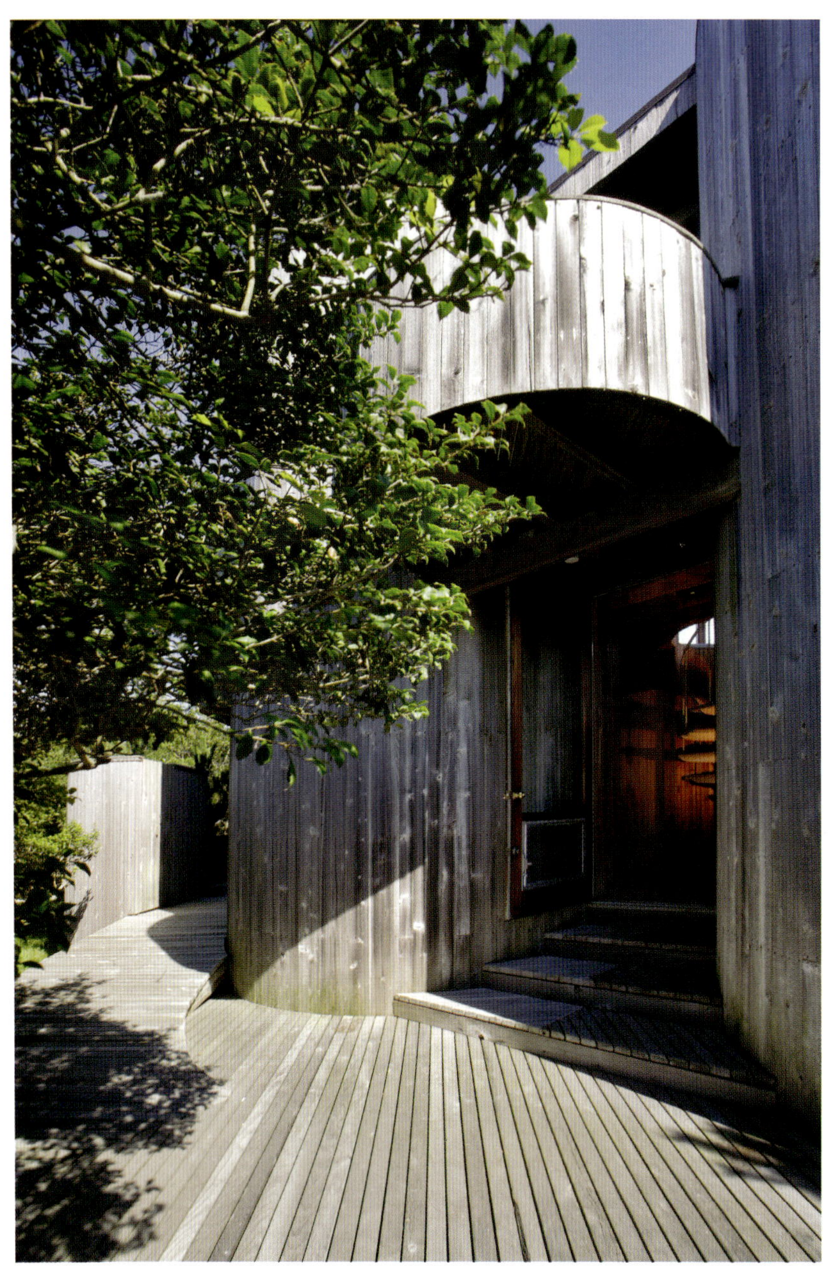

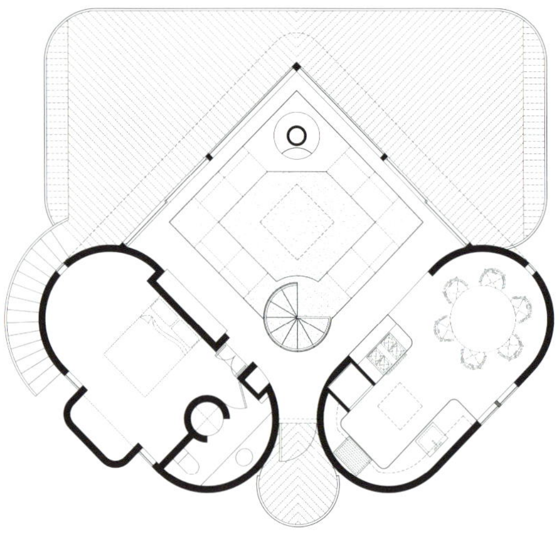

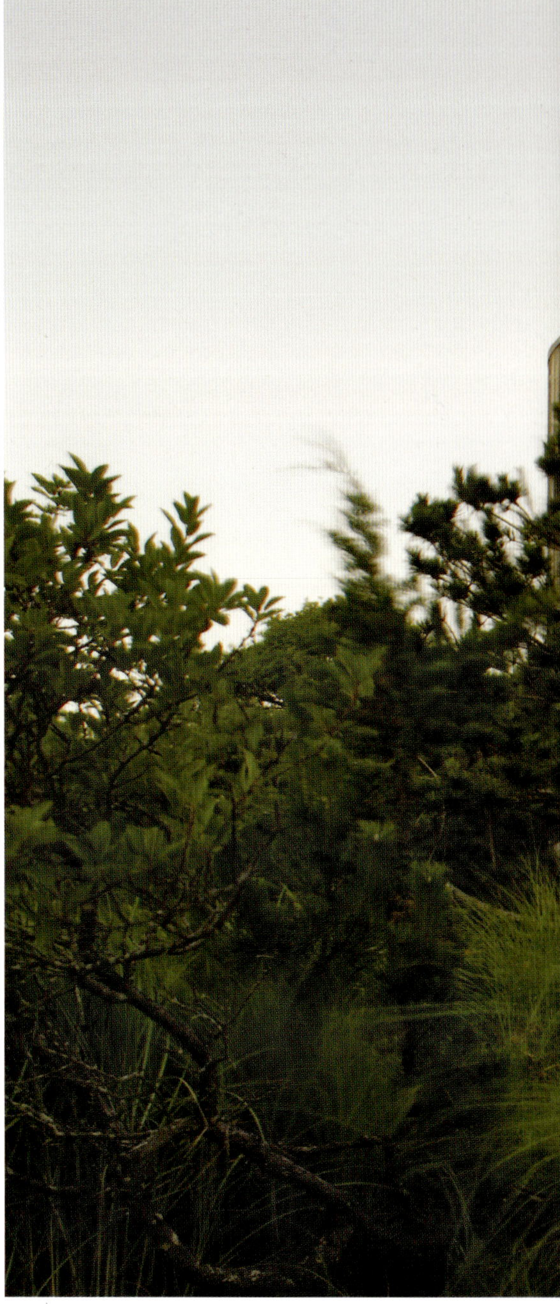

UPPER LEFT:
Rosenthal House, Seaview, NY, 1972, approach

LOWER LEFT:
Rosenthal House, upper-level floor plan

ABOVE:
Rosenthal House

PAGES 182–83:
Rosenthal House, living room

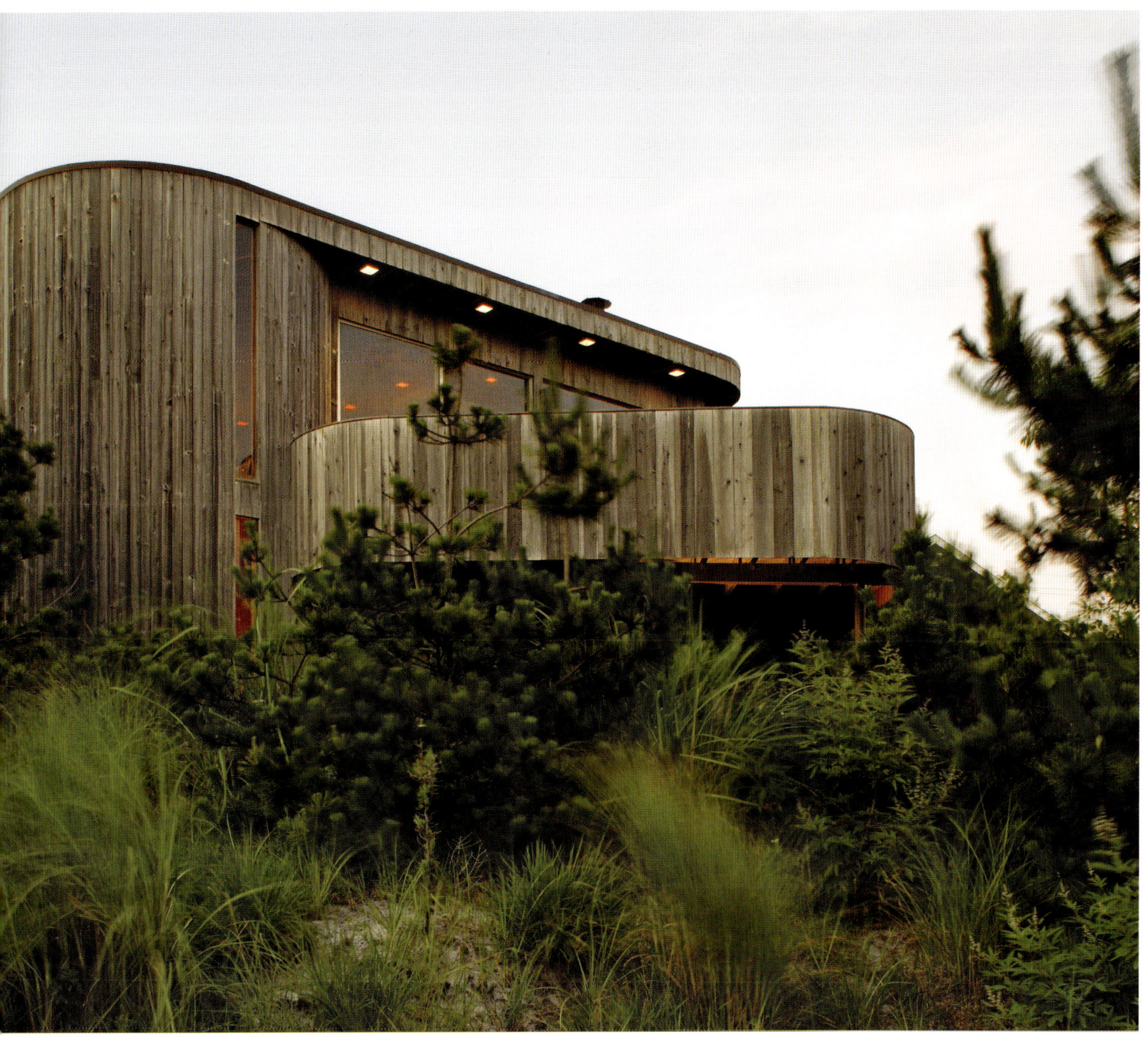

The Rosenthals were unfazed by his revelations and demands but struck by Gifford's appearance; at age forty, he was still turning heads. He rewarded their trust with a sleek composition nestled between two dunes. The Rosenthal House echoed the topography, with two tall elliptical spaces canted between a diamond-shaped, sunken living area with walls of glass. It was an exceptionally well-crafted home built by Gifford's favorite contractor, Joseph Chasas. The exposed ceiling framing formed a dazzling constellation unto itself. Cabinetry was curved with tiny pie-shaped wedges. Sliding walls transformed two triangular bedrooms for the Rosenthals' young sons into a spacious playroom. A brilliant orange fireplace punctuated the living room, and Gifford's telltale assortment of decontextualized utilitarian objects—including a sinuous wooden mold used to create toilet drains—adorned the walls.

Despite his divalike performance in securing the Rosenthal commission, Gifford's administration of the project was anything but theatrical. "He not only had a sense of design and function, but he was also very businesslike," Gladys Rosenthal recalled.[111] She was impressed by the architect's frequent on-site inspections and meticulous invoices. Forty years on, the home and the Rosenthals had weathered remarkably well. "We never had to replace anything. The original carpet is still here!"[112]

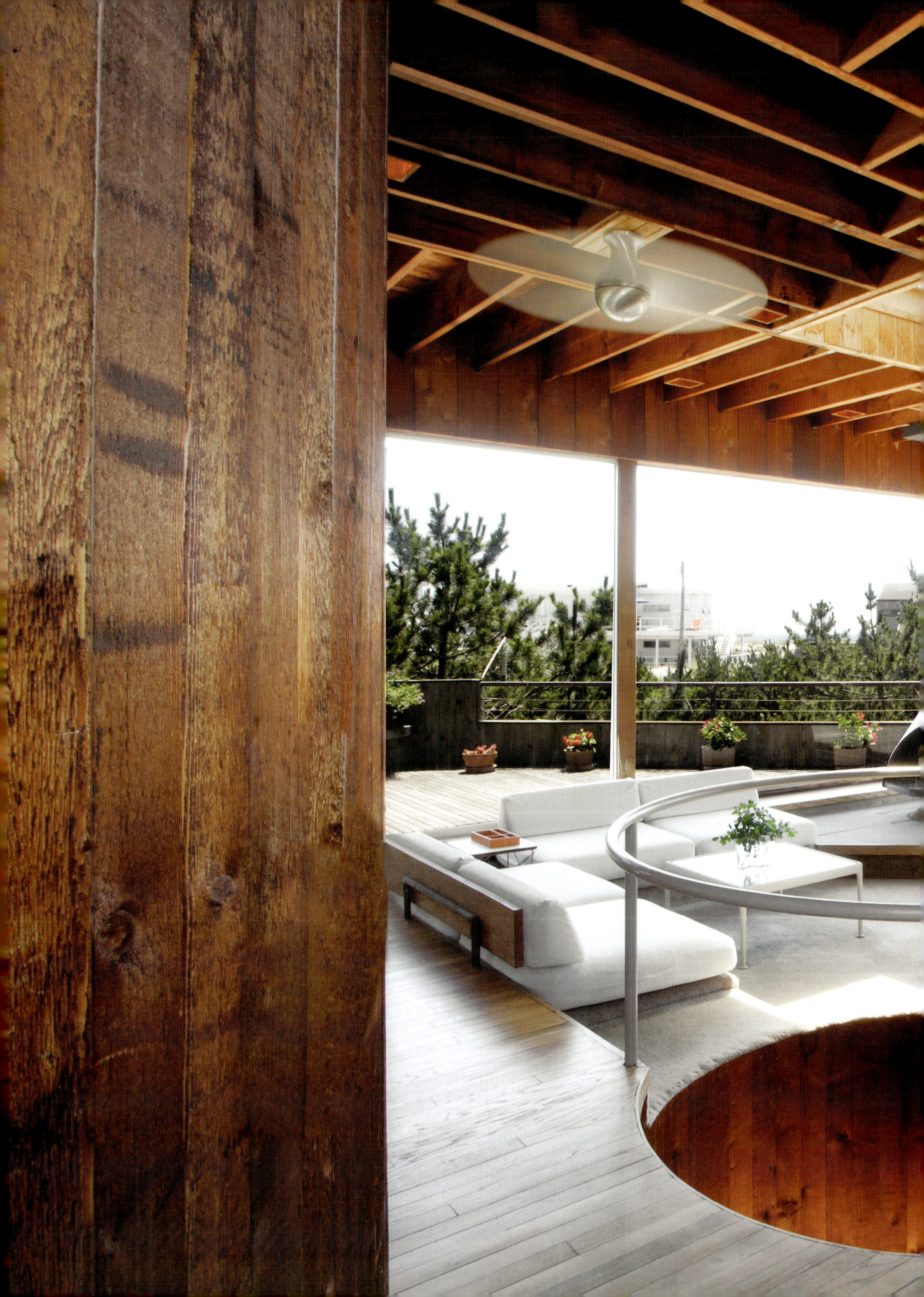

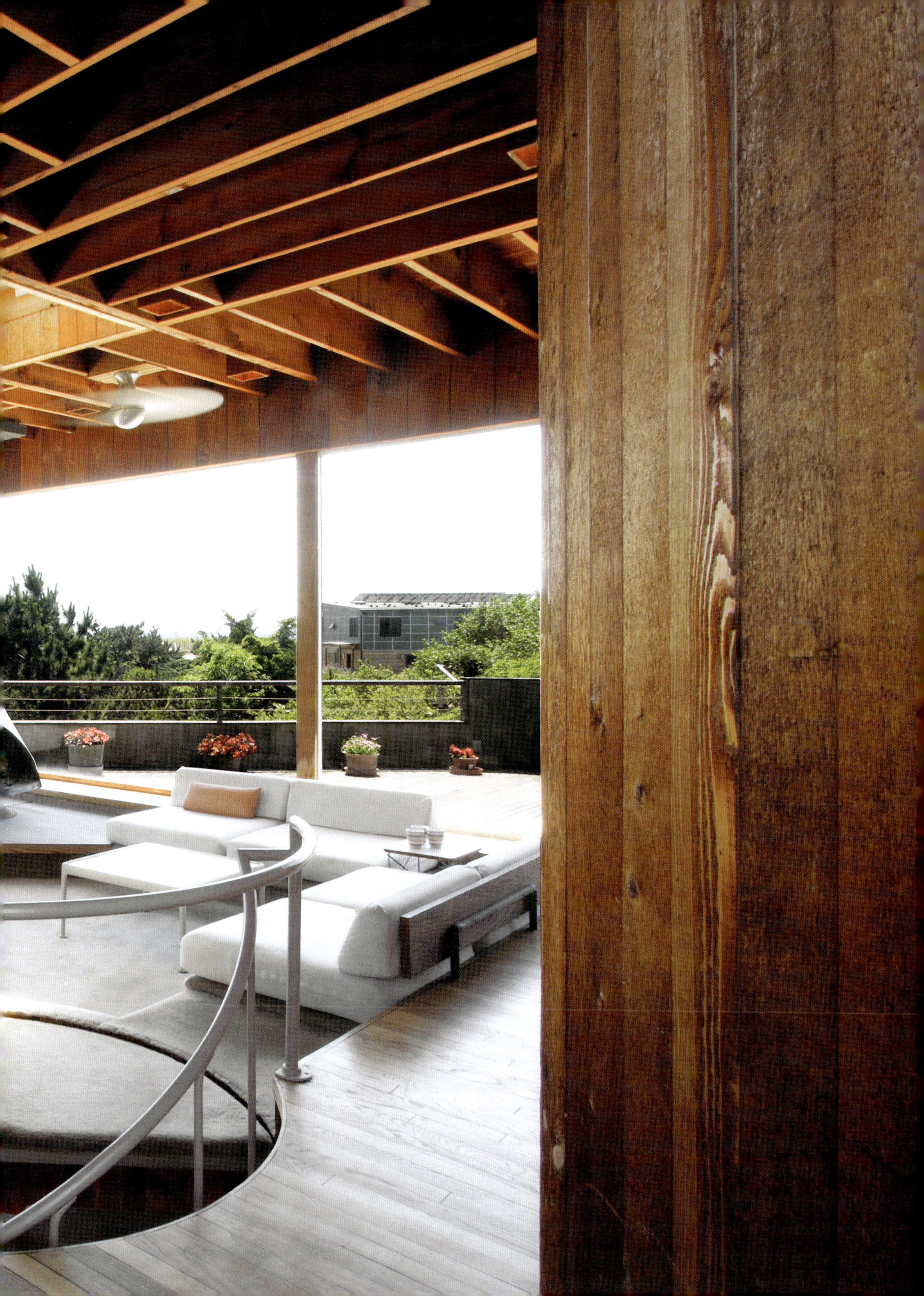

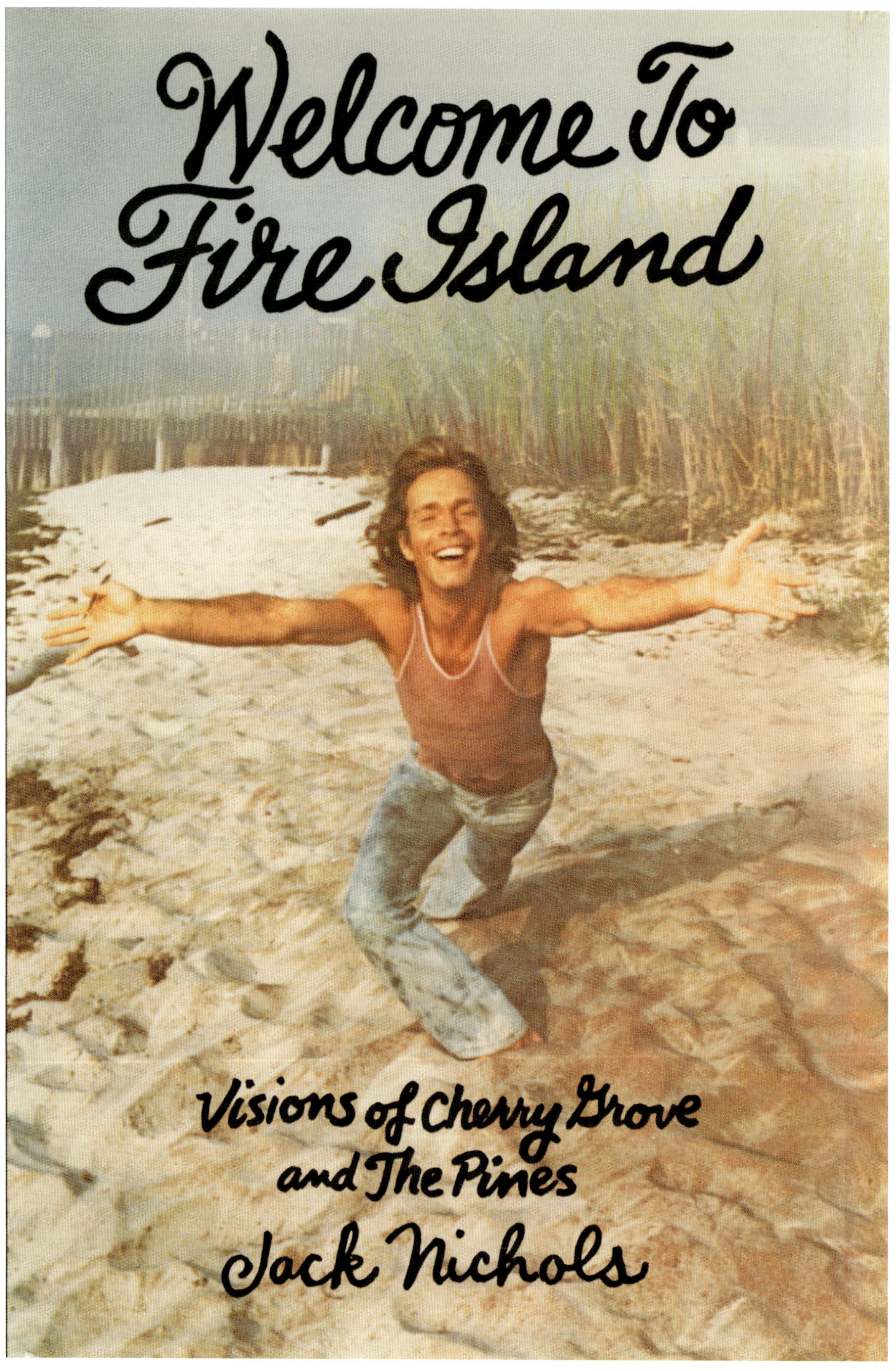
Welcome To
Fire Island
Visions of Cherry Grove
and The Pines
Jack Nichols

Fire Island's reputation as a testing ground for innovative architecture had been overshadowed by louder whispers about its libertine ways even before the sixties were in full swing. Sexual liberation and its discontents were hardly unique to the Pines, of course. John Updike's suburban Pennsylvania characters lamented where "all this fucking" was taking American culture in 1971.[113] But an added measure of scorn or titillation, depending on the commentator, was reserved for Fire Island. Summarizing thirteen summers spent in various communities there, Albert Goldman penned his infamous account for *New York* magazine in 1972, "I Have Seen the Future, and it's Fire Island."

> No, what I have seen again and again is your nice, mature, well-educated married couple entertaining other couples every weekend and making jokes about the "swinging singles" all around them. Then one weekend, after the beach and the Bloody Marys and the candlelit supper, the conversation turns to themes like wife-swapping and orgies, and somebody says: "The only things you regret are those you don't do." After that, it's mixed doubles for the rest of the night, the weekend, or the summer...Orgy is where it's all headed, and orgy is a grand old tradition on Fire Island.[114]

And that was only the straight communities! Sexual adventurism at a Roman scale could be found in the Pines and Cherry Grove. Their shared Meat Rack was the mecca toward which all erections faced. Even the cultural divide between the two reached a humorous detente in 1976. Thom "Panzi" Hansen, a Cherry Grove drag queen who was refused service at one of John Whyte's bars in the Pines, organized a small flotilla of friends for a drag "invasion" of the Pines by boat. Donning the most outrageous costumes they could muster, Panzi and his entourage grandly disembarked and performed a sit-in at the community's most popular bar. The spectacle inspired hilarity rather than hostility and became an annual event, fittingly held on Independence Day. The Invasion soon required the biggest ferryboat in service, which heaved under the weight of enormous high heels and entangled wigs. It remains the largest seasonal activity on Fire Island, drawing revelers of every orientation and proclivity.

A number of visual artists and writers emerged to come to grips with the new freedom. The Polaroid SX-70, the first easy-to-use instant camera, was released in 1972, to the annoyance of censorious film processors, and the camera played a central role in the sexual diary of a decade. Shapely men, lounging seductively astride the muscular architecture and glimmering pools of the Pines, graced artist Tom Bianchi's Polaroids. His subjects' nonchalance proved more shocking than the anatomy on display. Beyond their sensuality, the photos also captured the intense camaraderie of an upwardly mobile society free of the burdens of parenthood: Fire Island offered the promise of an indefinite extension of adolescence.

The literary response was more ambivalent. Jack Nichols' *Welcome to Fire Island: Visions of Cherry Grove and The Pines,* dedicated to his murdered lover, reserved its greatest appreciation for this utopia's "one ineffable grace: a virtual absence of physical violence, unless it is simulated or mutually agreed upon, as among the sadomasochists."[115] In perhaps the most celebrated

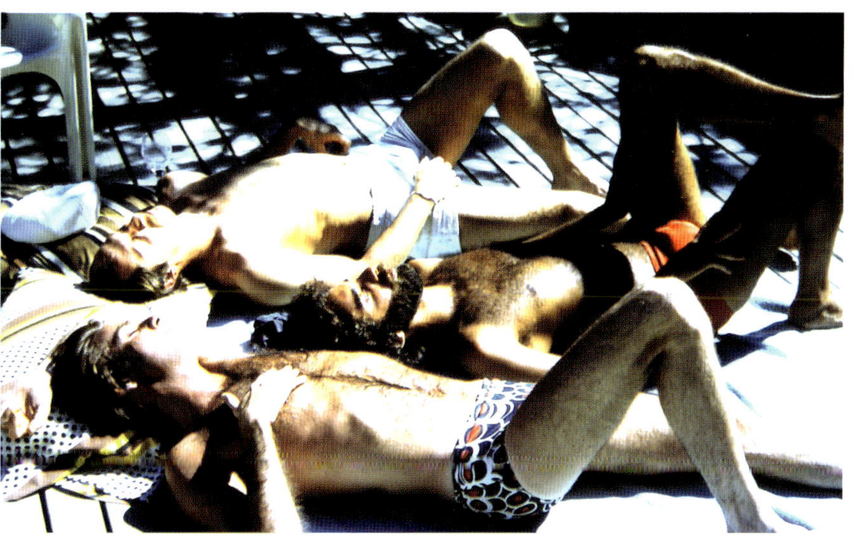

OPPOSITE:
***Welcome to Fire Island: Visions of Cherry Grove and the Pines*, by Jack Nichols, 1976**

RIGHT:
Men of the Pines, ca. 1973

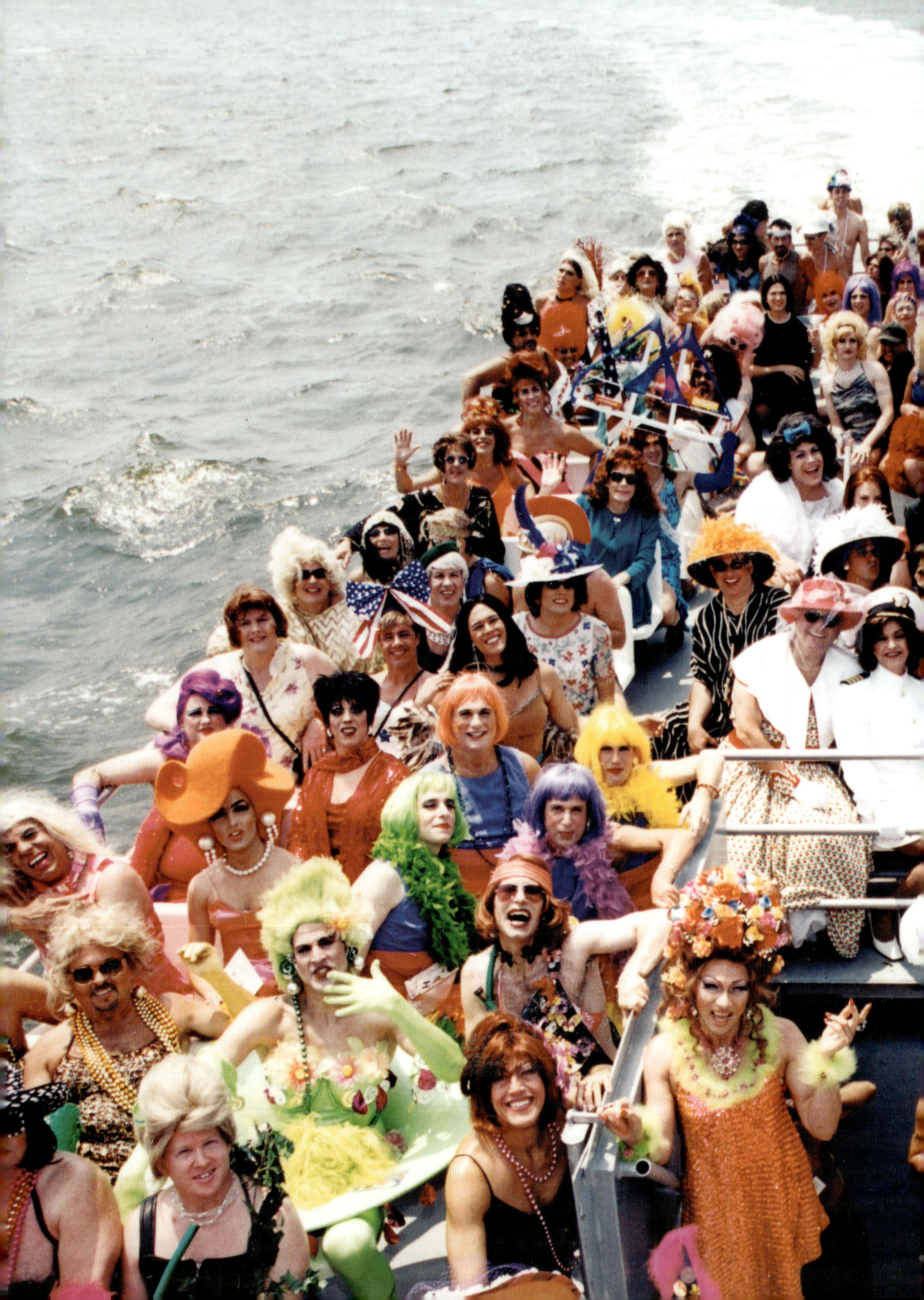

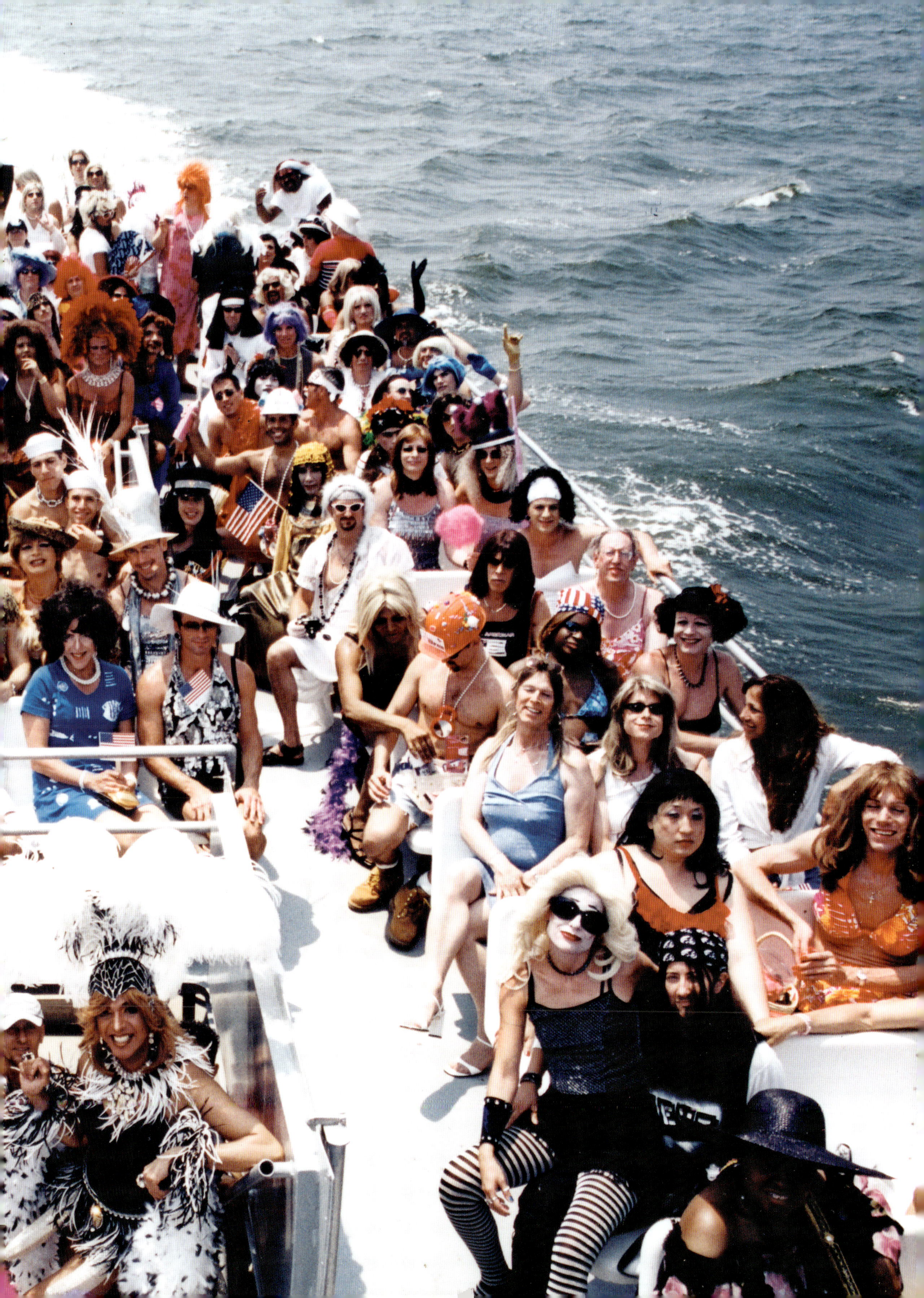

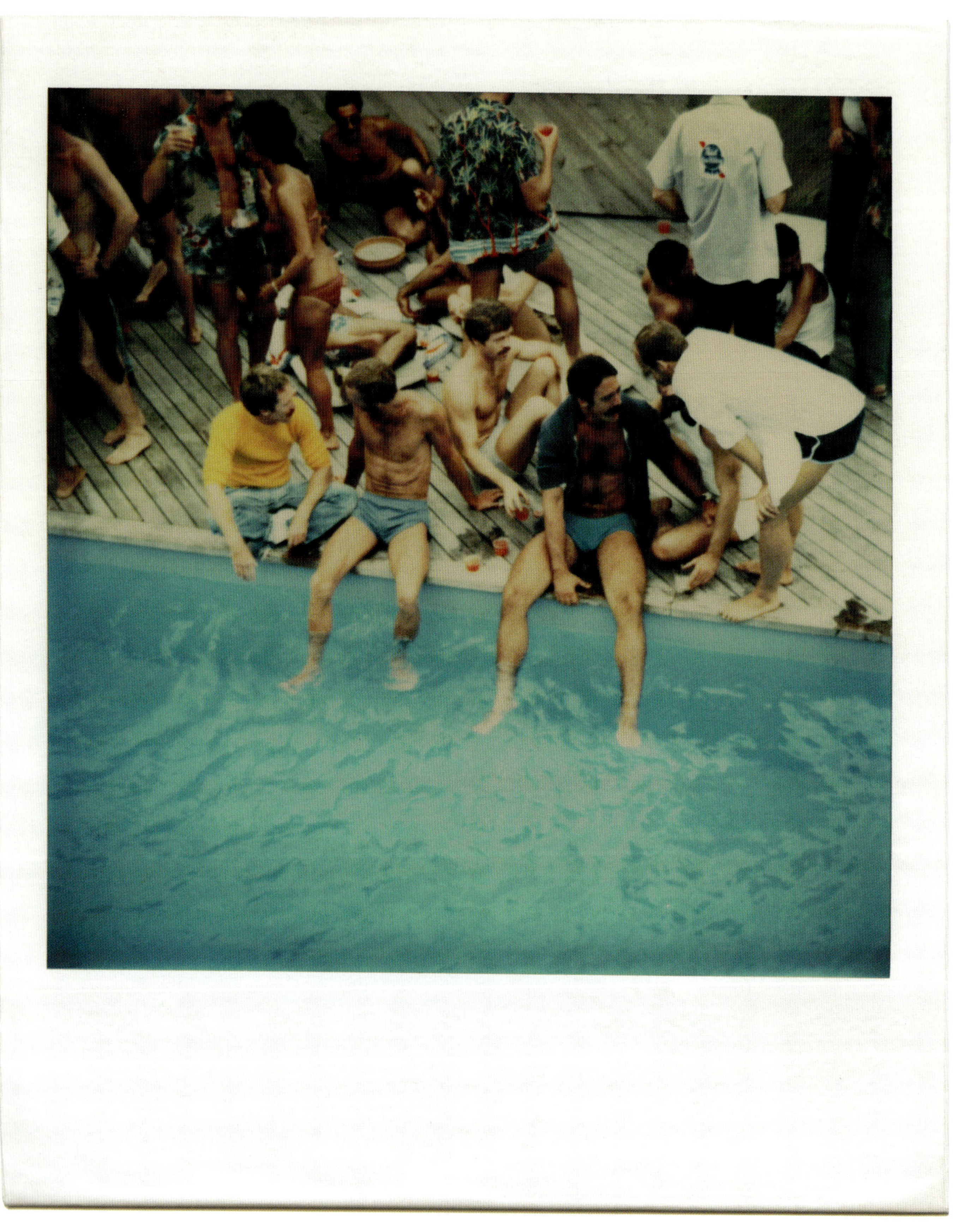

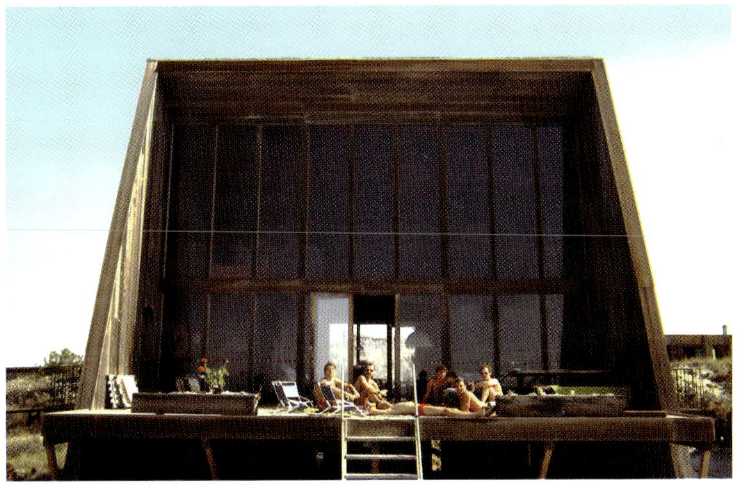

gay coming-of-age novel, Andrew Holleran's *Dancer from the Dance* contained an ode to the pleasures and perils of this brave new world. It follows the exploits of two friends who hunt for love but settle for sex in Fire Island Pines, "a national game preserve annually replenished by men who each summer arrived from every state in the Union via an Underground Railroad of a most peculiar sort...because nowhere else on earth was natural and human beauty fused; and because nowhere else on earth could you dance in quite the same atmosphere."[116] The novel is punctuated by hilarious scenes of debauchery yet permeated by a deep sense of unease. How much stimulation could the human psyche and the human body handle? One of the two protagonists dies of a drug overdose, and the other disappears mysteriously after delivering a jaded caution to a newcomer: "Never forget that all these people are primarily a visual people. They are designers, window dressers, models, photographers, graphic artists...and their sins, as Saint Augustine said, are sins of the eye...do not expect nourishment for anything but your eye—and you will handle it all beautifully."[117] *Faggots*, a 1978 novel by Larry Kramer, issued a finger-wagging takedown of the decadence to be found along the Manhattan–Fire Island axis. Kramer's hero, Fred Melish, confronts his ex-lover, who is en route to a sadomasochistic orgy with a "Nazi executioner" theme in the Meat Rack:

> ...why do faggots have to fuck so fucking much?!...all we do is live in our Ghetto and dance and drug and fuck...I'm tired of being a New York City–Fire Island faggot, I'm tired of using my body as a faceless thing to lure another faceless thing, I want to love a Person!...a Person who loves me, we shouldn't have to be faithful, we should want to be faithful![118]

Paradoxically, Horace Gifford grew shy just as his architecture embodied the extroversion of a newly liberated minority. He seemed like a neurotic actor who was radiant on the stage but skittish and withdrawn off of it. And the arenas of design and seduction were the two stages upon which Gifford could form connections to the outside world. He became a rare sight at conventional social gatherings. Most of his friendships came about as a result of his work as an architect. Sex was another matter. He liked it often, and he liked it in public. To shed his clothes was to shed the inhibitions that closed him down socially. He met his new partner Robert Greenfield at an infamous gay bathhouse in 1972.[119] In 1973, the architect hosted an elegant black-tie party. But that's all

PAGES 186–87:
The annual Invasion of the Pines by Cherry Grove drag queens

OPPOSITE:
Tom Bianchi, Untitled, SX-70 Polaroid, 1970s

ABOVE:
Men of the Pines, 1978

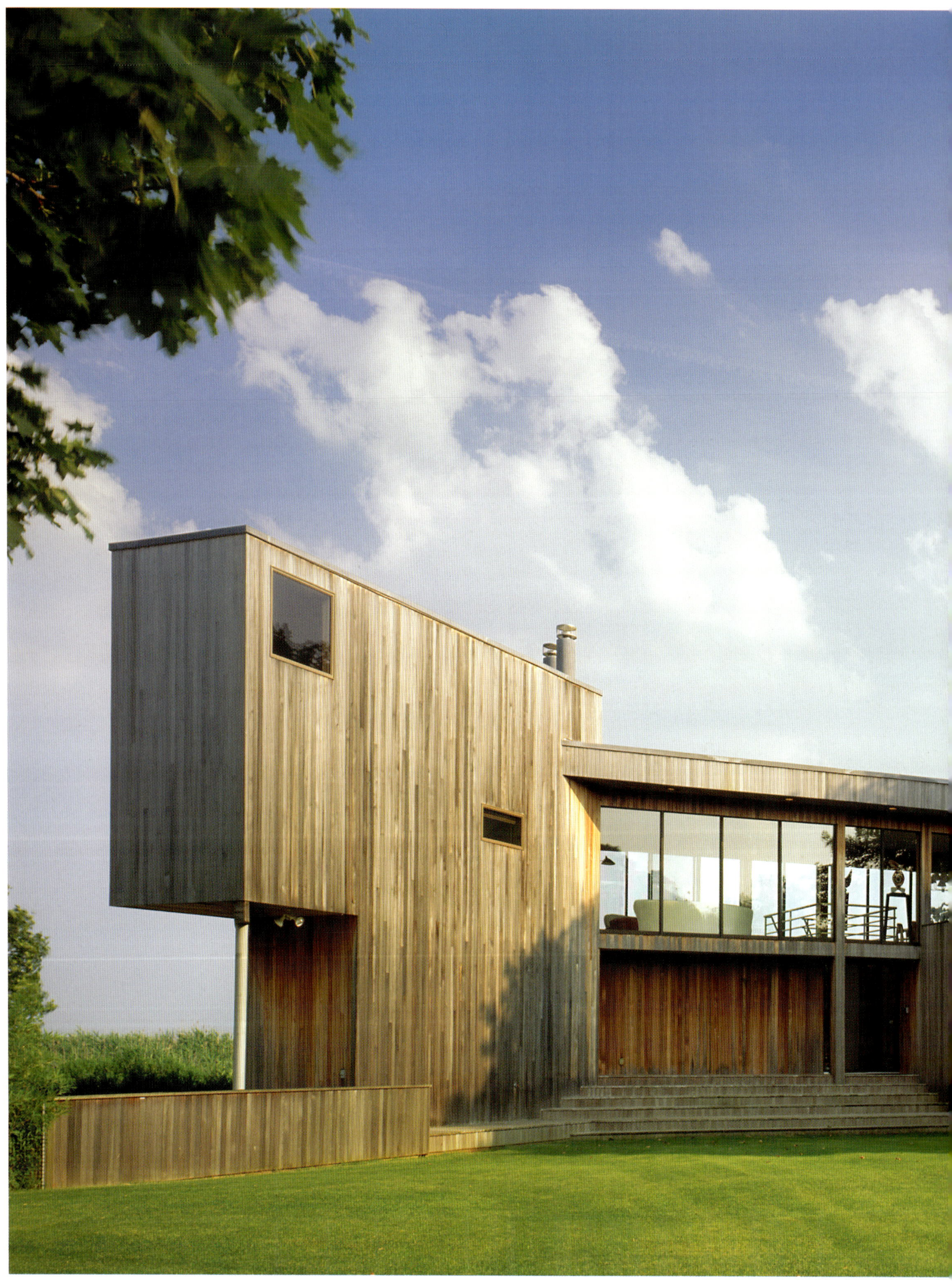

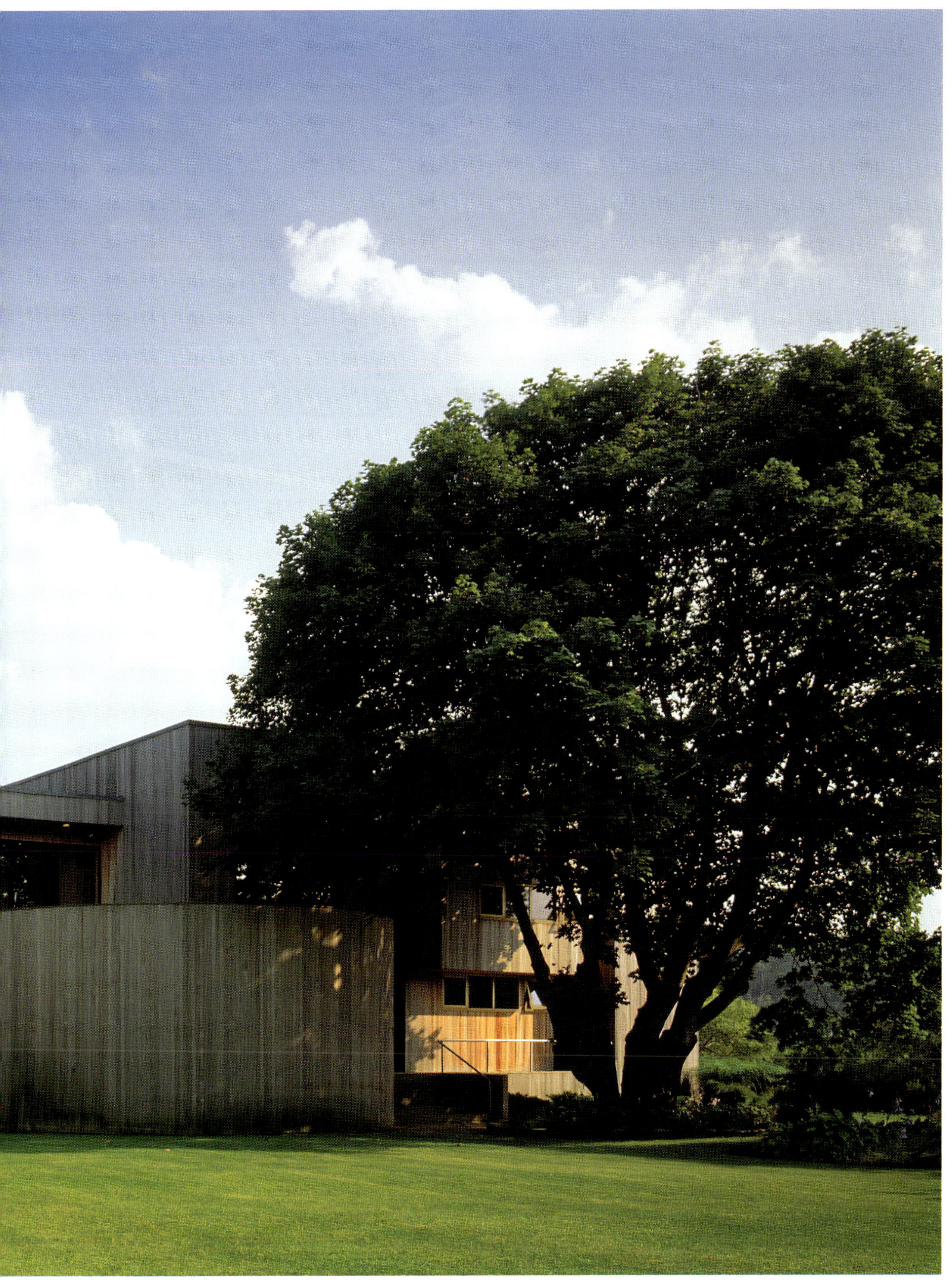

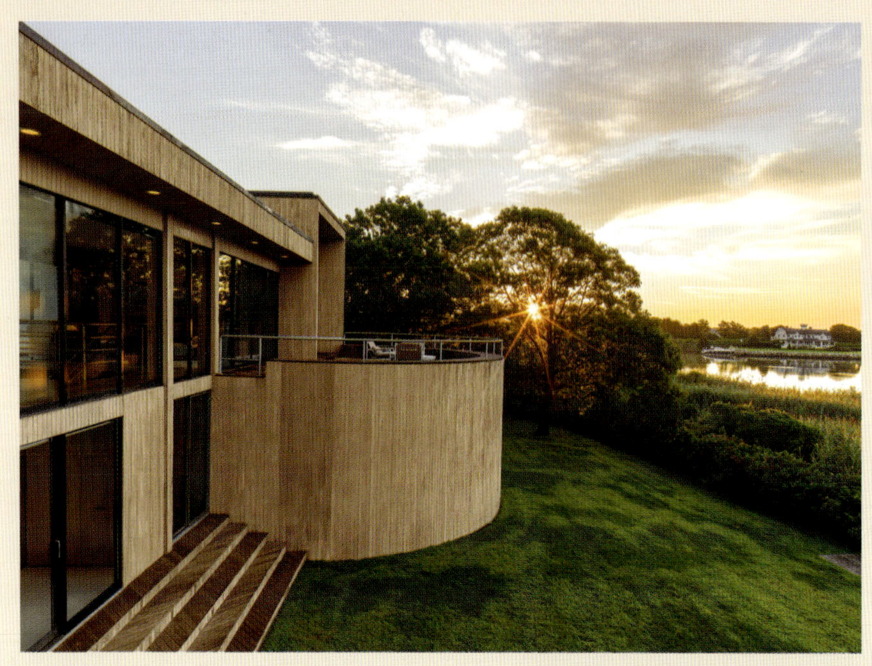

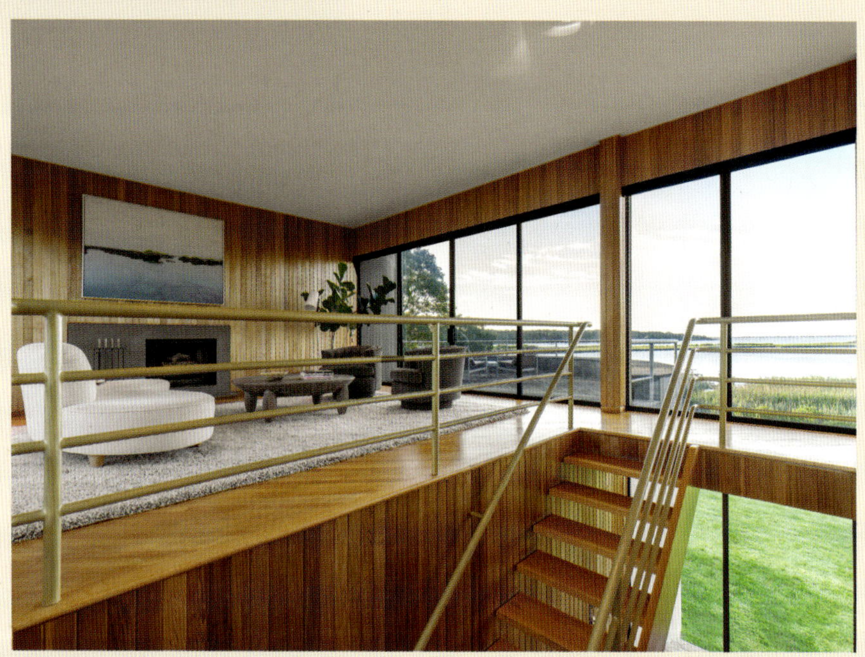

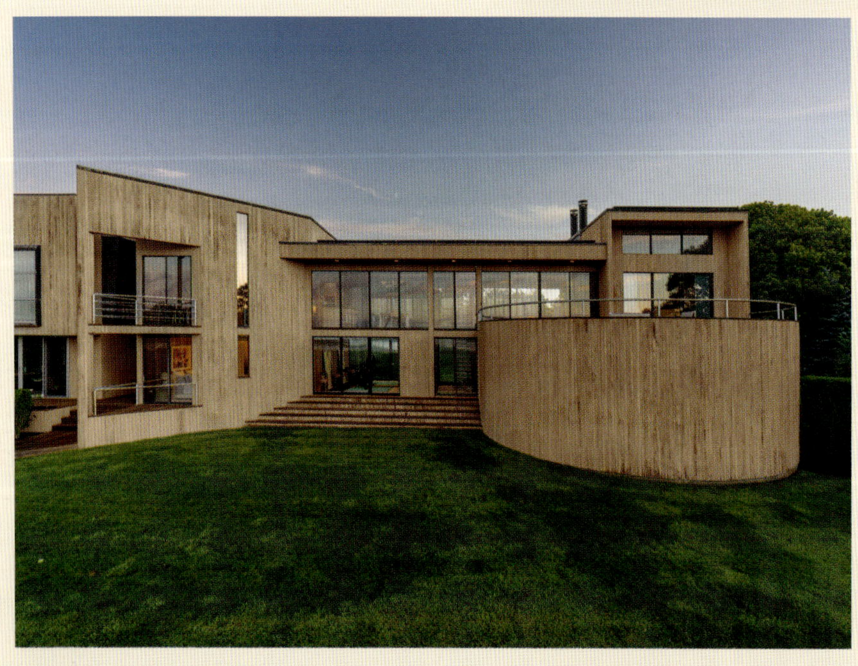

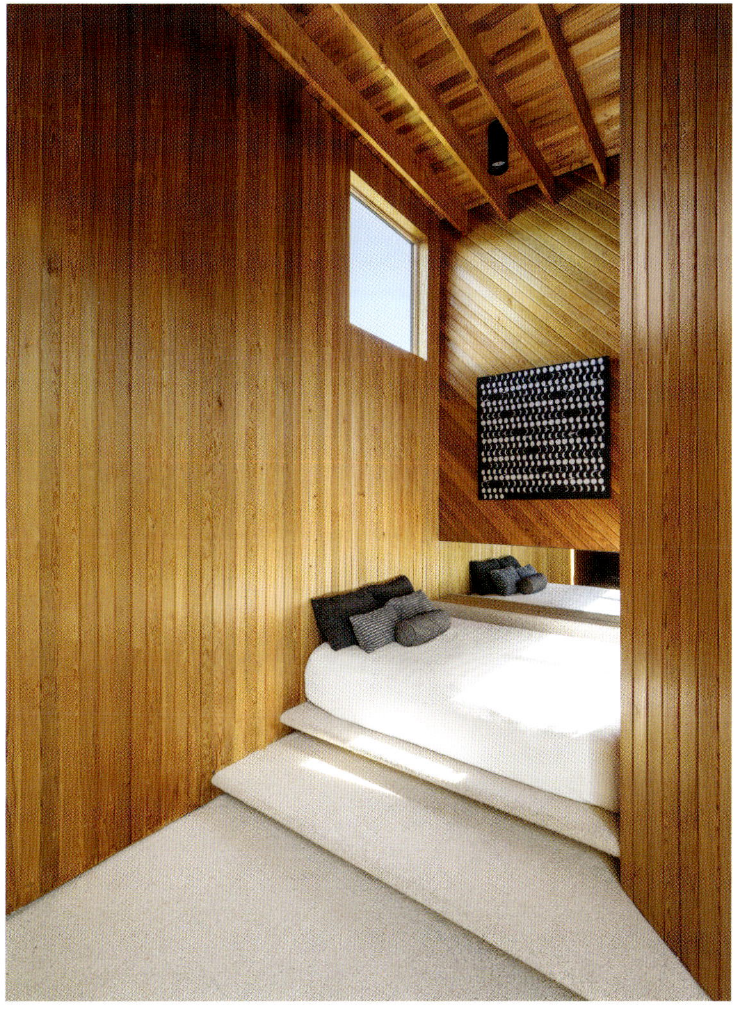

they wore: black ties.[120] Such wardrobe choices showed off Gifford's second most famous attribute, a robust endowment. Greenfield joked that he was going to have his boyfriend's penis pickled so that it could be admired in posterity.[121] More than one friend described Gifford as a sex addict. Yet heterosexual friends and clients consistently noted his shyness. It is rather fitting that the two realms in which he excelled would coalesce into a shapely architecture of seduction.

The Graham residence was commissioned by a Pines resident who camc out of the closet late in life but found his ideal beachfront property across the Great South Bay. His son Peter Graham, an environmentalist who would go on to found the eco-product empire Seventh Generation, persuaded his father to hire Gifford after an inspiring tour of his work in the Pines. Graham's expansive site, on an inlet in Eastport, New York, allowed for an elongated footprint, and Gifford elevated the house to capture views that resided above a stand of cattails. A winding approach to the home concluded with a circular drive spun around a magnificent tree. Like sheared continental plates, two semicircular decks contained a glass cube that bridged between solid shards at each end. A swimming pool, set within a circular plinth, powerfully restated the geometries of the main house.

The Sloan residence was the consummate example of Gifford's mature period. Norton and Marlo Sloan—one of many heterosexual couples who embraced the freewheeling culture of the Pines—commissioned a luxurious home whose smooth volumes appeared to have washed up on their site. Although any physical resemblance to Louis Kahn's work had receded, it still bore his "order of the castle," in which complex ancillary rooms surround a rectangular central space and endow the facade with a rippled presence.[122] Curved spaces extended, cloverlike, from a lofty living room animated by the painterly slash of a diagonal stairway. Mirrors created slivers of

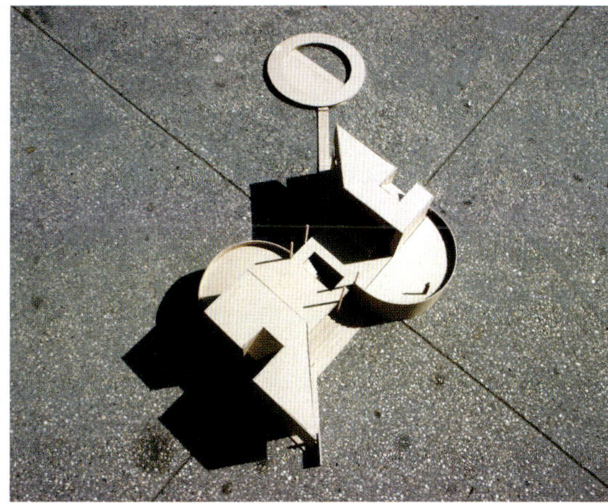

PAGES 190–91:
Graham House, Eastport, NY, 1978, approach

OPPOSITE:
Graham House, bayfront facade and Interior

ABOVE:
Graham House, bedroom

RIGHT:
Graham House, scale model

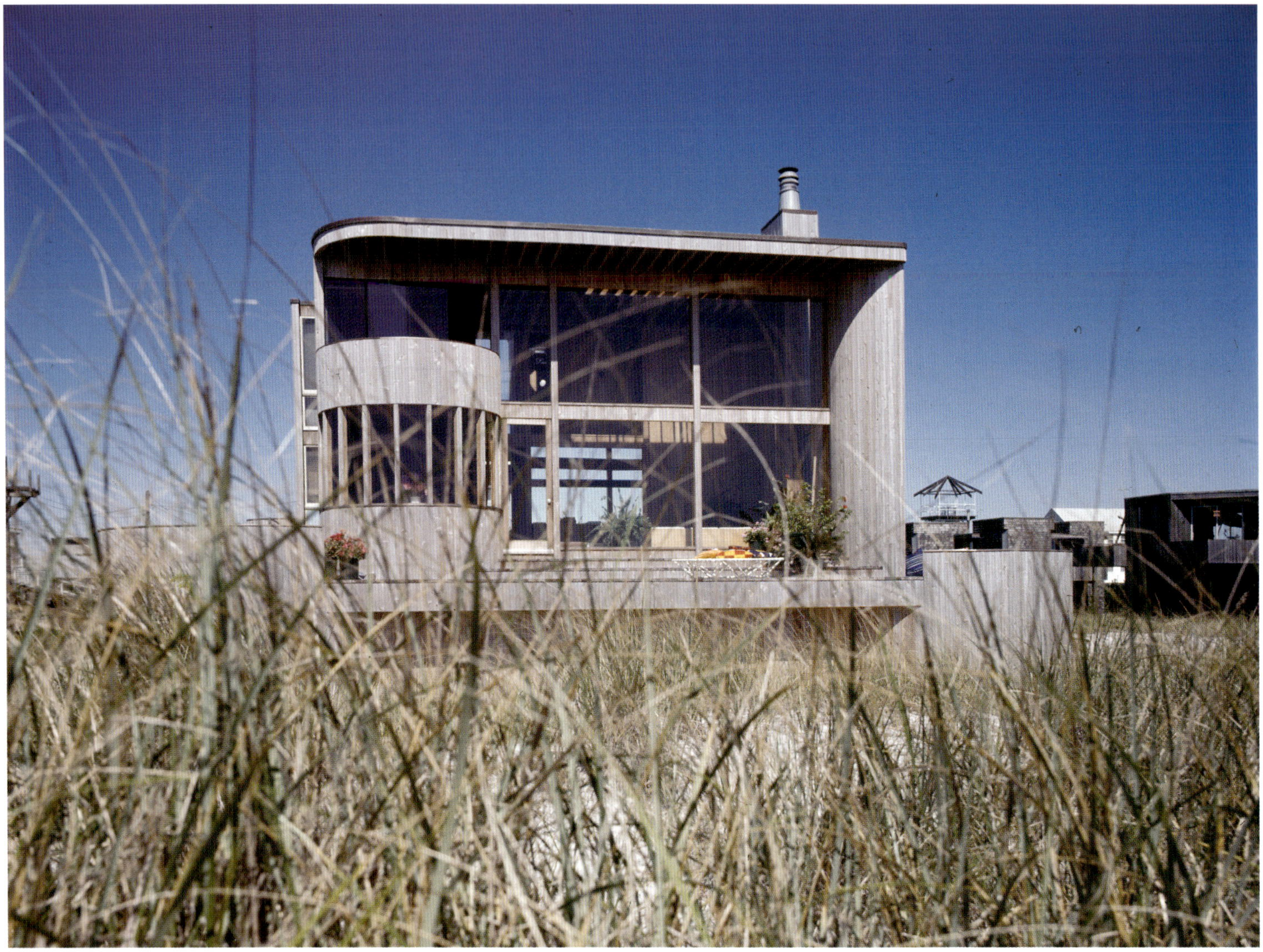

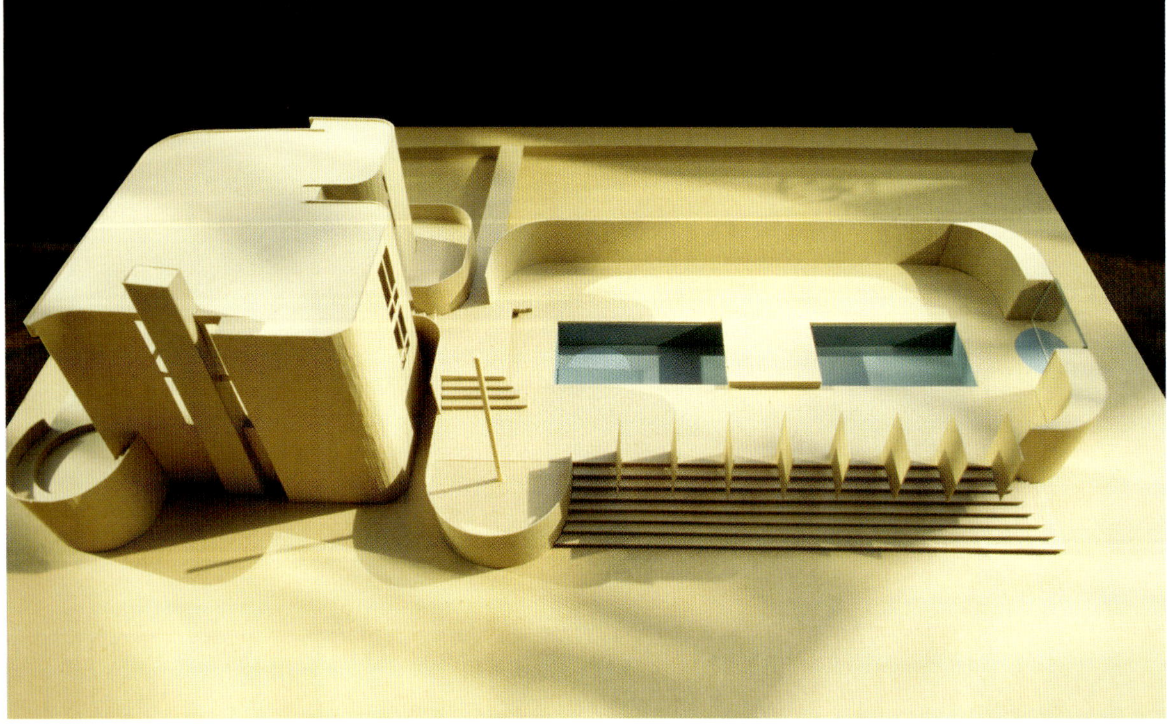

ABOVE:
Sloan House, Fire Island Pines, NY, 1972, view from ocean side

LEFT:
Sloan House, scale model of 1980 addition for Calvin Klein

OPPOSITE:
Sloan House, approach

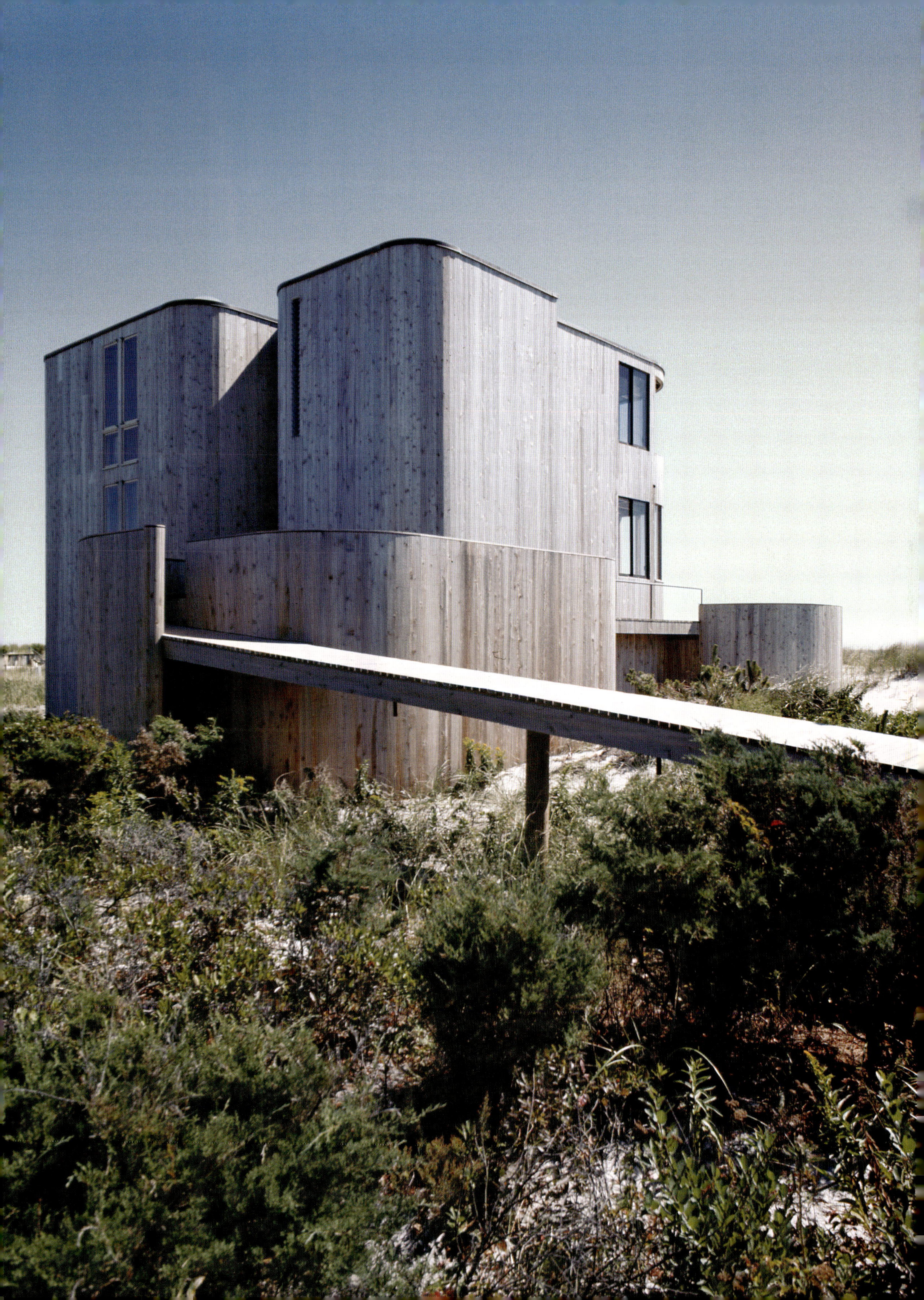

light above the fireplace. Positioned opposite full-height expanses of glass, a mirrored wall brought the ocean view to both sides of the space. A leather ottoman bridged the conversation pit. Outside, a lazy-Susan lounge rotated to catch the best rays for the sun-worshipping Marlo Sloan. Upstairs, a De Stijl–like composition of bunk beds housed the Sloans' four young children.

The hard-living Sloans divorced a few years after the house was built, and Calvin Klein became its new owner in 1977. At the height of his "Nothing comes between me and my Calvins" success, Klein acquired the lot to the rear of the home and hired Gifford to design a pool, a gym, a "pool boy's" quarters, and a garden. Gifford and his intern Ronald Bentley ventured to Fire Island by seaplane with Klein in March of 1980, braving the frigid waters to survey the property. Gifford lined the pool in black, with a mirror at one end to extend its apparent length. Doors to the east of the pool pivoted to expose a grand stair that led down to a grove of mature trees, helicoptered in for instant effect. In a 2013 interview with Marc Jacobs, Klein set the scene:

> CK: The house that I had on Fire Island was one of the sexiest houses I think I've ever owned.
> MJ: Well, it was also the sexiest times in the history of the world.
> CK: It was amazing. But the house was the ultimate hedonist house. I mean, it was made for sex.
> MJ: On the ultimate hedonist island.
> CK: I thought, God, this works perfectly—wave them in, whatever [both laugh].[123]

At the same time, Calvin Klein's daughter Marci had been kidnapped in 1978, and he was obsessed with security and privacy. Tall fences outfitted with security systems transformed the former Sloan residence into a compound rather than a house tucked into the dunes. And celebrities were not the only ones to screen themselves off from prying eyes. An increasing number of private swimming pools required fences. Other residents blocked off gardens filled with non-native, flowering plants to keep out the deer that once roamed with impunity. Such developments began to erode the open, free-flowing qualities that had made the Pines such a public space for private architecture. A certain intimacy was lost, but the Pines entered the 1980s as a renowned resort with an impressive architectural pedigree to match.

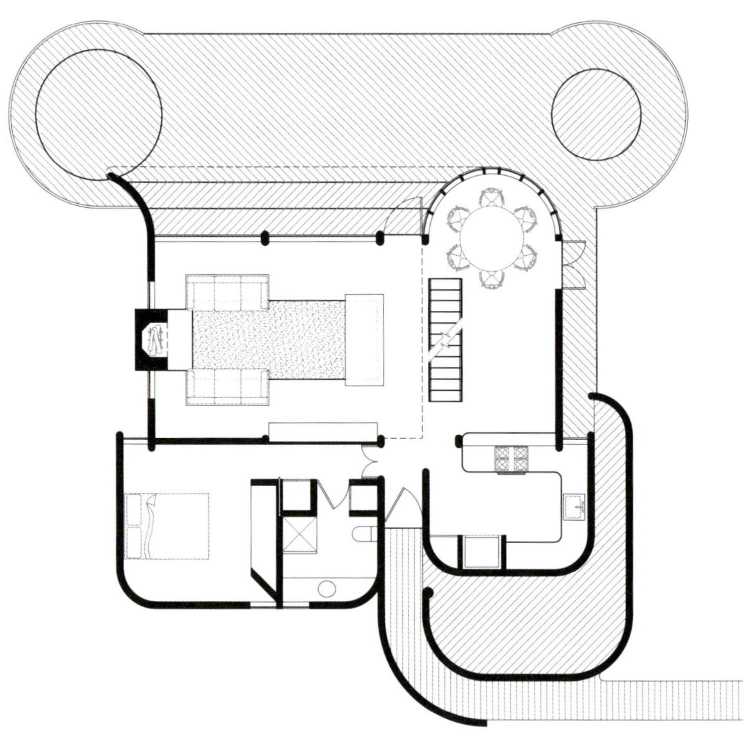

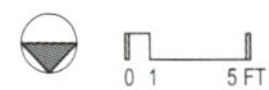

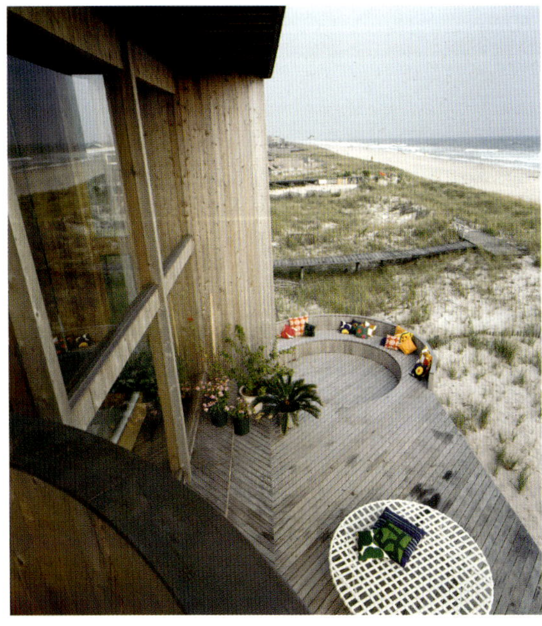

ABOVE:
Sloan House, floor plan

LEFT:
Sloan House

OPPOSITE:
Sloan House, living room

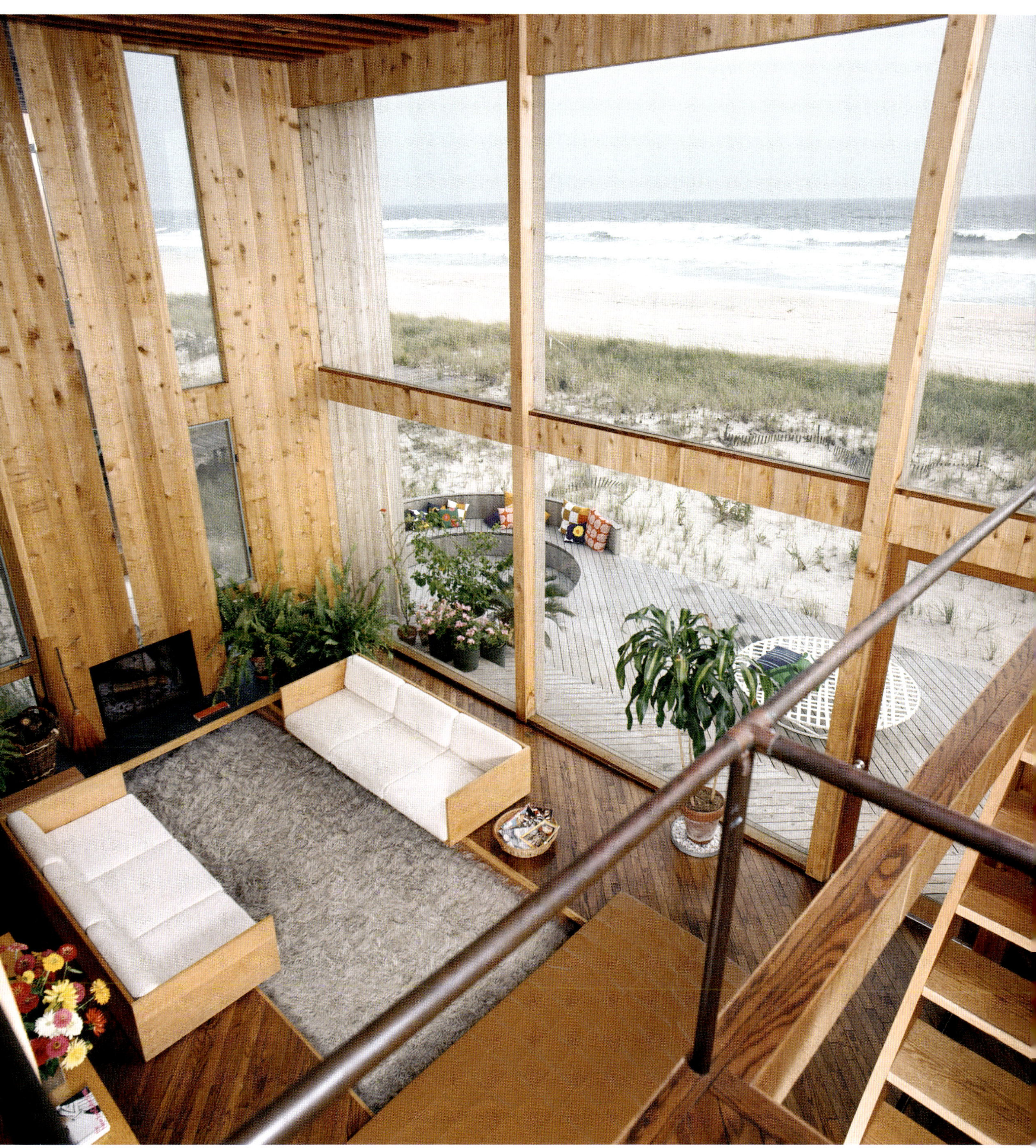

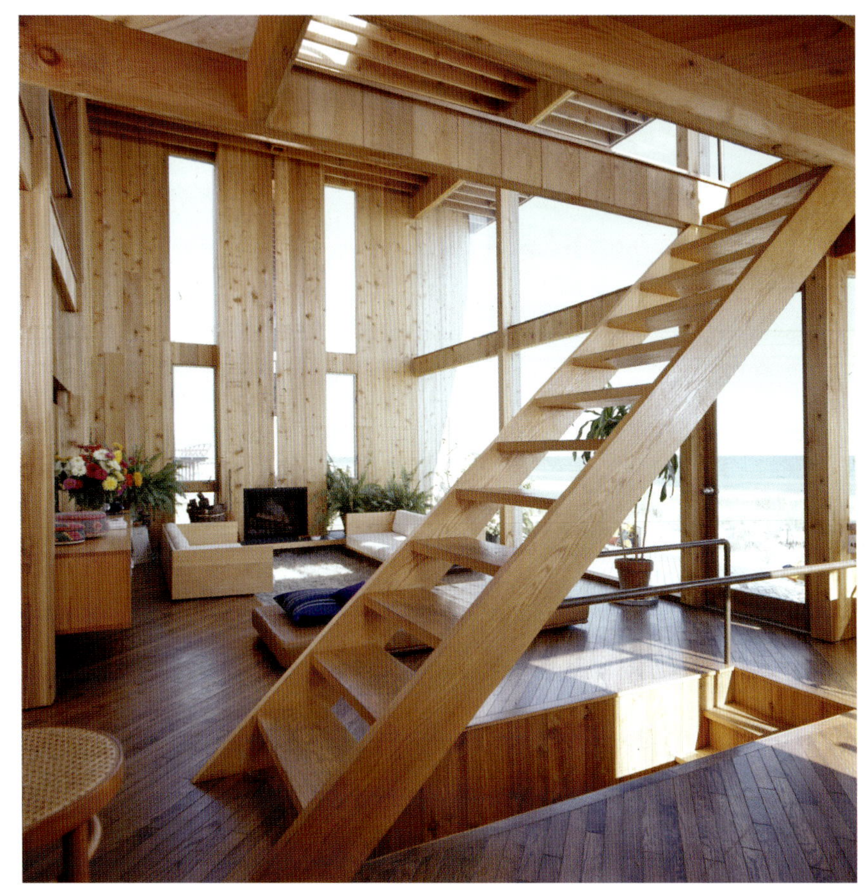

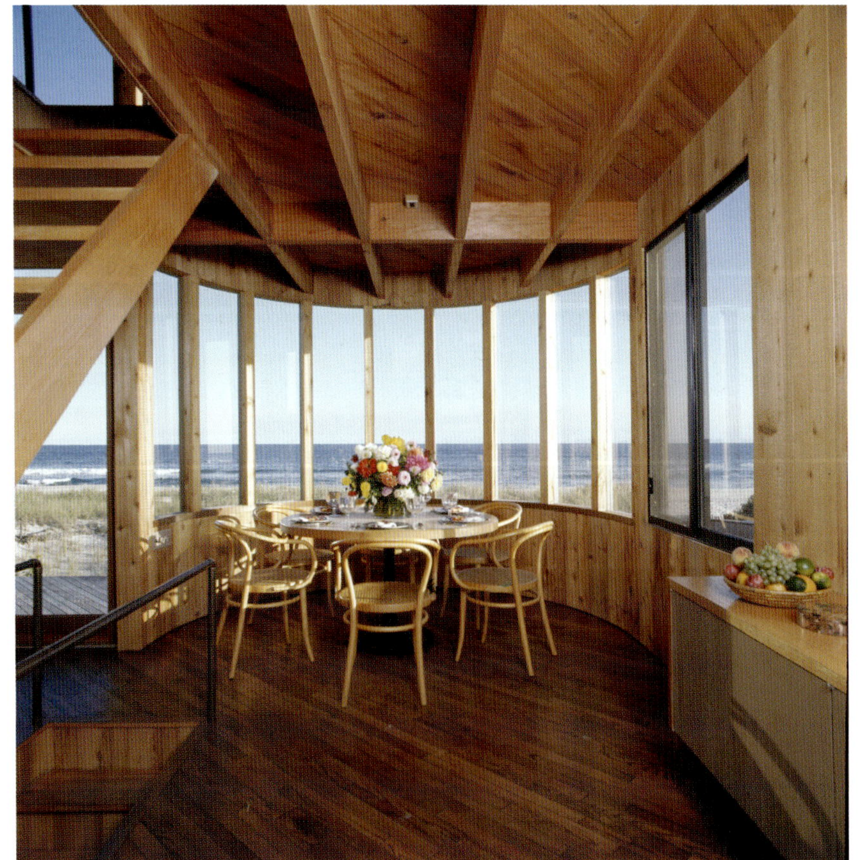

ABOVE:
Sloan House, living area

LEFT:
Sloan House, dining area

OPPOSITE:
ABOVE: **Calvin Klein at Sloan House, 1977;** BELOW, RIGHT: **Sloan House, primary bathroom;** BELOW, LEFT: **Sloan House, children's bedroom**

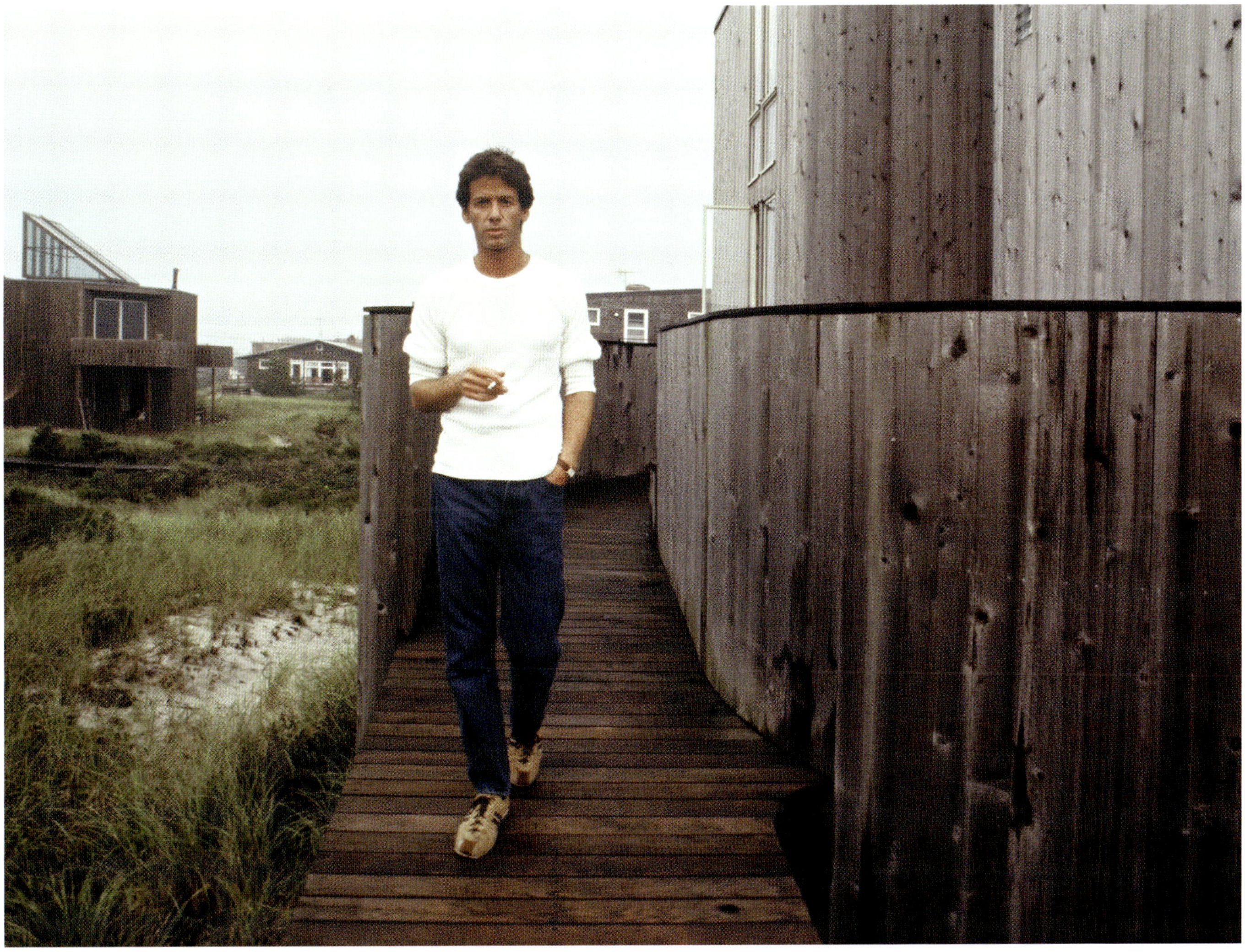

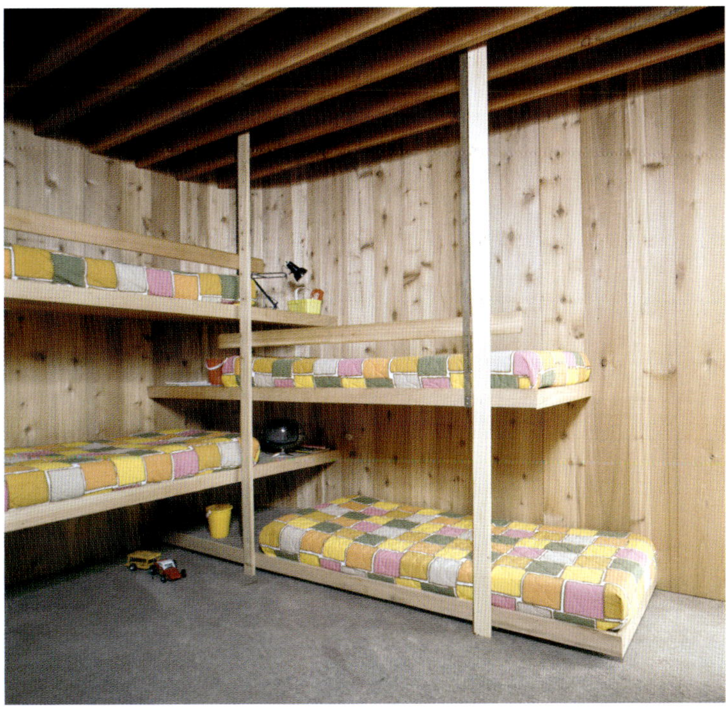

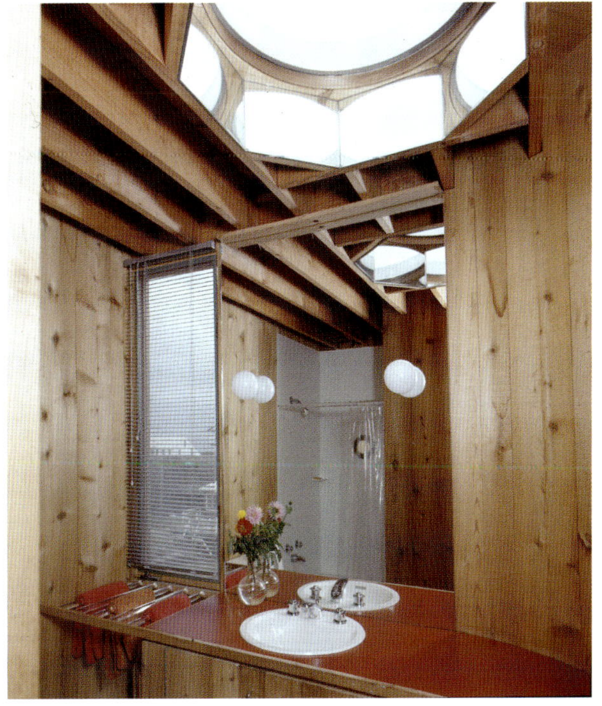

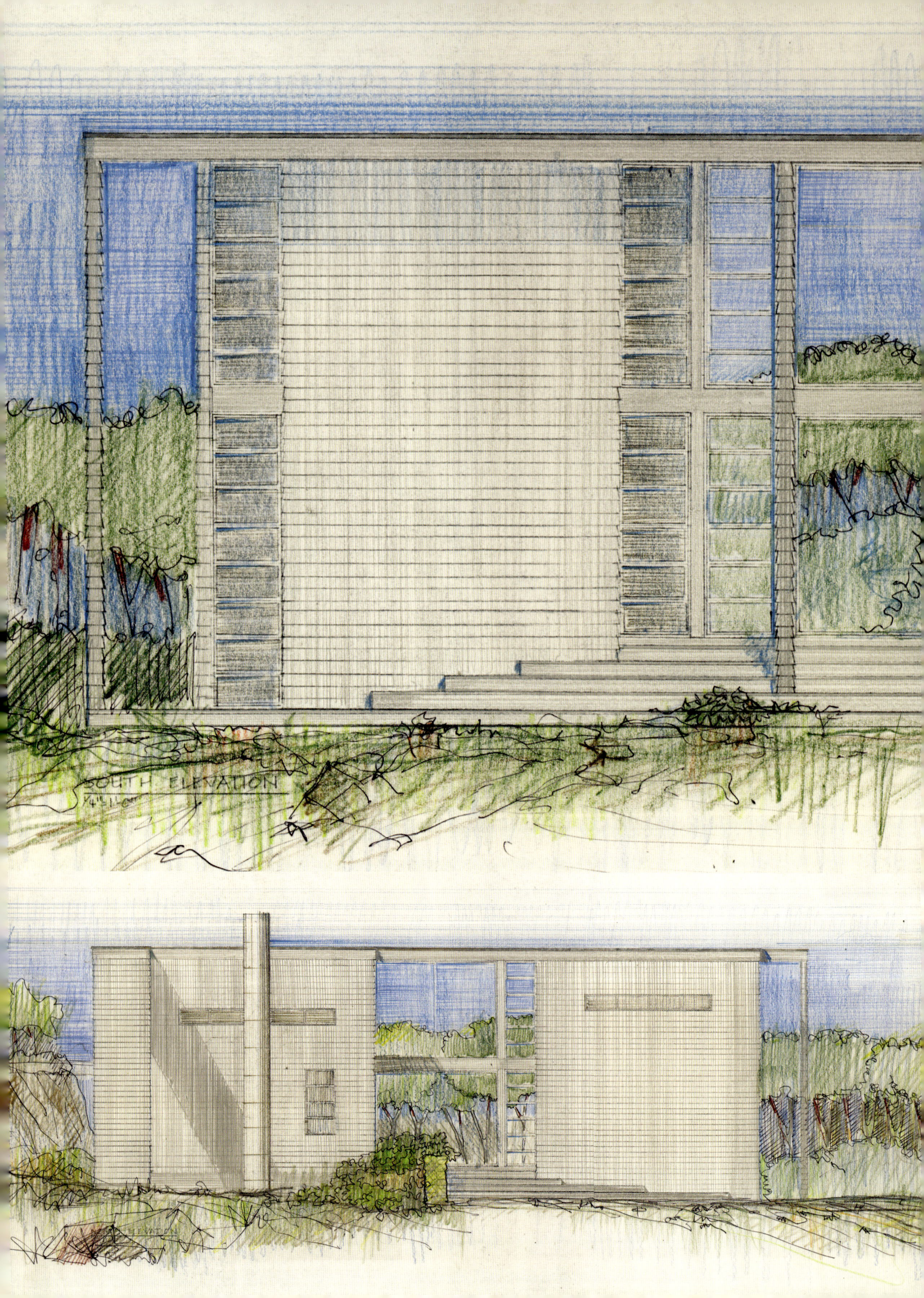
SOUTH ELEVATION
1/4" = 1'-0"

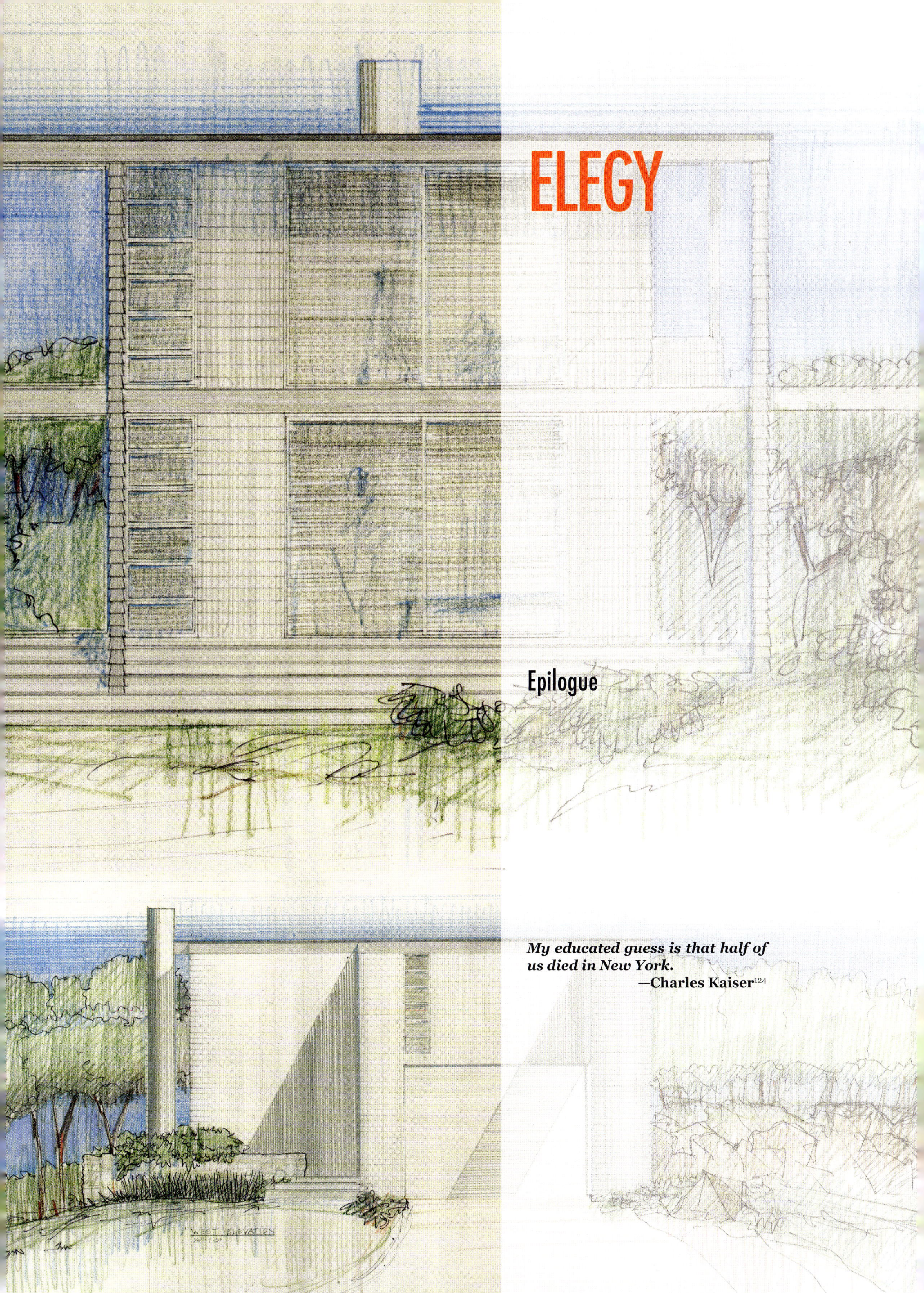

ELEGY

Epilogue

My educated guess is that half of us died in New York.
—Charles Kaiser[124]

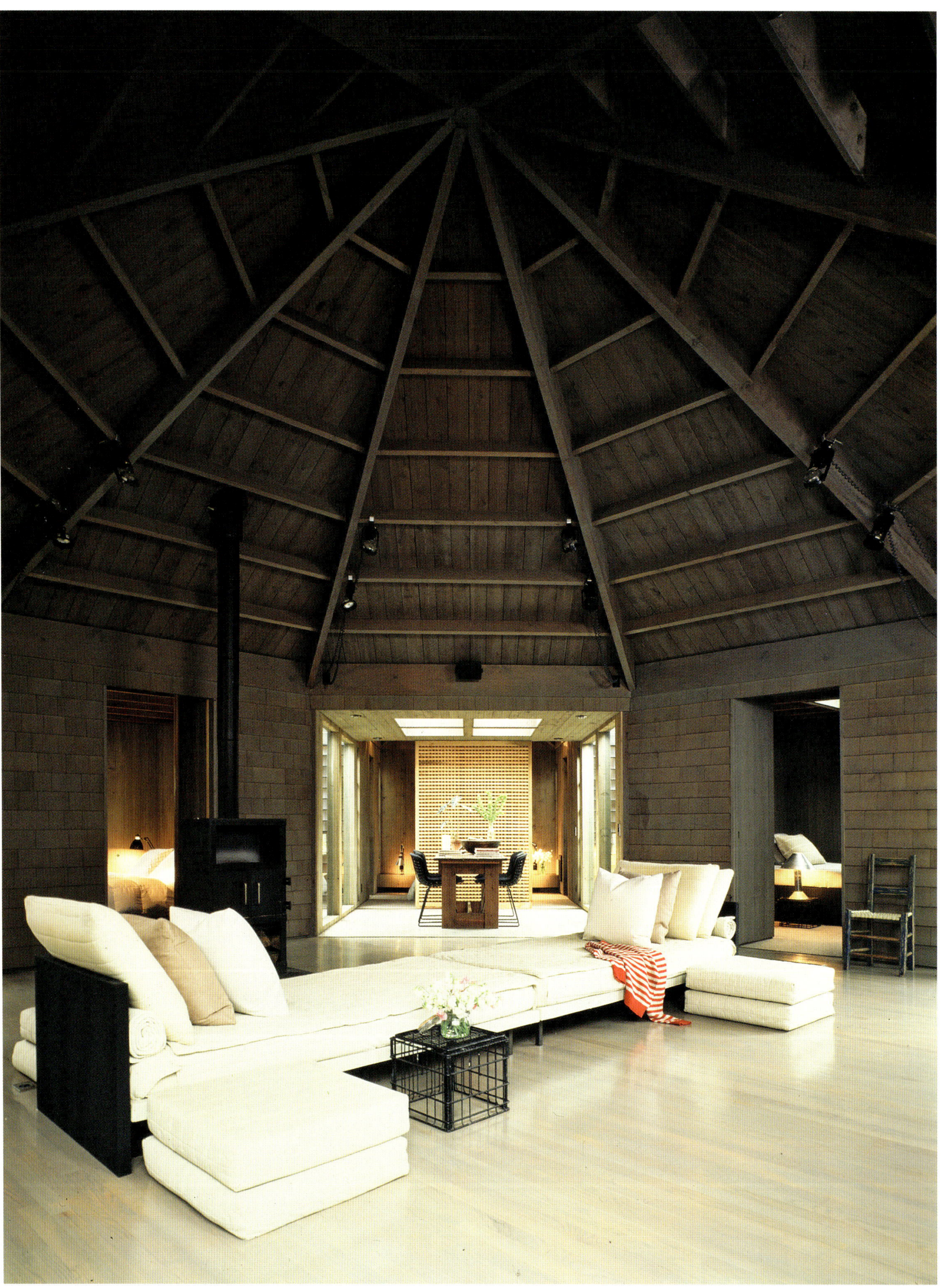

PAGES 200–01:

Silbert-Kiley House III (unbuilt), Roxbury, CT, 1987, elevations

OPPOSITE:

Living room of Wittstein-Miller House II, as enlarged by Scott Bromley in the early 1980s

PAGES 206–07:

Forstadt House, Ocean Beach, NY, 1989, an enlargement of the 1967 Moss House by Horace Gifford

On July 3 1981, the *New York Times* published an article entitled "Rare Cancer Seen in 41 Homosexuals." The idea of a sickness that somehow targeted gays seemed ludicrous to many, a fire-and-brimstone narrative that was easily laughed off. No one was laughing by the middle of the decade. For fifteen years, an HIV diagnosis equaled a painful death sentence, until protease inhibitors began to stem the epidemic in 1995. During this period, more people perished from AIDS in New York City alone than the total number of American soldiers who died in the Vietnam War.[125] "My educated guess is that half of us died in New York," wrote the journalist Charles Kaiser, author of *The Gay Metropolis: The Landmark History of Gay Life in America*.[126] For the two predominantly queer communities on Fire Island that were virtual extensions of New York City, AIDS was a massacre that emptied its homes and spread fear among gay and straight residents alike. Some people thought the virus might be airborne. A landscape beloved by naturists and hedonists alike, transformed so recently by gay liberation, morphed once again, this time into a site of loss, mourning, and a new activism that transcended the right to personal freedom. Under the cloud of a president who refused to utter the word AIDS, groups such as Gay Men's Health Crisis channeled Fire Island's love for a good party into effective fundraising platforms. The Calvin Klein residence, now owned by David Geffen, hosted GMHC's parties in the early 1990s. The same home became a principal setting for *Longtime Companion*, the first wide-release film to address the AIDS crisis. It traced the lives of a rapidly perishing group of friends; they begin as inveterate partiers and end up as dedicated caretakers.

Horace Gifford's post-Stonewall creations ranked among the most celebrated in his body of work. He reigned as the undisputed standard bearer of Fire Island in the 1970s, even as world-famous architects like Arthur Erickson touched down to design homes there. Yet the seeds of his personal and professional decline had already taken root at the peak of his influence. An early champion of Gifford's work was *The American Home*, a magazine that published lavish spreads of five Gifford homes, featuring one on the cover of its "vacation homes" issue in 1964. Its editor went so far as to proclaim Gifford "undoubtedly the top beach-house designer in the country."[127] But a management shakeup at the magazine in 1969 left Gifford out in the cold. By 1970, his romantic life was turned upside down when longtime partner Tom Prentiss left him for a woman. His friendship with C. Ray Smith, the gay *Progressive Architecture* editor, also suffered after Smith's brief marriage to a woman in 1971. *House and Garden* remained as the only publication to regularly feature Gifford's work, including a cover piece about the Travis-Wall residence in 1979.

In 1972, Gifford became romantically involved with a younger man named Robert Greenfield. Greenfield was impressed with the glamorous and well-off forty-year-old architect, who promptly whisked him off to Fire Island on a seaplane. Soon, there were first-class trips to Europe. The two men stood in stark contrast to one another. While Gifford's forthrightness was usually tempered by a reserved, Southern manner, Greenfield dispensed an undiluted brand of New York City chutzpah. At six feet, five inches tall, his physical presence was just as imposing as his personality. By all accounts, it was a tempestuous relationship. Greenfield was Gifford's junior by fifteen years and had no discernible career, arousing suspicion among the architect's protective friends that he was a "social climber."[128] While there might have been an element of truth to this critique, living with Gifford was not without its challenges.

Depression stalked Horace Gifford, most acutely during the dark winter months. When fashioning his own residence with "towers that reach out and grab for light,"[129] more was at stake for him than many ever knew. He was afflicted with a severe case of what is now known as seasonal affective disorder (SAD). The condition was an inheritance from both of his parents, with a manic component that may illuminate Gifford's astonishing output during the sixties. As the seventies dawned, his radiant demeanor became shadowed by periods of taciturnity and impulsiveness. No one was spared, not even the editors who championed his work. Late clients such as Peter Graham recalled a "very, very sensitive man who could be recalcitrant if he didn't get his way. You would have to seduce him out of it."[130] Clients were expected to accommodate these passing storms, as Gifford's uniformly frenetic pace gave way to fitful bursts of activity followed by retreats into oblivion. He completed nine homes in 1969 and only one in 1970. By the mid-1970s, he began to disappear for extended periods. During these withdrawals, locked in his bedroom with a telephone, he refused to speak with anyone but his sister, Jean, his lifelong confidante and first client. He tried everything to quiet the tremors in his mind, including electroshock therapy. Nothing worked.

Gifford cleverly established himself in the Pines as a leading architect before anyone else had thought to do so, yet some of his other choices may have hindered a wider success. By dropping out of the University of Pennsylvania, he denied himself the qualifications to spread his ideas through teaching. His 1965 arrest made him fearful of applying for his architecture license. In the late sixties, he turned down a $500,000 townhouse commission, reportedly for Halston,[131] complaining that "I'd have to set up an office, buy suits, be a real businessman."[132] Instead, he could be seen on the beach strolling to meetings in a Speedo. Embracing this carefree and humorous image of a happy, hippie modernist tending his own garden partially illuminates the man and his milieu. Yet Gifford was not lacking in larger visions, and he felt the sting of condescension from colleagues who dismissed his beach-house specialty as an unserious adjunct of the profession. As he approached his fortieth birthday in 1972, a creeping dissatisfaction with the narrowness of his career had set in. But the overwhelming sense of helplessness that afflicts the clinically depressed obscured a clear path forward.

At the same time, the broader public began to reject modern architecture. Modernism's political content had always been more muted in the United States than in Europe, where it enacted an explicit agenda to elevate the living conditions of the working class by harnessing industrial technologies. It owed its popular ascendance in the United States to a broadly shared prosperity and optimism about the future that was increasingly difficult to muster in the context of the Vietnam War, social unrest, and stagflation. As Horace Gifford turned inward, Americans turned on each other. This climate of scarcity and generational conflict contributed to the reactionary politics and callow nostalgia for "the good old days" that allowed postmodern architecture to proliferate.

Alas, the new vogue for premodern architectural referents was rarely accompanied by traditional craftsmanship. Ghostly silhouettes of historical architectural forms with the depth and substance of a child's drawing were soon plunked across countless subdivisions and skylines as the seventies digressed into the eighties. Facile symmetries and fantasias in Sheetrock steadily displaced the site-specific contours and robust materials of modern architecture. While enclaves like the Hamptons were running out of modernist steam by the advent of the 1973 Arab oil embargo, the Pines remained true to itself. For all of its problems, the seventies were a golden age for gays by the standards of the repression that had come before. With little to be nostalgic about, modern architecture suited them just fine, especially the hedonistic strain of it being perfected by Gifford. He could have bided his time on the safe shores of Fire Island while postmodernism ran its course. Instead, Gifford picked this inopportune moment to leave.

In 1976, feeling emotionally and physically exhausted, Gifford abruptly shuttered his Kips Bay Towers studio, sold his Fire Island home, and decamped to Houston with Robert Greenfield for a fresh start. He hoped that the proximity of his sister, the abundant Texas sunshine, and the promise of large commissions from developer contacts would reinvigorate his spirits and his practice. Once there, Gifford's Texan clients failed to deliver; none of the work came to fruition. Efforts to launch a beach-house revolution in Galveston netted a flattering profile in the *Houston Chronicle* but no commissions. By 1978, Gifford and Greenfield returned to New York. Their new multilevel home and studio in Manhattan's Turtle Bay Towers put a brave face on a faltering career.

Much had happened while they were away. Scott Bromley, a young protegé of Philip Johnson, began staking his claim as the go-to architect for the dwindling number of lots in the Pines. Bromley had achieved precocious fame as the designer of Studio 54 and knew how to maximize an opportunity. In his hands, a quaint fundraiser to purchase a fire truck for Fire Island Pines became Beach '79, an all-night oceanside party sheltered by an artful tangle of maypoles and billowing sails made of multicolored mosquito netting. Celebrity disco performers presided over a shirtless bacchanal, all under the eyes of a gushing press. The *New York Times* noted that the owner of Studio 54 struggled to get a ticket.[133] The "circuit party" was born, and residents vied to outdo one another for the most decadent event of the season. Arthur Erickson, a famous Canadian architect, came close in a party at his new home in the Pines nicknamed "Lincoln Center." Roberta Flack sang for the assembled guests. At the stroke of midnight, the ceiling retracted and hundreds of silver and gold balloons floated into a starlit sky. It was an era for spectacles. In this increasingly crowded, expensive, and flashy playground, Gifford's diminutive pavilions began to seem passé.

In 1981, Bromley purchased and set about enlarging Gifford's Wittstein-Miller House II. It was a handsome expansion, undertaken with far more grace than the hatchet jobs that would befall many other Gifford residences in the years to come. But its transformation marked a changing of the guard, as well as an era when small houses were synonymous with Fire Island's signature architecture. Things quickly got out of hand, as Fire Island's landscape wilted under fenced-in, gargantuan homes.

For a season after his return from Texas, Gifford rented the residence he had sold three years earlier but despaired of its unkempt condition. He counted many friends on Fire Island, even held a salon of sorts, but Gifford spurned the increasingly competitive milieu in which journalists were wooed and commissions were won. The prevalence of hard drugs, houses packed with renters, and a teeming party atmosphere were a far cry from the almost-secret society of small houses and candlelit dinner parties that the architect had joined two decades earlier. Suddenly, Gifford felt out of place in the very community that he'd helped to invent. In 1980, he left for good. His swan song to the Pines was his masterful work on the Calvin Klein residence. That same year, Samsonite Luggage recruited Gifford for a national advertising campaign. Samsonite's "rugged, organized, and classically handsome" attaché cases were extolled by the architect as he posed in front of his "architectural classics." With dozens of celebrated homes to his credit, national exposure, and famous clients, it might have been the moment for Gifford to graduate to the prestigious institutional commissions given to successful midcareer designers. Instead, an eighties media blitz marked the beginning of the end for the forty-eight-year-old architect.

In 1980, J. Hyde Crawford, a favorite client, invited Gifford to one of his homes in Bellport, a picturesque town on Long Island's South Shore. Bellport offered a lower-key ambience than the Pines and was reachable by train and car from New York. In an echo of the impulsiveness that caused him to build a home in the Pines after a single visit in 1961, Gifford and Greenfield bought a historic Bellport house, originally built for a ship's captain like Gifford's great-grandfather N. N. Penny. His interventions to the home were minimal. What most remember were the lavish gardens he created after rising at dawn each day. It was an odd inversion for a man who had spent two decades tucking modernist homes into virgin landscapes. But the activity was a form of self-medication: Gifford told his client Pete Roe that he needed to be "up with the sun" to control his depression.[134]

Changing public tastes, his own declining health, and the separation from his client base chipped away at modern house commissions. His attention and his convictions also drifted. With Greenfield, a fellow epicurean, he designed and comanaged Artichoke, a sleek and successful gourmet food shop in New York City, followed by a short-lived home furnishings shop in Bellport. He played the stock market. In this new locale, most design commissions were renovations of older homes. He had a brief and desultory flirtation with postmodernist themes but soon discarded this for a straightforward approach that paired historicist exteriors with whitewashed modernist interiors. Unlike the first two decades of Gifford's practice, many projects from the 1980s were never constructed. Few were published. The last Fire Island project was a reconstruction and enlargement of his 1967 Moss Residence, after a fire.

Occasionally, the fog lifted and great work was still possible. A 1987 house design layered a slender elegance onto a windswept, rocky ledge in Connecticut. Gene Silbert and John Kiley, clients who turned to Gifford during each decade of his career, asked for their home to be placed on top of the hill. Instead, Gifford sheltered it in the crook of the ledge, while a second-story bridge made a soft landing upon the preserved hilltop. But it was never built. The seventy-eight modern vacation homes he built between 1961 and 1981 were created for an audience largely lost to AIDS, and constitute his essential legacy.[135]

On a cold November day in 1991, Horace Gifford boarded a plane for Houston, carrying only a small valise and a few rolls of drawings. He was destined for the care of his sister, who lived in the first house he ever designed. And it was there that he died on April 6, 1992, of complications from AIDS. He was fifty-nine. Gifford's brother, an undertaker, prepared his body for burial in Vero Beach. Gifford's mother, Marie, outlived her son. Robert Greenfield, his recently estranged ex-partner, died of AIDS less than a year after Gifford. No formal provisions were made for Gifford's archive. But Greenfield's dying wish to preserve Gifford's original drawings and slides allowed this overlooked body of work to be interpreted by a new generation.

In his controversial screed about Fire Island in 1972, Albert Goldman interrupted his litany of scandals to reflect more thoughtfully on the Pines, a place whose 600 homes projected "the realization that life must be ordered and harmonious and benevolent if it is to be happy."[136] As the author of forty of these Pines homes and the inspiration for countless others, Gifford conferred a benevolent order upon a rapidly changing culture, one that turned to him to make sense of a world in which all the old constraints had fallen away. His work reminds us of the power of architecture to shape a culture, as well as its powerlessness to prevent its destruction. We cannot bring back that lost generation, but we can preserve its enduring artifacts.[137] In his last public statement, Horace Gifford said it best:

> In the end, the past is personal, and that is what makes its preservation so urgent. It is our own memories intermingled with the collective memory that we call history; it is not so much truth as interpretation; but in that interpretation we can find beauty and wisdom, inspiration for living and guidance for the future.[138]

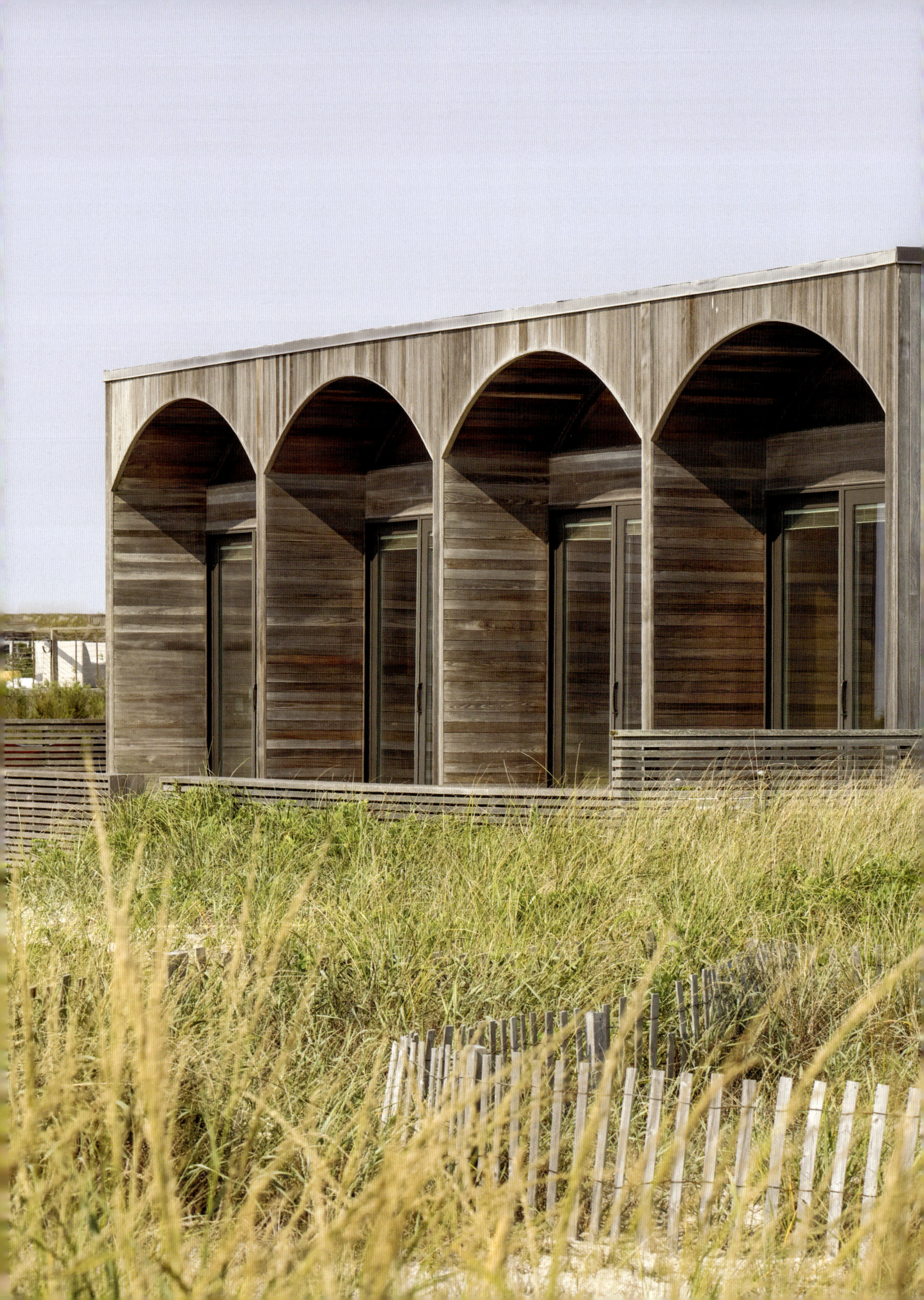

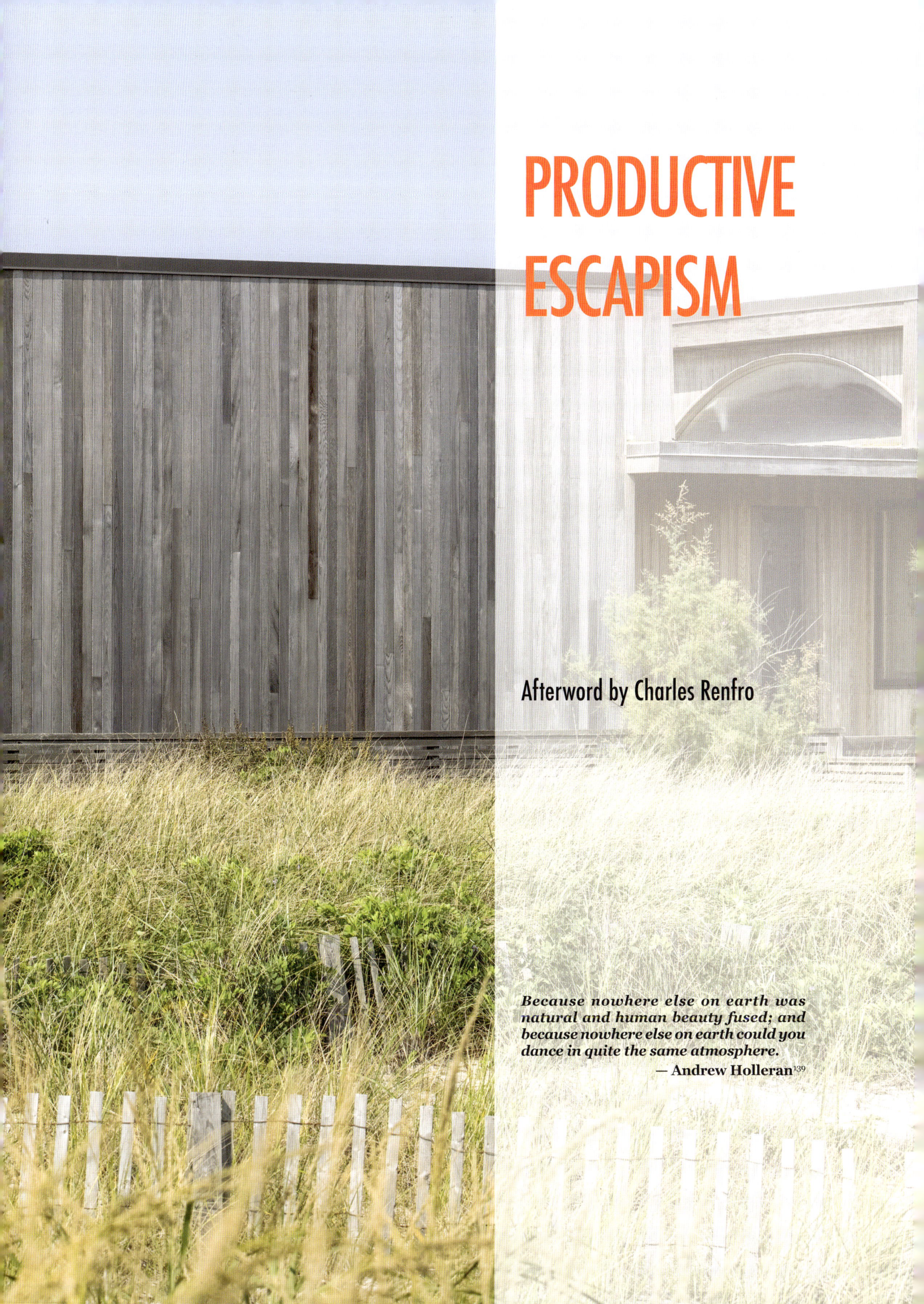

PRODUCTIVE ESCAPISM

Afterword by Charles Renfro

Because nowhere else on earth was natural and human beauty fused; and because nowhere else on earth could you dance in quite the same atmosphere.
— **Andrew Holleran**[139]

Years before I purchased a modest Horace Gifford house in the Pines, I would cry every time I left the island. They were tears of joy tinged with sadness and anxiety. Joy because I no doubt had an exhilarating and unscripted experience that I didn't think was possible. Sadness because I didn't know when I would feel so free and alive again (even if I was planning to come out the following weekend). And anxiety that all the living and loving that was packed into 48 hours wasn't quite real.

From the ferry, the sunset would dry the tears and bring me down to earth, forcing me to acknowledge that the Pines was indeed real, if completely unique. I realized that what makes Fire Island so special is its disarmingly simple merger of nature and architecture. Each is elevated by the other, a symbiotic and sublime relationship promoted by queer culture. Being on Fire Island made our queerness, our otherness, quite literally, natural. It legitimized our behaviors, enveloped them in waves and sand and branches of holly and pine trees. It helped wipe away years of stigma and trauma and fear in a place only 50 miles from where our successful "real" lives took place.

Fire Island also steeped us in modernism. The Pines is primarily a domestic environment—public space and commercial establishments play second fiddle to houses. Most of the transcendent experiences happen in houses, in the day, the night, or early morning if we are successful. By and large, these houses are simple affairs, rooted in mid-century modernism, the prevalent style at the time of the Pines' founding. But making modernist houses was not just about being au courant; it was about tricking the system. Among other talented peers, Horace Gifford, who was gay, understood that modernism was the Trojan Horse that would enable a new lifestyle on Fire Island to emerge. At the same time, it was a way to take back the freestanding house, long a typology associated with heteronormative, nuclear families, as ours: a typology that could reflect and inform the intentional families we were making.

Modernism embodied the idea of honesty in form and materials. It eschewed historical signifiers that referred to the past lives of other people and became a platform for—and by extension, an image of—each occupant's life. Modernism allowed a new lifestyle to flourish partly because it was untethered to the past. As with modernism generally, Gifford's houses were honest and simple. They were unadorned but elegant boxes that commune and conspire with nature, allowing the exterior setting to become the interior adornment. They enlisted nature as a theatrical partner: flowers come and go, leaves sprout and grow, tides rise and fall, all framed or revealed in the simple gestures of his houses. The beauty, the fragility, and even the hedonism of our lives is mirrored in the nature that surrounds our houses. With Gifford, we both become ourselves and become part of nature. We are validated in ways we could have never fathomed. Hence the tears.

As these pages so expertly detail, each of Gifford's houses is unique, but shares DNA. They use ample glazing and operable glass doors, often on parallel walls to create living spaces that merge with nature, both at the front and the rear. Glass sizes appear far too large to have been hauled by hand to their sites. They are bold and provocative, employing seemingly impossible cantilevers and spans in wood framing. An architect might marvel at these triumphs, but to most people they simply disappear. They were made to subtly elevate the experiences of their inhabitants rather than demand attention. The other materials he used, like cedar and pine, could have been sourced on the island. Programmatically, each of his houses rejected the hierarchy of traditional sleeping arrangements, eliminating the primary bedroom in favor of equally sized or lifestyle-oriented bedrooms, often with shared bathrooms. Sharing was at the center of Gifford houses: they nurtured collectivity while at the same time supporting radical individuality.

The house I purchased was Gifford's first design in the Pines. It was a modest affair, under 1,000 square feet and sold by *Better Homes and Gardens* as a plan that could be constructed cheaply by anyone, anywhere. Three were made in the Pines, and Gifford lived in one of them. Sadly, Gifford's house has been modified over the years, and the other one recently burned down, leaving mine as a kind of litmus test of Gifford's architectural prescience. Built around 1962, two years before I was born, my house has sheltered generations of gays, and I can safely say that it continues to inspire new generations of guests, including those raised on social media in a cultural environment accepting of queerness. They don't need Fire Island to feel like they can live their lives honestly, but they crave it nevertheless. These houses do more than just support beach living: they are an integral part of community-making, whether in the past, now, or into the future.

These houses are not fixed in resin. They can (and should) change to address their owner's needs, but they rarely need to. Most are examples of perfection that contemporary architects would

PAGES 206–07:
Forstadt House, Ocean Beach, NY, 1989, a reconstruction and enlargement by Horace Gifford of the 1967 Moss House

OPPOSITE:
Party at the Renfro House, Fire Island Pines, NY, 2024

PAGES 210–11:
Gifford House II, Fire Island Pines, NY, 1965

find challenging to alter. I snapped up 635 Fire Island Boulevard immediately when I saw the acre of undeveloped forest space directly behind the house, knowing that we could "expand" the house without touching it. Over the years, we (Daniel Gortler, my husband, and Alex Galan, my longtime housemate sister and best friend) have transformed the rear yard into a parallel, outdoor house—a watery Shangri-La even more embedded in nature than Gifford's houses. Our house has served as a kind of commons for a new generation of Pines visitors, most of whom become friends after a blissful afternoon or night there, bonded by the magic bones of Gifford's architecture.

As the Pines moves into middle age and the world around us changes, so too should our houses in the Pines. Gifford's vision is timeless in its celebration of intentional families and embrace of nature. Can it provide inspiration for a new architecture that helps to forestall the ravages of climate change while supporting the ever-changing definition of self-constructed identity and family? While the Pines is a place to escape, it has also been a place where architecture has engendered both freedom and care—for each other and for the environment. Let's call it a place of productive escapism.

The challenge to all of us who cherish Fire Island and Horace Gifford is to reenvision his aspirations for a new era: conceiving houses that secure their sand without obstructing natural shifts; that are truly off-grid, using wind and solar and harvested water; and that ditch air-conditioning in favor of natural ventilation, much in the way Gifford always designed his houses. Let's think about modularity and transformability. Let's grow or shrink or change our environments as our families and genders and predilections change. Let's think about houses that can move if needed and whose materials are entirely sustainable. These suggestions aren't revolutionary, they are evolutionary—and they began with Horace Gifford.

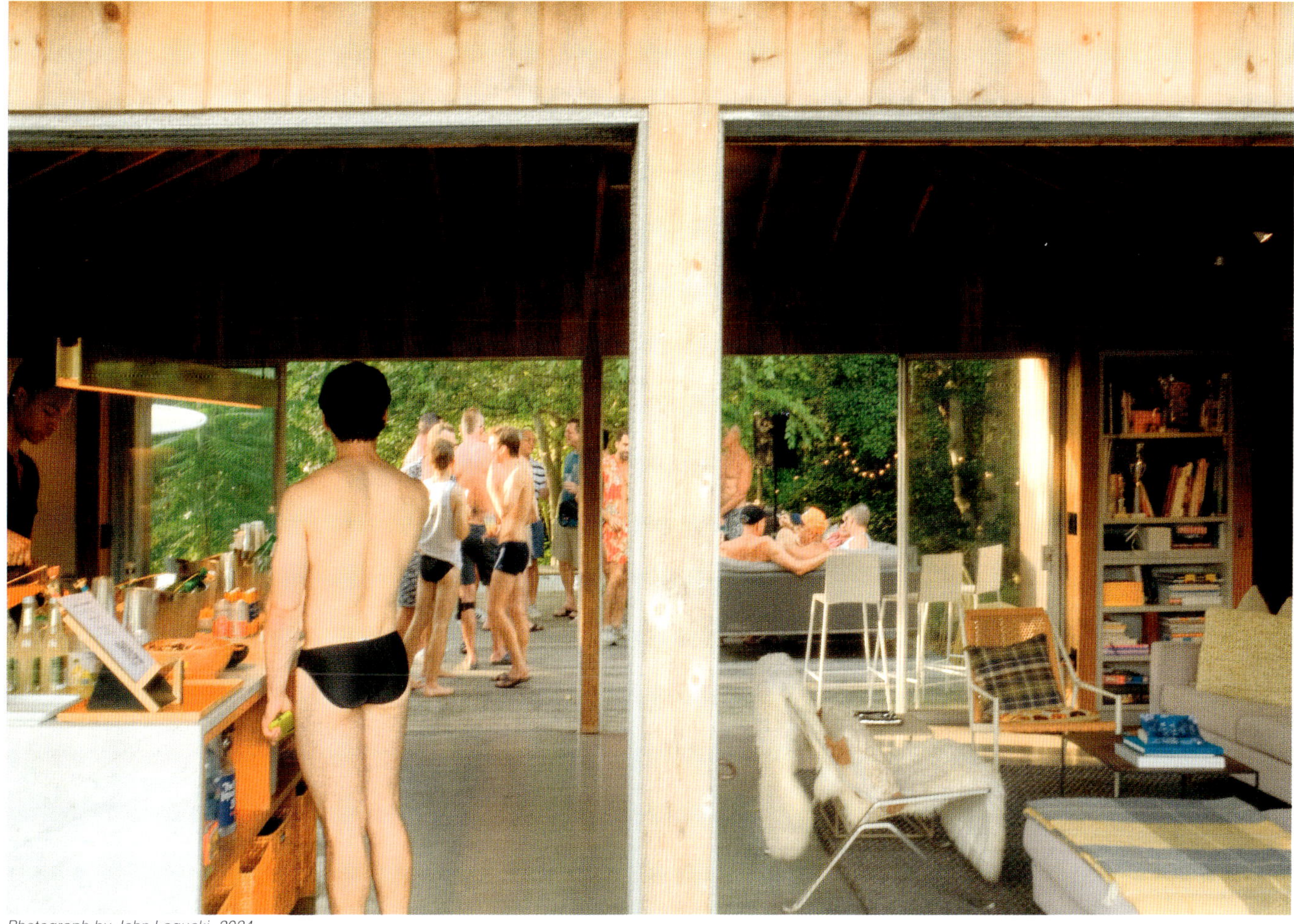

Photograph by John Lagucki, 2024

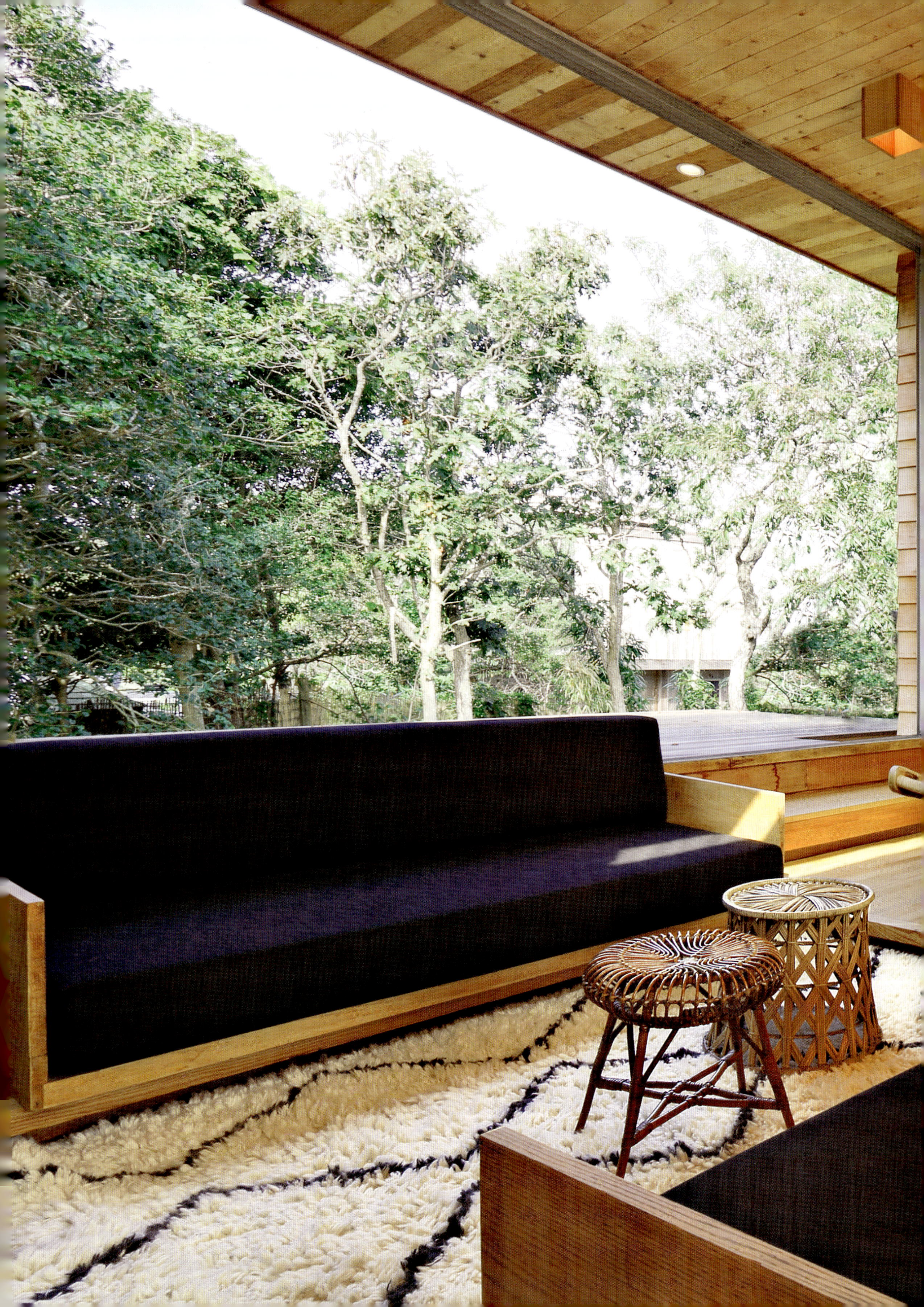

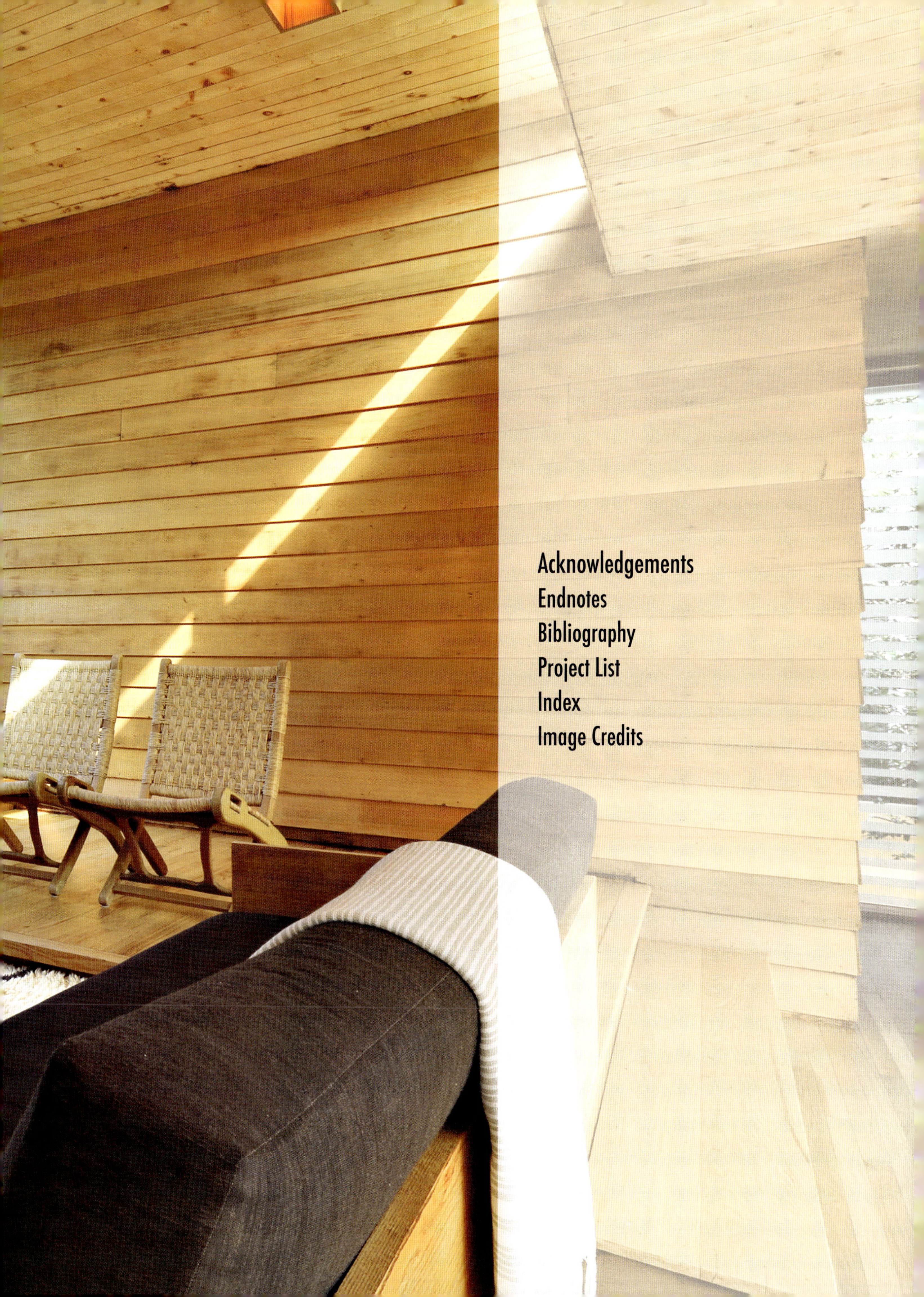

Acknowledgements

It is not every day that an untested writer gets to immortalize an obscure architect in the pages of an elegant hardcover book. Until now, I have practiced rather than written about architecture, and the distillation of all I have learned about Horace Gifford has been an adventure and an education. First, there was the not-insignificant matter of learning how to write. Then, there was the hunt for hundreds of vintage images, scattered across dozens of venues. Soon, we were commissioning new photo shoots for previously unpublished homes. Finally, Gifford's story had to break through a challenging publishing environment. At each of these junctures, this project might have come to a halt but for the assistance of the following people.

Special thanks are first and foremost given to Edward DiGuardia, who preserved Gifford's papers and provided unstinting access and encouragement. Peter Stamberg and Paul Aferiat, fellow Gifford enthusiasts, introduced me to key associates and clients. William Murphy patiently walked me through his twenty-year professional and personal affiliation with the architect. Gifford's niece Jane Slay shared moving personal recollections of her uncle, as did his longtime friend Robert Berlin. In Vero Beach, Pam Cooper of the Indian River County Main Library and Rebecca Rickey of the Heritage Center and Citrus Museum provided rich historical resources. William Whitaker and Nancy Thorne at the Architectural Archives of the University of Pennsylvania tirelessly fielded my inquiries. Photographers Michael Weber, Tom Sibley, and John Lagucki were generous with their time and talents. Robert Bonanno and Warren McDowell supplied many of the vintage Pines photographs that add contextual richness to what might have otherwise been a relentless parade of homes. Carl Saytor at Luxlab expertly guided the scanning of original slides. Michael Lugering, Tom Stoelker, and Gianfranco Lentini read early drafts and offered sage advice. Gianfranco also graces the cover of the new edition. Philip Monaghan, Cay Sophie Rabinowitz, and Christian Rattemeyer were consummate cheerleaders and behind-the-scenes fixers during my most harried moments. Paul Blackburn and Sebastien Queney's assistance in preparing the drawings was indispensable.

The following interviewees illuminated Horace Gifford and his milieu: Adele Applebaum, Leslie Armstrong, Harry Bates, Ferron Bell, Ronald Bentley, Robert Berlin, Lawrence Bonaguidi, Alan Borg, Jo Segal Bressler, Scott Bromley, Barry Browning, Fred Bruning, Elizabeth Burge, Robert Yale Burge, James Cashel, Peter Cott, J. Hyde Crawford, George Davis, Randy Davis, Barbara DiCarlo, Edward DiGuardia, Daniel Duhl, Florence Duhl, Michael Dunne, J. Charles Gifford, Ric Globus, Jake Gorst, Mel Dwork, Murray Fishman, Ron Fuzia, Alastair Gordon, Peter Graham, David Hatcher, Joyce Kahn, John Kiley, Kenneth Leedom, Carol Ferris-Lipkins, Richard Marek, Warren McDowell, Paul McGregor, Robert Miller, John Millman, Steve Molzon, Philip Monaghan, Paul Muldawer, William Murphy, Lee Naiman, Steve Navarro, Steve Perlo, Marlo Sloan Phillips, Felice Picano, Wakefield Poole, Elizabeth Reeves, Robert Rehbock, John "Pete" Roe, Ned Rorem, Jay Rosenberg, Gladys Rosenthal, J. Robert Rosenthal, Warren Rubin, Teresa Lee Rushworth, Susan Pilson Schreiner, Joerg Schwartz, Burt Seides, Gene Silbert, Jane Slay, Norton Sloan, Skyler Smith, Robert Sprague, Meg Switzgable, Mark Sylaj, Joseph Thal, William Trautman, Patrick Travis, William Wall, Barbara Weiser, Edwin Wittstein, and Harriet Wolfson.

Acquiring the rights to reproduce the many beautiful images in this book was an expensive proposition. Alas, raising the dead is not for the faint of heart or the slim of wallet! I thank Glen Wielgus and the Fire Island Pines Arts Project, who made me their first artist-in-residence and provided a start-up grant. The Architectural League of New York's fiscal sponsorship created a tax-deductible fund-raising vehicle, and I thank the league's Anne Rieselbach for her crucial support. As of October 2012, the following individuals and institutions contributed funding, via the Architectural League, to this project: the Robert Alfandre Foundation, Ronald Bentley and Salvatore LaRosa, Andrew Berman and Terry Todd, Marc Berman and John Yakubic, Lawrence Bonaguidi, Sully Bonnelly and Robert Littman, James and Susan Brady, Scott Bromley, Robert Yale Burge and Yale Burge Antiques Inc., James Cashel, Keith and Amanda Catanzano, J. Hyde Crawford and Charles Andrews, Jess and Deborah Eberhart, Carol Ferris-Lipkins, Goldman Sachs, Chuck Golod, James Guedry, Chuck and Mimi Greenlee, Michael Harrell, B. Thomas Henry, Lester and Carol Holt, Island Properties of the Pines, Wingate Jackson and Paul Trantanella, John Kiley and Gene Silbert, Kenneth Koen, Garry Korr, Mark Krayenhoff, Terence Law and Llewellyn Young, Edward Lewis, Williams Lewis, Andrew Lippman, Mark McGuire and Craig

Wilson, David Menkes, Thomas and Katherine Mike, John Millman, Sean Pierce, Milton Pike, Richard Pittelli and Gino Chiapparelli, Jay Rawlins, Eric Reinitz and Marc Blackwell, Dale and Sally Richter, Dale Riedl and Adam Dworkin, J. Robert and Gladys Rosenthal, Warren and Bernice Rubin, Joerg Schwartz, Michael Crisafulli and Morton Newburgh, William Murphy, Carlos Otero, Steve Tetreault, Nenad Lovric and Michael Wagner, the Leslie Setterholm Trust, the Joseph and Sheila Thal Foundation, William Trautman, Leonidas Vrondissis and Ellie Moschos, Richard Winger, Edwin Wittstein and Robert Miller, and Simon Yates and Kevin Roon. And I thank Jennifer Lippert, Andrea Truppin, and Anthony Viscardi for writing helpful recommendations for grants.

The following individuals and institutions generously donated images for this book: Harry Bates, Ferron Bell, *Better Homes and Gardens*, Tom Bianchi, Robert Bonanno and the Fire Island Pines Historical Preservation Society, Scott Bromley, J. Hyde Crawford, Charles Andrews, *House Beautiful*, the Indian River County Library of Vero Beach, Edward DiGuardia, Michael Dunne, Gilbert Emerson, the Andrew Geller Archives, J. Charles Gifford, Alastair Gordon, Gary Gunderson, the Library of Congress, Robert McCarter, Warren McDowell, David Menkes, Tad Mike, Lindsey Morris, Elizabeth Moulton, the National Register of Historic Places, Cynthia Peterson, the Pines Pantry, Wakefield Poole, Richard Reens, Eric Clarke Rhein, Tom Sibley, Sinclair Smith, Jane Slay, *Vero Beach Magazine*, Michael Weber, and Edwin Wittstein.

Current Gifford and Gifford-related homeowners cheerfully endured my impositions: Charles Andrews and J. Hyde Crawford, Marc Blackwell and Eric Reinitz, Sully Bonnelly and Robert Littman, Jo Segal Bressler, Scott Bromley, Thomas Brown and Meg Switzgable, Barry Browning, James Cashel, Beth Chase, Ari Fridkis, Jonathan and Maria Harber, Jean-Marc Houmard, John Kiley and Gene Silbert, Lucy Kneebone and David Stewart, Andrew Lippman, Nenad Lovric and Michael Wagner, David Menkes, John Millman, Carlos Otero, Steve Perlo, Milton Pike, Kevin Roon and Simon Yates, J. Robert and Gladys Rosenthal, Paul Rowe, Marina Schinz Rubin, and Jane Schube.

Others supplied critical visibility for this undertaking. The tristate chapter of DoCoMoMo and Fire Island Pines Ventures each sponsored a Horace Gifford lecture, while *Modernism* magazine published my survey of his work in its summer 2010 issue. I thank Jacques-Pierre Caussin, Mark Davis, and William Kopelk of Palm Springs Modernism Week for sponsoring a book launch lecture.

Diana Murphy of Metropolis Books and Alex Galan of ARTBOOK | D.A.P. took a chance on a new writer, and for that I am truly grateful. They partnered with Gordon DeVries Studio, a young and exciting imprint headed by Alastair Gordon and Barbara de Vries. I have often decried the lack of true mentorship in architectural practice, but I found a literary mentor in Alastair Gordon. Deliberately, and somewhat nervously, I modeled my text after Gordon's technique of crafting a seamless architectural narrative that is firmly situated within the larger culture. So I was delighted and flattered when Alastair offered to edit, copublish, and contribute the foreword to this book. The final result is immeasurably better for his involvement, matched only by Barbara de Vries' inspired book design. Thomas Evans deftly edited the second edition, while his calming influence neutralized the stress of a challenging schedule. Everything I love about Fire Island is distilled in the person of Charles Renfro. His moving afterword will show you why. I thank my parents and friends for their unwavering support, and my brother, John, for holding down the fort at my design practice. In a chronically distracted age, the pleasures of my total immersion in this research were immense. Yet it was also a melancholy business to encounter a generation so tragically cut down by AIDS. I hope this book, in its small way, does some justice to the accomplishments and remarkable spirit of that lost generation.

Endnotes

1 "For an Active Beach Life," *House and Garden* (July 1974): 24.
2 Ibid.
3 Gladys Rosenthal (client), interview with author, September 9, 2009.
4 Seaplane service was discontinued in the early 2000s but was influential in drawing an affluent crowd to the Pines during the 1960s and '70s.
5 Albert Goldman, "I Have Seen the Future, and It's Fire Island," *New York* (June 1972): 26–27.
6 Approximately 85 percent of Gifford's known construction drawings were in DiGuardia's possession, along with twelve slide carousels, several sketches, a modest amount of correspondence from magazine editors, and a self-penned project list and bibliography of published work up to 1977. Nearly all of Gifford's personal effects and correspondence were lost.
7 Ned Rorem, *The Later Diaries of Ned Rorem*, 1961–1972 (San Francisco: North Point, 1987), 181.
8 Warren Rubin, telephone interview with the author, May 27, 2009.
9 Madeleine McDermott Hamm, "Must All Beach Houses Look Alike?" *Houston Chronicle*, July 10, 1977.
10 Fred Bruning, "He Shoots Cutting Edges into the Sky," *Suffolk Sun*, May 5, 1968, 6.
11 Doris Herzig, "Designer's Home Rises Above It All," *Newsday*, June 16, 1966.
12 McDermott Hamm, "Must All Beach Houses Look Alike?"
13 Jack Parlett, *Fire Island: A Century in the Life of an American Paradise* (New York: Hanover Square, 2022). Jess Rothstein, narrator. *Finding Fire Island*, Spotify, 2023. John Dempsey, ed., *Fire Island: A Century of Art* (London: Phaidon, 2025).
14 As a practicing architect, I recognize the potential downsides of imposing more regulations on an already burdensome permit process. Execution and moderation are key, since historic preservation ordinances can be hijacked by NIMBY purists. And architecture is not truly modern if it cannot be changed.
15 Robert Berlin (Gifford friend), telephone interviews with author, November 18, 2009; April 23, 2010; and June 20, 2011.
16 Friend Charles Gifford, "What I Remember," *Stories of Life Along Beautiful Indian River*, ed. Anna Pearl Leonard Newman (Vero Beach: Anna Pearl Leonard Newman, 1953), 11.
17 Historic Property Associates, Inc, *Historic Properties Survey of the City of Vero Beach, Florida: A Study of the Historic Architectural Resources of Vero Beach and Recommendations for Their Preservation* (Saint Augustine: City of Vero Beach, 1990), xiv.
18 Berlin, interview.
19 Horace Gifford and Kay Wadtke, eds., *The Arrowhead 1950* (Vero Beach: Vero Beach High School Senior Class, 1950).
20 Teresa Lee Rushworth, "120 Years of the Giffords," *Vero Beach Magazine* (March 2008): 194–208. Charles Gifford (Gifford's brother), telephone interview with author, November 20, 2009.
21 Jane Slay (Gifford's niece), telephone interviews with author, September 24, 2008, and February 17, 2009. According to Slay, both Jean Gifford Slay and Horace Gifford Sr. suffered from depression.
22 Berlin, interview.
23 Paul Muldawer (Gifford's classmate at University of Florida), interview with author, November 18, 2009.
24 Ibid.
25 Ibid. Berlin became a psychologist.
26 Ibid.
27 Horace Gifford, letter to Robert Berlin, January 11, 1956.
28 Robert McCarter, *Louis I. Kahn* (London: Phaidon, 2005), 111.
29 Stephen Spender, *W. H. Auden: A Tribute* (London: Weidenfeld and Nicolson, 1975), 117. Cited in Esther Newton, *Cherry Grove, Fire Island: Sixty Years in America's First Gay and Lesbian Town* (Boston: Beacon, 1993), 46–47. Lee Koppelman and Seth Forman, *The Fire Island National Seashore: A History* (Albany: State University of New York Press, 2008), 13.
30 Koppelman and Forman, *The Fire Island National Seashore*, 2.
31 Charles Dickerson, "A Century at the Grove," *Fire Island News*, July 19, 1969. Cited in Newton, *Cherry Grove*, 15.
32 Koppelman and Forman, *The Fire Island National Seashore*, 13.
33 Philip Gefter, *What Becomes a Legend Most: A Biography of Richard Avedon* (Harper Collins, 2020), 108.
34 Ibid, 117.
35 Spender, *W. H. Auden*, 117.
36 Promotional poster for The Home Guardian Company of New York, ca. 1953.
37 "Follies Girl Recalls the Scent of The Pines," *Fire Island News*, July 21, 1988.
38 Richard Marek (son of George Marek), telephone interview with author, August 13, 2012.
39 "Ocean Bay Park," *Fire Island News*, July, 2, 1960. Cited in Alastair Gordon, *Beach Houses: Andrew Geller* (New York: Princeton Architectural Press, 2000), 56.
40 Edwin Wittstein and Robert Miller, interview with author, October 14, 2009.
41 Warren Rubin (client), telephone interview with author, May 27, 2009.
42 Horace Gifford, 1961 letter to Robert Berlin, read to author during telephone interview, April 23, 2010.
43 Horace Gifford, letter to Robert Berlin, December 27, 1955.
44 John D. Bloodgood, "Troubles Stay Behind," *Better Homes and Gardens* (August 1962): 5.

45 Bruning, "He Shoots Cutting Edges into the Sky."
46 Song was written by Malvina Reynolds in 1962; performed 1963 by Pete Seeger and released in 1963 by Folkways Records.
47 Wright built approximately sixty Usonian homes between 1936 and 1959.
48 Wittstein and Miller, interview.
49 *Interior Design: The New Freedom* (video course given by Barbaralee Diamonstein-Spielvogel at the Parsons School of Design, 1997), http://library.duke.edu/digitalcollections/dsva/.
50 The gated, haute-WASP community of Point O' Woods also has no Gifford homes. Architect David Leavitt designed a modernist home in Cherry Grove in 1956, but it burned down by the early 1960s. See Caroline Zaleski, *Long Island Modernism: 1930–1980* (New York: W. W. Norton, 2012), 67–69.
51 The author heard this nickname from several longtime Cherry Grove residents when he vacationed there during the summers of 2001 and 2002.
52 Bruning. "He Sends Cutting Edges into the Sky," 6.
53 Goldman, "I Have Seen the Future," 27.
54 Charles Gwathmey, cited in Alastair Gordon, *Weekend Utopia: Modern Living in the Hamptons* (New York: Princeton Architectural Press, 2000), 130.
55 "Opulence with a Single Motif," *House and Garden*, 106.
56 Gene Silbert (client), interview with the author, October 26, 2011.
57 Berlin, interview.
58 Newton, *Cherry Grove*, 92.
59 There have been rumors of a place called the Doughnut Hole, a lesbian version of the Meat Rack, but its existence seems to be apocryphal.
60 Murray Fishman (client), telephone interview with author, March 5, 2012.
61 "License Requirements," New York State Office of the Professions, n.d. See: http://www.op.nysed.gov/prof/arch/archlic.htm (accessed January, 7 2011).
62 William Trautman (Gifford friend), telephone interview with author, September 20, 2009. According to Trautman, Gifford never applied for his architectural registration because he believed that, because of his arrest, he was disqualified from obtaining his license. The New York State Office of the Professions did not respond to the author's inquiries regarding the disqualification of applicants with offenses of this nature.
63 Newton, *Cherry Grove*, 200.
64 Kurt Pressman, "The Night They Raided Fire Island," *Queens Quarterly* (Summer 1970): 14. Cited in Newton, *Cherry Grove*, 200.
65 Early projects were stamped by William Fuller, a Gifford associate, and some are credited to Gifford and Fuller in publications. Most projects from 1972 onward were stamped by longtime Gifford associate William Murphy.
66 Edward DiGuardia (friend and client), interview with author, March 15, 2010.
67 Herzig, "Designer Home Rises," 111.
68 Ibid.
69 William Murphy (associate and friend), interview with author, June 4, 2009.
70 Barbara DiCarlo (neighbor), interview with author, October 9, 2009. Confirmed by Ferron Bell (friend), telephone interview with author, April 8, 2012. Nan and Peter Schultz commissioned Gifford to design a Fire Island Pines home in 1964.
71 Goldman, "I Have Seen the Future," 27–28.
72 Art Directors Club, http://www.adcglobal.org/archive/hof/1984/?id=247 (accessed September, 10, 2011).
73 Scali, McCabe, Sloves was founded in 1967. In 1999, *Advertising Age* named the firm's Perdue Farms campaign one of the top 100 of the year.
74 "Sam Scali," Art Directors Club, 1984, http://www.adcglobal.org/archive/hof/1984/?id=247.
75 Rita Reif, "A 90-Minute Trip from Victoriana to Fire Island Modern," *New York Times Magazine* (October 18, 1967): 50.
76 Ibid.
77 Goldman, "I Have Seen the Future," 27.
78 Lawrence Bonaguidi (client), telephone interview with author, May 15, 2009.
79 Bruning, "He Shoots Cutting Edges into the Sky."
80 Patrick Travis and William Wall (clients), interview with author, March 15, 2010.
81 Ibid.
82 Ibid.
83 Ibid.
84 Wakefield Poole, *The Wakefield Poole Collection* (Philadelphia: TLA Entertainment Group, 2009). Quote by Jerry Walker as he interviewed Poole, commentary section of the DVD.
85 *Variety* (January 19, 1972), n.p.
86 See, for example, Fire Island Cruising 3, Lucas Films, New York, 2006, DVD.
87 Fishman, interview.
88 "Architects Speak Their Minds," *House and Garden* (June 1970): 44.
89 James Cashel (client), interview with author, July 2009.
90 John Kiley (client), e-mail interview with author, January 31, 2010.

91 Joseph Fried, "New Forms Emerge in Vacation Homes," *New York Times*, April 28, 1968.
92 Bruning, "He Shoots Cutting Edges into the Sky."
93 C. Ray Smith, "Variations on a Plan," *Progressive Architecture* (May 1968): 139.
94 Ibid, 134.
95 Kiley, interview.
96 McDermott Hamm, "Must All Beach Houses Look Alike?"
97 "House on a Sandy Island," *House and Garden* (June 1970): 95.
98 "Architects Speak Their Minds," 44.
99 Ibid.
100 Ibid.
101 Bruning, "He Shoots Cutting Edges into the Sky," 5–6.
102 Ibid.
103 Newton, *Cherry Grove*.
104 Jo Segal Bressler (Gifford client; Roeder friend), interview with author, September 2008. "Make-out loft" was the phrase invoked by Roeder in his request to Gifford.
105 *The Fire Island Kids*, British Film Institute, London, 1970, DVD release 2012.
106 Natalie Schram, "Tuned to Nature's Forces—and Man's Sociability," *House Beautiful* (July 1972): 65.
107 Ibid, 63.
108 Carol Ferris-Lipkins (client), telephone interview with author, March 6, 2010.
109 Gladys Rosenthal, interview.
110 Ibid.
111 Ibid.
112 Ibid.
113 John Updike, *Rabbit Redux* (New York: Random House, 1999), 411.
114 Goldman, "I Have Seen the Future," 27–28.
115 Jack Nichols, *Welcome to Fire Island* (New York: St. Martin's, 1976), 5.
116 Andrew Holleran, *Dancer from the Dance* (New York: Perennial, 1978), 207.
117 Ibid., 228.
118 Larry Kramer, *Faggots* (New York: Grove, 1978), 314–15.
119 Edward DiGuardia (friend), telephone interview with author, September 3, 2012.
120 Author interview with J. Robert Rosenthal, June 15, 2013.
121 DiGuardia, interview.
122 McCarter, *Louis I. Kahn*, 232.
123 Marc Jacobs, "The Visionary: Calvin Klein," *Interview* (August 28, 2013), https://www.interviewmagazine.com/fashion/calvin-klein#:~:text=JACOBS:%20But%20it%20was%20you,around%20the%20Studio%2054%20days.
124 Charles Kaiser, "Afterword," in Merle Miller, *On Being Different: What It Means to Be a Homosexual* (New York: Penguin, Kindle edition, 2012), 52.
125 According to the New York City HIV Epidemiology and Field Services Program, 62,281 people died in New York City of AIDS-related illnesses between 1981 and 1995; 58,282 Americans died in the Vietnam War.
126 Kaiser, "Afterword," 52.
127 Alan Borg, buildings editor of *The American Home*, letter to Horace Gifford, October 13, 1966.
128 Bert Seides (friend), interview with author, September 14, 2009.
129 Herzig, "Designer's Home Rises Above It All."
130 Peter Graham (client), interview with author, June 23, 2009.
131 Gene Silbert (client), e-mail interview with author, January 31, 2010. According to Silbert, Gifford turned down Halston and referred him to Paul Rudolph. Halston eventually purchased a Rudolph-designed townhouse in 1974. Bruning, "He Shoots Cutting Edges into the Sky," mentions this commission but does not mention Halston by name.
132 Bruning, "He Shoots Cutting Edges into the Sky."
133 Susanne Slesin, "Moonlit Benefit for the Pines," *New York Times*, July 9, 1979.
134 Pete Roe (client), telephone interview with author, September 9, 2012.
135 This figure is provisional due to the unknown status of some projects. Addresses were often omitted from drawings, so not all homes have been located. The cited number is the best estimate of built projects and significant additions during this period.
136 Goldman, "I Have Seen the Future," 30.
137 One home in the Pines is known to be demolished, two have burned down, and approximately one-quarter of Gifford's homes overall remain in original condition.
138 Horace Gifford, "Architecturally Bellport Is at a Crossroad," *Long Island Advance*, August 10, 1989.
139 Holleran, *Dancer from the Dance*, 207.

Selected Bibliography

"2 Faced House," *The American Home* (April 1964): Cover, 36–37. (Wittstein-Miller House)

"Another Smart Vacation Idea," *The American Home* (April 1965): 101. (Dell House)

"Architects Speak Their Minds," *House and Garden* (June 1970): 14, 42, 44. (Crawford House)

"Greek Cross: Panoramic Views," *House and Garden* (June 1966): 129–30. (Evans-DePass House)

"He likes outdoor sports, and so do the children, she likes to entertain a lot: so they built a house that can stand up to an active beach life," *House and Garden* (July 1974): 24–27. (Sloan House)

"House on a Sandy Island," *House and Garden* (June 1970): 92–95, 117–18. (Crawford House)

"Houses That Extend Summer," *House and Garden Building Guide* (Summer 1979): Cover, 84–87. (Travis-Wall House)

"How to enjoy the great outdoors in a house designed for living with Nature," *House and Garden* (May 1973): 114–17, 222. (Silbert-Kiley House)

"An Open and Shut Case for Privacy," *The American Home* (April 1964): 44–45. (Leedom House)

"Sand Castle Vacation House," *The American Home* (May 1966): 74–75. (Sprague-Geller House)

"Take it Easy Rooms," *House and Garden* (June 1966): 106–07. (Burge Pavilion)

"A View from the Top," *House and Garden Building Guide* (Summer 1969): 164–67. (Fishman House)

Wakefield Poole. *The Wakefield Poole Collection*. TLA Entertainment Group, 2009. DVD.

Bloodgood, John D. "Troubles Stay Behind," *Better Homes and Gardens* (August 1962): 5, 10. (Gifford House)

Borg, Alan C. "Towers, Decks, and a View," *The American Home* (Summer 1967): 68–71 (Gifford House II)

Bruning, Fred. "He Shoots Cutting Edges Into the Sky," *Suffolk Sun*, May 5, 1968, 4–6.

Clark, Sally and Lois Perschetz. *Making Space: How to Decorate and Renovate to Get the Space You Need from the Space You Have*. New York: Random House, 1983, 46–49. (Silbert-Kiley House II)

Dempsey, John, ed. *Fire Island: A Century of Art*. New York: Phaidon, 2025.

Domin, Christopher, and Joseph King. *Paul Rudolph: The Florida Houses*. New York: Princeton Architectural Press, 2002.

Drucker, Stephen. "Scott Free," *House Beautiful* (July 1994): 88–89, 101. (Wittstein-Miller House II, as renovated by Scott Bromley)

Goldman, Albert. "I Have Seen the Future, and It's Fire Island," *New York* (July 24, 1972): 26–30.

Gordon, Alastair. *Weekend Utopia: Modern Living in the Hamptons*. New York: Princeton Architectural Press, 2000.

Holleran, Andrew. *Dancer from the Dance*. New York: William Morrow, 1978.

Koppelman, Lee and Seth Forman. *The Fire Island National Seashore: A History*. New York: State University of New York Press, 2008.

Kramer, Larry. *Faggots*. New York: Grove, 1978.

McCarter, Robert. *Louis I. Kahn*. London: Phaidon, 2005.

McDermott-Hamm, Madeleine. "Must All Beach Houses Look Alike?" *Houston Chronicle*, July 10 1977: Section 8, Page 1.

Newton, Esther. *Cherry Grove, Fire Island: Sixty Years in America's First Gay and Lesbian Town*. Boston: Beacon, 1993.

Nichols, Jack. *Welcome to Fire Island: Visions of Cherry Grove and The Pines*. New York: St. Martin's, 1976.

Parlett, Jack. *Fire Island: A Century in the Life of an American Paradise*. New York: Hanover Square, 2022.

Reif, Rita. "A 90-Minute Trip from Victoriana to Fire Island Modern," *New York Times Magazine* (October 18, 1967): 50. (Scali House)

Rohan, Timothy. "Architecture in the Age of Alienation: Paul Rudolph's Postwar Academic Buildings." Dissertation, Harvard University, 2001.

Rothstein, Jess, narrator. *Finding Fire Island,* Spotify, 2023.

Saito, Yutaka. *Louis I. Kahn Houses*. Tokyo: Toto, 2003.

Schram, Natalie. "Tuned to Nature's Forces—and Man's Sociability." *House Beautiful* (July 1972): 62–65. (Roeder House)

Smith, C. Ray. "Variations on a Plan," *Progressive Architecture* (May 1968): 134–39.

Sverbeyeff, Elizabeth. "Pavilion in the Dunes," *New York Times Magazine* (June 20, 1965): 38–39. (Donghia House)

Project List

Horace Gifford's architectural associates were Ronald Bentley, William Fuller, David Hatcher, Louis Mueller, William Murphy, and Joerg Schwartz. Same-sex partners of clients were often deliberately excluded from the name of a residence in order to protect the clients' privacy at the time. Where it was evident that both partners participated in the creation of a home, and the partner's name was obtainable, both last names have been listed. Dates are keyed to completed construction documents.

1961
Gifford House, Fire Island Pines, NY
Slay House, Houston, TX

1962
Wittstein-Miller House, Fire Island Pines, NY
Rumley House, Fire Island Pines, NY
Jenkins House, Fire Island Pines, NY

1963
Wittstein-Miller House II, Fire Island Pines, NY
Leedom-Cott House, Fire Island Pines, NY
McGregor House, Fire Island Pines, NY
Dell House, Fire Island Pines, NY
Kreiger House, Ocean Bay Park, NY
Switzgable House, Fire Island Pines, NY

1964
Runnels House, Sagaponack, NY
Donghia House, Fire Island Pines, NY
Schultz House, Fire Island Pines, NY
Kauth House, Fair Harbor, NY
Miller House (unbuilt), Fire Island Pines, NY
Water Pumping Station, Fire Island Pines, NY

1965
Evans-DePass House, Fire Island Pines, NY
Gifford House II, Fire Island Pines, NY
Sprague-Geller House, Fire Island Pines, NY
Applebaum House, Seaview, NY
Burge Pavilion, Fire Island Pines, NY
Carey House (unbuilt), East Hampton, NY
Fishman House, Fire Island Pines, NY
Breslin House, Saltaire, NY
Ackert House (renovation), Fire Island Pines, NY
Photographic Studio for Mark Kauffman,
New York, NY

1966
Runnels House II, Bridgehampton, NY
Hillborn House, Fire Island Pines, NY
Hoernly House, Long Beach Island, NJ
Wolfson House, Fire Island Pines, NY
Globus House, Corneille Estates, NY
Naiman House, Fair Harbor, NY
Rehbock House, Fair Harbor, NY
Pike House, Saltaire, NY
Krieger House II (unbuilt), Ocean Bay Park, NY

1967
Luck House, Bridgehampton, NY
Kahn House, Saltaire, NY
Barnes House, Saltaire, NY
Moss House, Ocean Beach, NY
Bonaguidi House, Fire Island Pines, NY
Scali House, Fair Harbor, NY
Silbert-Kiley House, Redding, CT

1968
Runnels House III, Noyack, NY
Silverman House, Seaview, NY
Rubin House, Seaview, NY
DeSwaan House (unbuilt), Bridgehampton, NY
Crawford House, Fire Island Pines, NY
Rompapas House (with Harry Bates), Fire Island
Pines, NY
Bremeyer House, Fair Harbor, NY

1969
Cashel House, Fire Island Pines, NY
Slay House II, Vero Beach, FL
Basili House (unbuilt), Hawley, PA
Gracewood Lane Housing Development (unbuilt),
Vero Beach, FL
Masur House (unbuilt), Fire Island Pines, NY
Rubrum House, Fire Island Pines, NY
Kahan-Kaplan House, Fire Island Pines, NY
Roeder House, Fire Island Pines, NY
Kenmore House (addition, unbuilt), Fire Island
Pines, NY
Bellezza House (renovation), Putnam Valley, NY
Runnels Apartment (renovation), San Juan, PR

1970
Lipkins House, Fire Island Pines, NY
Rompapas House (addition, unbuilt), Fire Island
Pines, NY

1971
Bram House (addition, unbuilt) Fire Island
Pines, NY
Pilson House, Westhampton Beach, NY
Chasas House (unbuilt), Amagansett, NY
Raynor House, Kismet, NY
Barr House (unbuilt), Wilton, CT
Beldezza House (renovation), Putnam, NY
Silbert-Kiley Apartment, New York City, NY
Ayers House (addition), Fire Island Pines, NY

1972
Runnels House IV, Sagaponack, NY
Rosenthal House, Seaview, NY
Miller House, Seaview, NY
Essebag House, Seaview, NY
Sloan House, Fire Island Pines, NY
Globus House (addition), Corneille Estate, NY
Offices for John Kiley, New York City, NY
Shorin House (addition), Seaview, NY
Landau House (renovation), Englewood, NJ

1973
Duncan House (unbuilt), Danbury, CT
Runnels House V, Noyack, NY
Duhl House (renovation and addition), Fire Island Pines, NY
Ansel House (renovation), Water Island, NY
Rosenthal House (renovation), Fire Island Pines, NY

1974
Ross House (unbuilt), New Canaan, CT
Gifford Apartment (unbuilt), New York City, NY
Landau House (renovation), Englewood, NJ

1975
Duhl Townhouse, New York City, NY
Duffy House (unbuilt), Manursing Island, NY
Travis-Wall House, Fire Island Pines, NY
Bonaguidi House II, Fire Island Pines, NY
Runnels House V (unbuilt), Southampton, NY

1976
Chasas House, Amagansett, NY
Scali Guest House, Fair Harbor, NY
Fairway One Waterwood (unbuilt), Houston, TX
Marshall Street Townhouses (unbuilt), Houston, TX
Slay House (addition), Houston, TX
Meyers House (renovation, unbuilt), Fire Island Pines, NY

1977
Peden Avenue House (unbuilt), Houston, TX
Travis-Wall House (swimming pool addition), Fire Island Pines, NY

1978
Graham House, Eastport, NY
Silbert-Kiley Apartment II, New York City, NY
Bonaguidi Terraces, New York City, NY
Marlo Sloan Apartment, New York City, NY
Gifford-Greenfield House and Studio, New York City, NY
Rosenberg House (renovation), New York City, NY
EGR Travel International Offices (unbuilt), New York City, NY
Strafaci Apartment (renovation, unbuilt), New York, NY

1979
Thal House, Montauk, NY
Artichoke Gourmet Foods, New York, NY

1980
Silbert-Kiley House II, Roxbury, CT
Runnels House VI, Noyack, NY
Cortner House, Seaview, NY
Klein House (addition), Fire Island Pines, NY
Schwartz House (addition), Seaview, NY

1981
Seidner House, Fair Harbor, NY
Silverman House, Sagaponack, NY
Schneiderman House (unbuilt), Westhampton Beach, NY

1982
Zacharia House (addition), Sagaponack, NY
Lecktrecker House (renovation), Bellport, NY

1983
Orentreich House, Fair Harbor, NY

1984
Rosenberg House (renovation), Bellport, NY
Robbins Apartment (renovation), New York City, NY

1985
Orentreich House, Dunewood, NY
Roe House (renovation), Bellport, NY
Weiser House (renovation), Bellport, NY
Bellport Harbor Bayfront Park (unbuilt), Bellport, NY
Orentreich Medical Group, New York City, NY
Rosenberg House (renovation), New York City, NY
Cold Spring Dairy, Cold Spring, NY

1986
Bellport Memorial Library Landscape (unbuilt), Bellport, NY
15 Hulse Street (renovation, unbuilt), Bellport, NY
Perlo-Rosenberg House (renovation), Bellport, NY

1987
Silbert-Kiley House III (unbuilt), Roxbury, CT
Perlo Apartment (renovation), New York City, NY

1989
Hulse Street Neighborhood Preservation Plan (unbuilt), Bellport, NY
Forstadt House (addition), Ocean Beach, NY

Index

Image Credits

87,121,188—Tom Bianchi. 4, 8, 11t, 12m, 12b, 28ll, 64t, 67b, 72lr, 73b, 89–91, 97, 106c, 106b, 111, 113t, 125c, 132–33, 135t, 135ll, 136–37, 142–43, 147, 154–55, 160–62, 163b, 164–66, 168t, 169, 169–72, 173l, 175lr, 180lr, 193lr, 194b, 200–01—Horace Gifford, courtesy Christopher Rawlins. 6, 32–33—Paul Cadmus c/o VAGA. 9, 46–47—courtesy Gordon de Vries Studio Archives. 11lr, 11c, 112, 114–15—Louis Reens courtesy Lawrence Bonaguidi. 12t, 30, 34b, 35–37, 38c, 38b, 42r, 56l, 56ur, 186–87—courtesy Warren McDowell. 14, 72–7, 128–31, 138lr, 158t, 159, 174, 176–77—Michael Weber. 15, 17tr, 100–02, 106tl, 107,123, 126t, 127, 178–79, 180tl, 181–83, 192, 193t, 206–07, 210–11—Tom Sibley. 17tl, 62–63, 65, 70–71, 98t, 98m, 99—Bill Maris ©Esto. 17b, 202—John Hall, courtesy Scott Bromley. 19, 44ul, 44ll, 57, 86t, 86c, 92ul, 157, 168ll, 189—Fire Island Pines Historical Preservation Society. 20–21, 56ll—courtesy David Menkes. 22—Gilbert Emerson, courtesy Vero Beach Magazine/Heritage Center and Citrus Museum. 23l—courtesy J. Charles Gifford/Vero Beach Magazine. 23r, 31—courtesy Jane Slay. 24, 25—courtesy Indian River County Historical Society Collection, Archive Center, Indian River County Main Library. 26, 27—courtesy Library of Congress. 28ul, 56lr—University of Pennsylvania Architectural Archives. 28ur—© Robert C. Lautman, National Building Museum. 28r—University of Florida, courtesy Paul Muldawer. 29—courtesy National Register of Historic Places. 34t—Metropolitan Museum of Art. 41—© Estate of Paul Himmel. 42–43—courtesy Pines Pantry. 38t—Estate of Lincoln Kirstein, c/o Bridgeman Art. 40—Richard Avedon, © The Richard Avedon Foundation. 46—*House Beautiful*. 45, 68b,76, 86b, 92b, 98b, 103, 106ur, 110lr, 113b, 119b, 126b, 141t, 146, 153ll, 158b, 163t, 167ll, 175ll, 180, 196r,—Christopher Rawlins. 52–55, 59, 66, 67t, 68t, 69, 91ll— Edwin Wittstein. 56t—Vincent Lisanti/The Meredith Company. 69, 70t, 71—Hans Namuth, posthumous digital reproduction from original negative. Hans Namuth Archive, Center for Creative Photography, ©1991 Hans Namuth Estate. 76l, 78b—courtesy Donghia Inc. 94c—Suffolk County Police Department. 94c—Main Street Press. 95—*Mattachine Review*. 91r—Hugh Ferriss Collection, Avery Architectural and Fine Arts Library. 92–93, 124, 125t—Bill Maris. 104–05—Ricardo Labougle.108–09—Troy Caperton. 110t, 167t—Bill Aller/*New York Times*/Redux. 110ll—*Business Week*. 116–18, 119t, 194t, 195, 196l, 197–98, 199ll, 199lr—Tom Yee. 135lr—Michael Dunne/Elizabeth Whiting. com. 138t—*Progressive Architecture*. 138ll—*Suffolk Sun*. 144–45—Christopher Baker. 149, 153t—J. Hyde Crawford. 150–51—Yale Wagner/Horace Gifford (superimposed by author). 152—Richard Champion, courtesy estate of Charles Andrews. 153lr—Yale Wagner. 156—Ferron Bell. 173r—© BFI / Courtesy of the BFI National Archive. 184—R. Mandel. 190–91—© Peter Aaron/ESTO. 199t—Barbara Walz c/o Kevin Walz. 209—John Lagucki.

Design and production: Barbara de Vries, Gordon de Vries Studio

Copy Editors: Anne Thompson, Thomas Evans

Printed in China through Asia Pacific Offset

Gordon de Vries Studio
Editorial Director: Alastair Gordon
Creative Director: Barbara de Vries
www.barbaradevries.net

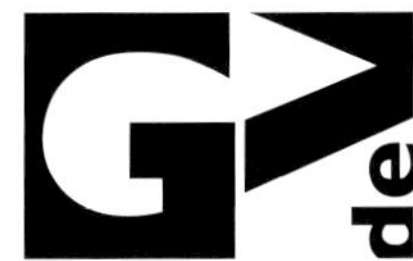

Copublished by Metropolis Books, ARTBOOK | D.A.P.
75 Broad St, Suite 630
New York, NY 10004
tel: 212 627 1999, fax: 212 627 9484
www.artbook.com

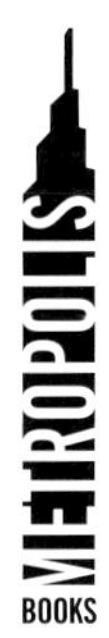

ISBN: 978-1-881616-99-3
Library of Congress Control Number: 2024944918

Second printing

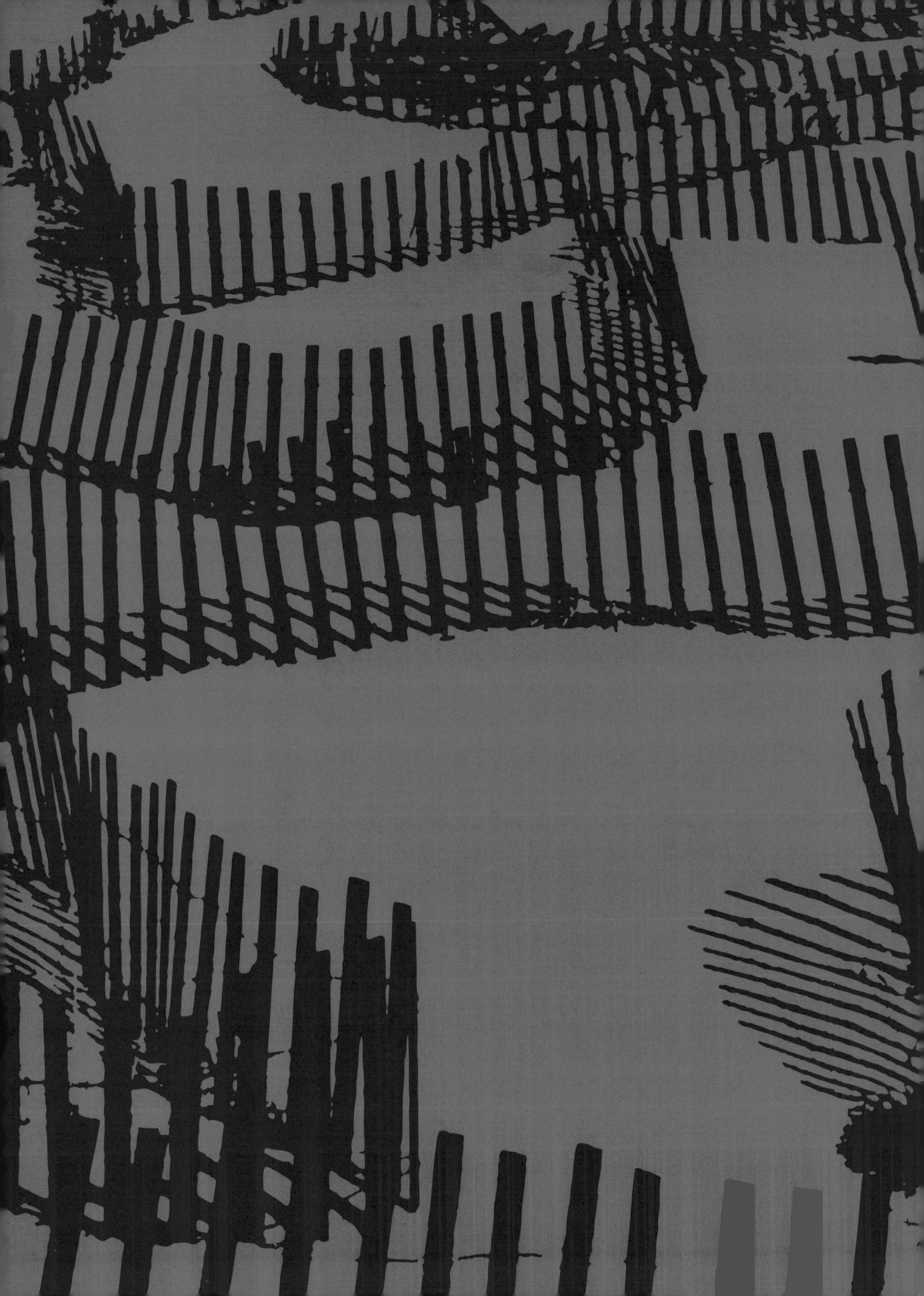